UNDERSTAND

SURVIVAL GUIDE

COVID-19

We have re-checked every business in this book before publication to ensure that it is still open after the COVID-19 outbreak. However, the economic and social impacts of COVID-19 will continue to be felt long after the outbreak has been contained, and many businesses, services and events referenced in this guide may experience ongoing restrictions. Some businesses may be temporarily closed, have changed their opening hours and services, or require bookings; some unfortunately could have closed permanently. We suggest you check with venues before visiting for the latest information.

SPECIAL FEATURES

Right: Montefrío (p279), Granada

FESUS ROBERT/SHUTTERSTOCK ©

WELCOME TO

Andalucía

I grew up in the Málaga-province mountain village of Cómpeta, dancing flamenco at local ferias, picking up a malagueño accent, navigating meat-mad Spanish menus as a life-long vegetarian and studying maps of Andalucian peaks, parks and rivers, then later lived in Cádiz province. Cádiz' Costa de la Luz remains my favourite place in the world (it's a close contest between Tarifa and Vejer de la Frontera) and, while Cádiz, Málaga, Córdoba and Seville are all fabulous, there's no city quite like magical Granada, with the edge-of-the-world villages of the Alpujarras just beyond. Andalucía, with its zest for life, will always be my home.

By Isabella Noble, Writer

@isabellamnoble isabellamnoble

For more about our writers, see p384

Andalucía

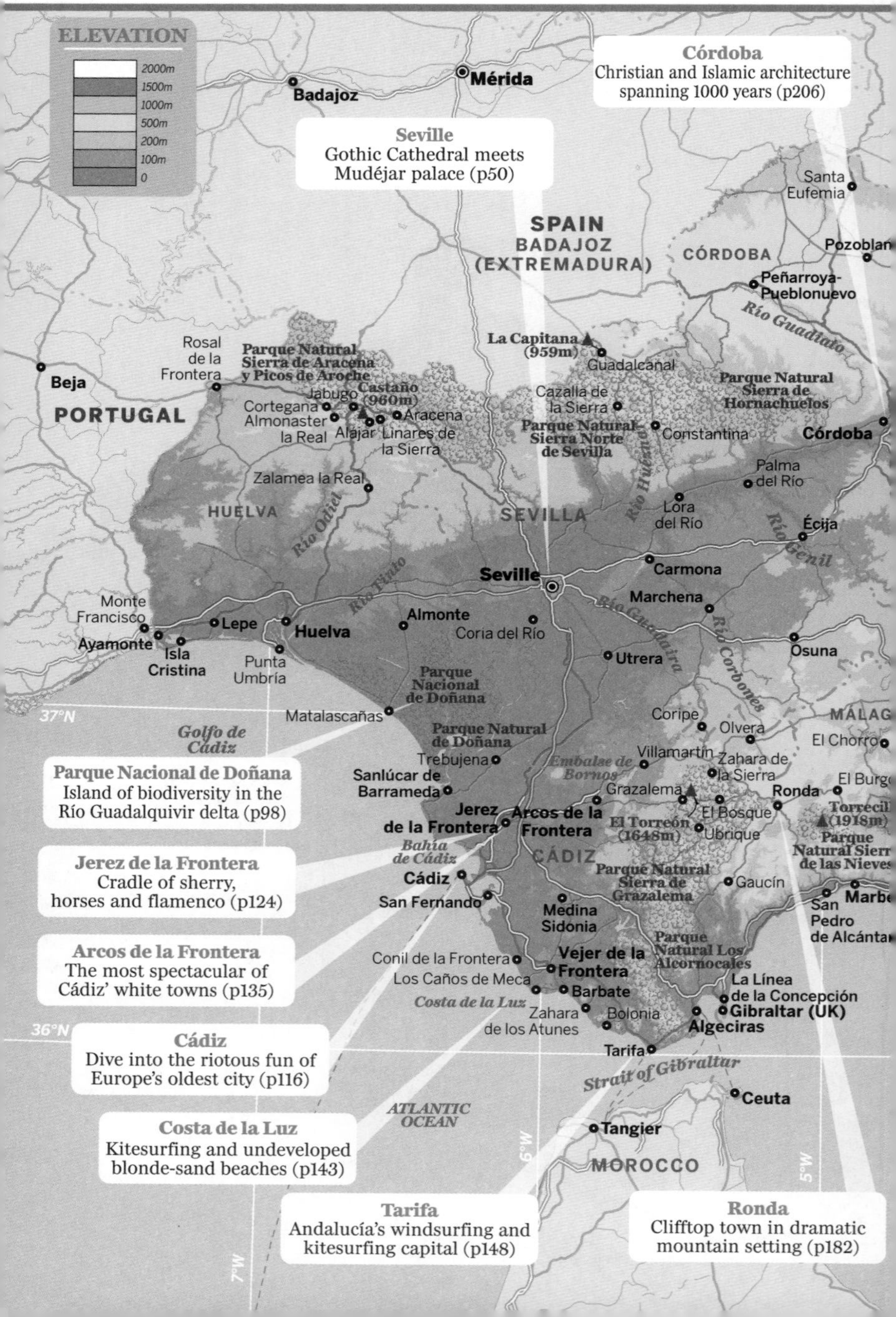

ELEVATION
2000m
1500m
1000m
500m
200m
100m
0
Córdoba
Christian and Islamic architecture spanning 1000 years (p206)
Seville
Gothic Cathedral meets Mudéjar palace (p50)
Parque Nacional de Doñana
Island of biodiversity in the Río Guadalquivir delta (p98)
Jerez de la Frontera
Cradle of sherry, horses and flamenco (p124)
Arcos de la Frontera
The most spectacular of Cádiz' white towns (p135)
Cádiz
Dive into the riotous fun of Europe's oldest city (p116)
Costa de la Luz
Kitesurfing and undeveloped blonde-sand beaches (p143)
Tarifa
Andalucía's windsurfing and kitesurfing capital (p148)
Ronda
Clifftop town in dramatic mountain setting (p182)
Mérida
Badajoz
SPAIN
BADAJOZ (EXTREMADURA)
CÓRDOBA
Santa Eufemia
Peñarroya-Pueblonuevo
Río Guadiato
La Capitana (959m)
Guadalcanal
Parque Natural Sierra de Hornachuelos
Rosal de la Frontera
Parque Natural Sierra de Aracena y Picos de Aroche
Beja
PORTUGAL
Jabugo
Castaño (960m)
Cortegana
Almonaster la Real
Alájar
Aracena
Linares de la Sierra
Cazalla de la Sierra
Parque Natural Sierra Norte de Sevilla
Constantina
Córdoba
Palma del Río
Zalamea la Real
HUELVA
Río Odiel
SEVILLA
Río Huéznar
Lora del Río
Écija
Río Genil
Carmona
Río Tinto
Seville
Marchena
Río Guadaira
Río Corbones
Monte Francisco
Ayamonte
Isla Cristina
Lepe
Huelva
Punta Umbría
Almonte
Coria del Río
Utrera
Osuna
Parque Nacional de Doñana
37°N
Golfo de Cádiz
Matalascañas
Parque Natural de Doñana
Coripe
Olvera
El Chorro
Trebujena
Embalse de Bornos
Villamartín
Zahara de la Sierra
El Burgo
Sanlúcar de Barrameda
Grazalema
Ronda
Jerez de la Frontera
Arcos de la Frontera
El Bosque
Torrecilla (1918m)
El Torreón (1648m)
Ubrique
Parque Natural Sierra de las Nieves
Bahía de Cádiz
CÁDIZ
Cádiz
Parque Natural Sierra de Grazalema
Gaucín
San Fernando
Medina Sidonia
San Pedro de Alcántara
Conil de la Frontera
Vejer de la Frontera
Parque Natural Los Alcornocales
Los Caños de Meca
Barbate
La Línea de la Concepción
Costa de la Luz
Gibraltar (UK)
36°N
Zahara de los Atunes
Bolonia
Algeciras
Tarifa
Strait of Gibraltar
Ceuta
ATLANTIC OCEAN
Tangier
MOROCCO
6°W
5°W
7°W

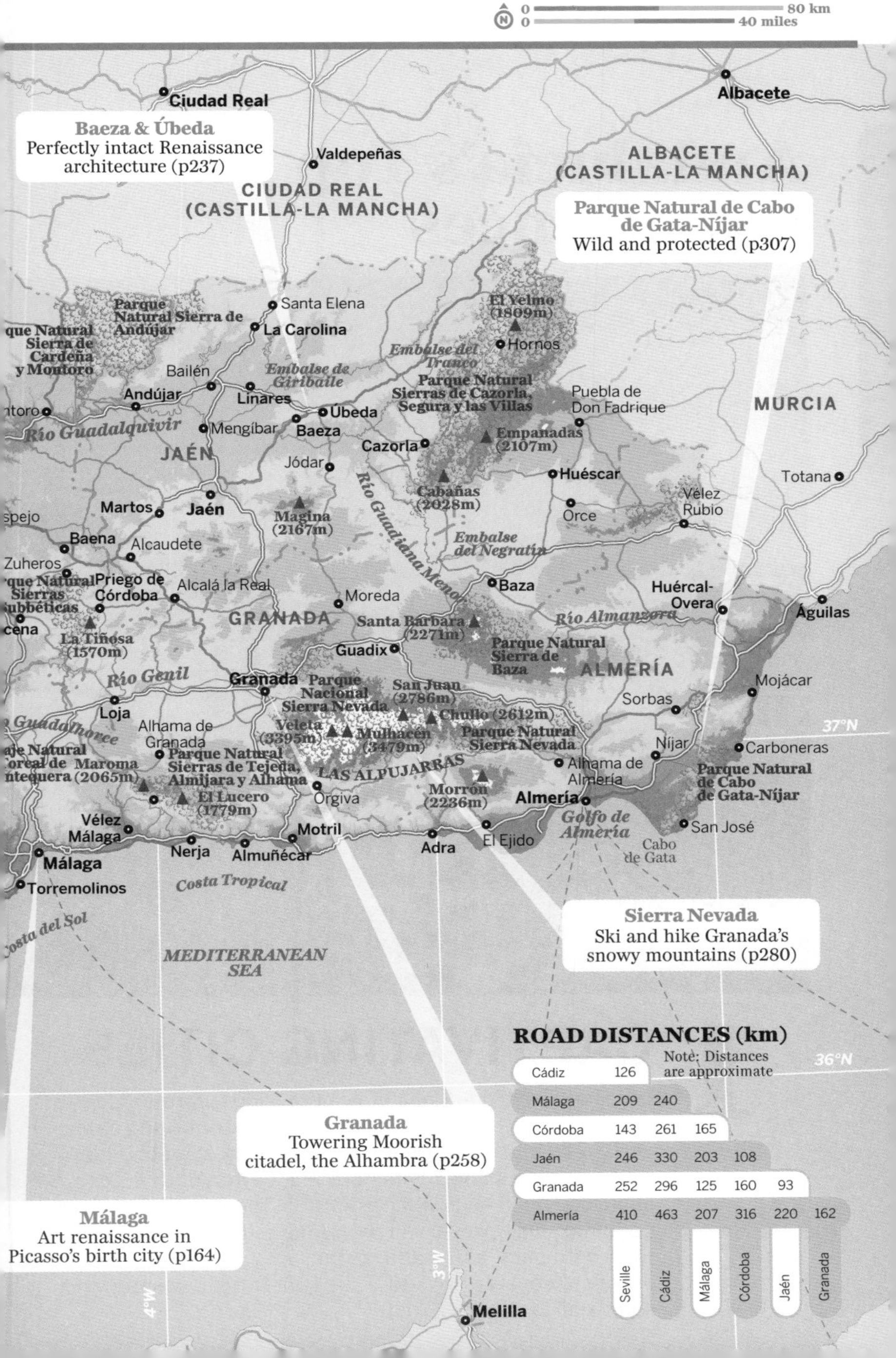

ROAD DISTANCES (km)

Note: Distances are approximate

	Seville	Cádiz	Málaga	Córdoba	Jaén	Granada
Cádiz	126					
Málaga	209	240				
Córdoba	143	261	165			
Jaén	246	330	203	108		
Granada	252	296	125	160	93	
Almería	410	463	207	316	220	162

Andalucía's Top Experiences

1 CAPTIVATING CITIES

Cities are where Andalucians' gregarious warmth is at its most intense. The noisy racket of mid-morning cafes and the festive atmosphere on after-dark streets equally affirm people's love of life here. Past often drab outer suburbs, you'll invariably reach a historic core of fine old buildings, well-preserved monuments and pretty parks, thick with bars, cafes and restaurants along palm- and orange-tree-lined streets. Take your time to wander and soak it all in. Seville (p50)

DAVID IONUT/SHUTTERSTOCK ©

Granada

There's nowhere quite like magical Granada, the final bastion (from 1249 to 1492) of Spain's Moorish culture. The Alhambra palace-fortress is among the world's most exquisite works of Islamic art, while contemporary Granada is a thriving Spanish city of culture, counterculture, tranquil teahouses and overflowing bars. p258

ZU SANCHEZ PHOTOGRAPHY/GETTY IMAGES ©

CGE2010/SHUTTERSTOCK ©

Seville

Stylish, ancient, proud, fun-loving and intimate, Seville flourished in both Moorish and Renaissance times and is home to magnificent Mudéjar, Gothic and baroque architecture. Being here today, among its flowery plazas and ebullient street life, is all about being part of that unique *sevillano* atmosphere. p50

Plaza de España (p66)

Córdoba

Córdoba is justly famed for its mesmerising Mezquita (mosque), one of the great works of Islamic architecture. Allow the medieval city to work its deep enchantment by wandering between gem-like little plazas along stone-paved lanes lined by golden-stone buildings, overhanging trees, potted plants and wrought-iron balconies. p206

Mezquita (p206)

2 SUN, SAND & SALTWATER

Most of Andalucía enjoys about 3000 hours of sunshine a year (twice as much as London), and Spaniards as well as foreigners flock to enjoy some of the best beach life in Europe. Your options range from the unspoiled strands of desert-like Cabo de Gata in the east through the busier, pebblier beaches of the central coast to endless golden stretches along the Atlantic.

Cabo de Gata

A volcanic, North Africa-like landscape backs the 60km coastline of this promontory, a protected *parque natural*. Cliffs and capes of surreal grandeur are interspersed with mostly undeveloped beaches, many of which can only be reached on foot, all lapped by azure waters. p307

Below: Faro de Cabo de Gata (p308)

NICK STUBBS/SHUTTERSTOCK ©

CORBIN ADLER/SHUTTERSTOCK ©

INIGOLAI-PHOTOGRAPHY/SHUTTERSTOCK ©

Costa de la Luz

Tall dunes, pine woods and Atlantic breakers lend an untamed, laid-back feel to the long, blonde beaches of western Andalucía. The strong breezes blowing through the Strait of Gibraltar have turned Tarifa (pictured above left), at Spain's southern tip, into a kitesurfing hotspot with a boho-cool vibe. p143

Costa Tropical

Granada province's coastline holds some pleasant, if pebbly, surprises. La Herradura's 2km-long beach (pictured above right), on a horseshoe bay, is a fine spot for kayaking and paddleboarding, with loads of semi-rustic restaurants too. Cliff-hemmed Playa Cantarriján is one of Andalucía's favourite, very laid-back, clothing-optional beaches. p291

3 MUSIC OF THE SOUL

From upbeat pop to the hiphop-influenced *reguetón*, Andalucian life is lived to an emotive, rhythmical soundtrack. The music that most of all says 'Andalucía' is of course flamenco, that passionate expression of both loss and joy which has its roots in Andalucía's Roma communities. Hear it live, whether at a *tablao* (tourist-oriented flamenco show, some of which are surprisingly good) or in a random bar or at one of the aficionados' clubs known as *peñas*.

Jerez de la Frontera

Perhaps the original cradle of the form, Jerez has a particularly fertile flamenco culture, with frequent performances in *peñas* and taverns, and a stellar annual flamenco festival. p130

ANIBAL TREJO/SHUTTERSTOCK ©

Granada

The lively flamenco scene here includes a top *peña*, La Platería (pictured above), and gigs in bars, courtyards and mansions in the old Muslim quarter, the Albayzín. p277

Seville

Deep in flamenco's western Andalucía heartland, Seville is home to many top-notch venues, including the Museo del Baile Flamenco (a museum too) and arguably the best of all *tablaos*, Los Gallos. p75

4 CELEBRATING LIFE

LINGLING7788/SHUTTERSTOCK ©

Andalucians' love of colour, noise, crowds, pageant and partying peaks at the countless local fiestas filling the calendar – often nominally celebrating a saint but, with the main exception of Semana Santa (Easter week) processions, usually far more festive than solemn in nature. Almost every city, town and village stages one major bash, often called a *feria* (fair), in the warmer months of the year. Expect loads of music, fireworks, fairgrounds, food, drink – and fun!

Noche de San Juan

Crowds flock to Andalucía's beaches for nocturnal partying with bonfires, barbecues and music on 23 June, traditionally the only night of the year when camping is allowed on Spanish beaches. p23

Cruces de Mayo

A charming early-May festival, celebrated particularly in Córdoba (pictured) and Granada, in which flower-bedecked crosses are set up in plazas and streets and become the focus of temporary bars, food stalls, music and dancing. p23

Romería de la Virgen de la Cabeza

Tens of thousands of people congregate round a remote hilltop north of Andújar for this passionate religious event on the last Sunday in April. Relatively under the radar as big festivals go. p237

5 MOORISH HERITAGE

Andalucía was all or partly under Moorish rule for nearly eight centuries (711 to 1492) and the imprint of that era runs deep. Granada's Alhambra palace-fortress and Córdoba's Mezquita (Mosque) are the two exquisite, not-to-be-missed monuments, but the Moorish stamp is everywhere – in church towers that were once minarets, the tangle of narrow village streets, the Andaucian love for fountains, the hillsides terraced for irrigated agriculture, the popular Arabic-style *hammam* bathhouses...

AKTURER/SHUTTERSTOCK ©

ANDIE_ALPION/SHUTTERSTOCK ©

Real Alcázar

Palacio de Don Pedro at the heart of Seville's grand palace-fortress was built under a Christian king in the 1360s, but much of its sumptuous decoration was crafted by Muslim artisans from Granada. p56

The Almonaster Mezquita

In the remote hill village of Almonaster la Real stands an almost mini version of Córdoba's great mosque (though Christianised centuries ago; pictured bottom left). p110

Almería's Alcazaba

This magnificent fortress (pictured above right), founded in the 10th century, lords it over the skyline of the eastern city that was once Moorish Spain's most important port and naval base. p298

6 VILLAGE VIBES

CARON BADKIN/SHUTTERSTOCK ©

JOSERPIZARRO/SHUTTERSTOCK ©

The Andalucian landscape is peppered with hundreds of enticingly picturesque villages – white-painted places of flowery balconies, proud old churches on angular plazas, and narrow, winding streets where you may have to make way for mules laden with produce from their owners' gardens. Many villages are popular escapes for city-dwellers so they're well endowed with rustic bars, restaurants doling out home-style cooking and cosy small hotels and guesthouses.

Capileira

Capileira (pictured top left) perches over 1400m high on the slopes of the dramatic Poqueira gorge, the white of its houses often matched by snow on the high Sierra Nevada above, for which it's an ideal jumping-off point. p286

Castaño del Robledo

The very name ('Chestnut tree in the oak wood') entices towards this tiny place (pictured bottom left) of a dozen streets overseen by two enormous churches – a perfect base for walking in the verdant Aracena hills. p110

Bolonia

A glorious, long, white beach, backed by the impressive ruins of Roman Baelo Claudia, culminates in a high, pine-covered dune. Enjoy super-fresh seafood at restaurants like Las Rejas. p148

7 PLEASURES OF THE PALATE

The seafood, ham and pork here among Spain's best. As of course is the olive oil (about one-third of the whole world's olive oil comes from Andalucía). Gazpacho is a cool delight for hot southern summers. Creative restaurant chefs concoct arty delights for demanding palates. But some of your most delicious moments will be in the bustling tapas bars, enjoying delectable combination mouthfuls alongside a glass of beer or wine.

Tapas in Seville

Andalucía's tapas capital, with wonderfully tasty bites in bars throughout the city. The Barrio de Santa Cruz (pictured below left), Plaza Alfalfa and Alameda de Hércules are all very happy hunting grounds. Don't miss Bar Eslava! p72

MARGARET STEPEIN/LONELY PLANET ©

Tasty Towns

A number of smaller cities and towns have become leaders in traditional and fusion food preparation. You'll love eating in Vejer de la Frontera (pictured top right; p143), Jerez de la Frontera (home of sherry; p124) or Úbeda (p240).

More Tapas

Almería and Málaga have particularly appealing tapas scenes: you can happily spend a evening touring half a dozen bars. In Almería, Granada and throughout Jaén province there's a free tapa with every drink!

8 HEAD FOR THE HILLS

ANTONIO LUIS MARTINEZ CANO/GETTY IMAGES ©

Andalucía is a delight for nature lovers. From the rocky wilderness of the Sierra Nevada to the rolling, woodland-clothed Sierra Morena along the region's northern fringe, from the stark desertscapes of Cabo de Gata to the vast Doñana wetlands, the variety is enormous. More than 30% of Andalucian territory is environmentally protected. The walking and cycling are marvellous and the landscapes always impressive however you're travelling.

Sierra Nevada & Las Alpujarras

The often snow-capped Sierra Nevada (pictured), south of Granada, holds three of Spain's six highest peaks. On its southern flank are the otherworldly Alpujarras valleys, dotted with white, Moorish-origin villages. p280

Parque Natural Sierras de Cazorla, Segura y Las Villas

This northeastern park, Spain's largest protected area at 2098 sq km, is rugged and mountainous, with great walking and abundant wildlife. p249

Doñana

The vast Doñana wetlands teem with countless water birds (including flamingos) and mammals such as deer and wild boar. All-terrain minibuses tour the core Doñana national park from El Rocío and Sanlúcar de Barrameda. p98

Need to Know

For more information, see Survival Guide (p351)

Currency

Euro (€), Gibraltar pound (£)

Language

Spanish (Castilian), English in Gibraltar

Visas

Generally not required for stays of up to 90 days per 180 days; not required at all for members of EU or Schengen countries. Most non-EU nationalities will need a pre-travel authorisation (ETIAS) from 2021. Some nationalities need a Schengen visa.

Money

ATMs widely available. Credit and debit cards accepted in most hotels, taxis, restaurants and shops.

Mobile Phones

Local SIM cards widely available (though may not be compatible with the Japanese system). EU phones have free roaming in Spain.

Time

Central European Time (GMT/UTC plus one hour)

When to Go

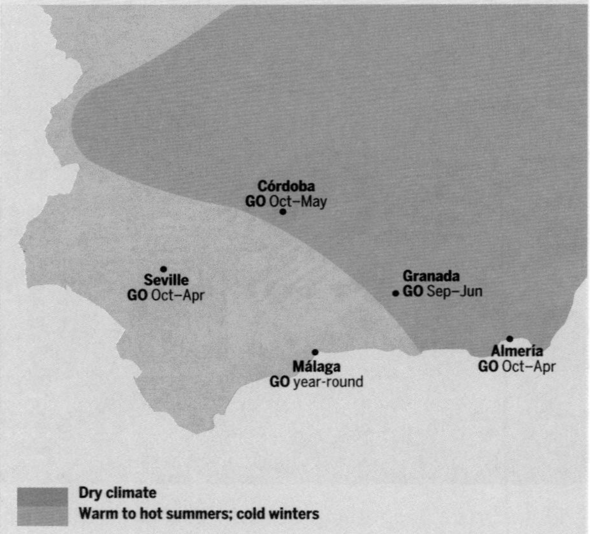

High Season (Jul–mid-Sep)

➡ Summer temperatures soar, and the climate is very dry.

➡ Most Spaniards holiday in July and, especially, August; expect sun, crowds and traffic jams, particularly along the coast.

➡ Many hotels hike prices; book ahead.

Shoulder (Apr, May & mid-Sep–Oct)

➡ Hotel prices can triple during Semana Santa and local ferias.

➡ Ideal weather: warm but not too hot (great for hiking).

➡ Spring brings a colourful cavalcade of Andalucian festivals.

Low Season (Nov–Mar)

➡ The coastal climate remains relatively warm and dry; it's cooler and rainier inland, especially higher up.

➡ Sierra Nevada ski season in full swing.

➡ Great hotel bargains (though some shut down).

➡ Sights and restaurants have reduced hours.

Useful Websites

Turismo Andalucía (www.andalucia.org) Encyclopaedic official Andalucía tourism site.

Spain (www.spain.info) Official Spanish tourist-board site.

Andalucia.com (www.andalucia.com) Handy guide to the region.

Lonely Planet (www.lonelyplanet.com/spain/andalucia) Destination information, hotel bookings, traveller forum and more.

Piccavey (www.piccavey.com) Excellent Andalucía coverage by a Granada-based blogger.

El País (www.elpais.com) Major newspaper with English-language section.

Important Numbers

Telephone numbers in Spain don't use area codes; simply dial the nine-digit number.

Country code	34
International access code	00
Ambulance	061
Emergency	112
National police	091

Exchange Rates

Australia	A$1	€0.59
Canada	C$1	€0.65
Japan	¥100	€0.86
Morocco	Dh1	€0.09
New Zealand	NZ$1	€0.55
UK	UK£1	€1.12
US	US$1	€0.91

For current exchange rates, see www.xe.com.

Daily Costs

Budget: Less than €75

- Hostel dorm: €15–40
- Budget-hotel double room: €45–65
- Eating at traditional tapas bars: €2–4 per tapa
- Bus transport: €23–30 (Seville–Granada)

Midrange: €75–175

- Boutique-hotel double room: €65–140
- Car hire: from €20
- Two-course meal with wine: €20–45
- Museums/attractions: €3–20

Top end: More than €175

- Room at *parador* or other upmarket hotel: from €140
- Meal at top-end restaurant: from €40
- Guided tour: from €20
- Car hire: from €20

Opening Hours

Opening hours in Andalucía have local and seasonal variations. Gibraltar businesses don't take a siesta: restaurants usually open 8am to 8pm and shops 10am to 6pm; most shops close after lunch on Saturday and reopen Monday.

Banks 8.30am–2pm Monday to Friday; some also open 4–7pm Thursday and 9am–1pm Saturday

Cafes 8am–11pm

Central post offices 8.30am–8.30pm Monday to Friday, 8.30am–2pm Saturday

Night-time bars and clubs 10pm–6am

Restaurants 1pm–4pm and 8pm–midnight

Shops 10am–2pm and 4.30pm–7.30pm or 5pm–8pm Monday to Friday or Saturday; big supermarkets and department stores 10am–10pm Monday to Saturday

Arriving in Andalucía

Seville Airport The EA shuttle bus (€4) leaves every 15 to 30 minutes throughout the day to the city centre. Taxis cost €23 to €32 (15 to 25 minutes).

Málaga Airport Suburban train C1 (€2.30) leaves every 20 minutes from Terminal 3, taking 11 minutes to the city centre. Bus A (€3, 20 minutes) leaves for the centre every 20 minutes from outside the Terminal 3 arrivals hall. Direct buses from the airport go to Granada, Marbella and Torremolinos. Taxis to the centre cost €22 to €25.

Granada Airport Alsa (p279) buses run between the airport and the city centre (€3, 20 to 40 minutes) at 6am and then hourly 9.20am to 10pm. Taxis cost €25 to €30.

Getting Around

Car Andalucía has an excellent road system. Having your own vehicle enables you to make the most of your time, as bus services to smaller villages rarely operate more than once a day and there are often no weekend services. Book car-hire online in advance for the best deals.

Bus With a more extensive network and cheaper prices than trains, buses travel to even the smallest Andalucian villages. Alsa runs most intercity routes. Various other companies service remoter areas.

Train High-speed AVE trains (book ahead) serve Seville, Córdoba, Málaga, Antequera and Granada. Slower but cheaper regional trains link most of Andalucía's other main towns and cities but aren't much use for smaller destinations.

For much more on **getting around**, see p362

What's New

Andalucía took years to work its way forward from the 2008 financial crisis, but by the late 2010s tourism was booming. The Covid-19 pandemic saw Andalucía's income from tourism (vital to its economy) fall by some 80% from 2019 to 2020. While the road back from this new blow will be long, Andalucians look forward to recovering the good times as quickly as possible.

Best in Travel

Cádiz province was awarded seventh place in Lonely Planet's list of top 10 regions in 2020, for its string of gastronomic triumphs (such as Jerez' first two Michelin stars), the exciting boutique-hotel scene developing in food-loving Vejer de la Frontera, and new flights launched to Jerez.

Jerez Stars

Hotshot Jerez chefs Juan Luis Fernández and Israel Ramos put the queen of the Sherry Triangle on Spain's culinary map with a Michelin star each – in 2019 for LÚ, Cocina y Alma (p128) and in 2020 Mantúa (p128), respectively – while the luxuriously converted 19th-century Casa Palacio María Luisa (p128) is now bringing boutique sparkle to the local accommodation scene.

Archaeological Jewels

Keen to see Europe's oldest known human remain? Granada's recently restored Museo Arqueológico (p266) displays the Orce tooth and other relics in a sweeping 16th-century riverside palace. Meanwhile, Jaén's new Museo Íbero (p233) is packed

LOCAL KNOWLEDGE

WHAT'S HAPPENING IN ANDALUCÍA?

Isabella Noble, Lonely Planet Writer

Spain was sadly one of the world's worst-hit countries during the Covid-19 crisis with, by official figures, nearly 70,000 deaths by the time the third wave of the virus was easing off in spring 2021. Andalucía had lower infection and death rates than many other parts of the country but the economic effects of the pandemic were severe here, notably in the key tourism sector where income fell by over three-quarters from 2019 to 2020 and an estimated 12,000 medium-size, small and self-employed businesses closed down. Before the pandemic, tourism in Andalucía was flourishing, with the region's unemployment rate down to under 25% in 2018, though it was still Spain's highest and many young Andalucians were still seeking work abroad. The post-Covid challenge is to get tourism back on its feet and the hope is that the visitors from key incoming countries like the UK and Germany will return.

Until recently, the reins of power in Andalucía had been held by the left-of-centre Partido Socialista Obrero Español (PSOE; Spanish Socialist Workers' Party) since 1982. But in the December 2018 Andalucian regional elections, the PSOE failed to win a majority, paving the way for a right-wing coalition government formed by the Partido Popular (PP) and Ciudadanos parties, supported by the emerging far-right Vox party.

As always, it can be hard to reconcile gloomy news stories with the warmth and colour of Andalucía. Family bonds remain strong; the music plays; the fiestas go on. With their optimism, warm nature and love of the good things, Andalucians have a time-tested recipe for making the very best of whatever fate throws at them.

with locally unearthed artefacts from the pre-Roman Iberian culture.

Natural Wines

Biodynamic, minimum-intervention, organic wines are soaring in popularity across Andalucía, from standout Córdoba shop-bar Jugo (p218) to ecoconscious Granada bar-meets-deli Al Sur de Granada (p276).

Food Culture

The best (and tastiest!) path to Andalucía's heart is, of course, through its gastronomy. Dive into the endlessly fascinating food-and-drink scene of Spain's sunny south on one of a fast-growing number of expert-led tapas tours and cooking classes in, say, Málaga, Granada, Seville, Córdoba, Cádiz or Jerez.

Emerging Destinations

Lesser-known spots across Andalucía are upping their game to entice visitors and tell their own stories – Almería city is feeling fresh and fabulously foodie after becoming Spain's 2019 culinary capital (Capital Española de la Gastronomía), while, over in Cádiz province, tiny whitewashed Setenil de las Bodegas is pulling in curious travellers with its smartened-up cave-homes and wonderful cave-restaurants.

Granada Wines

Though few outsiders seem to know it, Granada province produces some outstanding, international-award-winning wines. A huge milestone was the 2018 establishment of the Vinos de Granada Denominación de Origen Protegida (DOP; Denomination of Origin). And the region's bodegas have now thrown open their doors for tastings and visits, especially in the Contraviesa–Alpujarras hills.

Olive Oil

Jaén province's prized extra virgin olive oil was awarded IGP protected status by the EU in 2019, and olive-oil tourism is blossoming amid Andalucía's endless olive groves, with all kinds of exciting tours, tastings and events.

LISTEN, WATCH & FOLLOW

For inspiration and up-to-date news, visit www.lonelyplanet.com/spain/articles.

El País (www.elpais.com) Major print and digital newspaper with English-language section.

Piccavey (www.piccavey.com) Top Andalucía blog by Granada-based Molly Piccavey.

Twitter @Seville_Writer Journalist and translator Fiona Flores Watson shares Andalucía tips and updates from Seville.

Sur in English (www.surinenglish.com) Weekly selection of Spain and Andalucía news with an emphasis on Málaga province.

Instagram @lacosmopolilla Wide-ranging recommendations by travel journalist Patri Rojas, with a leaning towards Andalucí.

FAST FACTS

Food Trend Olive oil and natural wines

Andalucía Iberian Lynx Population 334 adults (in 2020)

Highest Peak Mulhacén (3479m)

Population 8.46 million

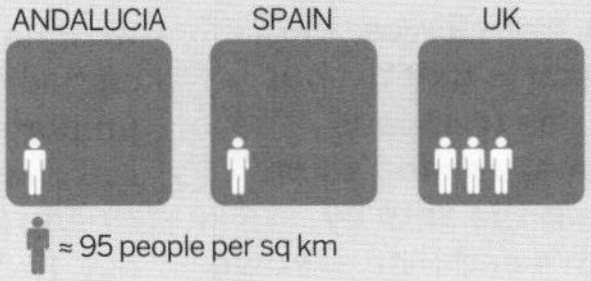

A New National Park

Known for its forests of rare *pinsapos* (Spanish firs) and populations of eagles and ibexes, Málaga's wild Sierra de las Nieves is becoming Spain's 16th national park – and only the third in Andalucía. Final parliamentary approval of the *parque nacional* (previously a less tightly protected *parque natural*) was expected in 2021.

La Geoda de Pulpí

Opened to the public in late 2019, the world's second-largest geode (p316) is an unforgettable sight: a mesmerising mass of sparkling subterranean crystals in Almería province.

Month by Month

TOP EVENTS

Carnaval February–March

Festival de Jerez February–March

Semana Santa March–April

Feria de Abril April

Feria del Caballo April–May

January

Apart from Reyes, the year starts quietly, but *romerías* (religious pilgrimages) and saints' days up the ante by month's end. The average Málaga temperature is 12°C, sometimes rising to 17°C. The Sierra Nevada ski season is well under way.

Día de los Reyes Magos

Three Kings' Day, on 6 January, is the highlight of any Spanish kid's calendar, with present-giving and family celebrations. Three local personalities dress up as the three wise men on 5 January and parade around throwing sweets in the Cabalgata de Reyes.

February

Cádiz' Carnaval and Jerez' flamenco festival lure people from far and wide. Andalucía's coolest month, February is also the best month for skiing in the Sierra Nevada.

Carnaval

Cádiz throws mainland Spain's largest Carnaval, with parades, fancy dress and a spectacle more famous for its wit and satire than its grandeur, best embodied by scathingly humorous *chirigotas* (satirical choral folk songs). The 10-day party ends the Tuesday 47 days before Easter Sunday, sometimes running into March. (p117)

Festival de Jerez

Each year, the self-styled *cuna* (cradle) of flamenco hosts what is claimed to be the world's most esteemed flamenco festival, over two weeks in late February or early March. (p130)

March

The best time to visit Andalucía starts now, with the arrival of spring flowers and warmer weather, especially in years when Easter falls early. This is a great season for hiking.

April

One of the top months to visit, April often has fine weather (though there's no guarantee!), not to mention Semana Santa parades and exuberant festivals headlined by the big one in Seville.

Semana Santa

There are few more elaborate manifestations of Christian Holy Week than in Seville (p69), where hooded *nazarenos* (penitents) carry huge *pasos* (floats) through the streets in ghostly solemnity. It's also spectacularly celebrated in Málaga (p170), Granada (p271), Córdoba (p214) and Arcos de la Frontera (p135). Semana Santa can also fall in March.

Feria de Abril

Seville's legendary week-long spring fair, held two weeks after Easter, is Andalucía's biggest fair. *Sevillanos* dress up in traditional gear, drink sherry, parade on horseback and dance *sevillanas* (flamenco-influenced folk dances). (p69)

Romería de la Virgen de la Cabeza

One of Spain's largest, most passionate religious events pulls in tens of thousands to see a small statue of the Virgin Mary carried around on the last Sunday in April, at the Santuario de la Virgen de la Cabeza, 31km north of Andújar town in Jaén province. (p237)

Feria del Caballo

Jerez' famous one-week horse fair in late April or early May dates back to medieval times and involves plenty of parades, music, dancing, competitions and makeshift bars serving the best local sherry. (p127)

May

The mountain slopes are strewn with wild blooms, the sun is out, and Andalucía buzzes in anticipation of *romerías* and summer fiestas. If Easter is early, the Romería del Rocío (Pentecost weekend) falls in May.

Cruces de Mayo

In the first week of May, squares and streets are decorated with crosses adorned with flowers, shawls, guitars and other traditional pieces, in honour of the cross on which Christ was crucified. Córdoba and Granada are great cities to see it, though other places are now reviving the tradition too. (p215)

Córdoba Festivals

Everything happens in Córdoba in May, from the vibrant flower festival (p215) to the later spring fair (p215). For the early-May floral homage to the city's gorgeous patios, homeowners open up around 50 private courtyards to compete for the 'best patio'.

Feria de la Manzanilla

Head to the unheralded, seafood-biased culinary town of Sanlúcar de Barrameda in Cádiz province for alfresco tapa tasting and *manzanilla* swilling during this May/June festival. Neighbouring El Puerto de Santa María also has a late-April/early-May sherry festival celebrating the local *fino*. (p134)

Tuna Festivities

In May and/or June, towns all along Cádiz' Costa de la Luz host Ruta del Atún festivals celebrating the *almadraba* season, including tuna-tapa competitions. Zahara de los Atunes has one of the liveliest. (p147)

Romería del Rocío

The greatest of all Spain pilgrimages, centred on Pentecost (Whitsunday) weekend, attracts over a million people to venerate the Virgin in Huelva province's El Rocío. They arrive in colourful parades on foot and horseback, by carriage and boat. Dates: 23 May 2021, 5 June 2022, 28 May 2023. (p102)

June

The summer fiesta season has fully kicked off, with temperatures rising and every town and village in Andalucía hosting its own party. The Romería del Rocío is sometimes held in June. Good hiking weather.

Noche Blanca del Flamenco

A night-long, top-class flamenco blowout, starring leading artists of the genre in free performances at picturesque venues around Córdoba, on a Saturday night around 20 June. (p215)

Ronda Guitar Festival

Ronda's six-day guitar fiesta celebrates all kinds of playing (not just flamenco) with concerts, conferences and wine tastings. (p188)

Corpus Christi

Another movable Catholic feast, celebrated eight-and-a-half weeks after Easter, Corpus Christi is particularly significant in Granada, where, despite the underlying solemnity, it has long been fused with the annual feria. Sometimes falls in May. (p271)

Orgullo de Andalucía

Seville throws southern Spain's largest LGBTQI+ Pride celebration over a party-filled week of concerts, exhibitions, drag shows and more, which wraps up with a packed-out Saturday-evening parade. (p356)

Noche de San Juan

The *andaluces* flock to the beach for a dawn-to-dusk party on 23 June, with swimming, drinking, dancing, barbecues and bonfires. Join the fun anywhere, perhaps in Nerja (p200) or Mojácar (p313).

July

Northern Europeans hit the Mediterranean beaches, and it gets hot (with average highs of 30°C in Málaga and 36°C in Córdoba and Seville). Linger by the coast, or escape to the mountain villages for (slightly) cooler air. The Spanish holiday season starts mid-month; reserve well ahead.

Jazz Vejer

Spanish and international musicians descend on the food-loving Cádiz white town of Vejer de la Frontera for this early-July jazz fest, which also includes 'gastro-jazz' events (www.jazzvejer.com).

Festival Internacional de Música y Danza

Top-notch contemporary and classical performances take place in the Alhambra and other historical settings around Granada during the three-week, international music and dance festival. (p271)

Festival de la Guitarra de Córdoba

Flamenco is a highlight of this 10-day guitar festival held in early July in the (by then) sizzling city of Córdoba, but you'll also hear live classical, rock and blues performances. (p215)

August

It's hot. Seriously hot. Hit Málaga's mid-month feria and the beaches for sea breezes. If you're on the *costas*, half of Spain (and much of Europe) will be joining you. Book ahead!

Feria de Málaga

In mid-August, Málaga hosts Andalucía's second-most-famous party after Seville's Feria de Abril. Celebrations are awash with all the usual calling cards: lights, dancing, sherry, fireworks, fairground rides. Mysteriously, few Costa del Sol tourists show up. (p170)

Noche del Vino

The whitewashed town of Cómpeta, in Málaga's Axarquía hills, celebrates the sweet local muscatel wine on 15 August, with a traditional treading of the grapes followed by fiery flamenco performances – and endless free cups of the tipple. (p196)

September

At last, a little relief from the heat (though not everywhere!). September promises great hiking and slightly cooler beach weather, and is harvest time for grapes.

Bienal de Flamenco

Seville shares this prestigious 30-day biennial flamenco festival with Málaga; Seville hosts in even-numbered years. Top-notch artists have graced the stages since 1980. (p69)

Fiestas de la Vendimia

Jerez' two-week September fair honours the grape harvest with horse riding, sherry, *bulerías* (a fast-paced flamenco song from Jerez), and the treading of the first grapes on the cathedral's steps. (p127)

October

Autumn brings the harvest, a tempting line-up of food festivals and milder temperatures (good for hiking). Keep an eye out for cheese tastings, soup and stew days, chestnut celebrations, ham-cutting contests and more.

November

A big month for agriculture, with peak olive harvests and, traditionally, pig slaughters. It's also the start of low season and, potentially, the Sierra Nevada ski season, though Seville still registers nearly 200 hours of sunshine.

December

The *andaluces* enjoy one last hurrah: Navidad (Christmas), with the festive season spilling into January. Otherwise, chilly December is low-key, apart from ski action in the Sierra Nevada.

Navidad (Christmas)

Families come together for feast-like dinners on 24 December (Nochebuena). Many Spaniards now celebrate Navidad, with Papá Noel bringing presents, though Three Kings' Day (6 January) is the traditional present-giving celebration.

Itineraries

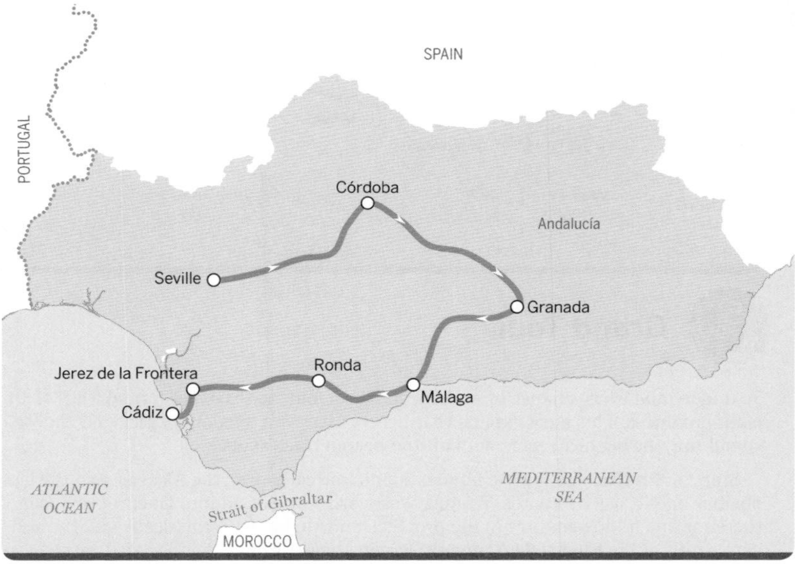

2 WEEKS Andalucía Highlights

You'd need months to poke into every corner of Andalucía, but two weeks will pack in the highlights. This greatest-hits itinerary is ideal for first-timers or those with limited time.

The best starting point is exceptional **Seville**, deserving of three days, where the Gothic cathedral and Mudéjar Alcázar stand side by side in surreal juxtaposition. Travel 150km northeast by train and several centuries back in time to **Córdoba**, home of flower-filled patios and the resplendent Mezquita. Free tapas, shadowy tearooms and the incomparable Alhambra beckon southeast in **Granada**, where you could fill at least three days reclining in Moorish-style bathhouses, wandering the Albayzín and deciphering the Lorca legend. Easily reached by bus, **Málaga** is understated by comparison; spend a couple of days enjoying the galleries, museums, fresh seafood and urban buzz. To the west (by bus or car), mountain-ringed **Ronda** is a dramatic contrast, doused in rebel-rousing history. West again (perhaps via some of Cádiz' white towns), **Jerez de la Frontera** is famous for its flamenco, festivals, horses and sherry bodegas. A 45-minute train trip southwest, **Cádiz** reveals a cheery mix of buzzy beaches, flamenco fun, seafood dining and surprising sights, including a romantic sea drive and a majestic cathedral.

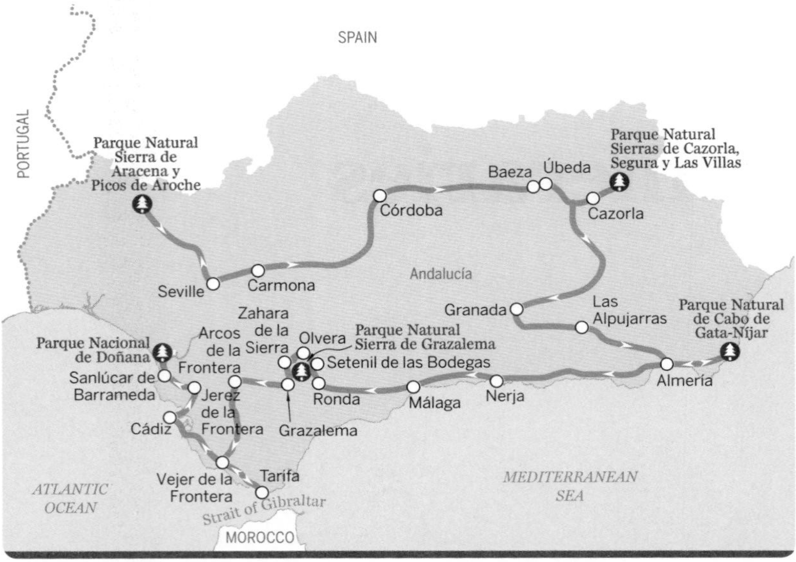

5 WEEKS Grand Tour

To understand every nuance of Andalucía, take a four- to five-week 'grand tour' of all eight provinces. This busy, expansive itinerary gives you freedom to pick and choose, combining the big headliners with off-the-beaten track spots.

Start in **Seville**, visiting the famous sights (the cathedral, the Alcázar) and the less-obvious ones (Casa de Pilatos, Triana). Westward sorties lead into Huelva province; there's prime hiking country in the province's north, between the sleepy villages and gentle hills of the **Sierra de Aracena**. Passing back through Seville, head east, stopping in history-rich **Carmona**. For week two, head to **Córdoba**, marvelling at its labyrinthine streets, hidden patios, Roman relics and splendid Mezquita. Tracking east into Jaén province takes you through olive groves to the Renaissance architecture of **Baeza** and **Úbeda**. Further east, **Cazorla** is the gateway to Andalucía's largest protected area, the **Parque Natural Sierras de Cazorla, Segura y Las Villas**.

Granada, at the start of week three, is an unmissable highlight, guarded by the marvellous Alhambra and heaving with soulful tapas bars. To visit all eight provinces, travel through the white mountain villages of **Las Alpujarras** to reach **Almería**, with its impressive Alcazaba, and the protected **Cabo de Gata**. Start week four by the coast at delightful **Nerja**, then hit **Málaga**, a provincial capital with booming art and food scenes. Next up: white-town 'capital' **Ronda**, on most itineraries since Hemingway visited. The white towns continue west across the border in Cádiz province; choose between **Olvera**, **Setenil de las Bodegas**, **Grazalema** and **Zahara de la Sierra** – or visit them all – and hike through the surrounding **Parque Natural Sierra de Grazalema**. Tracking west, **Arcos de la Frontera** reels in visitors with its spectacular clifftop setting.

Spend your final week kicking back along the beaches of Cádiz' Costa de la Luz, staying in **Tarifa** and **Vejer de la Frontera**, before delving into Andalucian culture in **Jerez de la Frontera** and **Cádiz**, two ancient cities packed with history, flamenco, sherry and worthwhile sights. Finally, swing by seafood-loving **Sanlúcar de Barrameda** and hop across the Río Guadalquivir to the ethereal **Parque Nacional de Doñana**.

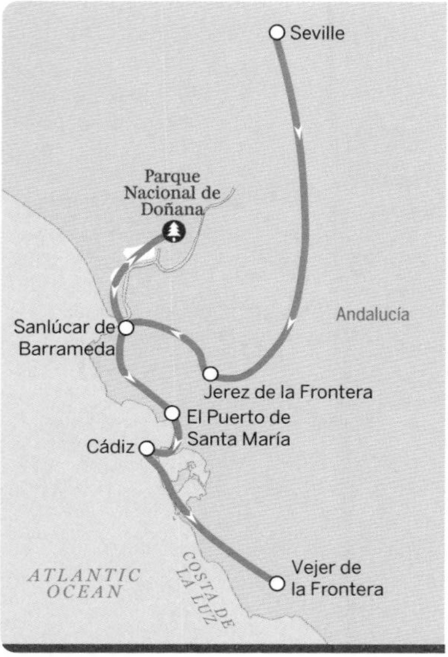

10 DAYS The Cultural Triangle

If you had to pick a region-within-a-region that best sums up Andalucía's essence, it would probably be the triangle taking in Seville, Cádiz and Jerez de la Frontera.

With excellent air, rail and bus connections, **Seville** is your best starting point. Lap up the Moorish-meets-Gothic architecture and seemingly limitless festivals for a day or two. Fast trains forge south to **Jerez de la Frontera**, first stop on the Sherry Triangle, where you can spend two days mixing bodega tours and tastings with horse shows, *tabanco* tapas, authentic flamenco and a *hammam* session. Continuing west (easily by bus) to **Sanlúcar de Barrameda** allows you to compare *fino* with *manzanilla* and savour some of Spain's finest seafood tapas. Sanlúcar is also a good base for Huelva's biodiverse **Parque Nacional de Doñana**. Buses link Sanlúcar with **El Puerto de Santa María**, home of more bodegas, festivals and fish restaurants. A catamaran ride across the bay, ancient **Cádiz** feels like the edge of Europe, with more superb seafood and a long history. The golden-white beaches here are famously broad and beautiful, and continue southeast along the Costa de la Luz. Explore them from **Vejer de la Frontera**, a dramatically perched white town with outstanding accommodation and dining.

3 WEEKS The West in Detail

Already seen the Alhambra and hiked the Sierra Nevada? Then go west to the self-styled cradle of Andalucian culture.

Start in Huelva province's **Parque Nacional de Doñana** – arguably Andalucía's finest natural attraction – basing yourself in either Sanlúcar de Barrameda or El Rocío. **Seville** broadcasts a wealth of well-known sights, while its provincial hinterland is less heralded. Visit **Carmona**, with its Alcázar, and **Osuna**, with its baroque architecture. South, rugged **Ronda** is well on the tourist map, though most visitors don't stay overnight. With time, you could sidestep west to white towns **Zahara de la Sierra**, **Olvera**, **Setenil de las Bodegas** and/or **Grazalema**, and hike in the **Parque Natural Sierra de Grazalema**. Exciting stops en route east to Málaga could be **El Chorro** gorge (home to the Caminito del Rey) and/or ancient **Antequera**. Lively port city **Málaga** has great seafood and excellent galleries and museums. To the southwest, **Gibraltar** lures visitors keen to meet its macaques. Stay in kitesurfer-cool **Tarifa**, before checking out the Costa de la Luz and overnighting in **Vejer de la Frontera**. Save time for culturally intense **Cádiz**, with detours to sherry-making **Jerez de la Frontera** and white-town queen **Arcos de la Frontera**.

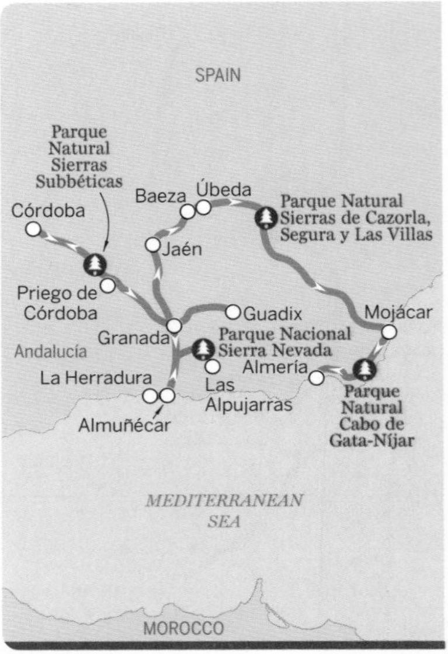

3 WEEKS The Andalucian Coast

Lapping five of its eight provinces, the Andalucian coastline is one of the region's great delights. Empires were once built here, though more recently resorts have colonised the shore. Most towns are linked by bus.

Start with Almería's protected, underdeveloped **Cabo de Gata**, a spectacular combination of cliffs, salt flats and sandy beaches. West, tapas-loving **Almería** is worth a stop for its Moorish Alcazaba. Granada's Costa Tropical is precipitous and authentic: **Almuñécar** makes a great base and low-key **La Herradura** is ideal for water sports. West again, Málaga province's **Nerja** has tempered its development, and excellent inland hiking beckons in **La Axarquía**. **Málaga** deserves three days; its reputation has skyrocketed in recent years thanks to its fine gastronomy and growing art and museum scene. **Marbella** is the most interesting stop on the over-touristed Costa del Sol, though **Mijas** merits a day trip. Southwest, **Gibraltar** guards the jaws of Europe. Northwest from kitesurfing capital **Tarifa**, Cádiz' Costa de la Luz offers water sports, coastal hikes, Roman ruins, white-sand beaches and international-flavoured cuisine. Stay in **Vejer de la Frontera**, visiting **Zahara de los Atunes** and **Los Caños de Meca**, before a grand two-day finale in **Cádiz**.

2 WEEKS The East in Detail

Spend three days in each of the two big-hitter cities, then branch out; you're best off with your own wheels.

Córdoba is an unmissable one-time Iberia capital graced by one of the finest mosques ever built. To the southeast, **Granada** showcases the later Nasrid era in its dazzling Alhambra, Albayzín and Moorish-style bathhouses. Beyond the cities, Córdoba-province highlights include the **Parque Natural Sierras Subbéticas** and elegant **Priego de Córdoba** (known for its olive oil), while Granada offers the **Parque Nacional Sierra Nevada** and **Las Alpujarras**, the village-dotted valleys that embellish the Sierra's southern slopes. Granada-province detours might include **Guadix**, with its inhabited caves, and coastal **Almuñécar** and **La Herradura**. North from Granada, amid olive groves, **Jaén** is a city of fine tapas bars, while **Baeza** and **Úbeda** are unique for their Renaissance architecture. Nature lovers should continue east to the **Parque Natural Sierras de Cazorla, Segura y Las Villas** for rugged mountain scenery, hilltop castles and abundant wildlife. Southeast, in Almería province, **Mojácar** promises a beachy vibe; **Cabo de Gata** is the region's most unspoiled coastal stretch; and **Almería** entices with its formidable Moorish Alcazaba.

Espetos (barbecued fish skewers)

Plan Your Trip

Eat & Drink Like a Local

Dining in Andalucía isn't just about what you eat; it's about how you eat, too. The culinary culture revolves around light breakfasts, leisurely lunches and late dinners spent grazing slowly from a selection of small tapas plates. If you're a visitor, adjust your body clock to a quintessentially Spanish groove.

The Year in Food

Andalucía is unusual in Europe in that, due to the balmy climate and extensive use of giant greenhouses, fruit and vegetables can be grown year-round, especially in Almería province and on Granada's Costa Tropical.

April–August

Spring and summer bring rice dishes and gazpacho, Andalucía's signature chilled soup, with regional variations such as *salmorejo* (Córdoba) and *ajo blanco* (Málaga).

August–October

The grape harvest ushers in a number of wine festivals, most notably Jerez de la Frontera's Fiestas de la Vendimia (p127) in September – the perfect opportunity to pair your *fino* with a good few tapas.

November–March

November is traditionally the start of the pig *matanza* (slaughter) and its accompanying pork-heavy feasts (though the tradition is disappearing in some areas). The olive-tree harvest is also under way. Winter is the time for hot roast chestnuts, and Huelva's strawberry season peaks from January to April.

Food Experiences

Meals of a Lifetime

Bar-Restaurante Eslava (p74) Creative contemporary tapas at renowned Seville hotspot.

La Brunilda (p73) One of Seville's best tapas bars.

Aponiente (p132) Andalucía's first three-Michelin-star restaurant, in El Puerto de Santa María.

Café Azul (p152) Best breakfasts in Andalucía.

El Jardín del Califa (p145) Outstanding Moroccan-Andalucian cooking in beautiful Vejer.

El Faro de Cádiz (p122) All the most exquisite Cádiz seafood tapas.

Misa de 12 (p245) Small Úbeda bar with a big culinary reputation.

Restaurante Arrieros (p108) Innovative mountain-sourced slow food in Huelva's Sierra de Aracena.

Bar-Restaurante El Acebuchal (p197) Fine Málaga country cooking and remote, end-of-the-road atmosphere.

Casa Balbino (p134) Andalucía's finest *tortillitas de camarones*? In Sanlúcar de Barrameda.

El Mesón de Cervantes (p172) Fabulous octopus and meats at an Argentine-run Málaga star.

Las Chimeneas (p289) Glorious organic local produce fuels outstanding Alpujarras cooking.

Picoteca 3Maneras (p274) Wonderfully creative cuisine in Granada's Realejo.

Óleo (p172) A *malagueño* chef meets a Japanese sushi master.

Palacio de Gallego (p240) Superb meat and fish dishes in a 16th-century Baeza house.

Casa Pepe de la Judería (p216) Historical Córdoba address excelling in meats and tapas.

Acánthum (p94) Michelin-star Huelva chef Xanty Elias' elaborate tasting menus.

LÚ, Cocina y Alma (p128) Juan Luis Fernández' Michelin-star gastronomy puts Jerez on the map.

Cheap Treats

Free tapas Granada, Jaén and Almería provinces serve a free tapa with every drink.

Chiringuitos Semipermanent shack-restaurants that specialise in fried seafood, often (not always) by the beach. The staples – *espeto de sardinas* (sardine skewers) and *boquerones fritos* (fried anchovies) – are best washed down with beer or *tinto de verano* (red wine with lemonade). Some only operate in summer.

Desayuno A typical Andalucian *desayuno* (breakfast) consists of a small strong coffee and a toasted roll topped with olive oil and/or crushed tomato. *Bocadillos* (filled rolls) are also cheap and tasty.

Menú del día Three-course, excellent-value restaurant lunch usually served with bread and wine. All-inclusive prices start at €10.

Dare to Try

Ortiguillas Croquette-sized sea anemones deep-fried in olive oil; a delicacy in the Cádiz area.

Callos A traditionally cheap leftover dish of tripe stew, particularly popular in Seville; it's recently been given a modern makeover by some of Andalucía's cutting-edge chefs.

Carrilleras de cerdo Pork cheeks, grilled or in a sauce as a delicacy.

Jabalí Wild boar (grilled or in sauces or stews) is common in rural Jaén and Córdoba.

Rabo de toro Oxtail stew.

Local Specialities

One of the most important influences over Andalucian chefs has always been the region's climate. The perfect antidote to the region's baking summers, for example, is chilled Andalucian gazpacho, while crunchy churros dunked in hot chocolate warm up winter afternoons.

Sevilla Province

Sevilla's Moorish past shines in several of its many, extraordinarily varied tapas, which arrive both in traditional and experimental form. Two great examples are *espinacas con garbanzos* (spinach, chickpeas and cumin) and *berenjenas con miel de caña* (fried aubergines drizzled with molasses), which are popular across Andalucía. *Huevos a la flamenca* is an ancient savoury dish of *morcilla* (blood sausage), garlic, onions and tomatoes topped with baked eggs. Sevilla also

Huevos a la flamenca

FOOD TOURS & COOKING COURSES

Annie B's Spanish Kitchen (p144) Popular cooking courses in Vejer de la Frontera, plus food and sherry tours across Cádiz province.

Taller Andaluz de Cocina (p68) Sherry tastings, cooking courses and food-market tours in Seville's Triana district.

Mimo Sevilla (p68) Wine tastings and food tours, including to Jerez.

Finca Buenvino (p106) Cooking at a country hotel in Huelva's Sierra de Aracena.

Las Chimeneas (p289) Alpujarras hideaway for cooking and baking retreats.

Spain Food Sherpas (p270) Local-focused food tours and cooking classes in Granada, Seville and Málaga.

Wanderbeak (p69) Tapas tours through Seville's centre and Santa Cruz district.

Granada Tapas Tours (p271) Fun, foodie small-group outings.

Foodie & Experiences (p214) All kinds of gastronomic goodness in Córdoba.

L'Atelier (p286) Vegetarian cooking classes in Granada's Alpujarras.

Cadizfornia Tours (p120) Uncover seafood-loving Cádiz through lively tapas tours.

Sanlúcar Smile (p134) Sherry tasting and tapas tours in Sanlúcar de Barrameda.

Devour Tours (www.devourtours.com) Terrific food experiences in Seville.

All Ways Spain (www.allwaysspain.com) Multiday gourmet-food trips.

Toma & Coe (www.tomaandcoe.com) Tapas tours and cookathons, including in Málaga.

produces some great sweets: *polvorones* are small, crumbly shortbreads from the town of Estepa, and *tortas de aceite* are sweet biscuits made from olive oil. Sevilla's bitter oranges are primarily used to make marmalade.

Huelva Province

Two gastronomic words define Huelva province: strawberries (the region grows 90% of the Spanish crop) and *jamón ibérico*. Huelva's famous *jamón* is the Champagne of Spain's cured meats, produced from black Iberian pigs that roam freely in the Sierra de Aracena feeding mainly on acorns. Sweeter and nuttier than the more ubiquitous *jamón serrano*, it is served sliced wafer thin and is notoriously expensive. *Chocos* (cuttlefish) are another local speciality, so much so that Huelva residents are known as *choqueros*.

Cádiz Province

Tuna headlines on Cádiz' Costa de la Luz, often caught using the ancient *almadraba* method; the town of Barbate (p148) claims the best catches. Prawns are similarly fabulous along the coast. *Pescaíto frito* (fried fish) is a Cádiz staple, and tapas of *tortillitas de camarones* are a Sanlúcar de Barrameda favourite. Other deep-fried stars include *chipirones* (baby squid) and *cazón en adobo* (marinated dogfish). Moroccan-influenced cooking is popular, too. Typical Cádiz cheeses include Manchego-like Grazalema, made from ewe's milk; *payoyo*, from the rare *payoya* goat in the Grazalema hills; and Cádiz, a strong goat's cheese from around Cádiz.

Cádiz province is also famously the home of sherry: Jerez de la Frontera and El Puerto de Santa María produce the best *fino* (dry) and *oloroso* (sweet, dark) varieties, while Sanlúcar de Barrameda makes its own unique *manzanilla*.

Málaga Province

The Mediterranean is all about fish and in Málaga this mean *boquerones* (anchovies) and *sardinas* (sardines). An *espeto de sardinas* (sardines grilled on a skewer) is best eaten on the beach at a *chiringuito*. *Ajo blanco* is Málaga's take on chilled gazpacho soup; the tomatoes are replaced by almonds, giving it a creamy white colour. *Porra antequerana* is Antequera's popular, thicker version of gazpacho. Málaga's grapes have a long history of producing sweet dessert wines (white and red), which have recently come back into fashion. Andalucians love cheese, and although many are imported from elsewhere in Spain, there are exceptions, including Málaga goat's cheese.

VEGETARIANS & VEGANS

Throughout Andalucía, fruit and vegetables are delicious and fresh, and eaten in season. Though local cuisine still indisputably revolves around meat, fish and seafood, things are slowly changing – in 2019, an estimated 10% of Spain's population followed a largely vegetarian or vegan diet. The number of specifically vegetarian or vegan restaurants in the region is on the up (especially in the bigger cities) and many restaurants now offer vegetarian options and/or can adapt dishes on request (less so in rural areas). Tarifa, Vejer, Granada, Córdoba, Seville and Málaga are some of Andalucía's better spots for meat-free dining.

Vegetarians will find that salads are a good bet (specify *'sin atún'* – 'without tuna'), as are gazpacho (chilled tomato soup), *ajo blanco* (a white gazpacho made from almonds and garlic), *parrillada de verduras* (grilled veggies) and *berenjenas con miel de caña* (fried aubergines drizzled with molasses). A word of warning: 'vegetable' dishes may not be meat-free (eg beans or soups sprinkled with bits of ham). Another reliable dish is *pisto* (ratatouille); or try *espárragos trigueros* (thin wild asparagus), *tagarninas* (thistles, popular in Cádiz) and *setas* (wild mushrooms), either grilled or in *revueltos* (scrambled eggs cooked with garlic). Tapas without meat include *pimientos asados* (roasted peppers), *aceitunas* (olives), *alcachofas* (artichokes), *espinacas con garbanzos* (chickpeas with spinach and cumin; may contain meat stock), *queso* (cheese; rarely fully vegetarian, however) and tortilla.

OLIVE OIL

Spain is the world's largest olive-oil producer and Andalucía's statistics are impressive: there are over 100 million olive trees in Andalucía; it is Spain's biggest producer of olive oil (around 80%!); and a remarkable 20% of the world's olive oil originates in Jaén province, which produces more olive oil than Greece. The seemingly endless olive groves of Córdoba, Jaén and Sevilla were originally planted by the Romans, but the production of *az-zait* (juice of the olive) – from which the modern generic word for oil, *aceite*, is derived – was further developed by the Moors. The most common type of olive is the full-flavoured and (sometimes) vaguely spicy *picual*, which dominates Jaén province and accounts for 50% of all Spanish olive production; also important is the *hojiblanca* olive (fruity, grassy and nutty), grown predominantly around Málaga and Sevilla provinces.

The best olive oils are those classified as 'virgin' (which must meet 40 criteria for quality and purity) and 'extra virgin' (the best olive oil, with acidity levels no higher than 1%). Accredited olive-oil-producing regions receive the designation Denominación de Origen (DO, which indicates the unique geographic origins, production processes and quality of the product). DO regions in Andalucía include Baena and Priego de Córdoba in Córdoba, and Sierra de Segura and Sierra Mágina in Jaén. In 2019, Jaén province became the first region in Spain to receive EU IGP 'protected origin' status for its extra virgin olive oil (p241).

Córdoba Province

Landlocked Córdoba grows copious chickpeas and olives, while its grapes are made into Montilla-Moriles wines, including the golden-amber, nutty-flavoured *amontillado* (not to be confused with *amontillado* sherry). Pedroches is a strong semicured sheep's-milk cheese from the Los Pedroches region in the north of the province. Córdoba specialities include *salmorejo* (a thick gazpacho-like soup topped with boiled eggs and ham), *rabo de toro* (stewed oxtail) and *flamenquín* (pork loin wrapped around *jamón serrano,* then coated in breadcrumbs and deep-fried).

Jaén Province

Jaén is the olive-oil capital of the world: the province alone accounts for around 40% of Spanish production and 20% of global production. Quality is understandably high; classic Jaén oils are bitter but fruity. The mountainous area of the Parque Natural Sierras de Cazorla, Segura y Las Villas has a strong hunting fraternity and is famous for its game, including partridge, venison and wild boar. Among Cazorla's local delicacies you'll find *rin-rán,* a mix of salted cod, potato and dried red peppers.

Granada Province

Few cuts of *jamón serrano* are better than those left to mature in the fresh mountain air of Trevélez village (p287) in Las Alpujarras. The mountains are also known for rabbit stews and the *plato alpujarreño,* a meat-heavy stomach-filler with eggs and potatoes. Down on the flat plains of La Vega, beans and asparagus grow in abundance, while the Costa Tropical yields luscious fruits. Granada is Spain's most strongly Moorish-influenced province, with fine tagines and *teterías* (teahouses), especially in Granada city. Granada's up-and-coming wines (p288), produced in the Guadix and Contraviesa–Alpujarras areas, were awarded Denominación de Origen Protegida (DOP) status in 2018.

Almería Province

Rather than deep-frying its fresh coastal fish, Almería tends to cook it *a la plancha* (on a metal grill), and also prepares staples like *ajo blanco* and *migas* (fried breadcrumbs, often with chorizo or peppers). Those ubiquitous greenhouses are filled with fruit and vegetables soaking up the southern sun. Almería is rightly famous for its plump year-round tomatoes and produces some tasty goat and cow cheeses.

CHURROS

Possibly invented by Spanish shepherds centuries ago, churros are long, thin, doughnut-like strips deep-fried in olive oil and then dipped in thick hot chocolate. In Andalucía, churros are enjoyed for breakfast, during the early-evening *merienda* (snack) or at sunrise as you stumble home from a night out. Good *churrerías* (churro cafes) abound, though Granada is often held up as Andalucía's churros capital, in particular on Plaza Bib-Rambla, and Málaga's Casa Aranda (p171) is a legendary churros spot. The *tejeringo* is a distinctively Andalucian version of the churro: a lighter, fluffier doughnut strip rolled into a large wheel.

How to Eat & Drink

Eating in Andalucía is all about timing, etiquette and a little insider knowledge.

When to Eat

Tip number one: get into the groove and feast on Spanish time. Wake up to a strong coffee accompanied by a light, sweet pastry, preferably taken standing up in a cafe. A more substantial *desayuno* can be procured at around 10am, often a *tostada* (toasted bread) drizzled with olive oil and topped with crushed tomatoes. Your first tapas window arrives at 1pm, when you can *picar* (graze) your way through a few small plates as a prelude to a larger *almuerzo* (lunch) at around 2pm. Some favour a full-blown meal with starter and main; others just order a selection of *medias raciones* (half-plate tapas servings) or *raciones* (full-plate servings).

Next comes the siesta. If you're up again by 5pm, consider having a revitalising *merienda,* a quick round of coffee and cakes (preferably in a cafe) to fill the hole between lunch and dinner. It's not impolite to start on tapas again around 8pm, or closer to 9pm in summer. Elbow your way to the bar and claim your *platillos* (small plates) as you sip a beer or perhaps a *tinto de verano. Cena* (dinner) rarely happens before 9pm and is usually less substantial than lunch, especially if you've warmed up with some tapas first. It's almost a faux pas to hit the sack before midnight, and at weekends people party until dawn.

Where to Eat

As elsewhere in Spain, Andalucía's bars are places to eat and socialise as much

SHERRY & FOOD PAIRINGS

Sherry, aside from being one of the world's most unappreciated wines (though it's now making a bit of a comeback), is also one of its most versatile, particularly the *fino* and *manzanilla* varietals, so you don't need a degree in oenology to pair it. You'll find strong sherry-pairing menus, along with bodega tours, in Jerez de la Frontera, Sanlúcar de Barrameda and El Puerto de Santa María.

TYPE OF SHERRY	SERVING TEMPERATURE	QUALITIES	FOOD PAIRINGS
Manzanilla	well chilled	dry, fresh, delicate, slightly salty essence	tapas, almonds, sushi, olives
Fino	chilled	very dry & pale	aperitif, tapas, soup, white fish, shellfish, prawns, oysters, a counterpoint for cheeses
Amontillado	cool but not chilled	off dry	aperitif, blue cheeses, chicken & white meat, cured cheese, foie gras, rabbit, consommé, rice dishes, asparagus, artichokes
Oloroso	cool but not chilled	dry, nutty, dark	red meat & game, mature cheeses
Pale Cream	room temperature	sweetened *fino*	fresh fruit, blue cheese
Cream	room temperature	sweet	dried fruit, cheesecake
Pedro Ximénez	room temperature	very sweet	dark chocolate, biscotti

JAMÓN

Unlike Italian prosciutto, Spanish *jamón* is a bold, deep red, well marbled with buttery fat. At its best, it smells like the forest and the field. Like wine and olive oil, Spanish *jamón* is subject to a strict series of classifications. *Jamón serrano,* which accounts for around 90% of cured ham in Spain, refers to *jamón* made from white-coated pigs introduced to Spain in the 1950s. Once salted and semidried by the cold, dry winds of the Spanish sierras, most now go through a similar process of around a year's curing and drying in a climate-controlled shed.

Jamón ibérico, also called *pata negra* (black leg), is more expensive and comes from a black-coated pig indigenous to the Iberian Peninsula and a descendant of the wild boar. Gastronomically, its star appeal is its ability to infiltrate fat into the muscle tissue, thus producing an especially well-marbled meat. Considered to be the best *jamón* of all is the *jamón ibérico* of Jabugo (p106), in Huelva province, which comes from pigs free-ranging in the Sierra Morena oak forests. The best Jabugo hams are graded from one to five *jotas* (Js). *Cinco jotas* (JJJJJ) hams come from pigs that have never eaten anything but acorns *(bellotas)*. If the pig gains at least 50% of its body weight during the acorn-eating season, it can be classified as *jamón ibérico de bellota,* the most sought-after designation for *jamón*.

as drink, but they come in many guises. These include bodegas (traditional wine bars), *cervecerías* (beer bars), *tascas* (tavern-like tapas bars), *taperías* (tapas bars) and *tabernas* (taverns). At many you can eat tapas at the bar, but there's often a *comedor* (dining room) for sit-down meals, too. You'll usually save 10% to 20% by eating at the bar rather than a table.

Restaurantes are more formal places where you sit down to eat. A *mesón* is a simple restaurant with homestyle cooking, while an *asador* specialises in roasted meats. A *venta* is a roadside inn (where food *can* be delicious and inexpensive). A *marisquería* is a seafood restaurant, and a *chiringuito* is a semi-open-air bar or kiosk, usually (not always) fronting the beach.

Ordering Tapas

Tapeando (going out for tapas) is a favourite Andalucian pastime and, while it may serve as the prelude to lunch, it's often also the main event in the evening, when Andalucians drag out their evening meal with tapas and drinks. Tapas often draw on the gastronomic peculiarities of their region. In Huelva, it would be a culinary crime to order anything but the local *jamón ibérico,* while in Granada North African–style tagine tapas reflect the city's history, and, in Cádiz province, seafood tapas are the real luxury.

A few *bar de tapas* tips:

- The best tapas times are from 1pm to 3pm and from 8pm onwards (9pm in summer).
- Tapas bars are often clustered together, enabling bar-hopping between bites.
- Good tapas places aren't always fancy, but they're invariably crowded. Be prepared to elbow your way to the bar.
- Don't worry about all those discarded serviettes on the floor – it's the Andalucian way to brush them off the table.
- Granada, Almería and Jaén provinces all offer a free tapa with every drink. Some places even allow you to choose!
- You can also eat tapas as *medias raciones* or *raciones,* which are great for sharing.

Menu Decoder

- Always ask for the house-special tapa/s.
- Andalucian paella is often made with almonds, sherry, chicken and sausages, as well as seafood.
- Olives and a bread basket accompany most meals. Olives are nearly always served green as opposed to black.
- Gazpacho is usually only available in spring and summer.
- Not that many Spaniards actually drink sangría; *tinto de verano* is more popular.
- Andalucians rarely drink sweet sherry; they prefer *fino* or *manzanilla,* especially with tapas.

Mountain biking, Sierra Nevada (p2

Plan Your Trip

Activities

One of the most epiphanic Andalucian experiences is discovering that most of the region remains traditional, untouristed and bursting with outdoor-adventure opportunities. Ancient walking trails link time-worn villages, cycling paths meander past ruined castles, and emblematic wildlife prowls the hills; or try diving, kitesurfing, horse riding, snowboarding or paragliding.

WESTEND61/GETTY IMAGES ©

Best Walking

Best Mountain Hikes
Sierra Nevada; Parque Natural Sierra de Grazalema

Best Hike-up Peaks
Mulhacén (Sierra Nevada); El Torreón (Sierra de Grazalema); El Lucero (Axarquía)

Best for Thrill-Seekers
Málaga province's unique Caminito del Rey

Best for Wildlife-Spotting
Parque Natural Sierras de Cazorla, Segura y Las Villas

Best Village-to-Village Hikes
Las Alpujarras; Sierra de Aracena

Best Pastoral Hikes
Sierra de Aracena; Sierra Norte de Sevilla; Sierras Subbéticas

Best Coastal Hikes
Parque Natural de Cabo de Gata-Níjar; Parque Natural de la Breña y Marismas del Barbate

Best Rivers & Canyons
Río Borosa Walk (Parque Natural de Cazorla, Segura y Las Villas); Garganta Verde (Parque Natural Sierra de Grazalema)

Best for Splendid Isolation
Parque Natural Sierra Norte de Sevilla; Parque Natural Sierra María-Los Vélez

Walking

Walking in Andalucía gets you to where 95% of visitors never go. If you're after some alone time while exercising your way through unblemished rural bliss, hit the *senderos* (footpaths).

All of Andalucía's *parques naturales* (natural parks) and *parques nacionales* (national parks) are criss-crossed by numerous well-marked trails, ranging from half-hour strolls to full-day mountain ascents and long-distance adventures. The scenery is rarely less than lovely and often majestic. You can sometimes string together day walks into multiday treks, sleeping along the way in hotels, *hostales* (budget hotels) and campgrounds, or the occasional mountain refuge.

Maps and signage are steadily improving but can still be iffy. The best markers are in the *parques naturales* and *nacionales,* and on major routes such as the long-distance GR7, identified by red-and-white paint splashes.

The two main categories of marked walking route in Spain are *senderos de gran recorrido* (GRs; long-distance footpaths) and *senderos de pequeño recorrido* (PRs; shorter routes of a few hours or one or two days).

When to Go

The best months for walking are generally May, June, September and October. July and August are ideal for the high Sierra Nevada but unbearably hot elsewhere; some trails close due to fire risk.

Information

The *parques naturales* and *nacionales* offer detailed walking information (in a growing number of languages) at their official visitor centres, and online at www.juntadeandalucia.es. Local tourist offices can be helpful, too, and there are plenty of locally based operators organising guided hikes and walking holidays. Among the best maps are those of Editorial Alpina (www.editorialalpina.com).

Cycling

Andalucía has more and more bike-hire opportunities, increasingly well-maintained and signposted touring and off-road trails, and a growing number of urban bike-sharing schemes and cycle paths – most notably in Seville (p80). Cycling tours are also on the up, especially in the big cities like Seville and Málaga (p170). Beware of hot weather, particularly in July and August.

Where to Go

The safest, flattest and most family-friendly paths are the greenways (p40) or *vías verdes* fashioned out of old railway lines.

Mountain-biking hotspots include the El Chorro and Ronda/Grazalema areas, the Parque Natural Sierras de Cazorla, Segura y Las Villas, La Axarquía and Las Alpujarras. The Parque Natural Sierra

Nevada maintains 13 mountain-bike trails, of which the king is the 450km Transnevada, which circles the entire mountain range between 1500m and 2000m, in eight stages.

Diving & Snorkelling

It's not quite the Caribbean, but Andalucía has some worthwhile spots for underwater exploration, mostly along its eastern coastline in Granada and Almería provinces. The Atlantic coast, with its strong currents, is best avoided (though there are some interesting wrecks around Gibraltar), and the western part of Andalucía's Mediterranean coast is of similarly limited interest to divers and snorkellers.

Practicalities

Most establishments offer PADI courses, plus dives for qualified divers (around €50) and introductory 'baptisms' (around €70). A four-day Open Water PADI course, for example, costs around €320.

Cabo de Gata, Almería (p308) Andalucía's top diving and snorkelling spot, with clear protected waters and a varied seabed of seagrass, sand and rock with caves, crevices, canyons and a wreck.

Costa Tropical, Granada (p291) Multicoloured fish, octopuses, corals and crustaceans, plus (relatively) warm waters make for excellent year-round diving and snorkelling; the gentle, shallow sea off La Herradura (p293) is ideal for beginners. Dive operators based in Málaga province's Nerja (p199) often head this way.

WILDLIFE-SPOTTING

Bounding deer, majestic sea mammals, flocks of migrating birds, the elusive Iberian lynx – Andalucía plays host to a fantastic array of wildlife (p338). A number of local companies run wildlife-spotting and birdwatching trips in the most popular areas.

Andalucía's famously endangered lynx population (p339), totalling 334 as of 2020, is split between the Parques Nacional and Natural de Doñana, and the Sierra Morena in and around the Sierra de Cardeña y Montoro, Sierra de Andújar and Despeñaperros natural parks. Local operators run 4WD trips into the Parque Natural Sierra de Andújar (Jaén province) and the Parques Nacional and Natural de Doñana (Huelva and Cádiz provinces), which are your best bet for spotting lynxes (though chances remain low).

PLACE	ANIMAL	TOUR OPERATOR
Parques Nacional & Natural de Doñana (p98)	Wild boar, Spanish imperial eagles, red & fallow deer, greater flamingos, waterbirds	Cooperativa Marismas del Rocío (p99), Doñana Reservas (p101), Doñana Nature (p101), Viajes Doñana (p134)
Parque Natural Sierras de Cazorla, Segura y Las Villas (p249)	Ibexes, red & fallow deer, wild boar, mouflons, red squirrels, bearded vultures, black vultures, golden eagles, peregrine falcons, lammergeier	Turisnat (p248)
Sierra Nevada (p280)	Andalucía's largest ibex population, wild boar, golden eagles, Bonelli's eagles, griffon vultures, kestrels	Nevadensis (p285), Spanish Highs (p284)
Parque Natural Sierra de Andújar (p236)	Ibexes, red & fallow deer, wild boar, wolves, mouflons, black vultures, black storks, Spanish imperial eagles, Iberian lynxes	IberianLynxLand (p237), Birds & Lynx Ecotourism (p237)
Parque Natural Sierra de Grazalema (p141)	Ibexes, griffon vultures	Independent visits recommended
Strait of Gibraltar (p157)	Marine mammals (Apr-Oct), over 300 species of migrating bird	FIRMM (p151)
Laguna de Fuente de Piedra (p194)	Birds, especially greater flamingos (Feb-Aug)	Centro de Visitantes José Antonio Valverde (p100)
Peñón de Zaframagón (p143)	Griffon vultures	Independent visits recommended

ALTERNATIVE ACTIVITIES

Vie Ferrate

Climbers might tackle Andalucía's increasingly popular vie ferrate – a form of fixed protection climbing using routes that are equipped with ladders, cables, bridges and, sometimes, zip lines. There are good beginner routes in Ronda and other more advanced routes in El Torcal, El Chorro and Comares, plus further options in the Sierra de Grazalema and near Cazorla. Several companies offer guided trips; try Andalucía Aventura (p186) and Vive Aventura (p195) in Málaga province, Tierraventura (p247) in Jaén province, Nevadensis (p285) in Granada's Sierra Nevada, and Horizon (p138) in Cádiz province.

Paragliding & Hang-Gliding

Parapente (paragliding) and, to a lesser extent, *ala delta* (hang-gliding) are popular in Andalucía year-round, with a growing number of launch points.

Little-known Algodonales, on the edge of Cádiz' Parque Natural Sierra de Grazalema, is among Andalucía's top free-flying centres, with an abundance of take-off points and strong enough winds to have attracted the World Hang-Gliding Championships in 2001. Locally based Zero Gravity (p142) offers one-week learn-to-fly paragliding courses (€885) and tandem flights (€90).

El Yelmo (p253), in Jaén's Parque Natural Sierras de Cazorla, Segura y Las Villas, is another major paragliding spot, attracting thousands of people with its June free-flying fair, the Festival Internacional del Aire (p253). Olivair (p253) does tandem paragliding here (€100).

The Sierra Nevada has some of Andalucía's highest launch sites.

Canyoning

Exciting Andalucian destinations for careering down canyons include Cádiz' Sierra de Grazalema with Horizon (p138), Granada's Las Alpujarras with Nevadensis (p285), Jaén's Parque Natural Sierra de Cazorla, Segura y Las Villas with Tierraventura (p247), or Málaga's La Axarquía region with Salamandra (p196).

Water Sports & Yoga

All along Andalucía's beautiful coastline, beachside operators enable you to venture off in a kayak, try stand-up paddleboarding (SUP) and wobble your way through SUP yoga. Join a class, take a course, or simply hire the gear and go.

Yoga is soaring in popularity; Granada's Alpujarras (p282) and the Tarifa area (p151) on Cádiz' Costa de la Luz have lively yoga scenes with classes and retreats.

Horse Riding

Beautiful horses define Andalucía as much as feisty flamenco, and an ever-growing number of *picaderos* (stables) offer guided rides and classes across the region.

Typical ride prices are €30 to €40 for one or two hours and around €100 for a half-day. Most stables cater to all levels, offering beginner lessons, challenging trail rides and even multiday expeditions.

Where to Go

The hub of Andalucía's horse culture is Jerez de la Frontera (Cádiz), home of the famous Real Escuela Andaluza del Arte Ecuestre (p129) and the spring Feria del Caballo (p127). The nearby Yeguada de la Cartuja – Hierro del Bocado (www.yeguadacartuja.com) breeding centre offers a fascinating insight into Andalucía's equestrian world.

Horse-riding highlights include:

- Beach and dune rides outside Tarifa (p149) on Cádiz' Costa de la Luz.
- Mountain trails around Lanjarón (p283) in Granada's Alpujarras and Grazalema (p138) in Cádiz.
- Woodland rides around Doñana (p102).
- Hillside routes through Málaga's Axarquía near Cómpeta (p196) and around Ronda (p182).
- Off-the-beaten track rides through Huelva's rippling Sierra de Aracena (p107).

GREENWAYS

One of Spain's greatest environmental ideas in the last 20 years are its *vías verdes* (greenways; www.viasverdes.com): disused railway lines that have been transformed into designated paths for cyclists, walkers, horse riders and other nonmotorised transport, including wheelchairs. Since 1993, 2800km of Spain's 7500km of abandoned railway track have been converted into *vías verdes*.

Andalucía currently has 29 (totalling over 700km), with the 36km Vía Verde de la Sierra (p143) in Cádiz province usually considered the finest. Two more leading lights are Sevilla's 18.7km Vía Verde de la Sierra Norte (p87) and the 128km Vía Verde del Aceite (p234) across Jaén and Córdoba.

As former railway lines, the *vías verdes* have relatively slight gradients, and preserve many original engineering features (bridges, tunnels, viaducts). They're well marked with kilometre posts and equipped with maps, lookouts, picnic spots, bike hire, and old stations reimagined as cafes and hotels.

Kitesurfing, Windsurfing & Surfing

Thanks to the strong winds that batter the Strait of Gibraltar, Cádiz' Costa de la Luz plays host to Europe's liveliest windsurfing and kitesurfing scene. Windsurfing, the original favourite, kicked off in the early 1980s. Kitesurfing, the cooler, more extreme younger sibling, is now overtaking it in popularity. The choppy seas off the Costa de la Luz aren't always beginners' territory. May, June and September are usually the best months (calmer water, fewer people).

Kitesurfing Full-day equipment hire €90; six-hour beginner course €250.

Windsurfing Half-day equipment hire €60; five-day beginner course €250 to €350.

Surfing Two-hour group class €30; full board and wetsuit hire €20.

Where to Go

Tarifa (p149) Europe's windsurfing and kitesurfing capital.

Los Caños de Meca (p147) Another surfing/kitesurfing hotspot, northwest of Tarifa.

El Palmar (p147) Andalucía's best board-riding waves.

Rock Climbing

Mention Andalucía to rock-climbing enthusiasts and they'll reply 'El Chorro'. This sheer limestone gorge (p189) above the Río Guadalhorce, 50km northwest of Málaga, contains hundreds of climbing routes, from easy to ultra-difficult. Many of them start in the vicinity of the infamous and now hugely popular Caminito del Rey (p191), a notoriously narrow path that clings to the rock face.

Other climbable limestone crags are El Torcal de Antequera and Archidona (both north of Málaga) and Los Cahorros gorge (Sierra Nevada).

Information

For El Chorro, you can organise rock-climbing trips and classes through Finca La Campana (p190) or Andalucía Aventura (p190). The season is October to April. A one-day taster costs around €55.

Skiing & Snowboarding

Granada's Sierra Nevada (p282) is Europe's most southerly ski area. Although its slopes lack the mega-steep, off-piste action of France or Switzerland, their skiing potential is fantastic. These are the highest mountains in Europe outside the Alps and the Caucasus, with cross-country routes, 110km of runs and a top skiing elevation of 3300m. Snow can fall as early as November and linger until early May, and the slopes are suited to beginners and families as well as advanced skiers.

Information

One-day adult ski passes cost €47 to €52, while equipment rental costs €25 per day. A one-day ski class costs around €65. Peak season is Christmas to New Year and early February to early March.

Plan Your Trip

Family Travel

Andalucía's sunny climate, fun beaches, easy-going attitude and many attractions make it ideal for families. Whole families, often including several generations, sitting around a restaurant or bar table eating and chatting is a fundamental element of the Andalucian lifestyle, and children are welcomed at all but the most formal restaurants, as well as at most bars and hotels.

Children Will Love...

Museums & Galleries

Museo Casa de la Ciencia (p66), **Seville** Interactive hands-on displays bring science alive.

Museo Picasso Málaga (p164), **Málaga** The perfect introduction to the art of Pablo Picasso.

Museo Lara (p185), **Ronda** Exhibitions on witchcraft and torture instruments!

Pabellón de la Navegación (p67), **Seville** Learn about seafaring at this maritime museum.

Museo de Cádiz (p116), **Cádiz** Presided over by a pair of marble Phoenician sarcophagi.

Museo del Baile Flamenco (p62), **Seville** Daily flamenco performances at 7pm.

Palacio de Viana (p214), **Córdoba** A feast of vibrant flowers in a Renaissance palace.

Muelle de las Carabelas (p95), **La Rábida** Scramble around three replica Columbus ships.

Caves & Castles

Gruta de las Maravillas (p104), **Aracena** Explore 12 caverns in far north Huelva, including stunning underground pools.

La Geoda de Pulpí (p316), **Almería province** Kids over eight will love descending deep underground to discover Europe's largest geode.

Cueva de Nerja (p198), **Nerja** Full of spooky stalactites and stalagmites.

Keeping Costs Down

Accommodation

Book well ahead to ensure the most varied options and prices, and to bag family/four-person hotel rooms. Self-catering apartments geared towards families abound across Andalucía.

Sights

There are child discounts for admission to most sights, and those under four usually get in free. Book well ahead for headliners such as Granada's Alhambra.

Transport

Children get 40% off tickets on the high-speed AVE train (free for kids under four) and often discounts on ferries, but pay full price on most buses. Hiring bikes (or joining a bike tour) is a great, fun way to see cities like Málaga without blowing the budget.

Eating

Plenty of restaurants have kids' menus or can rustle up half-portions for little ones; some even have a kids-only *menú del día*!

Activities

Kids typically pay reduced prices for tours and the like, and there are plenty of fun, free tours you can join.

St Michael's Cave (p156), **Gibraltar** Huge natural grotto with a lake and auditorium.

Guadix (p290), **Granada Province** Sleep in a cave-house and visit the cave-museum, northeast of Granada.

Cueva de la Pileta (p183), **Benaoján** Fascinating, uncommercial caves with narrow, low walkways, lakes and cave paintings, near Ronda.

Castles Jaén (p232), Segura de la Sierra (p253), Almodóvar del Río (p227), Olvera (p142), La Calahorra (p290) and Málaga (p164) have centuries-old castles to amuse all.

Wildlife

Parque Nacional de Doñana (www.miteco.gob.es) Look for deer, wild boar and elusive Iberian lynx in Spain's favourite national park.

Whale-watching (p149), **Tarifa** Spot whales and dolphins at one of Europe's top spots for this.

Dolphin-watching (p157), **Gibraltar** The strait of Gibraltar is home to several species of dolphin.

Mariposario de Benalmádena (p176), **Benalmádena** A butterfly park with 1500 fluttering beauties and a giant tortoise.

Parque Natural Sierras de Cazorla, Segura y Las Villas (p249) Glimpse wild boar, mouflon, ibex and deer, and there's a 5km mini train for kids around an animal-rescue centre.

Theme Parks

Tivoli World, Arroyo de la Miel (www.tivoliworld.net) As well as various rides and slides, there are daily dance, musical and children's events.

Isla Mágica (p68), **Seville** Pirate shows, roller coasters and more.

Oasys Mini Hollywood (p304), **Desierto de Tabernas** Wild West shows, stagecoaches, can-can dancers and a zoo at this former film set.

Other Adventures

Fairs & fiestas Annual town and village fairs always include a funfair with rides.

Windsurfing & kitesurfing (p149) Older children can take courses at Tarifa on the Cádiz coast.

Trip to Morocco (p154) Take a speedy ferry from Tarifa to Tangier for the day.

Aventura Amazonia (p180), **Marbella** Adventure playground with zip line circuits.

Cycling (p170) Cities like Málaga and Seville have great bike tours and rental for family fun.

Water sports (p293), **La Herradura** Granada's Costa Tropical is perfect for windsurfing, paddle-boarding, snorkelling and kayaking.

Vías Verdes (p40) Across Andalucía, 29 disused railways have been converted into flat, family-friendly cycling, walking and horse-riding tracks.

Region by Region

Sevilla Province

Seville city (p68) has great leafy parks, boat trips, the glittering Real Alcázar (p56) and a popular amusement park, Isla Mágica (p68).

Huelva Province

The big draw for families in Huelva province is the wonderful Parque Nacional de Doñana (p98), where you can head out on safari-style trips to spot deer, wild boar, birds and, if you're very lucky, Iberian lynx. For something off-the-beaten-track, head north to the cosy mountain hotels of the Sierra de Aracena (p107), and ride the old mining railway at Minas de Riotinto (p103).

Cádiz Province & Gibraltar

Older kids will love kitesurfing and windsurfing in Tarifa (p149), which is one of the major destinations for the sports in Europe and also has wonderful horse riding along blissful beaches. Tarifa is the launchpad for whale- and dolphin-spotting expeditions in the Strait of Gibraltar, too. You can hop on a ferry to Morocco for the day from Tarifa, head into the Parque Nacional de Doñana (p98) for wildlife-spotting from Sanlúcar de Barrameda, or visit the macaques on the Rock of Gibraltar (p156).

Málaga Province

The Costa del Sol's shallow waters, lively beaches and boat rides will have the whole family smiling, while Málaga city's (p164) museums and galleries will keep older kids entertained. The majority of Andalucía's family-oriented theme parks, resorts and entertainment are in Málaga province, especially around Fuengirola (p178), Benalmádena (p175) and Marbella (p179).

Córdoba Province

Kids of all ages are bound to delight in the shimmering Mezquita (p206) and flower-filled alleys of Córdoba city (p206), and there are some lovely country escapes for families across the province (though it gets very hot from June to mid-September!).

Jaén Province

Families heading for less-visited Jaén province are usually seeking out the wild expanses of the Parque Natural Sierras de Cazorla, Segura y Las Villas (p249), Spain's largest protected area and home to some of Andalucía's best wildlife-spotting: ibex, deer, mouflon, wild boar and the endangered lammergeier. You could combine this with Jaén's thrilling Parque Natural Sierra de Andújar (p236), where a lucky few may spot an Iberian lynx or a wolf.

Granada Province

Visitors of all ages will be mesmerised by Granada's Alhambra (p258). Horse riding and hillside rambles to suit all levels await in the Alpujarras, or hit the Sierra Nevada ski season (p282). The gentle beaches of the Costa Tropical (p291) are great for water sports.

Almería Province

Though Almería isn't Andalucía's most obvious region for families, the Wild West shoot-'em-up shows in the Desierto de Tabernas film locations (p311) are bound to knock kids' socks off, and there are glorious beaches around Cabo de Gata (p313), with good snorkelling and other watery pursuits.

Good to Know

Look out for the icon for family-friendly suggestions throughout this guide.

Accommodation Andalucía's accommodation caters to families of all kinds and sizes, and there are plenty of self-catering apartments. Most hotels provide cots and extra beds; enquire ahead.

Dining out It's rare to find a restaurant where children are not welcome. Even if restaurants do not advertise children's menus (though some do), they will normally be willing to prepare a small portion or suggest a suitable tapa or two. High chairs in restaurants are increasingly common. Take the kids for a 5pm *merienda* (afternoon snack) to tide them over until later-than-usual dinners.

Late nights Local children stay up late and at fiesta time it's commonplace to see even tiny kids toddling the streets at 2am.

Car travel You can hire car seats for infants and children from most car-rental firms; book ahead.

Prams & strollers Old city centres have narrow pavements and cobbled lanes, making navigating prams and strollers tricky, and some major sights (such as the core sections of Granada's Alhambra) don't allow them in. Best to bring a baby-carrier.

Breastfeeding Plenty of women in Spain breastfeed in public and you should feel comfortable doing so if you choose to.

Stuff for babies Pharmacies and supermarkets sell nappies, baby formula, sterilising solutions and ready-made food. Public baby-changing facilities are rare (bring your own changing mat).

When to go July and August are very busy in the main tourist resorts. In May, June, September and October, the weather is warm enough for paddling in the sea but hasn't yet hit serious sizzle.

Useful Resources

Lonely Planet Kids (www.lonelyplanetkids.com) Loads of activities and great family travel blog content.

Book: First Words Spanish (shop.lonelyplanet.com) A beautifully illustrated introduction to the Spanish language for ages five to eight.

Andalucia.com (www.andalucia.com) Excellent guide to the whole of Andalucía, with family-friendly tips.

Regions at a Glance

Sevilla Province

Food & Drink
Architecture
Music & Dance

Tapas

With an estimated 3000-plus bars, Seville is renowned for its terrific tapas scene. Traditional bars keep it simple while adventurous new-school outfits cook up a creative storm. Local cured hams, fresh seafood and slow-cooked meats shine across the province.

Catedral, Alcázar & More

Seville's cityscape is a thrilling patchwork of architectural styles, from the Arabesque Mudéjar of the Alcázar to the bombastic Gothic of the cathedral and the extravagant baroque of ancient churches. Beyond the capital, architectural jewels await in Osuna, Carmona and Écija.

Flamenco

Andalucía's greatest stash of flamenco venues lies in wait in soulful Seville. Triana reveals intimate *peñas* (clubs), while the Barrio de Santa Cruz hosts authentic *tablaos* (choreographed flamenco shows). During the raucous Feria de Abril, *sevillanas* (flamenco-influenced folk dances) steal the show.

p48

Huelva Province

Wildlife
Hiking
History

Doñana

The Parque Nacional de Doñana is one of Europe's most awe-inspiring protected spaces. Here, the Río Guadalquivir delta straddles Huelva and Sevilla provinces and treats visitors to sightings of rare birds and mammals: deer, wild boar and, if you're lucky, Iberian lynx. The gleaming pilgrimage hamlet of El Rocío makes an alluring base.

Pastoral Trails

Huelva's little-touristed northern reaches harbour the enchanting oak forests and highland *dehesa* (pastures where the region's famed black pigs forage for acorns) of the Parque Natural Sierra de Aracena y Picos de Aroche, a bucolic ancient region criss-crossed by easy trails between sleepy villages and secluded country hotels.

Columbus & the Moors

Huelva province unveils some surprising historical heirlooms, from Christopher Columbus relics to the Almohad town of Niebla and the exquisite miniature 9th-century *mezquita* (mosque) in remote Almonaster la Real.

p90

Cádiz Province & Gibraltar

Beaches
White Towns
Food & Drink

White-Sand Wonders

The sandy blonde Atlantic beaches that sweep along Cádiz' windblown Costa de la Luz are some of Spain's most beautiful and unspoilt. Go kitesurfing in Tarifa, soak up the sun beside Roman ruins in Bolonia, lounge in mellow Los Caños de Meca and hit the sunny *chiringuitos* (snack bars) in Cádiz city.

Hilltop Settlements

They're all here, the famous white towns, with their ruined hilltop castles, geranium-filled balconies, twisting alleys and somnolent churches. Arcos, Vejer, Zahara, Olvera...the ancient sentinels on a once-volatile frontier that divided Islamic and Christian Spain.

Sherry, Tuna & Fusion

Wild Atlantic bluefin tuna, caught using the Phoenician *almadraba* method, is the culinary star of Cádiz' Costa de la Luz, from rowdy tapas bars to Michelin addresses, while towns like Tarifa and Vejer put a deliciously international-influenced spin on glorious local produce. Locally made sherry is the perfect accompaniment.

p112

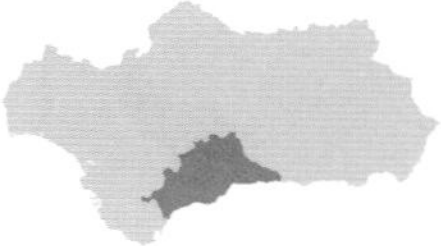

Málaga Province

Beaches
Art
Food & Drink

Coastal Resorts

Málaga province's popular beaches bag more tourist euros than the rest of Andalucía put together. Choose according to your style and budget – will it be easygoing Estepona, glitzy Marbella, party-hard Torremolinos, arty Málaga or charming (if touristed) Nerja?

Picasso & Beyond

Picasso may have left Málaga when he was only 10 years old, but the great master's birthplace continues to celebrate his legacy with the marvellous Museo Picasso and the intimate house where he was born in 1881. Meanwhile, an ever-growing slew of other museums and galleries bolster the city's claim to be Andalucía's 'art capital'.

Regional Dishes

Along Málaga's coastline, simple beachside *chiringuitos* and heaving tapas bars snuggle up against Michelin-starred seafood restaurants. Inland, Antequera serves fine soups and desserts, while Ronda is the home of mountain stews, meaty specialities and up-and-coming wines.

p160

Córdoba Province

Architecture
Food & Drink
Natural Spaces

Córdoba Caliphate

The 10th-century Córdoba caliphate defined Islamic architecture 1000 years ago. You can see it – intact – in all its glittering glory in Córdoba's famous Mezquita or elegantly ruined at Medina Azahara just outside the city.

Wine & Olive Oil

Step aside Jerez – southern Córdoba province produces its very own sweet, sherry-like Montilla-Moriles DO wines from Pedro Ximénez grapes, in ancient bodegas where local experts lead tours and tastings. And all those rippling olive groves yield some of the country's most prized olive oil, especially around Priego de Córdoba and Baena.

Off the Beaten Track

South from Córdoba city, the Parque Natural Sierras Subbéticas encompasses memorably beautiful emerald-green mountains riven by deep ravines and caves and surrounded by handsome white villages. North of Córdoba stretch the boundless horizons of the Los Pedroches region in the remote Sierra Morena.

p202

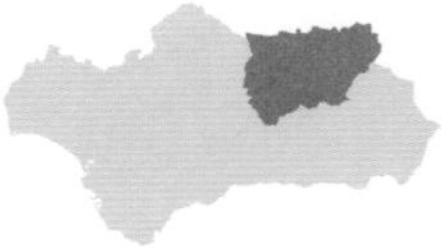

Jaén Province

Natural Spaces
Wildlife
Architecture

Andalucian Wilderness

Jaén province safeguards Spain's largest protected area, the dramatic Parque Natural Sierras de Cazorla, Segura y Las Villas, as well as the lesser-known, wildlife-rich Parque Natural Sierra de Andújar (home to the world's largest Iberian lynx population).

Rare Fauna

Lynx, wild boar, mouflon and endangered birds like the black vulture, Spanish imperial eagle and lammergeier are hardly ubiquitous in Andalucía. Your best chance of spotting these rare animals is in the quieter corners of Jaén province, where protected parks and craggy mountains break the never-ending expanse of olive groves.

Renaissance Towns

Renaissance architecture makes a cameo appearance in Andalucía courtesy of Jaén province's two Unesco-listed pearls – Úbeda and Baeza – plus its less-heralded provincial capital Jaén, whose grandiose cathedral is worthy of Granada or Seville.

p228

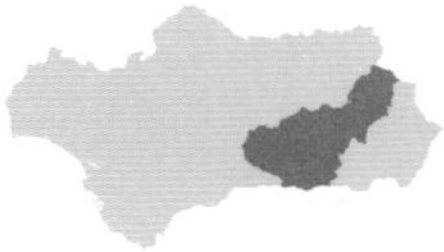

Granada Province

Architecture
White Villages
Outdoor Adventure

Alhambra & Granada

Lovely Granada city is a magnificent mix of just about every architectural style known to European building – from the hillside Moorish Albayzín quarter, the charming Realejo (the old Jewish district) and the baroque-Renaissance cathedral to the magical, unparalleled Nasrid-era Alhambra.

Las Alpujarras

Matching Cádiz province's white towns for spectacular beauty and fascinating history, Granada's villages soar higher, among the steep valleys of Las Alpujarras, where age-old artisan crafts, mountain recipes, tempting walking trails, delightful rural hotels and endless views await.

Hill Walks & Adrenalin

The mighty peaks of the Sierra Nevada and the lower, still-spectacular slopes of Las Alpujarras set an epic stage for exhilarating hiking of all levels, while this region's horse riding, skiing and mountain biking keep the adrenalin pumping.

p254

Almería Province

Beaches
History
White Towns

Protected Coast

Forgotten, lucky or perhaps just too arid to develop, the rugged cliffs and blissfully uncrowded beaches of Cabo de Gata have escaped overdevelopment and are now protected as a natural park, guarding the most precious flora and marine life in the southern Mediterranean.

Moorish Heritage

Often overlooked by Alhambra pilgrims, the city of Almería has plenty of its own stories to tell, many of them hailing from the pre-Christian era. Check out the old town and Alcazaba before treating yourself to a soothing *hammam* and some fabulous tapas.

The Remote North

Head to little-visited far northern Almería province for an off-the-beaten-track adventure to the isolated Los Vélez region, whose three white towns give way to Unesco-listed cave art and the wild Sierra de María mountains. Vélez Blanco's 16th-century Renaissance castle feels plucked from a fairy tale.

p294

On the Road

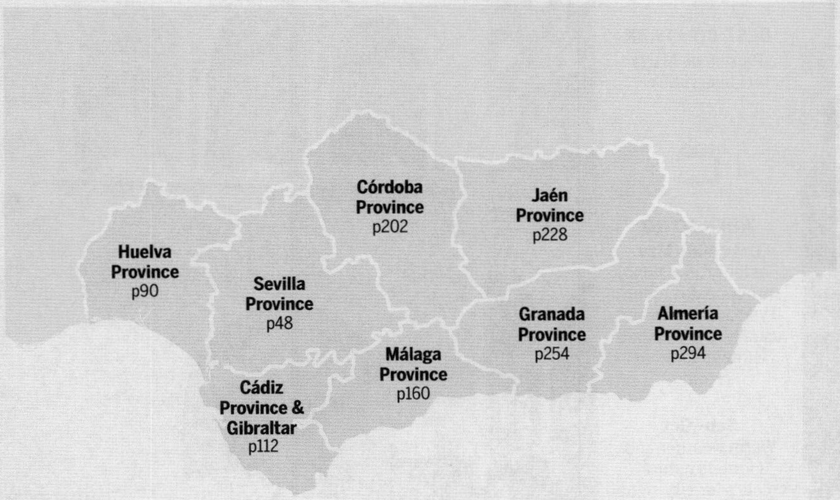

Córdoba Province p202
Jaén Province p228
Huelva Province p90
Sevilla Province p48
Granada Province p254
Almería Province p294
Málaga Province p160
Cádiz Province & Gibraltar p112

AT A GLANCE

POPULATION
1.95 million

CAPITAL
Seville

BEST URBAN MANSION
Casa de Pilatos (p62)

BEST BAROQUE
Iglesia de San Luis de los Franceses (p64)

BEST CITY PARK
Parque de María Luisa (p66)

WHEN TO GO

Late Mar–May
Easter processions, spring fiestas, countryside in bloom and usually fine weather, without summer crowds.

Sep–Oct
Warm weather and glorious natural colours for city sightseeing and country walking.

Dec–Feb
Low-season hotel rates, no crowds, chances of winter sun.

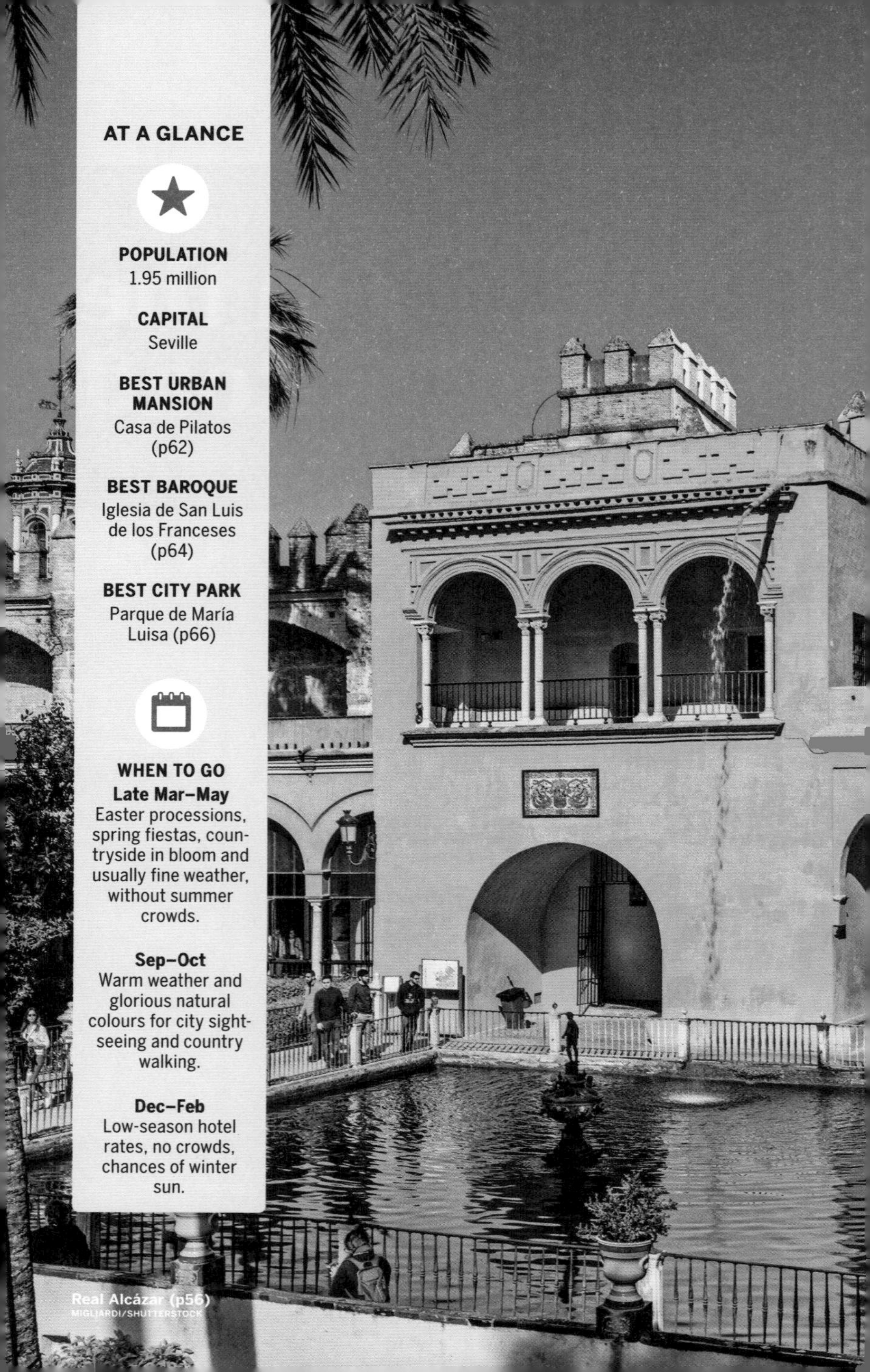

Real Alcázar (p56)
MIGLIARDI/SHUTTERSTOCK

Sevilla Province

From Moorish palaces and Roman ruins to sun-baked plains and bosky river valleys, Sevilla province boasts some of Andalucía's greatest hits and least-known treasures. Seville, the region's charismatic and high-spirited capital is famed for its artistic and architectural riches, flamenco clubs and teeming tapas bars; this heady riverside metropolis provides a dazzling introduction to the region. Just outside Seville, the ruins of ancient Itálica make for Andalucía's most thrilling Roman site. To the east, the vast, shimmering plains of La Campiña are punctuated by a string of handsome towns, most notably Carmona, Écija and Osuna, while to the north, the remote and little-visited Parque Natural Sierra Norte de Sevilla offers fine walking and hearty country food.

INCLUDES

SEVILLE

POP 688,710

Drenched in sunshine for much of the year, Seville is one of Spain's hottest and most seductive cities. Its historic centre, lorded over by a colossal Gothic cathedral, is an intoxicating mix of sumptuous Mudéjar palaces, baroque churches and romantic, orange-scented patios. Cramped flamenco clubs keep the intensity of this centuries-old tradition alive, while aristocratic mansions recall the city's past as a showcase Moorish capital and, later, a cosmopolitan metropolis rich on the back of New World trade.

But while history reverberates all around, Seville is as much about the here and now as the past. It's about eating tapas in a crowded bar or seeing out the day over a drink on a buzzing plaza. *Sevillanos* have long since mastered the art of celebrating and the city's Semana Santa and Feria de Abril festivities are among Spain's most heartfelt.

History

According to legend, Seville was founded by the Greek demigod Hercules. More plausibly, it probably started life as an Iberian settlement before growing to become an important Roman port (Hispalis). But it was under a succession of Islamic rulers that the city really came into its own. It enjoyed a heyday in the late 11th century as a major cultural centre under the Abbadid dynasty, and then again in the 12th century when the Almohads took control and built, among other things, a great mosque where the cathedral now stands. Almohad power dwindled after the disastrous defeat of Las Navas de Tolosa in 1212, and in 1248 the city fell to Castilla's Catholic king Fernando III (El Santo; the Saint).

Some 240-odd years later, the discovery of the Americas paved the way for another golden era. In 1503 the city was awarded an official monopoly on Spanish trade with the new-found continent. The riches poured in and Seville blossomed into one of the world's largest, richest and most cosmopolitan cities.

But it was not to last. A plague in 1649 killed half the city's population, and as the 17th century wore on, the Río Guadalquivir became more silted and difficult to navigate. In 1717 the Casa de la Contratación (Contracting House), the government office controlling commerce with the Americas, was transferred to Cádiz, and Seville went into decline.

The beginnings of industry in the mid-19th century saw a spate of major building projects in the city. Notably, the first iron bridge across the Guadalquivir, the Puente de Isabel II, was built in 1852, and in 1869 the old Almohad walls were knocked down to let the city expand. The city's hosting of the 1929 Exposición Iberoamericana led to further building projects.

The Spanish Civil War saw the city fall to the Nationalists in 1936 shortly after the outbreak of hostilities, despite strong resistance in working-class areas (which brought savage reprisals).

More recently, the city has undergone something of a roller-coaster ride. It was made capital of the autonomous Andalucía region in 1982, and in 1992 it hosted the Expo world fair, leading to major infrastructure improvements.

By the early 2000s, Seville's economy was on the up thanks to a mix of tourism, commerce, technology and industry. But the 2008 financial crisis hit the city hard and the economy tanked, reaching rock bottom in 2012. Recent years have seen growth returning to the Spanish economy and tourism taking off in Seville. However, unemployment, particularly among young people, remains a worrying issue.

Sights

Catedral & Barrio de Santa Cruz

Once Seville's medieval *judería* (Jewish quarter), Santa Cruz is a picturesque, tightly packed warren of cobbled alleyways, white buildings and plant-decked plazas perfumed with orange blossom. Nearby, Seville's immense Gothic cathedral dominates the city skyline and the Real Alcázar stuns with its Arabesque interiors and fabulous gardens.

★**Catedral & Giralda** CATHEDRAL
(Map p58; ☎902 09 96 92; www.catedraldesevilla.es; Plaza del Triunfo; adult/child incl Iglesia Colegial del Divino Salvador €10/free, incl rooftop guided tours €16, 4.30-6pm Mon free; ⏲11am-3.30pm Mon, to 5pm Tue-Sat, 2.30-6pm Sun Sep-Jun, 10.30am-4pm Mon, to 6pm Tue-Sat, 2-7pm Sun Jul & Aug) Seville's showpiece church is awe-inspiring in its scale and majesty. The world's largest Gothic cathedral, it was built between 1434 and 1517 over the remains of what had previously been the city's main mosque. Highlights include the Giralda, the mighty

Sevilla Province Highlights

1 **Real Alcázar** (p56) Revelling in the astonishing Mudéjar decor of Seville's royal palace complex.

2 **Catedral & Giralda** (p50) Admiring Christopher Columbus' tomb at the world's largest Gothic cathedral.

3 **Hospital de los Venerables Sacerdotes** (p61) Contemplating masterpieces by Golden Age maestro Diego Velázquez.

4 **Itálica** (p80) Roaming through the ruins of Seville's very own Pompeii.

5 **Museo Histórico Municipal** (p86) Marvelling at magnificent mosaics at Écija's terrific museum.

6 **Colegiata de Santa María de la Asunción** (p84) Browsing baroque treasures in Osuna's landmark church.

7 **Carmona** (p81) Strolling the town's historic centre, an attractive hilltop enclave of Moorish forts and Mudéjar churches.

Seville

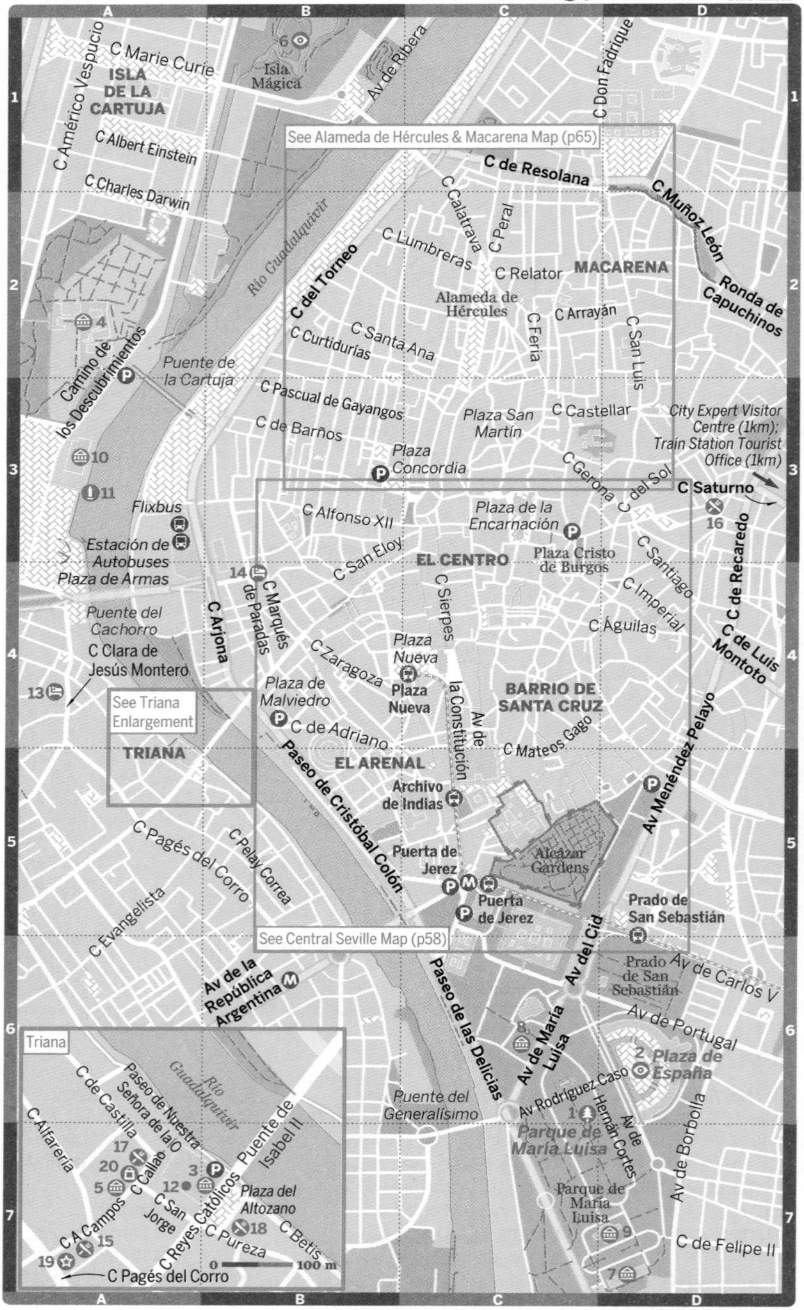
0 500 m
0 0.25 miles
A
B
C
D
1
2
3
4
5
6
7
C Marie Curie
ISLA DE LA CARTUJA
Isla Mágica
6
Av de Ribera
C Américo Vespucio
C Albert Einstein
C Charles Darwin
C Don Fadrique
See Alameda de Hércules & Macarena Map (p65)
C de Resolana
C Muñoz León
Ronda de Capuchinos
Río Guadalquivir
C Calatrava
C Peral
C Lumbreras
C del Torneo
C Relator
MACARENA
Alameda de Hércules
C Feria
C Arrayán
C San Luis
4
Camino de los Descubrimientos
Puente de la Cartuja
C Santa Ana
C Curtidurías
C Pascual de Gayangos
Plaza San Martín
C Castellar
City Expert Visitor Centre (1km); Train Station Tourist Office (1km)
C de Barños
10
Plaza Concordia
C Gerona
C del Sol
C Saturno
16
11
Flixbus
C Alfonso XII
Plaza de la Encarnación
Estación de Autobuses Plaza de Armas
C San Eloy
EL CENTRO
Plaza Cristo de Burgos
C Santiago
C de Recaredo
14
C Marqués de Paradas
C Arjona
C Sierpes
C Imperial
Puente del Cachorro
C Águilas
C Clara de Jesús Montero
C Zaragoza
Plaza Nueva
C de Luis Montoto
13
Plaza de Malviedro
Plaza Nueva
la Constitución
Av de
BARRIO DE SANTA CRUZ
See Triana Enlargement
TRIANA
C de Adriano
C Mateos Gago
Av Menéndez Pelayo
EL ARENAL
Paseo de Cristóbal Colón
Archivo de Indias
C Pagés del Corro
C Pelay Correa
Puerta de Jerez
Alcázar Gardens
Puerta de Jerez
Prado de San Sebastián
C Evangelista
See Central Seville Map (p58)
Av de la República Argentina
Paseo de las Delicias
Av del Cid
Prado de San Sebastián
Av de Carlos V
Av de Portugal
8
Av de María Luisa
2 Plaza de España
Puente del Generalísimo
Av Rodríguez Caso
1
Av de Hernán Cortés
Parque de María Luisa
Av de Borbolla
Parque de María Luisa
9
C de Felipe II
7
Triana
C de Castilla
Paseo de Nuestra Señora de la O
Río Guadalquivir
Puente de Isabel II
C Alfarería
17
20
C Callao
3
5
12
Plaza del Altozano
C San Jorge
18
C Reyes Católicos
C Pureza
C Betis
C A Campos
15
19
0 100 m
C Pagés del Corro

Seville

Top Sights
1 Parque de María Luisa......C6
2 Plaza de España......D6

Sights
3 Castillo de San Jorge......B7
4 Centro Andaluz de Arte Contemporáneo......A2
5 Centro Cerámica Triana......A7
6 Isla Mágica......B1
7 Museo Arqueológico......D7
8 Museo Casa de la Ciencia......C6
9 Museo de Artes y Costumbres Populares......D7
10 Pabellón de la Navegación......A3
11 Torre Mirador......A3

Activities, Courses & Tours
12 Taller Andaluz de Cocina......A7

Sleeping
13 Hotel Monte Triana......A4
14 La Parada del Marqués......B4

Eating
15 Alfarería 21......A7
16 Bar Casa Eme......D3
17 Casa Cuesta......A7
18 Manu Jara Dulcería......B7

Entertainment
19 Casa Anselma......A7

Shopping
20 Cerámica Triana......A7

bell tower, which incorporates the mosque's original minaret, the monumental tomb of Christopher Columbus, and the Capilla Mayor with an astonishing gold altarpiece.

The history of the cathedral goes back to the 15th century but the history of Christian worship on the site dates to the mid-13th century. In 1248 the Castilian king Fernando III captured Seville from its Almohad rulers and transformed their great 12th-century mosque into a church. Some 153 years later, in 1401, the city's ecclesiastical authorities decided to replace the former mosque, which had been damaged by an earthquake in 1356, with a spectacular new cathedral: 'Let's construct a church so large future generations will think we were mad', they quipped (or so legend has it).

The result is the staggering cathedral you see today, officially known as the Catedral de Santa María de la Sede. It's one of the world's largest churches and a veritable treasure trove of art, with notable works by Zurbarán, Murillo, Goya and others.

Audio guides cost €3. Note also that children under nine are not permitted on rooftop tours. You can also tour the cathedral's stained-glass windows – see the website for details and booking.

➡ Exterior

With its immense flying buttresses and Gothic embellishments, the cathedral's exterior provides a suitably dramatic shell for the treasures within. Pause to look at the **Puerta del Perdón** (now the cathedral's exit) on Calle Alemanes, which is one of the few remaining elements of the original mosque.

➡ Sala del Pabellón

Selected treasures from the cathedral's art collection are exhibited in this room, the first after the ticket office. Much of what's displayed here, as elsewhere in the cathedral, is the work of masters from Seville's 17th-century Golden Age.

➡ Tomb of Christopher Columbus

Once inside the cathedral proper, head right until you come to the tomb of Christopher Columbus (the Sepulcro de Cristóbal Colón) in front of the **Puerta del Príncipe** (Door of the Prince). The monument supposedly contains the remains of the great explorer, but debate continues as to whether the bones are actually his.

Columbus' remains were moved many times after his death (in 1506 in Valladolid, northern Spain), and there are those who claim his real bones lie in Santo Domingo. Certainly his bones spent time in the Dominican Republic after they were shipped to Spanish-controlled Hispaniola from their original resting place, the Monasterio de la Cartuja (p67), in 1537. However, they were later sent to Havana and returned to Seville in 1898.

DNA testing in 2006 proved a match between the bones supposed to be Columbus' and bones known to be from his brother Diego. And while that didn't conclusively solve the mystery, it strongly suggested that the great man really is interred in the tomb that bears his name.

➡ Sacristía de los Cálices

To the right of Columbus' tomb are a series of rooms containing some of the cathedral's

Seville Cathedral

THE HIGHLIGHTS TOUR

In 1402 the inspired architects of Seville set out on one of the most grandiose building projects in medieval history. Their aim was to shock and amaze future generations with the size and magnificence of the building. It took until 1506 to complete the project, but 500 years later Seville Cathedral is still the largest Gothic cathedral in the world.

To avoid getting lost, orient yourself by the main highlights. To the right of the visitor entrance is the grand 1 **Tomb of Columbus**. Continue into the southeastern corner to uncover some major art treasures: a Goya in the Sacristía de los Cálices, a Zurbarán in the 2 **Sacristía Mayor**, and Murillo's shining *La inmaculada* in the Sala Capitular. Skirt the cathedral's eastern wall past the often-closed 3 **Capilla Real**, home to some important royal tombs. By now it's impossible to avoid the lure of the 4 **Capilla Mayor** with its fantastical altarpiece. Hidden over in the northwest corner is the 5 **Capilla de San Antonio** with a legendary Murillo. That huge doorway nearby is the rarely opened 6 **Puerta de la Asunción**. Make for the 7 **Giralda** next, stealing admiring looks at the high, vaulted ceiling on the way. After looking down on the cathedral's immense footprint, descend and depart via the 8 **Patio de los Naranjos**.

TOP TIPS

- Don't try to visit the Alcázar and cathedral on the same day. There is far too much to take in.
- Take time to admire the cathedral from the outside. It's particularly stunning at night from the Plaza de la Virgen de los Reyes, and from across the river in Triana.
- Skip the line by booking tickets online or buying them at the Iglesia Colegial del Divino Salvador on Plaza del Salvador.

TRABANTOS / SHUTTERSTOCK ©

Capilla de San Antonio
One of 80 interior chapels, you'll need to hunt down this little gem notable for housing Murillo's 1656 painting, *Vision of St Anthony of Padua*. The work was pillaged by thieves in 1874 but later restored.

Patio de los Naranjos
Inhale the perfume of 60 Sevillan orange trees in a cool patio bordered by fortress-like walls – a surviving remnant of the original 12th-century mosque. Exit is gained via the horseshoe-shaped Puerta del Perdón.

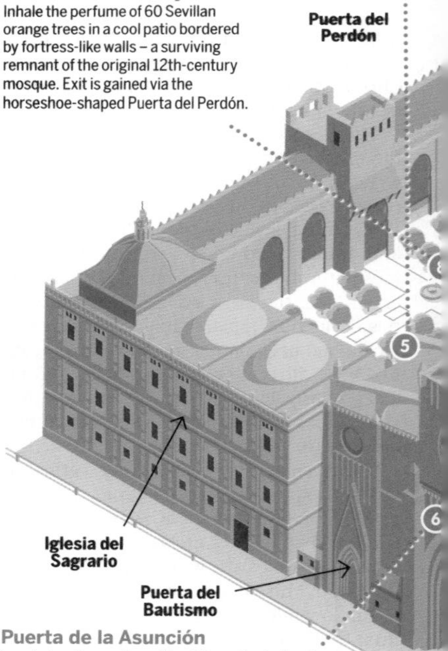

Puerta de la Asunción
Located on the western side of the cathedral and also known as the Puerta Mayor, these huge, rarely opened doors are pushed back during Semana Santa to allow solemn processions of Catholic *hermandades* (brotherhoods) to pass through.

DMITRY SHAKIN / GETTY IMAGES ©

MISTERVLAD / SHUTTERSTOCK ©

Giralda

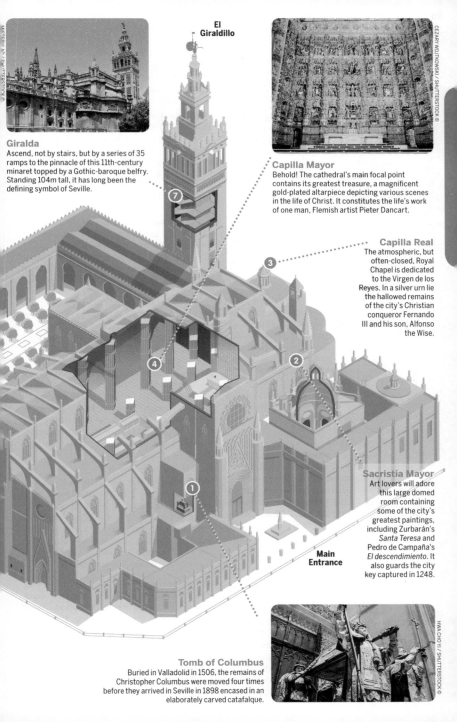

Ascend, not by stairs, but by a series of 35 ramps to the pinnacle of this 11th-century minaret topped by a Gothic-baroque belfry. Standing 104m tall, it has long been the defining symbol of Seville.

CEZARY WOJTKOWSKI / SHUTTERSTOCK ©

Capilla Mayor

Behold! The cathedral's main focal point contains its greatest treasure, a magnificent gold-plated altarpiece depicting various scenes in the life of Christ. It constitutes the life's work of one man, Flemish artist Pieter Dancart.

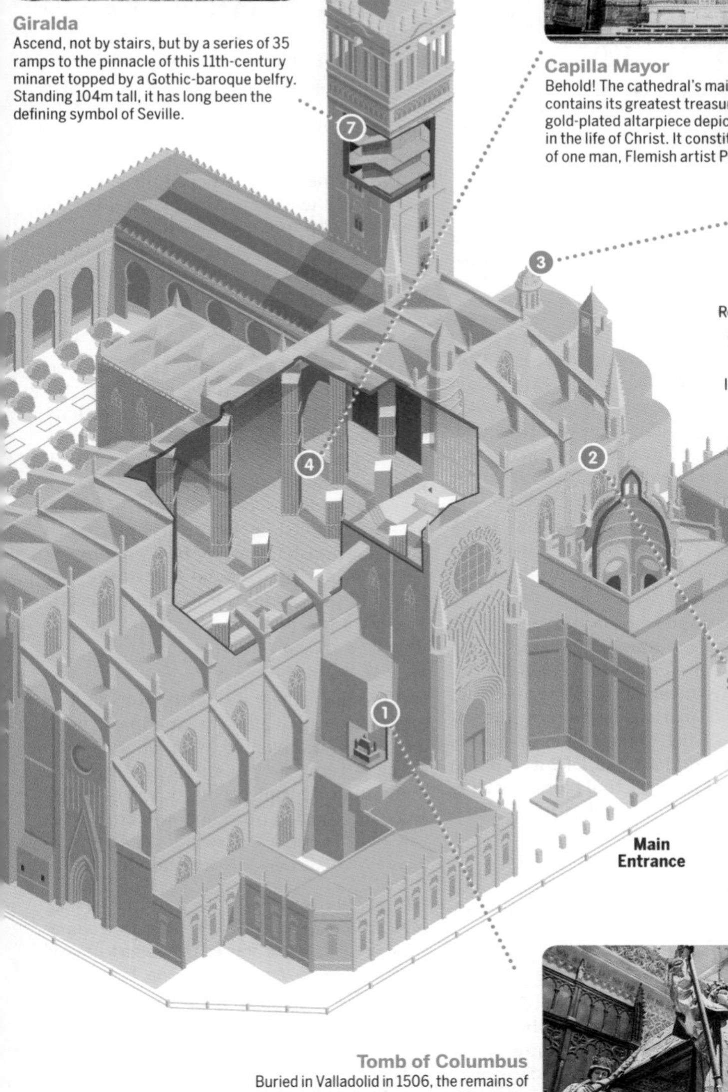

Capilla Real

The atmospheric, but often-closed, Royal Chapel is dedicated to the Virgen de los Reyes. In a silver urn lie the hallowed remains of the city's Christian conqueror Fernando III and his son, Alfonso the Wise.

Sacristía Mayor

Art lovers will adore this large domed room containing some of the city's greatest paintings, including Zurbarán's *Santa Teresa* and Pedro de Campaña's *El descendimiento*. It also guards the city key captured in 1248.

Tomb of Columbus

Buried in Valladolid in 1506, the remains of Christopher Columbus were moved four times before they arrived in Seville in 1898 encased in an elaborately carved catafalque.

HWA CHO YI / SHUTTERSTOCK ©

CATEDRAL TICKETS

To avoid queueing for tickets at the cathedral (p50), you can either book through the cathedral's website or buy tickets at the Iglesia Colegial del Divino Salvador (p62). There are rarely queues at this church, which sells combined tickets covering admission to the church, the cathedral and the Giralda. Note also that entry to the cathedral is free on Monday afternoons between 4.30pm and 6pm. Numbers are limited, though, so you'll need to reserve a slot on the website.

greatest masterpieces. First up is the Sacristy of the Chalices, behind the Capilla de los Dolores, where Francisco de Goya's painting of the Sevillan martyrs, *Santas Justa y Rufina* (1817), hangs above the altar.

➡ Sacristía Mayor

Next along is this large room with a finely carved stone cupola, created between 1528 and 1547. Pedro de Campaña's 1547 *El descendimiento* (Descent from the Cross), above the central altar at the southern end, and Francisco de Zurbarán's *Santa Teresa*, to its right, are two of the cathedral's most precious paintings. Also look out for the *Custodia de Juan de Arfe*, a huge 475kg silver monstrance made in the 1580s by Renaissance metalsmith Juan de Arfe.

➡ Sala Capitular

The circular chapter house, also called the Cabildo, features a stunning carved dome and a Murillo masterpiece, *La inmaculada*, set high above the archbishop's throne. The room, whose design was inspired by Michelangelo's Piazza del Campidoglio in Rome, was built between 1558 and 1592 as a venue for meetings of the cathedral hierarchy. Also impressive is the Antecabildo with its decorated vaulted ceiling.

➡ Capilla Mayor

Even in a church as spectacular as this, the Capilla Mayor (Main Chapel) stands out with its astonishing Gothic retable, reckoned to be the world's largest altarpiece. Begun by Flemish sculptor Pieter Dancart in 1482 and finished by others in 1564, this sea of gilt and polychromed wood holds more than 1000 carved biblical figures. At the centre of the lowest level is a tiny 13th-century silver-plated cedar image of the *Virgen de la sede* (Virgin of the See), patron of the cathedral.

➡ Coro

West of the Capilla Mayor and dominating the central nave is the 16th-century Coro (Choir). This giant box-like structure incorporates 114 elaborate wooden seats in Gothic-Mudéjar style and a vast organ.

➡ Capilla de San Antonio

The chapels along the sides of the cathedral hold yet more artistic treasures. Of particular note is the Capilla de San Antonio, at the western end of the northern aisle, housing Murillo's gigantic 1656 depiction of the *Visión de San Antonio de Padua* (Vision of St Anthony of Padua). The painting was the victim of a daring art heist in 1874.

➡ Giralda

In the northeastern corner of the cathedral you'll find the entrance to the Giralda. The climb to the top involves walking up 35 ramps, built so that the guards could ride up on horseback, and a small flight of stairs at the top. Your reward is sensational rooftop views.

The decorative brick tower, which tops out at 104m, was the minaret of the mosque, constructed between 1184 and 1198 at the height of Almohad power. Its proportions, delicate brick-pattern decoration, and colour, which changes with the light, make it perhaps Spain's most perfect Islamic building. The topmost parts – from bell level up – were added in the 16th century, when Spanish Christians were busy 'improving on' surviving Islamic buildings. At the very top is *El Giraldillo*, a 16th-century bronze weather vane representing 'faith', that has become a symbol of Seville.

➡ Patio de los Naranjos

Outside the cathedral's northern flank, this patio was originally the mosque's main courtyard. It's planted with 66 *naranjos* (orange trees), and has a small Visigothic fountain in the centre. Look out for a stuffed crocodile hanging over the courtyard's doorway – it's a replica of a gift the Sultan of Egypt gave Alfonso X in around 1260.

★ Real Alcázar PALACE

(Map p58; ☎954 50 23 24; www.alcazarsevilla.org; Plaza del Triunfo; adult/student/child €11.50/3/free, 6-7pm Mon Apr-Sep free, 4-5pm Mon Oct-Mar free; ⏲9.30am-7pm Apr-Sep, to 5pm Oct-Mar) A magnificent marriage of Christian and Mudéjar architecture, Seville's royal palace complex is a breathtaking spectacle. The site, which was originally developed as a fort in 913, has been revamped many times over the 11 centuries of its existence, most spectacularly in the 14th century when King Pedro added the sumptuous Palacio de Don Pedro, still today the Alcázar's crowning glory. More recently, the Alcázar featured as a location for the *Game of Thrones* TV series.

The Alcázar started life in the 10th century as a fort for the Cordoban governors of Seville but it was in the 11th century that it got its first major rebuild. Under the city's Abbadid rulers, the original fort was enlarged and a palace known as Al-Muwarak (the Blessed) was built in what's now the western part of the complex. Subsequently, the 12th-century Almohad rulers added another palace east of this, around what's now the Patio del Crucero. The Christian king Fernando III moved into the Alcázar when he captured Seville in 1248, and several later monarchs used it as their main residence. Fernando's son Alfonso X replaced much of the Almohad palace with a Gothic one and then, between 1364 and 1366, Pedro I created his stunning namesake palace.

Note that long entry queues are the norm here. To cut waiting time, it pays to pre-purchase tickets at www.alcazarsevilla.org.

➡ Patio del León

Entry to the complex is through the **Puerta del León** (Lion Gate) on Plaza del Triunfo. Passing through the gateway, which is flanked by crenellated walls, you come to the Patio del León (Lion Patio), which was the garrison yard of the original Al-Muwarak palace. Off to the left before the arches is the **Sala de la Justicia** (Hall of Justice), with beautiful Mudéjar plasterwork and an *artesonado* (ceiling of interlaced beams with decorative insertions). This room was built in the 1340s by the Christian king Alfonso XI, who disported here with one of his mistresses, Leonor de Guzmán, reputedly the most beautiful woman in Spain. It leads to the pretty **Patio del Yeso**, part of the 12th-century Almohad palace reconstructed in the 19th century.

➡ Patio de la Montería

Dominated by the facade of the Palacio de Don Pedro, the Patio de la Montería owes its name (the Hunting Courtyard) to the fact that hunters would meet here before hunts with King Pedro. Rooms on the western side of the square were part of the **Casa de la Contratación** (Contracting House), founded in 1503 to control trade with Spain's American colonies. The **Salón del Almirante** (Admiral's Hall) houses 19th- and 20th-century paintings showing historical events and personages associated with Seville. The room off its northern end has an international collection of beautiful, elaborate fans. The **Sala de Audiencias** (Chapter House) is hung with tapestry representations of the shields of Spanish admirals and Alejo Fernández' celebrated 1530s painting *Virgen de los mareantes* (Madonna of the Seafarers).

➡ Cuarto Real Alto

The Alcázar is still a royal palace. In 1995 it hosted the wedding feast of Infanta Elena, daughter of King Juan Carlos I, after her marriage in Seville's cathedral. The Cuarto Real Alto (Upper Royal Quarters), the rooms used by the Spanish royal family on their visits to Seville, are open for guided tours (€4.50; half-hourly 10am to 1.30pm; booking required). Highlights of the tours, which are conducted in either Spanish or English, include the 14th-century **Salón de Audiencias**, still the monarch's reception room, and Pedro I's bedroom, with marvellous Mudéjar tiles and plasterwork.

➡ Palacio de Don Pedro

This palace, also known as the Palacio Mudéjar, is Seville's single most stunning architectural feature.

King Pedro, though at odds with many of his fellow Christians, had a long-standing alliance with the Muslim emir of Granada, Mohammed V, the man responsible for much of the decoration at the Alhambra. So when Pedro decided to build a new palace in the Alcázar in 1364, Mohammed sent many of his top artisans. These were joined by others from Seville and Toledo. Their work, drawing on the Islamic traditions of the Almohads and caliphal Córdoba, is a unique synthesis of Iberian Islamic art.

Inscriptions on the palace's facade encapsulate the collaborative nature of the enterprise. While one, in Spanish, announces that the building's creator was the 'highest, noblest and most powerful conqueror Don Pedro, by God's grace King of Castilla and León', another proclaims repeatedly in Arabic that 'there is no conqueror but Allah'.

At the heart of the palace is the sublime **Patio de las Doncellas** (Patio of the Maidens), surrounded by beautiful arches, plasterwork and tiling. The sunken garden in the centre was uncovered by archaeologists in 2004 from beneath a 16th-century marble covering.

To the north of the patio, the **Alcoba Real** (Royal Quarters) features stunningly beautiful ceilings and wonderful plaster and tile

Central Seville

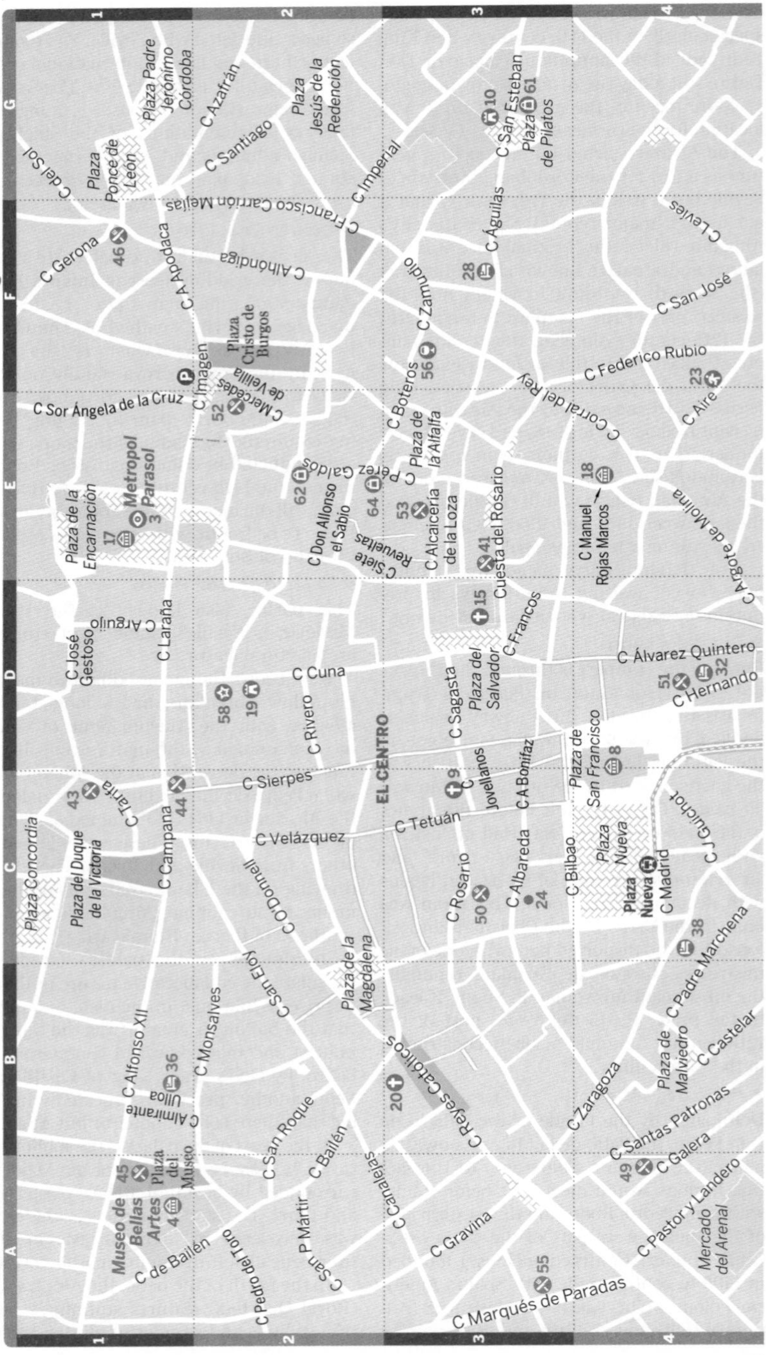

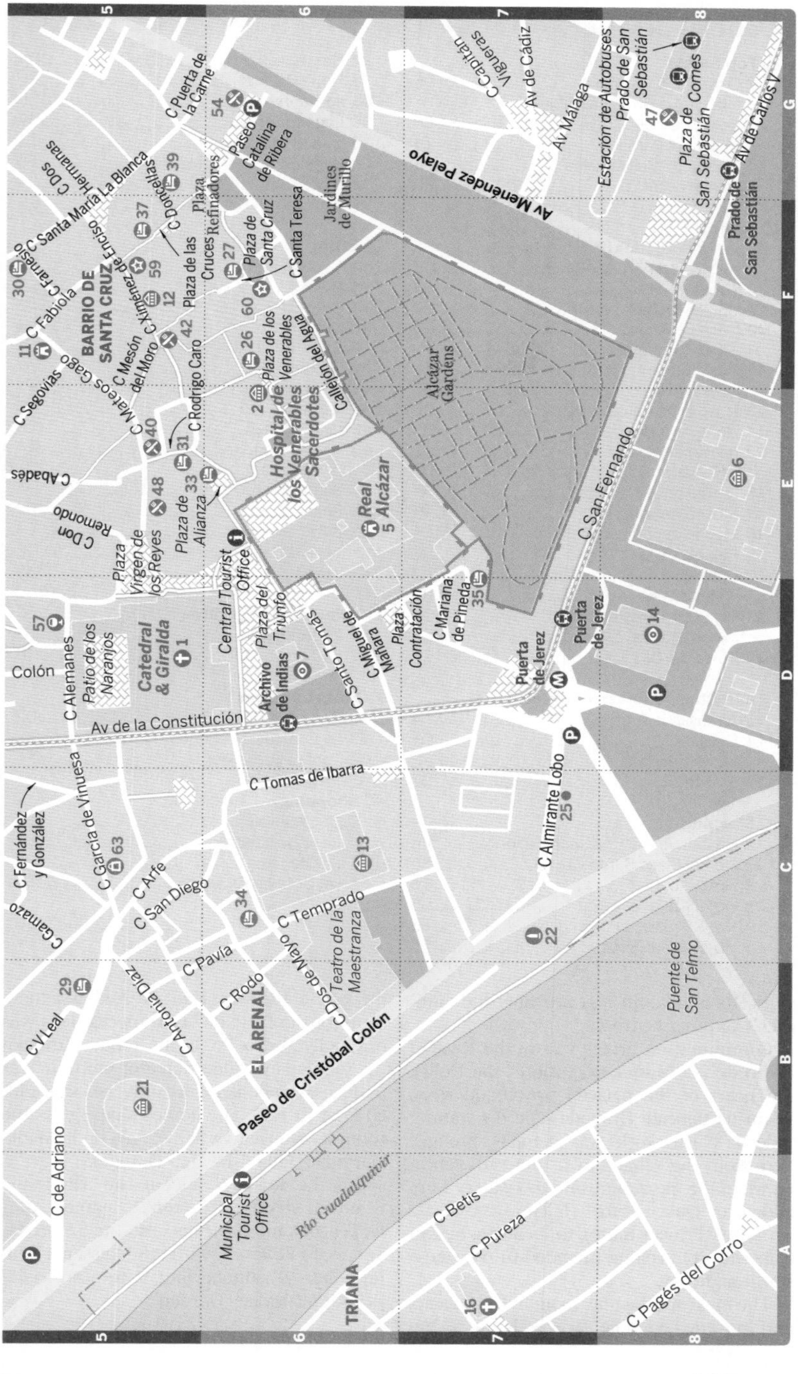
A
B
C
D
E
F
G
5
6
7
8
C Dos Hermanas
C Santa María La Blanca
C Farnesio
30
C Fabiola
11
C Segovias
C Mateos Gago
BARRIO DE SANTA CRUZ
C Ximénez de Enciso
C Mesón del Moro
C Doncellas
37
39
59
12
42
Plaza de las Cruces
Plaza Refinadores
C Puerta de la Carne
54
Paseo Catalina de Ribera
Plaza de Santa Cruz
27
60
26
C Santa Teresa
Jardines de Murillo
Av Menéndez Pelayo
C Capitán Vigueras
Av de Cádiz
Av Málaga
Estación de Autobuses Prado de San Sebastián
47
Plaza de San Sebastián
Comes
Prado de San Sebastián
Av de Carlos V
C Abades
C Don Remondo
40
31
C Rodrigo Caro
48
33
Plaza de Alianza
Plaza Virgen de los Reyes
Plaza de los Venerables
2
Hospital de los Venerables Sacerdotes
Callejón del Agua
Alcázar Gardens
Real Alcázar
5
Central Tourist Office
Plaza del Triunfo
C Santo Tomás
C Miguel de Mañara
Plaza Contratación
C Mariana de Pineda
35
C San Fernando
6
Puerta de Jerez
14
Colón
57
C Alemanes
Patio de los Naranjos
Catedral & Giralda
1
Archivo de Indias
7
Av de la Constitución
C Tomas de Ibarra
C Almirante Lobo
25
C Fernández y González
C García de Vinuesa
63
C Arfe
C San Diego
C Gamazo
34
13
C Temprado
Teatro de la Maestranza
C Pavía
C Rodo
C Dos de Mayo
22
29
C Antonia Díaz
EL ARENAL
C V Leal
21
Paseo de Cristóbal Colón
Puente de San Telmo
C de Adriano
Municipal Tourist Office
Río Guadalquivir
C Betis
C Pureza
TRIANA
16
C Pagés del Corro

Central Seville

Top Sights
1 Catedral & Giralda ... D5
2 Hospital de los Venerables Sacerdotes ... E6
3 Metropol Parasol ... E1
4 Museo de Bellas Artes ... A1
5 Real Alcázar ... E6

Sights
6 Antigua Fábrica de Tabacos ... E8
7 Archivo General de Indias ... D6
8 Ayuntamiento ... D4
9 Capilla de San José ... C3
10 Casa de Pilatos ... G3
11 Casa de Salinas ... F5
12 Centro de Interpretación Judería de Sevilla ... F5
13 Hospital de la Caridad ... C6
14 Hotel Alfonso XIII ... D8
15 Iglesia Colegial del Divino Salvador ... D3
16 Iglesia de Santa Ana ... A7
17 Museo Antiquarium ... E1
18 Museo del Baile Flamenco ... E4
19 Palacio de la Condesa de Lebrija ... D2
20 Parroquia de Santa María Magdalena ... B3
21 Plaza de Toros de la Real Maestranza ... B5
22 Torre del Oro ... C7

Activities, Courses & Tours
23 Aire Baños Árabes ... F4
24 CLIC ... C3
Mimo Sevilla ... (see 14)
25 Surf the City ... C7

Sleeping
26 Casual Sevilla Don Juan Tenorio ... F6
27 Hostal Plaza Santa Cruz ... F6
28 Hotel Abanico ... F3
29 Hotel Adriano ... B5
30 Hotel Amadeus ... F5
31 Hotel Casa 1800 ... E5
32 Hotel Casa de Colón ... D4
33 Hotel Palacio Alcázar ... E6
34 La Banda ... C6
35 Legado Alcázar ... D7
36 Oasis Palace Hostel ... B1
37 Pensión San Pancracio ... F5
38 Suites Sevilla Plaza ... C4
39 Un Patio en Santa Cruz ... G5

Eating
40 Bodega Santa Cruz ... E5
41 Bolas ... E3
42 Café Bar Las Teresas ... F5
43 Cocome ... C1
44 Confitería La Campana ... C1
45 Créeme ... A1
46 El Rinconcillo ... F1
47 Ispal ... G8
48 La Azotea ... E5
49 La Brunilda ... A4
50 Lobo López ... C3
51 Mamarracha ... D4
52 Palo Cortao ... E2
53 Sal Gorda ... E3
54 Vinería San Telmo ... G6
55 Zoko ... A3

Drinking & Nightlife
56 El Garlochi ... F3
57 La Terraza del Eme ... D5

Entertainment
58 Casa de la Memoria ... D2
59 La Casa del Flamenco ... F5
60 Tablao Los Gallos ... F6

Shopping
61 Coco Sevilla ... G3
62 La Importadora ... E2
63 La Oleoteca ... C5
64 Un Gato en Bicicleta ... E2

work. Its rear room was probably the monarch's summer bedroom.

Continuing on brings you to the covered **Patio de las Muñecas** (Patio of the Dolls), the heart of the palace's private quarters, featuring delicate Granada-style decoration; indeed, plasterwork was actually brought here from the Alhambra in the 19th century, when the mezzanine and top gallery were added for Queen Isabel II. The **Cuarto del Príncipe** (Prince's Suite), to its north, has an elaborate gold ceiling intended to recreate a starlit night sky.

The most spectacular room in the Palacio, and indeed the whole Alcázar, is the **Salón de Embajadores** (Hall of Ambassadors), south of the Patio de las Muñecas. This was originally Pedro I's throne room, although the fabulous wooden dome of multiple star patterns, symbolising the universe, was added later in 1427. The dome's shape gives the room its alternative name, Sala de la Media Naranja (Hall of the Half Orange).

On the western side of the Salón, the beautiful **Arco de Pavones**, named after its peacock motifs, leads onto the **Salón del Techo de Felipe II**, with a Renaissance ceiling (1589–91), and beyond, to the **Jardín del Príncipe** (Prince's Garden).

➡ **Palacio Gótico (Salones de Carlo V)**

Reached via a staircase at the southeastern corner of the Patio de las Doncellas is Alfonso X's much remodelled 13th-century Gothic palace. The echoing halls here were designed for the 16th-century Spanish king Carlos I and are now known as the Salones de Carlos V (after his second title as Holy Roman Emperor Charles V). Of the rooms, the most striking is the **Salone de los Tapices**, a vaulted hall with a series of vast tapestries.

➡ **Patio del Crucero**

Beyond the Salone de los Tapices, the Patio del Crucero was originally the upper storey of a patio from the 12th-century Almohad palace. Initially it consisted only of raised walkways along its four sides and two cross-walkways that met in the middle. Below grew orange trees, whose fruit could be plucked at hand height by the lucky folk strolling along the walkways. The patio's lower level was built over in the 18th century after it suffered earthquake damage.

➡ **Gardens**

On the other side of the Salone de los Tapices are the Alcázar's gardens. Formal gardens with pools and fountains sit closest to the palace. From one, the **Jardín de la Danza** (Garden of the Dance), a passage runs beneath the Salones de Carlos V to the photogenic **Baños de Doña María de Padilla** (María de Padilla Baths). These are the vaults beneath the Patio del Crucero – originally the patio's lower level – with a grotto that replaced the patio's original pool.

One of the gardens' most arresting features is the **Galeria de Grutesco**, a raised gallery with porticoes fashioned in the 16th century out of an old Islamic-era wall. There is also a fun hedge maze, which will delight children. The gardens to the east, beyond a long wall, are 20th-century creations, but no less heavenly for it.

Archivo General de Indias ARCHIVES

(Map p58; ☎954 50 05 28; Avenida de la Constitución; ⏲9.30am-5pm Tue-Sat, 10am-2pm Sun) FREE Occupying a former merchant's exchange on the western side of Plaza del Triunfo, the Archivo General de Indias provides fascinating insight into Spain's colonial history. The archive, established in 1785 to house documents and maps relating to Spain's American empire, is vast, boasting 7km of shelves, 43,000 documents, and 80 million pages dating from 1492 to the end of the empire in the 19th century. Most documents are filed away, but you can examine some fascinating letters and hand-drawn maps.

★ **Hospital de los Venerables Sacerdotes** MUSEUM

(Map p58; ☎954 56 26 96; www.hospitaldelosvenerables.es; Plaza de los Venerables 8; adult/student/child €10/8/free; ⏲10am-8pm Mar-Jun & Sep-Nov, 10am-2pm & 5.30-9pm Jul & Aug, 10am-6pm Dec-Feb) This gem of a museum, housed in a former hospice for priests, is one of Seville's most rewarding. The artistic highlight is the Focus-Abengoa Foundation's collection of 17th-century paintings in the Centro Velázquez. It's not a big collection, but each work is a masterpiece of its genre – highlights include Diego Velázquez' *Santa Rufina,* his *Inmaculada concepción,* and a sharply vivid portrait of *Santa Catalina* by Bartolomé Murillo.

Elsewhere, you can admire the hospital's ornately decorated chapel and delightful patio – a classic composition of porticoes, ceramic tiles and orange trees arranged around a sunken fountain.

Casa de Salinas PALACE

(Map p58; ☎619 254498; www.casadesalinas.com; Calle Mateos Gago 39; guided tours adult/child €8/4; ⏲10am-6pm Mon-Fri mid-Oct–mid-Jun, to 2pm mid-Jun–mid-Oct) Built during Seville's 16th-century golden age, this Santa Cruz mansion is like a micro-version of the Alcázar, just without the queues. And like several other city palaces (Casa de Pilatos, Palacio de Lebrija and Palacio de Las Dueñas), it's privately owned, with the family still in residence, hence visits are by guided tour only. You'll see stunning Mudéjar plaster arches and a Roman mosaic of Bacchanalian shenanigans, original ceramic tiles, and the family's drawing rooms with exquisite wooden ceilings.

Centro de Interpretación Judería de Sevilla MUSEUM

(Map p58; ☎954 04 70 89; www.juderiadesevilla.es; Calle Ximénez de Enciso 22; adult/student €6.50/5; ⏲11am-7pm) Dedicated to Seville's Jewish history, this small, poignant museum occupies an old Sephardic house in Santa Cruz, the one-time Jewish neighbourhood that never recovered from a brutal massacre in 1391. The massacre and other historical happenings are catalogued inside, along with a few surviving mementos including documents, costumes and books.

The museum also offers guided walks of Seville's Jewish sites for €22. Lasting two to 2½ hours, these require a minimum of two people and are available in Spanish, French or English. Call ahead if you're interested.

El Centro & El Arenal

★Museo de Bellas Artes MUSEUM
(Fine Arts Museum; Map p58; ☎955 54 29 42; www.museodebellasartesdesevilla.es; Plaza del Museo 9; EU/non-EU citizen free/€1.50; ⏱9am-9pm Tue-Sat, to 3pm Sun) Housed in a grand mannerist palace, the former Convento de la Merced, the Museo de Bellas Artes is one of Spain's premier art museums. Its collection of Spanish and Sevillan paintings and sculptures comprises works from the 15th to 20th centuries, but the focus is very much on brooding religious paintings from the city's 17th-century Siglo de Oro (Golden Age).

Works are displayed in chronological order, with the Golden Age masterpieces clustered in *salas* V to X. The most visually arresting room is the convent's former church (*sala* V), hung with paintings by masters of the Sevillan baroque, above all Murillo. His *Inmaculada concepción* (aka *La colosal*; 1650) at the head of the church displays all the curving, twisting movement so central to baroque art. Other artists represented include Pacheco (teacher and father-in-law of Velázquez), Juan de Valdés Leal, Zurbarán (look for his deeply sombre *Cristo crucificado,* c 1630–35) and sculptor Juan Martínez Montañés.

Elsewhere, look out for El Greco's portrait of his son Jorge Manuel (c 1600–05), Velázquez' *Cabeza de apóstol* (1620), and a portrait by Goya in *sala* XI.

For a change of subject matter, push on to *sala* XII where Gonzalo Bilbao's *Las cigarreras* (The Cigarette Makers; 1915) is one of several canvases depicting scenes of Sevillan life.

Iglesia Colegial del Divino Salvador CHURCH
(Map p58; ☎954 21 16 79; www.iglesiadelsalvador.es; Plaza del Salvador; adult/child €5/free, incl Catedral & Giralda €10/free; ⏱11am-5.30pm Mon-Sat, 3-7pm Sun Sep-Jun, 10am-5.30pm Mon-Sat, 3-7pm Sun Jul & Aug) Overlooking Plaza del Salvador, this baroque church was built between 1674 and 1712 on the site of Muslim Ishbiliya's main mosque. Its mannerist red-brick facade masks a cavernous, light-filled interior crowned by a soaring dome and filled with extravagant gold altarpieces. Particularly breathtaking is the *retablo* behind the main altar, a 21m-high composition crafted by the Portuguese artist Cayetano de Acosta between 1770 and 1779. A second, and earlier, Acosta altarpiece graces the Capilla Sacramental.

Museo del Baile Flamenco MUSEUM
(Map p58; ☎954 34 03 11; www.museoflamenco.com; Calle Manuel Rojas Marcos 3; adult/child €10/6, incl show €26/15; ⏱10am-7pm) The brainchild of *sevillana* flamenco dancer Cristina Hoyos, this museum illustrates the dance with interactive displays, paintings, displays of period dresses, and photos of revered erstwhile (and contemporary) performers. Even better are the fantastic nightly performances (at 5pm, 7pm and 8.45pm; €22) staged both in the courtyard and the more intimate basement space (€37 including a drink). Combined museum and show tickets are a good option.

Casa de Pilatos PALACE
(Map p58; ☎954 22 52 98; www.fundacionmedinaceli.org; Plaza de Pilatos; ground fl €10, whole palace €12; ⏱9am-7pm Apr-Oct, to 6pm Nov-Mar) The haunting Casa de Pilatos, which is still occupied by the ducal Medinaceli family, is one of the city's most glorious mansions. Originally dating to the late 15th century, it incorporates a wonderful mix of Mudéjar, Gothic and Renaissance decor, with some beautiful tilework and *artesonados*. The overall effect is like a mini-Alcázar.

The staircase to the upper floor has the building's finest tiles, and a great golden *artesonado* dome above. Visits to the upper floor, still partly inhabited by the Medinacelis, are guided. Of interest are several centuries' worth of Medinaceli portraits and a small Goya bullfighting painting.

Note there is free admission for EU citizens (take ID) on Monday (3pm to 7pm).

Palacio de la Condesa de Lebrija PALACE
(Map p58; ☎954 22 78 02; www.palaciodelebrija.com; Calle Cuna 8; adult/child incl guided tour €12/6, ground fl 6pm & 7pm Mon free; ⏱10.30am-7.30pm) This aristocratic 16th-century mansion, set around a beautiful Renaissance-Mudéjar courtyard, boasts an eclectic look that blends a range of decorative elements, including Roman mosaics, Mudéjar plasterwork and Renaissance masonry. Its former owner, the late Countess of Lebrija, was an archaeologist; she remodelled the house in 1914, filling many of the rooms with treasures from her travels.

Visits to the top floor are by guided tour only (in English or Spanish), though this is included in the ticket price.

Parroquia de Santa María Magdalena CHURCH

(Map p58; ☎954 22 96 03; Calle Bailén 5; ⏰7.45-11am & 6.30-9pm Mon & Fri, 7.45am-1.30pm & 6.30-9pm Tue-Thu, 8.45am-2pm & 6.30-9pm Sat & Sun) Behind a fairly unobtrusive exterior, this historic late-17th-century church opens to reveal an enormous baroque interior capped by an octagonal cupola. Its headline act is the colossal gold *retablo* behind the main altar (an 18th-century addition), but you'll also find several works by big-name baroque artists Francisco de Zurbarán and Juan de Valdés Leal.

Capilla de San José CHURCH

(Map p58; ☎954 22 32 42; Calle Jovellanos; ⏰9am-12.45pm & 6.30-8.30pm) FREE For a blast of full-on baroque glitz, pop into this small church hidden away on a side street between Calles Sierpes and Tetuán. Behind its 18th-century facade, it boasts some startlingly lavish decor, culminating in an extraordinary gold altarpiece centred on a sculpture of San José.

Ayuntamiento HISTORIC BUILDING

(Casa Consistorial; Map p58; https://casaconsistorialsevilla.sacatuentrada.es; Plaza de San Francisco; Mon-Thu €4, Sat free; ⏰tours 7pm Mon-Thu, 10am Sat) Sandwiched between Plaza de San Francisco and Plaza Nueva is Seville's striking city hall, the *ayuntamiento*. In its original form, the building dates to the 16th century, but a major 19th-century makeover saw the addition of an imposing neoclassical facade on the Plaza Nueva side. On its eastern walls you can see some ornate Renaissance carvings.

Visits, by 50-minute guided tour only, take in its richly furnished staterooms.

Plaza de Toros de la Real Maestranza MUSEUM

(Map p58; ☎954 21 03 15; www.realmaestranza.com; Paseo de Cristóbal Colón 12; tours adult/child €8/3, 3-7pm Mon free; ⏰9.30am-9pm Apr-Oct, to 7pm Nov-Mar, to 3pm bullfight days) In the world of bullfighting, Seville's white and yellow-trimmed bullring is the equivalent of football's Old Trafford or Camp Nou – if you're selected to fight here, you've made it. In addition to having almost religious significance to fans, it's also the oldest ring in Spain – construction started in 1761 and continued on and off until 1881 – and one of the biggest, with a capacity of up to 14,000. A visit enables you to learn about bullfighting's deep-rooted traditions without witnessing a fight.

LOCAL KNOWLEDGE

A HAMMAM HIDEAWAY

Hidden away in a centuries-old Mudéjar town house, the **Aire Baños Árabes** (Map p58; ☎955 01 00 24; www.beaire.com; Calle Aire 15; bath/bath with massage from €37/56; ⏰10am-10pm Sun-Tue, to 11pm Wed & Thu, to midnight Fri & Sat) are an oasis of calm in the heart of the Santa Cruz district. The smart, Arabic-style baths sport elegant Moroccan *riad*-style decor, and a long list of bath and massage packages are available; it's best to book a day or so in advance. See the website for further details.

Hospital de la Caridad MUSEUM

(Map p58; ☎954 22 32 32; www.santa-caridad.es; Calle Temprado 3; adult/child 7-17yr €8/2.50, 3.30-7.30pm Mon free; ⏰10.30am-7.30pm Mon-Sat, 10.30am-12.30pm & 2-7.30pm Sun) The Hospital de la Caridad, a sturdy building one block east of the river, was established in the late 17th century as a hospice for the poor and elderly. It was founded by Miguel de Mañara, by legend a notorious libertine who supposedly changed his ways after seeing a vision of his own funeral procession. The hospital's showpiece attraction is its gilded chapel, decorated with works by several Golden Age painters and sculptors, most notably Murillo, Valdés Leal and Roldán.

The hospital was famously pillaged by Napoleon's troops in 1810 when a French officer named General Soult helped himself to four Murillo paintings from the chapel's walls. These were never returned, though copies were made and hung up in place of the originals in 2008. See if you can spot the fakes.

Torre del Oro TOWER

(Map p58; ☎954 22 24 19; Paseo de Cristóbal Colón; adult/6-14 yr €3/1.50, Mon free; ⏰9.30am-6.45pm Mon-Fri, 10.30am-6.45pm Sat & Sun) This distinctive tower, one of Seville's signature landmarks, has been guarding the Río Guadalquivir since the 13th century. The original dodecagonal structure, built to bolster the city's fortified walls, was subsequently heightened, first in the 14th century and then again in the late 1700s. Over the centuries, the tower has served as a chapel, prison and naval office; nowadays it houses a small maritime museum and a rooftop viewing platform.

La Macarena & Alameda de Hércules

★Metropol Parasol LANDMARK
(Map p58; ☎606 635214; www.setasdesevilla.com; Plaza de la Encarnación; €3; ⊙9.30am-10.30pm Sun-Thu, to 11pm Fri & Sat) The Metropol Parasol, known locally as *Las Setas* (The Mushrooms), is one of Seville's iconic modern landmarks. Built in 2011 to a design by German architect Jürgen Mayer H, the colossal sunshade is a hypnotic sight with its undulating honeycombed canopy – said to be the world's largest wooden-framed structure – and massive support trunks. Lifts run up from the basement to the top, where you can enjoy killer views from a winding walkway.

The structure, six years in the making, covers a former dead zone in Seville's central district once filled by an ugly car park. Roman and Moorish ruins unearthed during excavation of the plaza were cleverly incorporated into the Parasol's foundations and are now on show at the **Museo Antiquarium** (☎955 47 15 80; ⊙10am-8pm Tue-Sat, to 2pm Sun) in the basement. The structure also houses the neighbourhood food market, the **Mercado de la Encarnación**, several cafes and tapas bars, and **Plaza Mayor**, a space designed to host open-air events and now a popular hang-out for local kids.

Palacio de Las Dueñas PALACE
(Map p65; ☎954 21 48 28; www.lasduenas.es; Calle Dueñas 5; adult/6-12yr €10/8; ⊙10am-8pm Apr-Oct, to 6pm Nov-Mar) This gorgeous 15th-century palace was the favourite home of the late Duchess de Alba, one of Spain's most prominent aristocrats. Renaissance in design, it boasts beautiful gardens and a lovely arcaded courtyard. Inside, you can admire paintings and tapestries, as well as the Duchess' collection of Semana Santa, bullfighting and football memorabilia (she was a Betis fan). A plaque commemorates famous Spanish poet Antonio Machado, who was born here in 1875.

Iglesia de San Luis de los Franceses CHURCH
(Map p65; ☎954 55 02 07; Calle San Luis 37; €4, 4-8pm Sun free; ⊙10am-2pm & 4-8pm Tue-Sun) The finest example of baroque architecture in Seville, this imposing (and deconsecrated) 18th-century church is a former Jesuit novitiate dedicated to King Louis IX of France. Designed by Leonardo de Figueroa, its unusual circular interior harbours four extravagantly carved and gilded altarpieces inset with paintings (Louis' image is topped by a huge crown), and a central cupola. You can also visit the chapel decorated with macabre reliquaries (saints' bones) in glass boxes, and the crypt.

The church was closed for decades, and only reopened after a major refurbishment in 2017. Don't miss the beautiful ceiling murals, which carry messages defending the Jesuits against criticisms – unsuccessfully, as they were expelled from Spain soon after the church was completed in 1731. The main cupola's decoration – use the cleverly angled mirror to study it, saving your neck – has the theme of continuity of worship: the old is represented by the Jewish Ark of the Covenant and seven-branched candlestick, and the new by the angels.

Palacio de los Marqueses de la Algaba PALACE
(Map p65; ☎955 47 20 97; Plaza Calderón de la Barca; ⊙10am-2pm & 6-9pm Mon-Fri, to 2pm Sat Apr-Oct, reduced hours Nov-Mar) FREE One of Seville's classic Mudéjar-style palaces, complete with a lovely central courtyard, this historic mansion houses the **Centro de la Interpretación Mudéjar**, a small museum showcasing Mudéjar pieces from the 12th to 20th centuries. Though the collection gets a little lost in the wonderfully restored mansion, the captions (in Spanish and English) do a good job of explaining the origins and distinguishing characteristics of the complex Mudéjar style.

Basílica de La Macarena BASILICA
(Map p65; ☎954 90 18 00; Calle Bécquer 1; basilica/museum free/€5; ⊙9am-2pm & 6-9.30pm Mon-Sat, 9.30am-2pm & 6-9.30pm Sun Jun–mid-Sep, 9am-2pm & 5-9pm Mon-Sat, 9.30am-2pm & 5-9pm Sun mid-Sep–May) This 20th-century neobaroque basilica is home to Seville's most revered religious treasure, the *Virgen de la Esperanza Macarena* (Macarena Virgin of Hope), known popularly as the Macarena. This magnificent 17th-century statue, a star of the city's fervent Semana Santa (Holy Week) celebrations, stands in splendour behind the main altarpiece, adorned with a golden crown, lavish vestments and five flower-shaped diamond and emerald brooches donated by the famous matador Joselito El Gallo in 1912.

Alameda de Hércules & Macarena

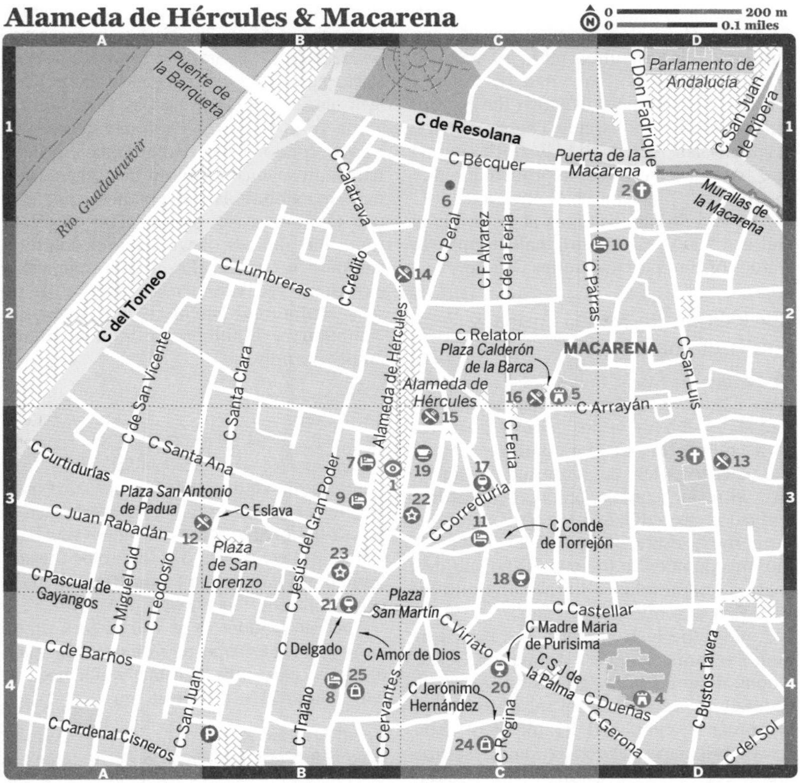

Alameda de Hércules & Macarena

Sights

1 Alameda de Hércules........B3
2 Basílica de La Macarena........D1
3 Iglesia de San Luis de los Franceses........D3
4 Palacio de Las Dueñas........D4
5 Palacio de los Marqueses de la Algaba........C2

Activities, Courses & Tours

6 Taller Flamenco........C1

Sleeping

7 Corner House........B3
8 Hotel Boutique Doña Lola........B4
9 Hotel Sacristía de Santa Ana........B3
10 Hotel San Gil........D2
11 One Shot Palacio Conde de Torrejón 09........C3

Eating

12 Bar-Restaurante Eslava........B3
13 conTenedor........D3
14 Duo Tapas........C2
15 Freskura........C3
16 Mercado de Feria........C2

Drinking & Nightlife

17 Bier Kraft........C3
18 Casa Vizcaíno........C3
Corner House Terraza........(see 7)
19 El Viajero Sedentario........C3
20 Gallo Rojo........C4
21 Maquila........B4

Entertainment

22 Fun Club........C3
23 Naima Café Jazz........B3

Shopping

24 Lama La Uva........C4
25 Tarico........B4

Alameda de Hércules SQUARE
(Map p65) Flanked by bars, cafes and restaurants, this tree-lined plaza is a hugely popular hang-out, frequented by families, tourists and students. It's also the historic hub of Seville's gay scene. The square was originally laid out in the late 16th century and became a fashionable promenade during the city's 17th-century Golden Age.

The two Roman columns at its southern end are 2000-year-old originals, topped by statues of Hercules and Julius Caesar.

Parque de María Luisa & South of the Centre

★Parque de María Luisa PARK
(Map p52; 8am-10pm Sep-Jun, to midnight Jul & Aug;) A glorious oasis of green, the 34-hectare Parque de María Luisa is the perfect place to escape the noise and heat of the city, with duck ponds, landscaped gardens and paths shaded by soaring trees. The land, formerly the estate of the Palacio de San Telmo, was donated to the city in the late 19th century and developed in the run-up to the 1929 Exposición Iberoamericana.

Amidst the lush gardens, the park contains several notable drawcards. Chief among them is **Plaza de España** (Avenida de Portugal), the most flamboyant of the building projects completed for the 1929 Expo. A vast brick-and-tile confection, it features fountains, mini-canals, and a series of gaudy tile pictures depicting historical scenes from each Spanish province. You can hire rowing boats to pootle around the plaza's canals for €6 (for 35 minutes).

In the south of the park, the **Museo Arqueológico** (955 12 06 32; www.museosdeandalucia.es/web/museoarqueologicodesevilla; Plaza de América; EU/non-EU citizens free/€1.50; 9am-9pm Tue-Sat, to 3pm Sun Sep-Jun, 9am-3pm Tue-Sun Jul & Aug) has some wonderful Roman sculptures, mosaics and statues – many gathered from the archaeological site of Itálica just outside Seville.

Opposite is the **Museo de Artes y Costumbres Populares** (955 54 29 51; www.museosdeandalucia.es/web/museodeartesycostumbrespopularesdesevilla; Plaza de América 3; EU/non-EU citizens free/€1.50; 9am-9pm Tue-Sat, to 3pm Sun Sep-Jun, 9am-3pm Tue-Sun Jul & Aug), dedicated to local customs, costumes and traditions.

The park is a great place for children to let off steam and families to bond over a bike ride – four-person quad bikes are available to hire for €14 per half hour.

Museo Casa de la Ciencia MUSEUM
(Map p52; 954 23 23 49; www.casadelaciencia.csic.es; Pabellón de Perú, Avenida de María Luisa; museum €3, incl planetarium €5; 10am-9pm Tue-Sun) Housed in the Peruvian Pavilion from the 1929 Expo, complete with carved condors and llamas, this excellent, hands-on science museum has several permanent exhibitions and a planetarium, plus two temporary exhibitions. The cetaceans room has models of whales and dolphins, common in the Straits of Gibraltar, while elsewhere you can peruse displays of insect sculptures, molluscs and minerals. Temporary exhibitions are interactive and family-friendly.

Antigua Fábrica de Tabacos HISTORIC BUILDING
(Map p58; 954 55 10 00; Calle San Fernando; 8am-9pm Mon-Fri, to 2.30pm Sat) FREE Now home to the University of Seville, this massive former tobacco factory – workplace of Bizet's fictional heroine, Carmen – was built in the 18th century and is said to be the second-largest building in Spain after the El Escorial monastery northwest of Madrid.

You can wander in at will or pick up an audio guide at the porter's office in the main entrance hall – it's free but you'll need to leave photo ID as a deposit.

Hotel Alfonso XIII LANDMARK
(Map p58; Calle San Fernando 2) As much a local landmark as an accommodation option, this striking, only-in-Seville hotel – conceived as the most luxurious in Europe when it was built in 1928 – was constructed for the 1929 world fair. Ring-fenced by towering palm trees, it sports a classic neo-Mudéjar look, complete with glazed tiles and terracotta bricks.

Triana

On the west bank of the Río Guadalquivir, Triana has long had a reputation as an 'outsider' neighbourhood. It was once home to Seville's Roma community and its past is littered with stories of sailors, ceramicists, bullfighters, flamenco artists, religious zealotry and working-class identity. Nowadays, it's a colourful area of churches, ceramic shops and waterfront bars.

Castillo de San Jorge MUSEUM
(Map p52; 955 47 02 55; Plaza del Altozano; 11am-5.30pm Tue-Sat, 10am-2.30pm Sun) FREE Adjacent to the Puente de Isabel

II, the Castillo de San Jorge is steeped in notoriety: it was here that the infamous Spanish Inquisition had its headquarters from 1481 to 1785. When the Inquisition fires were finally doused in the early 19th century, the castle was demolished and a market built over its ruins. These remains were subsequently rediscovered in 1990, and they now house a museum illustrating the Inquisition's activities and life in the *castillo*.

Centro Cerámica Triana MUSEUM
(Map p52; ☎954 34 15 82; Calle Antillano Campos 14; adult/child €2.10/free; ⏲11am-5.30pm Tue-Sat, 10am-2.30pm Sun) Housed in a former tile factory, this small museum provides a fascinating introduction to Triana and its industrial past. Exhibits, which include brick-lined kilns and a comprehensive collection of tiles, chart the methodology and history of ceramic production, cleverly tying it in with the wider history of the neighbourhood and its residents.

Iglesia de Santa Ana CHURCH
(Map p58; http://santanatriana.org; Plazuela de Santa Ana, Calle Pelay Correa; €2; ⏲10.30am-1.30pm & 4.30-7pm Mon-Thu, 11am-1.30pm & 4.30-7pm Fri) Known as the Cathedral of Triana, the 13th-century Iglesia de Santa Ana was the first church built in Seville after the 1248 Reconquista. Architecturally, it's Gothic-Mudéjar in style, with a high, vaulted interior and a wealth of religious imagery – look for statues of Santa Rufina and Santa Justa, Christian martyrs who were potters from this *barrio* (district). The saints are often depicted with the Giralda, which they allegedly saved during the 1755 Lisbon earthquake.

Isla de la Cartuja

Centro Andaluz de Arte Contemporáneo MUSEUM
(Map p52; ☎955 03 70 70; www.caac.es; Avenida Américo Vespucio 2; admission €3, 7-9pm Tue-Fri & all day Sat free; ⏲11am-9pm Tue-Sat, 10am-3.30pm Sun) Contemporary art goes hand in hand with 15th-century architecture at the Centro Andaluz de Arte Contemporáneo. The centre, sensitively housed in the **Monasterio de Santa María de las Cuevas**, hosts temporary exhibitions by Andalucian and international artists alongside some truly bizarre permanent pieces. Look out for *Alicia* by Cristina Lucas, a massive head and arm poking through two windows that was supposedly inspired by *Alice in Wonderland*. Elsewhere, several brick kilns testify to the monastery's past as a 19th-century ceramics factory.

The Monasterio de Santa María de las Cuevas, commonly known as the Monasterio de la Cartuja, or more simply La Cartuja, was founded in 1400. It later became a favourite Sevillan lodging place for Christopher Columbus, who prayed in its chapel before his voyage to the Americas and whose remains lay here from his death in 1506 to 1537.

In 1839 the complex was bought by an enterprising Englishman, Charles Pickman, who turned it into a porcelain factory – hence, the bottle-shaped kilns rising rather incongruously in the *claustrón* (large cloister). The factory ceased production in the 1980s and, following a restoration, served as the Royal Pavilion during the 1992 Expo.

Pabellón de la Navegación MUSEUM
(Map p52; ☎954 04 31 11; www.pabellondelanavegacion.com; Camino de los Descubrimientos 2; adult/child €4.90/3.50; ⏲11am-8.30pm Tue-Sat, to

TRIANA'S TILES

A distinctive feature of Seville's cityscape are the panels of brightly coloured tiles that adorn so many of its monuments, palaces, benches and bars.

The manufacture of ceramic tiles (*azujelos*) in Seville dates to ancient Roman times when potters set up shop in Triana, working clay extracted from the nearby Cartuja area.

Under the Moors, new glazing techniques were introduced and palaces across the city were tiled with *azulejos* painted with intricate geometric motifs. The subsequent expulsion of the Moors led to a shift in style as 16th-century Italian and Flemish ceramicists ushered in a trend for tile-pictures depicting religious and mythological subjects.

There followed a long period of decline, which lasted until an Englishman, Charles Pickman, opened a ceramics factory in the Monasterio de la Cartuja (p67) in the mid-19th century. However, a failure to modernise eventually forced this, and Triana's remaining potteries, out of business, and in 2012 the district's sole surviving factory, Cerámica Montalván, closed its doors for the very last time.

SEVILLE FOR CHILDREN

With leafy parks, a largely pedestrianised centre, brilliant food and a Disney-style amusement park, Seville is well set up for fun with the kids. Kids get into many sights free, though age limits vary – the Catedral (p50) is free for children up to 14; the Real Alcázar (p56) for under 16s. Both are accessible with strollers. Children under three travel free on city buses.

Kid-friendly sights and activities include:

Parque de María Luisa (p66) Seville's main park. Rowing boats are available for hire in the park at Plaza de España.

Isla Mágica (p68) Big amusement park targeted at kids over 10.

Museo Casa de La Ciencia (p66) Science museum with hands-on displays.

Pabellon de la Navegación (p67) Interactive exhibits on Seville's maritime history.

3pm Sun Apr-Jun, Sep & Oct, 10am-3.30pm Tue-Sun Jul & Aug, 10am-5pm Tue-Sat, to 3pm Sun Nov-Mar;) This boxy concrete-and-glass pavilion on the banks of the Río Guadalquivir revived a previous navigation museum that had been here from the 1992 Expo until 1999. Its permanent collection is split into four parts – navigation, mariners, shipboard life and historical views of Seville – and although its exhibits are interactive and kid-friendly, they might be a little underwhelming for adults. The ticket also covers admission to the adjacent **Torre Mirador** (Torre Schindler; adult/child incl Pabellón de la Navegación €4.90/3.50; noon-7.30pm Tue-Sat, to 2pm Sun Apr-Jun, Sep & Oct, 11am-2pm Tue-Sun Jul & Aug, 11am-4.30pm Tue-Sat, to 2pm Sun Nov-Mar).

Isla Mágica AMUSEMENT PARK

(Map p52; 902 16 17 16; www.islamagica.es; Camino de los Descubrimientos; full day adult/child €35/22; 11am-11pm mid-Jun–Aug, shorter hours Sep-Nov;) This Disney-does-Spanish-colonial amusement park provides an action-packed day out for kids and thrill-seekers with an array of white-knuckle rides, shows and attractions. Further aquatic fun awaits in the Agua Mágica section, accessible with a separate €9 ticket.

Hours vary by season – see the website for details. Buses C1 and C2 both stop near the park.

Courses

LaCasa Sevilla LANGUAGE

(666 882981; www.lacasasevilla.com; 2hr from €28) Fun and dynamic Spanish classes take students out and about in the city. Join Cristina, who hails from Cádiz and has lived in both the UK and US, to learn how to buy fruit and vegetables in a local market, or explore some of Seville's most beautiful and historic monuments while learning the language.

Taller Andaluz de Cocina COOKING

(Map p52; 955 31 25 74; www.tallerandaluzdecocina.com; Mercado de Triana, Plaza del Altozano; courses €44-60) Located in Triana Market, this cooking school offers a range of hands-on courses covering classic Spanish cuisine and tapas, as well as sherry tastings and market tours. Lessons and guided tours are all available in English – check the website for details.

Taller Flamenco DANCING

(Map p65; 954 56 42 34; www.tallerflamenco.com; Calle Peral 49) Offers flamenco dance courses, singing and guitar lessons, and language classes with the possibility of being taught in groups or on a one-to-one basis. Reckon on €102 for a one-week language course, €146 for a weekend flamenco course.

Tours

Pancho Tours TOURS

(664 642904; www.panchotours.com) FREE Runs excellent free tours, although you're welcome to tip the hard-working guide who'll furnish you with an encyclopaedia's worth of anecdotes, stories, myths and theories about Seville's fascinating past. The 2½-hour tours kick off daily at 11am – check the website for details. Pancho also offers bike tours (€25), skip-the-line cathedral (€21.25) and Alcázar visits (€17.50), and nightlife tours (from €17).

Mimo Sevilla FOOD & DRINK

(Map p58; 854 55 68 00; www.mimofood.com/en/location/sevilla; Calle San Fernando 2; tastings/tours/classes from €45/115/125) Based at its foodie shop in the lobby of the Hotel Alfonso XIII, Mimo runs wine tastings, cooking classes, tapas tours and day trips, including one to the sherry city of Jerez. Bank on €115 for a three-hour tapas tour, €45 for two hours of wine tasting.

Wanderbeak TOURS
(☎932 20 61 01; www.wanderbeak.com; tours €99) New to Seville, Wanderbeak runs evening food tours, taking in the Santa Cruz neighbourhood and a selection of traditional and modern tapas bars. The three-hour tours provide a good introduction to the city and its food culture, as well as teaching you the ins and outs of tapas-style dining.

Festivals & Events

Semana Santa RELIGIOUS
(www.semana-santa.org; ⏲Mar/Apr) Every day from Palm Sunday to Easter Sunday, elaborate, life-size *pasos* (floats carrying revered statues of Christ or the Virgin Mary) are paraded across town from their home churches to the cathedral. For the best views, park yourself near the cathedral in the early evening.

The processions are organised by more than 50 *hermandades* or *cofradías* (religious brotherhoods, some of which include women). Members, known as *nazarenos*, dress in white robes and pointed conical hoods, adding a sinister air to proceedings.

The week's highlight is La Madrugá, the early hours of Good Friday when several of the city's most venerated statues make their appearances.

Schedules are widely available during Semana Santa, or on the Semana Santa website.

Feria de Abril FERIA
(https://feriadesevilla.andalunet.com; El Real de la Feria; ⏲Apr) Seville's celebrated spring fair is held two weeks after Easter on the Real de la Feria fairground in the Los Remedios area west of the Río Guadalquivir. For six days and nights, *sevillanos* dress up in elaborate finery, parade around in horse-drawn carriages (the *paseo de caballos*), eat, drink and dance the *sevillana* (a popular style of fiesta dance).

Bienal de Flamenco FLAMENCO
(www.labienal.com; ⏲Sep) The big names of the flamenco world descend on Seville for this major flamenco festival. Held in September in even-numbered years, it features a comprehensive program of performances, exhibitions and workshops in venues across town.

Sleeping

Expect high-season rates from March to June and in September and October. Rates also skyrocket during Semana Santa and the Feria de Abril, for which you'll have to book well in advance.

Catedral & Barrio de Santa Cruz

Pensión San Pancracio PENSION €
(Map p58; ☎954 41 31 04; Calle Cruces 9; tr €90-100, q €120-130, without bathroom s €25-28, d €38-42, tr €60-75; ❄📶) An old-school family-run pension on a quiet Santa Cruz backstreet, this rambling house has plenty of room options and a pleasant flower-bedecked patio-lobby. Don't expect frills, just friendly staff and basic, spartan digs. Note that only the triples and quads with private bathrooms have air-con; all other rooms have fans.

★**Legado Alcázar** BOUTIQUE HOTEL €€
(Map p58; ☎954 09 18 18; www.legadoalcazarhotel.com; Calle Mariana de Pineda 18; d €124-150; ❄📶) Formerly part of the Alcázar royal palace, this stylish art-clad hotel looks onto the palace gardens, whose peacocks used to roost in one of the suites. Rooms range from bijou, with archaeological remains under the floor, to majestic, with wood-beamed ceilings, contemporary furniture, garden views and an outdoor balcony shower. Set-menu breakfasts (€15) are served in a pretty cafe-style room.

★**Hotel Amadeus** BOUTIQUE HOTEL €€
(Map p58; ☎954 50 14 43; www.hotelamadeussevilla.com; Calle Farnesio 6; d €92-195, tr €121-335, q €180-365; P❄📶) A soothing oasis of calm in the heart of the old *judería*, this delightful hotel boasts a ceramic-tiled lobby, period furniture and collection of musical instruments (which guests are free to play). Rooms, named after composers, are equally stylish, and there's a small rooftop terrace offering views over to the Giralda.

Un Patio en Santa Cruz HOTEL €€
(Map p58; ☎954 53 94 13; www.patiosantacruz.com; Calle Doncellas 15; s €55-210, d €65-220; ❄📶) This immaculate two-star has stark white walls hung with bright artworks and cascading plants. The sunny, light-filled rooms, complete with parquet, chandeliers and dashes of lilac, are good-looking and comfortable, staff are friendly, and there's a cool rooftop terrace with Moroccan-mosaic tables.

Casual Sevilla Don Juan Tenorio HOTEL €€
(Map p58; ☑ 955 54 44 16; www.casualhoteles. com; Plaza de los Venerables 5; r €45-155; ❄ 🛜) Atmospherically located off a Santa Cruz plaza, this bright hotel offers slick modern rooms, each themed after a character from *Don Juan Tenorio*, with quirky lights, stencils and stone-effect wall coverings. It has excellent wi-fi and hydromassage showers, and loans out useful mobile-phone packs with routers, chargers and selfie sticks (free if registered on the website, otherwise €2).

Hostal Plaza Santa Cruz HOTEL €€
(Map p58; ☑ 954 22 88 08; https://santacruz. alojamientosconencantosevilla.com; Calle Santa Teresa 15; d €40-120; ❄ 🛜) Offering a lovely location in the Barrio de Santa Cruz, this welcoming outfit has rooms spread over three buildings. Those in the main hotel, just off Plaza Santa Cruz, are fairly featureless with laminated parquet or marble floors and the occasional blast of colourful wallpaper, whilst the apartments are slightly more colourful with tiles, artworks and fully equipped kitchens.

⭐**Hotel Casa 1800** LUXURY HOTEL €€€
(Map p58; ☑ 954 56 18 00; www.hotelcasa 1800sevilla.com; Calle Rodrigo Caro 6; d €170-750; ste €360-1050; ❄ 🛜 ▦) A short hop from the cathedral and Alcázar, this stately *casa* (house) is positively regal. Setting the tone is the elegant, period decor – wooden ceilings, chandeliers, parquet floors and plenty of gilt – but everything about the place charms, from the helpful staff to the panoramic rooftop pool and complimentary afternoon tea.

Hotel Palacio Alcázar BOUTIQUE HOTEL €€€
(Map p58; ☑ 954 50 21 90; www.hotelpalacio alcazar.com; Plaza de Alianza 12; s €85-220, d €120-280; ❄ 🛜) Soothing, white minimalism on a cobbled Santa Cruz plaza, the four-star Palacio Alcázar sparkles in Seville's oldest quarter. It sports 12 lovely rooms, each in white and pearl grey with small oil paintings providing a dash of colour. Up top, you can enjoy drinks overlooking the Giralda at the wonderfully sited rooftop bar. Buffet breakfast costs €9.80 extra.

🛏 El Centro & El Arenal

⭐**La Banda** HOSTEL €
(Map p58; ☑ 621 012891, 955 22 81 18; www. labandahostel.com; Calle Dos de Mayo 16; dm €18-38; ❄ 🛜) Run by a young, sociable crew, this Arenal hostel ticks all the boxes. It's within easy walking distance of the big sights, the mixed dorms are clean and tidily furnished, and it has a great rooftop bar. Evening meals (€8, or €10 for Saturday paella and sangria) are available and a weekly program of events means there's always something going on.

Oasis Palace Hostel HOSTEL €
(Map p58; ☑ 955 26 26 96; www.oasissevilla. com; Calle Almirante Ulloa 1; dm €18-30, d €70-140; ❄ 🛜 ▦) A veritable oasis in the busy city-centre district, this buzzing hostel occupies a palatial 19th-century mansion. There are various sleeping options ranging from mixed 14-person dorms to doubles with en suite bathrooms, and excellent facilities, including a cafe-bar, fully equipped kitchen and rooftop deck with a small pool. Breakfast, not included in most rates, is available for €3.50.

⭐**Hotel Casa de Colón** BOUTIQUE HOTEL €€
(Map p58; ☑ 955 11 78 28; www.hotelcasade colon.com; Calle Hernando Colón 3; d €70-220; ❄ 🛜) A superb location, warm service and quirky decorative features combine to winning effect at this charming, family-run hotel. Look out for white cast-iron pillars, bedsteads made from old doors, and cobalt blue stained glass in the neo-Mudéjar windows. Some rooms have exposed-brick walls and side views of the cathedral, while top-floor *aticos* have private terraces. Continental breakfast is available for €9.

La Parada del Marqués BOUTIQUE HOTEL €€
(Map p52; ☑ 954 44 83 70; www.laparadadel marques.com; Calle Marqués de Paradas 45; d €100-150; ❄ 🛜) 🌿 Clean, contemporary styling, helpful staff and reasonable rates make this small hotel close to Plaza de Armas bus station an excellent midrange option. Eco touches include energy-saving keys and insulated windows (for keeping road noise out), while antique furniture, exposed-brick walls and original tiled floors feature in the high-ceilinged white rooms.

Suites Sevilla Plaza APARTMENT €€
(Map p58; ☑ 955 03 85 33; www.suitessevilla plaza.com; Calle Zaragoza 52; 1-bedroom €80-240, 2-bedroom €140-450; ❄ 🛜) With eight self-catering apartments and a central location handy for just about everywhere, Suites Sevilla Plaza is ideal for families, groups or longer stays. Apartments, which sleep from two to six, are spacious and tastefully attired in an unfussy modern style. Added bonuses include a laundry, bike hire (€10) and a rooftop space with views of the Giralda.

Hotel Abanico HOTEL €€
(Map p58; ☎954 21 32 07; www.hotelabanico.com; Calle Águilas 17; s €50-158, d €55-162; ❄📶) From the beautiful, columned lobby to the distinctive tile work, wrought-iron balconies and radiant religious art, this welcoming hotel has Seville written all over it. Rooms are simple affairs with pronounced colours and modest, old-school furniture. Breakfast is €7 extra.

Hotel Adriano HOTEL €€
(Map p58; ☎954 29 38 00; www.adrianohotel.com; Calle de Adriano 12; s €70-150, d €80-250; P❄📶) Near the bullring in the Arenal district, the traditional Adriano scores across the board with courteous staff, classically attired marble-floored rooms and a lovely coffee shop, Pompeia, on the ground floor. Garage parking is available for €21 per day.

La Macarena & Alameda de Hércules

Corner House HOTEL €€
(Map p65; ☎954 91 32 62; www.thecornerhousesevilla.com; Alameda de Hércules 11; d €45-120; ❄📶) This self-styled 'urban' hotel sits well with the buzzing bars and cafes on the Alameda de Hércules. Modern in look and upbeat in vibe, it offers sun-filled rooms with minimal white decor, hanging lamps and the occasional blast of designer colour. There's a ground-floor restaurant, El Disparate, and, up on the 3rd floor, a great rooftop bar (p78).

Hotel Boutique Doña Lola BOUTIQUE HOTEL €€
(Map p65; ☎954 91 52 75; www.donalolasevilla.com; Calle Amor de Dios 19; s €40-110, d €45-110, apt €75-190; ❄📶) A short hop from the bar action on the Alameda de Hércules, gay-friendly Doña Lola is well positioned for sorties pretty much everywhere. From the lobby, complete with a coloured chequered floor, stairs lead to rooms which, although small, are modern and minimally furnished. There are also mini-apartments over the road, and up top, a solarium with an alfresco Jacuzzi.

Hotel San Gil HOTEL €€
(Map p65; ☎954 90 68 11; www.hotelsangil.es; Calle Parras 28; d €65-180; ❄📶🏊) On a quiet street in the Macarena neighbourhood, San Gil's slightly out-of-the-way location is balanced by its proximity to the nightlife of the Alameda de Hércules. Behind the mustard-yellow colonial facade, an ostentatiously tiled lobby gives on to an elegant courtyard and comfortable, modern rooms.

SEVILLE'S LOGO

Walk around Seville and you'll see a curious symbol (NO8DO) emblazoned on everything from vans and buses to benches, bins and manhole covers.

According to local legend, the symbol, now Seville's logo, was granted to the city by King Alfonso X after it had backed him in a 13th-century power struggle against his rebellious son, Sancho IV of Castilla.

The elongated 8 in the middle of the word represents a skein of yarn, the Spanish word for which is *madeja*. So NO8DO becomes '*no madeja do*', which sounds like '*no me ha dejado*' or 'she (the city) hasn't abandoned me'.

Hotel Sacristía de Santa Ana BOUTIQUE HOTEL €€€
(Map p65; ☎954 91 57 22; www.hotelsacristia.com; Alameda de Hércules 22; d €60-250; ❄📶) Occupying an 18th-century town house on the Alameda de Hércules, this traditional hotel makes a fabulous first impression. On entering, you're greeted by a splendid red-tiled courtyard centred on a small fountain and overlooked by carved wooden balustrades. Up from here, hallways lead to old-fashioned rooms furnished with arty bedsteads, beamed ceilings and antique furniture.

One Shot Palacio Conde de Torrejón 09 DESIGN HOTEL €€€
(Map p65; ☎854 56 58 54; www.oneshothotels.com; Calle Conde de Torrejón 9; d €80-275; P❄📶🏊) This converted 18th-century palace cuts a contemporary dash near the Alameda de Hércules. It boasts 56 slickly styled rooms and suites with rain showers and 46-inch smart TVs, as well as a restaurant serving creative cuisine, and a small rooftop pool. The interior design encompasses a *celosia* (geometrically patterned Moorish screen) ceiling and sharp modern furniture, with quirky photography and art exhibitions.

Triana

Hotel Monte Triana HOTEL €€
(Map p52; ☎954 34 31 11; www.hotelesmonte.com; Clara de Jesús Montero 24; s €70-160, d €90-190; P❄📶) Escape the tourist hordes at this smart Triana hotel over the river from the historic centre. The polished black and white lobby sets the tone for spacious, good-value

rooms decorated in corporate shades of white and honey wood. Facilities also impress with a fitness room, bar, cafe and garage (€15 per night).

Eating

The city is brimming with bars, cafes, restaurants and markets. Hotspots include the Barrio de Santa Cruz, the streets around Plaza de la Alfalfa and the Alameda de Hércules. Note that some restaurants close for part of August.

Catedral & Barrio de Santa Cruz

Bodega Santa Cruz TAPAS €

(Map p58; 954 21 86 18; Calle Rodrigo Caro 1; tapas €2.50; 8am-midnight) This is as old-school as it gets, a perennially busy bar staffed by gruff waiters and frequented by Sevillans and visitors alike. Traditional tapas such as *montaditos de pringá* (bread rolls stuffed with slow-cooked pork and sausage) are best enjoyed alfresco with a cold beer as you watch the armies of tourists traipse past.

★La Azotea ANDALUCIAN €€

(Map p58; 954 21 58 78; www.laazoteasevilla.com; Calle Mateos Gago 8; tapas €3.50-6.50, mains €12-22; 9am-midnight) The best of the bars and restaurants in the cathedral area, this is one of several Azotea branches around town. It takes a contemporary approach to dining, offering sleek, modern design, energetic service and creative Andalucian cuisine. Particularly outstanding are its seafood dishes, such as grilled *calamar* (squid) and sea bass curry.

Vinería San Telmo TAPAS €€

(Map p58; 954 41 06 00; www.vineriasantelmo.com; Paseo Catalina de Ribera 4; tapas €3.50-6.50, medias raciones €6.90-15; 1-4.30pm & 8pm-midnight) San Telmo's innovative tapas continue to wow diners, and its tables, either outside or in the brick-tiled interior, are a prized commodity. Bag one, for which you'll either have to wait or book, and sit down to the likes of pan-fried octopus with red onions and grilled foie gras with apple compote.

Café Bar Las Teresas TAPAS €€

(Map p58; 954 21 30 69; www.lasteresas.es; Calle Santa Teresa 2; tapas €2.50-4.50, mains €8-24; 10am-1am) The hanging hams look as ancient as the bar itself, a sinuous wrap-around affair with a cheerfully cluttered interior. Locals congregate at the bar while tourists take to the wonky streetside tables for traditional tapas like *espinacas con garbanzos* (spinach with chickpeas) and hearty *salchichón ibérico* (sausage).

El Centro & El Arenal

Sal Gorda ANDALUCIAN €

(Map p58; 955 38 59 72; www.facebook.com/SalGordaSevilla; Calle Alcaicería de la Loza 23; tapas €3.20-8.50; 1-4.30pm & 8-11.30pm Wed-Mon) Incongruously located in an old shoe shop, this tiny, low-key place serves innovative takes on Andalucian dishes – try *ajo blanco* (white gazpacho soup) with *mojama* (salt-cured tuna), and a first-class version of the ubiquitous tuna tartare. Mushroom risotto with langoustines is a firm favourite, and the wine list features good local whites such as El Mirlo Blanco from Constantina. Reservations recommended.

Palo Cortao SPANISH €

(Map p58; 649 446120; www.palo-cortao.com; Calle Mercedes de Velilla 4; tapas €3.50-7, mains €6-12; 1-4.30pm Tue-Sun, 8.30-11.30pm Tue-Sat) This excellent sherry bar, tucked

ICE CREAM

In a city where summer temperatures regularly top 40 degrees, a coolling ice cream is always a good idea.

One of the city's best *heladerias* (ice-cream parlours) is **Créeme** (Map p58; 954 91 08 32; www.facebook.com/creemehelado; Plaza del Museo 2; cones & tubs €3-5; 12.30pm-1am), a modern outfit near the Museo de Bellas Artes that serves exquisite flavours such as *caramelo de mantequilla salada* (caramel with salted butter).

Other top choices include **Bolas** (Map p58; 954 22 74 11; Cuesta del Rosario 1; cones €2.20-4, tubs €2.80-5; 2pm-midnight Mon-Thu, to 12.30am Fri & Sat, to 11.30pm Sun), where you can enjoy exotic combos like its Medina sorbet of orange, ginger and cinnamon, and **Freskura** (Map p65; Calle Vulcano 4; cones & tubs €3-4.80; noon-1am), an Alameda outpost that specialises in smooth, Italian-style gelato.

away in a side street near the Metropol Parasol, offers excellent, knowledgeable service (Ana) and imaginative cooking (Angel). Choose from more than 30 sherries by the glass (*palo cortao* is a less common type), accompanied by premium *chacinas* (cold meat) and cheeses, plus tapas such as cuttlefish balls in red shrimp sauce.

Bar Casa Eme TAPAS €

(Map p52; Calle Puerta del Osario 5; tapas €2.70-4.90; ⌚12.30-4pm & 8.30pm-midnight Thu-Tue) With its red plastic tables and a neon-lit interior tiled with religious icons, you'd easily walk past this place without giving it a backward glance. But stop and you'll discover it's a real find, an authentic bar serving delicious tapas prepared by the gruff old boy who runs the place. Try the superb *solomillo al whisky* (pork loin in whisky sauce).

Confitería La Campana PASTRIES €

(Map p58; ☎954 22 35 70; www.confiterialacampana.com; Calle Sierpes 1-3; pastries from €2.50; ⌚8am-10pm) A landmark art deco patisserie and cafe, La Campana has been catering to Seville's sweet-toothed since 1885. Join the mixed crowd in its elegant interior for a *yema* (soft, crumbly biscuit cake wrapped like a toffee), or a coffee and *torta de aceite* (flat, crumbly biscuit made with olive oil).

★La Brunilda TAPAS €€

(Map p58; ☎954 22 04 81; Calle Galera 5; tapas €4-7.50, mains €6.50-15; ⌚1-4pm & 8.30-11.30pm Tue-Sat, 1-4pm Sun) Hidden away in an anonymous Arenal backstreet, this tapas hotspot is a guarantee of good times. The look is modern casual with big blue doors, brick arches and plain wooden tables, and the food is imaginative and brilliantly executed. Arrive promptly or expect long queues.

★Mamarracha TAPAS €€

(Map p58; ☎955 12 39 11; www.mamarracha.es; Calle Hernando Colón 1-3; tapas €2.50-12, mains €5.50-14; ⌚1-4.30pm & 8.30pm-midnight) Sharp decor, young staff in black T-shirts, cool tunes and an international menu, this is a fine example of the modern tapas bars that Seville so excels at. Its interior sports distressed cement, exposed vents and a vertical garden wall, while its menu reveals some slick combos, including a terrific focaccia with marinated Iberian pork.

Lobo López MEDITERRANEAN €€

(Map p58; ☎854 70 58 34; www.facebook.com/LoboLopezTapas; Calle Rosario 15; tapas €3-8, mains €10-19; ⌚8am-11.30pm Mon-Sat, from 12.30pm Sun; ❄📶🥗) From the hip-yet-historic decor (concrete-cast art, vertical garden, exposed-brick arches) to the cheeky waiters, this place rocks a cool vibe. The food doesn't disappoint, with a short but well-chosen menu, including some tasty international interpretations – Hawaiian tuna *poke*, Vietnamese pulled pork rolls. Unusually, it's open all day, so it's also an ideal mid-afternoon cake-and-smoothie stop.

Zoko ANDALUCIAN €€

(Map p58; ☎954 96 31 49; www.restaurante-zoko.com; Calle Marqués de Paradas 55; tapas €4.50-7.50; ⌚12.30-4pm & 8pm-midnight) Superb sustainably caught bluefin tuna *(atún de almadraba)* stars at this trendily casual restaurant near Plaza de Armas bus station. As well as the tenderest tuna, which comes in croquettes, salads and tataki, it also cooks up some superlative rice dishes.

La Macarena & Alameda de Hércules

Cocome CAFE €

(Map p58; ☎955 11 15 66; www.cocomefresco.com; Calle Tarifa 4; breakfasts €3.50-5.50; ⌚9am-noon & 1-5pm Mon-Sat; 🥗) Get your day off to a sunny start with breakfast at this cheery cafe near Plaza del Duque. Staff are delightful and there's an impressive selection of toast, fruit bowls, granola, yoghurts, cereals and smoothies. For lunch, there's soup, or make-your-own salads, wraps and sandwiches. Sit at the front window bar for street views, or the tables at the back.

Duo Tapas TAPAS €

(Map p65; ☎955 23 85 72; Calle Calatrava 10; tapas €3-5, medias raciones €8-12; ⌚12.30-4.30pm & 8.30pm-midnight) Exciting tapas go hand in hand with a casual, bustling vibe at this 'new-school' bar just off the Alameda de Hércules. Squeeze yourself into a table and eat your way through a menu that ranges from excellent pork cheeks in wine to fusion fare with an Asian twist, such as tempura veggies and shrimp spring rolls.

Mercado de Feria MARKET €

(Lonja de Feria; Map p65; www.mercadodelaferia.es; Plaza Calderón de la Barca; tapas & drink €6; ⌚12.30-6pm Tue & Wed, 1pm-midnight Fri & Sat, 1-6pm Sun) For an authentic bite in atmospheric surrounds, head to this Macarena market, the oldest in Seville. There are numerous tapas bars to try or you can opt for the central

Lonja de Feria food court where a €6 ticket buys you a beer and a daily dish, perhaps a portion of paella, fried fish or meatballs.

★ Bar-Restaurante Eslava TAPAS €€
(Map p65; ☎954 90 65 68; www.espacioeslava.com; Calle Eslava 3; tapas €2.90-4.50, restaurant mains €13.50-26; ⌚bar 12.30pm-midnight Tue-Sat, restaurant 1.30-4pm & 8.30pm-midnight Tue-Sat) You'll almost certainly have to wait for a table at the bar, but it's so worth it, especially if you use the time to start on the excellent wine list. The tapas are superb: contemporary, creative, brilliantly executed and incredible value for money. Standouts include slow-cooked egg served on mushroom puree, and a filo pastry cigar stuffed with cuttlefish and algae.

★ conTenedor ANDALUCIAN €€
(Map p65; ☎954 91 63 33; www.restaurantecontenedor.com; Calle San Luis 50; mains €9-22; ⌚1.30-4.30pm & 8-11.30pm Mon-Thu, 1.30-4.30pm & 8.30pm-midnight Fri & Sat, 1.30-4.30pm & 8.30-11.30pm Sun) The atmosphere at this slow-food restaurant in boho Macarena is arty and relaxed, with an open kitchen, mismatched furniture and colourful paintings by co-owner Ricardo on the walls. The food is equally appealing, with dishes composed to show off locally sourced organic produce. Try the duck rice, the house speciality, or keep it green with a creative salad.

Parque de María Luisa & South of the Centre

Ispal ANDALUCIAN €€
(Map p58; ☎955 54 71 27; www.restauranteispal.com; Plaza de San Sebastián 1; mains €12-25, tasting menus €49-75; ⌚1-4pm & 8pm-midnight Tue-Sat, 1-4pm Sun; ❄) Improbably located in the Prado de San Sebastián bus station, this celeb haunt flies the flag for regional Andalucian cuisine. Imaginative and impeccably presented tasting menus take diners on a culinary tour of Seville and province, featuring olives, *torrijas* (Spanish-style French toast) with orange blossom, sea bass from Isla Mayor, and suckling pig. Wines are all from Andalucía too.

Triana

★ Manu Jara Dulcería PASTRIES €
(Map p52; ☎675 873674; Calle Pureza 5; pastries €2-3.50; ⌚9.30am-2.30pm & 4.30-9pm Mon-Thu, 9.30am-9pm Fri & Sat, 10am-8.30pm Sun) No day in Triana would be complete without a stop at this exquisite patisserie. With its traditional wood and tiled interior, it sets the perfect backdrop for an array of artfully crafted cakes and pastries, including a sensational *milohajas* (*mille feuille* or vanilla slice). There's another branch in Nervión by the Sevilla FC stadium, and in the nearby Triana Market.

Alfarería 21 ANDALUCIAN €€
(Map p52; ☎955 83 48 75; www.facebook.com/alfarera21Triana; Calle Alfarería 21; tapas €2.80-4.50, mains €7-15; ⌚12.30-4pm & 8pm-midnight) This bar occupies an old Triana ceramic factory: Montalván's original brick-and-tile facade and *azulejo* wall tiles maintain the traditional feel, while the short menu veers towards the modern with updated twists on traditional Sevillan fare. Downstairs there's a casual vibe, with stools and low or high tables, while upstairs is more formal.

Casa Cuesta TAPAS €€
(Map p52; ☎954 33 33 35; www.casacuesta.net; Calle de Castilla 1; tapas €3, mains €7.50-15; ⌚8am-12.30am Mon-Sat, from 12.30pm Sun) A neighbourhood institution once frequented by local bullfighters, writers and artists, Casa Cuesta looks exactly the part with its large, plate-glass windows, ceramic tiling, bullfighting and flamenco memorabilia, and gleaming beer pumps. In keeping with the decor, the food is traditional with a good selection of tapas, rice dishes, and meat and fish *raciones* (full servings of tapas items).

Drinking & Nightlife

Popular drinking areas include Calle Betis in Triana, Plaza de Salvador, Barrio de Santa Cruz, and the Alameda de Hércules, host to a lively scene and the city's gay nightlife. In summer, dozens of *terrazas de verano* (open-air bars) pop up on the river's banks.

★ Bier Kraft CRAFT BEER
(Map p65; ☎955 12 41 80; Calle Correduría 35; ⌚6pm-2am Tue-Thu, 1pm-3am Fri & Sat, 1pm-2am Sun) Sporting high ceilings and a retro-industrial look, Bier Kraft has been flying the flag for craft beer since 2017. Its collection of national and international beers is one of the city's best, providing fuel for many happy hours of elbow-raising experimentation. For an easy start, try the hoppy blonde Río Azul.

El Viajero Sedentario CAFE
(Map p65; www.facebook.com/viajerosedentario; Alameda de Hércules 77; ⌚9.30am-1am Tue-Sat, 10.30am-11pm Sun) This inviting Alameda cafe is a lovely place to hang out with its bright

murals, shady courtyard and tiny book-stacked interior. Early evening is a good time for a relaxed pre-dinner beer, and it's not uncommon to find people dancing to low-key jazz tunes on sultry summer nights.

Maquila CRAFT BEER
(Map p65; 955 18 23 20; www.facebook.com/maquilabar; Calle Delgado 4; 1-4.30pm & 8pm-midnight) A leading light in Seville's craft beer scene since 2015, this cool, open-plan bar has six beers on tap and a small selection of bottled brews. Its in-house label, Son, is always a good bet, or you can go for one of the regularly rotated IPAs, pale ales, stouts or pilsners. To accompany the amber nectar, there's a full menu of tapas (€3.20 to €5.90).

Gallo Rojo CRAFT BEER
(Map p65; www.facebook.com/gallorojofactoriadecreacion; Calle Madre Maria de Purisima 9; 5pm-midnight Tue-Thu, to 2am Fri & Sat, to 10pm Sun) Housed in a former factory, arty Rojo is a lively yet laid-back spot that regularly hosts concerts, readings and flamenco performances. It's also a cool place to drink, with mismatched vintage furniture, huge plate glass windows and excellent craft beer – try the house Zurda golden ale or choose from the selection of guest Sevillan and European brews.

Casa Vizcaíno BAR
(Map p65; 954 38 60 57; Calle Feria 27; 10am-11.30pm Mon-Fri, to 4pm Sat & Sun) Sawdust on the floor, yellowing pictures of Jesus and a blue-tiled bar tended by veterans who chalk your tab on the counter, this no-frills watering hole is as authentic as it gets. Join the crowds that spill onto the pavement to gossip over vermouth and expertly poured beer.

El Garlochi BAR
(Map p58; Calle Boteros 26; 9pm-3am Mon-Sat, to midnight Sun) There are few weirder places to drink than this baroque temple of kitsch. Decked out in ultra-camp religious decor, it's dedicated entirely to the iconography, smells and sounds of the Semana Santa. To get in the mood, try the signature cocktail, a Sangre de Cristo (Blood of Christ), made from grenadine, sparkling wine and whisky.

☆ Entertainment

★Casa de la Memoria FLAMENCO
(Map p58; 954 56 06 70; www.casadelamemoria.es; Calle Cuna 6; adult/student/child €18/15/10; 11am-6pm, shows 7.30pm & 9pm) Occupying the old stables of the 16th-century Palacio de la Condesa de Lebrija, this cultural centre stages authentic, highly charged flamenco shows, as well as housing a small exhibition of flamenco memorabilia. The nightly shows are perennially popular, and as space is limited, you'll need to reserve tickets a day or so in advance by calling or visiting the venue.

LOCAL KNOWLEDGE

SEVILLE'S OLDEST BAR

El Rinconcillo (Map p58; 954 22 31 83; www.elrinconcillo.es; Calle Gerona 40; tapas €2.50-3.50, raciones €7.50-20; 1pm-1.30am), the blueprint for centuries' worth of imitators, is the oldest bar in Seville – and some say, Spain – dating to 1670. Over the centuries, it's become pretty touristy, but it's managed to retain a gnarled sense of authenticity. With its hanging hams, ceramic tiles and dark wood ceilings, it sets a memorable stage for classic tapas.

Tablao Los Gallos FLAMENCO
(Map p58; 954 21 69 81; www.tablaolosgallos.com; Plaza de Santa Cruz 11; adult/child €35/20; shows 8pm & 10pm) Located on a pretty Santa Cruz plaza, this is Seville's oldest *tablao* (choreographed flamenco show), dating from 1966. Its two-nightly shows feature a wider range of performers (all top-notch) than most set-ups, with four dancers, three singers and three guitarists – hence its above-average admission price. One for aficionados.

Naima Café Jazz JAZZ
(Map p65; 653 753976; Calle Trajano 47; 8pm-2am Mon-Wed, 4pm-2am Thu & Sun, 4pm-3am Fri & Sat) This mellow bar is an evergreen favourite for jazz and blues, staged most nights. Drinks are reasonably priced and its tiny interior – you could easily find yourself squeezed in next to the drummer with a hi-hat crashing inches from your nose – ensures a humming vibe. Gigs are free if you buy a drink, otherwise there's a €3 'donation'.

La Casa del Flamenco FLAMENCO
(Map p58; 955 02 99 99; www.lacasadelflamencosevilla.com; Calle Ximénez de Enciso 28; adult/student/child €20/15/10; shows 7pm winter & autumn, 7pm & 8.30pm spring, 8.30pm summer) A beautiful patio in an old Sephardic Jewish mansion in Santa Cruz is home to La Casa del Flamenco. Shows, performed on a stage hemmed in by seating on three sides, are mesmerising.

1

2

VDV/SHUTTERSTOCK ©

Tablao Cardenal (p218), Córdoba **2.** Peña La Platería (p277), ranada **3.** Castanets

Seeing Flamenco

The intensity and spontaneity of flamenco have never translated well onto studio recordings. Instead, to ignite the goosebumps and inspire the powerful emotional spirit known to aficionados as *duende*, you have to be there at a performance, stamping your feet and passionately yelling *'¡olé!'*.

Peñas

Peñas are private local clubs run by enthusiasts determined to preserve flamenco in its traditional form. Most are closed to non-members, but some open their doors to the public at particular times. To find a *peña*, ask in flamenco bars or tourist offices, check posters, and use your ears to follow any interesting sounds. Not surprisingly, *peñas* present some of the most authentic and passionate shows in Spain. They also incorporate flamenco's oft-overlooked fourth component, the *jaleo* (audience participation).

Tablaos

Tablaos are well-rehearsed flamenco shows that display the art in a highly professional and choreographed way. Unlike *peñas, tablao* shows are held in venues where drinks and sometimes dinner are included in the price of the ticket. *Tablaos* are sometimes derided by flamenco experts for lacking the spit and sawdust that makes the art so unique, and for catering to a visiting clientele, but the artistic talent at these events is of a high standard, and the venues are often eye-catching.

Bars & Tabancos

Local bars are your best bet for seeing flamenco on the cheap, and the atmosphere will certainly be informal, though the music and dancing may be more akin to mad jamming sessions than authentic *cante jondo* (an intense flamenco vocal style). Age-old flamenco neighbourhoods such as Triana in Seville or Santiago in Jerez are known as places where dancers and musicians come together to talk, drink and, if you're lucky, perform. In Jerez, the lively revitalised *tabancos* (bars pouring sherry from the barrel) often host flamenco performances and classes, while the Festival de Jerez (p130) is a top-tier celebration of the art in venues around town.

LOCAL KNOWLEDGE

ROOFTOP COCKTAILS

Seville's rooftops harbour some wonderful bars, ideal for cooling cocktails and captivating views. Two of the best are:

Corner House Terraza (Map p65; ☎954 91 32 62; www.thecornerhousesevilla.com; Corner House, Alameda de Hércules 11; ⏲5-11pm Wed-Sun Nov-Feb, 4pm-midnight daily Mar-Oct) With its wooden decking, handmade tables and grandstand views over the vibrant, tree-lined plaza below, the rooftop terrace at the Corner House is a top spot to kick back and enjoy a cool evening cocktail. The mojitos (€8) are particularly fine, sharply flavoured and packing a formidable punch.

La Terraza del Eme (Map p58; www.emecatedralmercer.com; Calle de los Alemanes 27; ⏲2pm-2am) Enjoy spectacular cathedral close-ups and classic cocktails at the chic roof terrace bar of the five-star EME Catedral Hotel. Drinks are on the pricey side at around €16 for a G&T, but DJs create a lively lounge vibe and the Catedral views really are special.

Casa Anselma FLAMENCO

(Map p52; ☎606 162502; Calle Pagés del Corro 49; ⏲11.45pm-2am Mon-Sat) True, the music is often more folkloric than flamenco, but this Triana institution is the antithesis of a showbiz flamenco *tablao*, with cheek-to-jowl crowds, zero amplification and spontaneous outbreaks of dancing. Doors don't open till around midnight, and there's an arbitrary admission policy, so you may be refused entry. Reservations recommended.

Fun Club LIVE MUSIC

(Map p65; ☎636 669023; www.facebook.com/SalaFUNCLUB; Alameda de Hércules 86; €6-12; ⏲9.30pm-7am Thu-Sat) The iconic Fun Club has been entertaining the nocturnal Alameda de Hércules crowd since the late 1980s. It still packs them in, drawing a young, energetic crowd to its club nights and regular gigs – indie, rock and hip-hop. Great for sweaty, late-night dancing.

Shopping

Seville's commercial shopping district is centred on Calles Sierpes, Velázquez/Tetuán and Cuna, north of Plaza Nueva. For a more alternative scene, head to the area around Calles Pérez Galdós and Regina or, to the north, around Calles Amor de Dios and Feria. Over the river, Triana is the place for ceramic ware.

★**La Oleoteca** FOOD

(Map p58; ☎954 86 91 85; www.oleotecasevilla.com; Calle García de Vinuesa 39; ⏲10.30am-2pm & 5-8pm Mon-Sat, 10.30am-2pm Sun) If you're looking to take some Spanish olive oil home, super-enthusiastic Andrés García is the person to help you. At his well-stocked shop, he'll talk you through the finer points of his collection and steer you to the blends that best suit your tastes and budget. Reckon on around €5 for a half-bottle, €7 to €20 for a full-sized one.

La Importadora CLOTHING

(Map p58; ☎954 56 18 29; www.laimportadora.es; Calle Pérez Galdós 2; ⏲10.30am-2pm & 5-8.30pm Mon-Fri, 11am-2.30pm & 5.30-8.30pm Sat) Part-boutique, part-gallery, La Importadora captures the hip Alfalfa vibe with its exposed white-brick walls, contemporary (and original) artworks, pot plants and racks of shabby-chic vintage clothes. You'll find everything from seasonal fashions, often by local designers, to bijou jewellery and cool shoes.

Un Gato en Bicicleta BOOKS

(Map p58; ☎955 29 56 51; Calle Pérez Galdós 22; ⏲9.30am-2pm & 4.30-9pm, closed Mon morning) This arty bookshop, gallery, cafe and ceramics studio is a hub for Seville's creative community. Look for painter Agustín Israel's irreverent takes on *nazarenos*, the hooded Holy Week penitents, and tomes covering cinema, fashion and architecture. It regularly hosts book presentations and there's coffee and cakes at its cafe. Find it on Instragram: @ungatoenbicicleta.

Tarico FOOD & DRINKS

(Map p65; ☎954 02 68 03; www.facebook.com/TiendaTarico; Calle Amor de Dios 14; ⏲10am-2.30pm & 5.30-10pm mid-Jul–mid-Oct, shorter hours mid-Oct–mid-Jul) From award-winning extra-virgin olive oil from Jaén to goat's milk cheese from Huelva, this airy food store showcases quality produce from small regional producers. Items have been personally selected by the owner, who's happy to guide you through his stock of craft beers, wines, cheeses, cured meats, pâtés, honeys and chocolates.

Coco Sevilla CERAMICS
(Map p58; ☎657 299470; https://facebook.com/cocosevilla; Plaza de Pilatos 3; ⏲11am-8pm) Run by friendly French owner Didier, this pretty shop stocks a range of colourful 19th-century *azulejos* (ceramic tiles) made across the river in Triana. Their typical geometric *alicatado* designs are also replicated on jewellery, notebooks, drinks mats and other eye-catching mementos, all imaginatively displayed. Other finds include printed cotton scarves, shawls and hand-painted fans.

Lama La Uva WINE
(Map p65; ☎601 494138; www.lamalauva.com; Calle Regina 1; ⏲11.30am-2.30pm & 7-11pm Tue-Sat) Overshadowed by the Metropol Parasol, Ana's shop has an eye-catching turquoise facade and an impressive range of wines from less well known Spanish regions, plus all eight Andalucian provinces. You can buy a bottle, or stop in the small bar for a tasting: she offers more than 40 sherries and knowledgeable pairings with cheeses and *jamón serrano*.

Cerámica Triana CERAMICS
(Map p52; ☎954 33 21 79; www.ceramicatriana.com; Calle Callao 14; ⏲10am-9pm Mon-Fri, to 8pm Sat) Seville specialises in distinctive *azulejos* and they are best bought in Triana, the historic hub of the city's ceramic industry. Cerámica Triana has been around for more than 50 years and its tiled shopfront is something of a local landmark. Inside, you'll find every inch of space crammed with decorative crockery, tiles, signs, crucifixes and figurines.

Information

MEDICAL SERVICES

Centro de Salud El Porvenir (☎954 71 23 23; Calle Porvenir; ⏲8am-8pm Mon-Fri) Public clinic with emergency services.

Hospital Virgen del Rocío (☎955 01 20 00; www.hospitaluvrocio.es; Avenida de Manuel Siurot) Seville's main hospital, 1km south of Parque de María Luisa.

TOURIST INFORMATION

Airport Tourist Office (☎954 78 20 35; www.andalucia.org; Seville Airport; ⏲9am-7.30pm Mon-Fri, 9.30am-3pm Sat & Sun)

Municipal Tourist Office (Map p58; ☎955 47 12 32; www.visitasevilla.es; Paseo Marqués de Contadero; ⏲9am-2.30pm Mon-Fri)

Central Tourist Office (Map p58; ☎954 21 00 05; www.turismosevilla.org; Plaza del Triunfo 1; ⏲9am-7.30pm Mon-Fri, 9.30am-7.30pm Sat & Sun; 📶)

Train Station Tourist Office (☎954 78 20 02; www.andalucia.org; Estación Santa Justa; ⏲9am-7.30pm Mon-Fri, 9.30am-3pm Sat & Sun)

Getting There & Away

AIR

Seville Airport (Aeropuerto de Sevilla; ☎913 21 10 00; www.aena.es; A4, Km 532), 7km northeast of the city, has flights to/from Spanish cities and destinations across Europe including London, Paris, Amsterdam, Dublin, Frankfurt and Rome.

It's served by international airlines such as Ryanair, easyJet and Vueling.

BUS

Estación de Autobuses Plaza de Armas (Map p52; ☎955 03 86 65; www.autobusesplazadearmas.es; Avenida del Cristo de la Expiración) Seville's main bus station. From here, **ALSA** (☎902 42 22 42; www.alsa.es) buses serve Málaga (€19 to €24, 2¾ to three hours, six to seven daily), Granada (€23 to €30, three hours, 11 to 12 daily), Córdoba (€12.65, 1¾ to two hours, seven daily) and Almería (€38 to €47, 5¼ to 8¾ hours, four daily). **Damas** (☎959 25 69 00; www.damas-sa.es) runs buses to Huelva province and **Flixbus** (Map p52; ☎919 01 06 32; www.flixbus.es) has international services to cities in Portugal including Faro, Lisbon and Porto.

Estación de Autobuses Prado de San Sebastián (Map p58; Plaza San Sebastián) Has services to many smaller towns in Andalucía. Damas operates buses to Ronda and Marbella, while **Comes** (Map p58; ☎902 19 92 08; www.tgcomes.es) runs to Cádiz, Jerez de la Frontera and some of the harder-to-reach *pueblos blancos* (white towns) in Cádiz province.

TRAIN

Seville's principal train station, **Estación Santa Justa** (Avenida Kansas City), is 1.5km northeast of the centre.

High-speed AVE trains go to/from Madrid (€50 to €88, 2½ to 3¼ hours, hourly) and Córdoba (€14 to €32, 45 minutes to 1¼ hours, up to 35 daily). Slower trains head to Cádiz (€17 to €24, 1¾ hours, 16 daily), Huelva (€13, 1½ hours, four daily), Granada (€31 to €61, 2½ to 4¼ hours, nine daily) and Málaga (€25 to €47, two to 3½ hours, 12 daily). Note that the cheapest services to Granada and Málaga involve travelling part of the way by bus.

Getting Around

TO/FROM THE AIRPORT

The **EA Bus** (☎955 01 00 10; www.tussam.es; one way/return €4/6) connects the airport to the city centre, running to/from Plaza de Armas bus station via Santa Justa train station and Prado de San Sebastián.

Departures from the airport are every 15 to 30 minutes between 5.20am and 1am; from Plaza de Armas between 4.30am and 12.10am. Services are reduced early in the morning and late at night.

Taxis charge set fares: €23 (daytime Monday to Friday); €25 (weekends, night-time Monday to Friday, daytime Easter and the Feria de Abril) and €32 (night-time Easter and the Feria de Abril). Note that these rates apply only to the journey to/from the airport – if you phone for a cab, you'll also be charged for the drive to your pick-up point.

BUS

Seville has an extensive bus network, operated by **Tussam** (☎955 01 00 10; www.tussam.es).

Buses run from around 6am to midnight. Night buses (buses A1 to A8) operate out of Prado de San Sebastián (p79) between midnight and 2am from Sunday to Thursday and until 5am on Fridays and Saturdays.

Useful routes include the following circular lines:

C1 and C2 External route around the centre.

C3 and C4 Internal route around the centre.

C5 Runs through the centre.

Tickets can be bought on buses, at stations, or at kiosks next to stops. A standard ticket is €1.40 but a range of passes are also available, including daily/three-day travel cards for €5/10.

CAR & MOTORCYCLE

Driving in Seville is generally not worth the hassle. Traffic restrictions are in force and the narrow streets of the historic centre are not car friendly. Parking is no fun either.

For car hire, there's **Avis** (☎902 11 02 83; www.avis.com; Estación Santa Justa; ⊙8am-11pm) or **Enterprise** (☎954 41 26 40; www.enterprise.es; ⊙7.30am-10pm Mon-Fri, to 9pm Sat & Sun) at Santa Justa train station, and all the normal firms at the airport.

CYCLING SEVILLE

Seville's bike-sharing scheme, **Sevici** (☎900 900722; www.sevici.es), is one of the largest of its kind in Europe with 2500 bikes and 250 docking stations.

Visitors can use bikes by getting a seven-day subscription directly at a docking station. This costs €15 (plus a €150 returnable deposit). Once you've saddled up, the first 30 minutes of usage are free. Beyond that, it's €1.03 for the first hour and €2.04 every hour thereafter.

Alternatively, a number of operators offer bike tours and rental, including **Surf the City** (Map p58; ☎693 261910; www.surfthecity.es; Calle Almirante Lobo 2, Edificio Cristina Local 15; kickscooter tours €20-50, bike tour €25; ⊙10am-8pm; 🚹) 🍃.

METRO

Seville's single metro line, run by the **Metro de Sevilla** (☎900 92 71 72; www.metro-sevilla.es), traverses the city south of the *casco antiguo* (old town). Useful stops include Prado de San Sebastián, Puerta de Jerez and Puerta de Cuba (for Triana).

A single ticket costs €1.35 to €1.80, depending on how far you go. A one-day travel card costs €4.50.

TAXI

- Taxis are white with a yellow diagonal stripe.
- You can hail a cab on the street, pick one up at a taxi rank or phone for one.
- A day-time journey in the centre will cost from around €8.

TRAM

Seville has a single tram line. T1 runs between Plaza Nueva and San Bernado via Avenida de la Constitución, Puerta de Jerez and Prado de San Sebastián.

The standard ticket is €1.40 but a range of passes are available if you're likely to use it a lot.

Buy tickets from the ticketing machines at the tram stops.

AROUND SEVILLE

Santiponce

POP 8440

Some 9km northwest of Seville, the white village of Santiponce is home to Andalucía's most thrilling Roman site, Itálica, as well as a grand Gothic-Mudéjar monastery. Just off the A66 and well served by buses from Seville, it makes for a fantastic day trip.

★Itálica ROMAN SITE

(☎600 141767; www.museosdeandalucia.es; Avenida de Extremadura 2; EU/non-EU citizens free/€1.50; ⊙9am-9pm Tue-Sat, to 3pm Sun Apr–mid-Jun, shorter hours Jul-Mar; Ⓟ) The ruins of ancient Itálica, the first Roman city founded on the Iberian Peninsula, are extensive and, in parts, quite spectacular. Broad paved streets lead to the remains of houses set around beautiful mosaic-laid patios and, best of all, a stunning 25,000-seat **amphitheatre**, one of the largest ever built. The city, founded in 206 BCE and later the birthplace of emperors Trajan and Hadrian, enjoyed a golden age in the 2nd century CE, when many of its finest buildings were constructed.

Highlights include the **Casa de los Pájaros** (House of the Birds), the **Edificio de Neptuno** (Building of the Neptune Mosaic), and the **Casa del Planetario** (House of the Planetarium), with a mosaic depicting the gods after whom the seven days of the week were named.

Monasterio de San Isidoro del Campo MONASTERY
(☎671 568517; Avenida de San Isidoro del Campo 18; 10am-3pm Tue-Thu, to 7pm Fri & Sat, to 2.30pm Sun Jan-Jun & Sep-Dec, 10am-3pm Tue-Sun Jul & Aug; P) FREE In the southern outskirts of Santiponce, this fortified Gothic monastery was founded in 1301 by Guzmán El Bueno (hero of the 1294 battle at Tarifa). Over the centuries it hosted a succession of religious orders, including, in the 15th century, the hermetic Hieronymites who embellished the Patio de Evangelistas with some striking murals and Mudéjar-style floral and geometric patterns. Also outstanding is the church's altarpiece by 17th-century Sevillan sculptor Juan Martínez Montañés.

The monastery also enjoys celebrity as the place where the Bible was first translated into Castilian in 1569.

Getting There & Away

From Seville's Plaza de Armas bus station, bus M170 (A or B) runs to Santiponce (€1.60, 25 minutes, at least half-hourly), making its final stop at the entrance to the Itálica archaeological site.

LA CAMPIÑA

Carmona

POP 28,620

Rising above a sea of golden, sun-baked plains 35km east of Seville, Carmona is a delight. Its hilltop centre is packed with noble palaces, majestic Mudéjar churches and two Moorish forts; nearby, a haunting Roman necropolis tells of the town's ancient origins.

The strategically sited town flourished under the Romans, who laid out a street plan that survives to this day: Via Augusta, running from Rome to Cádiz, entered Carmona by the eastern Puerta de Córdoba and left by the western Puerta de Sevilla. The Muslims subsequently built a strong defensive wall, but in 1247 the town fell to Fernando III. Later, Mudéjar and Christian artisans constructed grand churches, convents and mansions.

> **OFF THE BEATEN TRACK**
>
> **CUEVA DE LA BATIDA**
>
> A short, but in places steep, walk from Carmona's Puerta de Córdoba leads through the tough, sun-hardened plains to the Cueva de la Batida. This haunting spot, a series of caves cut into a rusty-brown rock face, is what remains of a quarry that was used to extract stone from Roman times through to the 15th century. The tourist office can provide a leaflet outlining two walking routes to/from the Cueva.

Sights

★**Necrópolis Romana** ROMAN SITE
(Roman cemetery; ☎600 143632; www.museosdeandalucia.es; Avenida de Jorge Bonsor 9; EU/non-EU citizens free/€1.50; 9am-9pm Tue-Sat, to 3pm Sun Apr–mid-Jun, 9am-3pm Tue-Sun mid-Jun–mid-Sep, 9am-6pm Tue-Sat, to 3pm Sun mid-Sep–Mar) This ancient Roman necropolis is one of the most important of its kind in Andalucía. The site, which is slightly let down by a lack of signage, contains hundreds of tombs, some elaborate and many-chambered, hewn into the rock in the 1st and 2nd centuries. Most of the inhabitants were cremated: in the tombs are wall niches for the box-like stone urns. You can enter the huge **Tumba de Servilia** and climb down into several others.

The site also features an interesting **museum** displaying objects found in the tombs. Across the street is what's left of a 1st-century-BCE **Anfiteatro Romano**.

Alcázar de la Puerta de Sevilla FORTRESS
(☎954 19 09 55; Plaza de Blas Infante; adult/child €2/1, Mon free; 10am-6pm Mon-Sat, to 3pm Sun Sep-Jun, 9am-3pm Mon-Fri, 10am-3pm Sat & Sun Jul & Aug) Carmona's signature fortress is a formidable sight. Set atop the Puerta de Sevilla, the imposing main gate of the old town, it had already been standing for five centuries when the Romans reinforced it and built a temple on top. The Muslim Almohads added an *aljibe* (cistern) to the upper patio, which remains a hawk-like perch from which to admire the typically Andalucian tableau of white cubes and soaring spires.

Buy tickets at the tourist office.

Carmona

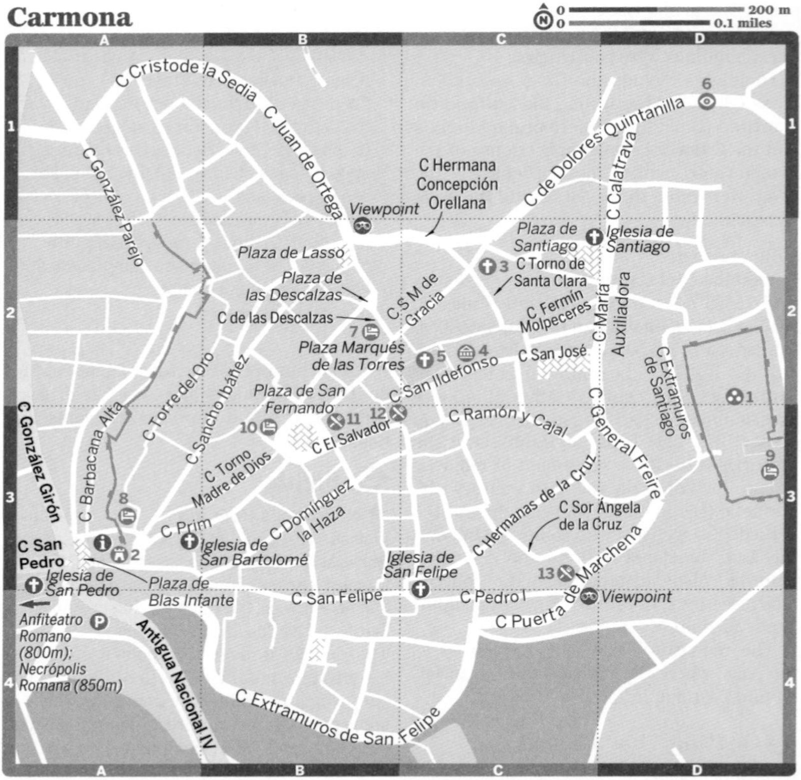

Carmona

Sights

1	Alcázar de Arriba	D2
2	Alcázar de la Puerta de Sevilla	A3
3	Convento de Santa Clara	C2
4	Museo de la Ciudad	C2
5	Prioral de Santa María de la Asunción	C2
6	Puerta de Córdoba	D1

Sleeping

7	El Rincón de las Descalzas	B2
8	Hostal Comercio	A3
9	Parador de Carmona	D3
10	Posada San Fernando	B3

Eating

11	Cervecería San Fernando	B3
12	Mingalario	B3
13	Molino de la Romera	C3

Prioral de Santa María de la Asunción CHURCH

(☎954 19 14 82; www.santamariacarmona.org; Plaza Marqués de las Torres; adult/child €3/1.80; ⏰9.30am-2pm & 5-7pm Tue-Fri, 9.30am-2pm Sat) This splendid church was built mainly in the 15th and 16th centuries on the site of Carmona's former mosque. The Patio de los Naranjos, through which you enter, has a Visigothic calendar carved into one of its pillars. The interior, crowned by high Gothic vaults, is centred on a towering altarpiece detailed to a mind-boggling degree with 20 panels of biblical scenes framed by gilt-scrolled columns.

Museo de la Ciudad MUSEUM

(☎954 14 01 28; www.museociudad.carmona.org; Calle San Ildefonso 1; adult/student/child €2.50/1.20/free, Tue free; ⏰11am-2pm Mon, to 7pm Tue-Sun Sep–mid-Jun, 10am-2pm mid-Jun–Aug) Carmona's history, from its origins as a Copper-Age settlement to the modern era, is charted at the city museum, housed in the aristocratic Palacio del Marqués de las Torres. The sections on the Tartessians and their Roman successors are highlights: the former includes a unique collection of large earthenware vessels with Middle Eastern decorative motifs, the latter several excellent mosaics.

Convento de Santa Clara CONVENT
(954 14 21 02; www.clarisasdecarmona.wordpress.com; Calle Torno de Santa Clara; adult/child €2/1; 11am-2pm & 4.30-6.30pm Thu-Mon) With its Gothic ribbed vaulting, carved Mudéjar-style ceiling and dazzling altarpiece – a shining example of Sevillan baroque – the Santa Clara convent appeals to both art and architecture buffs. Take in the bell tower, actually an 18th-century addition, and pretty, arch-lined cloister before picking up some cookies baked by the resident nuns.

Alcázar de Arriba RUINS
(Alcázar del Rey Don Pedro; Calle Extramuros de Santiago; adult/student/child €2/1/free; 11am-3pm Mon, Tue, Thu & Fri, to 3pm Sat & Sun) The stark, ruined fortress on the southeastern edge of Carmona was an Almohad fort that Pedro I turned into a country palace in the 13th century. It was brought down by earthquakes in 1504 and 1755, and its ruins now provide a memorable viewing platform and a backdrop to the luxurious Parador de Carmona hotel.

Puerta de Córdoba GATE
(Calle de Dolores Quintanilla; adult/child €2/1; 11am-3pm Mon, Tue, Thu & Fri, 10am-3pm Sat & Sun) With its two hexagonal towers and neoclassical decor, the result of an 18th-century facelift, this Roman gate originally controlled access to the city from the east. It's in a marvellous state of repair and makes for an excellent photo opportunity: you can either climb to the top and snap the surrounding landscape or use the arch to frame the golden countryside beyond.

Sleeping

Hostal Comercio HOSTAL €
(954 14 00 18; hostalcomercio@hotmail.com; Calle Torre del Oro 56; s €35, d €45-50, tr €70, q €94;) A warm welcome awaits at this traditional family-run *hostal*. It's a modest outfit but its location, just inside the Puerta de Sevilla, is ideal and its 14 simply furnished rooms, set around a plant-filled patio with Mudéjar-style arches, are good for the money with their brick-flagged floors and solid wood furniture.

★El Rincón de las Descalzas BOUTIQUE HOTEL €€
(954 19 11 72; www.elrincondelasdescalzas.com; Calle de las Descalzas 1; s €46-66, d €50-116, ste €121-178;) Discreetly sited in a revamped 18th-century town house, this delightfully sprawling hotel offers 13 colourful rooms and a picturesque, orange-hued patio. Each room is different, and some are better than others, but all sport a refined heritage look with carved-wood beds, exposed brick and sandstone, timber arches and the occasional fireplace.

Posada San Fernando BOUTIQUE HOTEL €€
(954 14 14 08; www.posadasanfernando.es; Plaza de San Fernando 6; s/d/tr €55/65/100;) This excellent-value hotel enjoys a prime location on Carmona's main square. It's a cosy affair with characterful and tastefully fitted rooms ensconced in a 16th-century building. Expect heavy, dark woodwork, antique furniture, hand-painted tiles and, in some rooms, windows overlooking the palm-lined plaza.

Parador de Carmona HISTORIC HOTEL €€€
(954 14 10 10; www.parador.es/en/paradores/parador-de-carmona; Alcázar del Rey Don Pedro, Calle Extramuros de Santiago; r €105-200; P) With jaw-dropping views of the surrounding valley, Carmona's luxurious *parador* (top-end state-owned hotel) occupies the 13th-century Alcázar del Rey Don Pedro. That means a gorgeous columned patio, divine terrace bar and understated terracotta-floored rooms. There's also a dining room serving high-end Andalucian fare, a seasonal outdoor pool and free parking.

Eating

Molino de la Romera ANDALUCIAN €€
(954 14 20 00; www.molinodelaromera.es; Calle Sor Ángela de la Cruz 8; tapas €3.50-6, mains €12-19; 1-4pm & 8.30-11.30pm Mon-Sat) Housed in a cosy, 15th-century olive-oil mill complete with panoramic terrace, a lovely courtyard and coolly rustic interior, this popular restaurant serves hearty, well-prepped meals with a splash of contemporary flair. Particularly good are its chargrilled meat dishes, including juicy cuts of tender Galician beef.

Cervecería San Fernando ANDALUCIAN €€
(661 654960; Plaza de San Fernando 18; tapas €2.50, mains €9-17; noon-5pm & 8pm-midnight Tue-Sun) With ringside seating on Carmona's vibrant central square, enthusiastic service and flavoursome food, Cervecería San

Fernando promises memorable dining. Get things rolling with a cold beer and plate of artichokes capped by lavish slices of *jamón* before moving onto a steak or perhaps some scrambled eggs with sausage.

Mingalario ANDALUCIAN €€
(☎954 14 38 93; Calle El Salvador 1; tapas €2-4.50, raciones €7-18; ⊙noon-4pm & 8pm-midnight, closed Tue & Sun dinner) This traditional tapas bar looks the part perfectly with its hanging hams, kitschy religious paintings and upturned barrels. In keeping with the look, the menu is defiantly old school, featuring regional favourites such as *carrillada de cerdo* (slow-cooked pork cheeks), and spinach with chickpeas (a Carmona speciality).

Information

Tourist Office (☎954 19 09 55; www.turismo.carmona.org; Alcázar de la Puerta de Sevilla; ⊙10am-6pm Mon-Sat, to 3pm Sun Sep-Jun, from 9am Mon-Fri, to 3pm Sat & Sun Jul & Aug)

Getting There & Around

BICYCLE

To explore the surrounding countryside, consider hiring a bike at **Carmona Bike Tours** (www.carmonabiketours.com; Calle Mimosa 15; bicycle hire per day €12; ⊙9.30am-2pm Mon-Sat & 5.30-8.30pm Mon-Fri).

BUS

Casal (☎954 99 92 90; www.autocarescasal.com) runs buses to Seville (€2.85, 1¼ hours, at least seven daily) from a stop on Paseo del Estatuto.

ALSA (☎902 42 22 42; www.alsa.es) has three daily buses to Córdoba (€9.83, 1½ hours) via Écija (€4.85, 35 minutes) leaving from a stop on the other side of Paseo del Estatuto.

CAR & MOTORCYCLE

There's 24-hour underground parking on Paseo del Estatuto (€13 per 24 hours).

Osuna

POP 17,620

The small rural town of Osuna is the unlikely setting for a cache of artistic and architectural treasures. Set in an otherwise empty landscape of vast, billowing plains, it boasts a series of grand baroque mansions and an attractive white centre crowned by a mighty Renaissance church. Most of the town's notable buildings were commissioned by the fabulously wealthy dukes of Osuna and built between the 16th and 18th centuries.

Sights

★Colegiata de Santa María de la Asunción CHURCH
(☎954 81 04 44; Plaza de la Encarnación; guided tours €5; ⊙tours 9.30am & hourly 10.15am-1.15pm Tue-Sun, plus 7pm & 8pm Thu mid-Jun–mid-Sep, hourly 10.15am-1.15pm plus 4pm & 5pm Tue-Sun mid-Sep–mid-Jun) Lording it over the town, this formidable Renaissance structure – two churches above a crypt – sits on the site of the town's medieval parish church. It contains a rich collection of baroque art, including several paintings by José de Ribera (El Españoleto) and a fine sculpture by Juan de Mesa.

Visits are by Spanish-language guided tours, which take in a finely decorated underground mausoleum (the *panteón ducal*), created in 1545 as the family vault for the Dukes of Osuna.

Monasterio de la Encarnación MUSEUM
(Plaza de la Encarnación; €3.50; ⊙9.30am-2.30pm Tue-Sun mid-Jun–mid-Sep, 10am-2.30pm & 4-6pm Tue-Sun mid-Sep–mid-Jun) This former monastery is now Osuna's museum of religious art. Its church boasts an impressive baroque altarpiece, while the patio features some wonderful 18th-century Sevillan tilework depicting various biblical, hunting, bullfighting, monastic and seasonal scenes. Entry is by guided tour only (in Spanish), led by one of the resident nuns.

Museo de Osuna MUSEUM
(☎954 81 57 32; Calle Sevilla 37; €2.50, Wed free; ⊙9.30am-2.30pm Tue-Sun & 7-9pm Thu mid-Jun–mid-Sep, 10am-2pm & 5-8pm Tue-Sun mid-Sep–mid-Jun) Housed in the 18th-century Palacio de los Hermanos Arjona y Cubas – along with the tourist office – this small municipal museum displays an eclectic mix of local relics, as well as exhibits and cast photos from *Game of Thrones,* whose fifth season was partly filmed in Osuna.

Sleeping

Five Gates Hostal HOSTAL €
(☎955 82 08 77, 626 620717; www.fivegates.es; Calle Carrera 79; s €30-35, d €45-55; ❄📶) Conveniently located on the main strip through Osuna's historic centre, this spic-n-span *hostal* offers comfortable, uncluttered rooms decorated in tasteful, low-key style, with colourful walls and blonde-wood floors. There's also a kitchen for guest use and a big communal lounge with games and DVDs.

DON'T MISS

OSUNA'S BAROQUE MANSIONS

Lined with pristine white buildings, the streets west of Calle Carrera, Osuna's central spine, are sprinkled with aristocratic mansions and florid baroque facades. Many are strung along two roads: Calle Sevilla, which leads west off central Plaza Mayor, and Calle San Pedro, a few blocks to the north. As a rule, the buildings are closed to the public, but even viewed from outside they are a splendid sight.

One of the most impressive mansions is the late-18th-century **Palacio de los Cepeda** (Calle de la Huerta 10; closed to the public). Now Osuna's courthouse, it boasts a central portal flanked by Churrigueresque columns and a pair of stone halberdiers holding the Cepeda family coat of arms.

Other standouts include the 18th-century **Palacio de Govantes y Herdara** (Calle Sevilla 44; closed to the public), characterised by twisted pillars encrusted with grapes and vine leaves, and the 1773 **Cilla del Cabildo Colegial** (Calle San Pedro 16; closed to the public) with a flamboyant facade (at the time of research hidden behind scaffolding) featuring a sculpted version of Seville's famous Giralda bell tower.

A short walk away, the pearly-white **Palacio del Marqués de la Gomera** (Calle San Pedro 20) sports elaborate pillars on its facade, with the family shield on top; it's now a hotel.

★ **Hotel Palacio Marqués de la Gomera** HISTORIC HOTEL €€
(954 81 26 32; www.hotelpalaciodelmarques.es; Calle San Pedro 20; s €51-70, d €56-89;) Live like nobility at this palatial four-star hotel, elegantly housed in one of Osuna's finest baroque mansions. Tiled floors and sandstone arches remain from the original building, decorating the sumptuous arched courtyard and spacious, individually styled rooms. There's even an ornate private chapel, as well as a smart restaurant and peaceful back patio. Rates are available with or without breakfast.

Eating

★ **Taberna Jicales** TAPAS €
(954 81 04 23; www.tabernajicales.es; Calle Esparteros 11; tapas €2-3.50, raciones €7.50-16; 8am-5.30pm Thu-Tue) Grilled chunks of tuna served on a bed of thick *salmorejo* (a cold tomato-based soup) seasoned with roasted red pepper; pork tenderloin slow cooked in sweet Pedro Ximénez wine – classic tapas don't get much better than these. Taberna Jicales is well known locally and it pays to take your cue from the townsfolk who pile in at lunchtime for a taste of superb regional cuisine.

Casa Curro TAPAS €€
(955 82 07 58; www.facebook.com/restaurantecasacurro; Plaza Salitre 5; tapas €2.50-3, mains €9-15; noon-midnight Tue-Sun) A favourite with the *Game of Thrones* cast when they were filming in town, this is one of Osuna's best-known tapas bars, frequented by locals and visitors alike. It certainly looks the part with its long polished bar, cluttered walls and blackboard menus, and the traditional food is reliably good.

Information

Tourist Office (954 81 57 32; www.osuna.es; Calle Sevilla 37; 9.30am-2.30pm Tue-Sun & 7-9pm Thu mid-Jun–mid-Sep, 10am-2pm & 5-8pm Tue-Sun mid-Sep–mid-Jun) Helpful office in the Museo de Osuna. Can provide a street map and a useful English-language guide to the town.

Getting There & Away

Osuna is 91km southeast of Seville, off the Granada–Seville A92.

The **bus station** (Avenida de la Constitución) is 1km southeast of Plaza Mayor. **Monbus** (www.monbus.es) runs eight daily buses (six on Sunday) to/from Seville (€8, 1½ hours).

By train, **Renfe** (912 32 03 20; www.renfe.com) services run to/from Seville (€11.50, 70 minutes, 10 daily) and Málaga (€14, 2¼ hours, five daily) from the **train station** (Avenida de la Estación), 1km west of Plaza Mayor. Note, however, that some services might involve taking the bus for sections of the journey.

Écija

POP 39,880

Écija, the least known of the Campiña towns, often slips under the radar. Many travellers overlook it, perhaps put off by its reputation as *la sartén de Andalucía* (the frying pan of Andalucía) – in July and August temperatures can reach a suffocating 45°C. But avoid high summer and you'll find

DON'T MISS

ÉCIJA'S CHURCHES & BELL TOWERS

Nicknamed *la ciudad de las torres* (the city of towers), Écija is famous for its spire-studded skyline. A series of baroque towers rises above the town's rooftops, most dating to the late 18th century, when many churches were rebuilt following a devastating earthquake in 1755.

One of the town's finest towers belongs to the **Iglesia de Santa María** (Plaza de Santa María; 9.30am-1.30pm & 5.30-8.30pm Mon-Sat, 10am-1pm Sun), an 18th-century church just off Plaza de España. A few blocks to the northeast, the fairy-tale belfry of the **Iglesia de San Juan** (Plaza de San Juan; tower €2; 10am-1pm Tue-Sun) is the only church tower in town you can actually climb. Nearby, the Gothic-Mudéjar **Iglesia de San Pablo y Santo Domingo** (Plaza de Santo Domingo; 6.30-7.30pm Tue-Fri, 7-8pm Sat, noon-1.30pm Sun) features an 18th-century brick tower.

Fronting a pretty plaza in the north of the old town, the **Parroquia Mayor de Santa Cruz** (Plazuela de Nuestra Señora del Valle; 9am-1pm & 5-8.30pm Mon-Sat, 10am-1pm & 6-9pm Sun) was once Écija's principal mosque and still has traces of Islamic features and some Arabic inscriptions. Beyond the roofless atrium, which retains a series of impressive Gothic arches from the original 13th-century church, the cavernous interior boasts a gold baroque *retablo* and an altar made from an early Christian sarcophagus.

it's a quietly confident town rich in architectural and historic interest.

Its compact centre is riddled with palaces, churches and ceramic-tiled towers – hence a second nickname, *la ciudad de las torres* (the city of towers) – many dating from an 18th-century baroque building boom. A few ancient ruins also survive, a legacy of its past as a wealthy Roman town. Known as Colonia Augusta Firma Astigi, it flourished in the 1st and 2nd centuries CE, supplying olive oil to markets across the Roman Empire.

Sights

★Museo Histórico Municipal MUSEUM
(954 83 04 31; http://museo.ecija.es; Plaza de la Constitución 1; €3; 10am-1.30pm & 4.30-6.30pm Tue-Fri, 10am-2pm & 5.30-8pm Sat, 10am-3pm Sun mid-Sep–May, 10am-2.30pm Tue-Fri, 10am-2pm & 8-10pm Sat, 10am-3pm Sun Jun–mid-Sep) FREE Écija's museum, housed in the 18th-century Palacio de Benamejí, is a true gem. It has rooms dedicated to the area's prehistory and protohistory, but its chief drawcard is its fabulous collection of local Roman finds. These include a graceful sculpture of a wounded Amazon (a legendary female warrior) and a series of stunningly preserved mosaics, mostly unearthed in and around the town. A highlight is the *Don del Vino* mosaic depicting scenes related to the mythical 'birth' of wine.

Palacio de Peñaflor PALACE
(Calle Emilio Castelar 26; €2; 10am-1.30pm & 4.30-6.30pm Mon-Fri, 10am-2pm & 5.30-8pm Sat, 10am-3pm Sun) The huge, 18th-century 'Palace of the Long Balconies' is Écija's most iconic image. Its curved facade is a florid example of baroque exuberance with its ornate, columned portal, wrought-iron balconies and traces of flamboyant frescoes. Inside, much of the palace is off-limits but you can take in the vaulted ground-floor stables, an impressive double staircase and the old marquis' office. Up yet more stairs, a mirador (viewing terrace) offers fine rooftop views.

Sleeping & Eating

★Hotel Palacio de los Granados HISTORIC HOTEL €€
(955 90 53 44; www.palaciogranados.com; Calle Emilio Castelar 42; d €60-70, ste €125-200;) Sections of this charming palace hotel date to the 15th century. Its interiors have been lovingly restored and its rooms, all of which are slightly different, reveal a stately look with wood-beamed ceilings, Mudéjar arches, 18th-century brick floors and even the occasional fireplace. Adding to the romance is a tiny courtyard where pomegranate trees grow over a tiny plunge pool.

Ágora TAPAS €
(955 31 70 77; Calle Barquete 38A; tapas €2-2.50, menú del día €9; 11am-4pm Mon, to 11pm Wed & Thu, to midnight Fri, noon-4.30pm & 7.30pm-midnight Sat, noon-4.30pm & 7.30-11.30pm Sun) A bit out from the historic centre, this buzzing spot is one of Écija's favourite tapas bars. Its outdoor tables, shaded by a gnarled olive tree, are much sought after, particularly at weekends, when crowds pour in to dine on traditional tapas, prepared with skill and served with practised efficiency by a young, energetic crew.

Hispania SPANISH €€
(☎954 83 26 05; www.hispaniacafe.com; Pasaje Virgen de Soterraño 3; mains €10-18; ⏰12.30-3.30pm & 8-10.30pm Tue-Sun) Stylish and perennially packed, this slick side-street operation ensures a full house with its contemporary approach to Spanish cooking. In line with the modern decor, dishes are creative and forward-looking, with everything from red tuna tataki to burritos of Iberian ham and wok-fried rice combos. Book ahead Thursday to Saturday.

Information

Tourist Office (☎955 90 29 33; www.turismoecija.com; Calle Elvira 1; ⏰10am-2pm & 4.30-6.30pm Mon-Sat, 10am-2pm Sun)

Getting There & Away

Écija is 53km east of Carmona on the A4 between Córdoba and Seville. From the **bus station** (Avenida del Genil), ALSA (p84) buses connect with Carmona (€4.85, 35 minutes, three daily), Córdoba (€5.15, one hour, six daily) and Seville (€7.53, 1¼ hours, three daily).

PARQUE NATURAL SIERRA NORTE DE SEVILLA

Cazalla de la Sierra

POP 4790 / ELEV 584M

This attractive little *pueblo blanco*, on a hilltop 85km northeast of Seville, sits in the heart of the Parque Natural Sierra Norte, making it the ideal base for exploring. There are some lovely walks in the surrounding woods; in town the action is focused on Plaza Mayor, which is overshadowed by the Iglesia de Nuestra Señora de la Consolación.

Activities

Sendero de Las Laderas HIKING
This 8km hiking trail leads down from Cazalla to the Huéznar valley, passing through typical Sierra Norte evergreen-oak woodlands, olive groves and small cultivated plots, as well as the odd chestnut wood and vineyard. It's rated as medium difficult and is quite hard work in places with some steep stretches. Allow about three hours to complete it.

Vía Verde de la Sierra Norte CYCLING
(www.viasverdes.com) This 18.7km cycling (and walking) route is one of the most popular of Andalucía's 30 *vías verdes* (greenways). Running along a disused mining railway, it leads north through the Huéznar valley below Cazalla to the village of **San Nicolás del Puerto** and on south to the old **Cerro del Hierro mines**.

Bike hire is available at **Bicicletas Verde Vía** (☎955 49 01 04; www.bicicletasverdevia.com; Carretera A455, Km 8; per day €8-12; ⏰9am-8pm) at the start of the *vía*, 8km east of Cazalla on the A455.

Sleeping

La Plazuela CASA RURAL €
(☎954 42 14 96, 661 335897; www.apartamentos-elpua.es; Calle Caridad 4; s €45-60, d €60-75, f €85; ❄📶) With a central location just off Cazalla's main pedestrian drag, this modest lodging makes a convenient base. Its nine spacious rooms are individually decorated in neo-rustic style with brightly coloured walls, tiled floors and basic wooden furniture. The owners offer a cheerful welcome but speak no English, which can make phone communication a bit hit and miss.

Paraíso del Huéznar COTTAGE €€
(☎609 512579, 955 49 01 04; www.paraisodelhueznar.com; Carretera A455, Km 8; cottages per person incl breakfast €30-40; P📶🏊) Some 8km down the windy A455 east of Cazalla (towards Constantina), the Paraíso has five comfortable, country-style *casitas* (cottages). Sleeping from two to 12 people, these come with fully equipped kitchens, log fires and private parking. There's also a communal swimming pool and handy on-site bicycle hire.

★**Las Navezuelas** CASA RURAL €€
(☎954 88 47 64; www.lasnavezuelas.com; Carretera A432, Km 43.5; s/d/ste incl breakfast €50/70/88, 4-person apt €140; ⏰late Feb-Dec; P📶🏊) Make it to this blissful rural retreat – signposted off the A432, 3km south of Cazalla – and you won't want to leave. Immersed in silence, it's housed in a 16th-century *cortijo* (farmhouse) and offers rustic, thick-walled rooms and three self-catering apartments. Outside, you can lounge by the pool and wander through the olive groves and cork oak woods that flourish on the 130-hectare estate.

Eating

★**Agustina** ANDALUCIAN €€
(☎954 88 32 55; Plaza del Concejo; mains €8.50-15.50; ⏰1-5pm & 8pm-midnight Wed-Mon) With its urban-style interior and alfresco seating on a lovely stone plaza, Agustina brings

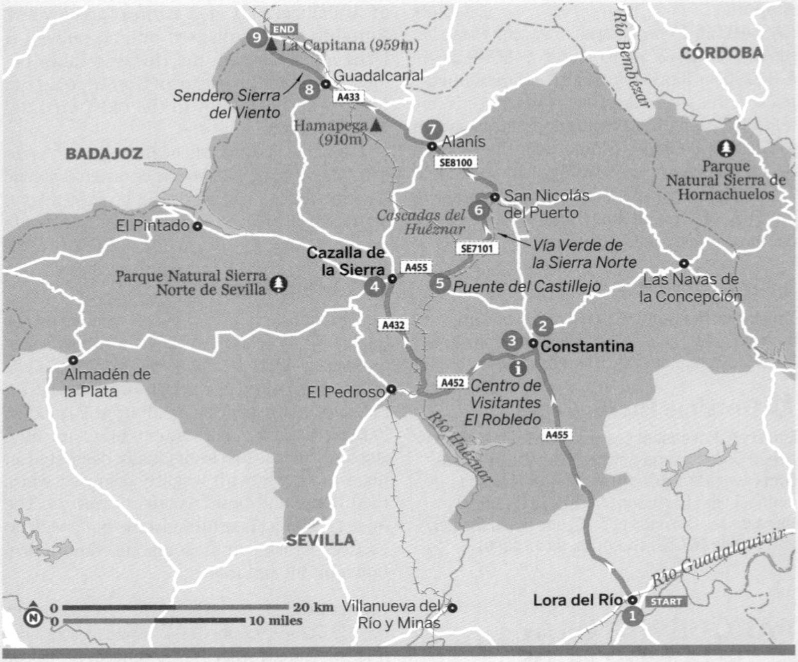

Driving Tour
Parque Natural Sierra Norte de Sevilla

START LORA DEL RÍO
END LA CAPITANA
LENGTH 105KM; TWO DAYS

Head up to the Parque Natural Sierra Norte de Sevilla for a taste of life in the slow lane and some wonderfully scenic driving. From Seville, follow the A4 and the A457 to 1 **Lora del Río**, then pick up the A455 for the climb up to 2 **Constantina**, the park's largest town. Stop off to explore its attractive old town and hilltop castle before continuing west on the A452 to the 3 **Centro de Visitantes El Robledo**, where you can pick up walking maps and look around its botanical garden. Push on along the A452 as it winds through the hilly countryside, mists clinging to the mountains as they recede into the distance. Shortly after crossing the Río Huéznar, where you can see part of an old aqueduct, turn right onto the A432 and drive 12km north to 4 **Cazalla de la Sierra** (p87). Lunch on contemporary cuisine at Agustina (p87), then spend the afternoon investigating the town's charming streets and nearby walking trails. Overnight at Las Navezuelas (p87), 3km to the south.

Next morning, pick up the A455 back towards Constantina. This road crosses the Río Huéznar just east of the Cazalla-Constantina train station. A bumpy 1km track leads downstream from here to the 5 **Puente del Castillejo** railway bridge. Next, follow the SE7101 as it parallels the river for 13km on the way to San Nicolás del Puerto. Just before getting to the village, take a moment for a quick detour to the 6 **Cascadas del Huéznar** (waterfalls). From riverside San Nicolás del Puerto, take the SE8100 northwest, ploughing on through the increasingly remote landscape to 7 **Alanís**, topped by a medieval castle. Keep going on the A433, along the edge of the park, to windswept 8 **Guadalcanal**. North of town, leave your car and hit the hiking trail: the 5km (two-hour) Sendero Sierra del Viento follows a ridge to 9 **La Capitana**, the park's highest peak (959m) and the perfect point to wrap up your tour.

a dash of the contemporary to Cazalla. Its culinary approach is similarly modern, featuring updated takes on traditional Sierra dishes and more adventurous compositions with international ingredients. Service is excellent, as is the local cherry liqueur the owner will happily whip out at the end of the meal.

Cortijo Vistalegre ANDALUCIAN €€
(☎954 88 35 13; www.cortijovistalegre.es; Carretera Real de la Jara, Km 0.5; mains €6-21; ⏰12.30-4.30pm & 8.30pm-12.30am Wed-Fri, 12.30pm-12.30am Sat & Sun) Italian pizzas star alongside classic cuts of Andalucian pork at this smartly rustic *cortijo* on the southwestern edge of town. Colourful wall hangings, candle-lit tables and an open log fire set the scene indoors, or you can dine on the sought-after outdoor terrace. Reservations recommended for the weekend.

Information

Oficina de Turismo (☎954 88 35 62; www.cazalla.org; Plaza Doctor Nosea 1; ⏰10am-2pm daily & 4.30-6.30pm Mon-Sat) Can provide maps and information on walks in the area.

Getting There & Away

Monbus (p85) runs buses between Cazalla de la Sierra and Seville (€6.74, 1¾ to two hours) four times daily Monday to Friday, and twice daily Saturday and Sunday.

Constantina

POP 5950 / ELEV 555M

Constantina, the Sierra Norte's largest town and unofficial capital, is a charming spot set amidst the rolling, tree-clad hills of the Huéznar valley. Narrow medieval lanes weave through its compact white centre lined with handsome 18th-century mansions and traditional cafes.

Castillo Árabe CASTLE
(⏰9am-9pm) FREE Looming over the western side of town, Constantina's ruined castle is worth the climb for the views alone. Below, you'll see the distinctive Mudéjar bell tower of the **Iglesia de Santa María de la Encarnación** towering above the huddled white houses of the **Barrio de la Morería**.

The castle, which has dominated the local skyline since the Islamic Almoravid era, is thought to stand over an earlier Roman fort.

Sendero Los Castañares HIKING
The 5.5km Sendero Los Castañares trail leads up through thick chestnut woods to a hilltop viewpoint, then loops back to Constantina (about two hours total). It's signposted from Paseo de la Alameda at the northern edge of town.

Asador Los Navarro ANDALUCIAN €€
(☎954 49 63 61; www.asadorlosnavarro.com; Paseo de la Alameda 39; tapas €2.50, mains €6.50-25; ⏰9am-11.45pm) Located at the head of the tree-lined Paseo de la Alameda, this warm, coffee-coloured bar-restaurant is a cheerful local haunt, appreciated for its barbecued meats, hearty tapas and quality local wines.

Information

Centro de Visitantes El Robledo (☎648 140091; Carretera Constantina-El Pedroso, Km 1; ⏰10am-2pm Wed-Sun Apr-Nov, hours vary rest of year) The park's main visitor centre, 1km west of Constantina off the A452, with hiking information and a botanical garden.

Oficina Municipal de Turismo (☎955 88 12 97; Avenida de Andalucía; ⏰9am-2pm Tue-Sun & 4-7pm Fri & Sat) On the main southern approach road to town.

Getting There & Away

Monbus (p85) runs buses from Seville to Constantina (€7.35, 1¾ hours) four times daily Monday to Friday, twice on Saturday and three times on Sunday.

El Pedroso

A sleepy village of broad cobbled streets and pristine white houses, El Pedroso lies 16km south of Cazalla de la Sierra on the A432 Seville road. There's little to detain you in the village itself but there's some fine walking in the surrounding bucolic countryside.

Sendero del Arroyo de las Cañas HIKING
This 10km (3½-hour) circuit through the flattish countryside west of El Pedroso is one of the prettiest walks in the area, it traverses a landscape strewn with granite boulders and, in spring, gorgeous wildflowers. The start point is opposite Bar Triana on the western side of the village.

Getting There & Away

Monbus (p85) buses run to El Pedroso from Seville (€5.53, 1¼ hours) up to five times daily Monday to Friday, twice on Saturdays and three times on Sundays.

AT A GLANCE

POPULATION
524,000

CAPITAL
Huelva

BEST REAL-TIME LYNX VIDEOS
Centro de Visitantes El Acebuche (p100)

BEST BEACH
Flecha del Rompido (p97)

BEST ECO-FRIENDLY HOTEL
Posada de San Marcos (p109)

WHEN TO GO

Apr
Prime time for walking in the Sierra de Aracena, with comfortable temperatures and abundant wildflowers.

May–Jun
Join the cavalcade of pilgrims at the Romería del Rocío, Andalucía's most colourful festival.

Nov
Witness the honking, quacking cacophony of countless overwintering waterbirds in Parque Nacional de Doñana.

Aracena (p104)
JAN WOLOSZCZUK/SHUTTERSTOCK

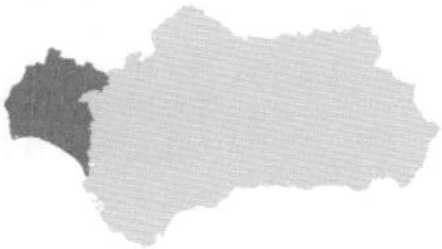

Huelva Province

Andalucía's most westerly, end-of-the-line destination, packs in a mix of historical intrigue, natural beauty and sun worship, but still remains largely off the beaten track for foreign visitors. Here you'll find sleepy hill villages, relics from Columbus' voyages, endless stretches of untainted coastline and Spain's most beloved national park.

Discover Parque Nacional de Doñana's vast marshes, dunes, beaches and woodlands; the attractive yet relatively undiscovered Costa de la Luz; and the enchanting Sierra de Aracena, dotted with cobblestoned villages, criss-crossed by some of Andalucía's finest walking trails; as well as some of the Iberian Peninsula's most prized pork products.

INCLUDES

HUELVA

POP 143,660

The capital of Huelva province is a modern, unpretentious industrial port set between the Odiel and Tinto estuaries. Despite its unpromising outskirts, Huelva boasts an appealingly lively pedestrianised centre, and the city's people – called *choqueros* because of their supposed preference for the locally abundant *chocos* (cuttlefish) – are noted for their warmth.

Huelva's history dates back 3000 years to the Phoenician town of Onuba. Onuba's river-mouth location made it a natural base for exporting inland minerals to the Mediterranean. The town was devastated by the 1755 Lisbon earthquake, but later grew when British company Rio Tinto developed mines in the province's interior in the 1870s. Today, Huelva has a sizeable fishing fleet and a heavy dose of petrochemical industry (introduced in the 1950s by Franco).

Sights

More a scene than a collection of dazzling sights, Huelva nevertheless offers a few worthwhile stops.

Muelle-Embarcadero de Mineral de Río Tinto HISTORIC SITE

An odd legacy of the area's mining history, this impressive iron pier curves out into the Odiel estuary 500m south of the port. It was designed for the Rio Tinto company in the 1870s by British engineer George Barclay Bruce. Equipped with boardwalks on upper and lower levels, it makes for a delightful stroll or jog to admire the harbour and ships. It's 1km southwest of Plaza de las Monjas.

Museo de Huelva MUSEUM

(959 65 04 24; www.museosdeandalucia.es/museodehuelva; Alameda Sundheim 13; EU/non-EU citizens free/€1.50; 9am-9pm Tue-Sat, to 3pm Sun) This wide-ranging museum is stuffed with history and art. The permanent ground-floor exhibition concentrates on Huelva province's impressive archaeological pedigree, with interesting items culled from its Roman and mining history; upstairs houses a collection of Spanish painting spanning seven centuries. Don't miss the stunning ancient Roman *noria* (waterwheel), the best preserved of its kind anywhere in the world.

Santuario de Nuestra Señora de la Cinta CHAPEL

(Avenida de la Cinta; 9am-1pm & 4-7pm; P) Of Gothic-Mudéjar origins but reconstructed in the 18th and 19th centuries, this pretty white sanctuary looks out across the Odiel estuary from its peaceful hillside spot 3km north of the centre. Columbus allegedly promised to pray here upon returning to Spain across the turbulent Atlantic in 1493; the story is depicted in tiles by artist Daniel Zuloaga. Take city bus 6 from outside the bus station.

Casa Colón HISTORIC BUILDING

(Plaza del Punto) Huelva's salmon-pink Casa Colón was constructed as the city's original luxury hotel in the 1880s to accommodate guests of the Rio Tinto company. It now contains the town's archives and hosts conferences.

Festivals & Events

Fiestas Colombinas CULTURAL

(late Jul/early Aug) Huelva celebrates Columbus' departure for the Americas (3 August 1492) with this six-day festival of music, dance, cultural events and bullfighting.

Sleeping & Eating

In a salty city such as Huelva, it's no surprise that seafood stars on most menus. Busy tapas bars line Avenida Pablo Rada, just north of the centre, and pedestrianised Calle Vázquez López to the south.

Senator Huelva Hotel BUSINESS HOTEL €

(959 28 55 00; www.senatorhuelvahotel.com; Avenida Pablo Rada 10; r from €59;) Catering to the business set, this impeccably maintained hotel is definitely your best bet in Huelva. Bright red banisters draped in greenery liven up the lobby, and staff are charmingly efficient. All 162 rooms are smartly outfitted with dark-wood desks and crisp white sheets. Huelva's central square is only a five-minute walk away.

★ **Restaurante Juan José** ANDALUCIAN €

(959 26 38 57; www.facebook.com/barrestaurantejuanjose; Calle Villa Mundaka 1; tapas €2-2.70, raciones €7.50-12; noon-5pm & 8pm-midnight Mon-Sat) Locals regularly pack into this humble, friendly neighbourhood restaurant 1.5km northeast of Plaza de las Monjas for its fabulously gooey *tortilla de patatas* (potato-and-onion omelette). The tuna (fresh from Isla Cristina) and *carne mechada*

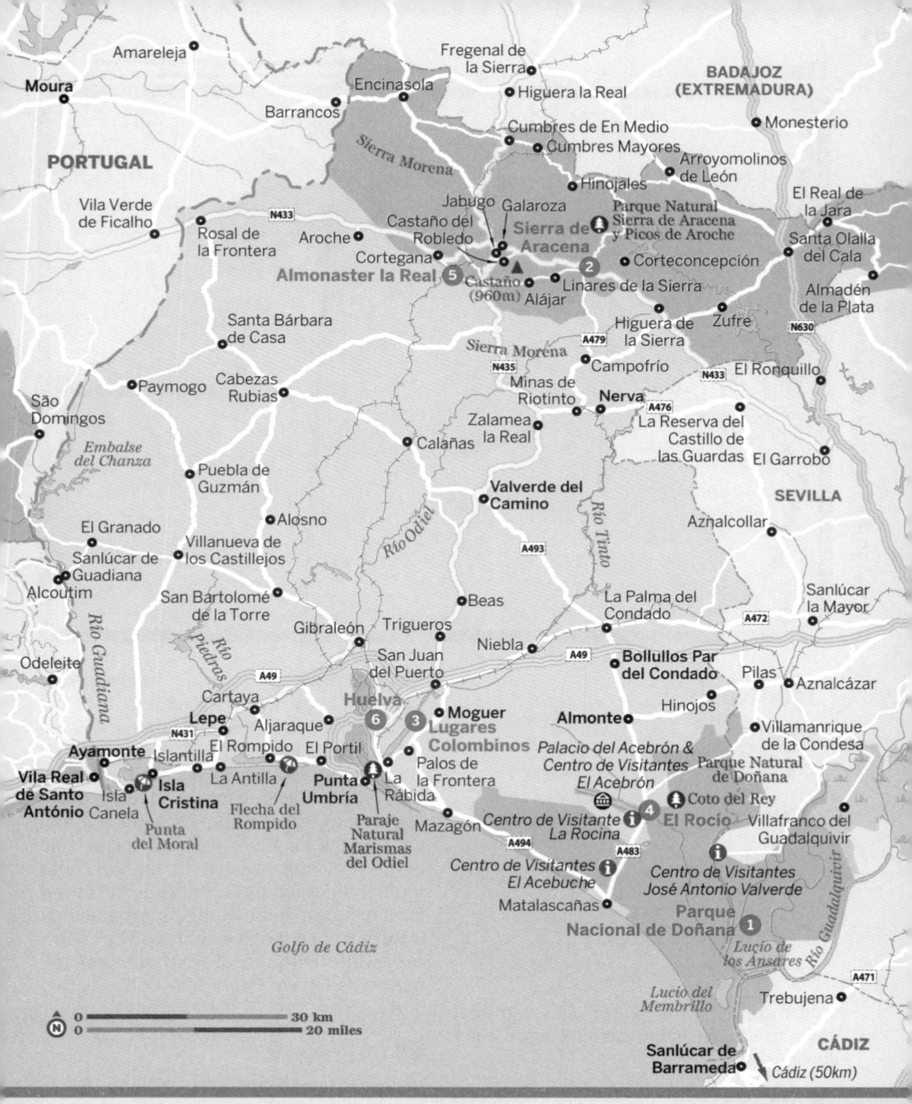

Huelva Province Highlights

1. **Parque Nacional de Doñana** (p98) Exploring the untrammelled wilderness of Europe's largest nature reserve.
2. **Sierra de Aracena** (p107) Hiking from one enchanted village to the next and tasting creative regional cooking in this off-the-radar rural hideaway.
3. **Lugares Colombinos** (p95) Retracing the steps of Christopher Columbus in La Rábida, Palos de la Frontera and Moguer.
4. **El Rocío** (p100) Feeling the festive fervour and delighting in the pageantry of Spain's largest religious pilgrimage.
5. **Almonaster la Real** (p110) Checking out 9th-century Islamic architecture in this remote mountain village.
6. **Huelva** (p92) Trawling for tapas and experiencing local life in the pedestrianised streets around Plaza de las Monjas.

Huelva

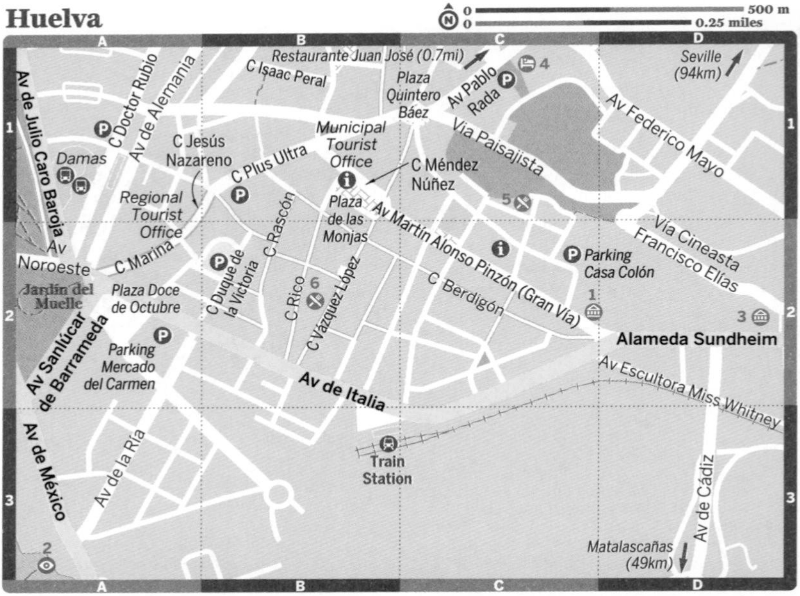

Huelva

Sights

1 Casa Colón C2
2 Muelle-Embarcadero de Mineral de Río Tinto A3
3 Museo de Huelva D2

Sleeping

4 Senator Huelva Hotel C1

Eating

5 Acánthum C1
6 Azabache B2

(meat stuffed with pepper and ham) are tasty, too. Arrive before 2pm to snag a lunch table.

★ **Azabache** TAPAS €€
(☎959 25 75 28; www.restauranteazabache.com; Calle Vázquez López 22; raciones €13-22; ⊙8.30am-midnight Mon-Fri, to 4pm Sat) Join the sophisticated local crowd squeezing into this narrow tiled tapas bar in the heart of Huelva's pedestrianised downtown. Busy, helpful waiters are quick to deliver cheese and *jamón* (ham) platters, scrambled *gurumelos* (local wild mushrooms), fried *chocos* and fresh fish specials. Beyond the front bar area is a more formal restaurant.

★ **Acánthum** GASTRONOMY €€€
(☎959 24 51 35; www.acanthum.com; Calle San Salvador 17; 11-/18-course tasting menu €65/85; ⊙1.30-3.30pm Tue-Sun, 9-11.30pm Thu-Sat) Celebrating the flavours of his native Huelva, Chef Xanty Elias' exuberant mutlicourse menus have earned him Michelin star status since 2015. Reserve ahead for a table in the sleek stone-walled dining room, and settle in for a feast that draws equally from Huelva's coast and mountains, prominently featuring the region's famous *gambas blancas* (white shrimp), *chocos* and Denominación de Origen Calificada (DOC) Iberian pork.

Information

Municipal Tourist Office (☎959 54 18 17; http://turismo.huelva.es; Plaza del Punto; ⊙10am-2pm daily, plus 5-8pm Mon-Sat)

Regional Tourist Office (☎959 25 74 67; www.turismohuelva.org; Calle Fernando el Católico 14; ⊙9am-2pm Mon-Fri) Helpful for the whole province.

Getting There & Around

BUS

Most buses from the **bus station** (Avenida Doctor Rubio) are operated by **Damas** (☎959 25 69 00; www.damas-sa.es; Avenida Doctor

Rubio). Destinations include Almonte (for El Rocío; €4, 1¼ hours), Aracena (€11.25, 2½ to three hours), Isla Cristina (€4, one to 1¼ hours), Moguer (€1.75, 45 minutes), Matalascañas (€4, 1¼ hours), Palos de la Frontera (€1.75, 30 minutes) and Seville (€8.95, 1¼ to two hours). Frequency is reduced on Saturday, Sunday and public holidays.

CAR & MOTORCYCLE

There's metered street parking around town (Monday to Saturday), indicated by blue and orange lines, and a pair of useful city centre parking lots at **Casa Colón** (Calle Arquitecto Monis) and **Mercado del Carmen** (Avenida de Italia).

TRAIN

From Huelva's new **train station** (Avenida de Italia), opened just south of the centre in 2018, Renfe runs three daily services to Seville (€12.70, 1½ hours) and one direct high-speed Alvia train to Córdoba (€38.50, 1¾ hours) and Madrid (€58, 3¾ hours).

LUGARES COLOMBINOS

The 'Columbian Sites' are the three townships of La Rábida, Palos de la Frontera and Moguer, along the eastern bank of the Tinto estuary. All three played a key role in Columbus' preparation for his journey of discovery and can be visited as an easy day trip from Huelva, Doñana or Huelva's eastern coast. As the countless greenhouses suggest, this is Spain's main strawberry-growing region (Huelva province produces 90% of Spain's crop).

La Rábida

POP 500

Sights

Monasterio de la Rábida MONASTERY
(☎959 35 04 11; www.monasteriodelarabida.com; Paraje de la Rábida; adult/student €3.50/3; ⏱10am-6pm Tue-Sun; P) In the pretty, peaceful village of La Rábida, don't miss this palm-fringed, hilltop Franciscan monastery, visited several times by Columbus before his great voyage of discovery. Highlights include a chapel with a 13th-century alabaster Virgin before which Columbus prayed, and a fresco-lined Mudéjar cloister, one of the few parts of the original structure to survive the 1755 earthquake.

Muelle de las Carabelas HISTORIC SITE
(Wharf of the Caravels; adult/reduced €3.60/1.50; ⏱10am-9pm Tue-Sun mid-Jun–mid-Sep, 9.30am-7.30pm Tue-Sun mid-Sep–mid-Jun; P) On the waterfront below the Monasterio de la Rábida is this pseudo 15th-century quayside, where you can board life-size replicas of the *Niña,* the *Pinta* and the *Santa María* – the three ships used by Columbus in his initial trans-Atlantic expedition. A single ticket grants access to all three ships and the attached museum, which features excellent bilingual (English-Spanish) displays tracing the history of Columbus' voyages. Here you can see instruments of navigation and get a glimpse of the indigenous experience at the time of the Spaniards' arrival.

Parque Botánico José Celestino Mutis GARDENS
(Paraje de La Rábida; ⏱10am-7.30pm Tue-Sun) FREE La Rábida's beautifully landscaped botanical garden sits on a hillside, with plants and trees from both New World and Old. The large park makes for a delightful ramble, featuring palm-lined canals, pools, a greenhouse containing tropical plants and a fine observation deck overlooking the Río Guadiana.

Getting There & Away

Damas (www.damas-sa.es) runs frequent buses from Huelva to La Rábida (€1.75, 20 minutes). Buses continue northeast from here to Palos de la Frontera (€1.40, 10 minutes) and Moguer (€1.75, 25 minutes).

Palos de la Frontera

POP 11,290

It was from the port of Palos de la Frontera that Columbus and his compatriots set sail into the unknown. The town provided the explorer with two of his ships, two captains (brothers Martín Alonso Pinzón and Vicente Yáñez Pinzón) and more than half his crew.

Damas (www.damas-sa.es) runs frequent buses from Palos de la Frontera to La Rábida (€1.40, 10 minutes), Moguer (€1.40, 15 minutes) and Huelva (€1.75, 30 minutes).

Iglesia de San Jorge CHURCH
(Calle Fray Juan Pérez; ⏱hours vary) Towards the northern end of Calle Colón is this 15th-century Gothic-Mudéjar church, where Columbus and his sailors took Communion before embarking on their great expedition. Water for their ships came from La Fontanilla well nearby.

THE FOUR VOYAGES OF CHRISTOPHER COLUMBUS

In April 1492, Christopher Columbus (Cristóbal Colón to Spaniards) finally won the Spanish royal support of the Reyes Católicos (Catholic Monarchs; Fernando and Isabel) for his proposed westward voyage of exploration to the spice-rich Orient. This proposal was to result in four great voyages and a fabulous golden age for Spain, though some historians now argue that Columbus' captains, the Pinzón brothers, really deserve the credit for finding the New World.

On 3 August 1492, Columbus embarked from Palos de la Frontera with 100 men and three ships. After a near mutiny as the crew despaired of finding land, they finally made landfall on the Bahamian island of Guanahaní on 12 October, naming it San Salvador. The expedition went on to discover Cuba and Hispaniola, where the *Santa María* sank. The *Niña* and the *Pinta* made it back to Palos on 15 March 1493.

Columbus – with animals, plants, gold ornaments and six Caribbean Indians – received a hero's welcome on his return, as all were convinced that he had reached the fabled East Indies (in fact, his calculations were some 16,000km off). Martín Alonso Pinzón died on arrival in Spain, supposedly having failed to beat Columbus back with the big news.

Columbus made further voyages in 1493 and 1498, discovering Jamaica, Puerto Rico, Trinidad and the mouth of the Orinoco River. But he proved a disastrous colonial administrator, enslaving the indigenous peoples and alienating Spanish settlers. Eventually he was arrested by a Spanish royal emissary and sent home in chains. In an attempt to redeem himself, Columbus embarked on his fourth and final voyage in May 1502. This time he reached Honduras and Panama, but then became stranded for a year in Jamaica, having lost his ships to sea worms.

Columbus died in 1506 in Valladolid, northern Spain – impoverished and apparently still believing he had reached Asia. His remains were eventually returned to the Caribbean, as he had wished, before being brought back to Seville. Or were they? The story of Columbus' posthumous voyages has become quite the saga itself.

Moguer

POP 22,090

The sleepy whitewashed town of Moguer, 8km northeast of Palos de la Frontera on the A494, is where Columbus' ship, the *Niña*, was built. The main Columbus site in town is the 14th-century Monasterio de Santa Clara.

Casa Museo Zenobia y Juan Ramón Jiménez MUSEUM

(☎959 37 21 48; www.casamuseozjrj.com; Calle Juan Ramón Jiménez 10; adult/concession €3.50/2.50; ⏰10am-2pm & 4-8pm Tue-Fri, 10am-2.30pm Sat & Sun mid-Jun–mid-Sep, reduced hours rest of year) Moguer has its own charming flavour of Andalucian baroque, and its sunny beauty was fulsomely expressed by local poet laureate Juan Ramón Jiménez (1881–1958), who won the Nobel Prize for literature in 1956. The old home of the poet and his writer wife, Zenobia Camprubí, is open for visits.

As you wander around town, keep an eye out for tiled quotes marking key locations from Jiménez' most famous poem *Platero y yo* (Platero and I), which was inspired by his beloved donkey Platero, and for sculptures of Jiménez' well-known characters.

Monasterio de Santa Clara MONASTERY

(☎959 37 01 07; www.monasteriodesantaclara.com; Plaza de las Monjas; guided tours adult/reduced €3.50/2.50, free Sun; ⏰tours 10.30am, 11.30am, 12.30pm, 5.30pm & 6.30pm Tue-Sat, 10.30am & 11.30am Sun) Columbus spent a night of vigil and prayer at this grand 14th-century monastery upon returning from his first voyage in March 1493. Highlights of the 45-minute guided visit include a lovely Mudéjar cloister, a 14th-century kitchen, the whitewashed Claustro de las Madres, illuminated manuscripts and a one-of-a-kind 14th-century Nasrid choir stall bearing images of Alhambra-inspired lions, columns and Arabic capitals.

ℹ Information

Tourist Office (☎959 37 18 98; Teatro Municipal Felipe Godínez, Calle Andalucía 17; ⏰10am-2pm & 5-7pm Tue-Sat) Excellent office inside the Teatro.

Getting There & Away

Damas (www.damas-sa.es) runs frequent daily buses (13 on weekdays, seven on weekends) from Moguer to Palos de la Frontera (€1.40, 15 minutes), La Rábida (€1.75, 25 minutes) and Huelva (€1.75, 45 minutes).

COSTA DE LA LUZ

Huelva province's modestly developed Costa de la Luz consists of beautiful broad white sands backed by dunes and pine trees. West of Huelva, the main beach hotspots are Punta Umbría, Flecha del Rompido, Isla Cristina and Ayamonte. All are friendly, unpretentious places, more popular with Spanish holidaymakers than with foreign visitors. The Costa de la Luz also continues southeast from Huelva, along almost the entire coastline of neighbouring Cádiz province.

Flecha del Rompido BEACH
Possibly the most spectacular beach on Huelva's Costa de la Luz, this 8km-long sandbar along the mouth of the Río Piedras can be reached only by ferry, which keeps the crowds away, even in midsummer. The waters on the inland side remain calm, while the south side faces the open sea. Part of the Río Piedras wetlands reserve, it's a place of great ornithological and botanical interest.

From April to October, hourly **Flechamar** (☎959 39 99 42; www.flechamar.com; return €4; ⏲mid-Apr–late Oct) boats go to the Flecha from the port at the western end of El Rompido (23km southwest of Huelva). At least two daily buses go from Huelva to El Rompido (€2.35, 50 minutes).

Isla Cristina

POP 21,260

Founded after the 1755 earthquake, Isla Cristina is first and foremost a bustling fishing port with a 250-strong fleet. Besides the tuna and sardines, it's famous for its lively Carnaval. To the south of town lies a pair of long sandy beaches popular with Spanish holidaymakers.

Sights

Playa Central BEACH
Along the rear of Playa de la Gaviota, a boardwalk trail heads east to Playa Central, the main tourism zone with a few hotels and restaurants. The beach here is a long unbroken swath of sand, popular for sunbathing and swimming in warm weather. Further east, a nature trail winds through forested marshlands, with good birdwatching opportunities.

Playa de la Gaviota BEACH
At the southern end of Avenida Federico Silva Muñoz (the continuation of the central Gran Vía), a bridge crosses a lagoon to reach the sprawling Playa de la Gaviota.

Sleeping & Eating

Hotel Sol y Mar HOTEL €€
(☎959 33 20 50; www.hotelsolymar.org; Paseo Maritimo, Playa Central; s/d from €48/66; ⏲late Mar-Oct; P❄📶) Possibly the best-value hotel on this coast, with perfect balconies overlooking a broad swath of beach and little else. It has plenty of style, and welcome extras such as rain showers and friendly service. The on-site **restaurant** (mains €12-15; ⏲12.30-11.30pm late Mar-Oct) serves mostly seafood on a lovely beachfront terrace.

Hermanos Moreno SEAFOOD €
(☎959 34 35 71; Avenida Padre Mirabent 39; raciones €6-12; ⏲noon-4pm & 8pm-midnight Apr-Sep, noon-4pm Oct-Mar) Beloved for its friendly service and reasonably priced daily specials, Moreno is one of several busy seafood spots on this square on the peninsula's northwest tip. It's opposite the seafood auction market, where you can watch restaurant buyers from across Spain bid for the day's catch. *Chocos, castañuelas* (small cuttlefish), *chipirones* (squid), stuffed tuna – it just doesn't get any fresher.

Information

Tourist Office (☎959 33 26 94; http://wp.islacristina.org/turismo; Calle San Francisco 12; ⏲10am-2pm) A block inland from the fishing port. Attached is a small (free) museum featuring prize-winning costumes from Isla Cristina's Carnaval.

Getting There & Away

Damas (www.damas-sa.es) runs at least five daily buses between Isla Cristina's **bus station** (Calle Manuel Siurot) and Huelva (€4, one to 1¼ hours).

Ayamonte

POP 20,950

Staring across the Río Guadiana to Portugal, Ayamonte has a cheerful border-town buzz.

OFF THE BEATEN TRACK

NIEBLA

Thirty kilometres east of Huelva on the A472 to Seville (4km north of the A49), the brilliantly preserved medieval town of Niebla makes a fascinating stop. Encircled by 2km of dusty-orange Moorish-era walls and with five original gates plus 46 towers, Niebla's old town and its narrow streets simmer with history.

Niebla's main attraction is the majestic 15th-century **Castillo de los Guzmán** (959 36 22 70; Calle Campo del Castillo; €4.50; 10am-3pm), probably of Roman origins but built up into a palace fortress under Moorish rule. It's set around two open patios; in the dungeon below there's a spine-chilling torture museum. Also here is Niebla's tourist office (959 36 22 70; www.turismoniebla.com; Calle Arrabal 36; 10am-6pm).

On the central Plaza de Santa María, the beautiful **Iglesia de Santa María de Granada** (mass 7pm Mon-Sat, noon Sun) was originally a Visigothic cathedral before becoming a 9th-century mosque, and then a Gothic-Mudéjar church in the 15th century.

Damas (www.damas-sa.es) runs three to five daily buses to Niebla from Seville (€6.20, 1½ hours) and three to seven daily buses from Huelva (€3.10, 30 minutes). From El Rocío, there's no direct bus service to Niebla, but it's an easy 35-minute drive if you've got your own wheels.

The riverside strip between the tourist office and the port makes for a pleasant stroll, as does the adjoining town centre. The local beaches, **Isla Canela** and **Punta del Moral**, are attractive enough, but quite a way south of town and marred by ugly high-rise development.

The old town, between Paseo de la Ribera and the ferry dock (400m west), is dotted with attractive plazas, old churches, cafes, boutiques and restaurants.

Information

Tourist Office (959 32 07 37; Plaza de España 1; 9am-8pm Mon-Fri Mar-Oct, to 3pm Nov-Feb, 10am-2pm Sat year-round)

Getting There & Away

There are no customs or immigration checks when crossing the Spain–Portugal border here, by road or ferry.

BUS

From the **bus station** (Avenida de Andalucía), five daily buses go to Isla Cristina (€1.75, 15 to 25 minutes), six to Huelva (€5.30, one to 1¼ hours) and one to Faro (Portugal; €15, 40 minutes).

FERRY

Portugal-bound romantics can skip the fast, modern A49 motorway and enjoy a slower 15-minute ferry trip across the Guadiana to Portugal's Vila Real de Santo António with **Transporte Fluvial del Guadiana** (652 525168; www.rioguadiana.net; Avenida del Muelle de Portugal 37; adult/child/bicycle/motorcycle/car €1.90/1.20/1.20/3.50/5.50; half-hourly departures 9.30am-9pm Jul–mid-Sep, hourly departures 10am-7pm mid-Sep–Mar, to 8pm Apr-Jun). The same operator runs cruises up the Guadiana, one of Spain's longest rivers, to Sanlúcar de Guadiana (nine hours). Check timings and buy tickets at the kiosk facing the ferry dock.

PARQUE NACIONAL DE DOÑANA & AROUND

The World Heritage–listed Parque Nacional de Doñana is a place of haunting natural beauty and exotic horizons, where flocks of flamingos tinge the evening skies pink above one of Europe's most extensive wetlands (the Guadalquivir delta), huge herds of deer and boar flit through *coto* (woodlands), and the elusive Iberian lynx battles for survival. Here, in the largest roadless region in Western Europe, and Spain's most celebrated national park, you can experience nature at its most raw and powerful.

The 601-sq-km national park extends 30km along or close to the Atlantic coast and up to 25km inland. Much of the perimeter is bordered by the separate **Parque Natural de Doñana**, under less strict protection, which forms a 682-sq-km buffer for the national park.

The national park and its surrounding natural park together provide a refuge for 360 bird species and 37 types of mammal, including endangered species such as the

Iberian lynx and Spanish imperial eagle (nine breeding pairs). It's also a crucial habitat for half a million migrating birds.

Since its establishment in 1969, the national park has been under pressure from tourism operators, farmers, hunters, developers and builders who oppose the restrictions on land use. Ecologists, for their part, argue that Doñana is increasingly hemmed in by tourism and agricultural schemes, roads and other infrastructure that threaten to deplete its water supplies and cut it off from other undeveloped areas.

Access to the interior of the national park is restricted, although anyone can walk or cycle along the 28km Atlantic beach between Matalascañas and the mouth of the Río Guadalquivir (which can be crossed by boat from Sanlúcar de Barrameda in Cádiz province), as long as they do not stray inland.

The towns of El Rocío (p100) and Matalascañas (p103), both with good accommodation and restaurants, are Huelva province's main bases for adventures into the Parques Nacional and Natural de Doñana.

Sights & Activities

Four-hour, land-based trips in eight- to 30-passenger all-terrain vehicles are the only way to get inside the national park from the western side. Bookings can be made directly with various accredited agencies, including El Rocío-based Doñana Nature (p101) and Doñana Reservas (p101), and Cooperativa Marismas del Rocío at the El Acebuche park visitors centre near Matalascañas. Especially in the larger vehicles, the experience can feel a bit theme park–like, but guides have plenty of in-depth information to share.

During spring, summer and holidays, book as far ahead as possible, but otherwise a week or less is usually sufficient notice. Bring binoculars (if you like), drinking water and mosquito repellent (except in winter). English-, German- and French-speaking guides are normally available if you ask in advance.

You can pretty much count on seeing deer, wild boar and numerous bird species. Serious ornithologists may be disappointed by the strict limits on access to the heart of the park, and you'd be very lucky to spot a lynx.

Playa del Parador BEACH

This stunning 6km stretch of cliff-backed sands at the western edge of Parque Natural de Doñana is one of the prettiest beaches in Huelva province. Access is from the Parador de Mazagón, just off the A494 about 25km west of Matalascañas.

Cooperativa Marismas del Rocío WILDLIFE

(☎959 43 04 32; www.donanavisitas.es; Centro de Visitantes El Acebuche; tours €30) Runs four-hour tours of the national park in 20- to 30-person all-terrain vehicles, with one morning and one afternoon departure daily from the Centro de Visitantes El Acebuche. Tours traverse 75km of the southern part of the park and cover all the major ecosystems

DOÑANA: LIFE CYCLES

The many interwoven ecosystems that make up the Parque Nacional de Doñana give rise to fantastic diversity. About 380 sq km of the park consists of *marismas* (marshes). These are almost dry from July to October, but in late autumn they fill with water, eventually leaving only a few islets of dry land. Hundreds of thousands of waterbirds arrive from the north to winter here, including an estimated 80% of Western Europe's wild ducks. As the waters sink in spring, greater flamingos, herons, storks, spoonbills, avocets, hoopoes, bee-eaters and albatrosses arrive for the summer, many of them to nest. Fledglings flock around the *lucios* (ponds) and, as these dry up in July, herons, storks and kites move in to feast on trapped perch.

Between the marshlands and the park's 28km-long beach is a band of sand dunes, pushed inland by the wind by 2m to 5m per year. When dune sand eventually reaches the marshlands, rivers carry it back down to the sea, which washes it up on the beach – and the cycle begins again.

Elsewhere in the park, stable sands support 144 sq km of *coto* (woodland and scrub). *Coto* is the favoured habitat of many nesting birds and the park's abundant mammal population – 37 species including red and fallow deer, wild boar, wildcats and genets.

DOÑANA WALKS

The walking trails near the park's visitor centres are easy enough to be undertaken by most. The March–May and September–November migration seasons are the most exciting for birdwatchers. The isolated, pond-side Centro de Visitantes José Antonio Valverde (p100) has particularly good birdwatching.

Sendero Lagunas del Acebuche From the Centro de Visitantes El Acebuche, the two Senderos del Acebuche (Acebuche Paths; 1.5km and 3.5km round trip) lead to birdwatching hides overlooking nearby lagoons (though these can get quite dry).

Sendero Charco de la Boca At the Centro de Visitantes La Rocina, the Sendero Charco de la Boca is a 3.5km return walk along a stream, then through a range of habitats, passing four birdwatching hides.

Raya Real The Raya Real, one of the most important routes used by Romería pilgrims on their journeys to and from El Rocío, can be accessed from the northeastern edge of that village by crossing the Puente del Ajolí and following the track into the woodland.

It crosses the Coto del Rey, a large woodland zone where you may spot deer or boar in the early morning or late evening.

– coast, dunes, marshes and Mediterranean forest. Trips start with a long beach drive, then head inland.

Sleeping

★ **Parador de Mazagón** HOTEL €€€
(☎959 53 63 00; www.paradores.es; Carretera San Juan del Puerto-Matalascañas, Km 31; d €150-334;) Perched above the sea in a pine forest at Doñana's western edge, Mazagón stands out among Spain's nationwide *parador* (luxurious state-owned hotels) network as a true haven for nature lovers. From the hotel's front door, it's a five-minute walk to the seemingly endless expanse of cliff-fringed sandy beach below. Alternatively, stay up top to enjoy the gardens, pool, spa and on-site bar-restaurant.

Information

The park has seven visitor centres. The most important four for visitors accessing the park from Huelva province are as follows:

Centro de Visitantes El Acebrón (☎600 144625; ⏲9am-3pm & 4-7pm Feb-Oct, to 6pm Nov-Jan) Located 6km along a minor paved road west of the Centro de Visitantes La Rocina, this centre offers a Doñana information counter and an ethnographic exhibition on the park inside a palatial 1960s residence, plus walking paths.

Centro de Visitantes El Acebuche (☎959 43 96 29; ⏲8am-3pm & 4-9pm May–mid-Sep, to 7pm mid-Sep–Mar, to 8pm Apr) Twelve kilometres south of El Rocío on the A483, then 1.6km west, El Acebuche is the national park's main visitor centre. It has paths to birdwatching hides and a live film of Iberian lynxes at its breeding centre.

Centro de Visitantes José Antonio Valverde (☎671 564145; ⏲10am-8pm Apr-Sep, to 7pm Mar & Oct, to 6pm Nov-Feb) The remote Centro de Visitantes José Antonio Valverde, on the eastern edge of the park, is generally an excellent birdwatching spot as it overlooks a year-round *lucio* (pond). The easiest way to reach the centre is by authorised tour from El Rocío; the alternative is to drive yourself on rough roads from Villamanrique de la Condesa or La Puebla del Río to the northeast.

Centro de Visitantes La Rocina (☎959 43 95 69; A483; ⏲9am-3pm & 4-7pm Feb-Oct, to 6pm Nov-Jan) Beside the A483, 1km south of El Rocío. Has a national park information desk and walking paths.

Getting There & Away

You cannot enter the national park in your own vehicle, though you can drive to the four main visitor centres. **Damas** (www.damas-sa.es) runs eight to 10 buses daily between El Rocío and Matalascañas (€1.40, 25 minutes), which stop at the El Acebuche turn-off on the A483 on request. Some tour companies will pick you up from Matalascañas with advance notice.

El Rocío

POP 1370

El Rocío, the most significant town in the vicinity of the Parque Nacional de Doñana, surprises first-timers. Its sand-covered streets are lined with colourful single-storey houses with sweeping verandahs, left empty half the time. But this is no ghost town: these are the well-tended properties of 115 *hermandades* (brotherhoods), whose pilgrims converge on the town every Pentecost (Whitsunday) weekend for the Romería del Rocío, Spain's largest religious festival.

Beyond its uniquely exotic ambience, El Rocío impresses with its striking setting in front of luminous Doñana *marismas* (wetlands), where herds of deer drink at dawn and, at certain times of year, flocks of flamingos gather in massive numbers.

Whether it's the play of light on the marshes, an old woman praying to the Virgin at the Ermita, a rider prancing through the streets on horseback or someone passing by in a flamenco dress, there's always something to catch the eye on El Rocío's dusky, sand-blown streets.

Sights & Activities

The marshlands in front of El Rocío, which have water most of the year, offer some of the best bird- and beast-watching in the entire Doñana region. Deer and horses graze in the shallows and you may be lucky enough to spot a big pink cloud of flamingos wheeling through the sky. Pack a pair of binoculars and stroll the waterfront promenade.

Ermita del Rocío CHURCH

(Calle Ermita; 8am-9pm Apr-Sep, to 7pm Oct-Mar) A striking splash of white at the heart of the town, the Ermita del Rocío was built in its present form in 1964. This is the permanent home of the celebrated Nuestra Señora del Rocío (Our Lady of El Rocío), a small wooden image of the Virgin dressed in long, jewelled robes, which normally stands above the main altar.

People arrive to see the Virgin every day of the year, and especially on weekends, when El Rocío's brotherhoods often gather for colourful celebrations.

Francisco Bernis Birdwatching Centre BIRDWATCHING

(959 44 23 72; www.facebook.com/centroFranciscoBernis; Paseo Marismeño; 9am-2pm & 4-6pm Tue-Sun) FREE Run by national bird conservation group SEO Birdlife (www.seo.org), this birdwatching facility backs onto the marshes about 700m east of the Ermita. Flamingos, glossy ibises, spoonbills and more can be spied through the rear windows or from the observation deck with high-power binoculars (free). Experts offer help identifying species and information about migratory birds and where to see them.

Tours

Doñana Nature WILDLIFE

(630 978216, 959 44 21 60; www.donana-nature.com; Calle Moguer 10; per person €30) Runs half-day, small-group (eight- to 15-person) tours of the Parque Natural de Doñana twice daily (one morning and one afternoon departure; binoculars provided). Specialised ornithological and photographic trips are also offered. English-speaking guides available on request.

Doñana Reservas WILDLIFE

(959 44 24 74, 629 060545; www.donanareservas.com; Avenida de la Canaliega; tours per person €30) Runs four-hour tours in 20- to 30-person all-terrain vehicles, focusing on the marshes and woods in the northern section of the park, and including a stop at the Centro de Visitantes José Antonio Valverde – usually an excellent birdwatching spot. There's one morning and one afternoon departure daily.

DOÑANA'S IBERIAN LYNX

For wildlife-watchers, the Iberian lynx is Doñana's most prized, yet elusive, animal. Lynx numbers in the Doñana area now fluctuate between 70 to 100 individuals (the official figure in 2018 was 94, up significantly from the 41 recorded in 2002). A slump in Doñana's population of rabbits (the lynx's main prey) has recently prompted park authorities to introduce 10,000 new rabbits into the area. There's also an increasingly successful captive breeding program – with Doñana's 27 breeding lynx pairs adding 35 new cubs to the resident population in 2019 (check out www.lynxexsitu.es for up-to-the-minute statistics). The Centro de Visitantes El Acebuche streams a live video of lynxes in its nearby breeding centre, which makes for pretty exciting viewing even when they're just stretching, yawning and grooming themselves – but you can't visit them. Some resident lynxes have been run over attempting to cross roads around Doñana (here in the park and elsewhere in Spain, some 29 lynxes perished in road accidents in 2019, which offers a compelling incentive to heed the posted speed limits).

DON'T MISS

SPAIN'S GREATEST RELIGIOUS PILGRIMAGE: ROMERÍA DEL ROCÍO

Every Pentecost (Whitsunday) weekend, seven weeks after Easter, El Rocío transforms from a quiet backwater into an explosive mess of noise, colour and passion. This is the culmination of Spain's biggest religious pilgrimage, the **Romería del Rocío**, which draws up to a million joyous pilgrims.

The focus of all this revelry is the tiny image of Nuestra Señora del Rocío (Our Lady of El Rocío), which was found in a marshland tree by a hunter from Almonte village back in the 13th century. When he stopped for a rest on the way home, the Virgin magically returned to the tree. Before long, a chapel was built on the site of the tree (El Rocío) and pilgrims started arriving.

Solemn is the last word you'd apply to this quintessentially Andalucian event. Participants dress in their finest Andalucian costume and sing, drink, dance, laugh and romance their way to El Rocío. Most belong to the 115 *hermandades* (brotherhoods) who arrive from towns all across southern Spain on foot, horseback and in colourfully decorated covered wagons.

The weekend reaches an ecstatic climax in the very early hours of Monday. Members of the Almonte *hermandad*, which claims the Virgin as its own, barge into the church and bear her out on a float. Violent struggles ensue as others battle for the honour of carrying La Paloma Blanca (the White Dove). The crush and chaos are immense, but somehow the Virgin is carried round to each of the *hermandad* buildings before finally being returned to the church in the afternoon. Upcoming dates are 24 May 2021, 6 June 2022 and 29 May 2023.

In recent years, Spaniards' rising concern for animal rights, spearheaded by animal-welfare political party PACMA (https://pacma.es), has drawn attention to mistreatment and neglect of animals, particularly horses and mules, during the Romería del Rocío festivities, and, despite the presence of voluntary veterinary services, seven horses died during the 2019 *romería*.

Doñana Horse Adventure HORSE RIDING
(☎626 784628; www.donanahorseadventure.com) Lovely French owner Sandrine offers a wide range of equestrian experiences, from two-hour private beginner's lessons (€45, in Spanish or English) to three-day horseback excursions through Parque Nacional de Doñana (€350).

Sleeping

Hotels get booked up to a year ahead for the Romería del Rocío.

La Fonda del Rocío HOSTAL €
(☎959 44 23 76; www.lafondadelrocio.es; Calle Sacrificio 34; r midweek €30-40, weekend €50-70; 📶) On a characteristic El Rocío lane lined with whitewashed houses, this friendly *hostal* makes a great budget option, with 19 simple but well-kept rooms surrounding a narrow patio filled with potted plants. Its sister enterprise across the street, Hostal Abuelo Eloy, has slightly smaller and cheaper rooms, complemented by pretty tiled common areas and a courtyard with lemon trees.

Hotel Toruño HOTEL €€
(☎959 44 23 23; www.toruno.es; Plaza Acebuchal 22; s €35-59, d €50-80, all incl breakfast; P ❄ 📶) This brilliantly white villa 350m east of the Ermita directly abuts the *marismas*, where you can spot flamingos going through their morning beauty routine. Inside, tile murals continue the wildlife theme. Interior rooms are uninspiring, especially on the ground floor; request one overlooking the marshes if available. Across the plaza, the hotel's Restaurante Toruño is among El Rocío's best.

★ **Hotel La Malvasía** HOTEL €€€
(☎959 44 27 13; www.hotellamalvasia.com; Calle Sanlúcar 38; s €100-110, d €120-170, ste €185-205; ❄ 📶) This idyllic hotel occupies a grand *casa señorial* (manor house) overlooking the marshes at the eastern end of town. Rooms have character: rustic tiled floors, vintage El Rocío photos and floral-patterned iron bedsteads. The top-floor sun terrace makes a spectacular bird-viewing perch, as does the suite, with its front-facing views of the lagoon.

Eating & Drinking

Restaurante Toruño ANDALUCIAN €€

(☎959 44 24 22; www.toruno.es; Plaza Acebuchal; mains €13-25; ⏲1-4pm & 8-11pm; 🖉) With its traditional Andalucian atmosphere, good food and huge portions, Toruño is a perennial El Rocío favourite. Menu highlights include the free-range Mostrenca calf, unique to Doñana; for noncarnivores, the *parrillada* (grilled assortment) of vegetables is fantastic. Dine in front of the restaurant by the 1000-year-old *acebuche* (olive) tree or out back overlooking the wetlands.

Aires de Doñana ANDALUCIAN €€

(La Choza; ☎959 44 22 89; www.airesdedonana.com; Avenida de la Canaliega 1; mains €15-22; ⏲1.30-4pm Tue-Sun, 8.30-11pm Tue-Sat) Affectionately nicknamed La Choza (the Hut), this thatched-roofed, whitewashed local institution has one big thing going for it: knockout views of La Ermita framed by horse pastures and bird-thronged wetlands. The menu includes everything from local Mostrenca beef to seafood; either way, you can't go wrong sipping drinks on the terrace at sunset.

Albero 36 BAR

(☎618 146555; www.facebook.com/Albero36El Rocio; Paseo Marismeño 36; ⏲noon-4.30pm & 8pm-midnight Wed-Sat, noon-7pm Sun) Cool blue-and-white decor, high ceilings, sandy floors and a spacious back patio create a relaxed, romantic Andalucian backdrop for drinks and tapas. At sundown, the chorus of birds flitting about the adjacent wetlands can be downright deafening.

Information

Tourist Office (☎959 44 23 50; www.almonte.es; Avenida de la Canaliega; ⏲9.30am-2pm) Relocated from the town hall to El Rocío's shoreline in 2020.

Getting There & Away

Damas (www.damas-sa.es) buses run from Seville's Plaza de Armas to El Rocío (€6.55, 1½ hours, two to three daily), continuing to Matalascañas (€1.40, 25 minutes). From Huelva, take a Damas bus to Almonte (€4, 1¼ hours, one to four daily), then another to El Rocío (€1.40, 20 minutes, eight to 10 daily).

Matalascañas

Abutting the Parques Nacional and Natural de Doñana, 50km southeast of Huelva, Matalascañas is a modern, purpose-built tourist resort (much like Mazagón to its west). Thanks to national park regulations, development is confined to a 4km by 1km space. The beach here is simply gorgeous.

Playa de Matalascañas BEACH

Matalascañas' long sandy beach stretches for 4km along the south edge of town, merging at either end into the wilder beaches of Parque Nacional de Doñana. To reach the best part of the beach, follow the main road east to a trail leading down along the edge of the park. From a control post on the beach below the Gran Hotel del Coto, a 1.5km boardwalk trail snakes through the dunes, here dotted with umbrella pine and maritime juniper.

Parque Dunar PARK

(A494, Km 52; ⏲8am-9pm) On the western edge of Matalascañas, the Parque Dunar is a 1.3-sq-km expanse of high, pine-covered dunes laced with a maze of sandy pathways and boardwalk trails.

Getting There & Away

Damas (www.damas-sa.es) runs two to three buses daily from Matalascañas to Seville (€7.95, two hours), plus twice-daily service Monday to Friday to Huelva (€4, 1¼ hours).

NORTHERN HUELVA PROVINCE

North of Huelva, straight highways are replaced by winding byways and you enter a more temperate zone, up to 960m higher than the coast. The rolling hills of Huelva's portion of the Sierra Morena are covered with a thick pelt of cork oak and pine, punctuated by winding river valleys, enchanting stone-and-tile villages, and the bustling 'capital' of the area, Aracena.

Word is slowly getting out about this still little-discovered rural world, threaded with walking trails. Most of the area lies within the 1870-sq-km **Parque Natural Sierra de Aracena y Picos de Aroche**, Andalucía's second-largest protected zone.

Minas de Riotinto

POP 3850 / ELEV 420M

Tucked away on the southern fringe of Huelva's Sierra Morena is one of the world's oldest mining districts; King Solomon of Jerusalem is said to have mined gold here for his famous temple, and the Romans were digging up silver by the 4th century BCE. The mines were then left largely untouched until the British Rio Tinto company made this one of the world's key copper-mining centres in the 1870s (leading, incidentally, to the foundation of Spain's first football club). The mines were sold back to Spain in 1954, and the miners clocked off for the last time in 2001. Nowadays it's a fascinating place to explore, with a superb museum, and opportunities to visit the old mines and ride the mine railway.

The Río Tinto itself rises a few kilometres northeast of town, its name ('red river') stemming from the deep red-brown hue of its iron- and copper-infused waters.

Sights & Activities

Museo Minero MUSEUM

(☎959 59 00 25; www.parquemineroderiotinto.es; Plaza Ernest Lluch; adult/reduced €5/4; ⊙10.30am-3pm & 4-8pm mid-Jul–mid-Sep, to 7pm rest of year; P) Riotinto's mining museum offers a sweeping overview of the area's unique history and geology, from the megalithic tombs of the 3rd millennium BCE to the British colonial era, and from impressively colourful locally quarried gemstones to ruddy rust-tinged Roman statues discovered on-site. Two of the most memorable displays are an elaborate 200m-long recreation of a Roman mine, and the *Vagón del Maharajah,* a luxurious train carriage built in 1892 for a tour of India by Britain's Queen Victoria.

Peña de Hierro MINE

(☎959 59 00 25; www.parquemineroderiotinto.es; adult/reduced €8/7; ⊙hours vary) These are old copper and sulphur mines 3km north of Nerva (6km east of Minas de Riotinto). Here you see the source of the Río Tinto and a 65m-deep opencast mine, and are taken into a 200m-long underground mine gallery. There are three guaranteed daily visits but schedules vary, so it's essential to book ahead through the Museo Minero (by phone or online).

Ferrocarril Turístico-Minero RAIL

(☎959 59 00 25; www.parquemineroderiotinto.es; adult/reduced €11/10; ⊙1.30pm & 5.30pm daily mid-Jul–mid-Sep, 1pm Mon-Fri, 1.30pm Sat & Sun mid-Feb–mid-Jul & mid-Sep–mid-Nov, 1.30pm Sat & Sun mid-Nov–mid-Feb) A fun way to see the area – especially with children – is to ride this historic railway through Riotinto's surreal landscape in restored early-20th-century carriages. The entire train journey (22km return) parallels the rust-red river, so you can appreciate its constantly shifting hues. Advance booking is required, either at the mining museum or the railway station 4km east of town.

Getting There & Away

Damas (www.damas-sa.es) runs three to five daily buses between Minas de Riotinto and Huelva (€7.10, 1¾ hours).

Aracena

POP 8110 / ELEV 673M

Sparkling white in its mountain bowl, the thriving old market town of Aracena is an appealingly lively place that's wrapped like a ribbon around a medieval church and ruined castle. With a stash of good places to eat and sleep, it's a popular destination for gastrotourism and an ideal base for exploring the surrounding Sierra de Aracena.

Sights

The handsome, cobbled **Plaza Alta** was originally the centre of the town. Here stands the elegant 15th-century **Cabildo Viejo**, the former town hall, with a grand Renaissance doorway (and a natural park information centre). From Plaza Alta, Calle Francisco Rincón descends the hill back towards town, passing a series of narrow streets attractively lined with humble whitewashed houses, before finally entering the main Plaza del Marqués de Aracena, a lively square fronted by a few cafe-restaurants.

★**Gruta de las Maravillas** CAVE

(Cave of Marvels; ☎663 937876; www.aracena.es/es/municipio/gruta; Calle Pozo de la Nieve; tours adult/child €10/7; ⊙10am-1.30pm & 3-6pm) Beneath Aracena's castle hill is a web of caves and tunnels carved from the karstic topography. An extraordinary 1.2km, 50-minute loop takes you through 12 chambers and past six underground lakes, all beautifully illuminated and filled with weird and wonderful rock formations, which provided a backdrop for the film *Journey to the Center of the Earth.*

Tours are in Spanish, with optional English-language audio guides available for €1.50. Frequency of departures varies ac-

Aracena

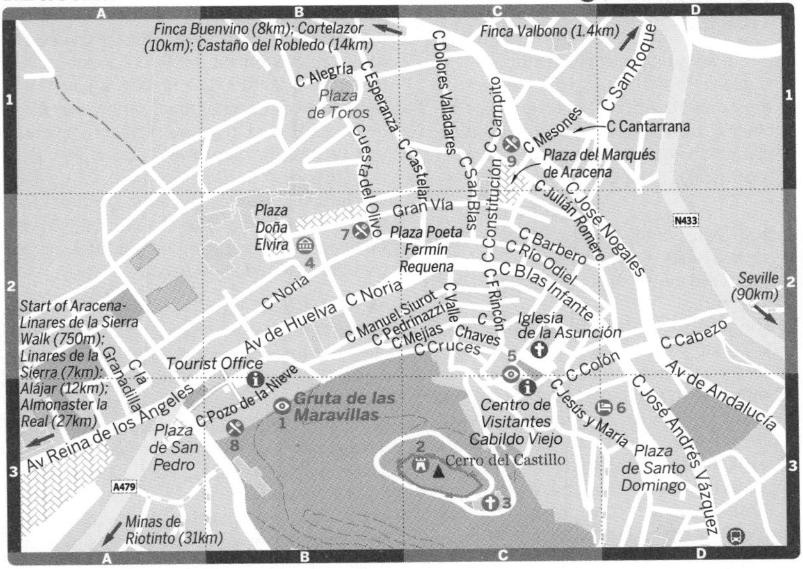

Aracena

Top Sights

1 Gruta de las Maravillas B3

Sights

2 Castillo C3
3 Iglesia Prioral de Nuestra Señora del Mayor Dolor C3
4 Museo del Jamón B2
5 Plaza Alta C2

Sleeping

6 Hotel Convento Aracena D3

Eating

7 Experience by Fuster B2
8 Jesús Carrión B3
9 Rincón de Juan C1

cording to demand. Tickets can sell out in the afternoons and on weekends when busloads of visitors arrive.

Museo del Jamón MUSEUM

(☎663 937870; www.aracena.es/es/municipio/museo; Gran Vía; adult/child €3.50/2.50; ⏲11am-2.30pm & 4-7.30pm) The *jamón* for which the sierra is famed gets due recognition in this modern museum. You'll learn why the acorn-fed Iberian pig gives such succulent meat, about the importance of the native pastures in which they are reared, and about traditional and contemporary methods of slaughter and curing. Displays are in Spanish, with free audio guides available in four other languages. Afterwards, the museum shop invites visitors to 'pig' out with a free tasting of local *bellota* ham.

Castillo CASTLE

(Cerro del Castillo; guided tour adult/child €2.50/1; ⏲tours 11.30am, 12.30pm, 1.30pm, 6pm, 7pm & 8pm Apr-Oct, 11.45am, 12.45pm, 1.45pm, 4pm, 5pm & 5.45pm Nov-Mar) Dramatically dominating the town are the tumbling, hilltop ruins of the *castillo,* built by the kingdoms of Portugal and Castilla in the 12th century atop the ruins of an earlier Islamic settlement. Directly adjacent is the Gothic-Mudéjar **Iglesia Prioral de Nuestra Señora del Mayor Dolor** (Plazoleta Virgen del Mayor Dolor; ⏲10am-5pm Sep-Jun, to 7.30pm Jul & Aug). Both are reached via a steep lane from Plaza Alta; guided tours grant access to the castle's interior, though it's honestly more impressive from the outside.

Activities & Tours

The hills and mountains around Aracena offer some of the most beautiful, and least known, walking country in Andalucía. Any time of year is a good time to hike here but

ARACENA DISCOUNT TICKET

If you're visiting multiple sights in Aracena, save 20% with the **Tarjeta Aracena Turística**, a combo ticket offering admission to the Gruta de las Maravillas, the Museo del Jamón and the Castillo (€12.50).

spring (April and May), when the meadows are awash with wildflowers and carnival-coloured butterflies, is the best time to hit the trails.

The Centro de Visitantes Cabildo Viejo (p107) can recommend walks of varying difficulty and give you basic maps; the tourist office (p107) sells the *Mapa Guía para Recorrer la Sierra de Aracena* (€4.50), a good map with dozens of suggested hikes. Also ask locally for the free brochure *10 Nordic Walking Routes: Parque Natural Sierra de Aracena,* which provides rough descriptions of 10 loop hikes in the area.

Aracena-Linares de la Sierra Walk WALKING

This sublime and fairly gentle 5km, two-hour ramble takes you down a verdant valley to sleepy Linares de la Sierra (p108). The signposted path (PRA48) is easy to find off the HU8105 on the southwestern edge of Aracena, 500m beyond the municipal swimming pool. You can extend the walk to Alájar (4km, 1½ hours), returning to Aracena by bus (except Sunday).

★**Jamones Eíriz Jabugo** FOOD & DRINK

(☎676 035827; www.rutadeljamondejabugo.com; Calle Pablo Bejarano 43, Corteconcepción; per person incl tasting €42.50) For a firsthand understanding of DOC Iberian ham production, nothing beats the two- to three-hour tours offered by this award-winning, fourth-generation, family-run operation. After an hour mingling with acorn-crazed pigs in their little patch of paradise under the oak trees, decamp to the maze of salting and curing chambers, where you'll witness hundreds of dangling hams developing their prized flavour.

Finish with a tasting of multiple meat products (ham, *lomito, salchicha* and chorizo). All tours must be booked in advance, and can be offered in English or other languages upon request. It's about a 6km drive northeast of Aracena.

Sleeping

Finca Valbono HOTEL €

(☎959 12 77 11; www.fincavalbono.com; Carretera Aracena-Carboneras, Km 1; d €50-70, 2-person apt €60-80, 4-person apt €100-120; P ❄ 📶 ≋) Just 1km northeast of Aracena, this lovingly run farmhouse immersed in greenery offers a splendid mix of country charm and convenient location. It has 20 *casitas* (cottages) set up with log fires, kitchenettes and supplementary sofa beds (perfect for groups or families), plus six rustic rooms. Other standout features include friendly staff and a lovely pool.

★**Finca Buenvino** INN €€

(☎959 12 40 34; www.fincabuenvino.com; Los Marines; s/d incl breakfast €90/140, 4-person cottage per week €600-850; 📶 ≋) For four decades, the Chesterton family has been welcoming guests to their spectacularly sited salmon-pink farmhouse on a hilltop 10 minutes west of Aracena. Six rooms in varying configurations (including a couple of family-friendly suites) all have high ceilings, charming decor and lovely views over the surrounding countryside. There's a grand living room and a sun porch with wraparound windows.

Optional dinners (€35 including wine) and occasional four-day cooking courses (€850 including meals and accommodation) feature recipes from the family's own *Buenvino Cookbook*. Down the hill are a pair of two-storey cottages sleeping up to four people each, surrounded by organic gardens where you can pick your own veggies. All in all, it's a dreamy base for exploring the Aracena area.

★**Hotel Convento Aracena** HISTORIC HOTEL €€€

(☎959 12 68 99; www.hotelconventoaracena.es; Calle Jesús y María 19; d €95-163, ste €195-243; P ❄ 📶 ≋) Glossy, modern rooms contrast with flourishes of original Andalucian baroque architecture at this thoughtfully converted 17th-century convent, Aracena town's finest lodging. Enjoy the on-site spa, sierra cuisine and year-round saltwater pool, with gorgeous village views and summer bar. Room 9 is fabulously set in the church dome (though be forewarned that it's windowless, save for the skylight in the cupola).

Eating & Drinking

Rincón de Juan TAPAS €

(Avenida de Portugal 3; tapas €2-3, raciones €10-14; ⏲7.30am-4pm Mon-Sat, 6.30pm-midnight

Wed-Sat) It's standing room only at this wood-beamed, stone-walled corner bar, indisputably Aracena's favourite local hangout for traditional tapas. Iberian ham is the star attraction and forms the basis for a variety of *montaditos* (small stuffed rolls) and *rebanadas* (sliced loaves for several people). The local goat's cheese is always a good bet.

★ **Experience by Fuster** FUSION €€
(☎634 682988; www.facebook.com/experiencebyfuster; Gran Vía 21; tapas €2.50-4, raciones €9-18; ⏲9am-midnight Mon, Tue, Thu & Fri, from 10am Sat & Sun) Aracena's home-grown celebrity chef Javier Fuster created an instant sensation when he opened this casual downtown restaurant in 2019. Sourcing ingredients largely from Huelva province, Fuster gives traditional Andalucian flavours a gourmet international twist in dishes like tempura battered pork tenderloin with cream of porcini mushrooms or seafood risotto with wakame seaweed.

★ **Jesús Carrión** TAPAS €€
(☎959 46 31 88; www.jesuscarrionrestaurante.com; Calle Pozo de la Nieve 35; tapas €6-13, mains €14-25; ⏲1.30-4pm Wed-Sun, 8.30-11pm Fri & Sat; 📶✍) Devoted chef Jesús heads up the creative kitchen at this wonderful family-run restaurant, which is causing quite the stir with its lovingly prepared, contemporary twists on traditional Aracena dishes. Try the Iberian ham carpaccio or the local boletus-mushroom risotto. Homemade breads come straight from the oven and salads are deliciously fresh – not a tinned vegetable in sight!

ℹ Information

Centro de Visitantes Cabildo Viejo (☎959 12 95 53; Plaza Alta; ⏲generally 9.30am-2pm year-round, plus 4-7pm Fri & Sat Mar-May & Oct-Dec) Gives out hiking information and maps, and has an exhibit on the Parque Natural Sierra de Aracena y Picos de Aroche. Hours vary by month.

Tourist Office (☎663 937877; www.aracena.es; Calle Pozo de la Nieve; ⏲10am-2pm & 4-6pm) Opposite the Gruta de las Maravillas; sells a good walking map.

ℹ Getting There & Away

The **bus station** (Calle José Andrés Vázquez) is 700m southeast of Plaza del Marqués de Aracena. **Damas** (www.damas-sa.es) runs two to three daily buses from Seville (€7.70, 1¼ hours), continuing to Cortegana via Alájar or Jabugo. From Huelva, there are two afternoon departures Monday to Friday, and one on weekends (€11.25, 2½ to 2¾ hours). There's also a local service between Aracena and Cortegana via Linares de la Sierra, Alájar and Almonaster la Real.

Sierra de Aracena

Stretching west of Aracena is one of Andalucía's most unexpectedly picturesque landscapes, a flower-sprinkled hill country dotted with old stone villages. Woodlands alternate with expanses of *dehesa* (evergreen oak pastures where the region's famed black pigs forage for acorns). The area is threaded by an extensive network of well-maintained walking trails, with ever-changing vistas and mostly gentle ascents and descents, making for some of the most delightful rambling in Andalucía.

Great hiking routes are particularly thick in the area between Aracena and Cortegana, making attractive villages such as Alájar, Linares de la Sierra, Castaño del Robledo, Cortelazor and Almonaster la Real perfect bases from which to set forth.

Locally available resources for hikers include the maps distributed by Aracena's tourist offices and information downloadable (in Spanish and English) from www.sierradearacena.com and www.ventanadelvisitante.es. Trickier to find but still worth seeking out are the guidebook *Sierra de Aracena Walk!* and its partner *Sierra de Aracena Tour & Trail Map*, both published by Discovery Walking Guides (www.dwgwalking.co.uk).

ℹ Getting There & Away

BUS

All buses are operated by **Damas** (www.damas-sa.es). Morning and afternoon buses travel the HU8105 daily from Aracena to Cortegana (€3.40, one hour). From Monday to Saturday, one daily bus also travels from Aracena to Linares de la Sierra (€1.20, 10 minutes), Alájar (€1.20, 30 minutes) and Almonaster la Real (€2.30, 50 minutes).

TRAIN

There's at least one daily train each way between Huelva and the stations of Almonaster-Cortegana (€9.85, 1¾ hours) and Jabugo-Galaroza (€10.90, two hours). Almonaster-Cortegana station is 1km off the Almonaster–Cortegana road, halfway between the two villages.

Sierra de Aracena

Linares de la Sierra

POP 260 / ELEV 505M

Just 7km west of Aracena along the HU8105, you'll bump into one of the area's cutest villages, Linares de la Sierra. Surrounded by a verdant river valley, its cobbled streets are renowned for their 300-odd *llanos* (front-patio mosaics) and are lined with oddly angled, tiled-roof houses. In the centre, behind the 18th-century Iglesia de San Juan Bautista, a minute bullring plaza is paved with concentric rings around a shield of flowers. From the village's fringes, signposted walking paths fan out into the hills towards Aracena and Alájar.

There's a little **visitors centre** (☎959 46 37 28; www.linaresdelasierra.com; Calle Blas Infante 1; ⏲9am-6pm Tue-Sun) with (limited) information on walks around Linares just south of the bullring plaza.

Linares de la Sierra-Alájar Loop WALKING
Starting from Linares de la Sierra's southwestern edge, this moderate, signposted 9.7km loop hike passes through high pastures and oak forest to the hamlet of Los Madroñeros, then climbs over the Puerto de los Madroñeros (618m) to Alájar village. The return route gently ascends the Barranco del Hoyo ravine to Puerto Linares (703m), before switching back steeply down to Linares.

★**Restaurante Arrieros** ANDALUCIAN €€€
(☎959 46 37 17; www.arrieros.net; Calle Arrieros 2; mains €15-21, tasting menus from €35; ⏲1-4pm Thu-Tue, closed mid-Jun–mid-Jul) The art of slow food is taken to the extreme here with meals normally spinning out over several lazy hours. The innovative approach to local pork products and wild mushrooms, such as the mushroom-and-apple stuffed *solomillo* (pork sirloin) and *carrilleras* (pig cheeks) in red wine, makes this one of the sierra's top places to eat.

Alájar

POP 760 / ELEV 570M

Five kilometres west of Linares de la Sierra is possibly the region's most picturesque village, Alájar, which retains its narrow cobbled streets and cubist stone houses along with a fine baroque church. Several good walking routes leave from or pass through here.

Sights & Activities

Peña de Arias Montano HISTORIC SITE
(HU8121; P) High above Alájar, this rocky spur provides magical views over the village. The site takes its name from remarkable 16th-century polymath and humanist Benito Arias Montano, who repeatedly visited this spot for retreat and meditation. The *peña's* 16th-century chapel is an important local pilgrimage site.

Ermita de Nuestra Señora Reina de los Ángeles CHURCH
(HU8121; ⏲11am-sunset) On the Peña de Arias Montano, the 16th-century Ermita de Nuestra Señora Reina de los Ángeles contains a small carving of the Virgin that is considered the patron of the whole Sierra de Aracena. In early September, the chapel is the focus of the area's biggest annual religious event, the **Romería de la Reina de los**

Ángeles, when people from all around the sierra converge here to honour their Virgin.

Outside the chapel are stalls selling local honey and cheeses, and an **info booth** (☎625 512442; ⏱Fri-Sun, hours vary) with displays about the local area.

Alájar-Castaño del Robledo Walk WALKING

Starting beside the bus stop on the western edge of Alájar, across the HU8105, this moderately difficult 5km uphill route leads you past the once deserted hamlet of El Calabacino, now an international artist/hippie colony, then on to the beautiful little village of Castaño del Robledo, passing through cork-oak and chestnut forest. Allow two hours.

Sleeping & Eating

★Finca La Fronda HOTEL €€

(☎959 50 12 47, 659 963510; www.fincalafronda.com; Carretera Cortegana-Aracena, Km 22; r incl breakfast €89-140; P ❄ 📶 🏊) Tucked away amid cork/chestnut forest, La Fronda makes the perfect hillside hideaway. Modern-rustic charm abounds in the bright lounge, Mudéjar-inspired patio and huge, flowery rooms with splashes of British character. Spectacular vistas of Alájar and the Peña de Arias Montano unfold from the rose-fringed pool, and the Saturday evening dinner concerts in the *finca's* dining room are not to be missed.

It's all under the loving care of the gracious Wordsworth family (yes, by the way, they are descendants of the poet), who are generous in sharing their love and knowledge of the local area; they can arrange *jamón* tastings, horse riding and hiking. It's signposted off the HU8105 at the top of the hill between Alájar and Linares de la Sierra.

★Posada de San Marcos INN €€

(☎959125712, 667906132; www.sanmarcosalajar.com; Calle Colón 12; s/d incl breakfast €67.50/95; P ❄ 📶 🏊) 🍃 Andalucía's first European Eco-Label hotel, this brilliantly restored 200-year-old house bordering a stream in the heart of Alájar runs on geothermal energy, rain harvesting and natural-cork insulation. The six comfortably rustic, airy rooms have big terraces, breakfast is home-made, and welcoming Spanish-English hosts Ángel and Lucy are experts on local hiking. The pool looks across the village to the *peña*.

The owners take pride in sharing Aracena's culture with guests, offering tastings of local olive oil, goat's cheese and DOC Iberian ham (per person €40), along with walking holiday packages. Lucy makes excellent three-course dinners upon request (per person €25, plus €12 per bottle of wine).

Molino Río Alájar COTTAGE €€€

(☎638 081415, 959 50 17 74; www.molinorioalajar.com; Finca Cabeza del Molino; house per day €125-183, per week €850-1275) Well-travelled Dutch owners Peter Jan and Monica rent out these six cottages on Alájar's western outskirts, ideal for families or anybody wanting a self-contained home in the heart of nature. Each unique unit is beautifully constructed of reclaimed wood, brick, stone and tile, equipped with a full kitchen and creatively decorated with vintage furniture, family heirlooms and flea-market finds.

Mesón El Molino ANDALUCIAN €€

(☎959 12 56 37; www.facebook.com/MesonElMolinodeAlajar; Calle Alta; mains €10-20; ⏱1pm-midnight Fri-Sun) Atmospherically housed in a historic olive mill with stone floors and a gigantic water wheel, El Molino specialises in hearty Aracena-style cuisine. Iberian pork holds centre stage, complemented by other mountain treats such as molasses-glazed baby lamb chops with aged Manchego cheese. It's only open on weekends, so plan ahead.

Cortelazor

POP 300 / ELEV 624M

About 10km northwest of Aracena via the N433 and HU8122, Cortelazor is a tiny whitewashed village with ancient Roman roots. Life here revolves around Plaza Andalucía, home to the parish church of Nuestra Señora de los Remedios and a pair of local bars. Just south of the square is the Olmo Milenario, an ancient elm tree whose spreading branches are said to have provided shade for town council meetings over the centuries. From the edges of town, some nice walking routes fan out into the surrounding hills.

Activities

Cortelazor-Alto de la Barquera Loop WALKING

Passing through a mix of pastures, oak woodland and creek valleys, this 12km loop affords some lovely views over the Sierra de

SIERRA DE ARACENA CUISINE

The hills around Aracena have given rise to some superb, and increasingly innovative, cuisine. Delights include the region's mushrooms; dozens of different varieties pop up out of the ground every autumn. And then there's the ham: the *jamón ibérico* of nearby **Jabugo** is considered the finest in the entire country; you won't fail to notice the providers of this bounty – contented-looking black pigs foraging in the forests for acorns.

Aracena. From Cortelazor's central Plaza Andalucía, walk down the right-hand side of the church, descend past a playground and bear left onto a path marked by posts with light blue stripes. After crossing a creek (Arroyo de la Guijarra), the trail climbs to a high promontory, Alto de la Barquera, before looping back west and north to Cortelazor.

Sleeping

★Casa Annette B&B €

(☎959 12 40 65; www.casaannette.com; Calle España 8; s/d without bathroom incl breakfast €35/45; ⓦ) A long-time labour of love for Scottish-Danish duo Stuart and Annette, this delightful guesthouse features four comfy and colourfully decorated (if mostly windowless) shared bathroom upstairs rooms. The owners graciously share advice on the local area and serve sumptuous breakfasts in the wood-beamed library, with fresh-baked bread, homemade jam and marmalade, local cheese and sausage, and coffee brewed Italian-style in moka espresso pots.

Castaño del Robledo

POP 220 / ELEV 740M

North of Alájar on the minor HU8114 road between Fuenteheridos and Jabugo, little Castaño del Robledo is a truly idyllic spot, surrounded by hazy green olive and cork forests. Its jigsaw of tiled terracotta roofs is overlooked by two large churches (one unfinished), either of which could easily accommodate the entire village population.

Activities

Castaño del Robledo-Galaroza Loop WALKING

A worthwhile 10km loop (three hours) can be hiked by taking the PRA38 trail from Castaño del Robledo to Galaroza village and returning via the alternative SLA129 riverside route. The walk traverses woodlands interspersed with long-distance panoramas. Wildflowers pop up in spring and you're likely to spot *pata negra* (black leg) pigs of Jabugo fame rooting about for acorns.

Sleeping

Posada del Castaño CASA RURAL €

(☎615 592854, 620 109331; www.posadadelcastano.com; Calle José Sánchez Calvo 33; s/d incl breakfast €40/50; ⓦ) This chilled-out converted village house, with its bendy roof beams, big book collection and colourful throws, has walkers foremost in mind. British owners Craig and Sasha (experienced travellers and hikers) are full of information, and offer self-guided walking tours and horse-riding holidays. Weather permitting, homemade breakfast is served on the back terrace overlooking the lush garden.

Almonaster la Real

POP 1820 / ELEV 613M

Set amid rolling hills covered in cork oak forest, Almonaster la Real is one of the Sierra de Aracena's most picturesque and appealingly authentic towns. Elderly locals loll about the peaceful village centre, while the hillside just above harbours a fabulous gem of Islamic architecture.

Sights & Activities

★Mezquita HISTORIC BUILDING

(Mosque; Calle Castillo 10; ⏲9am-dusk) FREE Dating to the 9th and 10th centuries, this rare jewel of a *mezquita* perches a five-minute walk above Almonaster's main square. The almost perfectly preserved structure is like a miniature version of Córdoba's great mosque. Despite being Christianised in the 13th century, it retains nearly all its original Islamic features: the horseshoe arches, the semicircular *mihrab* (prayer niche indicating the direction of Mecca; reputedly the Iberian Peninsula's oldest), an ablutions fountain and various Arabic inscriptions. Even older are the Roman and Visigothic columns nearest the mihrab.

The original square minaret adjoins the building. Just below is Almonaster's 19th-century bullring.

Iglesia de San Martín CHURCH

(Placeta de San Cristóbal; hours vary) The Mudéjar Iglesia de San Martín has a 16th-century portal in the Portuguese Manueline style, unique in the region.

Cerro de San Cristóbal Walk HIKING

From the eastern end of town, this circular hiking route (5.5km, about 2½ hours) leads up to the Cerro de San Cristóbal (912m) for fantastic views across the sierra.

Sleeping & Eating

Hotel Luz BOUTIQUE HOTEL €€

(638 870129; Calle Iglesia 3; standard/deluxe r €100/130;) Opened in 2019, this sleekly remodelled *casa señorial* enjoys an enviable position on Almonaster's church square. Its nine spacious rooms are packed with boutique-y features like four-poster beds, free-standing bathtubs and attractive woodwork. The downstairs lounge has cosy armchairs and a fireplace for chilly mountain evenings, while the backyard pool offers respite on a hot summer's day.

El Rincón de Curro ANDALUCIAN €€

(959 14 31 49, 676 780606; www.rincon.de.curro.la-colmena.org; Carretera Almonaster-Cortegana, Km 1; mains €13-27; 1.30-5pm) Look for this wonderful local restaurant in a whitewashed building on the main road just west of town. Since 2000, Señor Curro has been delighting discerning palates with his fine mountain cuisine. Local pork products get top billing, but plenty of dishes also feature seafood and vegetables – not to mention the deliciously crispy, cumin-y *patatas bravas* (potatoes in a spicy tomato sauce) offered as a free appetiser.

AT A GLANCE

POPULATION
1.27 million

CAPITAL
Cádiz

BEST BEACH BAR
Tangana (p152)

BEST FLAMENCO
Centro Cultural Flamenco Don Antonio Chacón (p130)

BEST NORTH AFRICA–INSPIRED HOTEL
La Casa del Califa (p144)

WHEN TO GO

Feb–Mar
Cádiz' riotous Carnaval and the flamenco-mad Festival de Jerez.

May–Jun
Good beach, hiking and kitesurfing weather; the Feria del Caballo brings horse mania to Jerez.

Sep–Oct
Warm but not sweltering; Jerez celebrates the grape harvest with the Fiestas de la Vendimia.

Tarifa (p148)
PAWEL KAZMIERCZAK/SHUTTERSTOCK

Cádiz Province & Gibraltar

If you had to pick just one region to attempt to explain Andalucía in its full, complex beauty, it would be Cádiz. Lying in wait across mainland Spain's southernmost province are oceans of olive trees, craggy mountains, thrillingly sited white towns (Arcos, Vejer, Zahara, Grazalema), glorious fortified sherry, flamenco in its purest incarnation, the font of Andalucian horse culture, and a dreamy blonde-sand coastline sprinkled with kitesurf-cool towns like Tarifa and Los Caños de Meca.

The expansive Sierra de Grazalema and Los Alcornocales natural parks are situated on the same lands as the once-contested frontier between Christian Spain and Moorish Granada, and that ancient border remains dotted with castle-topped, whitewashed towns.

INCLUDES

Cádiz Province & Gibraltar Highlights

1 **Tarifa** (p148) Kitesurfing, windsurfing or beach-lazing, with Morocco looming in the background.

2 **Jerez de la Frontera** (p124) Unravelling a world of flamenco, horses, sherry, bodegas and gastronomic triumph.

3 **Cádiz** (p116) Travelling through 3000 years of history as you wander Cádiz' sea-encircled old city.

4 **Vejer de la Frontera** (p143) Getting lost in white-town magic, Andalucian-fusion cooking and exquisite boutique hotels.

5 **Parque Natural Sierra de Grazalema** (p141) Hiking the sheer-sided Garganta Verde, or kayaking and canyoning between white villages.

6 **Arcos de la Frontera** (p135) Wandering the ultimate cliff-top *pueblo blanco*.

7 **Sanlúcar de Barrameda** (p133) Tucking into superfresh fish, strolling through *manzanilla* bodegas or the Parque Nacional de Doñana.

8 **Baelo Claudia** (p148) Turning back the clock at a ruined Roman seaside town.

9 **Los Caños de Meca & El Palmar** (p146) Sinking into white-sand-beach bliss.

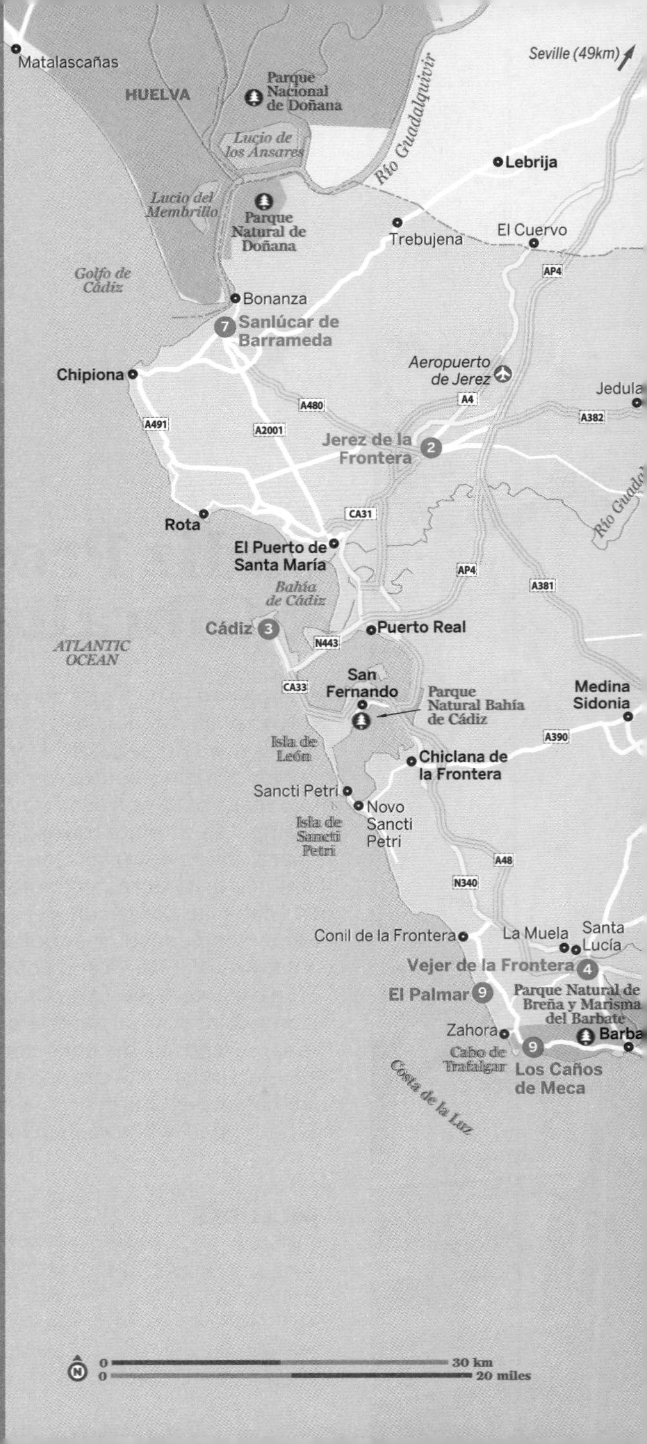

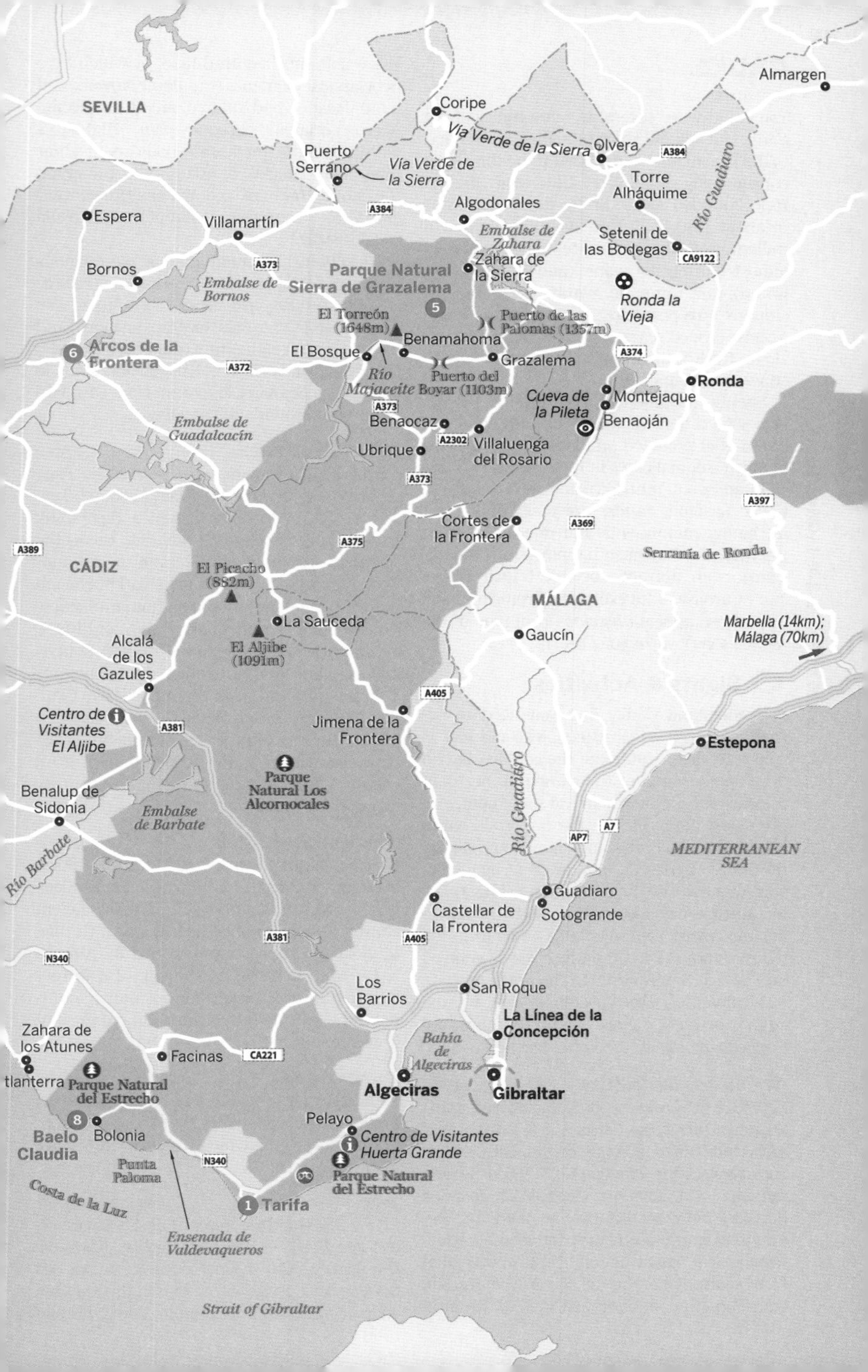
SEVILLA
Almargen
Coripe
Vía Verde de la Sierra
Olvera
A384
Puerto Serrano
Vía Verde de la Sierra
Torre Alháquime
Río Guadiaro
Algodonales
A384
Espera
Villamartín
Embalse de Zahara
Setenil de las Bodegas
CA9122
A373
Zahara de la Sierra
Bornos
Embalse de Bornos
Parque Natural Sierra de Grazalema
5
Ronda la Vieja
El Torreón (1648m)
Puerto de las Palomas (1357m)
Benamahoma
6
Arcos de la Frontera
El Bosque
Grazalema
A374
A372
Río Majaceite
Puerto del Boyar (1103m)
Ronda
Cueva de la Pileta
Montejaque
A373
Benaoján
Embalse de Guadalcacín
Benaocaz
A2302
Villaluenga del Rosario
Ubrique
A373
A397
Cortes de la Frontera
A369
A389
A375
Serranía de Ronda
CÁDIZ
El Picacho (882m)
MÁLAGA
La Sauceda
Gaucín
Marbella (14km); Málaga (70km)
Alcalá de los Gazules
El Aljibe (1091m)
A405
Centro de Visitantes El Aljibe
Jimena de la Frontera
A381
Estepona
Parque Natural Los Alcornocales
Benalup de Sidonia
Embalse de Barbate
Río Guadiaro
A7
AP7
Río Barbate
MEDITERRANEAN SEA
Guadiaro
Castellar de la Frontera
Sotogrande
A381
A405
N340
Los Barrios
San Roque
La Línea de la Concepción
Zahara de los Atunes
Bahía de Algeciras
Facinas
CA221
tlanterra
Parque Natural del Estrecho
Algeciras
Gibraltar
8
Bolonia
Baelo Claudia
Pelayo
Centro de Visitantes Huerta Grande
Punta Paloma
N340
Parque Natural del Estrecho
Costa de la Luz
1
Tarifa
Ensenada de Valdevaqueros
Strait of Gibraltar

CÁDIZ

POP 116,030

You could write several weighty tomes about Cádiz and still fall short of nailing its essence. Cádiz is generally considered to be the oldest continuously inhabited settlement in Europe, founded as Gadir by the Phoenicians in about 1100 BCE. Now well into its fourth millennium, the ancient centre, surrounded almost entirely by water (and originally an island), is a romantic, windswept jumble of sinuous streets where Atlantic waves crash against eroded sea walls, cheerful taverns sizzle up fresh fish, and salty beaches teem with sun-worshippers.

Spain's first liberal constitution (La Pepa) was signed here in 1812, while the city's urban model provided an identikit for fortified Spanish colonial cities in the Americas.

Enamoured return visitors talk fondly of Cádiz' seafood, sands, university buzz and intriguing monuments and museums. More importantly, they gush happily about the *gaditanos,* an upfront, sociable bunch whose crazy Carnaval is an exercise in ironic humour and whose upbeat *alegrías* (local type of flamenco song) warm your heart.

Sights & Activities

To understand Cádiz, first you need to befriend its *barrios* (districts). The old city is split into classic quarters: the cobbled Barrio del Pópulo, home of the cathedral, nexus of the once prosperous medieval settlement, and the oldest part of town; the Barrio de Santa María, the old Roma and flamenco quarter; the newer Barrio de la Viña, a former vineyard that became the city's main fishing quarter and Carnaval epicentre; and the Barrio del Mentidero (said to take its name from the many rumours spread on its streets), centred on Plaza de San Antonio in the northwest.

Meanwhile, often overshadowed by the city's historical riches, Cádiz' beaches are Copacabana-like in their size, feel and beauty.

★Catedral de Cádiz — CATHEDRAL

(☎956 28 61 54; www.catedraldecadiz.com; Plaza de la Catedral; incl Museo Catedralicio & Torre del Reloj adult/child €6/free; ⏲10am-9pm Mon-Sat, 1.30-9pm Sun Jul & Aug, 10am-2pm Mon-Sat, 1.30-8pm Sun Apr-Jun, Sep & Oct, 10am-7pm Mon-Sat, 1.30-7pm Sun Nov-Mar) Cádiz' beautiful yellow-domed cathedral is an impressively proportioned baroque-neoclassical construction, best appreciated from seafront Campo del Sur in the evening sun. Though commissioned in 1716, the project wasn't finished until 1838, by which time neoclassical elements (the dome, towers and main facade) had diluted architect Vicente Acero's original baroque plan. Highlights within are the intricate wood-carved choir (one of Andalucía's finest) and, in the crypt, the stone tomb of renowned 20th-century *gaditano* composer Manuel de Falla (1876–1946).

Tickets include audio guides, the religious treasures of the **Museo Catedralicio** (Plaza de Fray Félix; ⏲10am-4pm Mon-Sat Jul & Aug, to 3pm Apr-Jun, Sep & Oct, to 3pm Nov-Mar), just east, and a climb up the cathedral's (eastern) **Torre del Reloj** (Torre de Levante; ⏲10am-9pm Jul & Aug, to 8pm Apr-Jun, Sep & Oct, to 7pm Nov-Mar), with fabulous wraparound old-city views.

★Museo de Cádiz — MUSEUM

(☎856 105023; www.museosdeandalucia.es; Plaza de Mina; EU/non-EU citizen free/€1.50; ⏲9am-9pm Tue-Sat, to 3pm Sun) Set in a dusty-pink 19th-century neoclassical building, this is the province's top museum. Stars of the ground-floor archaeology section are two Phoenician marble sarcophagi carved in human likeness (uncovered a century apart in 1887 and 1980), along with lots of headless Roman statues and a giant marble 2nd-century Emperor Trajan (with head) from Bolonia's Baelo Claudia. Upstairs, the excellent fine-art collection (closed for renovation at research time) displays Spanish art from the 18th to early 20th centuries, including 18 superb 17th-century canvases by Zurbarán.

Iglesia de Santa Cruz — CHURCH

(Catedral Antigua; Plaza de Fray Félix; ⏲5.30-7.30pm Mon, 9.45am-12.45pm & 5.30-7pm Tue-Sat, 10.30am-12.30pm & 5.30-6.30pm Sun) Cádiz' most ancient church and original cathedral was a Gothic-Mudéjar creation commissioned by Alfonso X El Sabio in 1263, on the site of a former mosque. After suffering serious damage during the 1596 Dutch-British sacking of the city, it was rebuilt in the 18th century.

Campo del Sur — STREET

Flanked by pastel-painted houses, Cádiz' curving *malecón* (esplanade) is eerily reminiscent of Cuba's Havana, which it's believed to have inspired.

Teatro Romano — ARCHAEOLOGICAL SITE

(☎677 982945; Calle Mesón 11-13; EU/non-EU citizen free/€1.50; ⏲11am-5pm Mon-Sat, 10am-2pm Sun Apr-Sep, 10am-4.30pm Mon-Sat, to 2pm Sun Oct-Mar, closed 1st Mon of month) On the seaward edge of the Barrio del Pópulo, Cádiz' Roman

CÁDIZ' CARNAVAL

No other Spanish city celebrates Carnaval with as much spirit, dedication and humour as Cádiz. Here it becomes a 10-day singing, dancing and drinking fancy-dress street party spanning two alcohol-fuelled February weekends. The 300-odd officially recognised *murgas* (costumed group performers) are judged by a panel in the **Gran Teatro Falla** (☎956 22 08 34; www.facebook.com/TeatroFalla; Plaza de Falla); tickets are near-impossible to come by, but try your luck.

Costumed groups of up to 45 people, called *murgas*, tour the city on foot or on floats and tractors, dancing, drinking, singing satirical ditties or performing sketches. The biggest hits are the 12-person *chirigotas* with their scathing humour, irony and double meanings, often directed at politicians. Most of their famed verbal wit will be lost on all but fluent Spanish speakers. There are also plenty of *ilegales* – any singing group that fancies taking to the streets.

The heart of Carnaval, where you'll stumble across some of the liveliest scenes, is the working-class Barrio de la Viña, between the Mercado Central de Abastos and Playa de la Caleta, and along Calle Ancha and around Plaza de Topete, where *ilegales* tend to congregate.

theatre dates from the late 1st century BCE and, originally, had space for 10,000 spectators. A Moorish castle was later erected here, then rebuilt by Alfonso X El Sabio. You can access the excavated theatre via its modern interpretation centre, which has English- and Spanish-language displays detailing the site's history.

Plaza de Topete SQUARE
About 250m northwest of the cathedral, this triangular plaza is one of Cádiz' most intimate. Bright with flowers, it's usually talked about as Plaza de las Flores (Square of the Flowers). Beside is the revamped 1838 **Mercado Central de Abastos** (Plaza de la Libertad; 🕒9am-3pm), the oldest covered market in Spain (note the original pillars), now also a buzzing gastromarket (p121).

Oratorio de la Santa Cueva CHURCH
(☎956 22 22 62; Calle Rosario 10; adult/child €5/2, Sun free; 🕒10.30am-2pm & 5.30-8.30pm Tue-Fri Jun-Sep, 10.30am-2pm & 4.30-8pm Tue-Fri Oct-May, 10.30am-2pm Sat, 10am-1pm Sun year-round) Behind an unassuming door, the Santa Cueva conceals quite the surprise. Of its two superposed neoclassical 18th-century chapels, the bare, pillared subterranean **Capilla de la Pasión** is washed in white. Above is the richly adorned, oval-shaped **Capilla del Santísimo Sacramento**, with five religious canvases strung between its pillars – three of them important works by Goya.

Museo de las Cortes de Cádiz MUSEUM
(☎956 22 17 88; Calle Santa Inés 9; 🕒9am-6pm Tue-Fri, to 2pm Sat & Sun) FREE A fairly dry collection of portraits and maps focusing especially on the revolutionary Cádiz Parliament of 1812, which took place in the baroque **Oratorio de San Felipe Neri** (☎662 642233; Plaza de San Felipe Neri; adult/child €4/2; 🕒10.30am-2pm & 4.30-8pm Tue-Fri, 10.30am-2pm Sat, 10am-1pm Sun) next door, and the Napoleonic siege which the city was suffering at that time. The highlight is the 1770s model of 18th-century Cádiz, made in mahogany, silver and ivory by Alfonso Ximénez.

Playa de la Caleta BEACH
Hugging the western side of the Barrio de la Viña, this small, popular golden city beach catches the eye with its mock-Moorish *balneario* (bathhouse). It's flanked by two forts.

Torre Tavira TOWER
(www.torretavira.com; Calle Marqués del Real Tesoro 10; adult/child €6/free; 🕒10am-8pm May-Sep, to 6pm Oct-Apr) Northwest of Plaza de Topete, the 18th-century Torre Tavira is the highest point in town, opening up dramatic panoramas of Cádiz. It has a camera obscura that projects live, moving images of the city onto a screen. It's one of Cádiz' 160 watchtowers from the 18th century, 129 of which are still standing.

Puerta de Tierra GATE
(Plaza de la Constitución; 🕒9.30am-1.30pm & 3.30-6.30pm Tue-Fri, 10am-1pm Sat) FREE The imposing 18th-century 'Land Gate' guards the southeastern (and only land) entry to Cádiz' old town. You can wander the upper fortifications and defence tower, where Spanish- and English-language panels detail visible sights and the evolution of Cádiz' complex fortification system.

Cádiz

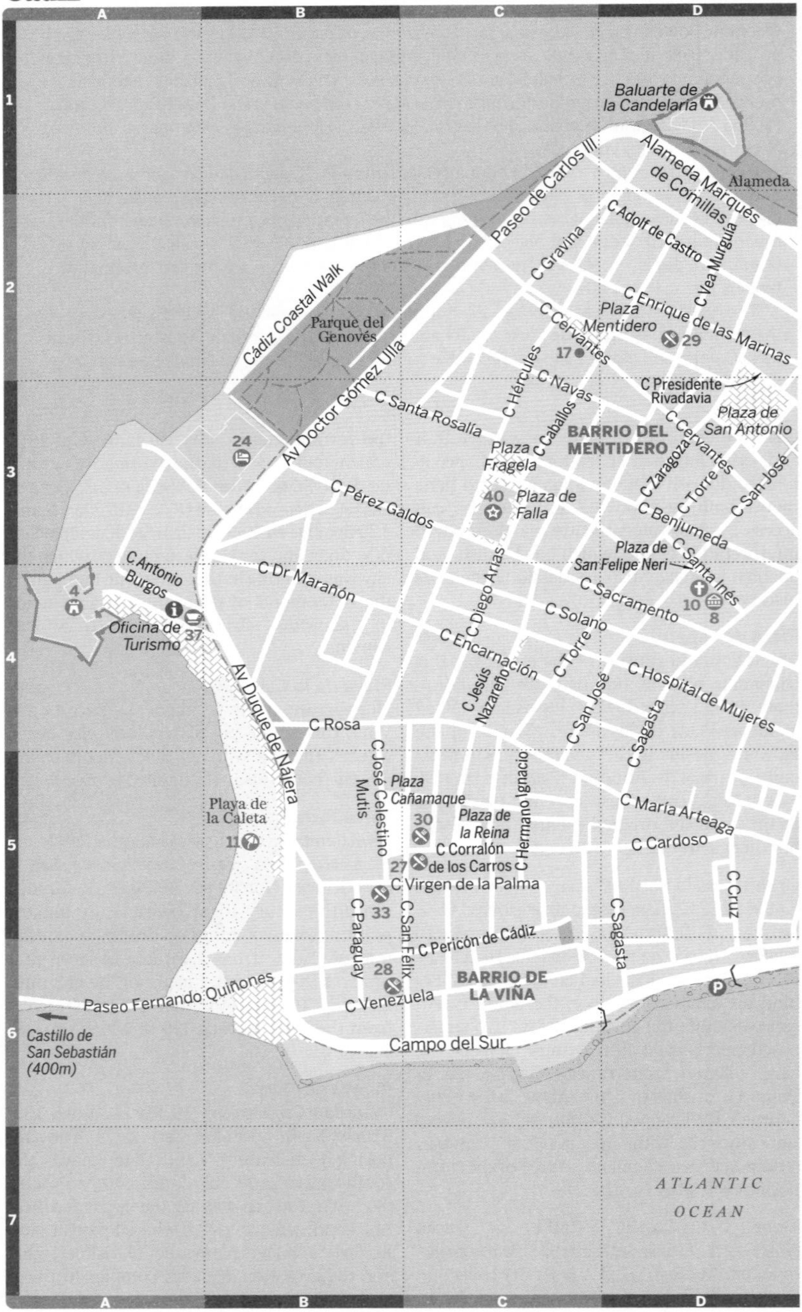
Baluarte de la Candelaria
Alameda
Alameda Marqués de Comillas
Paseo de Carlos III
C Adolf de Castro
C Gravina
C Vea Murguía
Cádiz Coastal Walk
Parque del Genovés
C Enrique de las Marinas
Plaza Mentidero
29
C Cervantes
17
Av Doctor Gómez Ulla
C Hércules
C Navas
C Presidente Rivadavia
C Santa Rosalía
C Caballos
BARRIO DEL MENTIDERO
Plaza de San Antonio
24
Plaza Fragela
C Zaragoza
C Torre
C San José
40
Plaza de Falla
C Pérez Galdos
C Benjumeda
Plaza de San Felipe Neri
C Santa Inés
C Antonio Burgos
C Dr Marañón
C Diego Arias
C Sacramento
4
Oficina de Turismo
37
10
8
C Solano
C Encarnación
C Torre
C Hospital de Mujeres
Av Duque de Nájera
C Jesús Nazareño
C San José
C Sagasta
C Rosa
C José Celestino Mutis
C Hermano Ignacio
Plaza Cañamaque
Playa de la Caleta
30
Plaza de la Reina
C María Arteaga
11
C Corralón de los Carros
27
C Cardoso
C Virgen de la Palma
33
C Paraguay
C San Félix
C Sagasta
C Cruz
C Pericón de Cádiz
28
BARRIO DE LA VIÑA
Paseo Fernando Quiñones
C Venezuela
Castillo de San Sebastián (400m)
Campo del Sur
ATLANTIC OCEAN

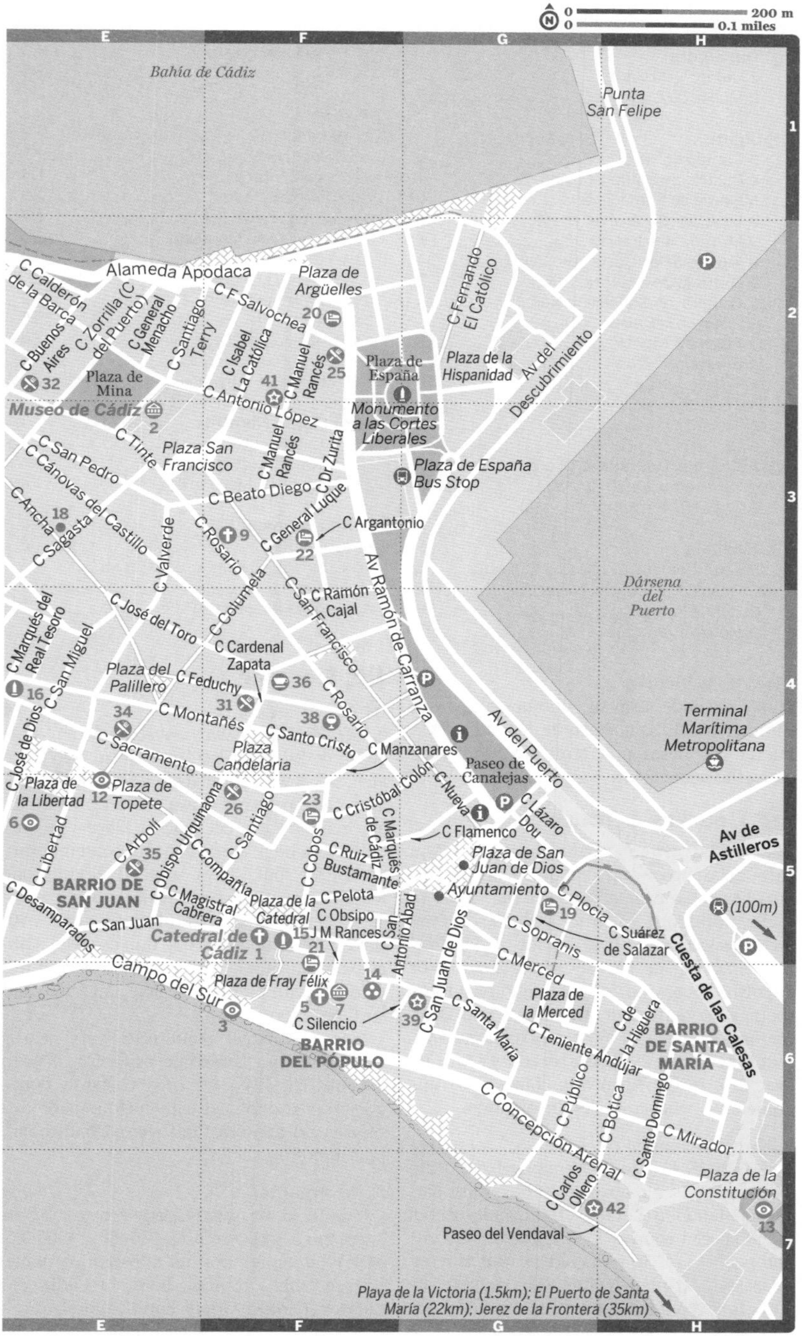
0 200 m
0 0.1 miles
Bahía de Cádiz
Punta San Felipe
Alameda Apodaca
Plaza de Argüelles
C Calderón de la Barca
C Buenos Aires
C Zorrilla (C del Puerto)
C General Menacho
C Santiago Terry
C Isabel La Católica
C F Salvochea
C Manuel Rancés
C Fernando El Católico
Plaza de España
Plaza de la Hispanidad
Av del Descubrimiento
Plaza de Mina
Museo de Cádiz
C Antonio López
Monumento a las Cortes Liberales
C Tinte
Plaza San Francisco
C San Pedro
C Cánovas del Castillo
C Beato Diego
C Dr Zurita
Plaza de España Bus Stop
C Ancha
C Sagasta
C Valverde
C Rosario
C General Luque
C Argantonio
C Columela
C San Francisco
C Ramón Cajal
Av Ramón de Carranza
Dársena del Puerto
C Marqués del Real Tesoro
C San Miguel
C José del Toro
C Cardenal Zapata
Plaza del Palillero
C Feduchy
C Montañés
C José de Dios
C Sacramento
Plaza Candelaria
C Santo Cristo
C Manzanares
Av del Puerto
Paseo de Canalejas
Terminal Marítima Metropolitana
Plaza de la Libertad
Plaza de Topete
C Cristóbal Colón
C Nueva
C Lázaro Dou
C Libertad
C Arbolí
C Obispo Urquinaona
C Santiago
C Cobos
C Marqués de Cádiz
C Flamenco
Plaza de San Juan de Dios
Av de Astilleros
C Compañía
C Ruiz Bustamante
BARRIO DE SAN JUAN
C Obispo
C Magistral Cabrera
Plaza de la Catedral
C Pelota
Ayuntamiento
C Plocia
(100m)
C Desamparados
C San Juan
C Obispo
Catedral de Cádiz
J M Rances
C San Antonio Abad
C San Juan de Dios
C Sopranis
C Suárez de Salazar
Cuesta de las Calesas
Campo del Sur
Plaza de Fray Félix
C Merced
C Silencio
C Santa María
Plaza de la Merced
C de la Higuera
BARRIO DE SANTA MARÍA
BARRIO DEL PÓPULO
C Teniente Andújar
C Público
C Botica
C Santo Domingo
C Concepción Arenal
C Mirador
C Carlos Ollero
Plaza de la Constitución
Paseo del Vendaval
Playa de la Victoria (1.5km); El Puerto de Santa María (22km); Jerez de la Frontera (35km)
1
2
3
5
6
7
9
12
13
14
15
16
18
19
20
21
22
23
25
26
31
32
34
35
36
38
39
41
42
E
F
G
H
1
2
3
4
5
6
7

Cádiz

Top Sights

1	Catedral de Cádiz	F5
2	Museo de Cádiz	E3

Sights

3	Campo del Sur	F6
4	Castillo de Santa Catalina	A4
5	Iglesia de Santa Cruz	F6
6	Mercado Central de Abastos	E5
7	Museo Catedralicio	F6
8	Museo de las Cortes de Cádiz	D4
9	Oratorio de la Santa Cueva	F3
10	Oratorio de San Felipe Neri	D4
11	Playa de la Caleta	B5
12	Plaza de Topete	E5
13	Puerta de Tierra	H7
14	Teatro Romano	F6
15	Torre del Reloj	F5
16	Torre Tavira	E4

Activities, Courses & Tours

17	K2 Internacional	C2
18	Las Bicis Naranjas	E3

Sleeping

19	Casa Caracol	G5
20	Casa de las Cuatro Torres	F2
21	Casa Piratas	F6
22	Hotel Argantonio	F3
23	Hotel Patagonia Sur	F5
24	Parador de Cádiz	B3

Eating

25	Almanaque	F2
26	Café Royalty	F5
27	Casa Manteca	C5
28	El Faro de Cádiz	B6
29	El Veedor	D2
30	Freidor Casa Manteca	C5
31	La Candela	F4
	La Cepa Gallega	(see 19)
32	La Marmita Centro	E2
33	La Tabernita	B5
34	La Tapería de Columela	E4
	Rincón Gastronómico	(see 6)
35	Taberna La Sorpresa	E5

Drinking & Nightlife

36	La Clandestina	F4
37	Quilla	A4
38	Taberna La Manzanilla	F4

Entertainment

39	El Pay Pay	G6
40	Gran Teatro Falla	C3
41	La Cava	F2
42	Peña Flamenca La Perla	G7

Playa de la Victoria BEACH

This fine, wide strip of Atlantic sand, with summer beach bars, starts 1km south of the Puerta de Tierra and stretches 4km back along the peninsula.

Courses & Tours

The **tourist office** (www.turismo.cadiz.es; Playa de la Caleta; noon-7pm Jun & Sep, 11am-9pm Jul & Aug) has a list of operators offering tours of Cádiz. **Cadizfornia Tours** (692 205412; www.cadizforniatours.com) has terrific twice-daily pay-what-you-like old-city tours (English or Spanish), plus wine-and-tapas and bike tours (both €25) and other itineraries. **Las Bicis Naranjas** (956 90 76 71; www.lasbicisnaranjas.com; Calle Sagasta 9; bike hire per hr/day €4/15, 3hr tours €29; 10am-9pm) hires bikes and runs guided two-wheel tours of the old town.

K2 Internacional LANGUAGE

(956 21 26 46; www.k2internacional.com; Plaza Mentidero 19) In a renovated 19th-century Barrio del Mentidero building, this old-city school offers special courses for long-term students and people over 50 years old, as well as regular classes. An intensive one-week course costs €175. It also organises tours, accommodation, and flamenco, cooking and surf courses.

Sleeping

★ **Casa Caracol** HOSTEL €

(956 26 11 66; www.casacaracolcadiz.com; Calle Suárez de Salazar 4; incl breakfast dm from €17, d from €48, d without bathroom €37;) Mellow, solar-powered Casa Caracol is Cádiz' original old-town backpacker. Cheery as only Cádiz can be, it has colourful, contemporary dorms for four, six or seven (including one female-only), with handmade bunks and individual lights, plugs and lockers, along with three private doubles (one duplex-style). Other perks include a social kitchen, a roof terrace/bar with hammocks, yoga, and bike and surfboard rental.

The on-the-ball team also runs nearby **Casa Piratas** (Callejón de los Piratas; d/studio from €44/55;), with five elegantly boutiquey rooms designed with custom-made furniture and artwork (and shared bathroom), plus a rooftop studio.

Hotel Argantonio HOTEL €€

(956 21 16 40; www.hotelargantonio.com; Calle Argantonio 3; incl breakfast s €80-150, d €100-180;) Rambling across an 18th-century home, this stylishly charming hotel in Cádiz' old quarter sparkles with its hand-painted, wood-carved doors, colourfully tiled floors adorning

bedrooms, bathrooms and corridors, and intricate Moorish-style arch and fountain in the lobby. The 1st floor is Mudéjar-inspired, the 2nd 'colonial romantic', the 3rd a mix. There's a tucked-away roof-terrace lounge, plus a cafe and good breakfasts.

Hotel Patagonia Sur HOTEL €€
(856 17 46 47; www.hotelpatagoniasur.es; Calle Cobos 11; s €86-135, d €95-135;) A glossy Argentine-run find offering clean-lined modernity and efficient yet friendly management just steps from the cathedral. The 16 rooms, all with tea-and-coffee sets, are smart, bright, fresh and snug. Bonuses include a glass-fronted cafe and sun-filled 5th-floor attic rooms with cathedral views and sun loungers on private terraces.

Casa de las Cuatro Torres BOUTIQUE HOTEL €€€
(956 90 31 33; www.casadelascuatrotorres.com; Plaza de Argüelles 3; d €135-185, apt €195-265;) Inhabiting part of a listed early-18th-century neoclassical *palacete* (mansion), in the northeastern old city, the Cuatro Torres is a design delight of original sky-reaching ceilings, wooden doors, beams, vaults, skylights and exposed-stone walls, all skilfully reimagined with boutique flair. From the pillared marble patio with a library lounge, you can head up to the rooftop terrace, bar and tower.

Parador de Cádiz LUXURY HOTEL €€€
(956 22 69 05; www.parador.es; Avenida Duque de Nájera 9; incl breakfast d €156-310, ste €254-330;) Bold, beautiful and right beside Playa de la Caleta, the so-called Parador Atlántico contrasts with Andalucía's other *paradores* (luxurious state-owned hotels) in that it's ubermodern and built from scratch. Sultry reds, ocean blues and bright turquoises throw character into the sleek rooms with balcony and floor-to-ceiling windows. Soak in four sea-view swimming pools, or seek out the spa.

Eating

Calle Virgen de la Palma, in the Barrio de la Viña, is the city's go-to fresh-seafood street. Calles Plocia and Sopranis, off Plaza de San Juan de Dios, are upmarket eat streets, and there are good options off Plaza de Mina in the Barrio del Mentidero.

★**Casa Manteca** TAPAS €
(956 21 36 06; www.facebook.com/tabernamanteca; Calle Corralón de los Carros 66; tapas €2.50, medias raciones €4-10; noon-4pm & 8.30pm-12.30am, may close Sun & Mon evenings Nov-Mar) The hub of the Barrio de la Viña fun, with every inch of its walls covered in flamenco, bullfighting and Carnaval paraphernalia, always-busy Casa Manteca is full of old tapas favourites. Ask the chatty waiters for mussels, *chicharrones* (pressed pork with a squeeze of lemon) or *payoyo* cheese with asparagus marmalade, and it'll fly across the bar on waxed paper.

Now there's a terrific Manteca *freidor* (fried fish specialist) **opposite** (956 21 36 03; www.facebook.com/freidorcasamanteca; Calle Corralón 59; raciones €7-10; 12.30-4pm & 8.30-11pm).

La Tapería de Columela TAPAS €
(956 07 42 97; www.facebook.com/lataperiadecolumela; Calle Columela 4; tapas €3-8; 1-4pm & 8-11pm Mon-Sat;) There's always a queue trailing out the door at wonderful Columela, where diners both local and international feast on delicately prepped tradition-meets-innovation tapas of local tuna, perhaps as tartare with mustard dressing. Squeeze in at the marble-top bar for respected local chef Agustín Campos' creations, which also include deep-fried aubergine drizzled with cane honey and slithers of *payoyo* cheese.

Taberna La Sorpresa TAPAS €
(956 22 12 32; www.tabernalasorpresa.com; Calle Arbolí 4; tapas €2.50-5.50; 11.30am-4.30pm & 8.30-11.30pm Tue-Sat, 11.30am-4.30pm Sun) Barrels of Pedro Ximénez, *manzanilla* (chamomile-coloured sherry) and *oloroso* (sweet, dark sherry) stack up behind the bar at this down-to-earth 1956 tavern, thoughtfully revamped and keeping Cádiz' old-school scene alive. Tapas focus on *almadraba* tuna, but there are plenty of other tasty bites, such as mussels, *chicharrones* and Iberian *bellota* ham, along with Cádiz-province wines and vermouth on tap.

Rincón Gastronómico TAPAS €
(Mercado Central de Abastos, Plaza de la Libertad; tapas €2-8; 9am-4pm Mon, 9am-3.30pm & 7pm-midnight Tue-Fri, 9am-4pm & 8pm-1am Sat;) Cádiz' neoclassical 1838 Mercado Central de Abastos is the setting for this ultra-buzzy globe-roaming gastromarket. Sample gloriously simple local specialities like *patatas aliñadas*, *payoyo* cheese and *ibérico* ham; pick your fresh fish and have it grilled before your eyes; venture into a plant-based world of vegan tortilla (convincingly delicious!); or hit the sherry stands.

La Cepa Gallega TAPAS €
(956 28 60 29; Calle Plocia 9; tapas €2-5; 10.30am-4pm & 8pm-late Mon-Sat, 10.30am-4pm Sun) Founded in 1920, this venerable

old *ultramarinos* (grocer) under keen new ownership does delectable wax-paper tapas of Cádiz cheeses, buttered anchovies, *ibérico* ham and tinned seafood to pair with its wide-roaming collection of Spanish wines and sherries. It's rustic-style, with wine-barrel tables and bottles lining the walls.

La Tabernita TAPAS €
(www.facebook.com/RafaTabernita; Calle Virgen de la Palma 32; tapas €2.50; 8.30-11.30pm Thu & Fri, 1.30-4pm & 8.30-11.30pm Sat & Sun;) Despite its limited opening times, La Tabernita gets immediately rammed for its superb homemade, family-style tapas. *Cazón al coñac* (dogfish in brandy), cuttlefish-in-ink 'meatballs' and *tortillitas de camarones* (shrimp fritters) are favourites to sample on the Barrio de la Viña's liveliest street.

El Veedor TAPAS €
(956 21 26 94; Calle Vea Murguía 10; tapas €2.50, medias raciones €6-10; 8.30am-4pm & 7.30pm-midnight) A long marble-top bar and tempting deli counter set the rustic tone at this classic-Cádiz *ultramarinos*. Try chunky home-cooked tortillas, *jamón de bellota, payoyo* cheese, local-style *chicharrones*, and sherry from the barrel.

Almanaque ANDALUCIAN €€
(956 80 86 63; Plaza de España 5; raciones €12-18; 1-4pm Mon & Sun, 1-4pm & 8.30-11pm Wed-Sat) A rustic-chic modern-day *casa de comidas* with open stone, tiled floors and bright-white walls creates an intriguing setting for sampling traditional, often-forgotten *gaditano* family recipes unlikely to be found elsewhere. Cram in alongside lunching locals for short, smartly prepared seasonal menus that might star *carabinero* prawns with fried eggs, *tagarninas* (thistles) with tuna belly, or pork, chickpea and turnip rice.

La Candela TAPAS €€
(956 22 18 22; www.facebook.com/LaCandelaTapasBar; Calle Feduchy 3; tapas €4-8, mains €8-12; 1.30-4pm & 8.30-11.30pm;) Like an arty cafe meets colourful tapas bar, La Candela surprises with its floral-stamped windows, rustic-industrial decor and brilliantly original Andalucian-Asian tapas and mains. From the busy little open kitchen at the back come bold creations with local inspiration – strawberry *salmorejo* (Córdoba-style thick gazpacho) with tuna tartare and fried *boquerones* (anchovies) topped with wasabi mayonnaise.

La Marmita Centro TAPAS €€
(956 21 52 27; www.grupolamarmita.com; Calle Buenos Aires 5-7; tapas €2-7; 1-4pm & 8pm-midnight;) Courtesy of Cádiz' popular La Marmita Group, this sleekly minimalist old-city spot thrills diners with its imaginative, intelligently presented Andalucian-international tapas. Border-crossing dishes focus on seasonal local produce, such as *salmorejo* with *payoyo* cheese or pad thai with garlicky prawns.

★El Faro de Cádiz TAPAS €€€
(956 21 10 68; www.elfarodecadiz.com; Calle San Félix 15; tapas €2.50-4; 1-4pm & 8.30-11.30pm) Ask any *gaditano* for their favourite Cádiz tapas bar and there's a good chance they'll choose El Faro. Seafood, particularly the *tortillitas de camarones* and superb *boquerones,* is why people come here, though the *rabo de toro* (oxtail) and vegetarian-friendly *patatas aliñadas* have their devotees. El Faro's upmarket restaurant (mains €17 to €24) gets mixed reviews.

Café Royalty CAFE €€€
(956 07 80 65; www.caferoyalty.com; Plaza Candelaria; tapas €4.50-10, mains €23-30; cafe 9.30am-11pm, restaurant 12.30-4pm & 8pm-midnight;) Originally opened in 1912 on the centenary of the 1812 constitution, the restored Royalty was once a discussion corner for the intellectuals of the day, including beloved *gaditano* composer Manuel de Falla. The frescoed, mirrored, intricately carved interior is – no exaggeration – breathtaking. It's fantastic for breakfast, tapas, cocktails, cakes and elegant updated-Andalucian meals: *almadraba* red-tuna sashimi, Sanlúcar king prawns, a two-person *chuletón.*

Drinking & Nightlife

The Plaza de Mina–Plaza San Francisco–Plaza de España triangle is the centre of the old city's late-night bar scene, especially Calle Beato Diego. More bars are scattered around the Barrio del Pópulo, east of the cathedral. Punta San Felipe (La Punta), on the northern side of the harbour, has a string of late-night drinks/dance bars. Cádiz' other nocturnal haunt, especially in summer, is down along Playa de la Victoria and the Paseo Marítimo, on and around Calle Muñoz Arenillas.

Quilla CAFE
(www.quilla.es; Playa de la Caleta; 11am-midnight Sun-Thu, to 2am Fri & Sat;) A bookish cafe-bar encased in what appears to be the rusty hulk

of an old ship overlooking Playa de la Caleta, with coffee, pastries, tapas, wine, art exhibitions, gratis sunsets and lightly modernised Andalucian dishes (burgers, salads, *tostas*, grilled fish; €8 to €13).

La Clandestina CAFE
(www.la-clandestina.com; Calle José del Toro 23; 9.30am-2pm & 5.30-9pm Mon-Fri, 10am-2pm Sat;) A cosy, boho bookshop-cafe and cultural space where you can flick through the day's papers over coffee, homemade cakes, fresh orange juice, and breakfast *tostadas* (€2 to €3) with artisan jams and olive oils served on pretty ceramic plates.

Taberna La Manzanilla WINE BAR
(www.lamanzanilladecadiz.com; Calle Feduchy 19; 11am-3.30pm & 7-10.30pm Mon-Fri, 11am-3.30pm Sat & Sun;) Family-run since the 1930s, La Manzanilla is a gloriously time-warped sherry tavern decked with bullfighting posters, on a spot once occupied by a pharmacy. The speciality, of course, is *manzanilla* from the giant oak barrel. Keep an eye out for tastings and other events.

☆ Entertainment

★ Peña Flamenca La Perla FLAMENCO
(956 25 91 01; www.laperladecadiz.es; Calle Carlos Ollero; €7) Paint-peeled, sea-splashed La Perla, set romantically next to the crashing Atlantic surf in the Barrio de Santa María, hosts flamenco at 9.30pm most Fridays, more often in spring and summer, for an audience full of aficionados. An unforgettable experience.

La Cava FLAMENCO
(956 21 18 66; www.flamencolacava.com; Calle Antonio López 16; €22) Cádiz' main *tablao* (choreographed flamenco show) happens in a rustically bedecked tavern on Tuesday, Thursday and Saturday at 9.30pm (schedules are reduced November to February).

El Pay Pay LIVE PERFORMANCE
(www.cafeteatropaypay.com; Calle Silencio 1; 8pm-3am Wed-Sat;) In the Barrio del Pópulo, this well-known, boundary-pushing 'cafe-theatre' runs a hugely varied arts program including drama, magic, storytelling, drag shows, stand-up comedy, and live jazz, blues and flamenco.

Information

Centro de Recepción de Turistas (956 24 10 01; www.turismo.cadiz.es; Paseo de Canalejas; 9am-7pm Mon-Fri, to 5pm Sat & Sun Jun-Sep, 8.30am-6.30pm Mon-Fri, 9am-5pm Sat & Sun Oct-May)
Oficina de Turismo Regional (956 20 31 91; www.andalucia.org; Avenida Ramón de Carranza; 9am-7.15pm Mon-Fri, 10am-2.45pm Sat & Sun)

Getting There & Around

BOAT

From Cádiz' **Terminal Marítima Metropolitana** (Muelle Reina Victoria), **Consorcio de Transportes Bahía de Cádiz** (CMTBC; 955 03 86 65; www.cmtbc.es) catamarans run to/from El Puerto de Santa María (€2.80, 30 minutes) at least 16 times daily Monday to Friday, and at least eight times daily at weekends.

BUS

All out-of-town buses leave from Cádiz' **bus station** (Avenida de Astilleros), on the eastern side of the train station (at the southeastern end of the old city). Most buses are operated by **Comes** (956 80 70 59; www.tgcomes.es), **Damas** (959 25 69 00; www.damas-sa.es), **Alsa** (952 52 15 04; www.alsa.es) or the CMTBC (p123), which runs to/from Jerez airport (p129).

BUSES FROM CÁDIZ

DESTINATION	COST (€)	DURATION	FREQUENCY
Arcos de la Frontera	6-7.50	1-1½hr	3-8 daily
El Puerto de Santa María	2.80	45min	every 30-60min
Jerez de la Frontera	3.90	50min	2-7 daily
La Barca de Vejer	6	1-1½hr	5-6 daily
Málaga	29	4½hr	4 daily
Ronda	16	3¼hr	1-2 daily
Sanlúcar de Barrameda	5.10	1hr	5-13 daily
Seville	13	1¾hr	9-10 daily
Tarifa	10	1¼-1¾hr	6 daily

Cádiz has a decent urban bus system, fanning out from Plaza de España. Useful routes include buses 1 and 7 for Playa de la Victoria; bus 7 also goes to Playa de la Caleta. Tickets cost €1.10.

CAR & MOTORCYCLE

There's lots of pricey underground parking, including on Paseo de Canalejas near the port (€25 per 24 hours). There's a cheap supervised car park on Avenida del Descubrimiento, on the northwestern side of the port (€8 per 24 hours).

TRAIN

From the train station, next to the bus station on the southeastern edge of the old town, frequent trains go to El Puerto de Santa María (€3.40 to €5.25, 35 minutes) and Jerez de la Frontera (€3.90 to €6.25, 45 minutes), as well as Seville (€17 to €24, 1¾ hours, 11 to 15 daily). Three daily high-speed Alvia trains go to Madrid (€47 to €65, 4¼ hours).

THE SHERRY TRIANGLE

North of Cádiz, Jerez de la Frontera, Sanlúcar de Barrameda and El Puerto de Santa María mark the three corners of Spain's famous 'sherry triangle'. Even if Andalucía's unique, smooth wine isn't your cup of tea (even with its recent renaissance?), you won't want to miss the history, the beaches, the handsome horses, the fabulous food, the feisty flamenco and the evocative environmental marvel that is the Parque Nacional de Doñana (p133).

Jerez de la Frontera

POP 191,790

Stand down, all other claimants. Jerez, as most savvy Hispanophiles know, *is* Andalucía. It just doesn't broadcast it in the way that Seville and Granada do. Jerez is the capital of Andalucian horse culture, stop one on the famed Sherry Triangle and – cue protestations from Cádiz, Seville and Granada – the cradle of Spanish flamenco. The *bulería,* Jerez' jokey, tongue-in-cheek antidote to Seville's tragic *soleá,* was first concocted in the legendary Roma *barrios* of Santiago and San Miguel. But Jerez is also a vibrant modern Andalucian city, where fashion brands live in old palaces and stylishly outfitted businesspeople sit down to distinctly contemporary, perhaps Michelin-star cuisine before moving on to bubbly *tabancos* (simple taverns serving sherry).

If you really want to unravel the eternal riddle that is Andalucía, start with Jerez.

Sights & Activities

Jerez (the word even means 'sherry') has around 20 sherry bodegas. Most require bookings for visits, but a few offer tours where you can just turn up. The tourist office (p129) has details.

★Bodegas Tradición WINERY
(☎956 16 86 18; www.bodegastradicion.com; Plaza Cordobeses 3; tours €35) An intriguing, evocative

THE SHERRY SECRET

Once sherry grapes have been harvested, they're pressed, and the resulting must is left to ferment in wooden barrels or, more commonly these days, in stainless-steel tanks. A frothy veil of *flor* (yeast) appears on the surface at the end of the fermentation, after which wines are fortified with a grape spirit, to 15% for finer wines and 17% or 18% for coarser.

Next, wine enters the *solera* (from *suelo,* 'floor') ageing process. The most delicate wines from palomino grapes are biologically aged under *flor* (becoming *finos* and *manzanillas*), while coarser palomino wines are matured by oxidation (becoming *olorosos*); an *amontillado* or *palo cortado* is produced by a combination of biological and oxidative ageing. Wine from the sweeter grapes, Pedro Ximénez and muscatel, is matured through oxidation.

In the *solera* system, American-oak barrels, five-sixths full, are lined up in rows at least three barrels high. Those on the bottom contain the oldest wine. From these, about three times a year (more for *manzanilla*), 10% to 15% of the wine is drawn out. This is replaced with the same amount from the barrels directly above, which is then replaced from the next layer – so you'll never know quite how old your sherry is. The wines age for at least three years and may be refortified before bottling.

In recent years, sherry has been making quite a comeback, with world-renowned Spanish chefs such as Ferran Adrià using it in their gastronomy, the arrival of fresh investment and international sherry bars and cocktails, and Cádiz' sherry producers innovating traditional methods.

bodega, not only for its extra-aged sherries (at least 20, mostly 30 years old) but also because it houses the **Colección Joaquín Rivero**, a private 14th- to 19th-century Spanish art collection that includes important works by Goya, Velázquez, El Greco and Zurbarán. Tours (1½ hours; in English, Spanish or German) require bookings and include a tasting session, and are well worth splashing out on.

Alcázar FORTRESS

(☎956 14 99 55; Alameda Vieja; Alcázar €5, incl camera obscura €7; ⏲9.30am-5.30pm Mon-Fri, 9.30am-2.30pm Sat & Sun Jul–mid-Sep, 9.30am-2.30pm daily mid-Sep–Jun) Jerez' muscular yet elegant 11th- or 12th-century fortress is one of Andalucía's best-preserved Almohad-era relics. It's notable for its octagonal tower, typical of Almohad defensive forts, reached through Islamic-style **gardens**, past a 12th-century **mosque-turned-chapel**, the sprawling **Patio de Armas** and the 17th- and 18th-century baroque **Palacio Villavicencio**, which unveils city views through its camera obscura.

Catedral de San Salvador CATHEDRAL

(☎956 16 90 59; www.catedraldejerez.es; Plaza de la Encarnación; incl Iglesia de San Miguel adult/child €6/free; ⏲10am-8pm Tue-Sat, to 6.30pm Mon, 1-7pm Sun Apr-Sep, 10am-6.30pm Mon-Sat, 1-6.30pm Sun Oct-Mar) Echoes of Seville colour Jerez' dramatic cathedral, a surprisingly harmonious mix of baroque, neoclassical and Gothic styles. Standout features are its broad flying buttresses and intricately carved stone ceilings. Behind the main altar, a series of rooms and chapels shows off the cathedral's collection of silverware, religious garments and art, including Zurbarán's *Virgen niña meditando* (Virgin Mary as a Child, Asleep). Across the square, the bell tower is 15th-century Gothic-Mudéjar on its lower half and 17th century at the top.

Bodegas González-Byass WINERY

(Bodegas Tío Pepe; ☎956 35 70 16; www.bodegastiopepe.com; Calle Manuel María González 12; tours from €16) Home to the famous Tío Pepe brand, 1835-founded González-Byass is one of Jerez' biggest sherry houses, just west of the Alcázar. There are several daily tours in Spanish, English and German; check schedules and book online (not essential). Basic visits include the Gustav Eiffel–designed La Concha bodega, and a sampling of two wines in the glossy designer tasting room; others add tapas and extra sherries. A luxe, on-site González-Byass hotel was in the works at research time.

Bodegas Lustau WINERY

(☎956 34 15 97; www.lustau.es; Calle Arcos 53; ⏲tours 11.30am & 1.30pm Mon & Sat, 10am, 11.30am, 1pm & 3pm Tue-Fri) Book ahead for the excellent-value tours (in Spanish or English) of the handsome, vine-shaded Lustau bodega, founded in 1896. 'Standard' visits (€18) include five wines and a vermouth, while 'complete tastings' (€28) take in seven wines and two vermouths.

Centro Andaluz de Flamenco ARTS CENTRE

(☎956 90 21 34; www.centroandaluzdeflamenco.es; Plaza de San Juan 1; ⏲9am-2pm Mon-Fri) FREE Both architecturally intriguing – note the entrance's original 15th-century Mudéjar *artesonado* (ceiling of interlaced beams with decorative inserts) and the intricate baroque courtyard – and a fantastic flamenco resource, this unique centre holds thousands of print and musical works. Flamenco videos are screened between 9.30am and 1.30pm, and staff provide lists of the city's many flamenco-hosting *tabancos* and *peñas* (small private clubs), plus information on upcoming performances and classes in flamenco dance and song.

Museo Arqueológico MUSEUM

(☎956 14 95 60; Plaza del Mercado; adult/child €5/free; ⏲9am-2.30pm Tue-Sun mid-Jun–mid-Sep, 10am-2pm & 4-7pm Mon-Fri, 9am-2.30pm Sat & Sun mid-Sep–mid-Jun) In the Santiago quarter, Jerez' modern archaeology museum houses fascinating local relics dating from Paleolithic to 20th-century times. Grab an audio guide and look for the 7th-century-BCE Greek bronze helmet found in the Río Guadalete, two cylindrical marble Copper Age idols from the 2nd or 3rd century BCE, and a fragment of a 15th-century Gothic-Mudéjar mural.

Iglesia de San Miguel CHURCH

(☎956 34 33 47; www.catedraldejerez.es; Plaza de San Miguel; incl Catedral de San Salvador adult/child €6/free; ⏲10am-7pm Mon-Sat Apr-Sep, to 6pm Oct-Mar) Built between the 15th and 18th centuries, this richly adorned church blends Gothic, Renaissance and baroque architecture, and was modelled on Seville cathedral (and possibly shared an architect). Its three-tiered, elaborately carved baroque bell tower is topped by a tile-patterned roof, while part of the main hall is graced by intricately sculpted, Portuguese-influenced late-Gothic pillars.

Hammam Andalusí HAMMAM

(☎956 34 90 66; www.hammamandalusi.com; Calle Salvador 6; baths €29, incl 15/30min massage

Jerez de la Frontera

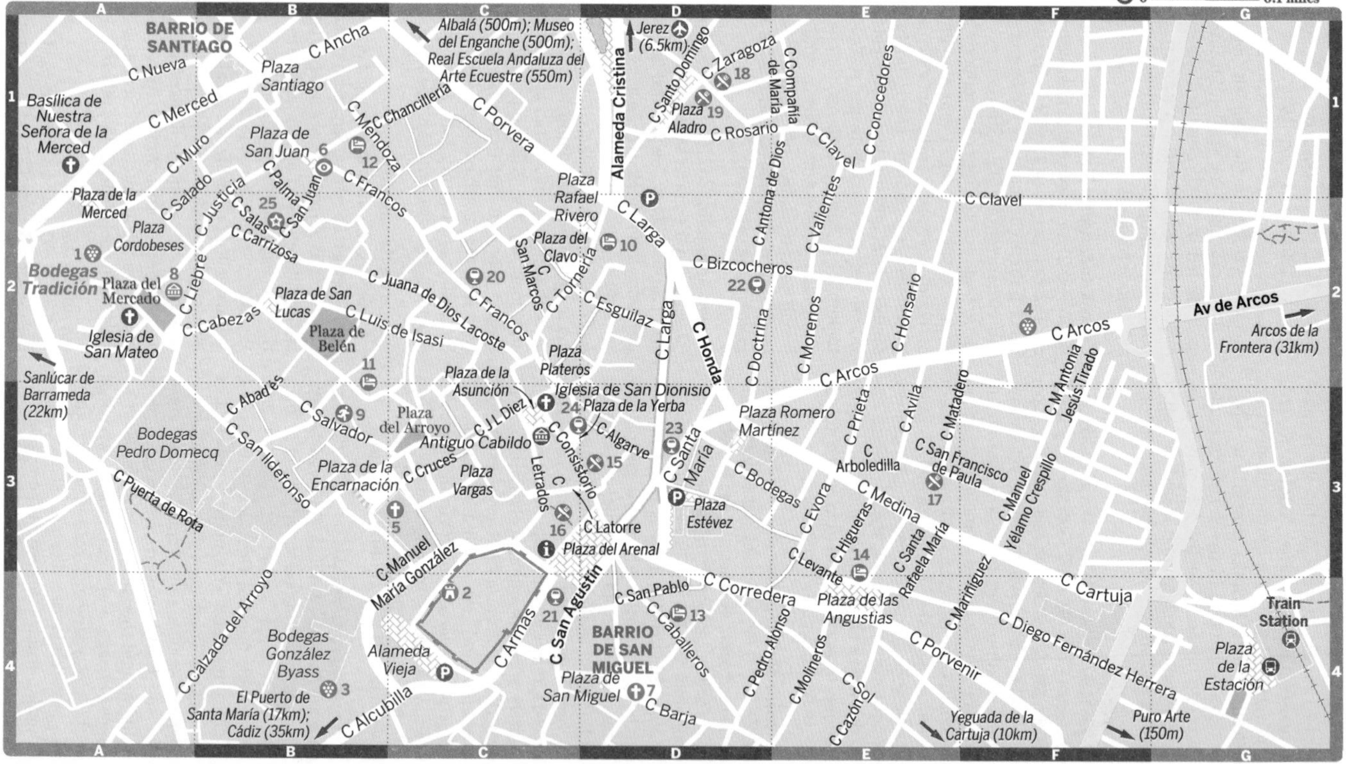

Jerez de la Frontera

Top Sights

1 Bodegas Tradición A2

Sights

2 Alcázar C4
3 Bodegas González-Byass B4
4 Bodegas Lustau F2
5 Catedral de San Salvador C3
6 Centro Andaluz de Flamenco B1
7 Iglesia de San Miguel D4
8 Museo Arqueológico A2

Activities, Courses & Tours

9 Hammam Andalusí B3

Sleeping

10 Casa Palacio María Luisa D2
11 La Fonda Barranco B2
12 Life Astuto Boutique B1
13 Nuevo Hotel D4
14 YIT Casa Grande E3

Eating

15 Albores D3
16 Bar Juanito C3
17 La Carboná E3
18 LÚ, Cocina y Alma D1
19 Mantúa D1
Mulai .... (see 16)

Drinking & Nightlife

20 Damajuana C2
21 Tabanco A la Feria C4
22 Tabanco El Guitarrón de San Pedro D2
23 Tabanco El Pasaje D3
24 Tabanco Plateros C3

Entertainment

25 Centro Cultural Flamenco Don Antonio Chacón B2

€39/60; ⏲10am-10pm) The magical Hammam Andalusí evokes Jerez' Moorish past. Incense, essential oils, fresh mint tea and the soothing sound of trickling water welcome you through the door, then you enjoy three turquoise pools (tepid, hot and cold) and, if you like, a massage. Book ahead.

Festivals & Events

Feria del Caballo FAIR

(⏲late Apr-early May) Jerez' week-long horse fair is one of Andalucía's grandest festivals, with music, dance, and equestrian competitions and parades. Bullfighting also features – but is seeing growing opposition from animal rights activists.

Fiestas de la Vendimia WINE

(⏲Sep) The biggest of Andalucía's *vendimia* festivals, this two-week autumn fiesta celebrates the grape harvest with flamenco, horse events and the traditional treading of the first grapes outside the cathedral.

Sleeping

Life Astuto Boutique HOSTEL €

(☎956 08 56 54; www.lifeapartments.es; Calle Chancillería 21; dm €12-14, d €40-70; ❄📶🏊) Set in a stylishly converted historical building, this great little hostel has crisp, contemporary shared-bathroom dorms (mixed or women-only) for four or six, with personal lockers, lamps, plugs and shelves, as well as private doubles. A dip pool graces the inner courtyard and garden, while a roof terrace unveils views across Jerez' rooftops.

Nuevo Hotel HOTEL €

(☎956 33 16 00; www.nuevohotel.com; Calle Caballeros 23; s €25-32, d €36-43; ❄📶) The Nuevo is a sweet 19th-century noble home filled with comfortable, simple, good-value rooms. The star is room 208, replete with Moorish-style stucco work and blue-and-white tiling creeping up the walls; you'll wake thinking you've taken up residence in Granada's Alhambra. Others rooms are plain, with antique furnishings. Cold breakfast (€5) available.

La Fonda Barranco BOUTIQUE HOTEL €€

(☎956 33 21 41; www.lafondabarranco.com; Calle Barranco 12; d €62-86; ❄📶) Dating back to at least 1865, this peaceful family-owned former merchant's house blends historical Moorish-inspired character with contemporary touches. You arrive into a cool patio (a glass of sherry is rustled up!), off which twisting staircases lead to a roof terrace and 10 charming, pristinely kept rooms with open-stone walls, wooden beams, carved doors, brick arches, pastel tones and decorative ceramic bowls.

YIT Casa Grande HOTEL €€

(☎956 34 50 70; www.hotelcasagrandejerez.com; Plaza de las Angustias 3; d €66-115; ❄📶) A beautifully restored 1920s mansion hosts 15 smartly classic rooms (marble floors, vintage furniture) over three floors surrounding a light-flooded, palm-dotted patio and a plush library lounge. Local-produce breakfasts are served in the courtyard, or beside the fantastic roof terrace with views across Jerez.

Casa Palacio María Luisa LUXURY HOTEL €€€
(☎956 92 62 63; www.casapalaciomarialuisa.com; Calle Tornería 22; r €250-310, ste €320-600; ❄📶🏊🐾) A five-star revamp of a dazzling 19th-century mansion has breathed fresh energy into Jerez' accommodation scene. The 21 luxe rooms are set around a marble-check patio fragrant with flowers; vertical gardens adorn interior courtyards; and there's a smart restaurant plus a tranquil open-air bar. Each room has its own soothing style, incorporating historical charm alongside bold wallpaper, velvet textures and original artwork.

Eating & Drinking

Jerez gastronomy combines Moorish heritage and maritime influences with international touches. Sherry, of course, flavours many traditional dishes such as *riñones al jerez* (sherry-braised kidneys) and *rabo de toro,* and there's also a notable turn towards creative contemporary cuisine in many of the city's top restaurants. Some of Jerez' most authentic and affordable eating and drinking spots are its *tabancos.*

Bar Juanito ANDALUCIAN €
(☎956 33 48 38; www.bar-juanito.com; Calle Pescadería Vieja 8-10; medias raciones €5-10; ⏲12.30-4pm & 8-11pm Mon-Sat, 12.30-4pm Sun) With its outdoor tables, rustic red chairs and check-print tablecloths, Juanito is like a slice of village Andalucía in the heart of the city, rustling up scrumptiously simple tapas since the 1940s. Its *alcachofas* (artichokes) are a past winner of the National Tapa Competition, but there's plenty more, all served with Cádiz wines. Live flamenco often happens on Saturday afternoon.

★**La Carboná** ANDALUCIAN €€
(☎956 34 74 75; www.lacarbona.com; Calle San Francisco de Paula 2; mains €15-21; ⏲1.30-4pm & 8-11pm Wed-Mon, closed Jul; 📝) 🌿 This cavernous, imaginative restaurant occupies an exquisite old bodega with a suspended fireplace. Delicately presented market-based specialities include grilled meats, fresh fish, boletus rice jazzed up with razor clams or *almadraba* tuna tartare with egg-yolk-and-*amontillado* (dry sherry) emulsion, plus outstanding local wines. Or go all-in with sherry-pairing menus (€45).

Albalá ANDALUCIAN, FUSION €€
(☎956 34 64 88; www.restaurantealbala.com; cnr Calle Divina Pastora & Avenida Duque de Abrantes; tapas €2-4, mains €9-20; ⏲noon-4pm & 8.30pm-midnight; 📶) Slide into blonde-wood booths amid minimalist decor for *jerezano* chef Israel Ramos' beautifully creative contemporary dishes fuelled by typical Andalucian ingredients. House specials include *rabo de toro* croquettes, fried eggs with truffle, *almadraba* red tuna tartare with guacamole, and deliciously crispy asparagus tempura dipped in soy aioli. It's 1km north of Plaza del Arenal.

Ramos is also behind highly innovative, Cádiz-rooted Michelin-starred restaurant **Mantúa** (☎856 65 27 39; www.restaurantemantua.com; Plaza Aladro 7; tasting menus €75-90, incl wines €110-140; ⏲1.30-3.15pm & 8.30-10.30pm Tue-Sat, 1.30-3.15pm Sun) 🌿.

Albores ANDALUCIAN €€
(☎956 32 02 66; www.restaurantealbores.com; Calle Consistorio 12; tapas €2-5, mains €8-19; ⏲8am-midnight) Pitching itself among age-old city-centre favourites, Albores brings a contemporary edge to local flavours and traditional recipes with its original, seasonally inspired tapas and plates. Chef Julián Olivares' show-stealing seafood includes clams in sherry-vinegar sauce and, in season, *almadraba* tuna specials, while other delectable bites range from goat's-cheese *tosta* to *papas aliñás*. One of Jerez' top breakfast spots.

Mulai FUSION €€
(☎695 251017; www.mulaijerez.com; Calle Pescadería Vieja 2; mains €12-18; ⏲1.30-4.30pm & 8.30-11.30pm Mon-Sat, 1.30-4.30pm Sun; 📝) 🌿 Fresh *gaditano* classics – Sanlúcar king prawns, *rabo de toro, camarones* – meet international inspiration at this stylish 2019 arrival, which brings a touch of (unlikely) Bali-chic to Jerez. Macrame wall hangings, bamboo lamps and photos of Indonesian fishers mingle with wooden beams and whitewashed walls, setting the tone for exquisite, original creations such as red-tuna tartare with truffle.

LÚ, Cocina y Alma GASTRONOMY €€€
(☎695 408481; www.universolu.com; Calle Zaragoza 2; tasting menus €90-150, incl wine €140-220; ⏲1-3pm & 8.30-10pm Tue-Sat, 1-3pm Sun) 🌿 Hotshot local chef Juan Luis Fernández, who trained at El Puerto's celebrated Aponiente, was awarded Jerez' first Michelin star in 2018 for his astonishing, wildly creative cookery, which reinvents superb Cádiz produce with effortlessly elegant French technique. The few tables overlook an open kitchen, chef's-table style, and there are three experimental, seasonal tasting menus, paired with Spanish and French wines.

DON'T MISS

THE GREAT TABANCO REVIVAL

Sprinkled across the city centre, Jerez' famous old *tabancos* are, essentially, simple taverns serving sherry from the barrel. Most date from the early 20th century and, although *tabanco* comes from the fusion of *tabaco* (tobacco) and *estanco* (tobacco shop), the focus is indisputably the local sherry. In danger of dying out just a few years ago, Jerez' *tabancos* have sprung back to life as fashionable modern-day hang-outs, reinvigorated by keen new ownership and frequented by crowds of stylish young *jerezanos* and curious visitors as much as old-timers. Several host regular flamenco (though you're just as likely to catch an impromptu performance) and sherry tastings. All are fantastic, cheap, down-to-earth places to get a real feel for Jerez – *fino* (dry and straw-coloured sherry) in hand.

The tourist office has information on the official **Ruta de los Tabancos de Jerez** (www.facebook.com/rutadelostabancosdejerez), though there are plenty of others, too.

Tabanco Plateros (☎956 10 44 58; www.facebook.com/tabanco.plateros; Calle Algarve 35; ⊙noon-4pm & 8pm-midnight Mon-Sat, 8pm-midnight Sun) Join the crowds spilling out from this lively *despacho de vinos* for a glass of *fino, oloroso* or *amontillado* alongside ingeniously simple tapas (€2 to €3) of, say, *jamón, payoyo* cheese and, on weekends, tortilla. Plateros is the original that kickstarted the *tabanco* comeback, and sometimes does sherry tastings too.

Tabanco El Pasaje (☎956 33 33 59; www.tabancoelpasaje.com; Calle Santa María 8; ⊙11am-3.30pm & 7pm-midnight Sun-Fri, 11am-4pm & 8pm-midnight Sat; Wi-Fi) Born in 1925, Jerez' oldest *tabanco* serves up its excellent sherry selection and pleasantly uncomplicated tapas (€2.50) with suitably raw twice-daily flamenco sessions (2pm and 9pm or 10pm). Flamenco legend Lola Flores is said to have performed here.

Tabanco El Guitarrón de San Pedro (☎649 656918; www.facebook.com/guitarrondesanpedro; Calle Bizcocheros 16; ⊙noon-4pm & 8pm-midnight Mon-Sat) Revitalised by sherry-loving owners (who offer pairings and tastings), El Guitarrón hosts regular flamenco dancing and singing, plus art exhibitions – all best enjoyed while feasting on uncomplicated tapas (€2 to €4) or sipping one of the many sherries.

Tabanco A la Feria (☎663 476542; www.facebook.com/Antoniocontrerascarava; Calle Armas 5; ⊙noon-4pm & 8pm-midnight) One of just a few venues offering daily shows, A la Feria gets taken over by fiery flamenco usually at 8pm and 10.30pm each night (less frequently in winter; check schedules online). Good sherries, tapas (€2) and *raciones* (€6).

☆ Entertainment

Jerez is home to one of Andalucía's liveliest flamenco (p130) scenes, with top-tier performances as well as outstanding classes in guitar, dance and song.

Real Escuela Andaluza del Arte Ecuestre LIVE PERFORMANCE
(☎956 31 80 08; www.realescuela.org; Avenida Duque de Abrantes; training sessions adult/child €11/6.50, shows adult €21-27, child €13-17; ⊙training sessions 10am-2pm Mon-Wed & Fri, shows noon Tue & Thu) Jerez' renowned Royal Andalucian School of Equestrian Art trains horses and riders. On 'thematic visits', you can watch them going through their paces in training sessions and visit the **Museo del Arte Ecuestre** and nearby **Museo del Enganche** (www.realescuela.org; Calle Pizarro; adult/child €4.50/2.50; ⊙10am-2pm Mon-Fri). The big highlight is the official *exhibición* (show), in which the beautiful horses show off their tricks to classical music. Book tickets online; schedules can vary.

Note that some animal rights advocates consider the training techniques for dressage and other similar horse performances cruel.

ℹ Information

Oficina de Turismo (☎956 33 88 74; www.turismojerez.com; Plaza del Arenal; ⊙8.30am-2pm & 4.30-6pm Mon-Fri, 8.30am-2.30pm Sat & Sun)

ℹ Getting There & Away

AIR

The **Aeropuerto de Jerez** (☎956 15 00 00; www.aena.es; Carretera A4), the only one serving Cádiz province, is 10km northeast of town on the A4, with flights to/from Barcelona, Madrid, Bilbao, Mallorca, London, Manchester and Berlin. Airlines include easyJet, Iberia, Ryanair and Vueling.

JEREZ' FERTILE FLAMENCO SCENE

Jerez' moniker as the 'cradle of flamenco' is regularly challenged by aficionados in Cádiz, Seville and Granada, but the claim has merit. This comparatively untouristed city harbours two Roma quarters, Santiago and San Miguel, which have produced numerous renowned artists, including Roma singers Manuel Torre and Antonio Chacón. Like its rival cities, Jerez has its own flamenco *palo* (musical form), the intensely popular *bulería*, a fast, rhythmic musical style with the same *compás* (accented beat) as Seville's *soleá*.

At the Centro Andaluz de Flamenco (p125) you can pick up information on *peñas* (small private clubs), *tabancos* (taverns that serve sherry from the barrel), performances, and song, dance and guitar lessons. From here, stroll down Calle Francos past a couple of legendary flamenco bars where singers and dancers still congregate. In the Santiago quarter, you'll find dozens of *peñas* known for their accessibility and intimacy; entry is normally free if you buy a drink. The *peña* scene is particularly lively during the flamenco-focused **Festival de Jerez** (www.facebook.com/FestivalDeJerez; late Feb-early Mar). Jerez' revitalised *tabancos* (p129) are also fantastic for flamenco; some, such as El Pasaje (p129) and A la Feria (p129), host regular performances, while others have more spur-of-the-moment flamenco.

Centro Cultural Flamenco Don Antonio Chacón (956 34 74 72; www.facebook.com/DAChaconFlamencoJerez; Calle Salas 2) One of the best *peñas* in town (and hence Andalucía), the Chacón, named for the great Jerez-born flamenco singer, often sees top-notch flamenco performers grace its stage. For upcoming events, check the Facebook page or contact the tourist office or the Centro Andaluz de Flamenco.

Puro Arte (647 743832; www.puroarteflamencojerez.com; Calle Madre de Dios 10; €30, incl tapas/dinner €45/49) Jerez' main *tablao* (choreographed flamenco show) stages popular local-artist performances two or three times daily. Options with drinks, tapas and/or dinner; advance bookings essential. Also offers flamenco dance classes.

Damajuana (www.facebook.com/damajuanajerez; Calle Francos 18; 8pm-3.30am Tue-Thu, 4pm-3.30am Fri-Sun) One of two historic bars on Calle Francos where flamenco singers and dancers have long met and drunk, with varied live music, tapas (€2 to €5.50) and a fun *movida flamenca* (flamenco scene) in a 16th-century mansion.

BUS

The **bus station** (956 14 99 90; Plaza de la Estación) is 1.3km southeast of the centre, served by CMTBC (p123), Comes (p123), Damas (p123) and **Monbus** (982 29 29 00; www.monbus.es).

Destination	Cost (€)	Time	Frequency
Arcos de la Frontera	3.10	40min	10-20 daily
Cádiz	3.90	45min	2-8 daily
El Puerto de Santa María	1.70	15-20min	2-7 daily
Ronda	13	2¾hr	1-2 daily
Sanlúcar de Barrameda	2	40min	7-13 daily
Seville	9	1¼hr	3-4 daily

CAR & MOTORCYCLE

There's 24-hour parking (€12) under the Alameda Vieja (beside the Alcázar).

TRAIN

Jerez' train station is beside the bus station.

Destination	Cost (€)	Time	Frequency
Cádiz	3-15	35-45min	20+ daily
Córdoba	25-35	2-3hr	7-14 daily
El Puerto de Santa María	2.80-12	8min	20+ daily
Seville	12-20	1¼hr	11-15 daily

Getting Around

TO/FROM THE AIRPORT

Taxis to/from the airport cost €15.

Eight to 10 daily trains run between the airport and Jerez (€1.10 to €2.55, seven to 11 minutes), El Puerto de Santa María (€1.70 to €3.80, 15 minutes) and Cádiz (€3.90 to €6.25, 45 minutes).

Local airport buses run three times on weekdays and once daily Saturday and Sunday to Jerez (€1.10, 30 minutes), once on weekdays to El Puerto de Santa María (€1.70, 50 minutes) and once daily to Cádiz (€3.90, 1½ hours).

El Puerto de Santa María

POP 43,100

When you're surrounded by such cultural luminaries as Cádiz, Jerez de la Frontera and Seville, it's easy to overlook the small print; such is the fate of El Puerto de Santa María, despite its collection of well-known icons, just across the bay from Cádiz. With its abundance of sandy blonde beaches, half a dozen sherry wineries (including renowned Osborne), seafood restaurants and a smattering of architectural heirlooms, El Puerto can seem like southern Andalucía in microcosm. It's an easy day trip from Cádiz or Jerez.

From the Cádiz catamaran dock, the castle and tourist office are 300m north, with the restaurant-filled old centre extending around. Several key bodegas are also within walking distance of the dock.

Sights

★ Bodegas Osborne WINERY

(☎956 86 91 00; www.osborne.es; Calle los Moros 7; tours from €15, tastings €10-55) Creator of the legendary black-bull logo still exhibited on life-size billboards all over Spain (now without the name), Osborne is El Puerto's best-known sherry winery. Set up by an Englishman, Thomas Osborne Mann, in 1772, it remains one of Spain's oldest companies run continuously by the same family.

The bodega offers tours with tastings at 10am (English), 11am (German) and noon (Spanish; plus 7.30pm in summer); book ahead. Some visits include sampling Huelva's much-lauded Cinco Jotas *jamón*.

Bodegas Gutiérrez Colosía WINERY

(☎607 450066, 956 85 28 52; www.gutierrezcolosia.com; Avenida de la Bajamar 40; tours €10) An intimate, family-run, 1838-founded sherry bodega, right beside the catamaran dock. Tours (1½ hours) end with a six-wine tasting, which can include tapas and flamenco on request, and run at 11.15am in English and 12.30pm in Spanish Monday to Friday, and at 1pm in both languages on Saturday; evening tours may happen July to September.

The Gutiérrez Colosía family also has a great nearby rustic-chic sherry and tapas bar, **Bespoke** (☎956 10 64 12; www.bespokepuerto.com; Avenida de la Bajamar 40; raciones €4-12; ⏲12.30-4pm & 8.30pm-late;) .

Castillo de San Marcos CASTLE

(☎627 569335; www.caballero.es; Plaza Alfonso X El Sabio; adult/child €10/5; ⏲tours 10am, 11.30am & 1pm daily, plus 6pm & 7.30pm Mon-Sat, reduced hours Oct-May) Heavily restored in the 20th century and now owned by Bodegas Caballero, El Puerto's castle was constructed over an Islamic mosque by Alfonso X El Sabio after he took the town in 1260. The original mosque inside, now converted into a church, is the highlight. Visits, in English or Spanish, last 1½ hours and end with a five-sherry tasting; book ahead.

Fundación Rafael Alberti MUSEUM

(☎956 85 07 11; www.rafaelalberti.es; Calle Santo Domingo 25; adult/child €4/2; ⏲10.30am-2pm Tue-Sun) Two blocks inland from Plaza Alfonso X El Sabio, this foundation has interesting, thoughtfully displayed exhibits on Rafael Alberti (1902–99), one of Spain's great Generation of '27 poets, in what was his childhood home. Free English, French or Spanish audio guides.

Sleeping

El Baobab Hostel HOSTEL €

(☎956 85 89 64; www.baobabhostel.com; Calle Pagador 37; per person €15-40; ⏲Apr-Oct;) In a converted 18th-century building near the bullring, this sunny 10-room hostel is El Puerto's budget pick, with a homey, friendly feel, simple interiors, and a communal kitchen and courtyard. Stripped-back, locker-equipped private rooms sleep two to eight.

Palacio San Bartolomé BOUTIQUE HOTEL €€€

(☎956 85 09 46; www.palaciosanbartolome.com; Calle San Bartolomé 21; r €68-170, ste €198-250;) Fancy a room with its own plunge pool, sauna, hot tub and deckchairs? It's all yours

EL PUERTO'S BEACHES

Drawing a predominantly Spanish crowd, El Puerto's white-sand beaches are among southern Spain's more popular coastal escapes. Pine-flanked **Playa de la Puntilla** is 1.5km southwest of the centre. Two kilometres further southwest is the swish **Puerto Sherry** marina, beyond which lie little **Playa de la Muralla** and 3km-long **Playa de Santa Catalina**, this last with beach bars (take bus 3 from the bullring bus stop). Bus 6 goes from the bullring 6km northwest of town to **Playa Fuentebravía** (Playa Fuenterrabía). On the eastern side of the Río Guadalete is popular **Playa de Valdelagrana**, backed by high-rise hotels.

A VERY BRITISH DRINK

The names give it away: Harvey, Sandeman, Terry, Humbert, Osborne. Andalucía's sherry industry might be Spanish in character, but it's firmly Anglo-Irish in origin. Francis Drake sacked Cádiz in 1587 and made off with over 3000 barrels of local *vino* – and a whole new industry was inauspiciously born.

Thomas Osborne Mann, from Exeter, befriended local winegrowers in El Puerto de Santa María in 1772 and set up what is today one of Spain's oldest family firms, Osborne (p131), famous for its black bull logo. George Sandeman, a Scotsman from Perth, founded his fledgling sherry empire in Tom's Coffee House in the City of London in 1790. John Harvey from Bristol began importing sherry from Spain in 1796 and his firm concocted the world's first cream sherry, Harvey's Bristol Cream, in the 1860s. Even Spain's most illustrious sherry dynasty, González-Byass (p125) – producers of the trademark Tío Pepe brand – was formed from an 1835 Anglo-Spanish alliance between Andalucian Manuel María González and his English agent Robert Byass.

with the Spa Suite at the deftly designed, welcoming San Bartolomé, set in a sensitively converted 18th-century palace. Rambling off a light-flooded patio, the 10 other rooms are equally enticing: four-poster beds, oversized showers, tile-carpeted floors, bright styling and contemporary elegance.

Eating & Drinking

El Puerto is famous for its outstanding seafood and tapas bars. Look along central Calles Luna and Misericordia, Calle Ribera del Marisco to the north, Avenidas de la Bajamar and Aramburu de Mora to the south, and Calle La Placilla near Plaza de España.

Toro Tapas TAPAS €€

(☎956 90 50 20; www.torotapaselpuerto.com; Calle los Moros 7, Bodegas Osborne; tapas €4-9, raciones & mains €7-18; ⏲8.30am-4.30pm & 8.30-11.30pm) An elegant, sprawling designer space beneath brick arches, the on-site trestaurant at renowned Bodegas Osborne is styled like a 'cathedral bodega'. Fresh, local produce is the key to the refined tapas and *raciones* (full-plate servings) here: top-tier Cinco Jotas *jamón* from Huelva, Cádiz cheeses served with Grazalema honey, *arroz meloso* (creamy rice) with Atlantic prawns.

★ **Aponiente** SEAFOOD €€€

(☎956 85 18 70; www.aponiente.com; Molino de Mareas El Caño, Calle Francisco Cossi Ochoa; 21-course menu €215, incl wine €315; ⏲1-4.30pm & 8-11.30pm Tue-Sat mid-Mar–Jun & Sep-early Dec, 1-4.30pm & 8-11.30pm Mon-Sat Jul & Aug) Audacious is the word for the bold experimentation of leading Spanish chef Ángel León, whose seafood-biased *nueva cocina* has won a cavalcade of awards, transforming Aponiente into Andalucía's first triple-Michelin-starred restaurant. Occupying a design-led 19th-century tide mill, Aponiente splits opinion in traditional El Puerto: some snort at its pretension, others salivate at the thought of its imaginative 21-course tasting menus.

Aponiente is 1.5km northeast of the centre. For a tapas-sized, town-centre taster of León's culinary magic, dine at creative sister venture **La Taberna del Chef del Mar** (☎956 11 20 93; www.latabernadelchefdelmar.com; Calle Puerto Escondido 6; tapas & raciones €6-22; ⏲1-4pm & 8.30-11.30pm Mon-Sat, 1-4pm Sun Apr-Oct) 🍃.

El Faro del Puerto ANDALUCIAN €€€

(☎956 87 09 52; www.elfarodelpuerto.com; Avenida de Fuentebravía, Km 0.5; tapas €4-15, mains €18-27; ⏲1.30-4.30pm & 8.30-11pm Mon-Sat, 1.30-4.30pm Sun; 🖉) Upmarket El Faro gets busy for its traditional-with-a-hint-of-innovation take on local seafood, excellent Spanish wine list, and classically smart, multiroom setting inside an old *casa señorial* (manor house). Menus change with the seasons; the *almadraba* tuna tartare is a highlight. The bar/tapas menu has some exciting vegetarian and gluten-free choices.

Bodega Obregón BAR

(☎956 85 63 29; Calle Zarza 51; ⏲9am-2pm & 6-10pm Mon-Fri, 9am-late Sat, 10am-2pm Sun) At this wood-beamed, family-run, spit-and-sawdust-style bar, the house sweet stuff is siphoned from woody barrels, and the home-cooked Saturday-lunch *guisos* (stews) are a firm local favourite.

Information

Oficina de Turismo (☎956 48 37 15; www.turismoelpuerto.com; Plaza de Alfonso X El Sabio 9; ⏲10am-8pm Jul & Aug, 10am-2pm & 5-7pm

Mon-Sat, 10am-4pm Sun May, Jun, Sep & Oct, reduced hours Nov-Mar) In the 16th-century Palacio de Aranibar.

Getting There & Around

BOAT

Catamarans (www.cmtbc.es; 7.10am-7.50pm Mon-Fri, 9.30am-9.15pm Sat, 9.30am-6.30pm Sun) run to/from Cádiz (€2.80, 30 minutes) at least 16 times daily Monday to Friday, and at least eight times daily on weekends.

BUS

El Puerto has two bus stops. CMTBC (p123) buses to Cádiz (€2.80, 45 minutes, every 30 to 60 minutes), Jerez de la Frontera (€1.70, 20 minutes, two to eight daily) and Sanlúcar de Barrameda (€2.05, 30 minutes, six to 14 daily) go from the **bus stop** (Plaza Elías Ahuja) outside the bullring. Comes (p123) buses to Seville (€11, 1½ to two hours, one to two daily) go from outside the train station.

CAR & MOTORCYCLE

There's supervised parking at the catamaran dock (€10 per 24 hours).

TRAIN

From the train station at the northeastern end of town, frequent trains go to/from Jerez de la Frontera (€1.80, 10 minutes), Cádiz (€3.40 to €5.25, 35 minutes) and Seville (€14, 1¼ hours).

Sanlúcar de Barrameda

POP 46,880

Sanlúcar is one of those lesser-known Andalucian towns that delight and enamour. Firstly, there's the gastronomy: Sanlúcar cooks up some of the region's best seafood on the hallowed waterside strip Bajo de Guía. Secondly, Sanlúcar's unique Atlantic-facing location at the northern tip of the esteemed Sherry Triangle enables its earthy bodegas, nestled in the somnolent, monument-strewn old town, to produce the much-admired one-of-a-kind *manzanilla*. Thirdly, sitting at the mouth of the Río Guadalquivir estuary, Sanlúcar provides a quieter, less touristed entry point into the ethereal Parque Nacional de Doñana than the more popular western access points in Huelva province.

Sights

Many of Sanlúcar's *manzanilla* bodegas are open for guided visits (usually in English or Spanish); the tourist office (p135) provides a list. The Barrio Alto, up Cuesta de Belén, is the most atmospheric part of town.

★ Bodegas Hidalgo–La Gitana WINERY

(669 663008; www.lagitana.es; Calle Banda de la Playa; tours €14; tours 1pm Mon-Sat, in English 11am Mon-Sat) Now run by the eighth generation, family-owned 1792-founded Bodegas Hidalgo still produces the famed La Gitana *manzanillas* that made its name, along with VORS sherries such as a small-scale *amontillado*. Detailed two-hour introductory tours are outstanding, while specialised visits include sunset tastings among the vines (€40) and summer night tours (€35).

Bodegas Barbadillo WINERY

(956 38 55 21; www.barbadillo.com; Calle Sevilla 6; tours €10; tours noon & 1pm Tue-Sun, in English 11am Tue-Sun) With its Barrio Alto 1821-founded bodega, Barbadillo was the first family to bottle Sanlúcar's famous *manzanilla* and also produces one of Spain's most popular *vinos*. Guided one-hour tours end with a four-wine tasting. This evocative 19th-century building also houses the **Museo de la Manzanilla** (10am-3pm) FREE.

Palacio de los Guzmán PALACE

(956 36 01 61; www.fcmedinasidonia.com; Plaza Condes de Niebla 1; tours €5; tours noon Thu, 11.30am & noon Sun) Just off the old town's Calle Caballeros, this rambling palace was the home of the Duques de Medina Sidonia, the aristocratic family that once owned more of Spain than anyone else. The mostly 17th-century house, of 12th-century origin, bursts with antiques, and paintings by Goya, Zurbarán and other Spanish greats. Stop for coffee and cakes in its old-world **cafe** (9am-9pm).

Iglesia de Nuestra Señora de la O CHURCH

(Plaza de la Paz; €4; 10.30am-2pm & 4.30-6.30pm) Fronting Calle Caballeros, this medieval church stands out among Sanlúcar's many others for its elaborate 1360s Gothic-Mudéjar portal and its rich interior embellishment, particularly the Mudéjar *artesonado*, one of the region's best preserved. The bell tower was built reusing a tower from the Moorish *alcázar* (fortress) that once stood here.

Castillo de Santiago CASTLE

(956 92 35 00; www.castillodesantiago.com; Plaza del Castillo 1; adult/child €7/5; 10.15am-3pm & 6.15-9pm Mon & Tue, 10.15am-7.30pm Wed, 10.15am-9pm Thu-Sun May-Oct, reduced hours Nov-Apr) Surrounded by Barbadillo bodegas, Sanlúcar's restored 15th-century castle has sprawling views across the Guadalquivir delta from its hexagonal Torre del Homenaje

(keep), and displays military uniforms and weapons and exhibits on the town's rich seafaring history.

🕝 Tours

Sanlúcar is a good base for exploring the Parque Nacional de Doñana (p98), which glistens just across the Río Guadalquivir.

Trips are run by the licensed **Visitas Doñana** (☑956 36 38 13; www.visitasdonana. com; Centro de Visitantes Fábrica de Hielo, Bajo de Guía; ☺9am-8pm Apr-Sep, to 7pm Feb-Mar & Oct-mid-Dec, to 6pm mid-Dec–Jan), whose boat, the *Real Fernando,* chugs up the river for wildlife-viewing. The best option is a 2½-hour boat/jeep combination (€35), which goes 30km through the park's dunes, marshlands and pine forests in 21-person 4WD vehicles, operated in conjunction with the Cooperativa Marismas del Rocío (p99), based in El Rocío, Huelva province; there are four trips a day. Book online or through the Centro de Visitantes Fábrica de Hielo (p135), as far ahead as possible; trips depart from Bajo de Guía.

Viajes Doñana (☑956 36 25 40; www. viajesdonana.es; Calle San Juan 20; ☺9am-2pm & 5-8.30pm Mon-Fri, 10.30am-2pm Sat) agency books 3½-hour tours (€40 per person) with the Cooperativa Marismas del Rocío in 21- or 29-person 4WDs, going 70km into the park, and private on-demand jeep tours for up to six people (€270 per jeep).

Sanlúcar Smile　WALKING
(☑669 663008; www.sanlucarsmile.com) A knowledgeable, engaging *sanluqueño* duo runs excellent three-hour walking tours of Sanlúcar (adult/child €25/5), typically including a *manzanilla* stop, as well as sherry bodega visits, tapas-and-wine tours, kayaking trips, adventures into Doñana, and more.

🎉 Festivals & Events

Romería del Rocío　RELIGIOUS
(☺7th weekend after Easter) Many pilgrims and covered wagons set out from Sanlúcar bound for El Rocío in Huelva province on Spain's largest religious pilgrimage, the Romería del Rocío (p102).

Feria de la Manzanilla　WINE
(☺late May/early Jun) A big *manzanilla*-fuelled fair kicks off Sanlúcar's summer.

🛏 Sleeping

★**La Alcoba del Agua**　BOUTIQUE HOTEL €€
(☑956 38 31 09; www.laalcobadelagua.com; Calle Alcoba 26; s €50-130, d €59-159; 🅿❄🛜❄) The laid-back, highly original, skilfully decorated 14-room Alcoba feels like something architect Frank Lloyd Wright might have conceived. Rooms styled with vintage pieces, rain showers and feature walls rise around a statement courtyard complete with loungers, hammock and lap pool. It's wonderfully homey, functional and central (just off Calle Ancha). Breakfast (€7) is a good buffet.

★**La Casa**　BOUTIQUE HOTEL €€
(☑617 575913; www.lacasasanlucar.com; Calle Ancha 84; d €50-85, q €100-120; ❄🛜) A friendly team manages this gorgeously fresh, outstanding-value boutique guesthouse. Custom-designed in blues, pinks and turquoises, the eight rooms are inspired by Doñana national park, blending traditional charm (19th-century shutters, marble floors) with contemporary style (see-through showers, geometric lamps, rectangular sinks), and have thoughtful touches including coffee kits. Breakfasts (€6) feature organic Huelva jams, fresh juice and other local goodies.

🍴 Eating

Sanlúcar is a culinary highlight of Andalucía. Strung out along **Bajo de Guía**, 1km northeast of the centre, is one of southern Spain's most famous eating strips, once a fishing village and now a haven of high-quality seafood restaurants that revel in their simplicity. Plaza del Cabildo is also a culinary hotspot.

★**Casa Balbino**　TAPAS €
(☑956 36 05 13; www.casabalbino.es; Plaza del Cabildo 14; tapas €2-3; ☺noon-5pm & 8pm-midnight) No matter when you arrive, Casa Balbino is always overflowing with people drawn in by its unbeatable seafood tapas. You'll have to elbow your way through and shout your order to a waiter. The options are endless, but the *tortillitas de camarones,* fried-egg-topped *tagarninas* and *langostinos a la plancha* (grilled king prawns) are the stuff of Andalucian dreams.

★**Casa Bigote**　SEAFOOD €€
(☑956 36 26 96; www.restaurantecasabigote. com; Bajo de Guía 10; mains €12-20; ☺1.30-4pm & 8pm-midnight Mon-Sat, closed Nov) A touch more elegant than its neighbours, long-established Casa Bigote is seafood-tastic Bajo de Guía's most renowned restaurant. House specials include *almadraba* tuna tataki with *salmorejo* sauce, cod in sour-citrus sauce and grilled squid with wild-mushroom rice, or fish of the day baked, grilled or salted. Waiters flit across

to permanently packed **Barra Bigote** (tapas €5 to €18), opposite.

El Espejo FUSION €€

(☎651 141650; www.elespejo-sanlucar.es; Calle Caballeros 11; mains €12-18, tasting menus €35-42; ⏲12.30-3.45pm & 8.30-11.30pm Wed-Sun Apr-Jul & Sep-Dec, 12.30-3.45pm & 8.30-11.30pm Thu-Sun, 8.30-11.30pm Mon-Wed Jul & Aug, reduced hours Jan-Mar) Flavours from Cádiz collide with international flair in imaginative, market-fuelled concoctions at this romantic patio restaurant up in the old town. Tables huddled between palms and geranium pots set the tone for elegantly prepped dishes such as delicate, little-known Sanlúcar-grown vegetables or *almadraba* red tuna tartare. Wine-pairing menus, and a swish bar.

Chef José Luis Tallafigo also runs smart courtyard restaurant **EntreBotas** (☎644 094252; www.facebook.com/restauranteentrebotas; Calle Banda de la Playa, Bodegas Hidalgo–La Gitana; raciones €7-25; ⏲12.30-4.30pm & 8.30pm-midnight), at Bodegas Hidalgo-La Gitana.

Information

Centro de Visitantes Fábrica de Hielo (☎956 38 65 77; www.juntadeandalucia.es; Bajo de Guía; ⏲9am-8pm Apr-Sep, to 7pm Feb-Mar & Oct–mid-Dec, to 6pm mid-Dec–Jan)

Oficina de Información Turística (☎956 36 61 10; www.sanlucarturismo.com; Avenida Calzada Duquesa Isabel; ⏲10am-2pm & 5-7pm Mon-Sat, 10am-2pm Sun)

Getting There & Away

From Sanlúcar's **bus station** (Avenida de la Estación), Damas (p123) goes to/from El Puerto de Santa María (€2.15, 30 to 45 minutes, six to 14 daily), Cádiz (€5.10, one hour, five to 13 daily) and Seville (€8.77, 1¼ to two hours, 10 to 12 daily). Monbus (p130) has seven to 13 daily buses to/from Jerez (€2, 40 minutes).

CÁDIZ' WHITE TOWNS

Arcos de la Frontera

POP 21,980

Everything you've ever dreamed a *pueblo blanco* (white town) could be miraculously materialises in Arcos de la Frontera (33km east of Jerez): a thrilling strategic clifftop location, a volatile frontier history, a low-key flamenco scene and a soporific old town full of mystery, with whitewashed arches soaring above slender, twisting alleys, grand old mansions and Roman-era pillars.

For a brief period during the 11th century, Arcos was an independent Berber-ruled *taifa* (small kingdom). In 1255 it was claimed by Christian king Alfonso X El Sabio for Seville and it remained literally *de la frontera* (on the frontier) until the fall of Granada in 1492.

Sights & Activities

Highly rated, multilingual **Infotur Arcos** (☎654 921792; www.visitasguiadasarcos.es; tours per person €5) runs guided tours.

Plaza del Cabildo SQUARE

Lined with fine ancient buildings, Plaza del Cabildo is the heart of Arcos' old town, its vertiginous **mirador** affording exquisite panoramas over the Río Guadalete. The Moorish-origin **Castillo de los Duques**, rebuilt in the 14th and 15th centuries, is closed to the public, but its outer walls frame classic Arcos views. On the square's eastern side, the Parador de Arcos de la Frontera (p137) is a reconstruction of a grand 16th-century magistrate's house; pop in for a drink.

Basílica Menor de Santa María de la Asunción BASILICA

(Plaza del Cabildo; €2; ⏲10am-12.45pm & 4-6.30pm Mon-Fri, 10am-1.30pm Sat Mar–mid-Dec) This Gothic-baroque creation is one of Andalucía's more beautiful, intriguing churches, built over several centuries on the site of a mosque. Check out the ornate gold-leaf altarpiece (a miniature of that in Seville's cathedral) carved between 1580 and 1608, the striking painting of San Cristóbal (St Christopher), the restored 14th-century Gothic-Mudéjar mural, the woodcarved 18th-century choir and the Isabelline ceiling tracery.

Iglesia de San Pedro CHURCH

(Calle San Pedro 4; €2; ⏲10am-12.45pm & 4-6.45pm Mon-Fri, 10am-1.30pm Sat) Containing a 16th-century main altarpiece said to be the oldest in Cádiz province, this Gothic-baroque confection contains one of Andalucía's most magnificent small-church interiors, behind an 18th-century facade, and may have been constructed atop an Almohad-era fortress.

Festivals & Events

Semana Santa RELIGIOUS

(⏲Mar/Apr) Dramatic Semana Santa processions see hooded penitents inching through Arcos' narrow streets.

Arcos de la Frontera

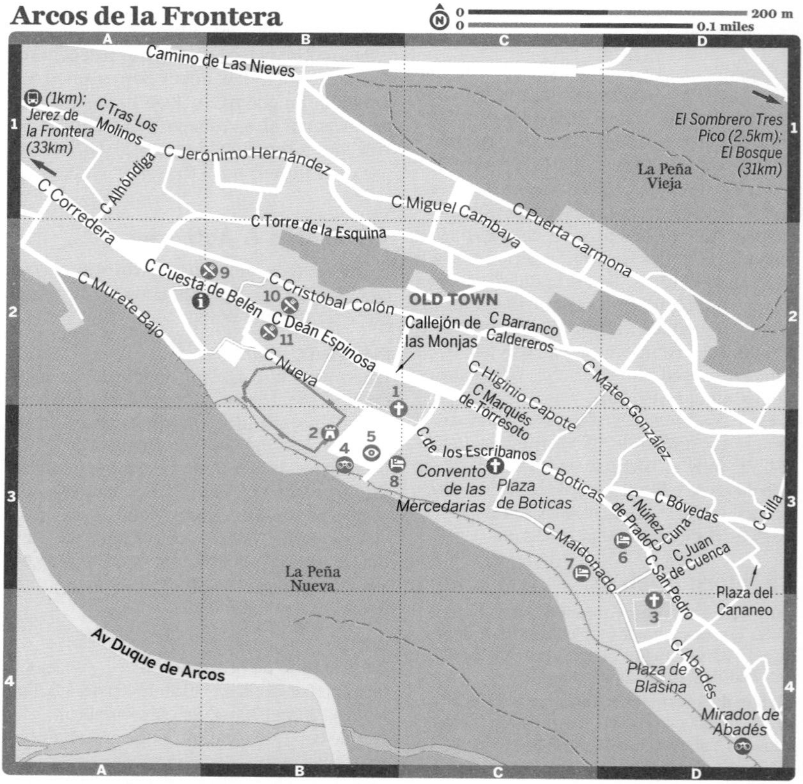

Arcos de la Frontera

Sights

1 Basílica Menor de Santa María de la Asunción B3
2 Castillo de los Duques B3
3 Iglesia de San Pedro D4
4 Mirador B3
5 Plaza del Cabildo B3

Sleeping

6 Casa Campana D3
7 La Casa Grande C3
8 Parador de Arcos de la Frontera B3

Eating

9 Aljibe B2
10 Bar La Cárcel B2
El Corregidor .... (see 8)
11 Taberna Jóvenes Flamencos B2

Sleeping

★ **La Casa Grande** HERITAGE HOTEL €€
(☎ 956 70 39 30; www.lacasagrande.net; Calle Maldonado 10; r €74-105, ste €110-125; closed 6-31 Jan;) This gorgeous, rambling, cliff-side mansion dating to 1729 once belonged to the great flamenco dancer Antonio Ruiz Soler, and still feels more arty home than hotel, with original tiling and arches. The seven rooms are individually styled with modern-rustic design and most have divine valley views. Great breakfasts (€10).

★ **Cortijo Bablou** AGROTURISMO €€
(☎ 691 016576, 620 759698; www.cortijobablou.com; Carretera Arcos-Algar, Km 4; incl breakfast r/yurt/caravan €115/85/135; Apr–mid-Oct; P) In flower-filled, lavender-scented grounds, 6km southeast of Arcos, French-owned adults-only Bablou comprises a creatively converted, four-room 19th-century farmhouse done with boho-chic style and decorative pieces collected from Morocco, as well as three glamping yurts (with bathroom) and a Romanian caravan. Breakfasts are a homemade treat, hammocks sway under the trees, the

pool overlooks rolling countryside, and open-air massages are arranged.

Casa Campana GUESTHOUSE €€
(☎600 284928; www.casacampana.com; Calle Núñez de Prado 4; d €70-95, apt €95-130;) One of several charming guesthouses in old Arcos, Casa Campana has two cosy doubles, a four-person room and a five-person apartment, all filled with character, in a house dating back at least 600 years. The patio is dotted with loungers and flowers, and the rooftop terrace is flooded with views. It's expertly run by knowledgeable owners who supply excellent walking-tour leaflets.

Parador de Arcos de la Frontera HERITAGE HOTEL €€
(☎956 70 05 00; www.parador.es; Plaza del Cabildo; r €120-150;) A rebuilt 16th-century magistrate's residence that combines classic *parador* luxury with a splendid setting and the best views in town. Eight of the traditional-style rooms have balconies opening onto sweeping clifftop panoramas; most others look out on Plaza del Cabildo. The elegant **cafe-restaurant** (mains €12-21; 8-11am, 1-4pm & 8-10.30pm;), with its sunny terrace, offers a smart menu rooted in local specialities.

Eating

★ Taberna Jóvenes Flamencos TAPAS €
(☎657 133552; www.facebook.com/pg/taberna.jovenesflamencos; Calle Deán Espinosa 11; tapas €2-4; noon-midnight Thu-Tue;) Along with oh-so-Andalucía flamenco/bullfighting decor, tiled floors and hand-painted tables, cheerful and popular Jóvenes Flamencos has an enticing menu of meat, seafood and vegetarian tapas and *raciones,* including chunky tortilla, goat's cheese drizzled with local honey and soul-warming onion soup topped with *payoyo* cheese. All ingredients and wines are from Cádiz province; service is impeccable; and music and dance break out regularly.

The team also runs nearby **Aljibe** (☎622 836527; Calle Cuesta de Belén; mains €10-19; 12.30-4pm & 7.30-11.30pm Wed-Mon;) , where Andalucian produce is laced with the influences of Moorish cuisine in the elegantly reimagined *aljibe* (cistern) of an 18th-century building.

El Sombrero de Tres Picos SPANISH €€
(☎956 70 03 18; www.facebook.com/RestauranteElSombrerodeTresPicos; Avenida El Sombrero de Tres Picos 3; tapas €2.50-4, mains €8-14; noon-late Tue-Sun;) Perched by the lake, 3.5km northeast of Arcos, this well-known restaurant has been revitalised by keen new owners, plating up traditional meats, stews and tapas prepared with creative flair and international influences, as well as classic Valencia-style paellas.

Bar La Cárcel TAPAS, ANDALUCIAN €€
(☎956 70 04 10; Calle Deán Espinosa 18; tapas €2-5, raciones €8-14; noon-1am Tue-Sun) A *cárcel* (prison) in name only, this welcoming, low-key bar-restaurant offers no-nonsense tapas – honeyed aubergine with goat's cheese, bacon-wrapped prawns, *tortillitas de camarones,* tuna with mushrooms in *oloroso* sauce – alongside ice-cold *cañas* (small draught beer) and *tinto de verano* (red wine with lemonade and ice).

Information

Oficina de Turismo (☎956 70 22 64; www.turismoarcos.com; Calle Cuesta de Belén 5; 9.30am-2pm & 3-7.30pm Mon-Sat, 10am-2pm Sun)

Getting There & Around

BUS

Buses from Arcos' **bus station** (Calle Los Alcaldes) in the new town (down to the west of the old town), off Avenida Miguel Mancheño, are operated by Comes (p123), Damas (p123) and/or the Consorcio de Transportes Bahía de Cádiz (p123). Frequency is reduced at weekends. For Seville, it's best to connect in Jerez.

CAR & MOTORCYCLE

There's underground parking below Paseo de Andalucía (€15 for 24 hours), west of the old town. A half-hourly 'microbus' (€0.90) runs up to the old

BUSES FROM ARCOS DE LA FRONTERA

DESTINATION	COST (€)	TIME	FREQUENCY
Cádiz	5.73-7.30	1hr	up to 11 daily
Jerez de la Frontera	2.05-3.10	30-40min	at least 20 daily
Ronda	9.93	2hr	2 daily Mon-Fri, daily Sat & Sun
Seville	8.90	2hr	2 daily

town from Plaza de España 8am to 9pm Monday to Friday and 8am to 2pm Saturday.

Grazalema

POP 1550 / ELEV 825M

Few white towns are as generically perfect as Grazalema, with its spotless whitewashed houses of rust-tiled roofs and wrought-iron window bars sprinkled on the steep, rocky slopes of its eponymous mountain range. Hikes fan out in all directions, making Grazalema the most popular base for adventures into the Parque Natural Sierra de Grazalema. The village is also an age-old producer of blankets, honey, cheese and meat-filled stews, and has its own special mountain charm.

◉ Sights & Activities

Plaza de España　　　　　　　　SQUARE
Grazalema centres on the 18th-century Plaza de España, overlooked by the Iglesia de la Aurora, begun in 1760 and completed 40 years later, and refreshed by a four-spouted Visigothic fountain.

Horizon　　　　　　　ADVENTURE SPORTS
(☑ 655 934565, 956 13 23 63; www.horizonaventura. com; Calle Las Piedras 1; ⊙ 10am-2pm & 5-8pm, reduced hours Oct-Apr) Just off Plaza de España, highly experienced Horizon offers all the most exciting activities in the Parque Natural Sierra de Grazalema, including hiking, kayaking, climbing, canyoning, caving, mountain biking, paragliding and vie ferrate, with Spanish-, English-, French- or German-speaking guides. A half-day walk costs €13 per person.

🛏 Sleeping & Eating

La Mejorana　　　　　　GUESTHOUSE €
(☑ 956 13 25 27; www.lamejorana.net; Calle Santa Clara 6; d incl breakfast €62; ❋ 🛜 ≋) An exceptionally welcoming house towards the upper end of Grazalema, La Mejorana has nine comfy rooms in colourful, updated rustic style. Some have private lounges and sky-blue Moroccan-style arches; others balconies, terraces, huge mirrors or wrought-iron bedsteads. A lounge, library and breakfast terrace, with gorgeous village views, overlook the leafy hammock-strung garden and twinkling pool.

Casa de las Piedras　　　　　HOTEL €
(☑ 956 13 20 14; www.casadelaspiedras.es; Calle Las Piedras 32; s/d €35/48, without bathroom

€35/40; ❋ 🛜) Mountain air and a homey feel create the perfect Grazalema setting at this rustic-design hotel with a snug lounge and masses of park activities information. The building dates from the 18th-century wool-splendour period and its simple, cosy rooms, in various shapes and sizes, are hidden off three charming patios and decorated with Grazalema-made blankets.

★ Tambor del Llano　　　　　HOTEL €€
(☑ 674 484885; www.tambordelllano.es; Cañada Grande-Los Alamillos; r incl breakfast €87-111; P ❋ 🛜 ≋ ⊛) / Named for a Lorca poem, this wonderful rural hideaway hosts 10 cosily contemporary rooms in a thoughtfully converted stable on a 32-hectare, middle-of-nowhere oak-forest estate 6km southeast of Grazalema. Organic homegrown produce and olive oil power meals, and the team runs yoga, Spanish-language and creative retreats, plus horse-riding excursions (including multinight trips). A pool was on the way at research time.

La Maroma　　　　　　　TAPAS €€
(☑ 956 13 22 79; www.facebook.com/gastrobar lamaroma; Calle Santa Clara; tapas €2-6, mains €6-16; ⊙ noon-5pm & 7.30-11pm Tue-Sun; 🛜 ✎) The cooking is more fun and inventive than the rustic check-cloth, beamed-ceiling, bull-festival-inspired decor suggests at this cosy gastrobar, run by a young family team. Creative local-inspired tapas and *raciones* throw mountain ingredients into tasty bites like mushrooms in honey-and-thyme sauce, wafer-thin chips, *huevos rotos* (fried eggs with potatoes), or *payoyo*-cheese salad with Grazalema-honey dressing. There's a dedicated vegan/vegetarian menu.

Restaurante El Torreón　　　ANDALUCIAN €€
(☑ 956 13 23 13; Calle del Agua 44; mains €7-18; ⊙ 1-4pm & 7-10.30pm Thu-Tue) This cosy, friendly restaurant with a roaring winter fire specialises in traditional mountain cuisine, from local chorizo and cheese platters to *tagarnina* scrambles (a Cádiz delicacy) and sirloin in green-pepper sauce. Vegetarians: there's a meat-free Andalucian-style menu (mushroom risotto, *tagarnina* croquettes, spinach scramble). Tables spill onto the street when it's sunny.

🛍 Shopping

Quesería La Abuela Agustina　　　FOOD
(☑ 686 250468; http://quesoslaabuelaagustina. com; Plaza Pequeña 7; ⊙ 10am-8pm) / Treasure

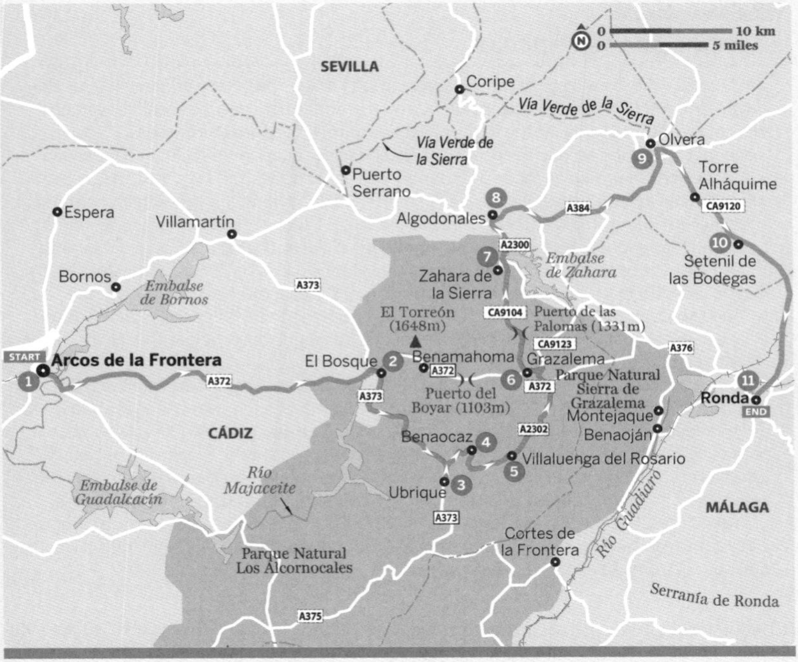

Driving Tour White Towns

START ARCOS DE LA FRONTERA
END RONDA
LENGTH 147KM; TWO DAYS

Rev up in dramatic 1 **Arcos de la Frontera** (p135), a Roman-turned-Moorish-turned-Christian citadel perched atop a sheer-sided sandstone ridge. Head 31km east along the A372 to 2 **El Bosque**, the western gateway to Parque Natural Sierra de Grazalema and site of the park's main information centre. The A373 takes you 13km south round to leather-making 3 **Ubrique** (supplier to some of the world's top designers), close to the borders of the Grazalema and Alcornocales natural parks. Mountains rise quickly as you drive 7km up the A2302 to tiny 4 **Benaocaz**, where several park hikes start/finish, then another 7km to equally diminutive 5 **Villaluenga del Rosario** with its artisanal-cheese museum. Plying the craggy eastern face of the sierra and then taking the A372 west brings you to 6 **Grazalema** , a red-roofed park-activity nexus famous for blanket making and honey; the perfect overnight stop. Steep CA9104 climbs to the 1357m Puerto de las Palomas and its lookout. Another 11km north is quintessential white town 7 **Zahara de la Sierra** (p140); its huddle of houses spreads around the skirts of a castle-topped crag above a reservoir at the foot of the Grazalema mountains. Nearby is the famous Garganta Verde hiking trail. The A2300 threads 10km north to 8 **Algodonales**, a white town on the edge of the natural park known for its guitar-making workshop and hang-gliding/paragliding. Take the A384 19km northeast from here past the Peñón de Zaframagón (an important refuge for griffon vultures) to 9 **Olvera** (p142), visible for miles around thanks to its Moorish castle. Following the CA9106 southeast, you'll pass the little-known white town of Torre Alháquime. From here, the CA9120 winds 11km southeast towards the border with Málaga province and 10 **Setenil de las Bodegas** (p140), a recently revitalised village instantly recognisable for its cave-houses. From Setenil, head 17km south and wrap up in beautiful gorge-top 11 **Ronda** (p182) in Málaga province.

WORTH A TRIP

SETENIL DE LAS BODEGAS

While most white towns sought protection atop lofty crags, the people of Setenil de las Bodegas (14km southeast of Olvera; p142) burrowed into the dark caves beneath the steep cliffs of the Río Trejo. Clearly, the strategy worked: it took the Christian armies a 15-day siege to dislodge the Moors from their well-defended positions in 1484. Setenil (population 2149) has long been known for its olive, honey and cured meats, but over the last few years, after decades off-map, the town has been smartened up, with rapidly growing tourism bringing new energy (and income) to its ancient streets. Many original cave houses (once used for storing wine) remain, and some have been converted into hotels and restaurants.

The **tourist office** (☎659 546626; www.setenil.com; Calle Villa 2; ⏲10.30am-2pm Tue-Sun) is near the top of the town in the 16th-century **Casa Consistorial** (with a rare wooden Mudéjar ceiling) and runs guided tours. Above is the 12th-century **castle** (Calle Villa; €1; ⏲11am-6pm), captured by the Christians just eight years before the fall of Granada; you can climb the 13th-century tower.

Setenil has some great tapas bars. Start with the cave bar-restaurants built into the rock along Calles Cuevas del Sol and Cuevas de la Sombra, and work your way up to Plaza de Andalucía and long-running **Restaurante Casa Palmero** (☎956 13 43 60; www.facebook.com/RestauranteCasaPalmero; Plaza de Andalucía 4; mains €8-19; ⏲1pm-late Fri-Wed; 📶), loved for its traditional village recipes rooted in local produce. And if you'd like to stay the night, there are plenty of cave-houses open to visitors, including some stylish interiors.

Autocares Sierra de las Nieves (☎952 87 54 35; http://grupopacopepe.com) runs six weekday buses and three Saturday buses to/from Ronda (€2, 45 minutes), plus a weekday bus to/from Málaga (€11, 3¼ hours).

trove of local produce, this prize-winning cheese specialist stocks mountain honeys and jams and small-scale olive oils from Olvera and Zahara, as well as its own goat- and sheep-milk cheeses made using traditional artisan methods.

Information

Oficina de Turismo (☎956 13 20 52; www.grazalema.es; Plaza de los Asomaderos; ⏲9am-3pm Tue-Sun Jun-Sep, 10am-2pm & 3-5.30pm Tue-Sun Oct-May) Excellent Parque Natural Sierra de Grazalema walking information, plus last-minute hiking permits (in person only, maximum one day ahead).

Getting There & Away

Damas (p123) runs two daily buses to/from Ronda (€3, 1½ hours); two to three daily to/from Ubrique (€2.32, 40 to 60 minutes), two of them via Benaocaz (€1.61, 10 to 30 minutes); and one daily Monday to Friday to/from El Bosque (€1.44, 40 minutes), where you can change for Arcos de la Frontera.

Zahara de la Sierra

POP 1200 / ELEV 550M

Strung around a vertiginous crag at the foot of the Grazalema mountains, overlooking the glittering turquoise Embalse de Zahara (Zahara Reservoir), rugged Zahara hums with Moorish mystery. For over 150 years in the 14th and 15th centuries, it stood on the old medieval frontier facing off against Christian Olvera, clearly visible in the distance. These days Zahara ticks all the classic white-town boxes, its streets framed by tall palms and hot-pink bougainvillea. It's also a great base for hiking the Garganta Verde, so it's popular. During the afternoon siesta, however, you could hear a pin drop.

Sights & Activities

El Mogote (☎610 049650; www.elmogote.com; Carretera A2300) offers guided two-hour kayaking trips (€15 per person), and rents kayaks and SUP boards (€12) from its base 3km north of town. Book ahead.

Castillo CASTLE
(⏲24hr) FREE A path opposite the Hotel Arco de la Villa leads to Zahara's 12th-century castle keep (it's a steep, steady 10- to 15-minute climb). The castle's recapture from the Christians by Emir Abu al-Hasan of Granada, in a night raid in 1481, provoked the Reyes Católicos (Catholic Monarchs) to launch the last phase of the Reconquista, ending with the 1492 fall of Granada.

Oleum Viride AGRICULTURAL CENTRE
(www.oleumviride.com; Finca Haza Las Lajas; tour €12) Learn all about inland Cádiz' age-old olive oil production at this enthusiastically run *almazara* (oil press), 1km northwest of central Zahara, whose sloping olive groves are still tended to by hand. The 1½-hour tour includes a four-oil tasting, or book in for local-produce tapas accompanied by the estate's own organic red wine (€25); minimum two people.

Sleeping & Eating

El Pantalán ANDALUCIAN €
(602 298232; www.elmogote.com; Carretera A2300; mains €7-15; 10am-11pm daily May-Sep, closed Tue & Wed Oct-Apr;) Fabulous Zahara views across the glassy reservoir make this relaxed restaurant and waterfront lounge bar, 3km north of town, hugely popular on warm days. Barbecued meats, seafood bites like fried *chocos* or *tortillitas de camarones,* and tapas of local cheese or *tagarnina* stew are among the classic dishes. It's attached to water sports outfitter El Mogote.

★**Al Lago** ANDALUCIAN €€
(956 12 30 32; www.al-lago.es; Calle Félix Rodríguez de la Fuente; mains €8-20; 12.30-4.30pm & 8-10.30pm Thu-Tue Mar-Oct;) At the foot of the village, overlooking Zahara's reservoir, British-American-run Al Lago serves Andalucian cuisine with an inventive, contemporary slant. Seasonal, often-organic regional ingredients star in creations ranging from beautifully prepared flatbread pizzas, mountain-cheese platters and local trout to chef Stefan's six-course tasting menus (€42), all expertly paired with Cádiz and Málaga wines. Excellent vegetarian and gluten-free options.

Also here are six subtly chic lake-view rooms and two kitchen-equipped **apartments** (incl breakfast d €85-117, f €98-110, apt €82-92; Mar-Oct;).

Information

Punto de Información Zahara de la Sierra
(956 12 31 14; Plaza del Rey 3; 10am-2pm Tue-Sun) Basic info on Zahara and the Parque Natural Sierra de Grazalema offered by a private agency.

Getting There & Away

Comes (p123) runs two daily weekday buses to/from Ronda (€4.60, 45 to 75 minutes).

Parque Natural Sierra de Grazalema

The rugged, pillar-like peaks of the Parque Natural Sierra de Grazalema rise abruptly from the plains northeast of Cádiz, revealing sheer gorges, rare firs, wild orchids and the province's highest summits, against a beautifully green backdrop at altitudes of 260m to 1648m. This is the wettest part of Spain – stand aside, Galicia and Cantabria, Grazalema village logs an average 2200mm annually. It's gorgeous walking country (best months: May, June, September and October), and, for the more intrepid, adventure activities abound.

The 534-sq-km park, named Spain's first Unesco Biosphere Reserve in 1977, extends into northwestern Málaga province, where it includes the Cueva de la Pileta (p183) near Benaoján.

Activities

Hiking, caving, canyoning, kayaking, rock climbing, cycling, birdwatching, horse riding, paragliding, vie ferrate – this beautiful protected area crams it all in. For the more technical stuff, go with a guide; Grazalema's Horizon (p138) is a respected adventure-activity outfits. Horse riding can be arranged through Tambor del Llano (p138), 6km southeast of Grazalema (one hour/day €30/120).

The Sierra de Grazalema is criss-crossed by 20 official marked trails. Four of the best – the Garganta Verde, El Pinsapar, Llanos del Rabel (6.2km) and El Torreón paths – enter restricted areas and require (free) permits from the **Centro de Visitantes El Bosque** (956 70 97 33; www.juntadeandalucia.es; Calle Federico García Lorca 1, El Bosque; 10am-2pm, closed Mon Jun-Sep). Ideally, book a month or two ahead. The centre will email permits with minimum 14 days' notice; communication may be in English or French, but permits are in Spanish. Additional (leftover) permits are sometimes available on the day; you can ask ahead by phone or email, but you'll have to collect them at the Centro or Grazalema's tourist office on the day (Garganta Verde permits are only available through the Centro in El Bosque). From 1 June to 15 October, some trails are fully or partly off limits due to fire risk; El Torreón is completely off limits, while the Garganta Verde and El Pinsapar are partly accessible on guided hikes with park-authorised operators.

The Centro de Visitantes El Bosque, Grazalema's tourist office and the unofficial Punto de Información Zahara de la Sierra (p141) have maps outlining the main walking possibilities. There's downloadable Spanish- and English-language hiking information online at www.juntadeandalucia.es.

★Garganta Verde HIKING

The 2.5km path that meanders into the precipitous Garganta Verde (Green Gorge), a lushly vegetated gorge over 100m deep, is one of the Sierra de Grazalema's most spectacular walks. Enormous griffon vultures, whose feathers ruffle in the wind as they whoosh by, make the one-hour descent even more dramatic (this is one of Europe's largest colonies). The best viewpoint is 30 minutes in.

At the bottom of the ravine, you follow the riverbed to an eerie cavern known as the **Cueva de la Ermita**. Then it's a 1½-hour climb back up. The trail starts 3.5km south of Zahara de la Sierra, at Km 10 on the CA9104 to/from Grazalema. You'll need a prebooked permit from the Centro de Visitantes El Bosque (p141); the route is partly off limits 1 June to 15 October.

El Pinsapar Walk HIKING

The 12km El Pinsapar route to Benamahoma starts from a car park 2km uphill (northwest) from Grazalema, 1km along the CA9104 to Zahara de la Sierra. Keep an eye out for the rare dark-green *pinsapo,* a relic of the great Mediterranean fir forests of the Tertiary period, which survives only in southwest Andalucía and northern Morocco. Allow 4½ hours one way.

El Torreón Walk HIKING

(⏲16 Oct-May) El Torreón (1648m) is Cádiz province's highest peak and, on clear days, from the summit you can see Gibraltar, Granada's Sierra Nevada and Morocco's Rif mountains. The challenging 3km route starts 100m east of Km 40 on the Grazalema–Benamahoma A372, 8km west of Grazalema. It's about 2½ hours to the summit.

Zero Gravity ADVENTURE SPORTS

(☎615 372554; www.paraglidingspain.eu; Avenida de la Constitución 44, Algodonales; 1-week courses €885) Little-known Algodonales, 6km north of Zahara de la Sierra, surprises as a major paragliding and hang-gliding centre of Andalucía. Long-standing Zero Gravity offers an extensive range of beginner and 'refresher' paragliding programs, plus 30-minute tandem flights with instructors (€90).

Olvera

POP 7930 / ELEV 643M

Topped by a Moorish-era castle, Olvera (27km northeast of Zahara de la Sierra) beckons from miles away across olive-tree-covered country. Reconquered by Alfonso XI in 1327, this relatively untouristed town was a bandit refuge until the mid-19th century. People (mostly Spaniards) come to Olvera to walk or cycle the Vía Verde de la Sierra, but, as a white town par excellence, it's also renowned for its olive oil (you may be able to visit local producers), two striking churches and history, which probably started with the Romans.

Sights

Castillo Árabe CASTLE

(Plaza de la Iglesia; incl La Cilla €2; ⏲10.30am-2pm & 4-8pm Tue-Sun Jun–mid-Sep, 10.30am-2pm & 4-6pm Tue-Sun mid-Sep–May) Perched on a crag 623m high above town is Olvera's late-12th-century castle, which later formed part of Nasrid-era Granada's defensive systems. The surrounding web of narrow streets, the Barrio de la Villa, was once the Moorish medina (narrow, maze-like old section of the town).

La Cilla MUSEUM

(Plaza de la Iglesia; incl Castillo Árabe €2; ⏲10.30am-2pm & 4-8pm Tue-Sun Jun–mid-Sep, 10.30am-2pm & 4-6pm Tue-Sun mid-Sep–May) The old grain store of the Duques de Osuna, next to the castle, houses the tourist office, the fascinating **Museo de la Frontera y los Castillos** (devoted to Olvera's turbulent history and the Reconquista), a small archaeological collection, and an exposition on the nearby Vía Verde de la Sierra cycling/hiking path.

Iglesia Parroquial Nuestra Señora de la Encarnación CHURCH

(Plaza de la Iglesia; €2; ⏲11am-1pm & 4-6pm Tue-Sun) Built over a Gothic-Mudéjar predecessor, Olvera's neoclassical top-of-the-town church was commissioned by the Duques de Osuna and completed in 1841.

Sleeping & Eating

No 31 B&B €€

(☎856 09 21 83; www.no31olvera.com; Calle Maestro Amado 31; r incl breakfast €70-75; ❄📶) A charming boutique conversion of a 19th-century townhouse, adults-only No 31 has three intimate rooms with original tiling, wooden beams and whitewashed walls. Just downhill from the castle (which you'll spy from the roof terrace); breakfasts are a delight.

DON'T MISS

VÍA VERDE DE LA SIERRA

The 36km **Vía Verde de la Sierra** (www.viasverdes.com) between Olvera and Puerto Serrano (to the west) is regularly touted as the finest of Spain's *vías verdes*, greenways that have transformed old railway lines into traffic-free thoroughfares for bikers, hikers and horse riders. It's one of 23 such *vías* in Andalucía, which together total 500km. Aside from the wild, rugged scenery, this route is notable for four spectacular viaducts, 30 tunnels (some with sensor-activated lighting) and three old stations transformed into hotel-restaurants, and is partly accessible for wheelchair users (see www.viasverdesaccesibles.es).

The **Hotel Vía Verde de la Sierra** (956 12 19 10; www.hotelviaverdedelasierra.es; Calle Pasadera 4; d/tr €60/70, 2-/6-person apt €90/130;), 1km north of Olvera, is the route's official eastern starting point. Here, **Sesca** (657 987432, 687 676462; www.sesca.es; regular/electric bike hire per day €10/20; 9am-2pm & 4-6pm Oct-May, reduced hours Jun-Sep;) rents bicycles, including tandems, kids' bikes, electric bikes and chariots, and you can check out the **Centro de Interpretación Vía Verde de la Sierra** (www.fundacionviaverdedelasierra.es; adult/child €2/1; 10am-2pm Mon & Fri, 9am-2pm Thu, 9am-5pm Sat & Sun). Bike hire is also available at Coripe (679 613069) and Puerto Serrano (678 107526) stations; call a day or two ahead. Note that the restaurants (but not the bike-hire facilities) close Monday in Olvera and Wednesday in Coripe.

A highlight of the Vía Verde is the **Peñón de Zaframagón**, a distinctive crag that's a prime breeding ground for griffon vultures. The **Centro de Interpretación y Observatorio Ornitológico** (956 13 63 72; www.fundacionviaverdedelasierra.es; Antigua Estación de Zaframagón; adult/child €2/1; 9am-3pm Mon-Wed, 10am-2pm Thu & Fri, 10am-2pm & 3-5pm Sat & Sun), in the former Zaframagón station building 16km west of Olvera, allows close-up observations by means of a high-definition camera placed up on the crag.

Information

Oficina de Turismo (665 940087, 956 12 08 16; www.olvera.es; Plaza de la Iglesia; 10.30am-2pm & 4-8pm Tue-Sun Jun–mid-Sep, 10.30am-2pm & 4-6pm Tue-Sun mid-Sep–May)

Getting There & Away

Damas (p123) runs one daily bus to/from Jerez de la Frontera (€9.12, 2½ hours) and Ronda (€5.55, 1¼ hours), and only daily weekday buses to/from Málaga (€12, 2¼ hours). Comes (p123) has one daily bus Monday to Friday to/from Cádiz (€15, 3¼ hours).

SOUTHEAST CÁDIZ PROVINCE & THE COSTA DE LA LUZ

Arriving on the Costa de la Luz from the Costa del Sol is like flinging open the window and breathing in the glorious fresh air. Bereft of tacky resorts and unplanned development, this is a world of flat-capped farmers, wind turbines and glugs of dry sherry with lunchtime tapas. Throw in beautiful blonde, windswept beaches and a string of spectacularly located white towns, and you're unequivocally in Andalucía. A buzzing surfing/kitesurfing scene and some of southern Spain's most thrilling hotels add to the appeal. Spaniards, well aware of this, flock to places like Tarifa, Zahara de los Atunes and Los Caños de Meca in July and August. It's by no means a secret, but the gleaming Costa de la Luz remains the same old laid-back beachy hang-out it's always been, admittedly with a little upmarket flair creeping in around Vejer de la Frontera.

The Costa de la Luz continues west into neighbouring Huelva province (p97), up to the Portugal border.

Vejer de la Frontera

POP 9090

Vejer – the jaw drops, the eyes blink, the eloquent adjectives dry up. Looming moodily atop a rocky hill above the busy N340, 50km south of Cádiz, this serene, compact white town is something special. Yes, there's a labyrinth of twisting old-town streets encircled by imposing 15th-century walls, some serendipitous viewpoints, a ruined castle, a booming culinary scene, a smattering of dreamy hotels and a tangible Moorish influence. But Vejer also has something special: an air of magic and mystery, an imperceptible touch of *duende* (spirit).

Sights & Activities

Plaza de España SQUARE

With its elaborate 20th-century, Seville-tiled fountain and perfectly white town hall, Vejer's palm-studded, cafe-filled Plaza de España is a favourite hang-out.

Castillo CASTLE

(Calle del Castillo; 10am-2pm & 5-9pm approx May-Sep, 10am-2pm & 4-8pm approx Oct-Apr) FREE Vejer's much-reworked castle, once home of the Duques de Medina Sidonia, dates from the 10th or 11th century. You can wander through the Moorish entrance arch, past the original rainwater *aljibe,* and climb the hibiscus-fringed ramparts for fantastic views across town to the white-sand coastline.

Estatua de la Cobijada STATUE

(Calle Trafalgar) Just below the castle is a lookout guarded by this statue of a woman dressed in Vejer's cloak-like, all-black traditional dress, the *cobijada,* which covers the entire body except the right eye. Despite its similarities to Islamic clothing, the *cobijada* is believed to be of 16th- or 17th-century Christian origin.

Iglesia del Divino Salvador CHURCH

(Plaza Padre Ángel; mass 8.30pm Mon-Wed & Fri, 9pm Sat & Sun) Built atop an earlier mosque, this unusual church is 14th-century Mudéjar at the altar end and 16th-century Gothic at the other. In the late afternoon the sun shines surreally through its stained-glass windows, projecting multicoloured light above the altar.

Museo de Vejer MUSEUM

(956 55 33 99; Calle Marqués de Tamarón 10; adult/child €2.50/free; 10am-2pm & 6-10pm Mon-Sat May-Sep, 10am-2pm & 4-6pm Oct-Apr) Housed in a 17th- to 18th-century mansion, Vejer's museum has a small, impressive history and archaeology collection, running from the area's early Paleolithic inhabitants to Roman and Moorish times to the civil war.

★ **Annie B's Spanish Kitchen** COOKING

(620 560649; www.anniebspain.com; Calle Viñas 11; 1-day course €155) Master the art of Andalucian cooking with sherry educator and local-cuisine expert Annie Mansion, whose popular day classes (Andalucian, Moroccan, seafood) end with lunch by the pool or on the roof terrace at her gorgeous old-town house. Annie also runs multiday cooking courses, Morocco day trips, and tapas, food and sherry tours of Vejer, Cádiz and Jerez.

Sleeping

Some of Andalucía's most fabulous hotels are tucked away in Vejer's old town and the surrounding countryside.

★ **La Casa del Califa** BOUTIQUE HOTEL €€

(956 44 77 30; www.califavejer.com; Plaza de España 16; incl breakfast r €100-165, ste €170-250; P) Rambling over several floors of labyrinthine corridors, this gorgeous hotel is Vejer's original hideaway, inhabiting a 16th-century building with its roots in the 10th century. The 20 calming rooms take inspiration from North Africa: antique furniture, original arches, terracotta-tiled floors. Special 'emir' service (€46) brings flowers, pastries and *cava* (sparkling wine). Breakfast is a local-focused feast in the fabulous Moroccan–Middle Eastern restaurant.

A Califa-team *hammam* is due in 2021.

★ **Casa Shelly** BOUTIQUE HOTEL €€

(639 118831; www.casashelly.com; Calle Eduardo Shelly 6; r €85-140; Mar-Oct;) All quiet, understated Scandi-Andalucian style, adults-only Casa Shelly feels as though it's wandered out of an interior-design magazine and into the thick of Vejer's old town. Beyond a peaceful lounge and fountain-bathed patio, the gorgeously converted mid-18th-century townhouse has seven design-led rooms with original wooden doors, antique-inspired tiles, wood-beamed ceilings, vintage Swedish furniture and queen-size beds, in dusty pinks, blues and greys. Coffee, tea and snacks included.

★ **La Fonda Antigua** BOUTIQUE HOTEL €€

(625 372616; www.chicsleepinvejer.com; Calle San Filmo 14; r incl breakfast €85-150;) A *jerezano* couple with an eye for interiors runs this adults-only boutique bolthole on the fringes of Vejer's old town. In the 11 all-different rooms, antique doors morph into bedheads, mismatched vintage tiles dot polished-concrete floors, and cheeky features include glass-walled showers and, for several, free-standing baths. The rooftop terrace, where Vejer-produce breakfasts are served, opens up sprawling old-town panoramas.

★ **Plaza 18** BOUTIQUE HOTEL €€€

(956 44 77 30; www.califavejer.com; Plaza de España 18; r incl breakfast €187-300; P) This 2019-opened boutique beauty is a luxe, six-room conversion of an 1896 merchant's house built atop a 13th-century home. The soothing entrance patio, with original check-print tiles and light well, sets the tone for boldly, indi-

vidually styled rooms with beamed ceilings, colour-feature walls, luxury furnishings, rain showers, international art and Vejer-scented toiletries. Solar power, organic building materials and aerothermal heating systems are key.

Breakfast nextdoor at La Casa del Califa.

V... BOUTIQUE HOTEL €€€
(☎956 45 17 57; www.hotelv-vejer.com; Calle Rosario 11-13; r €153-329; ❄📶) V... (for Vejer) is an exquisite creation: a beautifully restored 17th-century mansion set around a leafy patio, high above which a view-laden rooftop with sunbeds and hot tub awaits. Creative contemporary design (open-plan bathrooms, chic tubs, oversized mirrors) mixes with antiques in the 12 neutral-toned rooms, and breakfast (€10) arrives on enormous trays. The ancient *aljibe* is now a massage room.

Eating

Vejer has quietly morphed into a gastronomic highlight of Andalucía, where you can just as happily tuck into traditional, age-old recipes as Moroccan-fusion dishes.

Mercado de Abastos ANDALUCIAN €
(Calle San Francisco; dishes €2-8; ⏱noon-4pm & 8pm-midnight) Now glammed up gastrobar-style, Vejer's early-20th-century Mercado de San Francisco has become a buzzy foodie hotspot full of world-wandering stalls. Grab a *vino* and choose between Andalucian classics and contemporary twists: Iberian ham *raciones, tortilla de patatas,* fried fish in paper cups and popular sushi.

★**El Jardín del Califa** MOROCCAN €€
(☎956 45 17 06; www.califavejer.com; Plaza de España 16; mains €12-18; ⏱1-4pm & 8-11.30pm; ✎) Sizzling atmosphere and flawless cooking combine at this beautiful restaurant hidden within a cavernous 16th-century, Moorish-origin house where even finding the bathroom is a full-on adventure; it's also a fabulous hotel and *tetería* (teahouse). The seasonal, local-produce Moroccan–Middle Eastern menu – tagines, couscous, hummus, falafel – is crammed with Maghreb flavours (saffron, figs, almonds). Book ahead, for the palm-sprinkled garden or the moody interior.

★**Corredera 55** ANDALUCIAN €€
(☎956 45 18 48; www.califavejer.com; Calle de la Corredera 55; mains €11-22; ⏱noon-11.30pm; ✎) Exquisitely styled with boho-chic Vejer flair, Corredera 55 delivers elegant, inventive seasonal cuisine packed with local, organic ingredients and Cádiz-meets-international flavours. Andalucian wines pair perfectly with creations like mushroom-garlic risotto, cauliflower fritters with honey-yoghurt dressing, or *cava*-baked prawn-stuffed fish of the day.

> **DON'T MISS**
>
> **SANTA LUCÍA DINING**
>
> A 5km drive north of Vejer, the peaceful leafy hamlet of Santa Lucía, washed by a freshwater spring and some 15th-century water mills, hosts two of the area's top restaurants. With a lovely shaded terrace and thatched interior, family-owned 1945-founded **Venta El Toro** (☎956 45 14 07; www.facebook.com/ventaeltoro; tapas €2-3, mains €6-10; ⏱9.30am-9pm Wed-Mon) is loved for its fried farm-fresh eggs with hand-cut chips and other typically *vejeriego* goodies, including delicious breakfasts made with bread from Conil. Across the road at **Restaurante Castillería** (☎956 45 14 97; www.restaurantecastilleria.com; ⏱1.30-4pm Mar-Nov), courtesy of Juan and Ana Valdés, you can feast on succulent, expertly executed wood-fired meats sourced from responsible small-scale farms across Spain.

La Judería ANDALUCIAN €€
(☎956 90 74 71; www.facebook.com/laJuderiadeVejer; Calle Judería 3A; raciones €7-11, mains €10-25; ⏱noon-11.30pm Tue-Sun; 📶✎) Andalucian wines and fresh local produce take centre stage at this lively rustic-chic tapas bar/restaurant, with a sunny upstairs terrace and tables under the arches on one of Vejer's prettiest streets. Try local favourites such as *payoyo* cheese and *papas aliñás,* or international-inspired bites like falafel with tzatziki or flambéed tuna belly in black garlic.

Entertainment

Peña Flamenca 'Aguilar de Vejer' FLAMENCO
(☎956 45 07 89, 606 171732; Calle Rosario 29) Vejer's small-town flamenco scene is best experienced at this atmospheric bar and performance space founded in 1989. Free shows usually happen on Saturday at 9.30pm; book in for dinner (mains €12 to €23) or swing by for drinks and tapas (€6). The tourist office has schedules.

Information

Oficina Municipal de Turismo (☎956 45 17 36; www.turismovejer.es; Avenida Los Remedios 2;

WORTH A TRIP

MEDINA SIDONIA

An air of dwindling majesty sweeps through the wind-lashed, whitewashed streets of Medina Sidonia (population 10,170). This strategic hilltop town, 30km north of Vejer de la Frontera, was once the seat of the Duques de Medina Sidonia – one of Spain's most powerful families. Today, a slowly growing number of Spanish visitors are making their way here, yet Medina Sidonia remains largely off southern Andalucía's beaten track. With its fascinating historical sights, rich culinary heritage and guided tours (adult/child €6/3) with the ambitious tourism **team** (☎956 41 24 04; www.turismomedinasidonia.es; Calle San Juan; ⊙10.30am-2pm & 5.30-7.30pm Jun-Sep, 10.30am-2pm & 4.30-6.30pm Oct-May), it's very much worth exploring.

In the hilltop historic core, approached through the Moorish **Arco de Belén** (Calle Cilla) – one of three still-standing gates from this era – you'll find the 16th-century **Iglesia Santa María Mayor** (Plaza de la Iglesia Mayor; €2.50; ⊙11am-2pm & 5.30-8pm Mon-Fri, 11am-2pm & 4-8pm Sat Jun-Sep, 11am-2pm & 4-7pm Mon-Sat Oct-May); its Renaissance door gives way to a hushed Gothic-Mudéjar cloister, and the interior shines with a 22-image, plateresque main altarpiece, completed in 1584, and a 17th-century Cristo del Perdón (Christ of Forgiveness) carving by Sevillan baroque sculptor Pedro Roldán. Crowning Medina Sidonia is a Roman military fortress turned 11th-century Almoravid *alcázar* turned ruined 15th-century medieval **castle** (Calle Ducado de Medina Sidonia; adult/child €2/free; ⊙10am-2pm & 7pm-sunset Jun-Sep, 10am-2pm & 4-6pm Fri-Wed Oct-May). At the town-centre **Museo Arqueológico** (Calle Ortega 11; adult/child €3.50/free; ⊙10am-2pm & 6-9pm Jun-Sep, 10am-2pm & 4-6pm Thu-Tue Oct-May), you can see four well-preserved cryptoporticus and the excavated 1st-century *Cardo Maximus*, the main Roman street.

If you fancy staying overnight, **La Vista de Medina** (☎956 41 00 69; www.lavistademedina.com; Plaza de la Iglesia Mayor 2; d €60-110, q €80-110; ❄ 📶 🏊) has six rustic-chic, apartment-like rooms and two soothing pools in hibiscus-filled, fountain-washed gardens, plus a good Andalucian-international restaurant (mains €9 to €20) emphasising local produce and with horizon-reaching views.

Medina Sidonia has CMTBC (p123) buses to/from Cádiz (€5.25, 1¼ hours, two to three daily) and Jerez de la Frontera (€2.80, 45 minutes, three daily weekdays).

⊙10am-2.30pm & 4.30-9pm Mon-Sat, 10am-2pm Sun, reduced hours Oct-Apr)

Getting There & Away

Bus From Avenida Los Remedios, Comes (p123) runs buses to Cádiz, Zahara de los Atunes, Jerez and Seville. All other buses stop at La Barca de Vejer, on the N340 at the bottom of the hill; then it's a steep 20-minute walk or €6 taxi to town.

Destination	Cost (€)	Time	Frequency
Cádiz	5.96	1¼hr	5 daily
Jerez de la Frontera	8.01	1½hr	daily Mon-Fri
La Línea (for Gibraltar)	9.11	1¾hr	up to 6 daily
Seville	18	2¼hr	4 daily
Seville (from Ave Los Remedios)	17	3hr	daily
Tarifa	4.55	40min	8 daily
Zahara de los Atunes	2.57	25min	at least 1 daily

Los Caños de Meca & El Palmar

POP 150 (LOS CAÑOS DE MECA), 670 (EL PALMAR)

Little laid-back Los Caños de Meca, 16km southwest of Vejer, straggles along a series of spectacular white-sand beaches. Once a hippie haven, Caños still attracts beach lovers of all kinds and nations – especially in summer – with its alternative, hedonistic scene and nudist beaches, as well as kitesurfing, windsurfing and board-surfing opportunities. Immediately northwest is the beach resort of **Zahora** and, northwest again, the salt-white sands of surfer beach **El Palmar**, which gets busy in summer with surf schools, beach bars, yoga, horse riding and more.

Sights & Activities

Caños' **main beach** is straight in front of Avenida de Trafalgar's junction with the A2233. Nudists head to its eastern end for more secluded coves, including **Playa de las Cortinas**, and to **Playa del Faro** beside Cabo de Trafalgar. Broad, blonde **Playa de Zahora** extends northwest from Los Caños. About 7km northwest of Los Caños, lovely **El Palmar beach** has Andalucía's best board-surfing waves from October to May; at its southern end is nudist **Playa de la Mangueta**, accessible on foot.

★Parque Natural de la Breña y Marismas del Barbate NATURE RESERVE
(www.juntadeandalucia.es) This 50-sq-km coastal park protects important marshes, cliffs and pine forest from Costa del Sol–type development. Its main entry point is a 7.2km (two-hour) walking trail, the **Sendero del Acantilado**, between Los Caños de Meca and Barbate, along clifftops that rival Cabo de Gata in their beauty.

Cabo de Trafalgar LIGHTHOUSE
At the western end of Los Caños de Meca, a side road (often half-covered in sand) leads out to an 1860 **lighthouse** on a low spit of land. This is the famous Cabo de Trafalgar, off which Spanish naval power was swiftly terminated by a British fleet under Admiral Nelson in 1805.

Escuela de Surf 9 Pies SURFING, YOGA
(☎620 104241; www.escueladesurf9pies.com; Paseo Marítimo; board & wetsuit rental per 2/4hr €12/18, 2hr group class €28) A professional surf school offering board hire and surf classes for all levels, plus yoga sessions (€10) and SUP rental (€15 for two hours), towards the northern end of El Palmar beach.

Sleeping & Eating

Hotel Madreselva HOTEL €€
(☎956 43 72 55; www.califavejer.com; Avenida de Trafalgar 102; d €75-135; ⊙Apr–mid-Oct; P) Strung around a leafy courtyard, this mellow, peachy-orange hacienda-style hideaway has 18 charmingly rustic rooms with surfy vibes, vintage furniture and private terraces. There's a summer-only Spanish restaurant, all just a minute's walk from Caños' beach.

Las Dunas CAFE €
(☎956 43 72 03; www.barlasdunas.es; Carretera del Cabo de Trafalgar; dishes €4-12; ⊙9am-midnight Sep-Jun, to 3am Jul & Aug;) The ultimate relaxation spot, where kitesurfers kick back between sessions on the beach beside the Cabo de Trafalgar. There is Bob Marley on the speakers, great *bocadillos* (filled rolls), fresh juices, *platos combinados* and a laid-back, beach-shack feel, plus occasional concerts.

Casa Juan ANDALUCIAN €€
(☎956 23 20 99; www.barrestaurantecasajuan.com; Paseo Marítimo; raciones €8-12, mains €12-16; ⊙noon-midnight) Now a stylishly contemporary space looking out on southern El Palmar's beach, long-established Casa Juan specialises in elegant renditions of Atlantic bluefin *almadraba* tuna, from *atún encebollado* (stewed with onions) to grilled tuna belly. Other Cádiz favourites include *tortillitas de camarones*, *payoyo* cheese, grilled prawns and fresh fish.

Getting There & Away

Comes (p123) has at least two daily weekday buses from Los Caños de Meca to Cádiz (€6, 1½ hours) via El Palmar (€2, 15 minutes).

Zahara de los Atunes

POP 1060

About 20km southeast of Los Caños de Meca, Zahara de los Atunes fronts a fantastic 12km-long, west-facing sweep of white-gold sand. For years a traditional fishing village famous for its Atlantic bluefin *almadraba* tuna, today Zahara is a popular, easy-going summer beach hang-out that's forging its way into the local culinary scene, with several annual gastronomic festivals. Zahara's tiny old core of narrow streets and lively bars centres on the ruined 15th-century **Castillo de las Almadrabas** (Avenida Hermanos Doctores Sánchez Rodríguez), where the tuna catch was once processed. In summer, a few *chiringuitos* (beach bars) spill out onto the sand; the rest of the year, things are quiet.

Southeast of Zahara is the more developed resort of **Atlanterra**, from the south end of which you can walk to secluded Playa El Cañuelo (p148) via the Camarinal lighthouse.

Sleeping & Eating

Taberna de El Campero SEAFOOD €€
(☎956 43 90 36; www.latabernadelcampero.com; Calle María Luisa 6; tapas €5-9, raciones €14-25; ⊙Apr-Sep) From the super-star team behind Barbate seafood sensation El Campero (p148), this cheery contemporary tavern puts the spotlight on the region's famous Atlantic bluefin *almadraba* tuna, here served tapas-style with flair – everything from grilled tuna belly to tuna ceviche to beautiful sushi platters. The rest of the menu is also fired by local, seasonal ingredients: *payoyo* cheese, fried squid, grilled prawns.

THE GREAT ALMADRABA

One of the joys of Cádiz cuisine is the fresh Atlantic bluefin tuna caught using the traditional ancient *almadraba* method, introduced by the Phoenicians. The *almadraba* is considered one of the world's most sustainable fishing methods, with nets tied to the seabed and raised only once a day during wild-tuna migration season (May/June). **El Campero** (☎650 420792; www.restauranteelcampero.es; Avenida de la Constitución 5C; raciones & mains €11-25; ⏲12.30-5pm & 8pm-midnight Tue-Sun) in Barbate (9km southeast of Vejer) is known as 'the temple of tuna' for its superb contemporary-twist *almadraba* dishes such as tuna-back ceviche and *jamón marino* (salted tuna belly). But you'll find *almadraba* tuna on menus all over Cádiz, especially along the Costa de la Luz, and many towns host Ruta del Atún festivals in May or June, when restaurants compete for the best tuna tapa – the festival in Zahara de los Atunes (p147) is particularly popular. Vejer-based Annie B's Spanish Kitchen (p144) organises *almadraba* tours.

Restaurante Antonio SEAFOOD €€€
(☎956 43 95 42; www.restauranteantoniozahara.com; Bahía de la Plata, Km 1, Atlanterra; mains €15-30; ⏲1.30-4pm & 8-11pm Feb–mid-Dec) Prize-winning Antonio, 1km south of Zahara, is wildly recommended for its top-quality seafood, attentive staff and sparkling modern-design sea-view setting. *Almadraba* bluefin tuna, of course, is the star, dished up in incarnations from *atún encebollado* to sashimi. The tuna tartare is a speciality. It's also a hotel (well, two, technically), with beach-facing pool and bright rooms (including breakfast €100 to €212), many graced by Atlantic views.

Getting There & Away

Comes (p123) runs three daily buses to Vejer (€2.57, 25 minutes) and three to four to Cádiz (€8.40, two hours), and usually one daily weekday bus to/from Los Caños de Meca (€2, 30 minutes). Additional buses may run in summer.

Bolonia

POP 90

Tiny Bolonia village, off the N340 15km northwest of Tarifa, overlooks a gloriously white beach framed by a large dune, rolling pine-dotted or field-covered hills, and the impressive Roman remains of Baelo Claudia. From a small parking area 3km west of Baelo Claudia, along the CA8202, a 1.5km dirt track leads down to the Faro Camarinal, from where you can access quiet, nudist-friendly **Playa El Cañuelo**.

In July and August, three weekday Horizonte Sur (p149) buses run between Bolonia and Tarifa (€2.50, 30 to 40 minutes).

★Baelo Claudia ARCHAEOLOGICAL SITE
(☎956 10 67 97; www.museosdeandalucia.es; EU/non-EU citizens free/€1.50; ⏲9am-9pm Tue-Sat Apr–mid-Jun, 9am-3pm & 6-9pm Tue-Sat mid-Jun–Jul, 9am-3pm Tue-Sat Aug–mid-Sep, 9am-6pm Tue-Sat Sep-Mar, 9am-3pm Sun year-round) The ruined town of Baelo Claudia is one of Andalucía's most important Roman archaeological sites. These majestic beachside ruins – with views across to Morocco – include the substantial remains of a theatre, a paved forum, thermal baths, a market and the columns of a basilica, and the workshops that turned out the products that made Baelo Claudia famous in the Roman world: salted fish and *garum* (spicy seasoning made from leftover fish parts). There's a good museum.

Las Rejas SEAFOOD €€
(☎685 010274, 956 68 85 46; www.lasrejasrestaurante.com; El Lentiscal; raciones €8-20; ⏲12.30-5.30pm & 8.30-11.30pm Wed-Sun May–mid-Oct, 12.30-5.30pm & 8.30-11.30pm Sat & Sun mid-Oct–Apr) A well-established, smartish spot just back from Bolonia's beach, specialising in super-fresh fish, salty paellas and superb Cádiz seafood *raciones* like grilled prawns or *tortillitas de camarones*.

Tarifa

POP 13,640

Tarifa's southern-tip-of-Spain location, where the Mediterranean and the Atlantic meet, gives it a different climate and character to the rest of Andalucía. Atlantic winds draw surfers, windsurfers and kitesurfers who, in turn, lend this ancient yet deceptively small settlement a refreshing, laid-back, international vibe. Tarifa is the last stop in Spain before Morocco, and is also a taste of things to come. With its winding whitewashed streets and North African feel, the walled windswept old town could easily pass for Chefchaouen or Essaouira. It's no secret, however, and, in August especially, Tarifa gets packed (that's half the fun).

Tarifa may be as old as Phoenician Cádiz and was definitely a Roman settlement. It takes its name from Tarif ibn Malik, who led a Muslim raid in 710 CE, the year before the main Islamic arrival on the peninsula.

Sights

Tarifa's narrow old-town streets, mostly of Moorish origin, hint at Morocco. Wander through the fortified Moorish **Puerta de Jerez**, embellished after the Reconquista, then pop into the lively neo-Mudéjar **Mercado de Abastos** (Calle Colón; 8.30am-2pm Tue-Sat) before winding your way past the whitewashed, 18th-century baroque-neoclassical **Iglesia de San Francisco de Asís** (Calle Santísima Trinidad; 7-8pm Mon-Fri) to the mainly 16th-century **Iglesia de San Mateo** (Calle Sancho IV El Bravo; 8.45am-1pm & 6-8.30pm May-Sep, 8.45am-1pm & 5.30-8pm Oct-Apr). Head south along Calle Coronel Moscardó, then up Calle Aljaranda; atop part of the castle walls, the **Miramar** (607 984871; Calle Amargura; 10am-4pm) has spectacular views across to Africa and 851m Jebel Musa, one of the 'Pillars of Hercules' (Gibraltar is the other).

Castillo de Guzmán el Bueno CASTLE
(Calle Guzmán el Bueno; adult/child €4/free; 10am-4pm) Though built in 960 on the orders of Cordoban caliph Abd ar-Rahman III, this restored fortress is named after Reconquista hero Guzmán el Bueno. In 1294, when threatened with the death of his captured son unless he surrendered the castle to Merenid attackers from Morocco, El Bueno threw down his own dagger for his son's execution. Guzmán's descendants later became the Duques de Medina Sidonia, one of Spain's most powerful families. Above the interior entrance, note the 10th-century castle-foundation inscription.

Activities

Kitesurfing & Windsurfing

Tarifa's legendary winds have turned the town into one of Europe's premier windsurfing and kitesurfing destinations. The most popular strip is along the coast between Tarifa and Punta Paloma, 10km northwest. Dozens of schools offer equipment hire and classes, from beginner to expert level. The best months are May, June and September, but bear in mind that the choppy seas aren't always beginners' territory. Some schools also offer SUP sessions.

ION Club Valdevaqueros WATER SPORTS
(619 340913; www.ion-club.net; Carretera N340, Km 76, Playa de Valdevaqueros; 6hr group kitesurfing or windsurfing beginner course €250; 10.30am-8.30pm Jul & Aug, to 7pm Jun & Sep, to 6.30pm Mar-May & Oct-Dec) Recommended daily group/private windsurfing and kitesurfing classes with multilingual instructors at beginner, intermediate or advanced level, along with kit rental (€90 per day) and paddle-boarding sessions (two-hour €40), 10km northwest of town. Windsurfing is usually from the ION Club's centre at the Hurrican Hotel 7km northwest of Tarifa.

TARIFA: BEACH BLISS

Jazzed up by the colourful kites and sails of kitesurfers and windsurfers whizzing across turquoise waves, with Morocco looming behind, the exquisite bleach-blonde beaches that stretch northwest from Tarifa along the N340 are some of Andalucía's (and Spain's) most beautiful. In summer they fill up with sun-kissed beach lovers and chill-out bars, though the relentless winds can be a hassle. If you tire of lazing on the sand, kitesurfing, windsurfing and horse riding await.

In July and August, **Horizonte Sur** (699 427644; http://horizontesur.es) runs 11 to 14 daily buses Monday to Saturday from Tarifa's bus station to Punta Paloma via the beaches.

Punta Paloma One of Andalucía's most fabulous beaches, 10km northwest of Tarifa; famous for its huge blonde sand dune. At its far western end, you can lather up in a natural mud bath.

Playa de Valdevaqueros Sprawling between 7km and 10km northwest of Tarifa, to the great white dune at Punta Paloma, Valdevaqueros is one of Tarifa's most popular kitesurfing beaches, blessed with dusty alabaster-hued sand, aqua waters and a few summer beach bars.

Playa de los Lances This broad snow-white sandy beach stretches for 7km northwest from Tarifa. The low dunes behind it are a *paraje natural* (protected natural area).

Tarifa

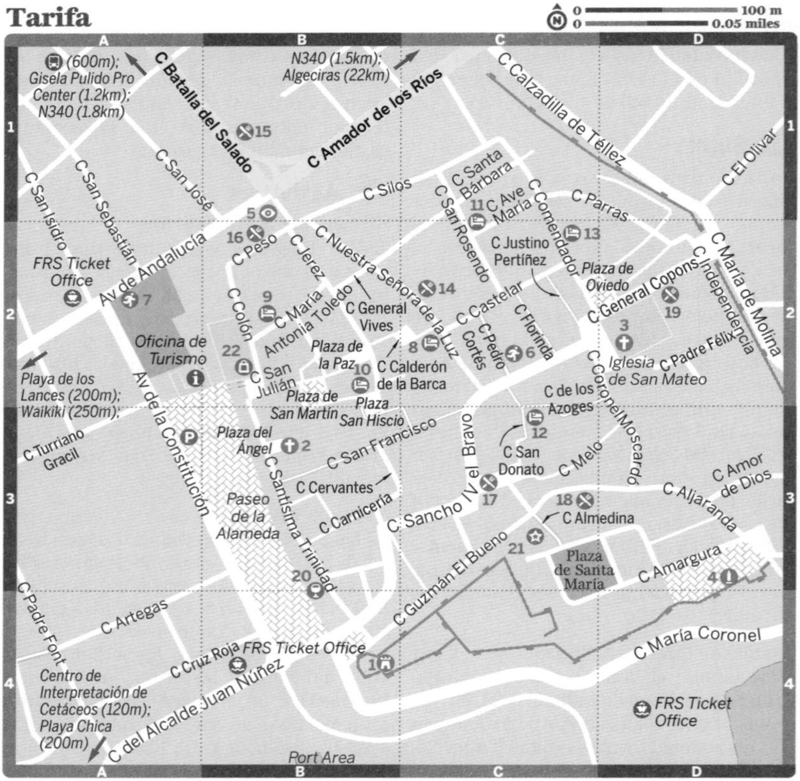

Tarifa

Sights

1 Castillo de Guzmán el Bueno B4
2 Iglesia de San Francisco de Asís B3
3 Iglesia de San Mateo D2
4 Miramar D3
5 Puerta de Jerez B1

Activities, Courses & Tours

6 FIRMM C2
7 OmShala A2

Sleeping

8 Aristoy Tarifa C2
9 Hostal África B2
10 La Casa de la Favorita B2
11 La Cocotera C2
12 Posada La Sacristía C3
13 Riad C2

Eating

14 Café 10 .... C2
15 Café Azul B1
16 Chilimosa B2
17 El Francés C3
18 El Lola C3
19 La Oca da Sergio D2

Drinking & Nightlife

20 La Ruina B3

Entertainment

21 Almedina C3

Shopping

22 Mercado de Abastos B2

Spin Out WATER SPORTS
(☎956 23 63 52; www.tarifaspinout.com; Carretera N340, Km 75.5, Playa de Valdevaqueros; 90min windsurfing class per person €59, board & sail rental per hr €30; ⏰10.30am-7pm Apr-Oct) Daily windsurfing classes and five-day courses (€349) for beginners, kids and experts, from a switched-on,

multilingual team, 11km northwest of town. There's also a kitesurfing school, plus SUP gear rental.

Whale-Watching

The waters off Tarifa are one of the best places in Europe to see whales and dolphins as they swim between the Atlantic and the Mediterranean from April to October; sightings of some kind are almost guaranteed during these months. In addition to striped and bottlenose dolphins, long-finned pilot whales, orcas and sperm whales, you may also spot endangered fin whales and common dolphins. Sperm whales swim the Strait of Gibraltar from April to August; the best months for orcas are July and August. Find out more at **Centro de Interpretación de Cetáceos** (956 68 29 65; www.facebook.com/CICAMTARIFA; Avenida Fuerzas Armadas 17; 10am-6pm Tue-Sun Apr-Oct) FREE.

FIRMM WHALE-WATCHING
(956 62 70 08; www.firmm.org; Calle Pedro Cortés 4; 2hr tours adult/child €30/20; Apr-Oct) Among Tarifa's dozens of whale-watching outfits, not-for-profit FIRMM is a good option. Its primary purpose is to study the whales and record data, which gives rise to environmentally sensitive two- or three-hour tours and week-long whale-watching courses. Book two to three days ahead.

Horse Riding

One-hour beach rides along Playa de los Lances cost €30 to €45 and two-hour beach-and-mountain rides cost €80. Excellent **Aventura Ecuestre** (626 480019, 956 23 66 32; www.aventuraecuestre.com; Carretera N340, Km 79.5, Hotel Dos Mares), 5km northwest of Tarifa, has multilingual guides and also offers pony rides for kids (30 minutes €20) and four-hour rides (€140) into the Parque Natural Los Alcornocales or across the Punta Paloma dunes. **Molino El Mastral** (679 193503; www.mastral.com; Carretera Santuario Virgen de la Luz; per hr €30), 5km north of Tarifa, is another reliable choice and also has modern-rustic self-catering apartments, €90 to €160, around a pool.

Yoga

Tarifa has an active yoga scene: **OmShala** (722 147636; www.omshalatarifa.com; Avenida de Andalucía 13; single class €15) is a popular hub, as is **Mandalablue Yoga** (644 772377; www.mandalablueyoga.es; single class €15), which specialises in open-air yoga on those blissful local beaches. Both centres offer drop-in sessions, plus in-depth workshops and retreats.

Sleeping

★ **Hostal África** HOSTAL €
(956 68 02 20; www.hostalafrica.com; Calle María Antonia Toledo 12; s €40-75, d €60-95, tr €90-120; Mar-Nov;) This mellow, revamped 19th-century house within Tarifa's old town is one of Cádiz province's best *hostales* (budget hotels). Full of potted plants and sky-blue-and-white arches, it's run by hospitable, on-the-ball owners, and the 13 unfussy, all-different rooms (including one triple) sparkle with bright colours. Enjoy the lovely roof terrace, with its loungey cabana and Africa views.

La Cocotera HOSTEL €
(956 68 22 19; www.lacocotera.com; Calle San Rosendo 12; dm €18-36, d €36-100, q €51-140;) At this popular hostel and coworking space full of digital nomads, the fruity-named, white-styled four-bunk dorms are crisp and spotless, with personal plugs and lights. Facilities include a well-equipped kitchen, two laptop-working spaces and a rooftop terrace with Morocco views; there are also private doubles.

Aristoy Tarifa BOUTIQUE HOTEL €€
(956 68 31 72; www.aristoytarifa.com; Calle Calderón de la Barca 3; r €90-225;) From the team behind several top Tarifa foodie ventures, the old-town Aristoy occupies a creatively revamped 18th-century building crowned by a terrace and plunge pool. Design combines the original beams and patio with polished concrete, bamboo touches and crisp white-on-white styling. A few rooms have terraces.

Posada La Sacristía BOUTIQUE HOTEL €€
(956 68 17 59; www.lasacristia.net; Calle San Donato 8; r incl breakfast €131-181;) A beautifully renovated 17th-century townhouse (once a Moorish stable) hosts this elegant historical-boutique find in the heart of town. Attention to detail is impeccable, with 10 stylishly updated rooms (four-poster beds, beamed ceilings, antique furniture) over two floors around a courtyard. Massages can be arranged, and, downstairs, there's a plush lounge for drinks and fuss-free tapas.

La Casa de la Favorita BOUTIQUE HOTEL €€
(690 180253; www.lacasadelafavorita.com; Plaza San Hiscio 4; r €85-125;) Sleek, all-white contemporary design sweeps through La Favorita's impeccable, boutique-inspired rooms, all with kitchenettes and coffee-makers. The best have balconies and/or terraces, while the suite is a two-level duplex-style affair. A small

library, a roof terrace and dynamic, colourful art add to the appeal.

Arte Vida HOTEL €€
(☎956 68 52 46; www.hotelartevidatarifa.com; Carretera N340, Km 79.3; r incl breakfast €95-170; P ❄ ☜) In a dreamy beachfront spot, 6km northwest of Tarifa, the Arte Vida has a deliciously laid-back feel and a handful of stripped-back, contemporary-design rooms with arty touches and cerulean walls. There's also a kitesurfing and windsurfing school, plus a good Mediterranean restaurant, a seasonal *chiringuito,* a lounge area and summer DJ sessions.

★**Riad** BOUTIQUE HOTEL €€€
(☎856 92 98 80; www.theriadtarifa.com; Calle Comendador 10; d €99-210) A seductively converted 17th-century townhouse, the Riad opens through a polished-concrete lobby adorned by an ornamental fountain/pool, fresh lilies and flickering candles. It's dressed with original architecture: exposed-stone walls, antique doors, red-brick arches, a frescoed facade. Off the patio are a *hammam*, a rooftop lounge and nine intimate rooms styled with *tadelakt* (waterproof plaster) walls, Morocco-made tiles and soothing Andalucía-meets-Morocco design.

Hotel Dos Mares HOTEL €€€
(☎956 68 40 35; www.dosmareshotel.com; Carretera N340, Km 79.5; r incl breakfast €95-250; P ❄ ☜ ≋) Opening onto blinding-white sands 5km northwest of town, Morocco-flavoured Dos Mares has bright, tile-floored rooms and bungalows washed in yellow, blue and burnt orange, some with sea-facing balconies. Other perks include a cafe, a gym, a pool, a kitesurfing school, a *chiringuito* and an excellent horse-riding school (p151).

Eating

Tarifa is full of good food with a strong international flavour: Italian, Moroccan and Middle Eastern in particular. Other Tarifa treats are smoothies, fusion food, organic ingredients, outstanding breakfasts and wonderful vegetarian/vegan meals.

★**Café Azul** CAFE €
(www.cafeazul-tarifa.com; Calle Batalla del Salado 8; dishes €2-9; ⊙9am-3pm; ☜ ✍) This long-established Italian-run cafe with eye-catching blue-and-white Morocco-inspired decor whips up some of the best breakfasts in Andalucía. You'll want to eat everything. The fruit salad with muesli, yoghurt and coconut, and the fruit-and-yoghurt-stuffed crêpe are works of art. It also serves Italian coffee, honey-sweetened teas, fresh smoothies and juices, *bocadillos* and cooked breakfasts, with delicious gluten-free and vegan options.

★**Surla** CAFE €
(☎956 68 51 75; www.facebook.com/surlatarifa; Calle Pintor Pérez Villalta 64; dishes €4-8; ⊙9am-5pm Mon-Fri, to 7pm Sat & Sun; ✍) Decorative surfboards, wall-mounted chairs and Balinese umbrellas fill the leafy, tropical-feel interior of this wonderful laid-back cafe, where the focus is on organic local, seasonal ingredients: *jamón* from Huelva's mountains, Granada olive oil, Cádiz' own free-range eggs, salt and *payoyo* cheese.

★**Tangana** INTERNATIONAL €
(☎606 415028; www.tanganatarifa.com; Carretera N340, Km 75.5, Playa de Valdevaqueros; dishes €6-12; ⊙10am-9pm Apr-Oct; ☜ ✍) Set around a boho-chic boutique and a series of chill-out lounges and self-catering bungalows, 11km northwest of Tarifa, this mellow bar-restaurant rustles up some of the best beachy bites in the Tarifa area. Turquoise-washed bench-style tables set a lazy-life scene for sipping mojitos and caipirinhas, or enjoying rustic *bocadillos,* creative salads, tuna tacos, seasonal paella and dreamy home-cooked breakfasts.

El Francés TAPAS €
(Calle Sancho IV el Bravo 21; raciones €7-13; ⊙12.30pm-midnight Fri-Tue Mar-Dec; ✍) Squeeze into the standing-room-only bar or battle for your terrace table at El Francés, which gives Andalucian classics a subtle twist. Tarifa's favourite tapas bar is a buzzing place, serving *patatas bravas* and *tortillitas de camarones* (shrimp fritters) alongside mini chicken-veg couscous or cheese-stuffed mushrooms. No reservations; pop in on the day to secure a table (dinner from 6.30pm only).

Café 10 CAFE €
(☎956 62 76 86; www.facebook.com/cafe10tarifa; Calle Nuestra Señora de la Luz 10; dishes €2-6; ⊙9am-2am, closed Jan; ☜ ✍) Old-town favourite Café 10 delivers the breakfast/snack goods in a snug, neo-rustic lounge with wall art and pink-cushioned chairs spilling out onto the sloping street. Tuck into homemade cakes, great coffee, fresh juices, sweet and salty crêpes, and *revueltos* (scrambles) and *molletes* (small toasted rolls). Later on, the G&Ts and mojitos come out.

Chilimosa VEGETARIAN €

(☎956 68 50 92; www.facebook.com/chilimosa; Calle Peso 6; mains €5-10; ⏲7pm-midnight Mon-Thu, 1-4.30pm & 7pm-midnight Fri-Sun, closed Jan-early Mar;) A cosy, casual vegetarian restaurant at the top of the old town, with just a handful of tables, Chilimosa is Tarifa at its low-key best. The unpretentious home-cooked Middle Eastern menu is fired by ingredients from the owners' garden, turning out such meat-free delights as spiced-vegetable samosas, falafel-hummus wraps, meze platters and tofu burgers. Takeaway, too.

El Lola TAPAS €€

(☎956 62 73 07; www.facebook.com/ElLolaTarifa; Calle Guzmán El Bueno 5; tapas €2-5, raciones €5-15; ⏲1-4pm & 7pm-midnight Apr-Oct;) With whitewashed walls and bright geraniums, busy El Lola is known for its delectable, lightly creative tapas and *raciones* of Atlantic bluefin *almadraba* tuna, from smooth tataki to a full degustation. Other temptations include just-cooked tortilla, grilled king prawns and croquettes stuffed with *ibérico* ham or spinach.

La Oca da Sergio ITALIAN €€

(☎615 686571; Calle General Copons 6; mains €8-19; ⏲1-4pm & 8pm-midnight daily Jun-Oct & Dec, reduced hours Jan-May) Amiable Sergio roams the tables Italian-style, armed with loaded plates and amusing stories, and presides over genuine home-country cooking at this popular spot tucked behind the Iglesia de San Mateo. Look forward to *caprese* salads, homemade pasta (try the truffle pappardelle), wood-oven thin-crust pizzas and after-dinner *limoncello.*

Drinking & Entertainment

Tarifa's busy bar scene centres on the old town's narrow Calles Cervantes, San Francisco and Santísima Trinidad. Summer *chiringuitos* get going with music/DJs on Playa de los Lances and the beaches northwest of town, particularly around sunset.

Tumbao LOUNGE

(www.facebook.com/tumbaotarifa; Carretera N340, Km 76, Playa de Valdevaqueros; ⏲10am-midnight Easter-Sep) The ultimate Tarifa-cool beach hang-out, Tumbao serves up cocktails, *tinto de verano,* and loungey sunset beats on a grassy, beanbag-strewn patch overlooking the kitesurfing action on Playa de Valdevaqueros, 10km northwest of town.

Waikiki LOUNGE

(☎956 79 90 15; https://waikikitarifa.com; Playa de los Lances; ⏲noon-late) Live music, DJ sets and sunny cocktails keep things busy at boho-cool beachfront lounge spot Waikiki, on the west side of the old town. Mojitos, daiquiris and other updated classics fill the menu, which also has excellent local-inspired dishes (€7 to €20) such as red-tuna tartare and goat's-cheese salad.

La Ruina CLUB

(www.facebook.com/LaRuinaTarifa; Calle Santísima Trinidad 2; ⏲midnight-3am Sun-Thu, to 4am Fri & Sat) One of Tarifa's favourite late-night haunts, this old-town ruin turned club amps things up with a steady early-hours diet of electro and house.

Almedina FLAMENCO

(☎956 68 04 74; www.facebook.com/almedina cafebar; Calle Almedina 3; ⏲8.30pm-midnight;) Built into the old city walls, cavernous bar Almedina squeezes a flamenco ensemble into its clamorous, stone-arched confines for its well-known Thursday sessions, usually at 10.30pm.

Information

Oficina de Turismo (☎956 68 09 93; www.turismodetarifa.com; Paseo de la Alameda; ⏲10am-1.30pm & 4-6pm Mon-Fri, 10am-1.30pm Sat & Sun)

Getting There & Away

BOAT

FRS (☎956 68 18 30; www.frs.es; Avenida de Andalucía 16; adult/child/car/motorcycle one way €45/15/125/33) runs six daily one-hour ferries between Tarifa and Tangier (Morocco). All passengers need a passport.

BUS

Comes (p123) operates from the **bus station** (☎956 68 40 38; Calle Batalla del Salado) beside the petrol station at the northwest end of town.

Destination	Cost (€)	Time	Frequency
Algeciras	2.45	30-60min	11-18 daily
Cádiz	11	1½hr	6 daily
Jerez de la Frontera	13	2½hr	2 daily
La Línea (for Gibraltar)	4.51	1hr	6 daily
Málaga	17-18	2½-3hr	3-4 daily
Seville	21	3-4hr	4 daily

ALGECIRAS: GATEWAY TO MOROCCO

The major port linking Spain with Africa is an ugly industrial fishing town famous for producing the greatest flamenco guitarist of the modern era, Paco de Lucía, who was born here in 1947 and died in 2014 in Playa del Carmen, Mexico. New arrivals usually leave quickly, by ferry to Morocco or bus to Tarifa or Málaga.

The **bus station** (Calle San Bernardo) is opposite the train station; the port is 600m east along Calle San Bernardo.

Buses from Algeciras

Destination	Price (€)	Time	Frequency
Cádiz	12	2hr	10-12 daily
Granada	27	3¾-5½hr	4 daily
Jerez de la Frontera	11	1-1½hr	6 daily
La Línea (for Gibraltar)	2.45	45min	every 30-45min
Málaga	15-19	1¾-3hr	19 daily
Málaga airport	18	2hr	3 daily
Seville	22	3½-4½	4 daily
Tarifa	2.45	30-60min	13-18 daily

Ferries from Algeciras

Ferries from Algeciras to Tangier drop you in Tangier Med, 40km east of Tangier itself, and are operated by **FRS** (☎956 68 18 30; www.frs.es) and **Trasmediterránea** (☎902 454645; www.trasmediterranea.es). Remember your passport when travelling to Tangier; no passport is required for trips to the Spanish Moroccan enclave of Ceuta, but you will need to show identification (such as a passport or national ID card) to board the ferry.

Destination	Ferry company	Price (one way) adult/child/car	Time	Frequency
Ceuta	FRS	€32/18/65	1hr	6 daily
Ceuta	Trasmediterránea	€34/20/114	1¼hr	5 daily
Tangier Med	FRS	€32/15/94	1½hr	8 daily
Tangier Med	Trasmediterránea	€20/15/109	1½hr	5 daily

Trains from Algeciras

Destination	Price (€)	Time	Frequency
Granada	32	4¼hr	3 daily
Madrid	40-60	6hr	3 daily
Ronda	12-20	1½hr	5 daily

Parque Natural Los Alcornocales

The 1736-sq-km Parque Natural Los Alcornocales is rich in archaeological, historical and natural interest, but it's still off Andalucía's beaten track. Stretching 75km north almost from the Strait of Gibraltar to the border of the Parque Natural Sierra de Grazalema (p141) and into Málaga province, it's a beautiful jumble of sometimes rolling, sometimes rugged medium-height hills, much of it covered in Spain's most extensive *alcornocales* (cork-oak woodlands), its fringes peppered by gorgeous white villages. There are plenty of rewarding walks (including along the long-distance Tarifa–Andorra GR7, part of the 10,000km cross-continental E4) and outdoor-activity options, but you'll need a car to explore the area properly.

Jimena de la Frontera, Cortes de la Frontera and Castellar de la Frontera, all along the park's eastern flank, make good bases (though the park is also easily accessible on day trips from nearby places like Tarifa). Jimena's romantically ruined 13th-century Nasrid **castle** (⏲9am-10pm Apr-Sep, to 8pm Oct-Mar) FREE, built on Roman ruins, once formed part of a defence line stretching from Olvera down through Setenil de las Bodegas, Zahara de la Sierra, Castellar and Algeciras to Tarifa.

Activities

Of the park's 22 official walking routes, five require (free) permits, including the 6.8km (3½-hour) trail up the park's highest peak Aljibe (1091m) and the 3.3km (two-hour) walk up the second-highest peak (El Picacho; 882m). The Travesía del Aljibe route, which also requires a permit, combines the two peaks with the 4.8km (three-hour) La Sauceda trail. All three trails start 12km northeast of Alcalá de los Gazules, at Km 30 on the A375.

Permits can be obtained in advance by email from the **Oficina del Parque Natural Los Alcornocales** (☎856 58 75 08; www.juntadeandalucia.es; Carretera Alcalá-Benalup, Km 1, Alcalá de los Gazules; ⏲8.30am-3.30pm Mon-Fri); write to request one at least a week ahead. On-the-spot permits are available on weekends from 10am to 2pm from the attached Centro de Visitantes El Aljibe (p155); on weekdays, the Oficina *might* issue last-minute permits. Downloadable hiking information (in English and Spanish) is available on its website.

Information

Centro de Visitantes El Aljibe (☎685 122686; www.juntadeandalucia.es; Carretera Alcalá-Benalup, Km 1, Alcalá de los Gazules; ⏲10am-2pm Tue-Sun)

Centro de Visitantes Huerta Grande (☎956 02 46 00; www.ventanadelvisitante.es; Carretera N340, Km 96; ⏲10am-2pm Wed-Sun Mar-Oct & Dec, 10am-2pm Thu-Sun Jan, Feb & Nov)

GIBRALTAR

POP 32,700

Red pillar boxes, fish-and-chip shops, creaky 1970s seaside hotels: Gibraltar – as British writer Laurie Lee once commented – is a piece of Portsmouth sliced off and towed 500 miles south. 'The Rock' overstates its Britishness, a bonus for pub-grub and afternoon-tea lovers, but a confusing double-take for modern-day British folk who thought the days of Lord Nelson memorabilia were long gone. Poised strategically at the jaws of Europe and Africa, Gibraltar, with its Palladian architecture, camera-hogging Barbary macaques, swashbuckling local history and spectacular natural setting, makes an interesting change to bordering Cádiz province.

The towering 5km-long limestone ridge rises to 426m, with cliffs on its northern and eastern sides. Gibraltarians speak English, Spanish and a curiously accented, sing-song mix of the two, often swapping mid-sentence. Signs are in English.

See the Directory A–Z (p358) for practicalities about visiting Gibraltar.

History

Both the Phoenicians and the ancient Greeks left traces here, but Gibraltar really entered the history books in 711 CE when Tariq ibn Ziyad, the Muslim governor of Tangier, made it the initial bridgehead for the Islamic invasion of the Iberian Peninsula, landing with an army of 10,000 men. The name Gibraltar derives from Jebel Tariq (Tariq's Mountain).

In 1704, an Anglo-Dutch fleet captured Gibraltar during the War of the Spanish Succession. Spain ceded the Rock to Britain by the 1713 Treaty of Utrecht, but it didn't give up military attempts to regain it until the failure of the Great Siege of 1779–83; Spain has wanted it back ever since.

In 1969, Francisco Franco (infuriated by a referendum in which Gibraltarians voted by 12,138 to 44 to remain under British sovereignty) closed the Spain–Gibraltar border. The same year a new constitution committed Britain to respecting Gibraltarians' wishes over sovereignty, and gave Gibraltar domestic self-government and its own parliament, the House of Assembly (now the Gibraltar Parliament). In 1985, just before Spain joined the European Community (now the EU), the border was reopened after 16 long years.

Gibraltarians believe in their right to self-determination and, in a 2002 vote, resoundingly rejected the idea of joint British-Spanish sovereignty. The thorny issue of the Rock's long-term future continues to hit headlines, with debates sparked by conflict over who controls its surrounding waters and, most recently, the still-unclear effects of the UK's decision to leave the EU.

In the UK's 2016 EU-membership referendum, Gibraltarians voted by 96% against Brexit (a higher pro-Remain percentage than anywhere else in Britain), but Gibraltar officially left the EU along with the rest of the UK in January 2020. While at the time of writing there are few visible changes on the ground, there are concerns (among other issues) that potential delays to crossings at a non-EU Spain–Gibraltar border would seriously complicate matters for the 15,000 Spain-based workers who cross into Gibraltar each day.

Sights

Gibraltar Town

Most Gibraltar sojourns start in Grand Casemates Sq, accessible through Landport Tunnel (at one time the only land entry through Gibraltar's walls), then continue along Main St, a slice of the British high street under the Mediterranean sun.

★Gibraltar Museum MUSEUM
(Map p158; ☎200 74289; www.gibmuseum.gi; 18-20 Bomb House Lane; adult/child £5/2.50; ⏲10am-6pm Mon-Fri, to 2pm Sat) Gibraltar's swashbuckling history unfolds in this fine museum, which comprises a labyrinth of rooms and exhibits ranging from prehistoric and Phoenician Gibraltar to the infamous Great Siege (1779–83). Don't miss the well-preserved 14th-century Islamic baths, and a 7th-century-BCE Egyptian mummy found in the bay in the 1800s.

> **CABLE CAR**
>
> The best way to explore the Rock is to whizz up on the **cable car** (Lower Cable-Car Station; Red Sands Rd; adult one way/return £16/14, child one way/return £7/7; ⏲9.30am-7.45pm Apr-Oct, to 5.15pm Nov-Mar) to the **top cable-car station**, then stop off at all the Upper Rock Nature Reserve sights on your way down. Note that the lower cable-car station stops selling tickets about two hours before the reserve closes. For the Apes' Den, hop out at the **middle station** (⏲closed Apr-Oct). Combined dolphin-watching and cable-car tickets (adult/child £41/19) are also available through dolphin-watching companies.

Nelson's Anchorage LANDMARK
(100-Tonne Gun; Map p157; Rosia Rd; incl Upper Rock Nature Reserve adult/child £13/8; ⏲9.30am-6.15pm Apr-Sep, 9am-5.45pm Oct-Mar) At the southwestern end of town, Nelson's Anchorage pinpoints the site where Nelson's body was brought ashore from the HMS *Victory* after the Battle of Trafalgar – preserved in a rum barrel, so legend says. A 100-tonne, British-made Victorian supergun commemorates the spot.

Upper Rock & Around

★Upper Rock Nature Reserve NATURE RESERVE
(Map p157; incl attractions adult/child £13/8, excl attractions pedestrian £5, combined ticket incl cable car adult/child £22/14; ⏲9.30am-6.45pm Apr-Sep, 9am-5.45pm Oct-Mar) The Rock is one of the most dramatic landforms in southern Europe. Most of its upper sections fall within the Upper Rock Nature Reserve. Tickets include admission to **O'Hara's Battery** (9.2 Gun; ⏲9.30am-7.15pm) on the Rock's summit, **St Michael's Cave** (St Michael's Rd), full of stalagmites and stalactites, the Apes' Den, the **Great Siege Tunnels** hewn out of the Rock during the siege of 1779–83, the 1333 **Moorish Castle** (Tower of Homage; Willis' Rd), the **Military Heritage Centre** (cnr Willis' & Queen's Rds), Nelson's Anchorage, and the spine-tingling **Windsor Suspension Bridge** and glass-floor, 340m-high **Skywalk** (St Michael's Rd).

The **WWII tunnels** (☎20071649; Willis' Rd, Hay's Level; tours adult/child £8/4; ⏲9am-6.15pm), where the Allied invasion of North Africa was planned, can also be visited, but you'll need to book ahead; you must have a nature-reserve ticket to access the tunnels, but they aren't included in that ticket. The Great Siege and WWII tunnels constitute only a tiny proportion of the Rock's more than 50km of tunnels, most of which remain off limits.

Apes' Den WILDLIFE RESERVE
(Map p158) The Rock's most famous inhabitants are its 160 tailless Barbary macaques. Many hang around the Apes' Den near the middle cable-car station, as well as at the top cable-car station and the Great Siege Tunnels. Legend has it that when the macaques (possibly introduced from North Africa in the 18th century) disappear from Gibraltar, so will the British. Summer is ideal for seeing newborns, but keep your distance to avoid run-ins with protective parents, and never feed or touch the macaques.

Gibraltar

Top Sights

1 Upper Rock Nature Reserve B3

Sights

2 Gorham's Cave Complex B5
3 Great Siege Tunnels B2
4 Military Heritage Centre B2
5 Nelson's Anchorage A4
6 O'Hara's Battery B4
7 Skywalk B3
8 St Michael's Cave B4
9 Windsor Suspension Bridge A3
10 WWII Tunnels A2

Activities, Courses & Tours

11 Dolphin Adventure A1
Dolphin Safari .... (see 11)
12 Mediterranean Steps B4

Gibraltar

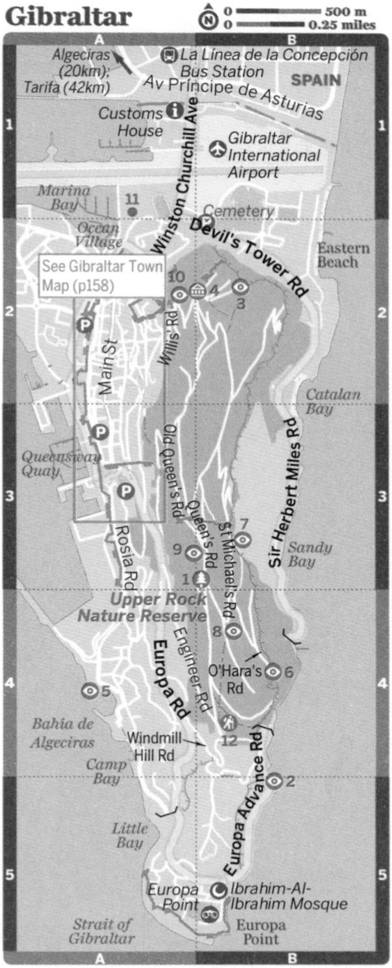

Gorham's Cave Complex CAVE

(Map p157; www.gibmuseum.gi; viewing platform adult/child £5/2.50; viewing platform 10am-2pm Mon-Fri) Inscribed on Unesco's World Heritage List in 2016, these four archaeologically rich cliffside caves on Gibraltar's southeastern coast were inhabited by Neanderthals from around 127,000 to 32,000 years ago. Though the caves themselves are off-limits, you can see them from the nearby viewing platform.

Activities

Hiking

★ **Mediterranean Steps** HIKING

(Map p157) Not the most well-known attraction in Gibraltar, but surely the most spectacular, this narrow, ancient path with steep steps – many hewn into the limestone – starts at the nature reserve's southern entrance at Jews' Gate and traverses the southern end of Gibraltar before steeply climbing the crag on the eastern escarpment to emerge on the ridge near O'Hara's Battery.

The views along the way are stupendous, though the 1.5km trail is mildly exposed; allow 45 minutes to an hour.

Dolphin-Watching

The Bahía de Algeciras has a sizeable year-round population of dolphins (striped, bottlenose and short-beaked common) and a Gibraltar highlight is spotting them. Responsible operators **Dolphin Adventure** (Map p157; 20050650; www.dolphin.gi; 9 The Square, Marina Bay; adult/child £25/13), led by marine biologists, and **Dolphin Safari** (Blue Boat; Map p157; 20071914; www.dolphinsafari.gi; 6 The Square, Marina Bay; adult/child £25/15) run dolphin-watching trips of one to 1½ hours. Most of the year each usually has two to three daily excursions. Dolphin Adventure also does summer whale-watching trips in the Strait of Gibraltar (adult/child £40/30). Advance bookings essential.

September to November are the best months for seeing dolphins, while March and April have the least sightings.

Birdwatching

The Strait of Gibraltar is a key point of passage for migrating birds between Africa and Europe; around 315 species (so far) have been recorded in the Gibraltar area. Soaring birds

Gibraltar Town

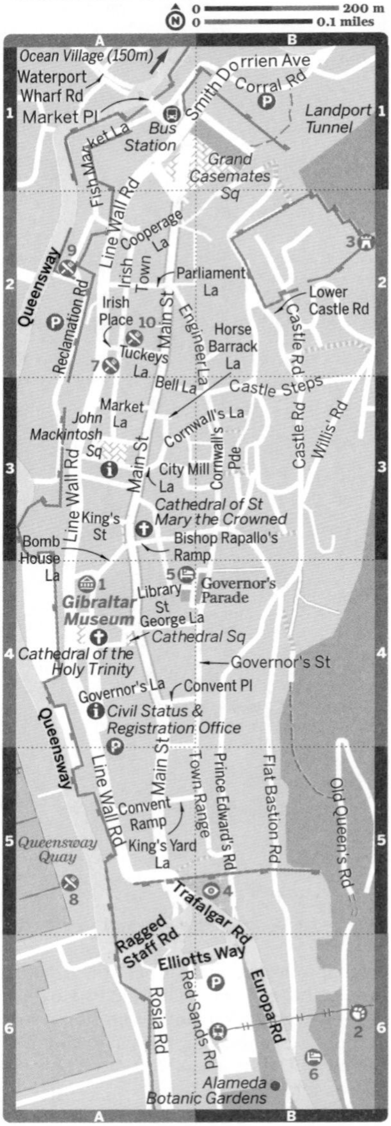

Gibraltar Town

Top Sights
1 Gibraltar Museum A4

Sights
2 Apes' Den B6
3 Moorish Castle B2
4 Trafalgar Cemetery B5

Sleeping
5 Eliott A4
6 Rock Hotel B6

Eating
7 Clipper A2
8 Lounge A5
9 My Wines A2
10 Sacarello's A2

such as raptors, black and white storks and vultures rely on thermals and updraughts for their crossings, and there are just two places where the seas are narrow enough for storks to get into Europe by this method: the Bosphorus and the Strait of Gibraltar. Northward migrations generally occur between mid-February and early June, southbound flights between late July and early November. The **Gibraltar Ornithological & Natural History Society** (www.gonhs.org) is an excellent resource.

Sleeping

Rock Hotel HOTEL €€€
(Map p158; ☎20073000; www.rockhotelgibraltar.com; 3 Europa Rd; incl breakfast r £105-170, ste £195-340; P ❄ 📶 🏊) As famous as the local monkeys, Gibraltar's grand old dame overlooks the botanical gardens and has 86 elegant yet cosy, creamy, wood-floored rooms with fresh flowers, tea/coffee kits, sea views and, for some, private balconies. Tick off gym, pool, welcome drink, writing desks, bathrobes, a sparkling terrace cafe-bar (open to all), winter Sunday roasts and summer barbecues.

Eliott HOTEL €€€
(Map p158; ☎20070500; www.eliotthotel.com; 2 Governor's Pde; r £124-215, ste £250-315; ❄ 📶 🏊) This super-central, four-star establishment has chicly updated, smartly contemporary rooms styled in warm blues, yellows and greys, some with capsule-coffee kits and/or balconies. Bonuses include a pool on the rooftop, where there's also a view-laden bar and an international restaurant.

Eating & Drinking

Goodbye tapas, hello fish and chips. Gibraltar cuisine is unashamedly British – and pretty pricey compared to Andalucía, just across the border. The staples are pub grub, beer, sandwiches, chips and stodgy desserts, though a few international flavours can be found at Queensway Quay, Marina Bay and Ocean Village (this last has lots of global chains). There's a cluster of good tapas bars and restaurants on Fish Market Lane, just outside Grand Casemates Sq.

My Wines TAPAS €
(Map p158; ☎20069463; www.mywinesgibraltar.com; 11-12 The Strip, Chatham Counterguard; tapas £3-11; ⏰7.30am-11pm Mon-Thu, to 2am Fri, 10am-3.30pm & 6pm-2am Sat; ✎) One of several buzzy Chatham spots, this wine boutique rustles up drops from 23 countries, served alongside a seasonally changing menu of lightly inventive Spanish-inspired tapas like mushroom croquettes, spicy *patatas bravas, huevos rotos* with ham or *pil pil,* or deep-fried goat's cheese. Live music, occasional wine pairings and a busy after-work scene.

Clipper PUB FOOD €
(Map p158; ☎20079791; www.theclipper.gi; 78B Irish Town; mains £7-9; ⏰9am-11pm Mon-Fri, 9am-4pm Sat, 10am-11pm Sun; 📶) Ask five…10…20 people in Gibraltar for their favourite pub and, chances are, they'll choose the packed-out Clipper. Looking sparklingly modern nowadays, the Clipper does real pub grub in traditionally large portions. British faves include jacket potatoes, chicken tikka masala, cheesy chips, Sunday roasts and that essential all-day breakfast.

Sacarello's INTERNATIONAL €€
(Map p158; ☎20070625; www.sacarellosgibraltar.com; 57 Irish Town; mains £8-15; ⏰9am-7.30pm Mon-Fri, to 4pm Sat; 📶✎) Founded in the 1980s, Sacarello's offers a great range of Spanish-international vegetarian food (pastas, quiches, soups) alongside pub-style dishes in an old multilevel coffee warehouse full of history. There's good house coffee, plus home-baked cakes, a salad bar and daily specials. From 3.30pm to 7.30pm, linger over cream tea (£6.20).

Lounge INTERNATIONAL €€€
(Map p158; ☎20061118; www.facebook.com/TheLoungeGastro; 17A & B Ragged Staff Wharf, Queensway Quay; mains £10-20; ⏰10am-4pm & 6-10pm Fri-Mon & Wed, 10am-11pm Tue & Thu; ✎) This popular, stylish waterside gastrobar and lounge, just south of the centre, serves a globetrotting, fresh-produce menu of salads, pastas, risottos, seafood, sandwiches and steaks, along with creative seasonal specials. Starters like king-prawn *pil pil* and goat's-cheese salad are followed by beer-battered cod or rib-eye steak with *chimichurri* sauce, all overlooking Queensway Quay's mega-yachts.

Information

Tourist Office (Map p158; ☎20045000; www.visitgibraltar.gi; Heritage Bldg, 13 John Mackintosh Sq; ⏰9am-4.30pm Mon-Fri, 9.30am-3.30pm Sat, 10am-1pm Sun)

Getting There & Away

AIR

Gibraltar's well-connected **airport** (Map p157; ☎20012345; www.gibraltarairport.gi) is at the northern end of the Rock, next to the Spanish border.

British Airways (www.britishairways.com) London (Heathrow).

EasyJet (www.easyjet.com) London (Gatwick/Luton), Bristol, Edinburgh, Manchester.

Royal Air Maroc (www.royalairmaroc.com) Casablanca, Tangier.

BUS

No buses go directly to Gibraltar, but the **bus station** (Map p157; Avenida de Europa) in La Línea de la Concepción (Spain) is only 400m north of the border. From here, regular buses go to/from Algeciras, Cádiz, Málaga, Seville, Tarifa and beyond.

CAR & MOTORCYCLE

Long vehicle queues at the border and congested streets in Gibraltar make it far less time-consuming to park in La Línea and walk south across the frontier (1.5km to Casemates Sq). To take a car into Gibraltar (free), you need an insurance certificate, a registration document, a nationality plate and a driving licence. Gibraltar drives on the right.

In Gibraltar, there are car parks on Line Wall Rd, Reclamation Rd and Devil's Tower Rd (£1.30 per hour). La Línea has some street parking, but it's easier and safer to use the underground car parks (from €11 per 24 hours) just north of Avenida Príncipe de Asturias.

Getting Around

Bus 5 runs between town and the border every 10 to 20 minutes. Bus 2 serves Europa Point, and bus 3 the southern town; buses 4 and 8 go to Catalan Bay. All these buses stop at **Market Place** (Map p158; www.gibraltarbuscompany.gi; Market Pl), immediately northwest of Grand Casemates Sq. Tickets cost £1.80, or £2.50 for a day pass.

AT A GLANCE

POPULATION
1.69 million

CAPITAL
Málaga

BEST CITY HOTEL
Palacio Solecio
(p171)

BEST SEAFOOD
La Escollera (p182)

BEST MOUNTAIN HIKE
El Lucero (p195)

WHEN TO GO

Apr–Jun
The best months for hiking, with wildflowers in bloom and bearable daytime temperatures.

Aug
Temperatures can hit 40°C so it's beach time; Málaga's feria is one of Spain's best parties.

Sep–Nov
Temperatures cool, prices drop, crowds thin. Most seasonal businesses stay open until October.

Puente Nuevo, Ronda (p183)
JOHN_SILVER/SHUTTERSTOCK

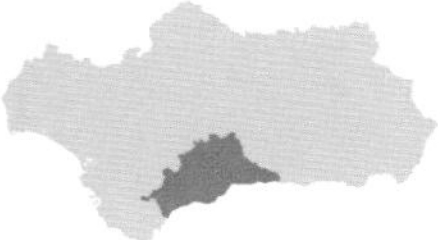

Málaga Province

After decades of being pointedly ignored, revitalised Málaga is now the Andalucian city everyone is talking about. Its 30-odd museums and edgy urban art scene are well matched by contemporary-chic dining choices, new boutique hotels and one of Spain's most stylish shopping streets. During the annual August feria, it sees a party atmosphere infused with flamenco, *fino* (dry, straw-coloured sherry) and carafe-loads of spirit.

Each region of the province has equally fascinating diversity, from the mountains of La Axarquía to the tourist-driven razzle-dazzle of the Costa del Sol. Inland are *pueblos blancos* (white towns) and the under-appreciated, elegant old town of Antequera.

INCLUDES

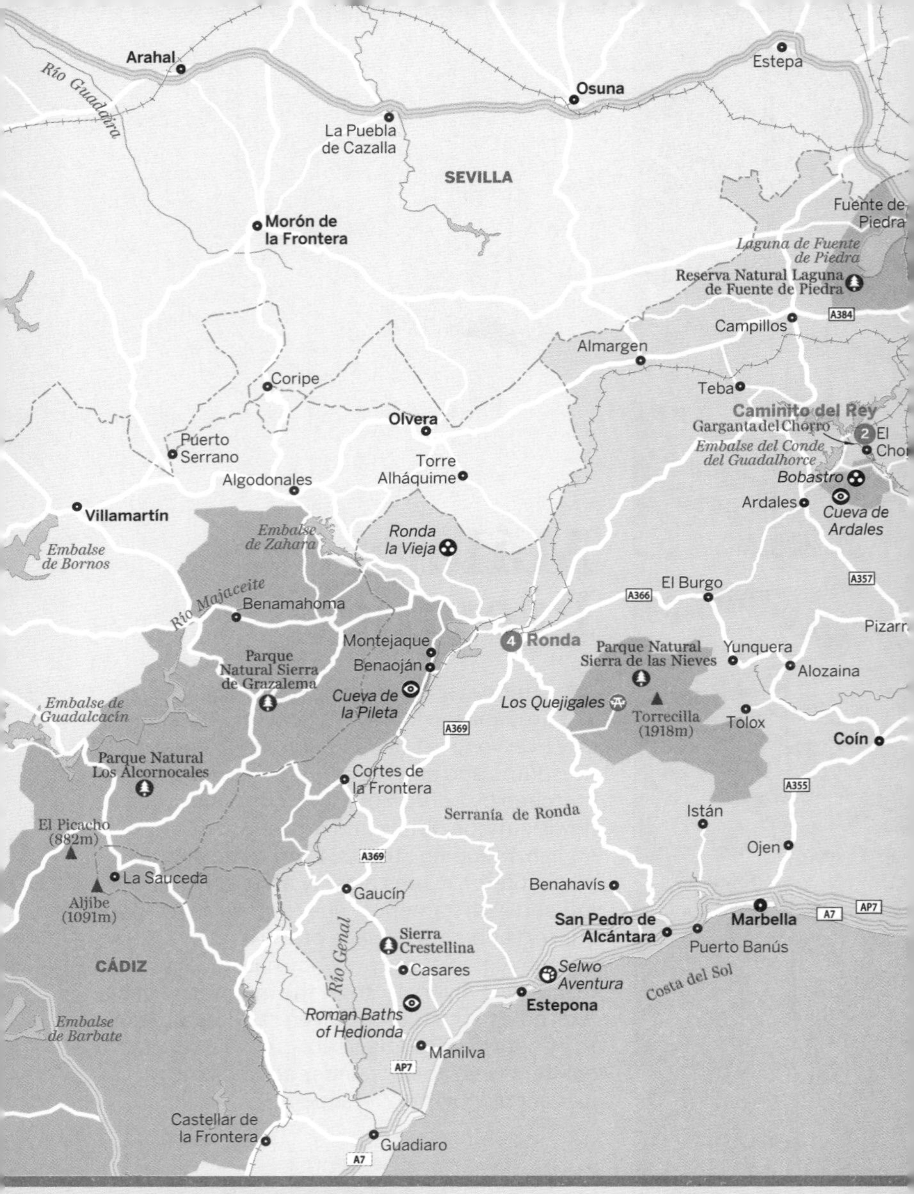

Málaga Province Highlights

1. **Málaga** (p164) Taking a trip from Picasso to the Pompidou Centre in Spain's ever-evolving art city.

2. **Caminito del Rey** (p191) Following a narrow 100m-high path through the jaws of El Chorro gorge.

3. **Cueva de Nerja** (p198) Delving into a subterranean world beneath the tourist bustle of Nerja.

4. **Ronda** (p182) Gazing into the Río Guadalevín canyon on a stroll from the bullring to the Arab baths in this amazingly picturesque town.

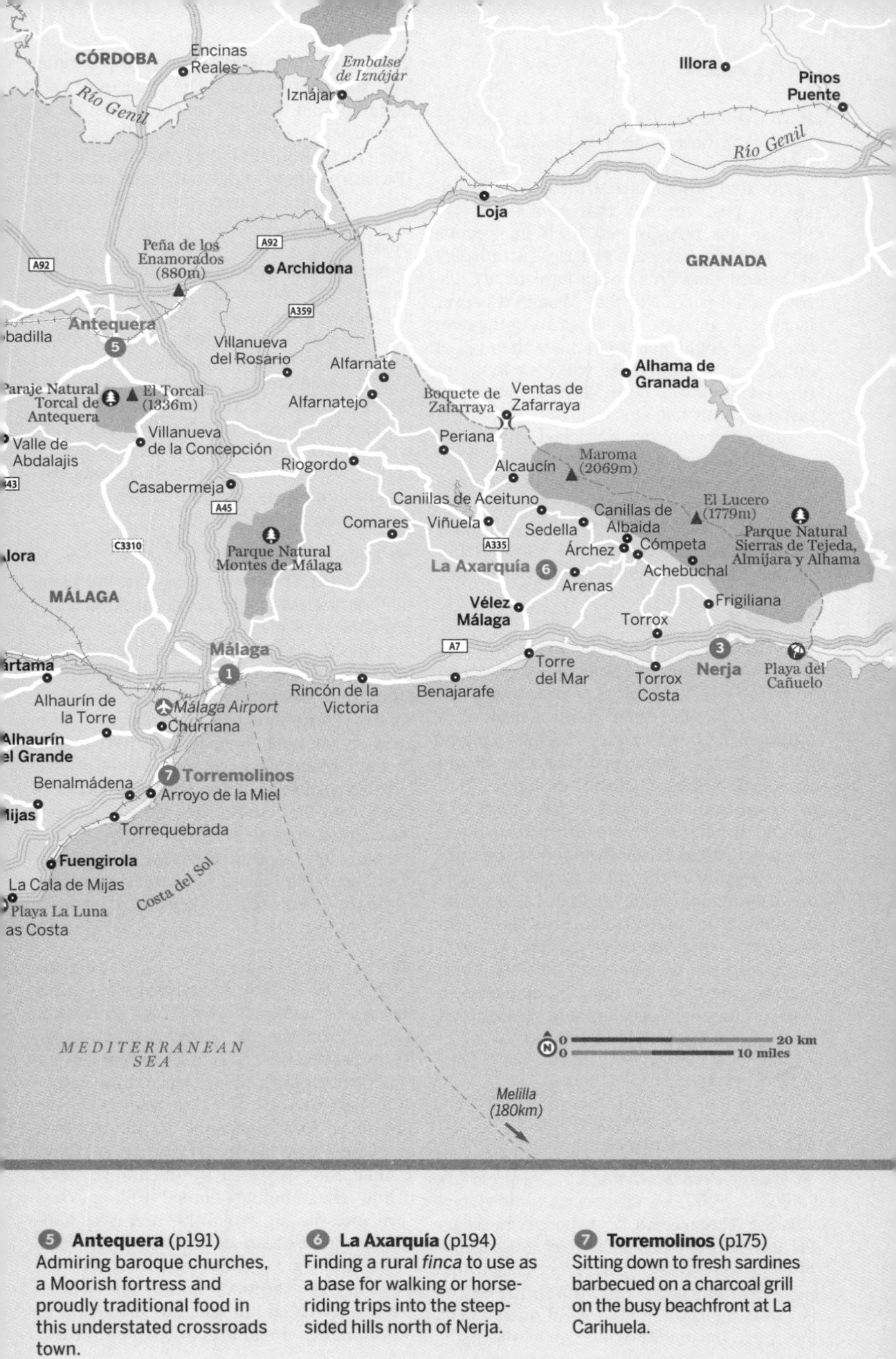

5 Antequera (p191)
Admiring baroque churches, a Moorish fortress and proudly traditional food in this understated crossroads town.

6 La Axarquía (p194)
Finding a rural *finca* to use as a base for walking or horse-riding trips into the steep-sided hills north of Nerja.

7 Torremolinos (p175)
Sitting down to fresh sardines barbecued on a charcoal grill on the busy beachfront at La Carihuela.

MÁLAGA

POP 574,654

If you think the Costa del Sol is soulless, you clearly haven't been to Málaga. Loaded with history and brimming with a youthful vigour that proudly acknowledges its multi-layered past, the city that gave the world Picasso has transformed itself in spectacular fashion, with art galleries, a radically rethought port area and a nascent art district called Soho. Not that Málaga was ever lacking in energy: the Spanish-to-the-core bar scene could put bags under the eyes of an insomniac *madrileño,* while the food culture encompasses both Michelin stars and tastefully tatty fish shacks.

Come here for tapas washed down with sweet local wine, and stay in a creative boutique hotel sandwiched between a Roman theatre, a Moorish fortress and the polychromatic Pompidou Centre, while you reflect on how eloquently Málaga has reinvented itself for the 21st century. Look out, Seville.

History

The name Málaga comes from *malaka,* meaning 'to salt': the appellation was given to the city by the Phoenicians in the 8th century BCE after their culinary custom of salting fish. The city grew to become a major port in Roman times, exporting olive oil and *garum* (fish paste), as well as copper, lead and iron from the mines in the mountains around Ronda. Málaga continued to flourish under Moorish rule from the 8th century CE, especially as the chief port of the emirate of Granada. The city held out against the invading Christian armies until 1487 and displayed equal tenacity against Franco's fascists during the Spanish Civil War. More recently the city has, happily, managed to stave off the mass development that typifies the adjacent Costa del Sol.

Sights

Historic Centre

★Museo Picasso Málaga MUSEUM

(952 12 76 00; www.museopicassomalaga.org; Calle San Agustín 8; €9, incl temporary exhibition €12, last 2hr before closing Sun free; 10am-8pm Jul & Aug, to 7pm Mar-Jun, Sep & Oct, to 6pm Nov-Feb) This unmissable museum in the city of Picasso's birth provides a solid overview of the great master and his work, although, surprisingly, it only came to fruition in 2003 after more than 50 years of planning. The 200-plus works in the collection were donated and loaned to the museum by Christine Ruiz-Picasso (wife of Paul, Picasso's eldest son) and Bernard Ruiz-Picasso (Picasso's grandson), and catalogue the artist's sparkling career with a few notable gaps (the 'blue' and 'rose' periods are largely missing).

Nonetheless, numerous gems adorn the gallery's lily-white walls. Highlights include a painting of Picasso's sister Lola undertaken when the artist was only 13; sculptures made from clay, plaster and sheet metal; numerous sketches; a quick journey through cubism; and some interesting late works when Picasso developed an obsession with musketeers. The museum, which is housed in the 16th-century Buenavista Palace, has an excellent cafe and holds revolving temporary exhibitions.

★Alcazaba CASTLE

(952 22 72 30; http://alcazabaygibralfaro.malaga.eu; Calle Alcazabilla 2; €3.50, incl Castillo de Gibralfaro €5.50; 9am-8pm Apr-Oct, to 6pm Nov-Mar) No time to visit Granada's Alhambra? Then Málaga's Alcazaba can provide a taster. The entrance is beside the Roman theatre, from where a meandering path climbs amid lush greenery: crimson bougainvillea, lofty palms, fragrant jasmine bushes and rows of orange trees. Extensively restored, this palace-fortress dates from the 11th-century Moorish period; the caliphal horseshoe arches, courtyards and bubbling fountains are evocative of this influential period in Málaga's history. The dreamy **Patio de la Alberca** is especially redolent of the Alhambra.

★Catedral de Málaga CATHEDRAL

(952 22 03 45; www.malagacatedral.com; Calle Molina Lario; cathedral & Ars Málaga €6, incl roof €10; 10am-6pm Sat, 2-6pm Sun year-round, 10am-8pm Mon-Fri Apr-Jun & Oct, to 9pm Jun-Sep, to 6.30pm Nov-Mar) Málaga's elaborate cathedral was started in the 16th century on the site of the former mosque. Of the mosque, only the **Patio de los Naranjos** survives, a small courtyard of fragrant orange trees. Inside, the fabulous domed ceiling soars 40m into the air, while the vast colonnaded nave houses an enormous cedar-wood choir. Aisles give access to 15 chapels with gorgeous 18th-century retables and religious art. It's worth taking the guided tour up to the *cubiertas* (roof) to enjoy panoramic city views.

DON'T MISS

LA MALAGUETA & THE BEACHES

At the end of the Paseo del Parque lies the exclusive residential district of La Malagueta, situated on a spit of land protruding into the sea. Apartments here have frontline sea views, and some of Málaga's best restaurants are found near the **Playa de la Malagueta** (the beach closest to the city centre). Head 2km east to reach the fabulous setting of seafood restaurant El Balneario de los Baños del Carmen (p172).

East of Playa de la Malagueta, sandy beaches continue to line most of the waterfront for several kilometres. Next along are **Playa de Pedregalejo** and **Playa el Palo**, El Palo being the city's original, salt-of-the-earth fishing neighbourhood. This is a great place to bring children and an even better place to while away an afternoon with a cold beer and a plate of sizzling seafood. To reach either beach, take bus 11 from Paseo del Parque.

Building the cathedral was an epic project that took some 200 years. Such was the project's cost that by 1782 it was decided that work would stop. One of the two bell towers was left incomplete, hence the cathedral's well-worn nickname, La Manquita (The One-Armed Lady).

Museo Carmen Thyssen MUSEUM
(www.carmenthyssenmalaga.org; Calle Compañía 10; €10, 2.30-4pm €6; ⏲10am-8pm Tue-Sun) Located in an aesthetically renovated 16th-century palace in the heart of the city's former Moorish quarter, this extensive collection concentrates on 19th-century Spanish and Andalucian art by painters such as Joaquín Sorolla y Bastida and Ignacio Zuloaga. It's particularly interesting for its almost cartoonish *costumbrismo* paintings that perpetuated a sentimental myth of 19th-century Spain as a place of banditry, flamenco, fiestas, bar-room brawls and bullfighting (and little else). There are also regular temporary exhibitions and a lovely patio cafe.

Castillo de Gibralfaro CASTLE
(☎952 22 72 30; http://alcazabaygibralfaro.malaga.eu; Camino de Gibralfaro; €3.50, incl Alcazaba €5.50; ⏲9am-8pm Apr-Sep, to 6pm Oct-Mar) One remnant of Málaga's Islamic past is the craggy ramparts of the Castillo de Gibralfaro, spectacularly located high on the hill overlooking the city. Built by 8th-century Cordoban emir Abd ar-Rahman I, and later rebuilt in the 14th century when Málaga was the main port for the emirate of Granada, the castle originally acted as a lighthouse and military barracks. Nothing much is original in the castle's interior, but the protective walkway around the ramparts affords superb views over Málaga.

There is also a **military museum**, which includes a small, scale model of the entire castle complex and the lower residence, the Alcazaba. The best way to reach the castle on foot is via the attractive Paseo Don Juan de Temboury, to the south of the Alcazaba. From here a path winds pleasantly (and steeply) through lushly gardened terraces with viewpoints over the city. Alternatively, you can drive up the Camino de Gibralfaro or take bus 35 from Avenida de Cervantes.

Casa Natal de Picasso MUSEUM
(www.fundacionpicasso.malaga.eu; Plaza de la Merced 15; €3, incl Sala de Exposiciones €4; ⏲9.30am-8pm, closed Tue Nov-Mar) For an intimate insight into the painter's childhood, head to the Casa Natal de Picasso, the house where Picasso was born in 1881. Now a study foundation, the house has striking photos and other memorabilia of young Picasso and his family, and a replica of his father's 19th-century artist's studio. The foundation also owns the small **Sala de Exposiciones** (€3; ⏲9.30am-8pm, closed Tue Nov-Mar) across the square, which shuffles an excellent deck of temporary shows, often including or heavily influenced by Picasso's work.

Teatro Romano LANDMARK
(Roman Theatre; ☎951 50 11 15; Calle Alcazabilla 8; ⏲10am-6pm Tue-Sat, to 4pm Sun) FREE The story of the unearthing of Málaga's Roman theatre is almost as interesting as the theatre itself. Dating from the time of Augustus (1st century CE), it was rediscovered in 1951 by workers building the foundations for a new Casa de Cultura. Today the theatre sits fully exposed beneath the walls of the Alcazaba. A small interpretive centre next door outlines its history and displays a few artefacts shovelled from its crusty foundations.

Málaga

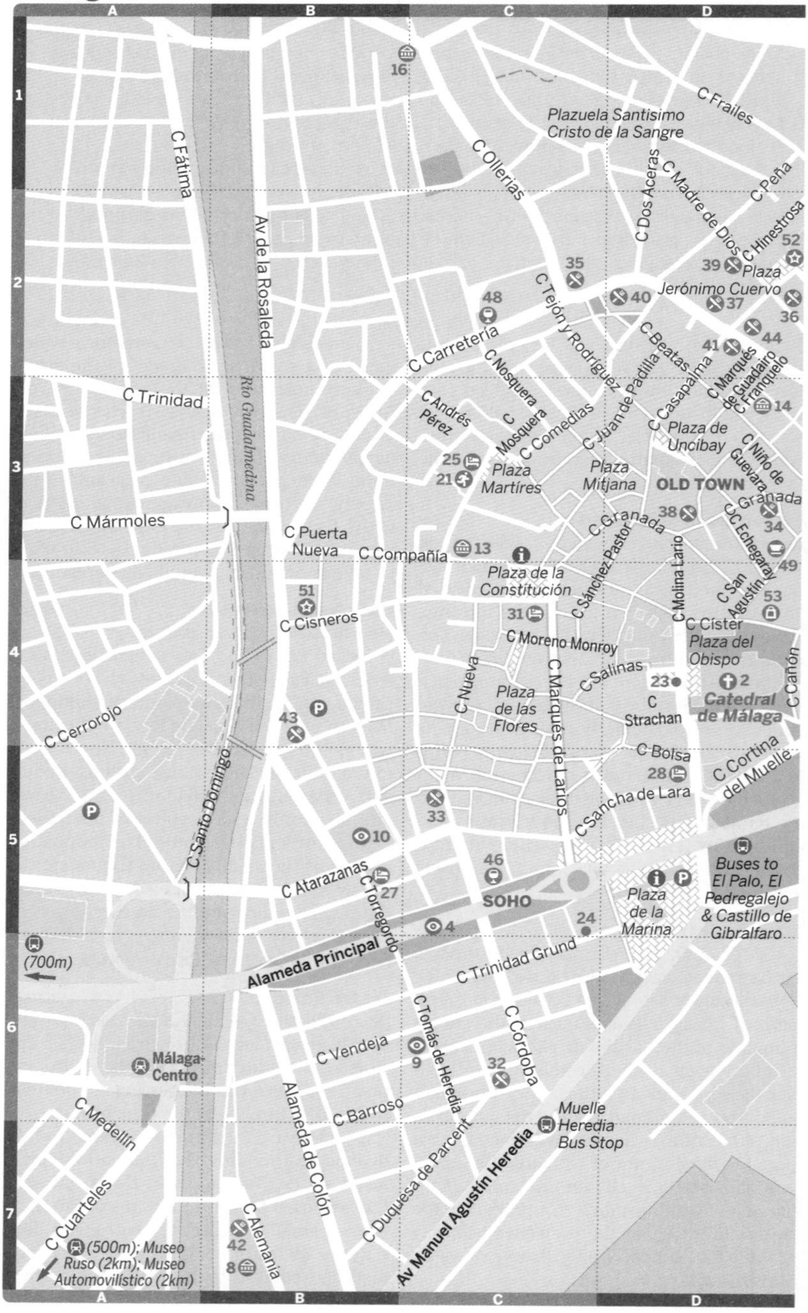

A
B
C
D
1
2
3
4
5
6
7
16
C Frailes
Plazuela Santisimo Cristo de la Sangre
C Ollerías
C Fátima
C Dos Aceras
C Madre de Dios
C Peña
C Hinestrosa
52
Av de la Rosaleda
35
39
Plaza Jerónimo Cuervo
C Tejón y Rodríguez
40
37
36
48
44
C Carretería
C Beatas
41
C Marqués de Guadalcázar
C Franquelo
14
C Nosquera
Río Guadalmedina
C Trinidad
C Andrés Pérez
C Mosquera
C Comedias
C Juan de Padilla
C Casapalma
Plaza de Uncibay
C Niño de Guevara
25
21
Plaza Mártires
Plaza Mitjana
OLD TOWN
C Granada
38
C Mármoles
C Granada
C Echegaray
34
C Puerta Nueva
C Compañía
13
C Sánchez Pastor
C Molina Lario
49
Plaza de la Constitución
51
C San Agustín
53
C Cisneros
31
C Císter
C Moreno Monroy
Plaza del Obispo
C Nueva
C Marqués de Larios
C Salinas
23
2
C Cañón
Catedral de Málaga
Plaza de las Flores
C Strachan
C Cerrorojo
43
C Bolsa
C Santo Domingo
28
C Cortina del Muelle
33
C Sancha de Lara
10
Buses to El Palo, El Pedregalejo & Castillo de Gibralfaro
46
C Atarazanas
27
C Torregorda
SOHO
Plaza de la Marina
24
4
(700m)
Alameda Principal
C Trinidad Grund
C Tomás de Heredia
C Córdoba
C Vendeja
9
Málaga-Centro
32
C Medellín
Alameda de Colón
C Barroso
Muelle Heredia Bus Stop
C Duquesa de Parcent
Av Manuel Agustín Heredia
C Cuarteles
C Alemania
42
8
(500m); Museo Ruso (2km); Museo Automovilístico (2km)

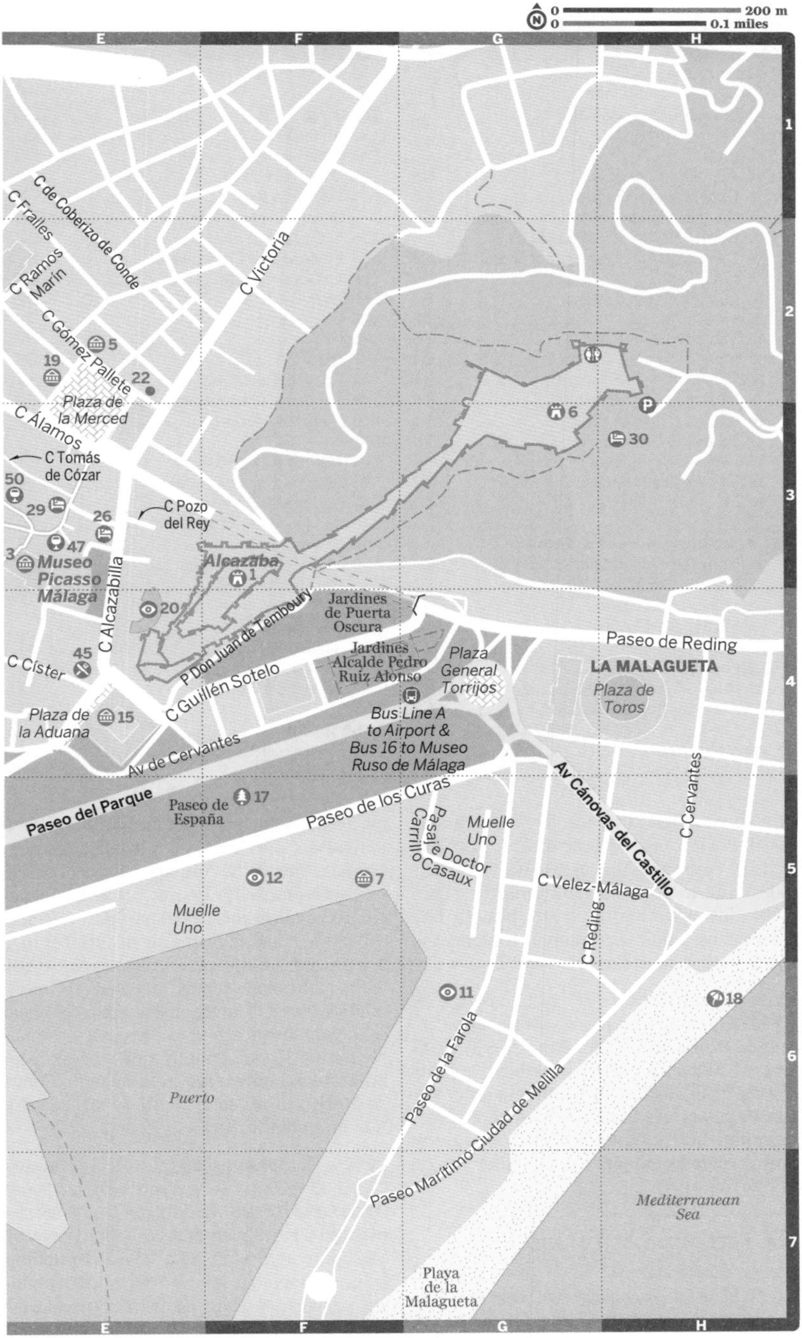
0 200 m
0 0.1 miles
C de Coberizo de Conde
C Fralles
C Ramos Marín
C Gómez Pallete
C Victoria
Plaza de la Merced
C Álamos
C Tomás de Cózar
C Pozo del Rey
Alcazaba
Museo Picasso Málaga
C Alcazabilla
P Don Juan de Temboury
Jardines de Puerta Oscura
Jardines Alcalde Pedro Ruiz Alonso
Plaza General Torrijos
Paseo de Reding
LA MALAGUETA
Plaza de Toros
C Císter
C Guillén Sotelo
Plaza de la Aduana
Bus Line A to Airport & Bus 16 to Museo Ruso de Málaga
Av de Cervantes
Paseo del Parque
Paseo de España
Paseo de los Curas
Pasaje Doctor Carrillo Casaux
Muelle Uno
Av Cánovas del Castillo
C Cervantes
C Velez-Málaga
C Reding
Muelle Uno
Puerto
Paseo de la Farola
Paseo Marítimo Ciudad de Melilla
Mediterranean Sea
Playa de la Malagueta
1
3
5
6
7
11
12
15
17
18
19
20
22
26
29
30
45
47
50
E
F
G
H
1
2
3
4
5
6
7

Málaga

Top Sights
1 Alcazaba F3
2 Catedral de Málaga D4
3 Museo Picasso Málaga E3

Sights
4 Alameda Principal C5
5 Casa Natal de Picasso E2
6 Castillo de Gibralfaro G3
7 Centre Pompidou Málaga F5
8 Centro de Arte Contemporáneo B7
9 MAUS C6
10 Mercado Atarazanas B5
11 Muelle Uno G6
12 Museo Aula del Mar F5
13 Museo Carmen Thyssen C3
14 Museo de Arte Flamenco D3
15 Museo de Málaga E4
16 Museo Jorge Rando B1
17 Paseo de España F5
18 Playa de la Malagueta H6
19 Sala de Exposiciones E2
20 Teatro Romano E4

Activities, Courses & Tours
21 Hammam Al-Andalus C3
22 Instituto Picasso E2
23 Málaga Adventures D4
24 Málaga Bike Tours C5

Sleeping
25 Dulces Dreams C3
26 Hotel Boutique Teatro Romano E3
27 The Lights Hostel B5
28 Molina Lario D5
29 Palacio Solecio E3
30 Parador Málaga Gibralfaro H3
31 Room Mate Larios C4

Eating
32 Al Yamal C6
33 Casa Aranda C5
34 Casa Lola D3
35 Colmado 93 C2
Dulces Dreams Cafeteria (see 25)
36 El Camerino D2
37 El Mesón de Cervantes D2
38 La Cosmopolita D3
39 La Peregrina Centro D2
40 La Tranca D2
41 Noviembre D2
42 Óleo B7
43 Recyclo Bike Café B4
44 Tapeo de Cervantes D2
45 Uvedoble Taberna E4

Drinking & Nightlife
46 Antigua Casa de Guardia C5
47 Bodegas El Pimpi E3
48 La Madriguera Craft Beer C2
49 La Tetería D3
50 Los Patios de Beatas E3
Mia Coffee Shop (see 21)

Entertainment
51 Kelipe B4
Peña Juan Breva (see 14)
52 Teatro Cervantes D2

Shopping
53 Alfajar D4

Museo de Arte Flamenco MUSEUM
(952 22 13 80; Calle Franquelo 4; €2; 10am-2pm Mon-Sat) Over two floors in the HQ of Málaga's oldest and most prestigious *peña* (flamenco club), this collection of photos, posters, costumes, fans, guitars and more is testament to the city's illustrious flamenco scene.

Museo Jorge Rando GALLERY
(952 21 09 91; www.museojorgerando.org; Calle Cruz del Molnillo 12; 10am-8pm Mon-Sat) FREE One of Málaga's newest museums exhibits the work of one of its most contemporary artists. Rando is now in his 70s, and his abstract paintings and sculptures focus on poverty and the environment, among other topics. It's stirring stuff.

Port Area & Around

Museo de Málaga MUSEUM
(951 91 19 04; www.museosdeandalucia.es/museodemalaga; Plaza de la Aduana; EU/non-EU citizen free/€1.50; 9am-9pm Tue-Sat, to 3pm Sun) Spread out over two floors in Málaga's neoclassical Palacio de Aduana, this vast, newly renovated museum houses art and archaeological collections. The 1st-floor fine-arts collection consists primarily of 19th-century Andalucian landscape and genre paintings, with additional rooms devoted to more modern work. The extensive archaeological collection, bequeathed to the city by the noble Loring-Heredia family, ranges from Neolithic shards uncovered in the nearby Cueva de Nerja (p198) to a headless statue of a Roman noblewoman.

Centre Pompidou Málaga MUSEUM
(951 92 62 00; www.centrepompidou.es; Pasaje Doctor Carrillo Casaux, Muelle Uno; €7, incl temporary exhibition €9; 9.30am-8pm Wed-Mon) Down by Málaga's port, this offshoot of Paris' Pompidou Centre is housed in a low-slung modern building crowned by artist Daniel Buren's playful multicoloured cube. Thought-provoking,

well-curated main exhibits rotate through on an annual or bi-annual basis, drawing on the museum's vast collection of contemporary art. There are also audiovisual installations, talking 'heads' and temporary exhibitions.

Centro de Arte Contemporáneo MUSEUM
(Contemporary Art Museum; ☎952 20 85 00; www.cacmalaga.org; Calle Alemania; ⏲9am-9.30pm Tue-Sun) FREE The contemporary-art museum is housed in a skilfully converted 1930s wholesale market on the river estuary. The bizarre triangular floor plan of the building has been retained, with its cubist lines and shapes brilliantly showcasing the modern art on display. Painted entirely white, windows and all, the museum hosts temporary shows featuring the work of well-known contemporary artists and has an obvious Spanish bias. It's usually filled with plenty of spectacularly weird exhibits.

Muelle Uno PORT
(P) The city's long-beleaguered port area underwent a radical rethink in 2013 and was redesigned to cater to the increase in cruise-ship passengers. Wide quayside walkways now embellish Muelle 1 and Muelle 2, which are lined by palm trees and backed by shops, restaurants, bars and a small kid-focused aquarium, the **Museo Aula del Mar** (☎951 60 01 08; www.auladelmar.info; Palmeral de las Sopresas, Muelle 2; adult/child/family €7/5/20; ⏲11am-2pm & 5-8pm Jul-early Sep, 10.30am-2pm & 4.30-6.30pm early Sep-Jun).

Paseo de España PARK
(Paseo del Parque; P) Looking like a mini-jungle when viewed from the Gibralfaro hill, this palm-lined extension of the **Alameda** was created in the 1890s on land reclaimed from the sea. The garden along its southern side is full of exotic tropical plants and trees, making a pleasant refuge from the bustle of the city. *Malagueños* stroll and take shelter in the deep shade of the tall palms, and on Sunday buskers and entertainers play to the crowds.

Mercado Atarazanas MARKET
(Calle Atarazanas; ⏲market 8am-3pm Mon-Sat; P) North of the city's main artery, the Alameda Principal, you'll find this striking 19th-century iron-clad building incorporating the original Moorish gate that once connected the city with the port. The magnificent stained-glass window depicts historical highlights of the city. The daily market here is pleasantly noisy and animated.

Other Areas

Museo Ruso de Málaga MUSEUM
(☎951 92 61 50; www.coleccionmuseoruso.es; Avenida de Sor Teresa Prat 15; €6, incl temporary exhibitions €8, 4-8pm Sun free; ⏲9.30am-8pm Tue-Sun; P) Housed in a former tobacco factory, this offshoot of St Petersburg's Russian State Museum is dedicated to Russian art from the 16th to 20th centuries. It features works by Ilya Repin, Wassily Kandinsky and Vladimir Tatlin, among others – though much of the focus is on Russian history rather than the art itself. From Málaga's Paseo del Parque, take bus 16 and get off at Avenida de Sor Teresa Prat. Alternatively, take the metro to Princesa-Huelin and walk the last 400m.

Museo Automovilístico Málaga MUSEUM
(☎951 13 70 01; www.museoautomovilmalaga.com; Avenida de Sor Teresa Prat 15; €9.50; ⏲10am-7pm) Fashion and old cars might seem like weird bedfellows, but they're an inspired combo when viewed through the prism of this slightly out-of-the-box museum in Málaga's erstwhile tobacco factory. The museum juxtaposes cars from the 1900s to the 1960s with haute couture from the same era. Imagine a 1936 Merc lined up next to a mannequin clothed in a Chanel jacket.

From Málaga's Paseo del Parque, take bus 16 and get off at Avenida de Sor Teresa Prat (€1.35, 10 minutes). Alternatively, take the metro to Princesa-Huelin and walk the last 400m.

Jardín Botánico Histórico La Concepción GARDENS
(☎951 92 61 80; www.laconcepcion.malaga.eu; Camino del Jardín Botánico 3; €5.20; ⏲9.30am-7.30pm Tue-Sun Apr-Sep, to 4.30pm Tue-Sun Oct-Mar) These exotic gardens were conceived in the mid-19th century by the Loring-Heredia clan, a noble family of railway builders and bankers who bequeathed the city its weighty archaeological collection, now on display in the Museo de Málaga. Laid out in 1855, the hillside grounds were updated by different owners in 1911. The state took over management of the gardens in 1990, and in 1994 they were opened to the public.

The gardens are 5km north of Málaga. Bus 2 will get you close, or you can take the five-times-a-day City Tour bus (€1.30) from the train station that'll drop you at the entrance.

MÁLAGA'S ARTISTIC REVIVAL

Befitting Picasso's birthplace, Málaga has an art collection to rival those of Seville and Granada, particularly in the field of modern art, where galleries and workshops continue to push the envelope. It wasn't always thus.

Little more than 15 years ago, Málaga's art scene was patchy and understated. The first big coup came in 2003, when, after 50 years of on-off discussion, the city finally got around to honouring its most famous son with the opening of the Museo Picasso Málaga (p164). More galleries followed, some focusing on notable *malagueños* such as Jorge Rando and Félix Revello de Toro, while others – such as the Museo Carmen Thyssen (p165), which shines a light on *costumbrismo* (Spanish folk art) – take in a broader sweep of Spanish painting. Then, in 2015, Málaga earned the right to be called a truly international art city when it opened offshoot galleries of St Petersburg's prestigious Russian State Museum and Paris' Pompidou Centre. The finishing touches to this colourful canvas were added in 2016: after 20 years in the dark, Málaga's 2000-piece-strong fine-arts collection was reinstated in the city's beautifully restored old customs house (p168) down by the port.

Málaga's vibrant artistic spirit is especially evident in the Soho neighbourhood, where street artists have launched **MAUS** (Málaga Arte Urbano en el Soho; www.mausmalaga.com), an edgy urban-renewal project that fosters a free creative space for street and graffiti artists.

Activities

★ **Málaga Bike Tours** CYCLING
(☎606 978513; www.malagabiketours.eu; Calle Trinidad Grund 5A; tours €25; ⏲10am-8pm Apr-Sep, to 7pm Oct-Mar; 👪) One of the best tours in town and certainly the best on two wheels. Málaga Bike Tours was a pioneer in city cycling when it was set up a decade ago. Its perennially popular excursions, including the classic **City Bike Tour**, are available in at least five languages, with kids' seats on offer if you're bringing the family.

Hammam Al-Andalus HAMMAM
(☎952 21 50 18; www.hammamalandalus.com; Plaza de los Mártires 5; baths €34; ⏲10am-midnight) These Moorish-style baths provide *malagueños* with a luxurious marble-clad setting in which to enjoy the same relaxation benefits as those offered by similar facilities in Granada and Córdoba. Massages are also available.

Málaga Adventures WALKING
(☎699 756864; www.malagaadventures.com; ⏲10am, noon & 6pm) FREE Free walking tours leave daily from the Plaza del Obispo opposite the cathedral (p164). Look out for the tour leaders in red T-shirts with red umbrellas. Tips are appreciated.

Courses

Instituto Picasso LANGUAGE
(☎952 21 39 32; www.instituto-picasso.com; Plaza de la Merced 20; 1-/2-/3-/4-week course €160/320/460/590) This private language school offers both group and individual instruction. Group classes include four 50-minute lessons a day and the price includes access to cultural activities such as flamenco and cooking courses. Accommodation is also available.

Festivals & Events

There's a whole host of festivals throughout the year in Málaga province. For details, see www.malagaturismo.com/en/events.

Semana Santa RELIGIOUS
Each night from Palm Sunday to Good Friday, six or seven *cofradías* (brotherhoods) bear holy images for several hours through the city, watched by large crowds.

Feria de Málaga FERIA
(www.feria.malaga.eu; ⏲mid-Aug) Málaga's nine-day feria, launched by a huge fireworks display, is the most ebullient of Andalucía's summer fairs. It resembles an exuberant Rio-style street party, with plenty of flamenco and *fino*; head for the city centre to be in the thick of it.

Sleeping

★ **Dulces Dreams** GUESTHOUSE €
(☎951 35 78 69; www.dulcesdreamshostel.com; Plaza de los Mártires 6; d with/without bathroom from €74/60; ❄📶) Managed by an enthusiastic young team and delightfully situated in a pedestrianised plaza overlooking a red-brick church, Dulces (sweet) Dreams

is a great budget option. The bright, high-ceilinged and whimsically decorated rooms are, appropriately, named after desserts: Cupcake is one of the best. Note that there's no lift, and street noise can be an issue for light sleepers.

Breakfast at the downstairs **cafe** (www.dulcesdreamshostel.com/cafeteria; Plaza de los Mártires 6; breakfast €6-9; ⏲9am-9pm) is healthy and cosmopolitan, with choices including avocado, cheese, fruit and muesli, plus organic coffee that guests say is the best in town.

The Lights Hostel HOSTEL €
(☎951 25 35 25; www.thelights.es; Calle Torregorda 3; dm €19-38; ❄📶) Never mind this hostel's rather bleak exterior. Ride the elevator up to reception and things brighten considerably, with a great roof terrace, a nice guest kitchen and air-conditioned four- to 10-bed dorms with thick mattresses and ample bedside conveniences (power outlets, reading lights, privacy curtains). Friendly staff organise frequent activities, from dinners to bar crawls to beach and cultural outings.

Hotel Boutique Teatro Romano BOUTIQUE HOTEL €€
(☎951 20 44 38; www.facebook.com/hotelteatroromano; Calle Zegrí 2; r €122-177; ❄📶) Reasonably priced for its ultra-central location, this boutiquey two-star overlooks the Roman theatre (p165), with eight family-friendly apartments and 13 sparkling white rooms so clean they look as if they've never been used. The whole place is modern, well managed, and studded with interesting design accents. The healthy breakfasts in the bright on-site cafe are a bonus.

★ **Palacio Solecio** BOUTIQUE HOTEL €€€
(☎952 22 20 00; www.palaciosolecio.com; Calle Granada 61; d €165-305, ste €320-415; ❄📶) Málaga's splashiest new boutique hotel opened in late 2019 in a sumptuously renovated 18th-century edifice, paces from the Museo Picasso in the heart of the pedestrian zone. Original architectural details are beautifully enhanced by modern designer touches in the luxurious rooms and suites. There's a colonnaded courtyard bar and an on-site restaurant presided over by Michelin-starred chef José Carlos García.

★ **Molina Lario** HOTEL €€€
(☎952 06 20 02; www.hotelmolinalario.com; Calle Molina Lario 20; d €198-325; ❄📶🏊) Situated within confessional distance of the cathedral, this four-star hotel has gracious service and a sophisticated, contemporary feel. The spacious, recently remodelled rooms are decorated in subdued tones of beige and white, with natural wood, crisp white linens and marshmallow-soft pillows. Topping it all off is a fabulous rooftop terrace and pool with views to the sea and the cathedral.

Room Mate Larios DESIGN HOTEL €€€
(☎952 22 22 00; www.room-matehotels.com; Calle Marqués de Larios 2; r from €162; ❄📶) Part of a small chain of Spanish-run design hotels, this central accommodation is housed in an elegantly restored 19th-century building. Rooms are luxuriously furnished with king-size beds and carpeting throughout; several rooms have balconies overlooking the sophisticated strut of shops and boutiques along Calle Marqués de Larios. The black-and-white rooftop bar comes with a lovely outdoor terrace.

Parador Málaga Gibralfaro HISTORIC HOTEL €€€
(☎952 22 19 02; www.parador.es; Castillo de Gibralfaro; r incl breakfast €180-225; P❄📶🏊) Perched next to Málaga's Moorish castle (p165) on the pine-forested Gibralfaro, the city's stone-built *parador* (luxurious state-owned hotel) hums with a sultan-like essence. Like most Spanish *paradores*, the kick is more in the setting and facilities than in the modern, businesslike rooms – though most do boast spectacular views from their terraces. Non-guests can dine at the excellent terrace restaurant.

Eating

Málaga has a staggering number of tapas bars and restaurants (more than 400 at last count), particularly around the historic centre.

★ **La Peregrina Centro** SEAFOOD €
(☎952 60 66 76; Calle Madre de Dios 17; tapas €2.50, raciones €5-12; ⏲1-4.30pm & 8.15-11.45pm Tue-Sat, 1-4pm Sun) A seafood lover's dream, this white-tiled shoebox of a tapas bar is a fantastic place to indulge your 'try-everything-on-the-menu' fantasies, with tapas-sized portions of every seafood item imaginable, from squid to shrimp to sardines. It's especially fun on a Sunday afternoon, when local families are out in force.

★ **Casa Aranda** CAFE €
(www.casa-aranda.net; Calle Herrería del Rey 3; churro €0.50, chocolate €1.95; ⏲8am-12.30pm

& 5-9pm) Casa Aranda is in a narrow alleyway next to the market and, since 1932, has been *the* place in town to enjoy chocolate and churros (tubular-shaped doughnuts). The cafe has taken over the whole street, with several outlets overseen by an army of mainly elderly, white-shirted waiters who welcome everyone like an old friend (and most are).

El Camerino MEDITERRANEAN €
(☎604 258810; http://elcamerinomalaga.es; Calle de la Madre de Dios 22; mains €10; ⏲noon-4pm Fri-Sun, 8pm-midnight Wed-Mon) An understated sense of style pervades this casual resto with stool and couch seating and a canopy of wine glasses dangling above the bar. The French chef gives his own unique twist to small plates including squid *cazuela*, pink rice with salmon and quiche of the day. The homemade bread is a delightful touch, the homemade ice cream even more so.

Noviembre CAFE €
(☎952 22 26 54; www.noviembrehealthyfood.com; Calle Álamos 18; breakfast from €4, sandwiches & salads €7-12; ⏲9am-2am;) With its purposefully aged wood, mismatched furniture and high-ceilinged interior, hip Noviembre offers excellent breakfast choices made with organic eggs, and the Big Apple burger provides a good lunch filler. Salads, juices and other healthy snacks round out the menu.

Recyclo Bike Café CAFE €
(www.recyclobike.com; Plaza Enrique García Herrera 16; breakfast/lunch from €3/6; ⏲9am-midnight Mon-Thu, to 2am Fri & Sat, 10am-midnight Sun;) Trendy cafe with affiliated bike shop where you can enjoy a 'Wiggins' salad or exceedingly cheap cakes, coffee and breakfasts. Old bikes adorn the walls and ceiling.

★El Mesón de Cervantes TAPAS €€
(☎952 21 62 74; www.elmesondecervantes.com; Calle Álamos 11; medias raciones €4-10, raciones €8-18; ⏲7pm-midnight Wed-Mon) Cervantes started as a humble tapas bar run by expat Argentine Gabriel Spatz, but has now expanded into four bar-restaurants (each with a slightly different bent), all within a block of each other. This one is the HQ, where pretty much everything on the menu is a show-stopper – lamb stew with couscous; pumpkin and mushroom risotto; and, boy, the grilled octopus!

★Óleo FUSION €€
(☎952 21 90 62; www.oleorestaurante.es; Edificio CAC, Calle Alemania; mains €14-22; ⏲1.30-4pm & 8.30pm-midnight Tue-Sat;) Located at the city's Centro de Arte Contemporáneo (p169) with white-on-white minimalist decor, Óleo provides diners with the unusual choice of Mediterranean or Asian food, with some subtle combinations such as duck breast with a side of seaweed with hoisin, as well as more purist Asian dishes and gourmet palate-ticklers such as candied roasted piglet.

Al Yamal MOROCCAN €€
(☎952 21 20 46; www.facebook.com/restaurante.alyamal; Calle Blasco de Garay 7; mains €14-20; ⏲noon-4.30pm & 7-11.30pm Mon-Sat) Moroccan restaurants are less common in Málaga than in Granada, but Al Yamal, family-run for four decades in the heart of the Soho district, serves the authentic stuff, including tagines, couscous and *kefta* (meatballs). The street profile looks unpromising, but the tiny dining room has six cosy booths decorated with vivid Moroccan fabrics and a trickling fountain.

El Balneario de los Baños del Carmen SEAFOOD €€
(☎951 90 55 78; www.elbalneariomalaga.com; Calle Bolivia 40, La Malagueta; mains €12-22; ⏲8.30am-1am Sun-Thu, to 2.30am Fri & Sat;) Enjoying front-row views of the beach at La Malagueta, El Balneario is a wonderful place to sit outside on a balmy evening and share a plate of prawns or grilled sardines, along with some long, cold beverages. Built in 1918 to cater to Málaga's bourgeoisie, it's rekindling its past as one of the city's most celebrated venues for socialising.

La Cosmopolita SPANISH €€€
(☎952 21 58 27; www.facebook.com/restaurantelacosmopolita; Calle José Denis Belgrano 3; mains €14-25) La Cosmopolita dependably draws a crowd with its sophisticated mix of time-tested classics (cured cheeses and Iberian meats, Gillardeau oysters, squid grilled with onions and saffron, anchovies in extra virgin olive oil) and Mediterranean-inspired fancies (guinea fowl in port wine sauce, tuna confit with aubergine stew).The cosy interior is complemented by chequered-cloth sidewalk tables spread across an intimate old town square.

Drinking & Nightlife

Málaga might not be as big as Madrid, but it's just as much fun. The pedestrianised old town is the main hive, especially around Plaza de la Constitución and Plaza de la Merced.

★La Tetería TEAHOUSE

(www.la-teteria.com; Calle San Agustín 9; speciality teas €2.70; ⏲9am-10pm Tue & Wed, to 11pm Thu & Sun, to 1am Fri, 3pm-1.30am Sat, 3-10pm Mon) There are numerous *teterías* in Málaga, but only one *La* Tetería. While it's less Moorish than some of its more atmospheric brethren, it still sells a wide selection of fruity teas, backed by a range of rich cakes. Along with the cafe's location next to the Museo Picasso Málaga (p164), this ensures that the place is usually close to full.

★Bodegas El Pimpi BAR

(www.elpimpi.com; Calle Granada 62; ⏲noon-2am; 📶) This rambling bar is an institution. The interior encompasses a warren of rooms, and there's a courtyard and open terrace overlooking the Teatro Romano (p165). Walls are decorated with historic feria posters and photos of visitors past, while the enormous barrels are signed by more well-known passers-by, including Tony Blair and Antonio Banderas. Tapas and meals are also available.

Antigua Casa de Guardia BAR

(www.antiguacasadeguardia.com; Alameda Principal 18; ⏲10am-10pm Mon-Thu, to 10.45pm Fri & Sat, 11am-3pm Sun) This atmospheric tavern dates to 1840 and is the oldest bar in Málaga. The peeling custard-coloured paintwork and black-and-white photographs of local boy Picasso look fittingly antique. Try the dark brown, sherry-like *seco* (dry), the romantically named *lágrima trasañejo* (very old teardrop), or any of the dozen other Málaga wines served from giant barrels running the length of the bar.

La Madriguera Craft Beer CRAFT BEER

(☎663 523577; www.facebook.com/lamadrigueracraftbeer; Calle Carretería 73; ⏲5pm-1am Wed & Thu, 5pm-3am Fri, noon-3am Sat, noon-5pm Sun) The 'Rabbit Hole', as its name translates, keeps the punters happy with daily listings of a dozen ever-changing craft beers and an equal number of more permanent light bites to soak them up.

Mia Coffee Shop COFFEE

(www.facebook.com/Miacoffeeshop; Plaza de los Mártires 4; ⏲9.30am-7.30pm Mon-Fri, 10am-6pm Sat) *¿Has sonreido hoy?* (Have you smiled today?) So reads the sign above the counter at this hole-in-the-wall coffee shop – and the answer will be an emphatic 'Yes!' when you squeeze through the door and sip a cup of

MÁLAGA TAPAS TRAIL

The pleasures of Málaga are essentially undemanding, easy to arrange and cheap. One of the best is a slow crawl around the city's numerous tapas bars and old bodegas (cellars).

La Tranca (www.latranca.es; Calle Carretería 92; tapas €1.60-3.90; ⏲12.30pm-2am Mon-Sat, to 4pm Sun) Drinking in this always busy bar is a physical contact sport, with small tapas plates passed over people's heads.

Colmado 93 (www.facebook.com/colmado93; Calle Carretería 93; tapas €1-3.50; ⏲noon-midnight Mon-Sat) The floor-to-ceiling shelves in this vintage ex-grocery create an atmospheric backdrop for sampling small plates of *mojama* (salt-cured tuna), sheep and goat's cheese, and *malagueña* sausage.

Casa Lola (www.tabernacasalola.com; Calle Granada 46; tapas €2.10-3.50; ⏲11am-4pm & 7pm-midnight) Fronted by traditional blue-and-white tiles, this ever-bustling spot serves a luscious range of *pintxos* (Basque-style tapas), accompanied by free-flowing vermouth on tap.

Tapeo de Cervantes (☎952 60 94 58; www.eltapeodecervantes.com; Calle Cárcer 8; medias raciones €4.50-8, raciones €8.50-14; ⏲1-3.30pm & 7.30-11.30pm Tue-Sun) This original Cervantes bar-restaurant (there are now four) is a bit more boisterous and intimate than the Mesón around the corner, yet the tapas line-up is virtually identical – ie among the best in the city.

Uvedoble Taberna (www.uvedobletaberna.com; Calle Císter 15; tapas €2.40-3.90; ⏲12.30-4pm & 8pm-midnight Mon-Sat; 📶) If you're seeking something a little more contemporary, head to this popular spot with its innovative take on traditional tapas.

TINTO DE VERANO

If you're visiting in summer, consider ordering a *tinto de verano* at any local bar. This long, cold drink is made with red wine, local lemonade (not too sweet), lashings of ice and a slice of lemon. It's refreshing, and it shouldn't make your head reel too much on a hot day.

their heavenly joe. Coffee in myriad forms is all you'll find here, but it's some of the best in Málaga.

Los Patios de Beatas WINE BAR
(952 21 03 50; www.lospatiosdebeatas.com; Calle Beatas 43; 1-4pm & 8pm-midnight Mon-Sat, 1-5pm Sun;) Two 18th-century mansions have metamorphosed into this sumptuous space where you can sample fine wines from a selection reputed to be the most extensive in town. Stained-glass windows and beautiful resin tables inset with mosaics and shells add to the overall art-infused atmosphere. Innovative tapas and *raciones* (full-plate servings) are also on offer.

Entertainment

The city has a strong flamenco legacy and its own *palo* (style) called *malagueñas*. There are several long-standing venues and a couple of new ones (though not as many as in Seville or Jerez).

★Peña Juan Breva FLAMENCO
(Calle Juan Franquelo 4; shows €15) You'll feel like a gatecrasher at this private *peña*, but persevere: the flamenco is *muy puro*. Watch guitarists who play as though they've got 24 fingers and listen to singers who bellow forth as if their heart was broken the previous night. There's no set schedule. Ask about dates at the on-site Museo de Arte Flamenco (p168).

Kelipe FLAMENCO
(665 097359; www.kelipe.net; Muro de Puerta Nueva 10; shows €25; shows 9pm Thu-Sun) There are many flamenco clubs springing up all over Andalucía, but few are as soul-stirring as Kelipe. Not only are the musicianship and dancing of the highest calibre, but the talented performers create an intimate feel and a genuine connection with the audience.

Teatro Cervantes THEATRE
(952 22 41 09; www.teatrocervantes.com; Calle Ramos Marín; Sep–mid-Jul) The handsome art-deco Cervantes has a fine program of music, theatre and dance, including some well-known names on the concert circuit. It also hosts a November jazz festival.

Shopping

The chic, marble-clad Calle Marqués de Larios is home to designer stores and boutiques. In the surrounding streets are family-owned small shops in handsomely restored old buildings, selling everything from flamenco dresses to local sweet Málaga wine. Don't miss the fabulous daily Mercado Atarazanas (p169).

Alfajar ARTS & CRAFTS
(www.alfajar.es; Calle Císter 1; 10am-9pm) Perfect for handcrafted Andalucian ceramics produced by local artisans. You can find traditional designs and glazes, as well as more modern, arty and individualistic pieces.

Information

Hospital Carlos Haya (951 29 00 00; www.hospitalregionaldemalaga.es; Avenida de Carlos Haya)

Municipal Tourist Office (951 92 60 20; www.malagaturismo.com; Plaza de la Marina; 9am-8pm Apr-Oct, to 6pm Nov-Mar) Offers a range of city maps and booklets. It also operates information kiosks at the Alcazaba entrance (Calle Alcazabilla), at the main train station (Explanada de la Estación), on Plaza de la Merced and on the eastern beaches (El Palo and La Malagueta).

Regional Tourist Office (951 30 89 11; Plaza de la Constitución 7; 9am-7.30pm Mon-Fri, 9.30am-3pm Sat & Sun) Located in a noble 18th-century former Jesuit college with year-round art exhibitions, this small tourist office carries a range of information on all of Málaga province, including maps of the regional cities.

Getting There & Away

AIR

Málaga's **airport** (AGP; 952 04 84 84; www.aena.es), the main international gateway to Andalucía, is 9km southwest of the city centre. It is a major hub in southern Spain, serving top global carriers as well as budget airlines.

BUS

The **bus station** (952 35 00 61; http://estabus.malaga.eu; Paseo de los Tilos) is 1km southwest of the city centre and has links to all major cities in Spain. The main bus line is **Alsa** (952 52 15 04; www.alsa.es). **Interbus** (www.interbus.es) runs to the Madrid airport.

Buses to the Costa del Sol (east and west) also usually stop at the more central Muelle Heredia bus stop.

Destinations include the following; note that the prices listed are the minimum quoted for the route.

Destination	Cost (€)	Duration (hr)	Frequency (daily)
Almería	20	2½-5	8
Córdoba	13	2¼-4	4
Granada	12	1½-2	23
Jaén	21	2¾-4¾	5
Madrid airport	17	6½	1
Seville	19	2¾	8

TRAIN

Málaga is the southern terminus of the Madrid–Málaga high-speed train line.

Málaga María Zambrano Train Station (☎902 43 23 43; www.renfe.com; Explanada de la Estación) is near the bus station, a 15-minute walk from the city centre. Destinations include Córdoba (€30 to €42, 45 minutes to one hour, 19 daily), Seville (€25 to €47, two to 3½ hours, 11 daily) and Madrid (€82, 2¾ hours, 14 daily).

ℹ Getting Around

TO/FROM THE AIRPORT

Bus

Bus Line A to the city centre (€3, 20 minutes) leaves from outside the arrivals hall every 20 to 25 minutes between 7am and midnight. The bus to the airport leaves from the eastern end of Paseo del Parque, and from outside the bus and train stations, with roughly the same frequency starting at 6.25am daily.

Car & Motorcycle

Numerous local and international car-hire agencies have desks at the airport.

Taxi

Taxis from the airport to the city centre cost between €22 and €25.

Train

Suburban train C1 (€2.30) runs from airport terminal T3 to María Zambrano station (eight minutes) and Málaga-Centro station beside the Río Guadalmedina (11 minutes) every 20 minutes between 6.44am and 12.54am. Departures from the city to the airport are every 20 minutes from 5.20am to 11.30pm.

BUS

EMT (Empresa Malagueña de Transportes) runs several useful buses around town (€1.30 for all trips around the centre), including buses 3 and 7 to the Museo Ruso de Málaga, bus 34 to El Pedregalejo and El Palo, and bus 35 to Castillo de Gibralfaro, all departing from points along Paseo del Parque and the Alameda Principal near Plaza Marina.

CAR & MOTORCYCLE

There are several well-signposted underground car parks in town. The most convenient are on Avenida de Andalucía, Plaza de la Marina and Plaza de la Merced – west, south and northeast of the centre, respectively.

METRO

Running west from María Zambrano train station, the clean and efficient two-line **Metro Málaga** (http://metromalaga.es) is of limited use to tourists, but can be handy for reaching the Museo Ruso and Museo Automovilístico.

TAXI

Taxi fares typically run between €6 and €8 for short trips (2km to 3km) within the city centre, including to the train and bus stations and Castillo de Gibralfaro.

TRAIN

Renfe (www.renfe.com) *cercanías* trains run from central Málaga to Fuengirola (€3.60), via the train station (€1.80), airport (€1.80) and Torremolinos (€2.05) every 20 minutes from 5.20am to 11.30pm.

COSTA DEL SOL

Regularly derided but perennially popular, Spain's famous 'sun coast' is a chameleonic agglomeration of end-to-end resort towns that were once (hard to believe) mere fishing villages. Development in the last 60 years has been far-reaching and not always subtle. Torremolinos is a popular gay resort, Benalmádena plugs theme parks and aquariums, Fuengirola draws families and water-sport lovers, Mijas poses as one of Andalucía's authentic white villages of yore and Marbella is loudly rich, while Estepona maintains a semblance of its former Spanish self.

Torremolinos & Benalmádena

POP 136,789

Once a small coastal village dotted with *torres* (towers) and *molinos* (watermills), 'Terrible Torre' became a byword for tacky package holidays in the 1970s, when it welcomed tourism on an industrial scale and morphed into a magnet for lager-swilling Brits whose command of Spanish rarely got beyond the words '*dos cervezas, por favor*'. But the times, they are a-changing.

Torre has grown up and widened its reach. These days the town attracts a far wider cross-section of people, including trendy clubbers, beach-loving families, gay visitors and, yes, even some Spanish tourists. Waiting for them is an insomniac nightlife, 7km of unsullied sand and a huge array of hotels, most of which subscribe to an architectural style best described as 'disastrous'.

Benalmádena, Torre's western twin, is more of the same with a couple of added quirks: a large marina designed as a kind of homage to Gaudí and a giant Buddhist stupa.

Sights & Activities

The centre of Torremolinos revolves around the pedestrian shopping street of San Miguel, from where several flights of steps lead down to the beach at Playamar; alternatively, take the **lift** (€0.50; 9am-midnight Jun-Sep, to 9pm Oct-May).

Benalmádena Pueblo has maintained a smidgen of traditional charm, with cobbled streets, orange trees and simple, flower-festooned houses. There's a magnificent view of the coast from the tiny church at the top of the village.

Casa de los Navajas HISTORIC BUILDING
(Calle del Bajondillo, Torremolinos; 11am-2pm & 6-8pm) FREE Impossible to miss in the concrete jungle of Torremolinos is this neo-Mudéjar beauty, a mini palace that formerly belonged to a local sugar baron, António Navajas. Originally constructed in 1925 in a style not dissimilar to that of Seville's Plaza de España, the house was renovated in 2014 and subsequently opened to the public. While there's no specific museum here, the terraced gardens, detailed architecture and sweeping views from the upstairs balconies are all impressive.

La Carihuela BEACH
(Torremolinos) Torremolinos' westernmost beach, stretching from a small rocky outcrop (La Punta) to Benalmádena, La Carihuela is a former fishing district and one of the few parts of town that hasn't suffered rampant overdevelopment. The beachside promenade is lined with low-rise shops, bars and restaurants, and is one of the most popular destinations for *malagueños* to enjoy fresh seafood at weekends.

Playamar BEACH
(Torremolinos) This long stretch of beach in Torremolinos is lined with reliably good *chiringuitos* (beach bars) and is also extremely family friendly, with playgrounds, and pedalos, sunbeds and parasols for hire. The wide promenade is popular with strollers and joggers, and in midsummer films are often screened.

Mariposario de Benalmádena BUTTERFLY PARK
(951 21 11 96; www.mariposariodebenalmadena.com; Calle Muérdago, Benalmádena Pueblo; adult/child €10/8.50; 10am-6.30pm; P) Next to the Buddhist stupa, in a quasi-Thai temple in Benalmádena (get off the train at Torremuelle station), this butterfly park is a delight. There are some 1500 fluttery creatures, including exotic subtropical species, moths and cocoons (in action), along with impressive plants and water features. Two iguanas, a wallaby and a giant tortoise are resident in the park.

Buddhist Stupa MUSEUM, MONUMENT
(www.stupabenalmadena.org; Benalmádena Pueblo; 10am-2pm & 4-6.30pm Tue-Sun; P) FREE The largest Buddhist stupa in Europe is in Benalmádena Pueblo. It rises up, majestically out of place, on the outskirts of the village, surrounded by new housing and with sweeping coastal views. The lofty interior is lined with exquisitely executed devotional paintings.

Sleeping & Eating

There's no shortage of greasy English-breakfast cafes and fish-and-chip shops, but fear not, Spain-o-philes: Torremolinos has arguably the finest clutch of beachside *chiringuitos* in the nation.

★**Hostal Guadalupe** HOSTAL €€
(952 38 19 37; www.hostalguadalupe.com; Calle del Peligro 15, Torremolinos; s €46-90, d €48-139, d/tr/q apt from €71/86/105;) At the bottom of the staircases that lead down to Torre's main beach is this nugget of old Spain that sits like a wonderful anachronism amid the concrete jungle. Enter through a delightful tiled tavern and ascend to plain but comfortable rooms, several with terraces overlooking the sea. There's also a couple of apartments with kitchen facilities for longer stays.

La Alternativa TAPAS €
(Avenida de la Constitución, Arroyo de la Miel; tapas from €2.50; 1pm-midnight Mon-Sat) A short walk from the Benalmádena-Arroyo de la Miel train stop, this large multiroomed place in an old-fashioned mall exudes a year-round feria atmosphere, its walls adorned

LGBTIQ+ TORREMOLINOS

Torremolinos is the most queer-friendly city in Andalucía. You'll see rainbow flags everywhere, from the moment you exit the subterranean train station in pedestrianised Plaza de la Nogalera, a rectangular square whose southern side is dotted with gay bars and clubs. Most of these places don't get going until 11pm at the earliest, with clubs filling up from 3am and running until 7am. A perennial favourite is **Parthenon** (www.facebook.com/parthenondisco; La Nogalera 716; ⌚midnight-6am Sun-Thu, to 7am Fri & Sat).

For some daytime action, hit Torrie's best-known gay-friendly bar-restaurant, El Gato Lounge, on Playa Beirola (sometimes known as 'El Gato Beach' or 'Gay Beach'), tucked just east of the rocky headland known as Punta de Torremolinos.

For more information on Torrie's gay life, visit www.gaytorremolinos4u.com. There's also a Torremolinos Gay Map available at many businesses in town.

with flamenco posters, matador pics and the occasional Virgin Mary. It's often packed and the tapas are superb. You can also have larger *raciones* like oxtail and Galician-style octopus.

★El Gato Lounge FUSION €€
(☎676 452504; www.elgatolounge.com; Paseo Marítimo 1K, Torremolinos; mains €5-10, tapas box menus €16-22; ⌚noon-late Feb-Oct) Don't expect the default sardines at this trend-setting fusion favourite across from Playamar beach's western end. Asian flavours abound in offerings like Sri Lankan curry, chicken satay, tuna tataki and Thai shrimp cakes – but the real showstopper is El Gato's 'tapas experience', featuring a flamboyant assortment of 12 Mediterranean-Asian tapas finished off with apple pie and cinnamon ice cream.

The relaxing beach-facing interior has a luxuriant allure, and the cocktails and highly attentive staff mean most people linger. The restaurant and the beach in front have long been favourite hang-outs for Torre's gay community.

Casa Juan SEAFOOD €€
(☎952 37 35 12; www.losmellizos.net; Calle San Ginés 20, La Carihuela; mains €14-22; ⌚1-4.30pm & 8pm-midnight Tue-Sat, 1-4.30pm Sun) The business dates back to the 1950s, but the fish is fresh daily at La Carihuela's most famous seafood restaurant, attracting shoals of *malagueños* on Sundays. It's been expanded into four dining spaces, so you can't go wrong provided you order carefully – some fish is sold by weight, so the bill can add up fast.

Drinking & Entertainment

Boomerang BAR
(☎665 455318; www.facebook.com/boomerang.torremolinos.bar; Plaza Tientos, Torremolinos; ⌚7pm-2am) It's always a party at this super-friendly bar with a devoted international and gay following up in Torremolinos' Pueblo Blanco neighbourhood. Great mixed drinks and an inviting space in an interior courtyard complete with fountain make it ideal for mingling and lingering late.

Clarence Jazz Club JAZZ
(☎951 91 80 87; www.clarencejazzclub.com; Calle Danza Invisible 8, Torremolinos; ⌚5pm-2am Wed & Thu, to 4am Fri & Sat, to midnight Sun) A great venue for live music five nights a week, this popular club recently reopened in spacious brand-new digs in Torremolinos. It hosts regular jam sessions, piano jazz nights and concerts by international acts.

Information

The main **tourist office** (☎951 95 43 79; www.turismotorremolinos.es; Plaza de Andalucía, Torremolinos; ⌚9.30am-6pm) is in the town centre. There are additional tourist kiosks at **Playa Bajondillo** (⌚10am-2pm) and **La Carihuela** (⌚10am-2pm).

Getting There & Away

BUS

Avanzabus/Portillo (☎955 03 86 65; http://malaga.avanzagrupo.com) runs services to Málaga (€1.50, 20 minutes, 21 daily), Marbella (€3.40, 30 minutes, 13 daily) and Ronda (€11.15, 2½ hours, six daily).

TRAIN

Trains run on the Renfe *cercanías* line to **Torremolinos** (Avenida Palma de Mallorca 53) and **Arroyo de la Miel-Benalmádena** (Avenida de la Estación 3) every 20 minutes from Málaga (€2.55, 18 minutes) from 5.20am to 11.30pm, continuing on to the final stop, Fuengirola (€2.55, 22 minutes).

Fuengirola

POP 80,309

Fuengirola is a crowded beach town decorated with utilitarian apartment buildings, but, despite half a century of rampant development, it retains a few redeeming qualities. Check out the beach – all 7km of it – adorned with a 10th-century Moorish castle. The town also has a large foreign-resident population, many of whom arrived in the '60s – and stayed.

Festivals & Events

Feria del Rosario CULTURAL
(6-12 Oct) Arguably the best and biggest on the Costa del Sol, Fuengirola's feria includes a *romería* (religious pilgrimage) during which locals head to the *campo* (countryside) for flamenco, paella and *cerveza* (beer). A flamenco Mass is held in the main church on 6 October, and is followed by drinking and dancing in the street, with most women in traditional flamenco attire.

Eating

★**Arte y Cocina** MEDITERRANEAN €€
(952 47 54 41; Calle Cervantes 15; mains €12-22; 6.30-10.30pm Tue-Thu & Sun, 7-11pm Fri & Sat;) The Italian-inflected food at this spot on Fuengirola's restaurant row is fresh as the decor. Expect artfully presented starters – from handmade ricotta-spinach tortelli to creamy porcini mushroom or seafood risotto – followed by honey-rosemary-marinated lamb chops or beef tagliata.

La Cepa Playa SEAFOOD €€
(692 623296; www.lacepaplaya.com; Paseo Maritimo; raciones €9-15; 10.30am-7pm) In business since 1959, when Fuengirola inhabited a different universe (both politically and economically), La Cepa is a *chiringuito* near the harbour serving a dizzying array of fish. Prawns, anchovies, cuttlefish, swordfish, clams, mussels, squid, sardines and hake are all on show. The paella's pretty good too.

Information

Tourist Office (952 46 74 57; http://turismo.fuengirola.es; Paseo Jesús Santos Rein 6; 9.30am-6pm Mon-Fri, 10am-2pm Sat & Sun;) One block northeast of the train station.

Getting There & Away

BUS

Avanzabus/Portillo (p177) runs bus services to Málaga (€2.35 to €3.35, 30 to 60 minutes, hourly), Estepona (€5.95, one hour, nine daily) and Marbella (€2.25 to €3.40, 30 minutes, 13 daily). Fuengirola's **bus station** (Calle Alfonso XIII) is half a block from the train station.

CAR & MOTORCYCLE

A toll road (AP7) connects Fuengirola with Estepona (€12.90), providing an alternative to the slower N340 coast road.

TRAIN

Trains (Avenida Jesús Santos Rein) on the Renfe *cercanías* line run every 20 minutes to Málaga (€4.10, 45 minutes) from 6.20am to 12.40am, with stops including the airport and Torremolinos (€2.55, 25 minutes).

Mijas

POP 82,742 / ELEV 428M

The story of Mijas encapsulates the story of the Costa del Sol. Originally a humble village, it's now the richest town in the province. Since finding favour with discerning bohemian artists and writers in the 1950s and '60s, Mijas has sprawled across the surrounding hills and down to the coast, yet it's managed to retain the throwback charm of the original *pueblo* (village).

Mijas has a foreign population of at least 40% and the municipality includes Mijas Costa and La Cala de Mijas, both located on the coast southwest of Fuengirola.

Sights & Activities

There are numerous trails leading out from Mijas. Call at the tourist office for maps. The fit can make for **Pico Mijas** (1151m) on a well-marked route. It's five hours return and a bit of a grunt.

Virgen de la Peña HISTORIC SITE
(Avenida Virgen de la Peña; 9.30am-6pm) If you walk past the *ayuntamiento* (town hall), you will reach this grotto where the Virgin Mary is said to have appeared to two children who were led here by a dove in 1586. Within the clifftop cave is a flower-adorned altar in front of an image of the Virgin, plus some religious vestments and silverwork in glass cases. It's a poignant spot despite the barrage of visitors.

Centro de Arte Contemporáneo de Mijas MUSEUM
(CAC; www.cacmijas.info; Calle Málaga 28; adult/child €3/free; 10am-6pm Mon-Sat) Notwithstanding its diminutive size, this museum houses the world's second-largest collection of Picasso ceramics, along with bronze figu-

rines, glassware, bas-reliefs, engravings and lithographs by Salvador Dalí, and a room dedicated to temporary exhibitions.

Coastal Footpath WALKING
(Playa La Luna, La Cala de Mijas, Mijas Costa;) Enjoy a gentle coastal stroll along a wooden promenade stretching 6km from La Cala de Mijas to Calahonda. The meandering walkway passes several beachside *chiringuitos*, quiet coves and rocky headlands. The path is in Mijas Costa, 20km southwest of the hilltop town of Mijas.

Sleeping

Casa Tejón APARTMENT €
(661 669469; www.casatejon.com; Calle Málaga 15; 2-person apt per day/week €50/325;) The small apartments here are cosily kitted out with a happy mishmash of furniture and textiles, and set around a small courtyard decorated with pots of scarlet geraniums. It's bang in the centre of the village, and the owners run a handy bar and restaurant next door.

TRH Mijas HOTEL €€€
(952 48 58 00; www.trhhoteles.com; Calle Tamisa 2; r €170-195;) High on a hillside just outside Mijas village, the TRH's top drawcards are the exceptional Costa del Sol panoramas from its long terrace bar, the big outdoor pool, and the newly refurbished Guinda spa, offering massages and a variety of other treatments. Downsides? It's a sprawling place that can feel a bit institutional when the tour buses roll in.

Eating & Drinking

Alboka Gastrobar INTERNATIONAL €€
(952 48 68 24; www.facebook.com/albokagastrobar; Avenida Virgen de la Peña 6; tapas €3-4.50, mains €9-17; noon-midnight Fri-Wed) A stone's throw from Mijas' central plaza, Alboka's fusion-themed menu encompasses creatively enhanced Spanish classics (Galician octopus with mango and raspberry coulis) and international offerings (veggie lasagne, Moroccan-spiced chicken skewers). It's all attractively presented in a sleek space with cushioned benches, mismatched vintage chairs and an eclectic soundtrack ranging from tango, jazz and sitar to Piaf, Dylan and Johnny Cash.

Aroma Cafe & Secret Garden INTERNATIONAL €€
(952 59 03 93; www.aromacafeandsecretgarden.com; Calle San Sebastián 8; mains €12-25; noon-1am) The house dates to 1872, but the real charmer here is the secret garden out the back: a divine dining space under mature orange, fig and olive trees with a well that dates from Moorish times. An Argentine barbecue is served nightly (weather permitting), while other dishes include traditional tapas, salads, pasta and seafood.

Museo del Vino WINE BAR
(www.museovinomijas.com; Calle San Sebastián 14; noon-4pm & 7-11pm) Located on the prettiest street in the village, this is more a wine bar than a museum, though it does have some literature and photographs relating to local viticulture. More striking is the sheer number of bottles lining the walls. Well-priced tasting offers invite you to sample a variety of wines accompanied by ham, cheese and other nibbles.

Information

Mijas Tourist Office (952 58 90 34; http://turismo.mijas.es; Plaza Virgen de la Peña; 9am-6pm Mon-Fri, 10am-2pm Sat & Sun) Helpful tourist office with a free map-dispensing machine outside.

Getting There & Away

The M112 bus runs four times daily to/from Málaga (€2.35, one to 1¼ hours), while the more frequent M122 serves Fuengirola (€1.55, 25 minutes) half-hourly. If you're driving, Mijas' centrally located 10-level car park is a bargain at €1 per day.

Marbella

POP 143,386

The Costa del Sol's bastion of bling is, like most towns along this stretch of coast, a two-sided coin. Standing centre stage in the tourist showroom is the 'Golden Mile', a conspicuously extravagant collection of star-studded clubs, shiny restaurants and expensive hotels stretching as far as Puerto Banús, the flashiest marina on the coast, where black-tinted Mercs slide along a quay populated by luxury yachts.

But Marbella has other, less ostentatious attractions. Its natural setting is magnificent, sheltered by the beautiful Sierra Blanca mountains, while its surprisingly attractive *casco antiguo* (old town) is replete with narrow lanes and well-tended flower boxes.

Long before Marbella started luring golfers, zillionaires and retired Latin American dictators, it was home to Phoenicians,

Visigoths, Romans and Moors. One of the joys of a visit to the modern city is trying to root out their legacy.

Sights & Activities

Marbella's tightly packed old town is chocolate-box perfect, with pristine white houses, narrow, mostly traffic-free streets and geranium-adorned balconies. You can easily spend an enjoyable morning or evening exploring the cafes, restaurants, bars, designer boutiques, and antique and craft shops.

Plaza de los Naranjos SQUARE
At the heart of Marbella's *casco antiguo* is the extremely pretty Plaza de los Naranjos, dating back to 1485, with tropical plants, palms, orange trees and, inevitably, overpriced bars.

Museo Ralli MUSEUM
(www.museoralli.es; Urbanización Coral Beach; 10am-3pm Tue-Sat) FREE This superb private art museum exhibits works by primarily Latin American and European artists in bright, well-lit galleries. Part of a nonprofit foundation with four other museums (in Chile, Uruguay and Israel), its wide-ranging, regularly rotating exhibitions include sculptures by Salvador Dalí, vibrant contemporary paintings by Argentinian surrealist Alicia Carletti and Peruvian artist Herman Braun-Vega, and works by heavyweights like Joan Miró, Henry Moore and Giorgio de Chirico. It's 6km west of central Marbella near Puerto Banús.

Aventura Amazonia ADVENTURE SPORTS
(952 83 55 05; www.aventura-amazonia.com; Avenida Valeriano Rodriguez 1; adult/child €24/22; 10am-6pm Tue-Fri, to 7pm Sat & Sun) Two dozen zip lines are located over six adventure circuits, the longest measuring 240m. Tots are catered to with an adventure playground, and there's even a day-care centre so that parents who want a quick escape can whiz through the trees.

Sleeping

Hostal El Gallo HOSTAL €
(952 82 79 98; www.hostalelgallo.com; Calle Lobatas 46; s/d from €40/55) In expensive Marbella, El Gallo – a traditional Spanish bar with a few rooms upstairs – is what you might call a rough in the diamond. Run by a welcoming family, it inhabits a narrow whitewashed street with flower boxes and throwback charm, and has all you need for a comfortable but economical stay.

★ **Claude** BOUTIQUE HOTEL €€€
(952 90 08 40; www.hotelclaudemarbella.com; Calle San Francisco 5; r €257-410) The former summer home of Napoleon III's wife has updated its regal decor to create a hotel fit for a 21st-century empress. Situated in the quieter upper part of town, the Claude's arched courtyards and shapely pillars successfully marry contemporary flourishes with the mansion's original architecture, while claw-foot bathtubs and crystal chandeliers add to the classic historical feel.

Eating

Marbella has a veritable Milky Way of restaurants that'd take aeons to sample in its entirety. Restaurants in the historic centre tend to be (over) priced for tourists; an exception is narrow Calle San Lázaro near the Plaza de los Naranjos, which is home to several excellent tapas bars generally frequented by locals.

El Estrecho TAPAS €
(www.barelestrecho.es; Calle San Lázaro 12; tapas €2.50-5, raciones €8-12; noon-midnight Mon-Sat) *Estrecho* (narrow) perfectly describes the tiny back alley that conceals this great little tapas bar, in business since 1954. Traditional tapas are the big draw here, from *albóndigas* (meatballs) and fried fish to *carne mechada* (slow-braised pork), *salmorejo* (Córdoba-style thick gazpacho) and seafood salad.

Mia Café TAPAS €
(952 76 66 75; Calle Remedios 7; tapas €2; noon-midnight) Tucked into a pretty old town square, this friendly newcomer wins accolades for its reasonably priced homemade tapas (six for €10), including vegan, veggie and gluten-free options. Grab a spot at a little tile-topped table and linger over salads, mini-burgers, spinach-laden tortilla Española and glasses of wine, enhanced by prime people watching in the heart of Marbella's pedestrian zone.

Garum INTERNATIONAL €€
(952 85 88 58; www.garummarbella.com; Paseo Marítimo; mains €12-23; noon-11.30pm) Finnish-owned and set in a dreamy location right on the 'Golden Mile' across from the beach, Garum has a menu that will please those seeking a little gourmet variety. Expect dishes ranging from smoked-cheese soup to Moroccan chicken samosas and red-lentil falafel.

★The Farm SPANISH **€€€**
(☎952 82 25 57; www.thefarm-marbella.com; Plaza Altamirano 2; mains €14-23; ⊙noon-11pm;) It's not a farm, but instead an exceptionally pretty restaurant in Marbella's old town, consisting of a patio, a terrace and a dining room furnished with modern 'chill-out' flourishes. The food's all farm fresh though, and there's a brilliant selection of set menus showcasing organic ingredients, including vegetarian and kids' options. Check the website calendar for occasional flamenco shows.

Drinking & Nightlife

For the most spirited bars and nightlife, head to Puerto Banús, 7km west of Marbella. In town, the best area is around the small Puerto Deportivo. There are also some beach clubs open only in summer.

Astral Coctelería COCKTAIL BAR
(www.astralmarbella.es; Muelle de Levante, Puerto Banús; ⊙10am-midnight Sun-Thu, to 1am Fri & Sat) If sipping flamboyantly colourful cocktails on a palm-fringed beachfront is your vision of Costa del Sol bliss, you've found your spot. Out in Puerto Banús, it's a fun and lively scene, with the bar area done up to look like the deck of a fully rigged three-masted ship.

Nikki Beach CLUB
(http://marbella.nikkibeach.com; Don Carlos Hotel, Carretera de Cádiz, Km 192; ⊙noon-late Apr-Oct;) Sprawl on white sofas overlooking the surf as you nibble haute tapas and enjoy live music or a DJ playing a riveting mix. It's a fixture on the glam clubbing scene: wear your best party clothes, shine those shoes and assume some attitude – it's that kind of place.

Shopping

Déjà Vu VINTAGE
(☎952 82 55 21; www.vintagemarbella.com; Calle Pedraza 8; ⊙11am-3pm & 5.30-9pm Mon-Fri, noon-3pm Sat) This is the place for designer and luxury vintage fashion from 1960s Chanel suits to classic Yves Saint Laurent three-piece suits. Also sells accessories, jewellery and some truly fabulous hats.

Information

Tourist Office (☎952 76 87 07; www.turismo.marbella.es; Plaza de los Naranjos; ⊙8am-8.30pm Mon-Fri, 10am-5pm Sat & Sun, to 9pm Jul & Aug) Has plenty of leaflets and a good town map. There are other tourist offices on the Paseo Marítimo and in Puerto Banús.

Getting There & Away

BUS

The **bus station** (☎952 82 34 09; Avenida del Trapiche) is 1.5km north of the old town just off the A7 *autovía* (toll-free dual carriageway).

Avanzabus/Portillo (p177) runs buses to Fuengirola (€3.40, 30 minutes, four daily), Estepona (€3.35 to €4.50, 30 to 40 minutes, hourly), Málaga (€6.50 to €8.85, 45 minutes to 1½ hours, half-hourly) and Ronda (€6.85, 1½ hours, nine daily).

CAR & MOTORCYCLE

Marbella's streets are clogged with traffic and parking is notoriously difficult. The most central underground car park is on Avenida del Mar (per hour/day €2.10/16.80). For free parking, try Calle Juan Alameda and Avenida Dr Maíz Viñals along Parque de la Represa.

Estepona

POP 68,286

Estepona was one of the first resorts to attract foreign residents and tourists almost 50 years ago and, despite the surrounding development, the centre of the town still has a cosy, old-fashioned feel. There's good reason for that: Estepona's roots date back to the 4th century. Centuries later, during the Moorish era, the town was an important and prosperous centre due to its strategic proximity to the Strait of Gibraltar.

Estepona is steadily extending its promenade to Marbella; at its heart is the pleasant Playa de la Rada beach. The Puerto Deportivo is the focal point of the town's nightlife, especially at weekends, and is also excellent for water sports.

Sights

Orchidarium GARDENS
(☎951 51 70 74; www.orchidariumestepona.com; Calle Terraza 86; adult/child €3/1; ⊙9am-2pm & 3-6pm Tue-Fri, 10am-2pm & 3-6pm Sat, 10am-2pm Sun) In an elegant glass-domed building surrounded by lush landscaping, Estepona's Orchidarium houses 1500 species of orchid – the largest collection in Europe – as well as 5000 subtropical plants, flowers and trees and an impressive artificial waterfall. It's a delightful oasis in the middle of town, perfect for an afternoon stroll.

Sleeping & Eating

Estepona has some good restaurants, particularly in the old town and port. Traditional places are usually the best bet: follow the aroma of fresh-off-the-boat fish and the sound of quick-fire Spanish.

Hotel Boutique Casa Veracruz BOUTIQUE HOTEL €€
(☎951 46 64 70; www.hotelboutiquecasaveracruz.com; Calle Veracruz 22; d €79-115; ❄📶) The 'boutique' label barely does this place justice. With its diminutive courtyard, trickling fountain, stately paintings and stylish antique furniture, it's like a little slice of historic Seville dispatched to the Costa del Sol – and all yours for a very economical sum. Extra touches include Nespresso machines, ample continental breakfasts, and complimentary tea, coffee and sweets available all day.

★**La Escollera** SEAFOOD €
(☎952 80 63 54; Puerto Pesquero; mains €8-14; ⏲1-4.30pm & 8-11.30pm Tue-Sat, 1-4.30pm Sun) Locals in the know – from dock workers swigging beers to families celebrating a first communion – flock to this port-side eatery to dine on arguably the freshest and best seafood in town. The atmosphere is agreeably bustling and no-frills basic, with plastic tables and paper cloths. But when the fish tastes this good and the beer is this cold, who cares?

La Cocina SPANISH €€
(☎952 79 63 20; www.facebook.com/RestauranteytapaslacocinA; Calle Blas Ortega 19; tapas €2.50-4, raciones €10-18; ⏲1-4pm & 7.30-11.30pm Tue-Thu, to midnight Fri-Sun) Half restaurant, half tapas bar, La Cocina serves delectable renditions of Spanish classics like *pulpo a la gallega* (Galcian-style octopus) and *gambas pil pil* (spicy, garlicky prawns). Especially charming is the informal *botica*, with its tiled interior and tall sidewalk tables on a pedestrianised square facing the church of Nuestra Señora de los Remedios.

Venta García EUROPEAN €€
(☎952 89 41 91; Carretera de Casares, Km 7; mains €12-20; ⏲12.30-4pm & 7.30-10.30pm Tue-Sat, 12.30-4.30pm Sun; Ⓟ) 🌿 Venta Garcia specialises in superbly conceived dishes using local produce, complemented by sublime countryside views. There's an emphasis on meat like venison (served with a red fruit sauce) and pork: the Montes de Málaga dish executes a local take on pork served with peppers, fried egg and chips. It's on the road to Casares, 7km from Estepona. Reserve at weekends.

🍷 Drinking & Nightlife

The Puerto Deportivo is the best place to head for late-night bars. Beach clubs also swing into action in summer. Check flyers around town to see what's on.

★**Siopa** CAFE
(www.facebook.com/siopaestepona; 80 Calle Real; ⏲7pm-late) Stamp-sized Irish-run bar-cafe on a pedestrian street near the historic centre specialising in bottled craft beers. You'll see no clichéd Gaelic-pub motifs here. Instead, you get a blackboard listing more than 40 craft beers and almost as many gins. It also serves the best coffee in town.

ℹ Information

Tourist Office (☎952 80 80 81; www.estepona.es; Plaza de las Flores; ⏲9am-3pm Mon-Fri, 10am-2pm Sat) Located on a historical square, this office has brochures and a decent map of town.

ℹ Getting There & Around

The **bus station** (Avenida Litoral) is 2km east of the town centre next to the Palacio de Exposiciones y Congresos. Avanza/Portillo (p177) buses run over a dozen times a day to Marbella (from €3.35, 30 to 45 minutes) and Málaga (from €9.25, 1¼ to two hours).

There are several well-signposted car parks along Avenida España, including the centrally located Parking Paseo Maritimo (per hour/day €2.10/17).

THE INTERIOR

Ronda

POP 33,877 / ELEV 744M

Built astride a huge gash in the mountains carved out by the Río Guadalevín, Ronda is a brawny town with a dramatic history littered with outlaws, bandits, guerrilla warriors and rebels. Its spectacular location atop El Tajo gorge and its status as the largest of Andalucía's white towns have made it hugely popular with tourists – particularly notable when you consider its relatively modest size. Modern bullfighting was practically invented here in the late 18th century, and the town's fame was spread further by its close association with American Europhiles Ernest Hemingway (a lover of bullfighting) and Orson Welles (whose ashes are buried in the town).

South of the gorge, Ronda's old town largely dates from Islamic times, when it was an important cultural centre filled with mosques and palaces. Further north, the grid-shaped 'new' town is perched atop steep cliffs, with parks and promenades looking regally over the surrounding mountains.

Sights

La Ciudad, the historic old town on the southern side of El Tajo gorge, is an atmospheric area for a stroll, with its evocative, still-tangible history, Renaissance mansions and wealth of museums. The newer town, where you'll be deposited if you arrive by bus or train, harbours the emblematic bullring and the leafy Alameda del Tajo gardens. Three bridges crossing the gorge connect the old town with the new.

Plaza de Toros NOTABLE BUILDING

(Calle Virgen de la Paz; €8, incl audio guide €9.50; ⏲10am-8pm Apr-Sep, to 7pm Mar & Oct, to 6pm Nov-Feb) In existence for more than 200 years, this is one of Spain's oldest bullrings and the site of some of the most important events in bullfighting history. A visit is a way of learning about this deep-rooted Spanish tradition without actually attending a bullfight. The on-site Museo Taurino is crammed with memorabilia such as blood-spattered costumes worn by 1990s star Jesulín de Ubrique. It also includes artwork by Picasso and photos of famous fans such as Orson Welles and Ernest Hemingway.

Built by Martín Aldehuela, the bullring is admired for its soft sandstone hues and galleried arches. At 66m in diameter, it is also the largest and, therefore, most dangerous bullring in Spain, yet it only seats 5000 spectators – a tiny number compared with the huge 50,000-seat bullring in Mexico City. Behind the Plaza de Toros, spectacular clifftop views open out from Paseo de Blas Infante and the nearby Alameda del Tajo park.

Puente Nuevo BRIDGE

(New Bridge; interpretive centre adult/reduced €2.50/2; ⏲interpretive centre 10am-6pm Mon-Fri, to 3pm Sat & Sun) Straddling the dramatic gorge of the Río Guadalevín (Deep River) is Ronda's most recognisable sight, the towering Puente Nuevo, so named not because it's particularly new (building started in 1759) but because it's newer than the **Puente Viejo** (Old Bridge). A rather lacklustre interpretive centre documenting the bridge's history sits directly underneath. You'll get better bridge views from above, or from the Sendero Los Molinos (p186), which runs along the bottom of the gorge. The bridge separates the old and new towns.

Casa del Rey Moro GARDENS

(House of the Moorish King; ☎617 610808; www.casadelreymoro.org; Calle Cuesta de Santo Domingo 9; adult/reduced €6/3; ⏲10am-9.30pm May-Sep, to 8pm Oct-Apr) Several landscaped terraces give access to La Mina, an Islamic stairway of nearly 200 steps cut into the rock all the way down to the river at the bottom of the gorge. These steps enabled Ronda

OFF THE BEATEN TRACK

CUEVA DE LA PILETA

Twenty kilometres southwest of Ronda la Vieja are some of Andalucía's most ancient and fascinating **caves** (☎666 741775; www.cuevadelapileta.org; Benaoján; adult/child €10/6; ⏲tours 10am-1pm & 4-6pm May-Sep, to 5pm Oct-Apr) . Torchlit guided tours into the dark belly of the cave system reveal Stone Age paintings of horses, goats and fish from 20,000 to 25,000 years ago. Beautiful stalactites and stalagmites add to the effect. The tours are given by English-speaking members of the Bullón family, whose great-great-grandfather discovered the paintings in 1905.

The fact that the caves are so uncommercial is a real plus. Although the family is finding the upkeep a battle, they are loath to give in to pressure from the local authorities to turn the caves over to its administration.

Benaoján village is the nearest you can get to the Cueva de la Pileta by public transport. The caves are 4km south of the village, about 250m off the Benaoján–Cortes de la Frontera road; you'll need your own transport from the village, or you can walk. The turn-off is signposted. Benaoján is served by two Los Amarillos buses (from Monday to Friday) and up to four daily trains to/from Ronda. Walking trails link Benaoján with Ronda and villages in the Guadiaro Valley.

Ronda

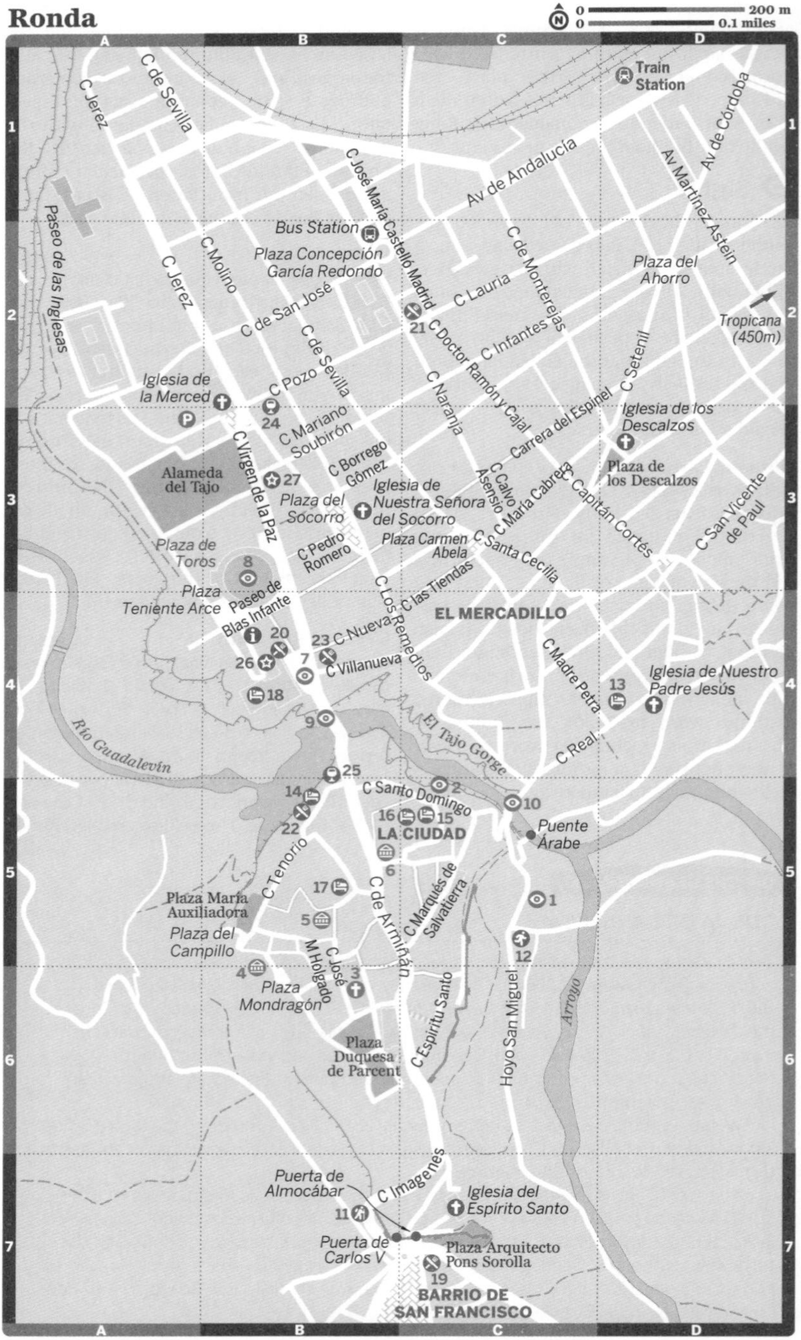

0 200 m
0 0.1 miles
Train Station
C Jerez
C de Sevilla
Av de Andalucía
Av de Córdoba
Av Martínez Astein
C José María Castelló Madrid
Bus Station
Plaza Concepción García Redondo
Paseo de las Inglesas
C Molino
C de Monterejas
Plaza del Ahorro
C Lauria
C de San José
C Doctor Ramón y Cajal
Tropicana (450m)
C Infantes
C Setenil
Iglesia de la Merced
C Pozo
C Naranja
Iglesia de los Descalzos
C Mariano Soubirón
Carrera del Espinel
C Virgen de la Paz
C Borrego Gómez
Plaza de los Descalzos
Alameda del Tajo
C Calvo Asensio
C María Cabrera
C Capitán Cortés
Iglesia de Nuestra Señora del Socorro
Plaza del Socorro
C San Vicente de Paul
Plaza de Toros
C Pedro Romero
Plaza Carmen Abela
C Santa Cecilia
C las Tiendas
Plaza Teniente Arce
Paseo de Blas Infante
C Los Remedios
EL MERCADILLO
C Nueva
C Villanueva
C Madre Petra
Iglesia de Nuestro Padre Jesús
Río Guadalevín
El Tajo Gorge
C Real
C Santo Domingo
LA CIUDAD
Puente Árabe
C Tenorio
C de Armiñán
C Marqués de Salvatierra
Plaza María Auxiliadora
Plaza del Campillo
C José M Holgado
Plaza Mondragón
C Espíritu Santo
Hoyo San Miguel
Arroyo
Plaza Duquesa de Parcent
Puerta de Almocábar
C Imagenes
Iglesia del Espírito Santo
Puerta de Carlos V
Plaza Arquitecto Pons Sorolla
BARRIO DE SAN FRANCISCO

Ronda

Sights

1 Baños Árabes C5
2 Casa del Rey Moro C5
3 Iglesia de Santa María La Mayor B6
4 Museo de Ronda B6
5 Museo Joaquín Peinado B5
6 Museo Lara B5
7 Plaza de España B4
8 Plaza de Toros B3
9 Puente Nuevo B4
10 Puente Viejo C5

Activities, Courses & Tours

11 Sendero Los Molinos B7
12 Spa-Hammam Aguas de Ronda C5

Sleeping

13 Aire de Ronda D4
14 Hotel Montelirio B5
15 Hotel Ronda C5
16 Hotel Ronda Nuevo C5
17 Hotel Soho Boutique Palacio San Gabriel B5
18 Parador de Ronda B4

Eating

19 Almocábar C7
20 Bardal B4
21 Bodega San Francisco C2
22 Restaurante Albacara B5
23 Tragatá B4

Drinking & Nightlife

24 Entre Vinos B2
25 Tabanco Los Arcos B4

Entertainment

26 El Quinqué B4
27 Ronda Guitar House B3

to maintain water supplies when it was under attack. It was also the point where Christian troops forced entry in 1485. The steps are dark, steep and wet in places. Take care.

Baños Árabes HISTORIC SITE
(Arab Baths; Calle San Miguel; €3.50, Tue free; 10am-3pm Sat & Sun year-round, to 7pm Mon-Fri Apr-Sep, to 6pm Mon-Fri Oct-Mar) Backing onto Ronda's river, these 13th-century Arab baths are among the best preserved in all of Andalucía, with horseshoe arches, columns and clearly designated divisions between the hot and cold thermal areas. An excellent 10-minute video (in Spanish and English) helps you visualise the baths in their heyday. Enjoy the pleasant walk down here from the centre of town.

Plaza de España SQUARE
The town's main square was made famous by Ernest Hemingway in *For Whom the Bell Tolls*. Chapter 10 tells how, early in the civil war, the 'fascists' of a small town were rounded up in the *ayuntamiento*, clubbed, and made to walk the gauntlet between two lines of townspeople before being thrown off a cliff. The episode is based on events that took place here in the Plaza de España. What was the *ayuntamiento* is now Ronda's *parador* (p186).

Museo Lara MUSEUM
(952 87 12 63; www.museolara.org; Calle de Armiñán 29; adult/child €4/2; 11am-8pm Jun-Oct, to 7pm Nov-May) This crazy, cluttered museum is the private collection of Juan Antonio Lara Jurado, who has been a collector since the age of 10. Now in his 80s, he still lives above the museum. You name it, it's here: priceless, historic collections of clocks, weapons, radios, gramophones, sewing machines, telephones, typewriters, smoking pipes, opera glasses, Spanish fans, scales, cameras, carriages and far, far more.

Iglesia de Santa María La Mayor CHURCH
(Calle José M Holgado; adult/child €4.50/2; 10am-8pm Apr-Sep, to 7pm Mar & Oct, to 6pm Nov-Feb, closed 12.30-2pm Sun) The city's original mosque metamorphosed into this elegant church. Just inside the entrance is an arch covered with Arabic inscriptions that was part of the mosque's *mihrab* (prayer niche indicating the direction of Mecca). The church has been declared a national monument, and its interior is a riot of decorative styles and ornamentation. A huge central cedar choir stall divides the church into two sections: aristocrats to the front, everyone else at the back.

Museo de Ronda MUSEUM
(Palacio Mondragón, Plaza Mondragón; €3.50; 10am-7pm Mon-Fri, to 3pm Sat & Sun Apr-Sep, shorter hours Oct-Mar) This somewhat faded city museum displays artefacts and information spanning several millennia of Andalucian history. Of even more interest to some will be the palatial setting. Built for Abomelic, ruler of Ronda in 1314, the palace has retained its colonnaded internal Mudéjar courtyard, from where a horseshoe arch leads to a clifftop garden with fountains and splendid views.

Museo Joaquín Peinado MUSEUM
(952 87 15 85; www.museojoaquinpeinado.com; Plaza del Gigante; adult/reduced €4/2; 10am-5pm Mon-Fri, to 3pm Sat) Native Ronda artist Joaquín Peinado was an amigo and contemporary of Picasso's, a fact reflected in his work, with its strong abstract lines, flirtations with cubism and seeming obsession with female nudes. Nearly 200 of his pieces are displayed in the 18th-century Palacio Marqueses de Moctezuma, a typically Andalucian space that's been fitted with a plush minimalist interior.

Activities

Spa-Hammam Aguas de Ronda HAMMAM
(627 596847; www.hammamaguasderonda.com; Calle Molino de Alarcón; baths €18, incl massage €23; noon-8pm Mon, 10am-9pm Tue-Thu, 10am-10pm Fri & Sat) Joining numerous other Andalucian cities, Ronda has opened its own Moorish-style hammam. Book a two-hour slot ahead; massages also available.

Hiking

Several well-marked hikes, ranging in distance from 2.45km to 9.1km, leave from the city limits. If you only have time for one, try **Sendero Los Molinos**, which takes you down to the mouth of the gorge and offers classic views back up to the Puente Nuevo.

The tourist office (p188) sells the 1:45,000 Serranía de Ronda hiking map (€5) published by Colecciones Topográficas de Andalucía, along with similar maps for the nearby Sierra de Grazalema and Sierra de las Nieves.

Climbing

The Serranía de Ronda has developed over half a dozen vie ferrate (fixed-protection climbing routes). The two most popular are on the cusp of the town. The **Tajo de Ronda I**, which climbs up the gorge for 56m, is rated difficult. The **Tajo de Ronda II**, which parallels it, is considered easy and ideal for beginners. Various companies, including **Andalucía Aventura** (627 100469; www.alandalusactiva.com), offer guided via ferrata climbs from around €30.

Sleeping

Ronda has some of the most atmospheric, historically interesting and well-priced accommodation in Málaga province – in fact, in all of Spain. In the first half of May and from July to September, you must book ahead.

★**Aire de Ronda** BOUTIQUE HOTEL €€
(952 87 59 82; www.airederonda.com; Calle Real 25; r €125-170; P) Located in a particularly tranquil part of town, this hotel is one of those old-on-the-outside, super-modern-on-the-inside places that Spain does so well. Smart minimalist rooms come in punchy black and white, and fabulous bathrooms have shimmering silver- or gold-coloured mosaic tiles, walk-in showers and, in one romantic couples' room, a glass partition separating the shower from the bedroom.

★**Hotel Soho Boutique Palacio San Gabriel** HOTEL €€
(952 19 03 92; www.sohohoteles.com; Calle Marqués de Moctezuma 19; d incl breakfast from €90;) Despite new chain-hotel management, this heavyweight historic edifice retains its age-old charm, filled with antiques and faded photographs that offer an insight into Ronda's history – bullfighting, celebrities and all. Ferns hang down the huge mahogany staircase, and there's a billiard room, a cosy living room stacked with books, and a DVD-screening room with 10 velvet-covered seats rescued from Ronda's theatre.

Hotel Ronda BOUTIQUE HOTEL €€
(952 87 22 32; www.hotelronda.net; Ruedo Doña Elvira 12; s/d €53/70;) With its geranium-filled window boxes and whitewashed *pueblo* exterior, Hotel Ronda offers relatively simple (for Ronda) contemporary rooms painted in vivid colours and accentuated by punchy original abstracts. Several rooms overlook the beautiful Mina gardens across the way. It's a bargain for the price. Just up the street, its brand-new sister **Hotel Ronda Nuevo** (Ruedo Doña Elvira 6; r €100-160;) offers three spacious modern rooms.

Parador de Ronda HOTEL €€€
(952 87 75 00; www.parador.es; Plaza de España; r €143-326; P) Acres of shining marble and deep-cushioned furniture give this modern *parador* a certain appeal, but really it's all about the views. The terrace is a wonderful place to drink in the sight of the gaping gorge with your coffee or wine, especially at night.

Hotel Montelirio HOTEL €€€
(952 87 38 55; www.hotelmontelirio.com; Calle Tenorio 8; r €132-190;) Hugging El Tajo gorge, the Montelirio has magical views. The converted *palacio* has been sensitively

WORTH A TRIP

GAUCÍN

Gaucín is a picturesque whitewashed village located on the edge of the Serranía de Ronda mountain range with views to Gibraltar and Morocco. The village was impoverished until the late 1970s, from which time it was gradually discovered by a group of footloose bohemians and artists, mainly from chilly northern-European climes. Since then Gaucín has continued to grow as an artists' colony.

Gaucín is also an excellent spot for birdwatchers and there are handy identification plaques throughout the meandering narrow lanes; look skywards and you may spy vultures and booted eagles circling above.

Gaucín is on the Ronda–Algeciras bus route operated by Comes (p189) that runs once a day in either direction. Gaucín also has a tiny train station, served thrice daily from Ronda (€6.25, 45 minutes), but be advised that it's a 25-minute uphill taxi ride from here to Gaucín village.

Ask to see the photo album that documents the Belgian owners' loving restoration of **La Fructuosa** (617 692784; www.lafructuosa.com; Calle Luís de Armiñán 67; r with street/valley view from €70/90;), an exquisite small hotel. Original features have been retained as far as possible, and exposed stone, original beams, terracotta tiles and dark-wood antiques complete the high-end rustic look. Downstairs off the breakfast room is a glorious terrace with bucolic valley views.

The hotel's **restaurant** (mains €12-20; 8-10pm Mon, Tue, Fri & Sat, from 7.30pm Wed, 1-3pm Sun), housed in a former bodega complete with ancient wine press, serves a creative menu that ranges from fennel velouté with toasted pistachios, to asparagus and lemon risotto, to braised lamb with Moroccan spices. It really shines on Wednesday nights, when tapas and live music draw a local crowd, and on occasional Sunday evenings when guest chefs are brought in for special international dinners.

refurbished and rooms are sumptuous. The lounge has retained its gorgeous Mudéjar ceiling and opens onto a terrace complete with plunge pool. The on-site **Restaurante Albacara** (952 16 11 84; www.hotelmontelirio.com/restaurant; Calle Tenorio 8; mains €19-25; 12.30-4pm & 7.30-11pm) is similarly excellent.

Eating

Typical Ronda food is hearty mountain fare, with an emphasis on stews (called *cocido, estofado* or *cazuela*), *trucha* (trout), *rabo de toro* (oxtail stew) and game such as *conejo* (rabbit), *perdiz* (partridge) and *codorniz* (quail).

Bodega San Francisco TAPAS €

(www.bodegasanfrancisco.com; Calle Comandante Salvador Carrasco; tapas €1-2, raciones €6-10; noon-5pm & 7pm-midnight Fri-Wed) This is one of Ronda's cheapest and most Spanish tapas bars, with a remarkable variety of dirt-cheap tapas, plus a full line-up of grilled meats and Iberian hams. It's just north of the centre.

Tragatá TAPAS €€

(952 87 72 09; www.tragata.com; Calle Nueva 4; mains €12-25; 1.15-3.45pm & 8-11pm;) A small outpost for Ronda's gourmet guru, Benito Gómez, who runs the nearby Bardal (p188), Tragatá allows you to sample some of the same *cocina alta* (haute cuisine) at a fraction of the price. The eruption of flavours ranges from tomato salad with mint and basil to Japanese tatakis to pig's trotter and pig's snout stew.

Tropicana ANDALUCIAN €€

(952 87 89 85; www.facebook.com/tropicanaronda; cnr Avenida Málaga & Calle Acinipo; mains €12-20; 12.30-3.30pm & 7.30-10pm Wed-Sun) A little off the trail in Ronda's new town, the Tropicana has nonetheless garnered a strong reputation for its certified-organic food, served in a small but handsome restaurant with the feel of a modern bistro.

★ **Almocábar** ANDALUCIAN €€

(952 87 59 77; Calle Ruedo Alameda 5; tapas €2, mains €15-25; 12.30-4.30pm & 8-11pm Wed-Mon) Tapas here include *montaditos* (small pieces of bread) topped with delicacies like duck breast and chorizo. Mains are available in the elegant dining room, where meat dominates – rabbit, partridge, lamb and beef cooked on a hot stone at your table. There's a bodega upstairs, and wine tastings and dinner can be arranged for a minimum of eight people (approximately €50 per person).

WORTH A TRIP

PARQUE NATURAL SIERRA DE LAS NIEVES

Southeast of Ronda lies the virtually uninhabited Parque Natural Sierra de las Nieves, noted for its rare Spanish fir (the *pinsapo*), large caves, and fauna including some 1000 ibex and various species of eagle. The *nieve* (snow) after which the mountains are named usually falls between January and March. **El Burgo**, a remote but attractive village 10km north of Yunquera on the A366, makes a good base for visiting the east and northeast of the park. The spa town of **Tolox**, 35km southeast of El Burgo, is another good option.

The park is crossed by a network of trails. The most rewarding walk is an ascent of the highest peak in western Andalucía, **Torrecilla** (1918m). Start at the Área Recreativa Los Quejigales, which is 10km east by unpaved road from the A376 Ronda–San Pedro de Alcántara road. The turn-off, 12km from Ronda, is marked by signs. From Los Quejigales there's a steepish 470m ascent by the **Cañada de los Cuernos gully**, with its tranquil Spanish-fir woods, to the high pass of **Puerto de los Pilones**. After a fairly level section, the final steep 230m to the summit rewards you with marvellous views. The walk is five to six hours return, and is easy to moderate in difficulty.

There's a **tourist office** (☎663 346620; www.sierranieves.com; Calle del Pozo 17; ⏲10.30am-2pm & 6-8pm Sat, 10.30am-2pm Sun) in Yunquera, and other offices in Tolox and El Burgo. You should also be able to pick up some park information at the tourist office in Ronda.

Buses run by **Autobuses Paco Pepe** (☎952 23 12 00; www.grupopacopepe.com) depart from Ronda's bus station (p189) bound for the villages of El Burgo (€3.50, 45 minutes) and Yunquera (€3.50, one hour) up to three times a day.

Bardal GASTRONOMY €€€
(☎951 48 98 28; www.restaurantebardal.com; Calle José Aparicio 1; 15-/19-course tasting menu €115/140; ⏲noon-4.30pm & 8-11.30pm Tue-Sat) You'll need to reserve ahead in order to enjoy a meal at Bardal, the flagship restaurant of celebrity chef Benito Gómez. The astounding 15- to 19-course menu is a whistle-stop tour through oyster stew, yellow-tomato gazpacho, frozen apple water, monkfish foie gras and other such uncommon dishes. Hold onto your hat – and fork.

Drinking & Entertainment

Ronda's traditionally low-key flamenco scene has expanded in recent years, with the opening of several distinctly different venues.

★**Entre Vinos** WINE BAR
(Calle Pozo 2; ⏲12.30-4.30pm & 8pm-12.30am Tue-Sat; ᯤ) Frequented mainly by locals, this stylish small wine bar with exposed-brick and wood panelling is a great place to taste local Ronda wines, accompanied by superb, well-priced and creative tapas.

Tabanco Los Arcos WINE BAR
(Calle Armiñán 6; ⏲12.30-11.30pm Tue-Sun) Adjacent to Ronda's famous bridge, this wine bar under the arches makes a relaxing mid-afternoon break. Snag a stool with gorge views at one of the tall tables in back, and sample drops from a dozen local wineries, served with a nice mix of tapas.

Ronda Guitar House CONCERT VENUE
(☎951 91 68 43; www.rondaguitarhouse.com; Calle Mariano Soubirón 4; tickets €15; ⏲concerts 7pm) A little different to the standard flamenco venues, this small performance space offers guitar recitals rather than full-blown shows. Virtuoso performer Paco Seco covers a multitude of acoustic genres: classical, flamenco, jazz or a fusion of all three. The same venue hosts the **Ronda Guitar Festival** (www.rondaguitarfestival.com; ⏲Jun) every summer.

El Quinqué LIVE PERFORMANCE
(☎633 778181; Paseo de Blas Infante; tickets €12-21; ⏲shows 2pm & 8.30pm Tue-Sun) For a traditional flamenco show employing a three-pronged attack of voice, guitar and dance, come to El Quinqué. Entry prices are very reasonable for the 45-minute lunchtime shows. Evening shows are double the length. Food and drink are available at the bar-restaurant.

Information

Tourist Office (☎952 18 71 19; www.turismoderonda.es; Paseo de Blas Infante; ⏲9.30am-

6pm Mon-Fri, to 5pm Sat, to 2.30pm Sun) Opposite the Plaza de Toros; provides information on the town and region.

Getting There & Around

BICYCLE

You can rent a bike from **Cycle Ronda** (654 869946; www.cycleronda.com; 3-day rental hybrid/road bike/e-bike €60/75/95) or **Center-Bikes** (951 46 95 03; www.centerbikes.com; Calle Sevilla 50; bike hire per day €20; 10am-2pm & 5-8.30pm Mon-Fri, 10am-2pm Sat).

BUS

From the town's **bus station** (Plaza Concepción García Redondo 2), **Comes** (956 80 70 59; www.tgcomes.es) runs to Cádiz (€18, 3½ hours). **Damas** (959 25 69 00; www.damas-sa.es) goes to Seville (€12.75, 1¾ to 2¾ hours) via Algodonales (€3.60, 40 minutes) and Grazalema (€3, 50 minutes). **Avanzabus/Portillo** (912 72 28 32; www.avanzabus.com) has four daily buses to Málaga (€12.70, 2¾ to three hours) and eight to Marbella (€6.85, 1¼ hours).

CAR & MOTORCYCLE

There are a number of underground car parks charging €2.40 per hour or €18 per day. Some hotels offer parking deals for guests, and there's also free street parking on the periphery of town.

TRAIN

Ronda's **train station** (952 87 16 73; www.renfe.com; Avenida de Andalucía) is on the line between Bobadilla and Algeciras. Trains run to Algeciras (€11.50 to €20.10, 1½ to two hours, five daily) via Gaucín and Jimena de la Frontera. This train ride is one of Spain's finest and worth taking just for the views. Other trains depart for Málaga (€12, two to 2¾ hours, one daily), Madrid (€55.70, four hours, three daily) and Granada (€16.65, 2½ to three hours, three daily). For Seville, change at Bobadilla or Antequera-Santa Ana. It's less than 1km from the train station to most accommodation. A taxi will cost around €7.

Serranía de Ronda

Curving around Ronda's south and southeast, the Serranía de Ronda may not be the highest or most dramatic mountain range in Andalucía, but it's certainly among the prettiest. Any of the roads through the range between Ronda and southern Cádiz province, Gibraltar or the Costa del Sol make a picturesque route. Cortes de la Frontera, overlooking the Guadiaro Valley, and Gaucín, looking across the Genal Valley to the Sierra Crestellina, are among the most beautiful spots to stop.

To the west and southwest of Ronda stretch the wilder Sierra de Grazalema and Los Alcornocales natural parks. There are plenty of walking and cycling possibilities. More recently, the region has developed nearly a dozen vie ferrate, making it one of the best areas in Spain for fixed-protection climbing. Ronda's tourist office can provide details of outdoor activities as well as maps.

Acinipo ARCHAEOLOGICAL SITE
(www.facebook.com/acinipoenclavearqueologico) FREE Some 20km northwest of Ronda, off the A374, is the relatively undisturbed Roman site of Acinipo at Ronda la Vieja. Although completely ruined, with the exception of its partially reconstructed theatre, it's a wonderfully wild site with fantastic views of the surrounding countryside. You can happily while away an hour wandering among the fallen stones and trying to guess the location of various baths and forums. Hours vary month to month – check the Facebook page for details.

★**El Molino del Santo** HOTEL €€€
(952 16 71 51; www.molinodelsanto.com; Estación de Benaoján, Benaoján; incl breakfast d €139-199, ste €219; Mar-Nov; P) Located near the well-signposted Benaoján train station, this British-owned hotel has a stunning setting next to a rushing stream; the main building is a former olive mill. Rooms are set amid pretty gardens and have private terraces or balconies. The restaurant is popular with locals and serves contemporary international cuisine.

El Chorro

Fifty kilometres northwest of Málaga, the Río Guadalhorce carves its way through the awesome **Garganta del Chorro** (El Chorro gorge). Also called the Desfiladero de los Gaitanes, the gorge is about 4km long, as much as 400m deep and sometimes just 10m wide. Its sheer walls, and other rock faces nearby, are a magnet for rock climbers, with hundreds of bolted climbs snaking their way up the limestone cliffs.

While Ardales (population 2700) is the main town in the area, most people use the hamlet of El Chorro, with its train station, hiking trails and decent hotel, as a base. Lying 6km west is the serene **Embalse del Conde del Guadalhorce**, a huge reservoir that dominates the landscape and is noted for its carp fishing. This is also the starting point for the legendary and recently revitalised Caminito del Rey path. The whole area is protected in a natural park.

Sights & Activities

Bobastro RUINS

(€3; 10am-3pm Mon-Fri, to 6pm Sat & Sun Apr-Oct, 10am-3pm Tue-Fri, to 5pm Sat & Sun Nov-Mar) Bobastro was the hilltop redoubt of 9th-century rebel Omar ibn Hafsun, who led a prolonged revolt against Cordoban rule. At one stage he controlled territory from Cartagena to the Strait of Gibraltar. It's thought that he converted from Islam to Christianity (thus becoming what was known as a Mozarab) before his death in 917 and was buried here. When Córdoba conquered Bobastro in 927, the poor chap's remains were taken for grisly posthumous crucifixion outside Córdoba's Mezquita.

From El Chorro village, drive up the far (western) side of the valley and after 3km take the signed Bobastro turn-off on your left. The ticket booth is another 3km up the hill; from here, follow a 500m path to the remains of a remarkable little Mozarabic church cut from the rock, the shape so blurred by time that it appears to have been sculpted by the wind alone.

Alternatively, you can hike 4km to Bobastro from El Chorro village. Take the road downhill from the station, cross the dam and turn left after 400m at the GR7 trail signpost. The first 2km are steep uphill, and then it's flat and slightly downhill. The views of El Chorro gorge are marvellous.

At the top of the hill, 2.5km up the road from the ticket booth and with unbelievable views, are faint traces of Ibn Hafsun's rectangular *alcázar* (Muslim-era fortress).

Climbing

Andalucia Aventura (www.andalucia-aventura.com; climbing course/via ferrata per person from €55/75) organises rock climbing and abseiling in El Chorro for various levels of skill, from a one-day taster (€55) to a four-day course (from €250 excluding accommodation). Its website has a calendar showing upcoming courses. Book online.

The fixed-protection climbing route **Via Ferrata de los Albercones** can be found close to the southern exit of the Caminito del Rey. It's rated 'medium' difficulty and comes with a couple of Himalayan-style bridges and a short zip line. You can rent gear and ask about guided trips at Finca La Campana.

Hiking

The most thrilling hike in the area (and probably the whole of Spain) is the vertigo-inducing Caminito del Rey.

A couple of easy circular hikes start from the Conde del Guadalhorce reservoir next to **Bar-Restaurante El Kiosko** (952 11 23 82; www.restauranteelkiosko.com; Parque de Ardales; mains €7.50-13; 8.30am-midnight), including the 4.2km **Sendero del Guaitenejo**, which offers the opportunity to branch off on a spur path leading up to a good viewpoint over the Chorro gorge.

An uphill 4km (one-way) hike to the Muslim-era ruins of Bobastro starts from just outside El Chorro village, following the long-distance GR7 path, which carries on to the village of Ardales.

The GR248 path south to the town of Álora (17.5km) passes through El Chorro and is clearly signposted from the train station.

Sleeping & Eating

Finca La Campana HOSTEL, HOTEL €

(626 963942; www.fincalacampana.com; camping per person €9, dm/d €14/38, 2-/4-/6-person cottages €56/78/88; P) A 2km uphill hike from the train station, but worth it, La Campana is a favourite for outdoor types, especially climbers. There are various sleeping configurations, including dorms, doubles, campsites and cottages, plus a pool, a kitchen and even a small climbing wall.

Complejo Turístico Rural La Garganta HOTEL €€

(952 49 50 00; www.lagarganta.com; Barriada El Chorro; r without/with gorge view from €81/90; P) It's amazing what you can make out of an old flour mill. La Garganta sits right next to El Chorro station, its former milling installations now hosting a pleasant rural hotel with pool, restaurant and comfortable rooms, including several family-friendly duplexes. It's well worth paying extra for a room with views of the river gorge.

Getting There & Away

Trains run twice daily from Málaga to El Chorro (€6.25, 40 minutes), continuing north from El Chorro to Seville (€20.80, 2¾ hours).

A half-hourly shuttle bus (€1.55, 20 minutes) runs between the train station and the starting point of the Caminito del Rey (p191).

DON'T MISS

EL CAMINITO DEL REY

The **Caminito del Rey** (King's Path; www.caminitodelrey.info; self-guided/guided visit €10/18; ⏲9.30am-5pm Tue-Sun Apr-Oct, to 3pm Nov-Mar) – so named because Alfonso XIII walked along it when he opened the Guadalhorce hydroelectric dam in 1921 – consists of a 2.9km boardwalk that hangs 100m above the Río Guadalhorce and snakes around the cliffs, affording breathtaking views at every turn. Required walks to/from the northern and southern access points make the total hiking distance 7.7km.

The *caminito* had fallen into severe disrepair by the late 1990s, and it became known as the most dangerous pathway in the world; it officially closed in 2000 (though some daredevils still attempted it). Following an extensive €5.5-million restoration, it reopened in 2015; it is now safe and manageable for anyone with a reasonable head for heights, and has become one of Andalucía's top tourist attractions.

The boardwalk is constructed with wooden slats; in some sections the old crumbling path can be spied just below. The walk can only be done in one direction (north–south), and it's highly advisable to book a time slot online; tickets often sell out days or even weeks in advance.

Buses run half-hourly from El Chorro train station to the starting point, where there are a couple of restaurants. From here you must walk 2.7km to the northern access point of the *caminito*, where you'll show your ticket and be given a mandatory helmet to wear. At the end of the *caminito* there's another 2.1km to walk from the southern access point back to El Chorro. Allow three to four hours total for the walk and connecting bus ride, as the views are made for savouring.

The most convenient public transport to the area is the twice-daily train from Málaga to El Chorro station. If you're driving, you can park at either end of the gorge and use the bus to make your connection.

Antequera

POP 41,239 / ELEV 577M

Known as the crossroads of Andalucía, Antequera sees plenty of travellers pass through but few lingering visitors. But those who choose not to stop are missing out. The town's foundations are substantial: two Bronze Age burial mounds guard its northern approach and Moorish fables haunt its grand Alcazaba. The undoubted highlight here, though, is the opulent Spanish-baroque style that gives the town its character and that the civic authorities have worked hard to restore and maintain. There's also an astonishing number of churches – more than 30, many with wonderfully ornate interiors.

Sights

The substantial remains of the Alcazaba, a Muslim-built hilltop castle, dominate Antequera's historic quarter and are within easy (if uphill) reach of the town centre.

★Antequera Dolmens Site — ARCHAEOLOGICAL SITE

(⏲9am-3pm & 8-10pm Tue-Sat, 9am-3pm Sun Jul–mid-Sep, hours vary rest of year) FREE Antequera's two earth-covered burial mounds – the **Dolmen de Menga** and the **Dolmen de Viera** – were built out of megalithic stones by Bronze Age people around 2500 BCE. When they were rediscovered in 1903, they were found to be harbouring the remains of several hundred bodies. Considered to be some of the finest Neolithic monuments in Europe, they were named a Unesco World Heritage site in 2016.

Prehistoric people of the Bronze Age transported dozens of huge slabs from the nearby hills to construct these burial chambers. The stone frames were covered with mounds of earth. The engineering implications for the time are astonishing. Menga, the larger, is 25m long, 4m high and composed of 32 slabs, the largest of which weighs 180 tonnes. In midsummer the sun rising behind the Peña de los Enamorados hill to the northeast shines directly into the chamber mouth.

The dolmens are located 1km from the town centre in a small, wooded park beside the road that leads northeast to the A45. Head down Calle Encarnación from the central Plaza de San Sebastián and follow the signs. A third chamber, the **Dolmen del Romeral** (Cerro Romeral; ⏲9am-3.30pm Tue-Sun mid-Jun–mid-Sep, hours vary rest of year) FREE, is 4km further out of town.

Alcazaba FORTRESS
(adult/child €4/2, incl Colegiata de Santa María la Mayor €6/3; ⌚10am-6pm) Favoured by the Granada emirs of Islamic times, Antequera's hilltop Moorish fortress has a fascinating history and covers a massive 62,000 sq metres. The main approach to the hilltop is from Plaza de San Sebastián, up the stepped Cuesta de San Judas and then through an impressive archway, the **Arco de los Gigantes**, built in 1585 and formerly bearing huge sculptures of Hercules. All that's left today are the Roman inscriptions on the stones.

The admission price includes a multilingual audio guide, which sets the historical scene as you meander along tidy pathways, flanked by hedges and the remains of a Gothic church and some 6th-century Roman dwellings.

Climb the 50 steps of the **Torre del Homenaje** for great views, especially towards the northeast and of the **Peña de los Enamorados** (Rock of the Lovers) – a rock whose profile resembles a human face, long the subject of local legends.

Colegiata de Santa María la Mayor CHURCH
(Plaza Santa María; adult/child €3/1.50, incl Alcazaba €6/3; ⌚10am-6pm) Just below the Alcazaba is the large 16th-century Colegiata de Santa María la Mayor. This church-college played an important part in Andalucía's 16th-century humanist movement, and flaunts a beautiful Renaissance facade, lovely fluted stone columns inside and a Mudéjar *artesonado* (a ceiling of interlaced beams with decorative insertions). It also plays host to some excellent musical events and exhibitions. Just outside the church entrance, don't miss the ruins of Roman baths dating from the 3rd century CE.

Museo de la Ciudad de Antequera MUSEUM
(Museo Municipal; Plaza del Coso Viejo; ⌚10am-2pm & 4.30-6.30pm Tue-Fri, from 9.30am Sat, 9.30am-2pm Sun) FREE Antequera's town-centre municipal museum displays an impressive collection of Roman artefacts from the surrounding area, including glassware, jewellery, stone carvings and fragmentary mosaics. Its pride and joy is an elegant and athletic 1.4m bronze statue of a boy, *Efebo*. Discovered on a local farm in the 1950s, it's possibly the finest example of Roman sculpture found in Spain.

Iglesia del Carmen CHURCH
(Plaza del Carmen; €2; ⌚11am-1.30pm Tue-Sat Jul–mid-Sep, hours vary rest of year) Only the most jaded would fail to be impressed by the Iglesia del Carmen and its marvellous 18th-century Churrigueresque *retablo* (altarpiece). Magnificently carved in red pine by Antequera's own Antonio Primo, it's spangled with statues of angels by Diego Márquez y Vega, and saints, popes and bishops by José de Medina. While the main altar is unpainted, the rest of the interior is a dazzle of colour and design, painted to resemble traditional tilework.

Museo Conventual de las Descalzas MUSEUM
(Plaza de las Descalzas; €3.30; ⌚10am-1.30pm & 5-7pm Tue-Fri, 9am-noon & 5-6.30pm Sat, 9am-noon Sun) This museum, in the 17th-century convent of the Carmelitas Descalzas (barefoot Carmelites), approximately 150m east of the town's Museo de la Ciudad de Antequera, displays highlights of Antequera's rich religious-art heritage. Outstanding works include a painting by Lucas Giordano of St Teresa of Ávila (the 16th-century founder of the Carmelitas Descalzas), a bust of the Dolorosa by Pedro de Mena and a *Virgen de Belén* sculpture by La Roldana.

Festivals & Events

Antequera's religious processions during **Semana Santa** (Holy Week; ⌚Mar/Apr) are among the most traditional in Andalucía. The city celebrates the harvest with bullfights, dancing and street parades during **Real Feria de Agosto** (⌚mid-Aug).

Sleeping & Eating

Antequera specialities include *porra antequerana* (a thick and delicious garlicky tomato soup that's similar to gazpacho), *bienmesabe* (literally 'tastes good to me'; a sponge dessert) and *angelorum* (a dessert incorporating meringue, sponge and egg yolk).

Hotel Coso Viejo HOTEL €
(☎952 70 50 45; www.hotelcosoviejo.es; Calle Encarnación 9; d incl breakfast €43-56; P ❄ ☎) This converted 17th-century neoclassical palace is right in the heart of Antequera, opposite Plaza Coso Viejo and the town museum (p192). The simply furnished rooms are set around a handsome patio with a fountain, and the excellent Mesón Las Hazuelas tapas bar and restaurant is just next door.

Parador de Antequera HISTORIC HOTEL €€
(☎952 84 02 61; www.parador.es; Paseo García del Olmo 2; d €95-160; P ❄ ☎ ≋) This *para-*

dor is in a quiet area of parkland north of the bullring and near the bus station. It's comfortably furnished and set in pleasant gardens with wonderful views, especially at sunset.

★**Arte de Cozina** ANDALUCIAN €€
(952 84 00 14; www.artedecozina.com; Calle Calzada 27; tapas €2.80-3.50, mains €15-24; 1-11pm;) It's hard not to notice the surrounding agricultural lands as you approach Antequera, and this fascinating little hotel-restaurant combo is where you get to taste what they produce. Slavishly true to traditional dishes, it plugs little-known Antequeran specialities such as gazpacho made with green asparagus or *porra* (a cold, thick tomato soup) with oranges, plus meat dishes that include *lomo de orza* (preserved pork loin).

Recuerdos Tapas Bodega TAPAS €€
(951 35 63 65; Calle Laguna 5; tapas €1.85-3.90, raciones €8-16; 12.30-5pm & 8pm-midnight) Classy, casual Recuerdos stands out for its innovative home cooking, backed by a varied line-up of wines and cocktails. Three dozen flavourful offerings – Iberian pork loin with pineapple, homemade partridge pâté with rosemary oil and Seville orange marmalade, shrimp fritters with avocado aioli – all come as tapas, *medias raciones* and *raciones*. It's a 10-minute walk north of the tourist office.

Information

Municipal Tourist Office (952 70 25 05; http://turismo.antequera.es; Calle Encarnación 4; 9.30am-7pm Mon-Sat, 10am-2pm Sun) A helpful tourist office with information about the town and region.

Getting There & Around

BICYCLE

Bikes are a good way of getting around town or – if you're fit – up into the mountains of El Torcal (p193). Rent bikes from **Ciclos 2000** (695 180706; Calle San José 6; mountain/road bike per day €10/20; 10am-2pm & 5-9pm Mon-Fri, 10am-2pm Sat).

BUS

The **bus station** (Paseo García del Olmo) is 1km north of the centre. Alsa (p174) runs buses to Seville (€14, 2½ hours, five daily), Granada (€9, 1½ hours, five daily), Córdoba (€11, two hours 40 minutes, one daily), Almería (€23, six hours, one daily) and Málaga (€6, one hour, five daily).

CAR & MOTORCYCLE

There's underground parking on Calle Diego Ponce north of Plaza de San Sebastián (per hour €1.50, 12 to 24 hours €18).

TAXI

There are convenient taxi stands along Calle Calzada and Calle Infante Don Fernando, or you can call **Taxi Radio Antequera** (952 84 55 30). Most rides within town (for example, from the train station to the Alcazaba) cost no more than €6 or €7.

TRAIN

Antequera has two train stations. Closest to town is the **Antequera-Ciudad train station** (Avenida de la Estación), 1.5km north of the centre. At research time, work was still under way on a new high-speed train tine that will eventually connect Antequera-Ciudad with Granada. In the meantime, Antequera-bound train passengers must disembark at **Antequera-Santa Ana station**, 18km northwest of the town, and catch a free Renfe bus transfer into town.

High-speed AVE trains travel from Antequera Santa Ana to Málaga (€27, 25 minutes, eight daily), Córdoba (€34, 35 minutes, 13 daily) and Madrid (€76, 2½ hours, 10 daily).

Paraje Natural Torcal de Antequera

South of Antequera are the weird and wonderful rock formations of the Paraje Natural Torcal de Antequera. This 12-sq-km area of gnarled, serrated and pillared limestone formed as a sea bed 150 million years ago and now rises to 1336m (El Torcal). Not surprisingly, this other-worldly landscape fanned by fresh mountain breezes was declared a Unesco World Heritage site, along with Antequera's dolmens (p191), in 2016.

The park has an impressive visitor centre, which is the starting point for various hiking routes.

Activities

Hiking

There are three marked walking trails that you can do unguided. The 1.5km **Ruta Verde** (Green Route) and the 3km **Ruta Amarilla** (Yellow Route) both start and end at the **Centro de Visitantes** (952 24 33 24; www.torcaldeantequera.com; 10am-7pm Apr-Oct, to 5pm Nov-Mar) and take in the full sweep of rocky surrealism. Be prepared for plenty of rock-hopping. The 3.6km **Ruta**

Naranja (Orange Route) runs between the upper and lower car parks, tracking below the road. Gentler options are the miradors (lookouts) near the Centro de Visitantes and about 500m down the road.

Several guided hikes are organised on the more restricted routes. These last for approximately three to five hours and cover 3km to 8km; the cost is €10 to €16 per person. The visitor centre website has a regularly updated itinerary. Book in advance, and wear shoes with good tread as the trails are rocky.

Climbing

The park contains Andalucía's oldest via ferrata, known as the **Camorro route**. Laid out in 1999, it actually consists of four separate vie ferrate: Escalenuela, Alto Antigua, Crestera and Techo. Various companies, including Andalucia Aventura (p190), offer guided climbs. Book in advance.

Getting There & Away

There's no public transport to El Torcal. If you're travelling by car, leave central Antequera along Calle Picadero, which soon joins the Zalea road. After 1km or so you'll see signs on the left to Villanueva de la Concepción. Take this road and, after 12km (before entering Villanueva), turn right and head 3.75km uphill to the information centre. By bike it's a tough uphill cycle, but a joy coming down, with killer views. Rent bikes from Ciclos 2000 (p193) in Antequera.

Laguna de Fuente de Piedra

About 25km northwest of Antequera, just off the A92 *autovía*, is the Laguna de Fuente de Piedra. When it's not dried up by drought, this is Andalucía's biggest natural lake and one of Europe's two main breeding grounds for the greater flamingo (the other is the Camargue wetlands in southern France). After a wet winter as many as 20,000 pairs of flamingos will breed at the lake.

The birds arrive in January or February, and the chicks hatch in April and May. The flamingos stay until about August, when the lake, which is rarely more than 1m deep, no longer contains enough water to support them. They share the lake with thousands of other birds of some 170 species.

The small village of Fuente de Piedra sits at the northeastern corner of the lake and has a useful **visitor centre** (☎952 71 25 54; www.visitasfuentepiedra.es; ⏲10am-3pm mid-Dec–Feb & mid-Jun–mid-Sep, to 4pm mid-Sep–mid-Dec, to 5pm Mar–mid-Jun), where you can rent binoculars.

A couple of short trails lead out from the visitor centre to various lookouts and observatories. The longest trail is the 2.5km **Sendero de las Albinas**.

Getting There & Away

Alsa (p174) buses stop in the village of Fuente de Piedra, an easy 1.5km walk from the visitor centre. There are three daily buses to Seville (€12.30, 2½ hours) and two to Málaga (€8.10, 1¾ hours) via Antequera (€2.50, 30 minutes).

EAST OF MÁLAGA

The coast east of Málaga (the Costa del Sol Oriental) is less developed than its western counterpart. Málaga's sprawl extends through a series of unremarkable seaside towns before culminating in more attractive Nerja.

This area's main redeeming feature is the rugged mountain region of La Axarquía, almost as beautiful as Granada's Las Alpujarras yet less known. The Parque Natural Sierras de Tejeda, Almijara y Alhama protects 407 sq km of these mountains.

La Axarquía

The Axarquía region is riven by deep valleys lined with terraces and irrigation channels that date to Islamic times – nearly all the villages dotted around the olive-, almond- and vine-planted hillsides were founded in this era. The wild inaccessible landscapes, especially around the Sierra de Tejeda, made it a stronghold of *bandoleros* who roamed the mountains without fear or favour. Nowadays, its chief attractions include fantastic scenery; pretty white villages; strong, sweet wine made from sun-dried grapes; and good walking in spring and autumn.

The 'capital' of La Axarquía, **Vélez Málaga**, 4km north of Torre del Mar, is a busy but unspectacular town, although its restored hilltop castle is worth a look.

Some of the most dramatic La Axarquía scenery is up around the highest villages of **Alfarnate** (925m) and **Alfarnatejo** (858m), with towering, rugged crags such as Tajo de Gomer and Tajo de Doña Ana rising to their south.

You can pick up information on La Axarquía at the tourist offices in Málaga (p174), Nerja (p201), Torre del Mar or Cómpeta (p197). Prospective walkers should ask for the leaflet on walks in the Parque Natural Sierras de Tejeda, Almijara y Alhama. Good maps for walkers are *Mapa topográfico de Sierra Tejeda* and *Mapa topográfico de Sierra Almijara* by Miguel Ángel Torres Delgado, both at 1:25,000. You can also follow the links at www.axarquia.es for walks in the region.

Comares

POP 1315

Comares sits like a snowdrift atop its lofty hill. The adventure really is in getting there: you see it for kilometre after kilometre, before a final twist in an endlessly winding road lands you below the hanging garden of its cliff. From a little car park you can climb steep, winding steps to the village. Look for ceramic footprints underfoot and simply follow them through a web of narrow, twisting lanes past the **Iglesia de la Encarnación** and eventually to the ruins of Comares' **castle** and a remarkable summit **cemetery**.

The village has a history of rebellion, having been a stronghold of Omar ibn Hafsun, but today there is a tangible sense of contented isolation, enjoyed by locals and many newcomers. Visitors are often of the adventurous variety. The village has established itself as a nexus for climbing and hiking excursions, and has what is reputedly Spain's longest zip line.

Activities

Comares has three vie ferrate, all located in close proximity to each other on the northern side of the village close to the **zip line** (1/2 rides €15/20). The easiest is the **Fuente Gorda**, which takes about 45 minutes and involves 50m of ascent. Slightly more difficult are the **Cueva de la Ventana**, which includes a 30m-long zip line, and the **Puerta del Agua**, which has a couple of wire 'tightrope' bridges with hand supports. Guided climbs with the correct equipment can be organised with **Vive Aventura** (☎697 218289; www.viveaventura.es).

The crags north of Comares have more than two dozen marked climbing routes, graded 6a+ to 8a+.

Sleeping & Eating

Hotel Atalaya HOTEL €
(☎952 50 92 08; www.facebook.com/AtalayaComares; Calle las Encinillas 7; s/d €30/50; P 📶) Welcoming, if simple, rural-style hotel on the southern approach to hilltop Comares. There's an on-site restaurant and sweeping views, and it's highly economical for what you get.

Getting There & Away

Alsa (p174) runs one bus daily from Málaga to Comares (€3.30, 1¾ hours) at 6.15pm, returning at 7am the next morning. There's no service on Sunday.

Cómpeta

POP 3922

This instantly attractive whitewashed village, with its panoramic views, steep, winding streets and central bar-lined plaza overlooking a 16th-century church, has long attracted a large foreign population. This has contributed to an active cultural scene, and Cómpeta is home to one or two above-*pueblo*-average restaurants serving contemporary cuisine. The village also has a couple of charity shops (rare in Spain) and a big following among organised walking groups. Not surprisingly, Cómpeta is a good base for hiking and adrenalin-fuelled activities.

Activities

The Cómpeta region is walking heaven and has become increasingly popular in recent years with nature-seeking visitors (especially Brits), who come here on organised walking holidays. There's even a **walking festival** (www.walkspain.co.uk/walking-festival; ⏲Sep) in September.

Free guided walking tours of the town set out every Saturday at 10.30am from the tourist office (p197).

For more information on guided and self-guided walks in the area, check out www.walkspain.co.uk.

El Lucero WALKING
An exhilarating long walk from Cómpeta is up the dramatically peaked El Lucero

(1779m), from whose summit, on a clear day, you can see both Granada and Morocco. This is a demanding full-day return walk from Cómpeta, but it's possible to drive as far up as Puerto Blanquillo pass (1200m) via a slightly hairy mountain track from Canillas de Albaida.

From Puerto Blanquillo a path climbs 200m to another pass, the Puerto de Cómpeta. One kilometre down from there, past a quarry, the summit path (1½ hours), marked by a signboard, diverges to the right across a stream bed. Total return walking time to the summit from Puerto Blanquillo is 4½ to five hours. The mountain is also sometimes known as Raspón de los Moriscos.

Salamandra OUTDOORS
(☎952 55 34 93; www.malaga-aventura.es; Avenida de Sayalonga 13; potholing/kayaking/canyoning per person from €25/20/45; ⊙9am-8pm Mon-Fri, 10am-2pm Sat) This is a one-stop centre that organises a wide range of activities, including guided hikes, potholing, canyoning and kayaking, plus themed tours, such as orchid trips in spring, mushroom picking and historical routes. The routes include the former merchants' pathway linking Cómpeta with Játar and covering some 20km (on foot).

Los Caballos del Mosquín HORSE RIDING
(☎608 658108; www.horseriding-andalucia.com; Canillas de Albaida; half-day trek €90-100) Specialises in guided horse-riding treks in the mountains of La Axarquía ranging from one hour to three days (including full board and accommodation). Located up a steep road between Cómpeta and Canillas de Albaida.

Festivals

Noche del Vino WINE
(Night of the Wine; ⊙15 Aug) Cómpeta has some of the area's best local wine, and the popular Noche del Vino features a program of flamenco music and dance and *sevillanas* (a flamenco-influenced folk dance) in the central and pretty Plaza Almijara, plus limitless free wine.

Sleeping

★Finca El Cerrillo HOTEL €€
(☎952 03 04 44; www.hotelfinca.com; Canillas de Albaida; s/d incl breakfast €90/100; ⊙closed mid-Jan–Feb; P❄📶🏊) The kind of cathartic rural retreat that'll make you want to up sticks and come live in Andalucía, Finca El Cerrillo is a longtime labour of love for British owners Sue and Gordon Kind. It inhabits an old olive-oil mill on the northern side of Canillas de Albaida (4km from Cómpeta), attracting art- and walking-focused groups and indie travellers.

Rooms are comfortable without sacrificing authenticity, and there's ample space around the rambling building to do yoga, paint, take in the view or just bask in the sun. Inviting common areas include a stately lounge, a magically illuminated tree house bar, and a flowery terrace with a cool pool where you'll want to spend 10 minutes admiring the view before jumping in. Dinner is available most nights (and breakfast daily).

Almijara Residence B&B €€
(☎642 950269; www.almijararesidence.com; Plaza Almijara 3; d incl breakfast €60-75, with balcony €75-90; ❄📶) Owners Paul and Maurice pull out all the stops to make guests comfortable at this cosy B&B with dramatic views over Cómpeta's central square. Perks include complimentary local wine, almonds, cookies, coffee and tea, Apple TV, Netflix and high-speed fibre internet. Breakfast is a gourmet affair, tailored to guests' dietary needs and served on a lovely sun terrace.

Eating

Taberna-Tetería Hierbabuena MOROCCAN €
(☎630 916553; www.facebook.com/restaurantetabernahierbabuena; Avenida de la Constitución 35; mains €6-13; ⊙9am-midnight Tue-Sun) Though it has its share of low-slung tables, shapely lampshades and silver teapots, the Hierbabuena isn't your average *tetería*: it offers English breakfasts, 'curry nights' and mushy peas, as well as teas and tagines. The combination seems to satisfy the food urges of its largely expat clientele.

★El Pilón INTERNATIONAL €€
(☎952 55 35 12; www.restaurantelpilon.com; Calle Laberinto 3; mains €11-20; ⊙7-11pm; 🖉) This former carpenter's workshop is the village's most popular restaurant – and rightly so. Dishes are created using locally sourced ingredients whenever possible, and the eclectic options include tandoori chicken, swordfish with olive tapenade and some truly creative vegetarian dishes. There's a

OFF THE BEATEN TRACK

ACEBUCHAL: A VILLAGE LOST & FOUND

Etched like a splash of white paint at the head of a steep-sided valley halfway between Cómpeta and Frigiliana, tiny Acebuchal is a one-time 'ghost village' that got a second chance.

Founded as a pit stop on an old mule trail between Granada and the coast in the 17th century, Acebuchal got into trouble during the civil war when it was suspected of harbouring Republican resistance fighters working against Franco's forces. When Franco took power in 1939, the resistance went underground, forming a guerrilla group called the Maquis that operated in mountainous areas like the Axarquía where it could find safe cover and an element of local support. Suspected of collaboration, Acebuchal was targeted in a government-led mopping-up campaign that resolved that the best way to root out Maquis opposition was to evacuate Acebuchal entirely and pack its 200 or so inhabitants off to Cómpeta, Frigiliana and beyond.

Cleared in 1948, the village quickly fell into ruin, a decline that appeared to be terminal. But when democracy returned to Spain in the 1980s, some of the old families, feeling homesick for their mountain nirvana, began planning a return. The dream became reality in 1998 when a former inhabitant named Antonio 'El Zumbo' came back with his family and rebuilt one of Acebuchal's derelict houses as a bar practically with his bare hands. Inspired by his example, more families followed. Electricity and water mains were connected to Acebuchal in 2003, and in 2005 the village celebrated its first Mass in 60 years in its refurbished chapel. By the 2010s discerning tourists had begun to trickle into the former ghost village, most of them on foot, as the settlement isn't on a paved road.

Today Acebuchal is a vibrant hub of rural Spanish life, with all 30-plus of its houses renovated (some as holiday rentals) and Antonio's bar – now run by his son – thriving once again as one of the best mountain pit stops in Andalucía.

The wonderful **Bar-Restaurante El Acebuchal** (☎951 48 08 08; www.facebook.com/bar-el-acebuchal-360441977305565; mains €11-16; ⏲10am-6pm, kitchen 12.30-4pm; 📶) is the focal point of Acebuchal village. It's a favoured stop for walkers and lovers of rural tranquillity and plies some of the best food in Málaga province. It's worth hiking in for the homemade bread alone, not to mention the cakes.

cocktail lounge with sweeping views, regular entertainment, and sticky toffee pudding for homesick Brits.

Taberna-Restaurante Casa Paco ANDALUCIAN €€
(☎952 51 60 77; www.facebook.com/casapacocompeta; Plaza Almijara 6; mains €10-26; ⏲9am-midnight Tue-Sat, from 10am Sun) One of three restaurants with alfresco seating under a cluster of umbrellas in the main square, Paco – the one nearest to the church – is the best, with strong coffee, traditional tapas, speedy waitstaff and good crêpes.

ℹ Information

Tourist Office (☎952 55 36 85; Avenida de la Constitución; ⏲10am-2.30pm Mon-Sat, to 2pm Sun) Beside the bus stop at the foot of the village.

ℹ Getting There & Away

Loymer (☎952 54 11 13) runs three daily buses from Málaga to Cómpeta (€5, 1¾ hours), stopping in Torre del Mar. The buses stop next to the tourist office in Avenida de la Constitución.

Frigiliana

POP 3009

In the beauty pageant of Spanish villages, Frigiliana, 7km north of Nerja, has won plenty of awards – and no wonder. With its multicultural history, handsome civic buildings and pretty, whitewashed houses kept impeccably clean by a proud populace, it's far from an ugly duckling.

But, like all beauty, the prettiness here comes with a price: you won't have the place to yourself. Coaches pull up daily and disgorge their cargo into the sinuous streets adorned with pots of blood-red geraniums.

Like most small Andalucian towns, Frigiliana is split into two parts: old and new. The steeply banked old town is scattered with pictorial signage directing you from castle to church to fountain. However, the real exhibit is the town itself. Wander around. Get lost. Find yourself.

The old town's sturdy 16th-century Renaissance palace, **El Ingenio**, today processes molasses from sugar cane.

El Fuerte, the hill that climbs above the village, was the scene of the final bloody defeat of the *moriscos* (Muslim converts to Christianity) of La Axarquía in their 1569 rebellion, and where they reputedly plunged to their death rather than be killed or captured by the Spanish. You can walk up here if you follow the streets to the top of the town and then continue along the dusty track.

Frigiliana is on the GR249 long-distance footpath. You can walk south down to the Cueva de Nerja (14.6km) or head north into the Almijara Mountains and Cómpeta. Another shorter route heads to Cómpeta via the recently repopulated village of Acebuchal (7km).

The **tourist office** (☎952 53 42 61; www.turismofrigiliana.es; Calle Cuesta del Apero; ⏲10am-2.30pm & 5.30-9pm Mon-Sat, 10am-2.30pm Sun Jul–mid-Sep, hours vary rest of year) is next to the bus stop.

Getting There & Away

Regular buses link Frigiliana with Nerja (€1.15, 15 minutes, 12 daily). They leave from the taxi rank near the tourist office.

Nerja

POP 21,091

With the Sierra Almijara rising behind it, the dramatically sited seaside community of Nerja has succeeded in rebuffing developers, allowing its centre to retain a low-rise village charm despite the proliferation of souvenir shops and the large number of visitors it sees. At its heart is the perennially beautiful Balcón de Europa, a palm-lined promontory built on the foundations of an old fort that offers panoramic views of the cobalt-blue sea flanked by honey-coloured coves.

Just 56km east of Málaga, the town is increasingly popular with package holidaymakers and 'residential tourists', which has pushed it far beyond its old confines. There's significant urbanisation, especially to the east. The holiday atmosphere, and seawater contamination, can be overwhelming from July to September, but the place is more *tranquilo* the rest of the year.

Spaniards of a certain age remember Nerja as the setting for *Verano azul*, a hugely popular TV series filmed in the town in the early 1980s.

Sights & Activities

The town centres on the delightful **Balcón de Europa**, which juts out over the deep blue Mediterranean and is *the* place for the local *paseo* (promenade) on a languid summer's evening.

★Cueva de Nerja CAVE

(www.cuevadenerja.es; adult/child €14/12; ⏲10am-4.30pm Sep-Jun, to 7pm Jul & Aug) It's hard to imagine the surreal world that lies beneath the mountain foothills 4km east of Nerja, and it's even harder to believe that these vast caverns weren't discovered until five local *chicos* (young men) who had gone out looking for bats stumbled across an opening in 1959. Hollowed out by water around five million years ago and once inhabited by Stone Age hunters, this theatrical wonderland of extraordinary rock formations, subtle shifting colours, and stalactites and stalagmites is evocative of a submerged cathedral.

About 14 buses run daily from Málaga and Nerja, except on Sunday. Alternatively you can take a mini tourist train from Nerja's museum, or you can walk (there's pavement all the way).

The whole site is well organised for visitors, with restaurants, a car park and a short walking trail above the caves. A full tour of the caves takes about 45 minutes. Note that there's no extra charge for guided tours.

Playa Burriana BEACH

(P) This is Nerja's longest and best beach, with plenty of towel space on the sand. From Balcón de Europa, walk east down bleached-white Calle Carabeo and continue about 15 minutes to the beach. Burriana is backed by a line of *merenderos* (open-sided restaurants). You can rent kayaks or paddleboards here for €6 per hour.

Playa Calahonda BEACH

This small, pretty cove is just east of the Balcón de Europa. You can rent sunbeds and

Nerja

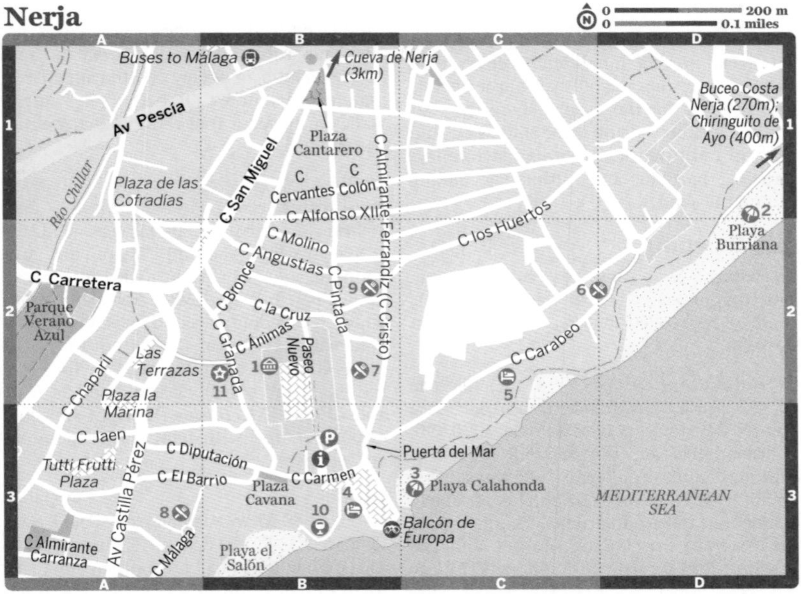

Nerja

Sights
1 Museo de Nerja B2
2 Playa Burriana D1
3 Playa Calahonda C3

Sleeping
4 Hotel Balcón de Europa B3
5 Hotel Carabeo C2

Eating
6 Bakus C2
7 La Piqueta B2
8 Lan Sang A3
9 Pápalo B2
Restaurante 34 .... (see 5)

Drinking & Nightlife
10 Cochran's Irish Bar B3

Entertainment
11 Centro Cultural Villa de Nerja B2

parasols here, though it does get busy at the height of summer, especially with guests from the nearby Hotel Balcón de Europa (p200).

Playa del Cañuelo BEACH
East of Nerja the coast becomes more rugged; with your own wheels you can head to some great beaches reached by tracks down from the A7. Playa del Cañuelo, immediately before the border with Granada province, is one of the best, with a couple of summer-only restaurants.

Museo de Nerja MUSEUM
(☎952 52 72 24; www.cuevadenerja.es/museum; Plaza de España 4; adult/child €3/2; ⏲10am-4.30pm Sep-Jun, to 7pm Jul & Aug) Nerja's museum traces the history of the town from the cave dwellers of Palaeolithic times to the tourist-boom years of the '60s, and is well worth a browse – preferably before you visit the Cueva de Nerja. The museum's highlights centre on artefacts found in the caves and range from the thought-provoking skeleton of an adult cave dweller to a fascinatingly mundane prehistoric cheese dish.

Buceo Costa Nerja DIVING
(☎952 52 86 10; www.nerjadiving.com; Playa Burriana; snorkelling €37.50, dives incl gear from €55; ⏲9am-7pm) Diving can be especially rewarding here due to the Atlantic stream, which results in highly varied marine life. This reputable outfit organises courses for most levels, from a basic Discover Scuba try-out (€70) to a full-blown Open Water course (€450).

Festivals & Events

Noche de San Juan CULTURAL

(23 Jun) Nerja's inhabitants celebrate St John's Day by dusting off their barbecue kits and heading for the beach. There they eat sizzling seafood, drink wine and beer, and stay up until the next morning swimming, dancing, partying and, ultimately, flaking out on the sand.

Sleeping

Nerja has a huge range of accommodation, but in summer rooms in the better hotels tend to be booked at least two months in advance.

★Hotel Carabeo HOTEL €€

(952 52 54 44; www.hotelcarabeo.com; Calle Carabeo 34; d/ste incl breakfast from €100/210; mid-Mar–mid-Nov;) Full of stylish antiques and wonderful paintings, this small, family-run seafront hotel is set above manicured terraced gardens. There's a pool on a terrace overlooking the sea, and the on-site **Restaurante 34** (mains €17-27.50; 1-3pm & 7-11pm Tue-Sun Mar-Nov;) is excellent. The building is an old schoolhouse and is located on one of the prettiest pedestrian streets in town, festooned with pink bougainvillea.

Hotel Balcón de Europa HOTEL €€

(952 52 08 00; www.hotelbalconeuropa.com; Paseo Balcón de Europa 1; d with breakfast/half board from €144/180;) This terraced hotel sticks out on a small promontory like a boat departing for Africa. Outside it's usually mayhem (this is Nerja's popular tourist playground), but inside the mood is surprisingly tranquil, with private room balconies overlooking a snug section of beach lapped by the translucent Mediterranean. A pool, sauna, piano bar and restaurant with a view all add value.

Eating

Nerja has an abundance of restaurants and bars, most geared towards the undiscerning. In general, avoid any that advertise all-day English breakfasts or that have sun-bleached posters of the dishes. Playa Burriana, Nerja's best beach, is backed by an animated strip of restaurants and bars.

★Chiringuito de Ayo SEAFOOD €

(www.ayonerja.com; Playa Burriana; all-you-can-eat paella €8; 8am-7pm; P) The menu is listed in nine languages, but the only word you need to understand at beachside Ayo is 'paella'. They cook the rice dish every day in a huge pan atop an open wood-burning fire. A plateful is yours for €8; better yet, you can walk on up for a free refill as many times as you like.

La Piqueta TAPAS €

(www.facebook.com/LaPiquetaTaperia; Calle Pintada 8; tapas €2.50, raciones €5-12.50; 10am-midnight Mon-Sat) There are two good reasons why this is the most popular tapas bar in town: first, the house wine is excellent; second, you get a free tapa with every drink in a tradition that's more Granada than Málaga province. On the menu are sturdy classics such as tripe and *huevos estrellados* (literally, smashed eggs) prepared with ham, garlic, potatoes and peppers.

Lan Sang THAI, LAO €€

(952 52 80 53; www.lansang.com; Calle Málaga 12; mains €13-18; 1-3pm & 7.30-11pm Mon-Sat) The owner and chef are both from Laos, so the dishes here are a subtle combination of Thai and Lao cuisines. As well as curries, stir-fries and soups, there's an emphasis on fresh local fish and seafood, prepared with spices including tamarind, ginger, kaffir-lime leaves and chilli. Soups and salads are similarly based on delicate, fragrant flavours.

Pápalo FUSION €€€

(951 50 52 39; Calle Almirante Ferrándiz 53; mains €17-24; 1-3.30pm & 7-10.30pm) On a busy corner in the heart of the pedestrian zone, Pápalo is the newest venture of one of Nerja's long-standing star chefs. Artistic presentation and international flavours are the constants in a menu that ranges from tagliatelle with prawns, octopus, white wine and chives to duck breast with sweet potatoes in a molasses, kaffir lime and lemongrass reduction.

Bakus BISTRO €€€

(952 52 71 79; Calle Carabeo 2; mains €20-26; 12.30-3.30pm & 7-10pm Tue-Sun) On a sunny day – that is, almost *any* day in Nerja – head straight for this sprawling terrace overlooking pristine Playa Carabello. The menu abounds with intriguing flavour combinations such as prawn and mango salad with orange vinaigrette, *malagueño* kid goat with pine nuts, rack of lamb with sage, balsamic and pink peppercorns, or

pork belly with roasted new potatoes in apricot sauce.

Drinking & Entertainment

Cochran's Irish Bar IRISH PUB

(www.cochransirishpub.com; Calle Salón 12; 11am-midnight Sun-Thu, to 3am Fri & Sat) Cochran's has Guinness, Murphy's and Jameson's on tap, great live music kicking off around 11pm on weekends, and – bonus – a shockingly good view over the Mediterranean from its terrace, which is open during the day.

Centro Cultural Villa de Nerja LIVE PERFORMANCE

(952 52 38 63; http://cultura.nerja.es; Calle Granada 45) This well-run centre organises an ambitious annual program of classical music, theatre, jazz and flamenco, featuring international and Spanish musicians and performers.

Information

Tourist Office (952 52 15 31; http://turismo.nerja.es; Calle Carmen 1; 10am-2pm & 4.30-8pm Mon-Fri, 10am-1.30pm Sat & Sun)

Getting There & Away

Alsa (p174) runs regular buses to/from Málaga (€4.65, 1¼ to 1½ hours, 23 daily), Antequera (€9.30, 2½ hours, three daily), Almería (€14.65, 2½ to four hours, five daily) and Granada (€11.10, 2¼ hours, six daily).

There's no bus station, just a ticket office and bus stop on the main roundabout on Carretera N340.

AT A GLANCE

POPULATION
781,000

CAPITAL
Córdoba

BEST BRIDGE
Puente Romano (p211)

BEST COUNTRY HOTEL
Casa Olea (p224)

BEST FLAMENCO
Noche Blanca del Flamenco (p215)

WHEN TO GO

Apr–May
Delightful weather, festival season in Córdoba city and other towns, and the countryside blossoms.

Jul–Aug
Hot, hot, hot, but good rates at many lodgings. Look for one with a pool!

Sep–Oct
Warm but not too warm - a fine time to be in both city and countryside.

Alcázar de los Reyes Cristianos (p212)
PERNELLE VOYAGE/SHUTTERSTOCK

Córdoba Province

Straddling the Río Guadalquivir, historic Córdoba city is the main magnet of Andalucía's northernmost province. The city is rich in historical interest with a charming old town and a wealth of museums and monuments, culminating in the mighty Mezquita (Mosque). It's not all high culture, though, and you'll find plenty of bars, restaurants and cafes.

To the north and west of the city rises the Sierra Morena, a rolling expanse of remote villages, ruined castles and hillside forests. To the south, olive trees and vines cloak the rippling landscape, yielding some of Spain's best olive oils and unique wines. The crag-perched village of Zuheros and nearby Priego de Córdoba make ideal bases for exploring the caves and canyons of the beautiful Sierras Subbéticas.

INCLUDES

Córdoba Province Highlights

1. **Mezquita** (p206) Marvelling at Córdoba's mesmerising mosque, one of Andalucía's great must-see sights.

2. **Palacio de Viana** (p214) Strolling through the elegant patios of this stately Renaissance mansion.

3. **Zuheros** (p222) Taking in this charming white village with its rocky backdrop, landmark castle and walks in the Sierras Subbéticas.

4. **Priego de Córdoba** (p223) Lapping up baroque fantasy architecture and some of the world's best olive oil.

5. **Montilla Wines** (p221) Tasting the province's most celebrated tipple, found everywhere but best experienced at one of Montilla's historic wineries.

6. **Medina Azahara** (p217) Trawling through the hillside ruins of what was once a caliph's showpiece capital.

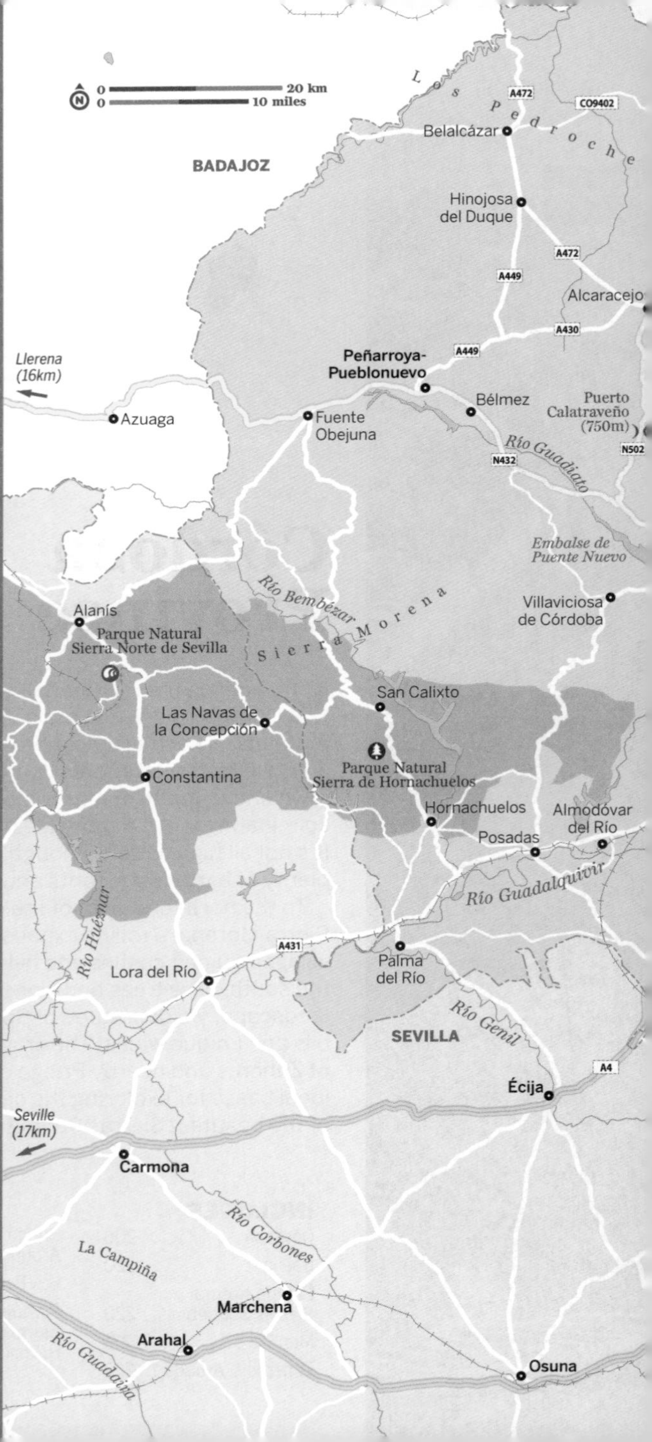

Puertollano
502
Santa Eufemia
CIUDAD REAL
Río Jándula
Viso
Fuencaliente
Pozoblanco
A424
Villanueva de Córdoba
N420
Cardeña
Parque Natural Sierra de Andújar
Río Jándula
Sierra Morena
Parque Natural Sierra de Cardeña y Montoro
CÓRDOBA
A420
Bailén
N432
Adamuz
Montoro
Andújar
A4
Villa del Río
JAÉN
Medina Azahara
6
El Carpio
1 2
Córdoba
A431
Bujalance
A306
Porcuna
N432
Río Guadajoz
N331
Jaén
Martos
Castro del Río
La Carlota
A45
Montemayor
Espejo
La Rambla
Vía Verde del Aceite
Baena
Vía Verde del Aceite
A316
5 Montilla
Alcaudete
Santaella
Aguilar de la Frontera
Doña Mencía
Luque
3 Zuheros
A318
Lobatejo (1380m)
A333
CO7204
El Cañuelo
Ermita de la Virgen de la Sierra
Alcalá la Real
Parque Natural Sierras Subbéticas
Zagrilla
Monturque
Cabra
Priego de Córdoba
4
Moriles
Puente Genil
Lucena
Bermejo (1476m)
La Tiñosa (1570m)
N331
A45
Rute
Montefrío
Jauja
Encinas Reales
Benamejí
Granada (10km)
Iznájar
Embalse de Iznájar
Río Genil
A333
GRANADA
MÁLAGA

CÓRDOBA

POP 325, 710 / ELEV 110M

One building alone is reason enough to set your sights on Córdoba. The astounding, multi-arched Mezquita is one of the world's greatest Islamic buildings, an enduring symbol of Córdoba's golden age as capital of Islamic Spain and Western Europe's largest and most cultured city. Of course, there's more to the city than its star attraction, and it merits far more than the fleeting visit many travellers give it. Its medieval centre is a charming pocket of winding lanes, white buildings and flower-bedecked patios, while nearby, bars and restaurants line its lively riverside. A short walk to the north, the vibrant modern town offers a more local vibe and yet more excellent eating and drinking options. The best time to visit is between mid-April and mid-June, when the city stages most of its major fiestas. September and October are also excellent months.

History

Córdoba's origins date back to the late Bronze Age when a settlement was set up on the Río Guadalquivir in the 8th or 9th century BCE. However, the city proper was founded in the 2nd century BCE as a strategic provisioning post for Roman troops. In about 25 BCE, Emperor Augustus made it capital of Baetica, one of the three Roman provinces on the Iberian Peninsula, heralding an era of prosperity and cultural ascendancy that saw it produce the famous writers Seneca and Lucan. But by the 3rd century, when Christianity reached Córdoba, the Roman city was in decline, and in 711 CE it fell to Islamic invaders.

Over the next few centuries, Córdoba grew to become the greatest city in Islamic Spain. In 756 Abd ar-Rahman I established himself here as the emir of Al-Andalus (the Muslim-controlled parts of the Iberian Peninsula), founding the Umayyad dynasty, which more or less unified Al-Andalus for two and a half centuries, and building the great Mezquita. However, it was under Abd ar-Rahman III (r 912–61) that the city, and Al-Andalus, enjoyed its greatest period. In 929 Abd ar-Rahman declared himself caliph (the title of the Muslim successors of Mohammed), ushering in the Córdoba caliphate.

Córdoba was by now the largest city in Western Europe with a population of around 250,000 and a flourishing economy. It boasted hundreds of dazzling mosques and public baths, while its university, library and observatories made it a centre of learning whose influence was still being felt many centuries later. Muslims, Jews and Christians coexisted peaceably.

Towards the end of the 10th century, Al-Mansur (Almanzor) wrested power from the caliphs. But after the death of his son in 1008, the caliphate descended into anarchy. Berber troops terrorised the city and, in 1031, Umayyad rule collapsed. Córdoba became a minor part of the Seville *taifa* (small kingdom) in 1069, and has been overshadowed by Seville ever since.

Twelfth-century Córdoba did, however, produce Al-Andalus' two most celebrated scholars – Muslim Averroës (1126–98) and Jewish Maimonides (1135–1204), whose magnum opus, the *Mishne Torah*, summarised the teachings of Judaism and systematised all Jewish law.

After Córdoba was taken by Castilla's Fernando III in 1236, the city's economic and cultural power waned and it fell into decline. The birth of Luis de Góngora (1561–1627), one of Spain's greatest poets, led to a brief cultural revival in the 17th century but it wasn't until the arrival of industry in the late 19th century that Córdoba's fortunes started to look up again.

Sights

Mezquita & Around

★Mezquita MOSQUE

(Mosque; ☎957 47 05 12; www.mezquita-catedraldecordoba.es; Calle Cardenal Herrero 1; adult/child €10/5, 8.30-9.30am Mon-Sat free; ⏲10am-7pm Mon-Sat, 8.30-11.30am & 3-7pm Sun Mar-Oct, 10am-6pm Mon-Sat, 8.30-11.30am & 3-6pm Sun Nov-Feb) A medieval mosque with a Christian cathedral set inside it, Córdoba's Mezquita is one of the world's greatest works of Islamic architecture. It was originally built in the 8th century but enlargements over the next couple of centuries saw it become one of the largest and most architecturally sophisticated mosques of its age. Some five centuries on and it remains an astonishing sight with its serene columned interior, lustrous decoration and extraordinary *mihrab* (prayer niche).

The history of worship on the site actually predates the Mezquita, going back to the mid-6th century when a small Visigoth church, the Basilica of San Vincente, stood here. Arab chronicles recount how Abd ar-Rahman I purchased half of the church for the Muslim community's Friday prayers, and then, in 784 CE, bought the other half as a site for a new mosque. His original structure, built between 786 and 788, subsequently underwent three extensions, increasing its size fivefold and bringing it to the form you see today – with one major alteration: a Christian cathedral was added to the middle of the mosque in the 16th century (hence the often-used description 'Mezquita-Catedral').

➡ Patio de los Naranjos

This lovely courtyard, with its orange, palm and cypress trees and fountains, was the site of ritual ablutions before prayers in the mosque. There are several entrances (it's free to go in and have a look around), the most impressive of which is the **Puerta del Perdón**, a 14th-century Mudéjar archway next to the bell tower. The Mezquita's ticket offices are just inside here.

➡ Bell Tower (Torre Campanario)

You can climb the 54m-high bell tower for fine panoramas and an interesting bird's-eye angle on the main Mezquita building. Originally built in 951–52 as the Mezquita's minaret, the *torre* was encased in a strengthened outer shell and heightened by the Christians in the 16th and 17th centuries. You can still see some caliphal vaults and arches inside. The original minaret, which would have looked very similar to Seville's Giralda, influenced all minarets subsequently built in the western Islamic world.

Up to 20 people are allowed up the tower every half hour between 9.30am and 6.30pm from March to October (to 5.30pm November to February, to 2.30pm July and August). Note, however, that there are no admissions at 11.30am and 1pm on Sundays. Tickets (€2) are sold at the ticket offices near the tower: they often sell out well ahead of visit times, so it's worth buying early in the day.

➡ Interior

Though stunning from the outside, it's really only by stepping into the Mezquita's mind-blowing interior that you get the full measure of its beauty. To help you navigate, there are free leaflets available just inside the visitor entrance.

The Mezquita's architectural importance lies in the fact that, structurally speaking, it was a revolutionary building for its time. Earlier Islamic buildings such as the Dome of the Rock in Jerusalem and the Great Mosque in Damascus placed an emphasis on verticality, but the Mezquita was intended as a simple, democratically horizontal space, where the spirit could roam freely and communicate with God – a kind of glorious refinement of the original Islamic prayer space (usually the open yard of a desert home).

Men prayed side by side on the *argamasa,* a floor made of compacted, reddish slaked lime and sand. The flat roof, decorated with gold and multicoloured motifs, was supported by striped arches suggestive of a forest of date palms. The arches rested on, eventually, 1293 columns (of which 856 remain today).

Abd ar-Rahman I's initial prayer hall – the area immediately inside the entrance – was divided into 11 'naves' by lines of arches striped in red brick and white stone. The columns of these arches were a mishmash of material collected from the earlier church on the site, Córdoba's Roman buildings and places as far away as Constantinople. To raise the ceiling high enough to create a sense of openness, inventive builders came up with the idea of a two-tier construction, using taller columns as a base and planting shorter ones on top.

Later enlargements, southward by Abd ar-Rahman II in the 9th century and Al-Hakim II in the 960s, and eastward by Al-Mansur in the 970s, extended the mosque to an area of nearly 14,400 sq metres, making it one of the largest mosques in the world.

The final Mezquita had 19 doors along its north side, filling it with light and creating a sense of openness. Most of these doorways have since been closed off, dampening the vibrant effect of the red-and-white double arches. Christian additions to the building, such as the cathedral and the many chapels around the fringes, further enclose the airy space.

➡ Mihrab & Maksura

In the southern wall, opposite the visitor entrance, the *mihrab* and *maksura* (royal prayer enclosure) are the Mezquita's decorative highlights. They were both created as part of an extension commissioned by Al-Hakim II in the 960s. The naves of the prayer hall were lengthened and a new *qiblah* wall (indicating the direction of Mecca) and *mihrab* were added.The bay in front of

Mezquita

TIMELINE

6th century AD Foundation of a Christian church, the Basilica of San Vicente, on the site of the present Mezquita.

786-87 Salvaging Visigothic and Roman ruins, Emir Abd ar-Rahman I replaces the church with a *mezquita* (mosque).

833-48 Mosque enlarged by Abd ar-Rahman II.

951-2 A new minaret is built by Abd ar-Rahman III.

962-71 Mosque enlarged, and superb new 1 **mihrab** added, by Al-Hakim II.

991-4 Mosque enlarged for the last time by Al-Mansur, who also enlarged the courtyard (now the 2 **Patio de los Naranjos**), bringing the whole complex to its current dimensions.

1236 Mosque converted into a Christian church after Córdoba is recaptured by Fernando III of Castilla.

1271 Instead of destroying the mosque, the Christians modify it, creating the 3 **Capilla de Villaviciosa** and 4 **Capilla Real**.

1523 Work on a Gothic/Renaissance-style cathedral inside the Mezquita begins, with permission of Carlos I. Legend has it that on seeing the result the king lamented that something unique in the world had been destroyed.

1593-1664 The 10th-century minaret is reinforced and rebuilt as a Renaissance-baroque 5 **belltower**.

2004 Spanish Muslims petition to be able to worship in the Mezquita again. The Vatican doesn't consent.

TOP TIPS

➡ The Patio de los Naranjos can be enjoyed free of charge at any time.

➡ Entry to the main Mezquita building is offered free every morning, except Sunday, between 8.30am and 9.30am.

➡ Group visits are prohibited before 10am, meaning the building is quieter and more atmospheric in the early morning.

INU/SHUTTERSTOCK ©

The Mihrab
Everything leads to the mosque's greatest treasure – the beautiful prayer niche, in the wall facing Mecca, that was added in the 10th century. Cast your eyes over the gold mosaic cubes crafted by sculptors imported from Byzantium.

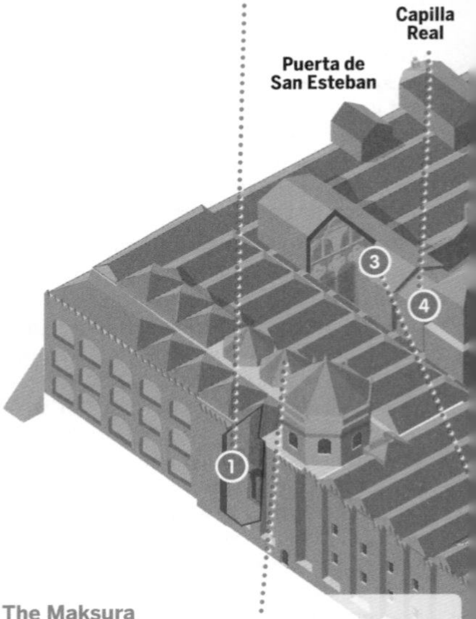

The Maksura
Guiding you towards the mihrab, the *maksura* was the former royal enclosure where the caliphs and their retinues prayed. Its lavish, elaborate arches were designed to draw the eye of worshippers towards the mihrab and Mecca.

RENATA SEDMAKOVA/SHUTTERSTOCK ©

Capilla Mayor

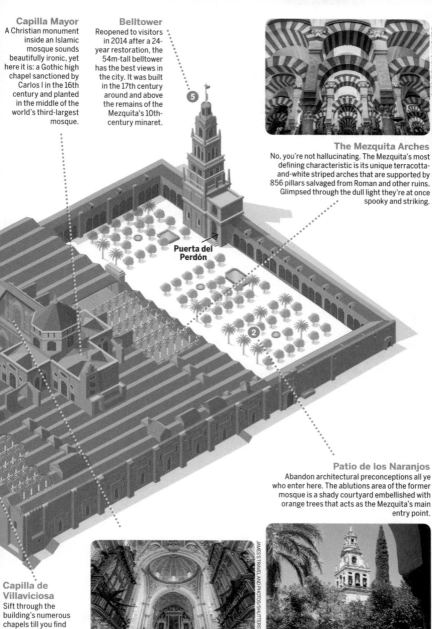

A Christian monument inside an Islamic mosque sounds beautifully ironic, yet here it is: a Gothic high chapel sanctioned by Carlos I in the 16th century and planted in the middle of the world's third-largest mosque.

Belltower

Reopened to visitors in 2014 after a 24-year restoration, the 54m-tall belltower has the best views in the city. It was built in the 17th century around and above the remains of the Mezquita's 10th-century minaret.

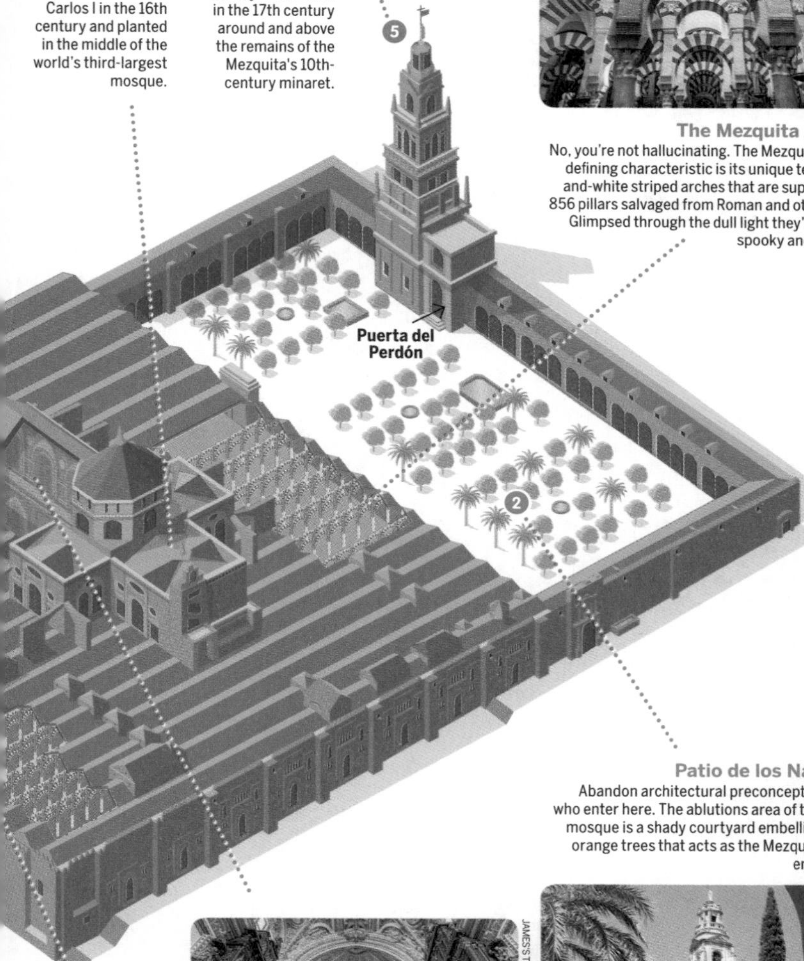

BILL PERRY/SHUTTERSTOCK ©

The Mezquita Arches

No, you're not hallucinating. The Mezquita's most defining characteristic is its unique terracotta-and-white striped arches that are supported by 856 pillars salvaged from Roman and other ruins. Glimpsed through the dull light they're at once spooky and striking.

Patio de los Naranjos

Abandon architectural preconceptions all ye who enter here. The ablutions area of the former mosque is a shady courtyard embellished with orange trees that acts as the Mezquita's main entry point.

Capilla de Villaviciosa

Sift through the building's numerous chapels till you find this gem, an early Christian modification which fused existing Moorish features with Gothic arches and pillars. It served as the Capilla Mayor until 1607.

JAMES'S TRAVEL AND PHOTOS/SHUTTERSTOCK ©

The Cathedral Choir

Few ignore the impressive *coro* (choir), built in the 16th and 17th centuries. Once you've admired the skilfully carved mahogany choir stalls depicting scenes from the Bible, look up at the impressive baroque ceiling.

MATT TROMMER/SHUTTERSTOCK ©

Córdoba

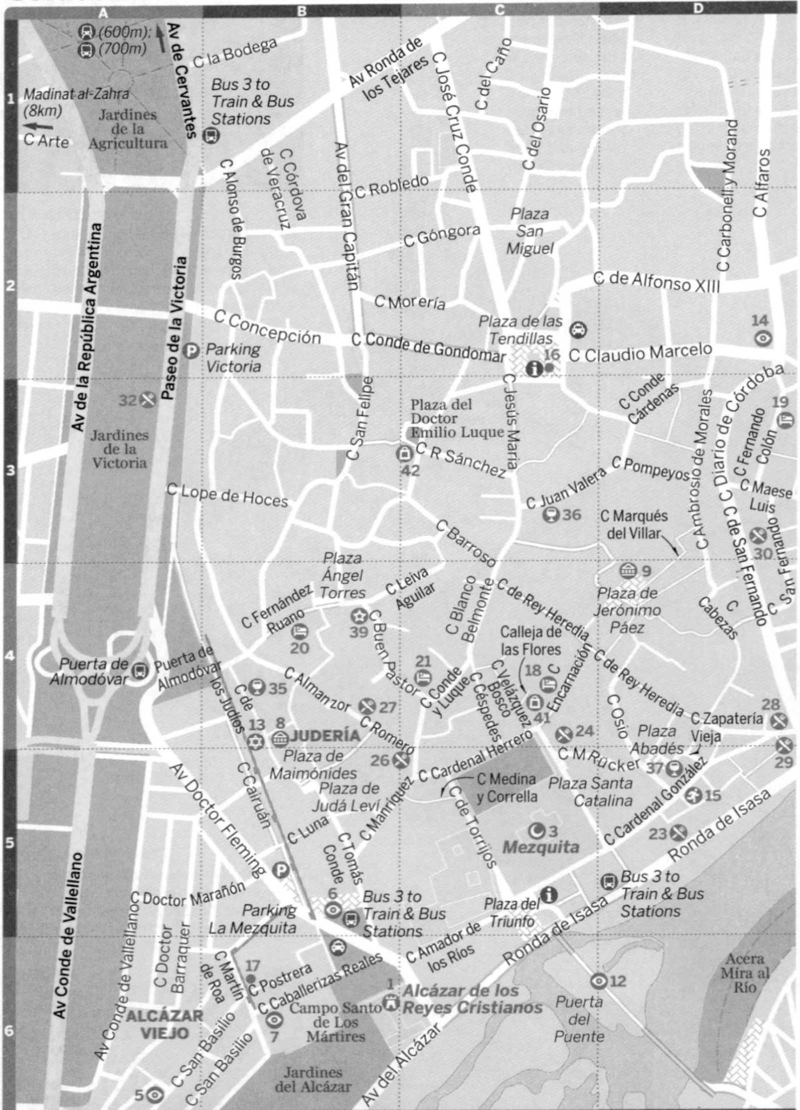

the *mihrab* and the bays to each side of it form the *maksura,* the area where the caliphs and courtiers would have prayed.

Particularly spectacular is the *mihrab's* **portal** – a crescent arch with a rectangular surround known as an *alfiz.* To decorate this, Al-Hakim asked the emperor of Byzantium, Nicephoras II Phocas, to send him a craftsman capable of imitating the mosaics of the Great Mosque of Damascus, one of the great Syrian Umayyad buildings. In response, the Christian emperor sent a mosaicist along with 1600kg of gold mosaic cubes. And it's this gold, shaped into

unbelievably intricate flower motifs and inscriptions from the Quran, that gives the portal its magical glitter. Inside the *mihrab*, a single block of white marble sculpted into the shape of a scallop shell, a symbol of the Quran, forms the dome that once amplified the voice of the imam throughout the mosque.

The arches of the *maksura* are the mosque's most intricate and sophisticated, forming a forest of interwoven horseshoe shapes. Above them the *maksura*'s sky-lit domes are a spellbinding sight, with their star-patterned stone vaulting. Each **dome** is held up by four interlocking pairs of parallel ribs, a highly advanced technique for 10th-century Europe.

➡ Cathedral

Following the Christian conquest of Córdoba in 1236, the Mezquita was used as a cathedral but remained largely unaltered for nearly three centuries. However, in the 16th century King Carlos I gave the cathedral authorities permission to construct a new Capilla Mayor (main altar area) and *coro* (choir) in the centre of the Mezquita.

Legend has it that when the king saw the results of the work he was horrified, exclaiming that the builders had destroyed something unique in the world. The church, which is still today Córdoba's official cathedral, took nearly 250 years to complete (1523–1766) and exhibits a range of architectural styles, from Gothic and plateresque to late Renaissance and Spanish baroque. Among its standout features are the Capilla Mayor's rich 17th-century jasper and red-marble **retable** (altar screen), and the fine mahogany stalls in the **choir**, carved in the 18th century by Pedro Duque Cornejo. Capping everything is a towering 16th-century **dome**.

➡ Night Visits

A one-hour sound-and-light show ('El Alma de Córdoba'), in nine languages via audio guides, is presented in the Mezquita twice nightly except Sundays from March to October, and on Fridays and Saturdays between November and February. Tickets are €18 (senior or student €9). Further details are available on the website.

Puente Romano BRIDGE

Spanning the Río Guadalquivir just below the Mezquita, this handsome 16-arch bridge originally formed part of Via Augusta, the ancient Roman road that connected Girona in Catalonia with Cádiz. It has been rebuilt several times since the 1st century CE and now makes for a lovely traffic-free stroll.

For a classic Córdoba view, cross the bridge and from the far riverside path look back to the Mezquita dominating the skyline.

Córdoba

Top Sights
1 Alcázar de los Reyes Cristianos B6
2 Centro Flamenco Fosforito E4
3 Mezquita C5
4 Palacio de Viana E1

Sights
5 Asociación de Amigos de los Patios Cordobeses A6
6 Baños del Alcázar Califal B5
7 Caballerizas Reales B6
8 Casa de Sefarad B4
9 Museo Arqueológico D4
10 Museo Julio Romero de Torres E4
11 Plaza de la Corredera E3
Plaza del Potro .... (see 10)
12 Puente Romano D6
13 Sinagoga B4
14 Templo Romano D2

Activities, Courses & Tours
15 Hammam Baños Árabes D5
16 Oway Tours C2
17 Patios de San Basilio B6

Sleeping
18 Balcón de Córdoba C4
19 Casa de los Azulejos D3
20 Hospedería Alma Andalusí B4
21 Hospedería del Atalia C4
22 Patio del Posadero F4

Eating
23 Amaltea D5
24 Bar Santos C4
25 Bodegas Campos E4
26 Casa Pepe de la Judería C5
27 El Churrasco B4
28 Garum 2.1 .... D4
29 La Bicicleta D4
30 La Boca D3
31 La Tinaja E4
32 Mercado Victoria A3
33 Taberna Salinas E3

Drinking & Nightlife
34 Amapola E4
35 Bodega Guzmán B4
36 Califa C3
37 El Barón D5
38 Jugo E2

Entertainment
39 Tablao Cardenal B4

Shopping
40 Mercado de la Corredera E3
41 Meryan C4
42 Ostin Macho C3

★ **Alcázar de los Reyes Cristianos** FORTRESS

(Fortress of the Christian Monarchs; ☎957 42 01 51; https://cultura.cordoba.es; Calle Caballerizas Reales; adult/student/child €5/2.50/free; ⏱8.30am-2.30pm Tue-Sun mid-Jun–mid-Sep, 8.15am-8pm Tue-Fri, 9.30am-6pm Sat, 8.15am-2.45pm Sun mid-Sep–mid-Jun) This formidable fort-palace dates to the 14th century when it was commissioned by King Alfonso XI and built over an earlier Moorish palace. It was Córdoba's main royal residence and it was here that Fernando and Isabel met Christopher Columbus in 1486. Inside, the highlight is a series of Roman mosaics, discovered under Plaza de la Corredera in the 1950s, while outside, the exquisite Moorish-style gardens are a joy to explore.

Nearby, you can visit the **Baños del Alcázar Califal** (☎608 158893; www.banosdelcalifal.cordoba.es; Campo Santo de los Mártires; adult/student/child €3/1.50/free, from 6pm Thu free; ⏱8.30am-2.30pm Tue-Sun mid-Jun–mid-Sep, 8.15am-8pm Tue-Fri, 9.30am-6pm Sat, 8.15am-2.45pm Sun mid-Sep–mid-Jun), the impressive 10th-century bathhouse of the Moorish Alcázar.

To see the Alcázar in a different light, a popular multimedia show, **Noches Mágicas en el Alcázar** (Magic Nights in the Alcázar; adult/child €6.50/free), is held here most nights. This had been temporarily suspended at the time of research, so check with the tourist office for the latest situation.

Caballerizas Reales STABLES

(Royal Stables; ☎671 949514; www.cordobaecuestre.com; Calle Caballerizas Reales 1; adult/child training €5/1, show €16.50/11.50; ⏱10am-1.30pm daily plus 4-7pm Tue, 4-6.30pm Wed-Sat, show 9pm Wed-Sat mid-Apr–mid-Sep, 7.30pm mid-Sep–mid-Apr) These elegant stables were built on the orders of King Felipe II in 1570 as a centre for developing the tall Spanish thoroughbred warhorse *(caballo andaluz)*. The centre still breeds these fine horses as well as running riding courses. You can watch training from 11am in the morning, or attend the 70-minute show that sets equestrian manoeuvres to flamenco music and dance.

Judería

The Judería, Córdoba's old Jewish quarter, forms the heart of the city's historic centre. Narrow cobbled streets weave through the area, which extends west and northwest of the Mezquita, leading past whitewashed buildings and wrought-iron gates, allowing glimpses of plant-filled patios. Some streets are choked with gaudy souvenir shops and touristy restaurants, but others remain quiet and unblemished.

Sinagoga SYNAGOGUE

(957 74 90 15; Calle de los Judíos 20; EU/non-EU citizen free/€0.30; 9am-9pm Tue-Sat, to 3pm Sun) Constructed in 1315, this small, probably private or family synagogue is one of the few surviving testaments to the Jewish presence in medieval Andalucía, though it hasn't been used as a place of worship since the expulsion of Jews in 1492. Its light-filled main hall, accessed through a small courtyard, is decorated with extravagant stucco work that includes Hebrew inscriptions and intricate Mudéjar star and plant motifs. Upstairs, the Galería de Mujeres was reserved for women.

Casa de Sefarad MUSEUM

(957 42 14 04; www.casadesefarad.es; cnr Calles de los Judíos & Averroes; adult/child €4/3; 11am-6pm Mon-Sat, to 2pm Sun) In the heart of the Judería, and once connected by tunnel to the synagogue, the Casa de Sefarad is an interesting museum devoted to the Sephardic (Iberian Peninsula Jewish) tradition. Exhibits are displayed thematically illustrating domestic life, music, traditions and the city's Jewish quarter. There's also a section on the women intellectuals (poets, artists and thinkers) of Al-Andalus.

East & North of the Mezquita

Museo Arqueológico MUSEUM

(957 35 55 17; www.museosdeandalucia.es; Plaza de Jerónimo Páez 7; EU/non-EU citizen free/€1.50; 9am-9pm Tue-Sat, to 3pm Sun Sep-Jun, 9am-3pm Tue-Sun Jul & Aug) Córdoba's excellent archaeological museum traces the city's many changes in size, appearance and lifestyle from pre-Roman to early Reconquista times. Its collection, one of Spain's largest, includes some fine sculpture, an impressive coin collection, and an array of finds relating to domestic life and religion; explanations are provided in English and Spanish. In the basement, you can walk through the excavated remains of the city's Roman theatre.

Plaza del Potro SQUARE

This historic square, formerly the site of a livestock market, takes its name from the colt (*potro*) that rears atop the 16th-century stone fountain. On the western flank, you'll find the **Posada del Potro**, a legendary inn that Cervantes describes in *Don Quijote* as a 'den of thieves'. The beautifully maintained building, set around a narrow courtyard, now houses the Centro Flamenco Fosforito. Opposite, in what was once a Franciscan charity hospital, is the Museo Julio Romero de Torres.

★ **Centro Flamenco Fosforito** MUSEUM

(Posada del Potro; 957 47 68 29; www.centroflamencofosforito.cordoba.es; Plaza del Potro; 8.45am-3.15pm Tue-Sun mid-Jun–mid-Sep, 8.15am-8pm Tue-Fri, 9.30am-6pm Sat, 8.15am-2.45pm Sun mid-Sep–mid-Jun) FREE Charmingly housed in a historic inn, this passionately curated museum is a must for anyone with even a passing interest in flamenco. Exhibits, which include photos, film footage, recordings and instruments, are combined with information panels in English and Spanish to chart the history of the art form and its great exponents.

Free concerts and flamenco performances are occasionally held here – check the website for upcoming events.

Museo Julio Romero de Torres MUSEUM

(957 49 19 09; Plaza del Potro 1; adult/child €4/free; 8.45am-3.15pm Tue-Sun mid-Jun–mid-Sep, 8.15am-8pm Tue-Fri, 9.30am-6pm Sat, 8.15am-2.45pm Sun mid-Sep–mid-Jun) Occupying the former Hospital de la Caridad, along with the Museo de Bellas Artes, this marvellous little museum is dedicated to the much-loved local painter Julio Romero de Torres (1874–1930). Its six scarlet rooms are hung with paintings vividly illustrating the artist's lifelong passions for flamenco and Andalucian female beauty.

Plaza de la Corredera SQUARE

Once the site of big public spectacles – bullfights, executions, Inquisition *autos-da-fé* – this vast Castilian-style plaza makes quite an impression with its arched porticoes and 17th-century buildings. Its assorted bars and cafes are a popular hang-out while, on the southern flank, the **Mercado de la Corredera** (Plaza de la Corredera; 8am-3pm Mon-Thu, to 3.30pm Fri & Sat) is a busy food market.

CÓRDOBA'S PATIOS

A striking characteristic of Córdoba's historic centre are the patios that appear in so many houses and *palacios*. These much-loved courtyards, typically centred on a trickling fountain and studded with pots of blazing geraniums and cascading bougainvillea, have provided sanctuary from the searing summer heat for centuries.

The best time to enjoy them is spring, when dozens are opened for free public viewing during the popular Fiesta de los Patios de Córdoba.

Palacio de Viana This aristocratic palace boasts 12 gorgeous patios, each with its own character and mood.

Asociación de Amigos de los Patios Cordobeses (Calle San Basilio 44; ⏲10.30am-1.30pm & 5-8pm) FREE This classic white-walled patio can be visited free year-round. Its colourfulness depends on the season, but you can always browse its craft workshops.

Patios de San Basilio (☎654 530377; www.patiosdesanbasilio.com; Calle Martín de Roa 2; tours €10; ⏲tours 10am, noon & 5.30pm Mar-Jun & Sep-Oct, 10am, noon & 4.30pm Nov-Feb, closed Wed, Sun afternoon & Jul, 10am & noon daily Aug) Runs guided visits to five well-tended patios in the charming *barrio* of San Basilio (also known as the Alcázar Viejo district) near the Alcázar de los Reyes Cristianos.

Templo Romano TEMPLE

(Calle Claudio Marcelo) Though generally not open to visitors, this 1st-century CE Roman temple can be viewed perfectly well from the street. Its 11 tall white columns make a striking sight, especially when floodlit after dark. The temple, dedicated to the cult of emperor worship, is thought to have looked eastwards towards a huge Roman circus (for horse races and other spectacles).

★ **Palacio de Viana** MUSEUM

(☎957 49 67 41; www.palaciodeviana.com; Plaza de Don Gome 2; whole house/patios €8/5, 2-5pm Wed free; ⏲10am-7pm Tue-Sat, to 3pm Sun Sep-Jun, 9am-3pm Tue-Sun Jul & Aug) A noble Renaissance palace, the Palacio de Viana is a particular delight in spring when its 12 plant-filled patios are awash with colour. The much-modified 14th-century mansion was home to the aristocratic Marqueses de Viana until 1980, and its stately rooms are crammed with art and antiques. Visits to the palace are by guided tour only, but you're free to explore the pretty courtyards on your own.

Activities

Hammam Baños Árabes HAMMAM

(☎957 48 47 46; http://cordoba.hammamalandalus.com; Calle del Corregidor Luis de la Cerda 51; baths & steam room €32, incl massage €45-99; ⏲10am-midnight) Follow the lead of the medieval Cordobans and treat yourself to a soak in the warm, hot and cold pools of these beautifully renovated Arab baths. You can also enjoy a range of massages.

Tours

A vast array of guided tours is available in Córdoba – see www.reservasturismodecordoba.org for a selection.

Foodie & Experiences TOURS

(☎662 525431; www.foodieandexperiences.com) Eat your way around Córdoba with a knowledgeable local guide. Foodie & Experiences offers a range of packages, including cooking classes, excursions to olive-oil mills, and a three-hour tapas tour (€82.50 for a single person, €55 per person for two to four people). Custom-made private tours are also available on request.

Oway Tours TOURS

(☎688 376581; www.owaytours.com) FREE Oway does an entertaining free 2½-hour walking introduction to the city, with enthusiastic guides proffering interesting snippets of history along the way. Find the guides with blue umbrellas in Plaza de las Tendillas at 10.30am daily: participants are divided into English-, Spanish- and French-speaking groups.

Festivals & Events

Semana Santa RELIGIOUS

(Holy Week; www.hermandadesdecordoba.es; ⏲Mar/Apr) Every evening from Palm Sunday to Good Friday, trains of robed penitents take to the streets to accompany ornate *pasos* (floats bearing sacred statues) to and from the cathedral in the Mezquita. The sombre processions draw large crowds, particularly around the Mezquita, where most *pasos* arrive between 7pm and 11pm.

Cruces de Mayo FIESTA
(May Crosses; early May) Crosses adorned with flowers and manila shawls are put up in plazas and streets that are themselves decorated for the occasion. Drinks and tapas stalls are set up, and the whole thing turns into a neighbourhood party with music and dancing. It lasts from the Wednesday to the Sunday of the first week in May, peaking on the Friday night and Saturday.

Fiesta de los Patios de Córdoba FIESTA
(http://patios.cordoba.es; May) This 'best patio' competition sees 50 or more of Córdoba's private courtyards open for free public viewing for two weeks in early May. Some of the best are on and around Calle San Basilio and in the Alcázar Viejo area 400m southwest of the Mezquita. Flamenco and concerts are staged in patios and plazas across town.

Feria de Mayo FERIA
(May Fair; late May) A massive week-long party takes over the Arenal area east of the centre. There's music, *sevillana* dancing, parades of horse-drawn carriages, dressing up, fireworks and loads of fun.

★ **Noche Blanca del Flamenco** MUSIC
(http://nocheblancadelflamenco.cordoba.es; mid-Jun) This all-night fest of top-notch flamenco features free performances by leading artists in picturesque venues such as Plaza del Potro and the Mezquita's Patio de los Naranjos.

Festival de la Guitarra de Córdoba MUSIC
(https://guitarracordoba.es; early Jul) A 10-day celebration of the guitar. Theatres across town stage concerts of classical, flamenco, rock, blues and more by top Spanish and international names.

Sleeping

The most atmospheric area to stay is the Judería and historic centre, but there are also good options in the area east of the Mezquita and up in the modern part of town around Plaza de las Tendillas.

Booking ahead is advisable for April, September and October, and essential for Semana Santa, the May festivals and national holidays.

Hospedería Alma Andalusí HOTEL €
(957 20 04 25; www.almaandalusi.com; Calle Fernández Ruano 5; s €38-65, d €76-128;) This cosy hotel in a quiet section of the Judería makes a great base. Rooms are small but attractive, with thoughtfully chosen furnishings, large photos of Córdoba's sights, and polished-wood or traditional-tile floors. The room rates we quote are fully refundable but there are also cheaper, non-refundable rates.

★ **Patio del Posadero** BOUTIQUE HOTEL €€
(957 94 17 33; www.patiodelposadero.com; Calle Mucho Trigo 21; r incl breakfast €95-155;) It's not the easiest to find – down a side alley 1km east of the Mezquita – but this refined hideaway is well worth the search. Housed in a converted 15th-century building, it marries contemporary design with traditional Córdoba-Moorish touches. From its brick-arched patio, stairs lead up to a salon and terrace with a small plunge pool, and six handsome, individually styled rooms.

Viento10 BOUTIQUE HOTEL €€
(957 76 49 60; www.hotelviento10.es; Calle Ronquillo Briceño 10; s €81-150, d €100-172;) An inspired conversion of a 15th-century hospital, Viento10 has just eight rooms, whose modern, clean lines and understated decor harmonise perfectly with the ancient pillars in its central courtyard. A strong sense of light suffuses the building, not least on the roof terrace with its sun loungers and Mezquita views. A small spa and excellent breakfasts (€8.80) add to the mix.

Casa de los Azulejos HOTEL €€
(957 47 00 00; www.casadelosazulejos.com; Calle Fernando Colón 5; incl breakfast s €59-90, d €67-151;) With its Andalucian-Mexican look, sunny, plant-filled patio, and basement micro-brewery, there's a lot to like about this stylish nine-room hotel. Its attractive rooms (named after Mexican plants) feature lilacs, lemons and sky blues, and jazzy bathroom tiles that complement the traditional Spanish floor *azulejos* (tiles) that give the place its name.

Hospedería del Atalia BOUTIQUE HOTEL €€
(957 49 66 59; www.hospederiadelatalia.com; Calle Buen Pastor 19; r €50-200;) Entered through a pretty white patio in the heart of the Judería, the low-key Atalia sports 20 tastefully styled rooms in burgundies, russets and olive greens. Good breakfasts are available for €6, and there's a sunny roof terrace with chairs and a view of the Mezquita tower.

★**Balcón de Córdoba** BOUTIQUE HOTEL €€€
(☎957 49 84 78; www.balcondecordoba.com; Calle Encarnación 8; d incl breakfast €142-427; ❄📶) Offering top-end boutique luxury a stone's throw from the Mezquita, the Balcón is a magazine spread waiting to happen. Its effortlessly cool decor blends a muted contemporary approach with historic touches, such as heavy wooden shutters, brick-arched patios and ancient stone relics. Service doesn't miss a beat and there are memorable Mezquita views from the rooftop terrace.

Eating

Córdoba's signature dish is *salmorejo*, a thick, chilled soup, sprinkled with hard-boiled egg and strips of ham. Along with *rabo de toro* (oxtail stew), it appears on every menu. Another city speciality is *flamenquín*, a roll of breaded pork wrapped around slices of ham. Don't miss the sweet local Montilla-Moriles wine.

★**La Bicicleta** CAFE €
(☎666 544690; Calle Cardenal González 1; dishes €4.95-15.95; ⏲noon-1am Mon & Fri, 10am-1am Tue-Thu & Sun, 9am-1am Sat; 📶📝) 🍃 Locals and visitors enjoy the shabby-chic Bicicleta, an inviting, laid-back cafe where you can sip on fruit juices and cocktails, dig into delish cakes or sit down to avocado-and-ham toasties or light meals such as hummus with salad.

Mercado Victoria FOOD HALL €
(www.mercadovictoria.com; Paseo de la Victoria; items €2-19; ⏲11am-1am Sun-Thu, to 2am Fri & Sat mid-Jun–mid-Sep, 10am-midnight Sun-Thu, to 2am Fri & Sat mid-Sep–mid-Jun) If you fancy a tasty fill-up without the formality of a restaurant meal, this buzzing food hall is ideal. Occupying a 19th-century pavilion in the Victoria gardens just west of the old city, its stalls cook up everything from Argentine empanadas and Mexican burritos to sushi, pizzas and classic Spanish seafood.

Taberna Salinas ANDALUCIAN €
(☎957 48 29 50; www.tabernasalinas.com; Calle Tundidores 3; mains €7.75-11; ⏲12.30-3.30pm & 8-11pm Mon-Sat, closed Aug) A historic bar-restaurant (since 1879) with a patio and several rooms, Salinas is adorned in classic Córdoba fashion with tiles, wine barrels, art and photos of bullfighter Manolete. It's popular with tourists, but it retains a traditional atmosphere and its classic regional food is reliably good (and served in huge helpings).

Bar Santos TAPAS €
(Calle Magistral González Francés 3; tapas €2.30-5; ⏲10am-midnight Mon-Fri, from 11am Sat & Sun) For one of Córdoba's signature eating experiences, join the queues at this legendary bar and order a *tortilla de patatas* (potato omelette). You'll be handed a paper plate weighed down by a thick wedge of the stuff, deftly cut from a giant yellow ball. Balancing this and your plastic cutlery, cross the street and eat under the Mezquita's walls.

★**Casa Pepe de la Judería** ANDALUCIAN €€
(☎957 20 07 44; www.restaurantecasapepedelajuderia.com; Calle Romero 1; tapas €3.60-14, mains €12-39; ⏲1-4pm & 7.30-11pm; 📶) Expertly prepared Andalucian fare, on a sunny roof terrace or in rooms adorned with Cordoban art, keeps Pepe's high in the popularity charts. Whether you go for tapas or the more expensive restaurant menu, quality is high, culminating in some fabulous meat dishes – try the sensational *presa ibérica* (steak of Iberian pork). Service remains attentive and friendly, even when it's packed.

Garum 2.1 TAPAS €€
(☎957 48 76 73; Calle de San Fernando 122; tapas €3.90-7.90, mains €9.90-16.90; ⏲1-4pm & 8-11pm) Blending a bistro-style approach with gourmet tapas, Garum 2.1 touts itself as a bistronomic tapas bar. This sounds faintly ridiculous but there's nothing off-putting about its tapas, which are creatively presented and often quite inspired. A case in point are its churros, here filled with oxtail and chocolate, and the award-wining octopus served with smoked pig's ears. Excellent wine too.

Bodegas Campos ANDALUCIAN €€
(☎957 49 75 00; www.bodegascampos.com; Calle de Lineros 32; mains €12-26; ⏲1-4pm & 8.30-11pm) This atmospheric warren of rooms and patios is a local institution, popular with *cordobeses* and visitors alike – including ex-Brit PM Tony Blair. The restaurant and more informal *taberna* (tavern) specialise in creatively updated regional dishes such as avocado puree and beef tenderloin with foie gras. It also produces its own house Montilla wine.

La Boca FUSION €€
(☎957 47 61 40; www.facebook.com/restaurante.laboca; Calle de San Fernando 39; mains €12.50-18.50; ⏲noon-midnight Wed-Mon, to 5pm Tue; 📶) Local ingredients are given an international makeover at this inventive restaurant, appearing in dishes such as Iberian pork-cheek

WORTH A TRIP

MEDINA AZAHARA

Some 8km west of Córdoba stand the ruins of **Medina Azahara** (Madinat al-Zahra; ☎957 10 49 33; www.museosdeandalucia.es; Carretera Palma del Río Km 5.5; EU/non-EU citizen free/€1.50, shuttle bus adult/child €2.50/1.50; ⏲9am-9pm Tue-Sat Apr–mid-Jun, to 3pm mid-Jun–mid-Sep, to 6pm mid-Sep–Mar, 9am-3pm Sun year-round; P), the 10th-century palace-city built by Caliph Abd ar-Rahman III. Only about a tenth of the original city has been excavated and visits, which start in a modern museum some 2km below the hillside ruins, are limited to the central section of the Alcázar, the quarter that comprised the caliph's palace and attendant offices and residential blocks.

Legend has it that Abd ar-Rahman III commissioned Medina Azahara for his favourite wife, Az-Zahra. More realistically, it was probably his declaration of the caliphate of Córdoba in 929 that spurred him to build a new capital. Work started in 940 and chroniclers record some staggering statistics: 10,000 labourers set 6000 stone blocks a day, eventually building a city whose outer walls stretched 1518m east to west, and 745m north to south.

Construction took 35 years, yet only a few years after the city was completed, it fell into rapid decline. In 981 the usurper Al-Mansur transferred his government to a new palace complex. Then, between 1010 and 1013, Berber soldiers sacked it during the violent power struggle that preceded the caliphate's demise. Over succeeding centuries its ruins were repeatedly plundered for building materials.

Get your entrance tickets at the modern **museum** by the car park. Here you can also watch an interesting introductory film (in Spanish with English subtitles) and browse informative displays illustrating Medina's planning and construction, its inhabitants and eventual downfall.

From the car park, a shuttle bus ferries you up to the ruins, which you enter through the city's original northern gate. Highlights include the arched **Edificio Basilical Superior**, which housed the main state admin offices, a row of **red-striped arches** from the Grand Portico, and the **Casa de Yafar**, believed to have been residence of the caliph's prime minister.

The site's crown jewel, the royal reception hall known as the **Salón de Abd ar-Rahman III** (or Salón Rico), has been closed for restoration since 2009 (with no expected completion date at the time of research).

To get to Medina Azahara by car from Córdoba, head west on the A431, exiting after about 6km. Alternatively, a bus runs to the site from Glorieta Cruz Roja at 10.15am, 11am and 11.45am Tuesdays to Sundays, plus 2.40pm on Saturdays – check these times as seasonal variations apply. Buy tickets (adult/child €9/5 return including the shuttle bus to/from the ruins) on the bus or at Córdoba's tourist office – buying in advance is sensible for weekends and public holidays. The bus then starts back from Medina 3¼ hours after it leaves Córdoba.

loaf in red curry or tuna tataki with soy mayo. Complementing the fusion cuisine, its *taberna* rooms and more formal restaurant section sport an arty, casually stylish look. Reservations advisable at weekends.

Amaltea FUSION €€
(☎957 49 19 68; Ronda de Isasa 10; mains €12-16; ⏲1-4pm & 8-11pm Mon-Sat, 1-4pm Sun; 📶🌿) One of a string of riverside restaurants, Amaltea impresses with its good-looking dining room and imaginative, international-inspired menu. Vegetarians are well catered to, while seafood aficionados can try butterfish tartar with wakame and wasabi ice cream, and carnivores can dig into tandoori lamb with rice.

La Tinaja ANDALUCIAN €€
(☎957 04 79 98; www.latinajadecordoba.com; Paseo de la Ribera 12; raciones €8-18; ⏲1.30-4pm & 8-11pm, later in summer) With its cool rustic interior and candlelit terrace (ignore the nearby bins), La Tinaja is one of the best of the riverside restaurants. Food-wise the onus is on local regional cooking, both traditional and modern, with evergreen crowd-pleasers such as *flamenquín*, a breaded pork loin wrapped around *jamón ibérico* (Iberian ham). Portions aren't for giant appetites.

El Churrasco GRILL €€€
(☎957 29 08 19; www.elchurrasco.com; Calle Romero 16; tapas €2-6.15, mains €12-34; ⏲1-4pm & 8-11.30pm Sun-Thu, to midnight Fri & Sat) Renowned for its char-grilled meats, including its signature *churrasco cordobés* (pork tenderloin grilled over oak charcoal, with Arabic sauces), this busy bar-restaurant stands out in the touristy Mezquita area. Service can be a bit gruff at the bar, but the expert grillers know their stuff and the food is consistently good – mainly steaks and traditional meat dishes but also some fish options.

Drinking & Entertainment

The bars and cafes on and around Plaza de las Tendillas are a favourite evening hang-out for many *cordobeses*. Another popular area is the riverfront Pasero de la Ribera where'll you'll find a string of bars. For a more alternative scene, head to streets such as Calles Alfonso XIII and Alfaros northeast of Plaza de las Tendillas.

★ **Jugo** WINE BAR
(www.facebook.com/quierojugovivo; Plaza San Andres 5; ⏲noon-1.45pm & 6-10pm Mon-Thu, noon-1.45pm & 6-11pm Fri, noon-3.30pm & 7-11pm Sat, noon-3pm Sun) A bit of a hike from the main tourist haunts, Jugo is a real find, a natural wine shop doubling as a bar. Run with welcoming cheer by English-speaking Javi and Gaby, it's a great place to escape the hordes and enjoy a tranquil glass or two, either in the woody, rustic interior or on the pretty plaza outside.

El Barón BAR
(Plaza de Abades 4; ⏲12.30pm-midnight) Set on a charming old town plaza, the outside tables at this unassuming bar are a lovely place for a relaxed drink. It has Montilla wines and *cava* (sparkling wine), craft beers, and a choice of sweet and savoury snacks (€2.50 to €9), including a rich house pâté and lush chocolate cake.

Amapola BAR
(www.facebook.com/amapolabarcordoba; Paseo de la Ribera 9; ⏲4pm-2.30am, from noon Fri-Sun) With Elvis Costello providing the soundtrack, beer served in pints, and a retro feel about the sparsely furnished interior, everything is in place to make this riverside bar your go-to drinking hang-out. There's a terrace looking down to the river and cool music, either spun by DJs or live most Friday and/or Saturday nights.

Califa CRAFT BEER
(www.cervezascalifa.com; Calle Juan Valera 3; ⏲noon-4pm & 6.30pm-12.30am Mon-Thu, noon-2am Fri & Sat, noon-4.30pm Sun; 📶) One of Andalucía's longest-running craft beer bars, with its own-label brews fermented on the premises. There's a blackboard's worth of pale ales, IPAs and stouts to choose from, including eight on tap, and a short menu of light dishes to soak it all up with.

Bodega Guzmán WINE BAR
(Calle de los Judíos 7; ⏲noon-4pm & 8.30-11.30pm Fri-Wed) This cavernous Judería bar, frequented by both locals and tourists, is straight out of central casting with its ceramic tiling, bullfighting memorabilia and giant wine barrels. Get into the groove by sipping on a bone-dry Montilla *fino*, perhaps accompanied by a tapa of sheep's cheese in olive oil.

Tablao Cardenal FLAMENCO
(☎691 217922; www.tablaocardenal.es; Calle Buen Pastor 2; shows incl 1 drink €23; ⏲shows 8.15pm Mon-Thu, 9pm Fri & Sat) A 17th-century aristocratic house in the Judería provides the atmospheric setting for professional, passionate flamenco shows featuring song, music and dance.

Shopping

Córdoba's craft specialities include silver jewellery, pottery, and colourful embossed leather *(cuero repujado),* known as *guadamecí* (if it's sheepskin) or *cordobán* (goatskin).

Ostin Macho CONCEPT STORE
(☎957 94 20 55; Plaza del Doctor Emilio Luque 2; ⏲10.30am-1.30pm & 5.30-8.30pm Mon-Fri, 11am-2pm Sat) Forget the obvious touristy shops, this appealing concept store is a much better bet for an original memento. Owner Ruben stocks a colourful collection of illustrated mugs and bowls, diaries, lamps, graphic books, artworks and prints, some designed by students at a local art school.

Meryan FASHION & ACCESSORIES
(☎957 47 59 02; www.meryancor.com; Calleja de las Flores 2; ⏲9am-8pm Mon-Fri, 9am-2pm Sat) This long-standing shop near the Mezquita has a good range of embossed leather goods: jackets, wallets, bags, boxes, notebooks, leather-covered wooden chests, all in a range of colours and prices.

Information

Information on Córdoba and its province is available at www.cordobaturismo.es.

Centro de Visitantes (Visitors Centre; ☎902 20 17 74; www.turismodecordoba.org; Plaza del Triunfo; ⏲9am-7pm Mon-Fri, 9.30am-2.30pm Sat & Sun) The main tourist office near the Mezquita; can provide maps and printed material in English and Spanish.

Municipal Tourist Information Kiosk (www.turismodecordoba.org; Plaza de las Tendillas; ⏲9am-1.30pm & 5-7.15pm) On Plaza de las Tendillas in the modern part of town.

Getting There & Away

BUS

The **bus station** (☎957 40 40 40; www.estacionautobusescordoba.es; Avenida de la Libertad) is behind the train station, 1.3km northwest of Plaza de las Tendillas.

Alsa (☎902 422242; www.alsa.es)

Autocares Carrera (☎957 50 16 32; www.autocarescarrera.es)

Autocares San Sebastián (☎957 42 90 30; www.autocaressansebastian.es)

Cambus (☎679 730134; www.cambusautocares.com)

Socibus (☎902 22 92 92; www.socibus.es)

TRAIN

Córdoba's modern **train station** (☎902 320 320; Plaza de las Tres Culturas), 1.2km northwest of Plaza de las Tendillas, is served by fast AVE services and slower regional trains.

Destination	Cost (€)	Duration	Frequency (daily)
Andújar	9.85	50min	4
Antequera (Santa Ana)	17-34	30-40min	17-18
Granada	25-49	1½-2¼hr	6
Jaén	15	1¾hr	4
Madrid	39-63	1¾-2¼hr	33-34
Málaga	21-42	1hr	16-17
Seville	14-32	45min-1¼hr	29-35

Getting Around

BICYCLE

There are bicycle lanes throughout the city, though they're underused.

Elektrik.es (☎671 417814; www.rentabikecordoba.com; Calle María Cristina 5; per 3hr/half-day/full day bicycle €6/10/14, electric bicycle €10/14/19; ⏲shop 10am-2pm & 5.30-8.30pm) Rents bikes for city and out-of-town riding.

BUS

Bus 3 (☎957 76 46 76; www.aucorsa.es) runs every 14 to 20 minutes (€1.30) from Avenida Vía Augusta (the street between the train and bus stations) down Calle de San Fernando to the riverside Paseo de la Ribera, east of the Mezquita. For the return trip, catch it on Ronda de Isasa near the main tourist office, or from Campo Santo de los Mártires, Glorieta Cruz Roja or Avenida de Cervantes.

BUSES FROM CÓRDOBA

DESTINATION	BUS COMPANY	COST (€)	DURATION	FREQUENCY (DAILY)
Almodóvar del Río	Autocares San Sebastián	2.05	30min	up to 10
Baena	Autocares Carrera	5.60	1hr	3-8
Baeza	Alsa	11.80	2¼hr	2
Granada	Alsa	15.25	2¾-4hr	9-11
Hornachuelos	Autocares San Sebastián	4.50	1-1¼hr	2-5
Jaén	Cambus	11	2hr	4-7
Madrid	Socibus	18-25	4¼-5hr	7-8
Málaga	Alsa	12.35	2½-3hr	3-4
Montilla	Autocares Carrera	3.90	45min	8 or more
Priego de Córdoba	Autocares Carrera	9.45	2hr	3-7
Seville	Alsa	12.65	1¾-2hr	7
Úbeda	Alsa	12.60	1¾-2½hr	4-5
Zuheros	Autocares Carrera	6.65	1¾hr	2-4

CAR & MOTORCYCLE

Driving in Córdoba is no picnic – the one-way system is nightmarish and cars are banned from most of the historic centre unless unloading or parking at a hotel.

There is free, unmetered parking south of the river across the Puente de Miraflores, and a mixture of free and metered parking on Paseo de la Victoria. Expect to pay around €0.85 per hour in a metered zone (marked with blue lines), though you can generally stop for free between 2pm and 5pm, overnight from 9pm to 9am, and from 2pm Saturday to 9am Monday. Convenient car parks include **Parking Victoria** (Paseo de la Victoria; per 24hr €12.65; 24hr) and **Parking La Mezquita** (Avenida Doctor Fleming; per 24hr €15; 24hr).

TAXI

Taxis from the bus or train stations to the Mezquita cost around €7. In the centre, you'll find taxi ranks on Campo Santo de los Mártires and just off Plaza de las Tendillas.

SOUTHERN CÓRDOBA PROVINCE

The rolling countryside south of Córdoba, known as the Campiña de Córdoba, is almost entirely swathed in olive trees and grapevines, yielding some of Spain's finest olive oils and the unique, sherry-like Montilla-Moriles wines. Back in the 13th to 15th centuries, this was frontier country, its undulating peaks straddling the border between Islamic- and Christian-controlled territories – hence the many towns and villages clustered around hilltop castles. In the province's southeastern reaches, the mountainous Parque Natural Sierras Subbéticas is a highlight, an unspoiled and sparsely populated area of rocky summits, canyons, caves and wooded valleys.

Baena

POP 19,340 / ELEV 430M

Baena, a busy market town 66km southeast of Córdoba, sits at the heart of a historic olive-oil producing area, designated with its own Denominación de Origen (DO; a certification guaranteeing provenance and quality control). It has no great must-see sights but if you're passing through, you can see how oil is produced at a working mill and enjoy fine views from the town's heavily restored castle.

Almazara Núñez de Prado OLIVE OIL MILL

(957 67 01 41; Avenida Cervantes 5; 9am-2pm Mon-Fri Jan-Jun, 4-5.30pm Mon-Fri Jun–mid-Sep) FREE To see how Baena produces its liquid gold, stop off at this working olive-oil mill, run by a family who own around 100,000 olive trees. Olives are hand-picked to prevent bruising, then pulped in ancient stone mills. Núñez de Prado is one of the few operations in Spain that still uses this traditional pulping method, and is famous for its *flor de aceite,* the oil that seeps naturally from the crushed olives.

Visits are by 40-minute tours.

Castillo de Baena CASTLE

(Plaza del Palacio; adult/child €2/1; 10.30am-1.30pm Tue-Sun & 4.30-7.30pm Thu-Sat winter, longer hours summer) This heavily restored 15th- to 16th-century castle sits at the top of Baena's hilltop centre. Neglect and the construction of water tanks in the 20th century have taken a toll and little remains of the castle's original interior. You can, however, climb its towers and walk along the battlements to admire sweeping views.

Information

Tourist Office (957 67 17 57; www.baena.es; Calle Virrey del Pino 5; 8am-2.30pm Mon-Fri & 4.30-7.30pm Wed-Fri) Helpful office with current information on all Baena's attractions.

Getting There & Away

Autocares Carrera (p219) Daily buses to/from Córdoba (€5.60, one hour, three to eight daily) and Priego de Córdoba (€4, one hour, three daily Monday to Friday, one on Sunday).

Monbus (982 29 29 00; www.monbus.es) Services to/from Zuheros (€1.43, 30 minutes, three to five daily).

Parque Natural Sierras Subbéticas

Although only about 70km southeast of Córdoba, the silent expanses of the Parque Natural Sierras Subbéticas feel a world away. The park, which encompasses some 320 sq km of craggy, emerald-green hills pocked with caves, springs and streams, is made for slow touring and there's some wonderful hiking in its valleys, canyons and peaks (including the highest, the 1570m La Tiñosa). Most visitors base themselves in picturesque Zuheros or Priego de Córdoba. The ideal months for walking are April, May, September and October.

WORTH A TRIP

MONTILLA & ITS WINES

The rolling countryside south of Córdoba is home to the wines of the Montilla-Moriles Denominación de Origen. Endlessly compared to sherry, to the irritation of local vintners, these highly drinkable wines are produced exclusively from the Pedro Ximénez grape.

The most delicate of Montilla wines is the pale, straw-like *fino*. Then there's *amontillado*, a golden-amber wine with a nutty flavour, and *oloroso*, a darker, full-bodied wine with an 18% to 20% alcohol content. The sweetest is the almost black *Pedro Ximénez*, made from grapes that have been sun-dried before pressing.

Montilla wines go very well with tapas or as an aperitif or dessert wine. The lighter ones also make a good accompaniment for soups and seafood starters. If you're feeling brave, try ordering a *fiti* (fifty-fifty), a powerful mix of *fino* and PX!

To learn more about these wines, the wineries in and around Montilla are far less visited than the sherry bodegas of Jerez, but equally as appealing.

Montilla's **Oficina de Turismo** (☎672 780521, 957 65 23 54; www.montillaturismo.es; Castillo de Montilla, Calle Iglesia; ⏲9am-2pm Mon-Thu, 9am-2pm & 4.30-6.30pm Fri, 10am-1pm & 4.30-6.30pm Sat, 10am-1pm Sun) is on the ball about winery visits and everything else in the area. The Spanish-language website Ruta del Vino Montilla Moriles (www.turismoyvino.es) is also helpful.

Montilla is 50km south of Córdoba, about 45 minutes by car. By bus, there are services to/from Córdoba (€3.90, 45 minutes, at least eight daily), Málaga (€11.40, 1¾ to two hours, four daily) and Priego de Córdoba (€4.70, 1½ hours, two to three daily).

Bodegas Alvear (☎957 65 29 39; www.alvear.es; Avenida María Auxiliadora 1; tours €12; ⏲tours without reservation 12.30pm Mon-Sat, by arrangement other times) Bodegas Alvear is the most renowned of Montilla's winemakers and one of Spain's oldest, with a range of PX vintages. Tours, which last around 90 minutes and include tastings, are available in Spanish, English, French or German. Get tickets at the Alvear shop at Avenida Boucau 6.

Bodegas Pérez Barquero (☎957 65 05 00; www.perezbarquero.com; Avenida de Andalucía 27; tours in Spanish €5, in English, French or German €10; ⏲tours with reservation noon Mon-Sat, by arrangement other times; P) The vast warehouses here are stacked high with oak barrels of highly acclaimed wines, with five-wine tastings held in an atmospheric former chapel. It is walkable from Montilla's centre – in the western part of town near the N331.

Bodegas Lagar Blanco (☎628 319977; www.lagarblanco.es; Carretera Cuesta Blanca Km 4.4; tour incl 2/5 wines €12/18, 5 wines plus tapas €40; ⏲tours Mon-Sat by arrangement; P) Owner Miguel Cruz gives excellent 1½-hour tours (in English or Spanish) of his winery in the Sierra de Montilla, 10km east of Montilla (about €10 by taxi). You'll see the vineyards and *tinaja* (fermentation vessels) as well as modern winemaking technology. Visits must be booked in advance, either by phoning or emailing lagarblanco@lagarblanco.es.

Castillo de Montilla (Calle Iglesia; ⏲9am-2pm Mon-Thu, 9am-2pm & 4.30-6.30pm Fri, 10am-1pm & 4.30-6.30pm Sat, 10am-1pm Sun) Little remains of Montilla's castle, which fell into ruin after its towers were demolished in 1508. You can see a few ruins scattered around the panoramic hilltop site but most of the area is now occupied by an 18th-century granary known as the Alhorí.

Las Camachas (☎957 65 00 04; Avenida de Europa 3; mains €14-25; ⏲1.30-5pm & 9-11.30pm) In a roadside house on the western edge of town, this long-standing Montilla choice specialises in traditional regional fare. Its stone-walled dining halls pair well with dishes such as *rabo de toro* (oxtail) and flavoursome grilled meats. Excellent local wine too.

Park information is available at the **Centro de Visitantes Santa Rita** (☎957 50 69 86; Carretera A339, Km 11.2; ⏲9am-2pm Wed-Sun, 6-8pm Sat & Sun May-Aug, 9am-2pm Wed-Sun Sep, 9am-2pm Wed-Sun, 4-6pm Sat & Sun Oct-Apr), 15km west of Priego de Córdoba on the road to Cabra. Also useful is the website www.turismodelasubbetica.es.

Zuheros & Around

POP 640 / ELEV 660M

Tiny Zuheros is the most picturesque of the villages in the Parque Natural Sierras Subbéticas. A jumble of white, red-roofed houses capped by a crag-top castle, it crouches in the lee of towering hills surrounded by olive groves stretching as far as the eye can see. Approached by twisting roads up from the A318, it has a delightfully relaxed atmosphere.

Sights

Castillo de Zuheros CASTLE
(☎957 69 45 45; Plaza de la Paz; adult/child incl Museo Arqueológico €2/1.25; ⊙10am-2pm & 5-7pm Tue-Fri, tours 11am, 12.30pm, 2pm, 5pm & 6.30pm Sat & Sun Apr-Sep, 10am-2pm & 4-6pm Tue-Fri, tours 11am, 12.30pm, 2pm, 4pm & 5.30pm Sat & Sun Oct-Mar) Grafted onto a rocky pinnacle, Zuheros' castle is of 9th-century Moorish origin, but most of what survives is a Christian construction from the 13th and 14th centuries, with remains of a 16th-century Renaissance palace attached. It's small but panoramic, with fine views from the top. Visits on weekends and holidays are guided; other days, you're free to visit on your own. Tickets are sold at the small **Museo Arqueológico** (Archaeological Museum; ⊙10am-2pm & 5-7pm Tue-Fri, tours 11am, 12.30pm, 2pm, 5pm & 6.30pm Sat & Sun Apr-Sep, 10am-2pm & 4-6pm Tue-Fri, tours 11am, 12.30pm, 2pm, 4pm & 5.30pm Sat & Sun Oct-Mar), just across the square, which also doubles as Zuheros' tourist office.

Cueva de los Murciélagos CAVE
(Cave of the Bats; ☎957 69 45 45; adult/child €7.50/6; ⊙12.30-5.30pm Tue-Fri, tours 11am, 12.30pm, 2pm, 5pm & 6.30pm Sat & Sun Apr-Sep, 12.30-4.30pm Tue-Fri, tours 11am, 12.30pm, 2pm, 4pm & 5.30pm Sat & Sun Oct-Mar; P) Carved out of the limestone massif 4km above Zuheros is this extraordinary cave. From the vast hall at the start of the tour, it's a 415m loop walk (with 700 steps) through a series of corridors filled with fantastic rock formations and traces of Neolithic rock paintings showing abstract figures of goats. Visits are by guided tour only: reserve by phoning between 10am and 1.30pm Tuesday to Friday or by emailing turismo@zuheros.es.

Activities

Zuheros offers excellent walking with several trails leading through the surrounding slopes. For a gentle warm-up, you can stroll round the village's lower periphery through the **Parque Periurbano**, taking in lookout points and a hanging bridge. Hotel Zuhayra has good hiking information and can put you in contact with an English-speaking guide, Clive Jarman, who lives in Zuheros.

Cerro Bramadero Walk HIKING
Behind Zuheros village lies a dramatic rocky gorge, the **Cañón de Bailón**. A beautifully scenic circular walk of about 4½ hours takes you up the canyon and round Cerro Bramadero hill then back to Zuheros via the road descending from the Cueva de los Murciélagos. The distance is around 13km, with a total ascent and descent of some 600m.

Vía Verde del Aceite CYCLING
(Vía Verde de la Subbética; www.viasverdes.com;) The area's easiest and best marked trail is the *vía verde* (greenway; a disused railway converted to a cycling and walking track). Running for 58km through the western and northern fringes of the Parque Natural Sierras Subbéticas, this local stretch of the 128km-long *vìa* – which, in its entirety, traverses Córdoba and Jaén provinces – is ideal for a relaxed, easy-going workout.

Centro Cicloturista Subbética CYCLING
(☎672 605088, 691 843532; www.subbeticabikesfriends.com; per half-/full day bikes €12/18, electric bikes €12/25; ⊙10am-12.30pm Sat & Sun mid-Jun–mid-Sep, 10am-2pm Mon-Fri, to 7pm Sat & Sun mid-Sep–mid-Jun;) The nearest bike-rental spot to Zuheros is the Centro Cicloturista Subbética at Doña Mencía station, 4km downhill from the village. It has a range of different bikes, including children's and electric bikes, and can provide local tourist information as well as showers and other services for cyclists.

Sleeping & Eating

★ **Hotel Zuhayra** HOTEL €
(☎957 69 46 93; www.zercahoteles.com; Calle Mirador 10; incl breakfast s €43-55, d €53-70;) An arrow's shot from Zuheros' castle, this sunny hotel has breathtaking views of the countryside from each of its white, tile-floored rooms. You can hire bikes here (€10 for four hours, €15 for longer) and the welcoming proprietors, the Ábalos brothers (who speak English), are a mine of local information.

★ **Restaurante Zuhayra** ANDALUCIAN €€
(www.zercahoteles.com; Calle Mirador 10; mains & raciones €7-18.50; ⏲1-3.30pm & 8-10.30pm) On the 1st floor of the Hotel Zuhayra, this excellent restaurant, open to all, serves pizzas, hamburgers and uncomplicated but super-tasty versions of local and Andalucian favourites, such as *berenjenas a la miel* (diced cubes of aubergine sweetened with honey) and grilled lamb chops with thyme. In good weather you can sit in a charming patio set beneath a natural rock face.

Mesón Atalaya ANDALUCIAN €€
(☎957 69 47 65; Calle Santo 58; mains €6-19; ⏲1-4pm & 9-11pm Tue-Sun) One of the first buildings you come to when entering Zuheros from the east, this rustic, family-run establishment does a fine line in filling country fare – no-nonsense meat dishes and *cazuelas* (types of stew), local cheeses and homemade desserts. There are two plant-filled patios and a small sunny terrace out front.

Information

Tourist Office (☎957 69 45 45; www.zuheros.es/turismo; Plaza de la Paz 1; ⏲10am-2pm & 5-7pm Tue-Fri, 11am-2pm Sat & Sun Apr-Sep, 10am-2pm & 4-6pm Tue-Fri, 11am-2pm Sat & Sun Oct-Mar)

Getting There & Away

BUS

Buses depart from Mesón Atalaya at the village's eastern entrance.

Autocares Carrera (p219) Runs two to four daily buses to/from Córdoba (€6.65, 1¾ hours).

Monbus (p220) Operates three or more daily buses to/from Doña Mencía (€1.18, 10 to 20 minutes), Baena (€1.43, 30 minutes) and Seville (€17.37, 3¾ hours).

CAR & MOTORCYCLE

There are parking areas near Mesón Atalaya restaurant at the upper entrance to the village: follow 'Cueva de los Murciélagos' signs as you approach Zuheros.

Priego de Córdoba & Around

POP 22,590 / ELEV 650M

Priego de Córdoba, perched on an outcrop above the Río Salado valley, is a prosperous market town founded in 745 CE and now renowned for its olive oil and showy baroque churches. It found itself on the Granada emirate's frontline against its Christian enemies until its definitive conquest by Alfonso XI in 1341. It later enjoyed prosperity as an important silk and velvet manufacturer, culminating in an 18th-century boom that gave rise to many of the town's flamboyant baroque buildings.

Sights

Note that the opening hours of Priego's churches and other sights have a habit of changing frequently: they are updated weekly on the website of the tourist office (p226).

★ **Parroquia de la Asunción** CHURCH
(Plaza Santa Ana 1; €2; ⏲11am-1.30pm Tue-Sat, 11am-noon Sun) The most visually stunning of Priego's churches, the Parroquia de la Asunción represents a high point in Andalucian baroque. The church was originally built to a Gothic-Mudéjar style in the 16th century but a comprehensive 18th-century makeover transformed it into a baroque tour de force. Its great masterpiece is the Sagrario (Sacristy), a soaring octagonal chamber where whirls of frothy white stucco surge upwards to a luminous cupola – all the work of local artist Francisco Javier Pedrajas in the 1780s.

For further lavish church ornamentation, head to the **Iglesia de la Aurora** (Carrera de Álvarez; €1.50; ⏲10.30am-1.30pm Tue-Sun) and **Iglesia de San Francisco** (Plaza de San Francisco; ⏲10am-1pm & 6-8pm Mon-Fri, 10am-1pm Sat, 9am-12.45pm Sun) FREE, both of which also feature 18th-century baroque decor.

Castillo CASTLE
(Plaza Abad Palomino; admission €1.50, Wed free; ⏲10.30am-2pm & 4-6.30pm Tue-Sat, 10.30am-2pm Sun) Priego's austere medieval castle, complete with square towers and forbidding ramparts, proudly overlooks Plaza Abad Palomino in the Barrio de la Villa. Originally an Islamic fortress, it was thoroughly remodelled by the town's Christian overlords between the 13th and 15th centuries. You can climb to the top of the keep (Torre del Homenaje) for aerial views of the white town spread beneath you.

Barrio de la Villa OLD TOWN
Priego's original Moorish quarter, the Barrio de La Villa extends to the northeast of the town centre. Narrow, geranium-hung lanes weave through the pristine white *barrio* (district), leading to the clifftop Paseo del Adarve, a panoramic promenade overlooking the Salado valley. Nearby, the elegant Paseo de Colombia is a landscaped plaza with fountains, flower beds and pergola.

Fuente del Rey FOUNTAIN

(Fountain of the King; Calle del Río) Occupying an entire plaza southwest of the centre, this splendid baroque fountain was completed in 1803. Water flows through 139 pipes, many sprouting from carved masks, to fill a three-tiered basin centred on a statue of Neptune and Amphitrite on a horse-drawn carriage.

Centro Cultural Adolfo Lozano Sidro MUSEUM

(☎957 54 09 47; Carrera de las Monjas 16; admission €2, Wed free; ⏱10.30am-1.30pm Tue-Sun, 6-8.30pm Tue-Fri, 5-7pm Sat) You get three museums for your money here: a history museum with well-displayed archaeological finds from the Priego area; a gallery with modern Spanish landscape paintings; and two floors dedicated to painter Adolfo Lozano Sidro (1872–1935), whose family lived in the building. His realistic art covered the spectrum of social life in his era.

Sleeping

★**Casa Olea** CASA RURAL €€

(☎696 748209; www.casaolea.com; Carretera CO7204, near El Cañuelo; s/d incl breakfast €121/132; P❄📶≋) Set amidst olive groves in an unspoiled river valley 12km north of Priego, this rustic farmhouse set-up has a beautifully spacious and relaxed feel. It makes a delightful base for exploring the region, with six simply attired rooms, soothing views, easy access to walks in the Sierras Subbéticas and mountain bikes to rent (€15 per day). Córdoba and Granada are both within 1½ hours' drive.

There's a lovely pool, and excellent dinners (two/three courses €21/26) are available five nights a week. Your British hosts, Tim and Claire, are full of information and tips on where to go and what to do. No children under seven and a minimum stay of two nights.

Casa Baños de la Villa BOUTIQUE HOTEL €€

(☎957 54 72 74; www.casabanosdelavilla.com; Calle Real 63; s/d incl breakfast €71/99; P❄📶≋) A big draw of this welcoming hideaway in the Barrio de la Villa is its *baños árabes,* a Moorish fantasy of baths and arches – indeed, room rates include a 90-minute session plus sauna. Its individually decorated rooms are all comfy with homey bric-a-brac and carved wood bedsteads, and there's a fine roof deck.

PRIEGO'S OLIVE OIL

Priego de Córdoba's extra virgin olive oil (*aceite de oliva virgen extra*) is prized across Spain. It has been a source of wealth since ancient Roman times and still today the area's small-scale producers turn out some of the country's finest blends. Oils such as Venta del Barón from the Mueloliva company and Rincón de la Subbética from Almazaras de la Subbética are known internationally and regularly win awards.

When buying, go for oils carrying the Denominación de Origen Priego de Córdoba designation, proof that they were produced locally.

Eating

La Pianola Casa Pepe ANDALUCIAN €

(☎957 70 04 09; Calle Obispo Caballero 6; mains €6-12; ⏱12.30-4pm & 8pm-12.30am Tue-Sun) Often busy, this animated corner restaurant wins you over with its efficient service and classic regional cuisine – nothing fancy, just well prepared local favourites ranging from *revueltos* (scrambled-egg dishes) to honey-sweetened aubergines and *flamenquín,* a deep-fried roll of *jamón* wrapped in pork meat.

★**Zyrah** FUSION €€

(☎957 54 70 23; www.facebook.com/zyrahpriego; Calle del Río; tapas €3-8.50, raciones €6-16; ⏱8am-midnight Tue-Sun) Bringing a dash of contemporary flair to Priego's traditional restaurant scene, Zyrah is a good-looking gastro bar whose experimental local cuisine hits the mark more often than not. You'll find classic regional ingredients on the menu but they're often incorporated into unusual compositions: *presa ibérica,* for example, is cut into strips and mixed with wok-fried Chinese noodles.

Vaquena ANDALUCIAN €€

(☎662 391278; www.vaquena.com; Carretera Co-612, Km 5.5; mains €8-20.50; ⏱12.30-6pm Tue-Sun autumn, winter & spring, from 8pm Tue-Sun summer) Diners tackle the vertiginous drive up to this remote restaurant for two reasons: to enjoy uplifting views from its lofty hillside setting and to feast on superlative beef, produced from the restaurant's own-reared cattle. The prized meat appears in various guises, in rice dishes, in croquettes and as hamburgers, but the star of the show is the butter-soft steak. Reservations recommended.

OFF THE BEATEN TRACK

LOS PEDROCHES

Stretching across Córdoba's far northern reaches, Los Pedroches is a still, silent area of big landscapes and long vistas. Castles and remote villages lie scattered across the verdant landscape, which ranges from picturesque river valleys and wooded hills in the Sierra Morena to endless swathes of flat farmland.

The area is renowned for its high-quality ham, *jamón ibérico de bellota*. This comes from the black Iberian pigs that graze freely on the extensive *dehesas* (woodland pastures) feasting on *bellotas* (acorns). Salted and cured for six to 12 months, the dark-pink ham is typically served wafer-thin with bread and Montilla wine.

The main approach to Los Pedroches is the N502, which branches off the northbound N4332 before passing over the 750m-high Puerto Calatraveño pass en route to **Alcaracejos**. This sleepy village is the area's main southern gateway and home to the district tourist office, the **Oficina Comarcal de Turismo** (957 15 61 02; www.turismolospedroches.org; Plaza de Andalucía 1, Alcaracejos; 9.30am-2.30pm Mon-Fri).

Twenty kilometres to the northwest, **Hinojosa del Duque** boasts a couple of worthwhile sights: the 16th-century **Catedral de la Sierra** (Plaza de la Catedral; 10.30am-1.30pm year-round, 7.30-9.30pm Apr-Sep, 6.30-8.30pm Oct-Mar) FREE with a Renaissance facade and a bell tower that supposedly inspired the *torre* of the Mezquita in Córdoba; and a **Museo Etnológico** (Ethnological Museum; 957 14 10 56; www.hinojosadelduque.es; Calle Cánovas del Castillo 3; noon-2pm & 5-8pm Wed-Fri, 11am-2pm Sat & Sun, 5-8pm Tue) FREE dedicated to the area's rural way of life – the latter also functions as a tourist office. Cafes on the cathedral plaza can provide refreshments.

From Hinojosa, it's 9km north to **Belalcázar**. This remote white town is guarded by a formidable 15th-century castle, the **Castillo de los Sotomayor**, whose main tower rises 45m above its hilltop perch. Following a recent restoration project, it's hoped the castle will shortly be open to visitors. In the town, near the **Iglesia de Santiago de Mayor**, is a statue of Sebastián de Belalcázar, a famous conquistador during Spain's New World expeditions.

Continuing east along the lonely CO9402 for 27km leads to **Santa Eufemia**, Andalucía's northernmost village. The main drawcard here is the **Castillo de Miramontes** FREE, a ruined Islamic castle that commands stunning 360-degree views from its lofty position 2.5km above the village.

Before returning to civilisation, there's excellent walking to be enjoyed in the **Parque Natural Sierra de Cardeña y Montoro** (www.ventanadelvisitante.es), a 384 sq km reserve of rolling hills, pastures and woodland. Trails meander through the bucolic landscape with several branching out from Aldea del Cerezo, 6km east of **Cardeña** village. Information and maps are available from the **Centro de Visitantes Venta Nueva** (685 957187; Junction N420 & A420; 9am-2pm Wed-Sun, 5.30-7.30pm Sat & Sun May & Sep, 9am-2pm Wed-Sun, 4.30-6.30pm Sat & Sun Jan-Apr & Oct-Dec, 9am-2pm Fri-Sun, 5.30-7.30pm Sat & Sun Jun, 9am-2pm Sat & Sun Jul, closed Aug), 1km south of Cardeña.

To stay in the area, **Villanueva de Córdoba** makes a good base. A lively market town 50km southeast of Santa Eufemia, it offers stylish contemporary accommodation at the **Hotel la Casa del Médico** (957 12 02 47; www.hotellacasadelmedico.com; Calle Contreras 4; r €70-125, ste €120-150;), and hearty hill-country food at the cheerful **La Puerta Falsa** (957 12 01 10; Calle Contreras 8; mains €10-25; 8am-midnight).

For more basic digs, the **Albergue Camino de Santiago** (617 715129; www.caminodesantiagobelalcazar.blogspot.com.es; Calle Pilar; dm incl breakfast €12; P) in Belalcázar is a modest *cortijo* (farmhouse) hostel intended primarily for walkers on the Camino Mozárabe (a pilgrim route to Santiago de Compostela), but open to all for good-value food and lodging.

Autocares San Sebastián (p219) provides bus service between Córdoba and Los Pedroches.

To find Vaquena, follow signs for the Ermita de la Virgen de la Sierra off the Priego de Córdoba–Cabras road and follow up the hairpin bends until you see a sign near the top for Caballos Valuenzela.

ⓘ Information

Oficina de Turismo (☑ 957 70 06 25; www.turismodepriego.com; Plaza de la Constitución 3; ⊙10am-2pm & 4.30-7pm Mon-Fri, 10am-2pm & 4.30-6.30pm Sat, 10am-2pm Sun) Very helpful and enthusiastic.

ⓘ Getting There & Around

BUS

Priego's **bus station** (☑ 957 70 18 75; Calle Nuestra Señora de los Remedios) is about 1km west of the centre. Autocares Carrera (p219) runs buses to/from Montilla (€4.70, 1½ hours, two or three daily) and Córdoba (€9.45, two hours, three to seven times daily). Alsa (p219) buses connect with Granada (€7.60, 1½ to two hours, two to four daily) via Alcalá la Real.

CAR & MOTORCYCLE

Parking can be a headache in Priego. Useful central car parks include **Parking Plaza de Abastos** (Calle Doctor Pedrajas; per hour/night €0.90/10; ⊙9am-11pm Sun-Thu, to midnight Fri & Sat, shorter hours winter) and **Aparcamiento Palenque** (Carrera de las Monjas; per day €1.50; ⊙7.30am-9.30pm Mon-Sat).

WESTERN CÓRDOBA PROVINCE

West of Córdoba, the Río Guadalquivir cuts through a sparsely inhabited landscape dotted with villages and castles, the most formidable of which looms high over Almodóvar del Río. Further west, the rural village of Hornachuelos acts as a gateway to the Parque Natural Sierra de Hornachuelos, a remote range of forested hills interspersed with pastureland and populated by deer, wild boar, otters and birds of prey.

Parque Natural Sierra de Hornachuelos

The Parque Natural Sierra de Hornachuelos is a 600-sq-km area of rolling hills in the western Sierra Morena. Its gentle slopes are densely wooded with poplars, ash trees,

holm and cork oaks, and pierced by a number of thickly wooded river valleys. The park is also renowned for its birdlife, hosting colonies of black and griffon vultures, eagles and rare black storks.

The small town of **Hornachuelos** on the park's southern fringe, standing above a small reservoir on the Río Bembézar, is the obvious base for enjoying the area's quiet charms.

Walking trails start from Hornachuelos village and the natural park visitors centre (p226), 1.5km to the north.

Sendero de Los Ángeles   WALKING

This path runs 4km (1½ hours) from the foot of Hornachuelos along the Bembézar reservoir to a huge, abandoned seminary, the Seminario de los Ángeles (open only to occasional guided visits). You may well spy griffon vultures from a colony a little further up the valley.

Sendero Guadalora   WALKING

(⊙closed Jun-Sep) This moderately demanding but rewarding walk starts at the visitors centre, then wends its way 6km (about 2½ hours) through evergreen oaks and olive trees and down a thickly wooded river valley to emerge onto the CO5310 road. You'll need a free permit to access the walk – this is easily obtained at the visitors centre.

From the CO5310, you must retrace your steps, if you haven't organised a taxi.

Hostal El Álamo   HOSTAL €

(☑957 64 04 76; www.complejoelalamo.com; Carretera San Calixto, Km 7.5, Hornachuelos; d incl breakfast €60, apt €160; ❉ ⏵ ▨) Motel-style El Álamo, on the main road through Hornachuelos, sports a faux *cortijo* (farmhouse) style, with tiled roofs and wagon wheels strewn about. Accommodation is in rustic-style double rooms or self-catering cottages sleeping up to six. Its popular **cafe/bar/restaurant** (mains €15-21; ⊙1-4pm & 8-11.30pm; ℗) is also a reliable choice for earthy country food.

ⓘ Information

Centro de Visitantes Huerta del Rey (☑957 57 96 56; www.ventanadelvisitante.es; Carretera Hornachuelos-San Calixto, Km 1.5; ⊙9am-2pm Wed-Fri, 4-6pm Sat & Sun) On the A3151 road, 1.5km north of Hornachuelos, the natural park visitors centre has displays and information for visitors, including individual walk maps for €0.80. No English spoken.

WORTH A TRIP

CASTILLO DE ALMODÓVAR

Almodóvar del Río's sinister-looking **castle** (957 63 40 55; www.castillodealmodovar.com; Calle del Castillo, Almodóvar del Río; adult/senior/child €9/7/5; 11am-2.30pm & 4-8pm Mon-Fri, 11am-8pm Sat & Sun Apr-Sep, to 7pm Oct-Mar; P) dominates the view from far and wide, rising cinematically above the town's steep hillside centre. It was founded in the 8th century but owes most of its present appearance to post-Reconquista rebuilding. You can climb several of its nine towers and see a film on its history in the chapel. You can also catch it on celluloid in the seventh series of *Game of Thrones* for which it doubled as Casterly Rock and Highgarden. There's free parking 600m below the castle. From there you can either walk up or take a shuttle bus (€1).

Oficina de Turismo (%957 64 07 86; www.turismohornachuelos.es; Recinto Ferial; h10am-2pm Tue-Sun) Enthusiastic and helpful tourist office in the feria grounds (near the Piscina Municipal), off the main A3151 road.

Getting There & Away

Autocares San Sebastián (p219) runs buses to/from Córdoba (€4.50, one to 1¼ hours, five daily Monday to Friday, two on Saturday). These leave from Carretera San Calixto (the A3151), just below the police station.

AT A GLANCE

POPULATION
631,000

CAPITAL
Jaén

BEST CASTLE
Castillo de La Iruela (p247)

BEST DAY WALK
Río Borosa Walk (p250)

BEST PATIO RESTAURANT
Palacio de Gallego (p240)

WHEN TO GO

Apr–mid-Jun
Warm but not too warm, and the countryside blooms; book rooms ahead for Úbeda and Baeza.

Jul
Bluescazorla, a rare Spanish blues festival, reverberates through the country town of Cazorla.

Sep–Oct
Mellow post-summer weather with autumn colours; male deer battle for mates in the Cazorla hills.

Jaén (p232)
MEGAPIXELES.ES/SHUTTERSTOCK

Jaén Province

For anyone who loves culture, nature, history and good food, this relatively little-visited province is one magical combination. Endless lines of olive trees – producing one-fourth of all the world's olive oil – carpet much of the landscape. Castle-crowned hills are a reminder that this was once a frontier zone between Christians and Muslims, while the gorgeous Renaissance architecture of Unesco World Heritage towns Úbeda and Baeza showcases the wealth amassed by the Reconquista nobility.

Beyond the towns and olive groves, Jaén has wonderful mountain country. The Parque Natural Sierras de Cazorla, Segura y Las Villas is a highlight for nature lovers, with rugged mountains, deep green valleys, prolific wildlife and dramatically perched villages.

INCLUDES

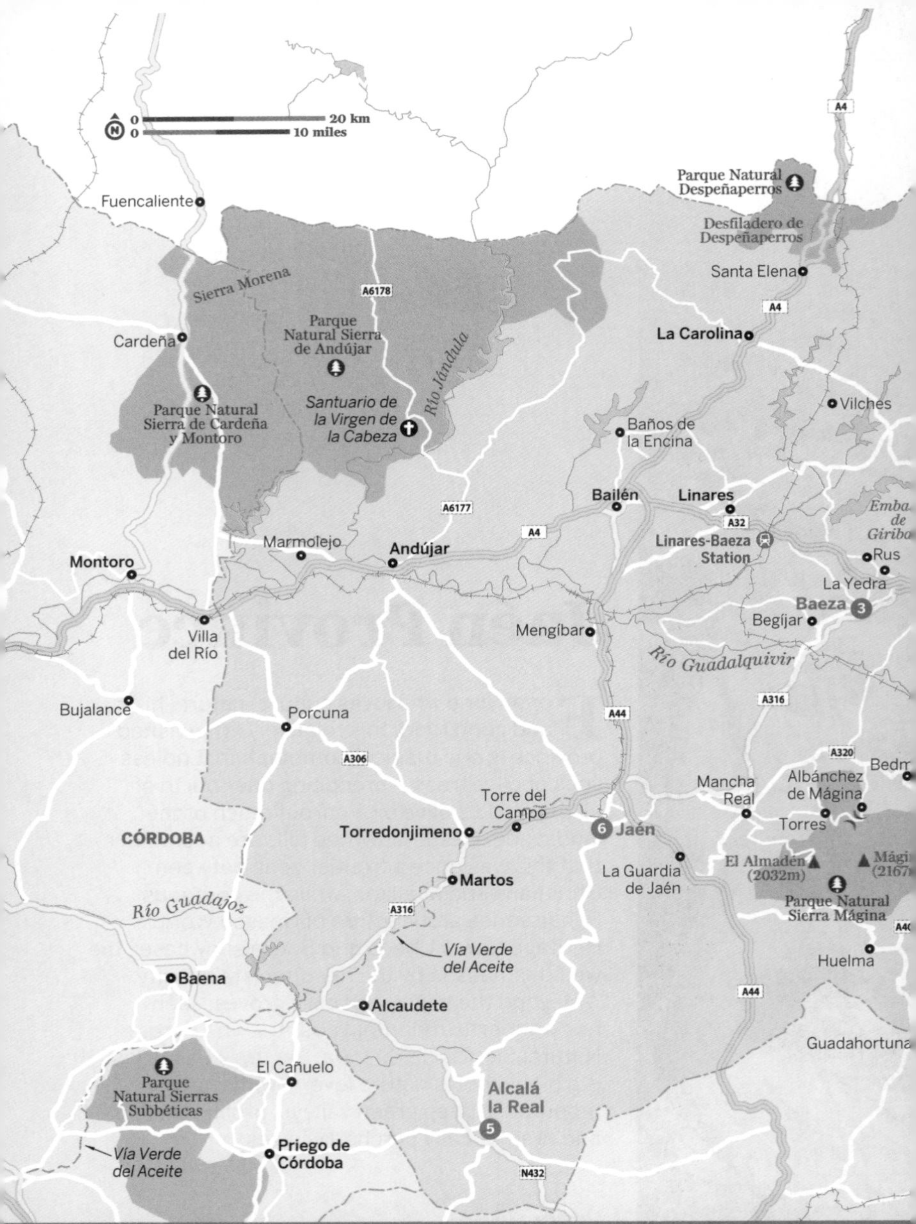

Jaén Province Highlights

1 **Úbeda** (p240) Indulging the senses with inspired architecture and cuisine.

2 **Parque Natural Sierras de Cazorla, Segura y Las Villas** (p249) Roaming the park's green valleys, craggy mountains and scenic villages, with an eye open for the plentiful wildlife.

3 **Baeza** (p237) Investigating the tangle of stone lanes lined with

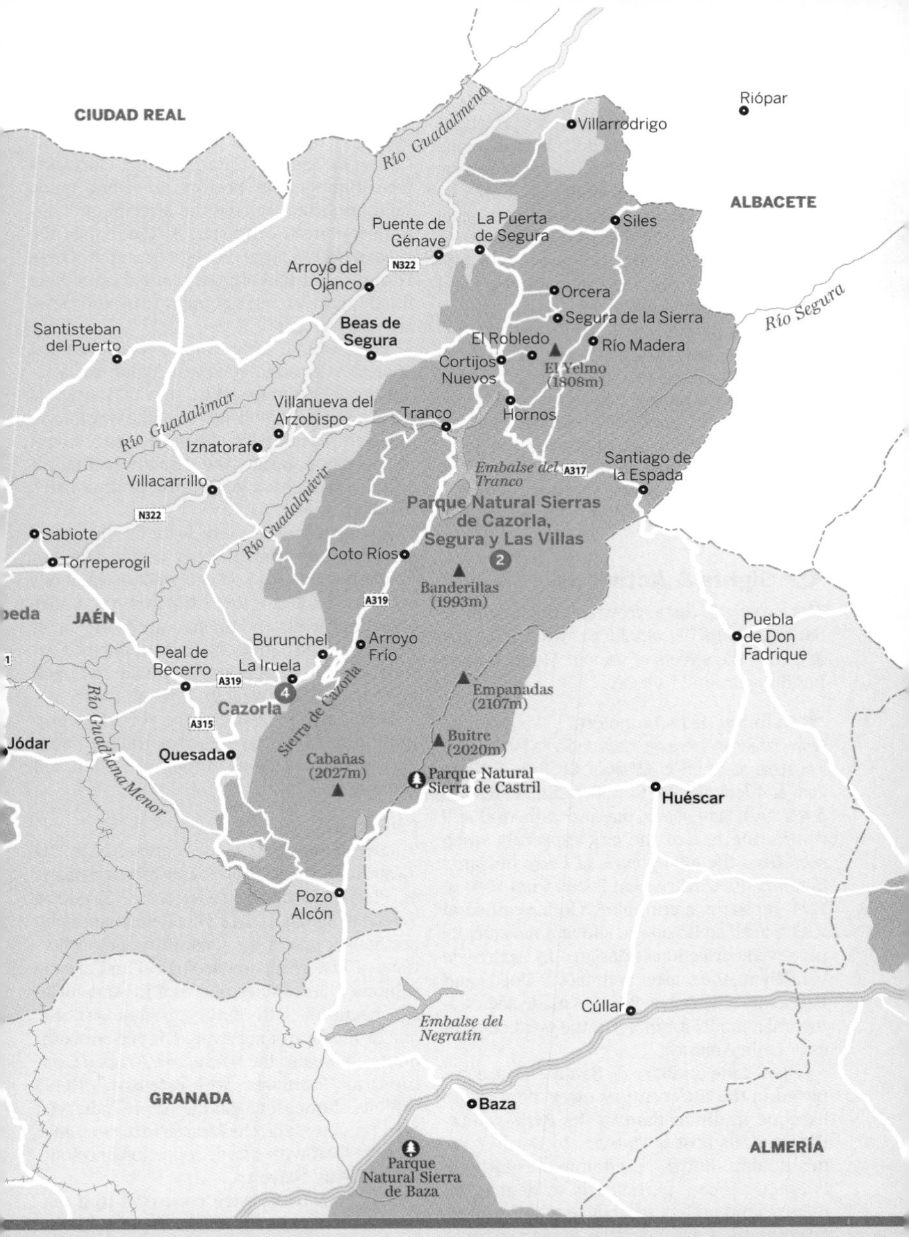

beautiful Renaissance buildings.

4 Cazorla (p246) Soaking up the atmosphere of this lively foothill town backed by lofty escarpments and crag-top castles.

5 Alcalá la Real (p236) Climbing up to a fascinating hilltop castle and medieval town, still under excavation.

6 Jaén (p232) Exploring traditional tapas bars and a historic castle and cathedral.

JAÉN

POP 112,999 / ELEV 575M

Set amid vast olive groves, upon which its precarious economy depends, Jaén is somewhat overshadowed by the beauty of nearby Úbeda and Baeza, and is often passed over by visitors to the province. But once you make it into town you will discover a charming, if mildly dilapidated, historic centre with hidden neighbourhoods, excellent tapas bars and a grandiose cathedral.

Muslim Yayyan was a significant city before its conquest by Castilla in 1246. For 2½ centuries Christian Jaén remained important thanks to its strategic location near the border with Nasrid Granada – until the Muslims were finally driven out of Granada in 1492. Jaén then sank into a decline with many of its people emigrating to the Spanish colonies – hence the existence of other Jaéns in Peru and the Philippines.

Sights & Activities

The wooded, castle-crowned hill Cerro de Santa Catalina defines Jaén's western boundary, with the streets of the old Moorish town huddling around its base.

★Catedral de la Asunción CATHEDRAL

(www.catedraldejaen.org; Plaza de Santa María; adult incl audio guide €5, child/senior €1.50/2; 10am-2pm & 4-7pm Mon-Fri, to 5.30pm Sat, 10-11.30am & 4-5.30pm Sun) Jaén's massive cathedral still dwarfs the rest of the city, especially when seen from the hilltop eyrie of Cerro de Santa Catalina. Its construction lasted from 1540 to 1724, replacing a crumbling Gothic cathedral which itself stood on the site of a mosque. Its perceived perfection of design – by Andrés de Vandelvira, the master architect of Úbeda and Baeza, and his father Pedro – made Jaén Cathedral a model for many of the great churches of Latin America.

The facade on Plaza de Santa María, completed in the 18th century, owes more to the baroque tradition than to the Renaissance, thanks to its host of statuary by Seville's Pedro Roldán. But the predominant aesthetic is Renaissance – particularly evident in its huge, round arches and clusters of Corinthian columns. A great circular dome rises over the crossing before the main altar. From the sacristy antechamber, south of the crossing, a 57-step staircase leads up to corridors along the cathedral's south and west sides yielding impressive views down into the cathedral.

★Castillo de Santa Catalina CASTLE

(Cerro de Santa Catalina; adult/reduced €3.50/1.50, 3-6pm Wed free; 10am-6pm Mon-Sat, to 3pm Sun; P) High above the city, atop cliff-girt Cerro de Santa Catalina, this fortress's near-impregnable position is what made Jaén important during the Muslim and early Reconquista centuries. At the end of the ridge stands a large cross, on the spot where Fernando III had a cross planted after Jaén finally surrendered to him in 1246; the views are magnificent.

The Moorish fortress here was revamped after the Christian conquest. What exists today is only about one-third of what there was – the rest was demolished to make way for the adjacent *parador* (state-owned luxury hotel) in the 1960s. Inside, the displays in English and Spanish give a good sense of the castle's history.

If you don't have a vehicle for the circuitous 5km drive up from the city centre, you can take a taxi (€7), or you can walk up in about 40 minutes from the cathedral via Calles Maestra, Parrilla and Buenavista. At the top of Buenavista, go 50m to the right along the Carretera de Circunvalación, then take the track up to the left and walk up through the trees.

If you aren't staying at the *parador*, drop in for a drink to see the extraordinary vaulted, decorative ceilings in the main salon and restaurant.

Palacio de Villardompardo BATHHOUSE, MUSEUM

(Centro Cultural Baños Árabes; www.bañosarabesjaen.es; Plaza de Santa Luisa de Marillac; 9am-10pm Tue-Sat, to 3pm Sun) FREE This Renaissance palace houses one of the most intriguing collections of historical, archaeological and artistic exhibits found under one roof in Andalucía: the beautiful 11th-century **Baños Árabes**, one of the largest surviving Islamic-era bathhouses in Spain; the **Museo de Artes y Costumbres Populares**, with extensive, diverse exhibits showcasing the life of pre-industrial Jaén province; and the **Museo Internacional de Arte Naïf** with a large collection of colourful and witty Naïve art.

The Arab baths were converted to a tannery after the Reconquista, then built over completely when the Conde de Villardompardo constructed his handsome palace over them in the 16th century. They were rediscovered in 1913. Of their four rooms (two cold, one warm, one hot), the warm room, with its multiple horseshoe arches, is the finest. On the way out, glass flooring reveals part of a

Jaén

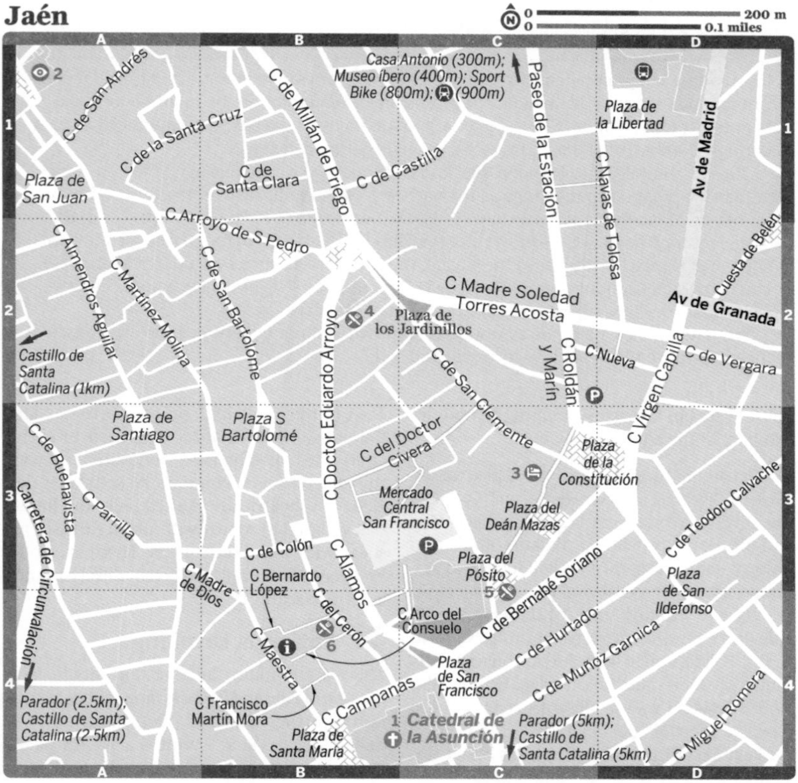

Jaén

Top Sights

1 Catedral de la Asunción B4

Sights

2 Palacio de Villardompardo A1

Sleeping

3 Hotel Xauen C3

Eating

4 Bar Bomborombillos B2
5 Panaceite C4
6 Taberna La Manchega B4

Roman street. A 10-minute film with English subtitles helps explain all about the baths.

The Museo de Artes y Costumbres Populares, spread over several floors, covers everything from horse carts to olive oil production to pig-slaughtering *(matanza)*. There's an antique doll's house, a fine collection of hand-painted ceramics and a recreation of rooms from an early-20th-century rural home, but perhaps most evocative are the photos of country life a century ago, showing just how tough and basic it was. The Naïve art museum is based on the work of its founder, Manuel Moral. You can spend a long time lost in the everyday detail so playfully depicted in these works.

Museo Íbero MUSEUM

(☎953 00 16 96; www.museosdeandalucia.es/museoibero; Paseo de la Estación 41; EU/non-EU citizen free/€1.50; ⊙9am-9pm Tue-Sat, to 3pm Sun Sep-Jun, to 3pm Tue-Sun Jul & Aug) Opened in 2017, Jaén's newest museum has a permanent exhibit focused on the importance of four archetypal figures in pre-Roman Iberian culture: the prince, the princess, the hero and the goddess. Each is illustrated by archaeological artefacts discovered around Jaén province, including arresting statues of a hero battling a wolf, a warrior in full double armour and the *Diosa del los Carneros*, a goddess holding a

OFF THE BEATEN TRACK

JAÉN TO ÚBEDA SCENIC DRIVE

If you prefer long, scenic routes to short, unexciting ones, consider driving from Jaén to Úbeda via Albánchez de Mágina. The journey takes you through the mountainous and beautiful Parque Natural Sierra Mágina, and Albánchez' little castle is arguably the most daringly perched of all Jaén province's daringly perched castles.

Turn off the A316 into Mancha Real and continue to the pretty village of Torres. Now comes the most dramatic stage as the narrow JA3107 winds up over the 1250m-high Puerto de Albánchez pass and down to Albánchez de Mágina. The leaning tower of the 14th-century **Castillo de Albánchez** (24hr) FREE stands on top of a single rock on a sheer cliff rising directly above the village. You can, surprisingly, walk up to it in about 20 steep minutes from the central Plaza de la Constitución. The bird's-eye views over the whitewashed village and surrounding mountains are stunning.

From Albánchez, continue to Úbeda via Jimena, Bedmar (where you can investigate the remains of a 15th-century fortress) and Jódar.

pair of rams in her arms. Rotating temporary exhibits fill the adjoining rooms.

Vía Verde del Aceite CYCLING, WALKING
(Olive Oil Greenway; www.viasverdes.com) Crossing the olive-strewn countryside of southern Jaén and Córdoba provinces, 128km of disused railway – including tunnels, viaducts and stations – have been converted to a well-surfaced cycling and walking track, with gentle gradients and refreshment stops en route. Start off at the Polideportivo Las Fuentezuelas sports centre on Jaén's northwest edge. **Sport Bike** (953 27 44 76; www.sportbikejaen.com; Calle San Francisco Javier 14; per day €10; 10am-2pm & 5-8.30pm Mon-Fri, 10am-2pm Sat), near Jaén train station, rents 24-speed mountain bikes.

Festivals & Events

Semana Santa RELIGIOUS
(Mar/Apr) The week leading up to Easter Sunday sees statue-bearing processions through the old city by 30 *cofradías* (brotherhoods).

Sleeping

Hotel Xauen HOTEL €
(953 24 07 89; www.hotelxauenjaen.com; Plaza del Deán Mazas 3; incl breakfast s €46-66, d €56-82;) The Xauen has a superb location in the centre of town. Communal areas are decorated with large colourful photos on a range of themes, while the rooms are a study in brown and are moderately sized, but comfy and well cared for. The rooftop sun terrace has stunning cathedral views. Parking nearby is €14.

★ **Parador Castillo de Santa Catalina** LUXURY HOTEL €€
(953 23 00 00; www.parador.es/parador-de-jaen; Castillo de Santa Catalina; d €120-183; P) Next to the castle high on the Cerro de Santa Catalina, Jaén's *parador* reopened in spring 2020 after an exhaustive renovation. Beyond the allure of its incomparable setting, it dazzles with theatrically vaulted halls and luxuriously dignified rooms with plush furnishings, some with four-poster beds. There is also an excellent restaurant and a bar with panoramic terrace seating.

Eating & Drinking

There aren't many fancy restaurants in Jaén, but one of Andalucía's best tapas zones is here, north of the cathedral, along and between Calles Maestra and Cerón. There are plenty of bars to choose from, but in the tiny alleys between the two streets, you'll find a couple of particularly cherished establishments that have been going strong for well over a century.

Here, and throughout Jaén province, bars will give you a free tapa with every drink. You only pay for any extra tapas you order.

Taberna La Manchega ANDALUCIAN €
(Calle Bernardo López 8; bocadillos €2-3, platos combinados & raciones €6-12; 10am-4pm & 8pm-midnight Wed-Mon) La Manchega has been in action since 1886; apart from enjoying the *bocadillos* (long bread rolls with fillings including five types of tortilla) and *raciones* (full servings of tapas items) such as *chorizo de ciervo* (venison chorizo), *conejo al ajillo* (rabbit in garlic) and *solomillo* (pork tenderloin), you can drink wine and practise your Spanish with the old-time bartenders.

★ **Panaceite** SPANISH €€
(953 24 06 30; Calle de Bernabé Soriano 1; tapas €3-6, raciones €6.50-23.50; 7am-2am) Always packed, this corner bar near the cathedral has

a semicircle of outside tables. It serves some seriously good tapas and *raciones*, such as pork tenderloin with a choice of four sauces or aubergines in sugar-cane syrup, as well as salads, *bocadillos* and wines by the glass.

Bar Bomborombillos TAPAS €€

(☎691 941918; www.facebook.com/bomborombillos; Pintor Carmelo Palomino 12; tapas €5-17; ⏰1-4pm Wed-Sun & 8pm-midnight Tue-Sat; ✎) There's lots to love at this trendy back-alley tapas joint. Step through the old stone archway into an intimate, artsy space adorned with funky wooden chairs and flowers in multicoloured wine bottles. The menu abounds in creative adaptations of traditional Jaén favourites, including many vegan and gluten-free offerings.

Casa Antonio SPANISH €€€

(☎953 27 02 62; www.casantonio.es; Calle Fermín Palma 3; mains €19-24; ⏰1-4pm & 8.30-11.30pm Tue-Sat, 1-4pm Sun, closed Aug) This elegant little restaurant, in an unpromising street off Parque de la Victoria, prepares top-class Spanish fare rooted in local favourites, such as partridge in *escabeche* (an oil-vinegar-wine marinade), lamb chops or roast shoulder of kid goat. There's also excellent seafood. Nothing over complicated, just top ingredients expertly prepared. Service is polished and attentive.

ℹ Information

Oficina de Turismo (☎953 19 04 55; www.turjaen.org; Calle Maestra 8; ⏰9am-7.30pm Mon-Fri, 10am-3pm & 5-7pm Sat, 10am-3pm Sun) Combined city and regional tourist office with helpful multilingual staff.

ℹ Getting There & Around

CAR & MOTORCYCLE

Jaén's one-way street system is no fun, but the way to most hotels is well signposted. There are a couple of central 24-hour underground car parks: **Parking Constitución** (Calle Roldán y Marín; per hour/day €1.45/15.75) and **Parking San Francisco** (Calle de las Flores; per hour/day €1.45/15.75).

TRAIN

Jaén's **train station** (www.renfe.com; Plaza Jaén por la Paz) has four trains a day to Cádiz (€39, five hours), via Córdoba (€15, 1¾ hours) and Seville (€29, three hours), and four to Madrid (€37, 3¾ hours). For Málaga (€37, three hours), make connections in Córdoba.

NORTHWEST JAÉN PROVINCE

North of Jaén you pass across indifferent countryside until the Sierra Morena appears on the horizon. This range of rolling, green wooded hills stretching along Andalucía's northern border is little visited, but has a mysterious, lonely magic all its own.

Desfiladero de Despeñaperros & Santa Elena

The Desfiladero de Despeñaperros, a dramatic gorge cutting through the Sierra Morena, is straddled by the hilly and beautiful **Parque Natural Despeñaperros** (www.ventanadelvisitante.es; Ⓟ) 🍃. The gorge is traditionally considered the main gateway to Andalucía from the north. The A4 highway and the Madrid–Jaén railway zip quickly through by viaducts and tunnels. To get a better look at its rocky pinnacles, take the old N-IVa road, which has a mirador (viewpoint) and restaurant where you can stop and take in the

BUS

Alsa (☎902 42 22 42; www.alsa.es), **Cambus** (☎679 730134; www.cambusautocares.com) and **Autocares Samar** (☎902 25 70 25; www.samar.es) run services from the **bus station** (☎953 23 23 00; www.epassa.es/autobus; Plaza de la Libertad).

DESTINATION	COMPANY	COST (€)	DURATION (HR)	FREQUENCY (DAILY)
Baeza	Alsa	4.60	1	10-16
Cazorla	Alsa	9.50	2-2½	3
Córdoba	Cambus	11.25	2	6-9
Granada	Alsa	9.15	1¼	11-14
Madrid	Samar	27	4-5	3-4
Málaga	Alsa	21	2¾-4¾	4
Úbeda	Alsa	5.55	1-1¾	10-17

WORTH A TRIP

ALCALÁ LA REAL

From a distance the **Fortaleza de la Mota** (www.tuhistoria.org; Alcalá la Real; adult/child €6/3; ⌚10.30am-7.30pm Apr–mid-Oct, 10am-6pm mid-Oct–Mar; P) looks more like a city than a mere fort, with its high church tower and doughty keep rising above the surrounding walls. And in a sense that's what it was, for back in the Middle Ages this fortified hill now looming over the town of Alcalá la Real *was* Alcalá la Real. It's a marvellous stop if you're heading along the Granada–Córdoba road across southwestern Jaén province, and well worth a detour even if you're not.

The modern town below only came into being in the 17th century, when fortified towns on hills had passed their use-by date. Today the fortress is as much archaeological site as monument, for what were houses, palaces, stables and streets are now lines of low ruins. The fortress was founded around 1000 CE then largely rebuilt after being wrested from Nasrid Granada by Castilla's Alfonso XI in 1341. One of the most remarkable features is the inside of the church, where the floor has been removed to lay bare dozens of graves carved out of the rock beneath.

If you're here on a Saturday, Sunday or public holiday, budget an extra 45 minutes and €2 per person for a tour of the Ciudad Oculta (Hidden City), a system of tunnels cut inside the rock for access to an all-important well. The story goes that the fortress only fell to Alfonso XI after the besieging Christians found the way to this well and poisoned it.

scenery. From the north, take exit 243 from the A4 and follow the park signs; from the south, take exit 257 into Santa Elena town then head out past the signposted Camping, and from the bottom of the gorge follow 'Venta de Cárdenas' signs. For information on the park and walking routes, visit the **Centro de Visitantes Llano de las Américas** (☎610 282531; Carretera JA7102, Km 2; ⌚10am-2pm Thu year-round, 9am-2pm & 4-6pm Fri-Sun Sep-Jun, 8am-3pm Fri-Sun Jul & Aug), 2km west of exit 257 towards Miranda del Rey.

Museo Batalla de las Navas de Tolosa MUSEUM

(☎953 10 44 35; www.museobatallanavas.es; Carretera JA7102, Santa Elena; adult/reduced €3/2; ⌚10am-2pm & 3.30-6.30pm Sun year-round, 10am-2pm & 5-8pm Tue-Sat Jun-Sep, 10am-2pm & 4-7pm Tue-Sat Oct-May; P) The course of Spanish history changed 2km west of Santa Elena on 16 July 1212, when Christian armies defeated the Muslim Almohad army in the battle of Las Navas de Tolosa, which opened the doors of Andalucía to the Reconquista. This museum, a few hundred metres west from A4 exit 257, tells the fascinating story and has a viewing tower from which you can see the (now-overgrown) battle site. After the battle the Christians are believed to have tossed Muslim captives off the cliffs of the Desfiladero de Despeñaperros. It's commonly believed this is the origin of the name Despeñaperros, which means 'overthrow of the dogs'.

Getting There & Away

Samar (p235) runs two to five daily buses between Jaén and Santa Elena (€6.20, 1½ hours), but your own vehicle is by far the easiest way of getting to and around the area.

Parque Natural Sierra de Andújar

This large (748-sq-km) natural park north of Andújar town has the biggest expanses of natural vegetation in the Sierra Morena, as well as plenty of bull-breeding ranches. It's an exciting destination for wildlife-spotters, with numerous large mammals and birds, including five emblematic endangered species: the Iberian lynx, wolf, black vulture, black stork and Spanish imperial eagle. The Iberian lynx population is the largest in the world, with around 460 here and in the neighbouring Sierra Morena. There are also 21 breeding pairs of Spanish imperial eagle in the park (one-tenth of of this mighty bird's total population, found only in the Iberian Peninsula).

Sights & Activities

Staff at the park visitors centre, the **Centro de Visitantes Viñas de Peñallana** (☎953 53 96 28; Carretera A6177, Km 13; ⌚10am-2pm Thu-Sun plus 3-6pm Fri-Sun, closed afternoons mid-Jun–mid-Sep, closed Thu Jul & Aug), 13km north of Andújar town, can tell you the best areas for wildlife sightings, though you also need luck on your side. The best months for spotting lynxes are December and January, the mating season. Local guiding outfits can take you onto private land where sighting prospects are often higher: they include **Birds & Lynx Ecotourism** (☎659 936566; www.birdslynxecotourism.com; Centro de Visitantes Viñas de Peñallana; 1-/2-/3-/4-person tour per person €150/100/80/70), **IberianLynxLand** (☎636 984515, English 626 700525; www.iberianlynxland.com; 2-/3-/4-person tour per person €80/65/55) and **Turismo Verde** (☎628 916731; www.lasierradeandujar.com; tour per person €75). Tours range in price from €55 to €120 per person.

Santuario de la Virgen de la Cabeza CHAPEL
(Carretera A6177, Km 31, Cerro del Cabezo; P) On a hilltop in the heart of the park, 31km up the A6177 from Andújar, this chapel is the focus of one of Spain's biggest religious events, the **Romería de la Virgen de la Cabeza** (Apr), on the last weekend in April. The original 13th-century shrine here was destroyed during the civil war, when it was seized by pro-Franco troops and then captured by the Republicans after eight months of determined bombardment.

Sleeping & Eating

★**La Caracola** HOTEL €€
(☎640 758273; www.lacaracolahotelrural.com; Carretera A6177, Km 13.8; s/d incl breakfast €42.50/70; P) A great base for wildlife-watchers, La Caracola sits among woodlands and offers bright, contemporary rooms, comfortable common areas (including a cosy fireplace), and good meals (lunch or dinner €15). They'll serve breakfast as early as you like, and they can prepare picnics. It's 1.4km off the A6177: the signed turn-off is 800m north of the park visitors centre.

Getting There & Away

Andújar town is served by several daily trains from Jaén (€6.25, 45 minutes) and Córdoba (€9.85, 50 minutes), and by buses from Baeza (€6.05, 1½ hours) and Úbeda (€7, 1¾ hours). There are buses to the sanctuary on Saturday and Sunday.

EASTERN JAÉN PROVINCE

This part of the region is where most visitors spend their time. Less than an hour east of Jaén, the World Heritage–listed towns of Baeza and Úbeda, 9km apart, scupper any notion that there is little of architectural interest in Andalucía apart from Moorish buildings. The historic centres here guard a treasure trove of superb Christian Renaissance buildings from a time when a few local families managed to amass huge fortunes and spent large parts of them beautifying their home towns. Further east lie the picturesque villages, mountains and hiking trails of Spain's biggest protected area – the Parque Natural Sierras de Cazorla, Segura y Las Villas – for which Cazorla town makes a great starting point.

Baeza

POP 15,841 / ELEV 760M

With its beautiful historic centre enshrined as a Unesco World Heritage site, Baeza (ba-*eh*-thah) is easily visited on a day trip from its larger sister city Úbeda – though it has some good restaurants and accommodation of its own that may just tempt you to stick around. Here a handful of wealthy, fractious families, rich from grain-growing and cloth and leather production, left a marvellous catalogue of perfectly preserved Renaissance churches and civic buildings.

Baeza was one of the first Andalucian towns to fall to the Christians (in 1227), and little is left today of the Muslim town of Bayyasa after so many centuries of Castilian influence.

Sights

Baeza's main sights mostly cluster in the narrow streets south of the central Plaza de España and the broad Paseo de la Constitución (once Baeza's marketplace and bullring).

★**Catedral de Baeza** CATHEDRAL
(Plaza de Santa María; adult/child €4/1.50, 9.30-11am Mon free; 9.30am-2pm & 4-7pm Mon, 10am-2pm & 4-7pm Tue-Fri, 10am-7pm Sat, 10am-6pm Sun) As was the case in much of Andalucía, the Reconquista destroyed Baeza's mosque and in its place built a cathedral. It's a stylistic melange, though the predominant style is 16th-century Renaissance, visible in the facade on Plaza de Santa María and in the basic design of the three-nave interior (by Andrés de Vandelvira).

You can climb the tower for great views over the town and countryside. The tower's base dates from the 11th century and was part of the minaret of the mosque. The cathedral's next oldest feature is the 13th-century Gothic-Mudéjar Puerta de la Luna (Moon Doorway) at its western end – now the visitor entrance – which is topped by a 14th-century

Baeza

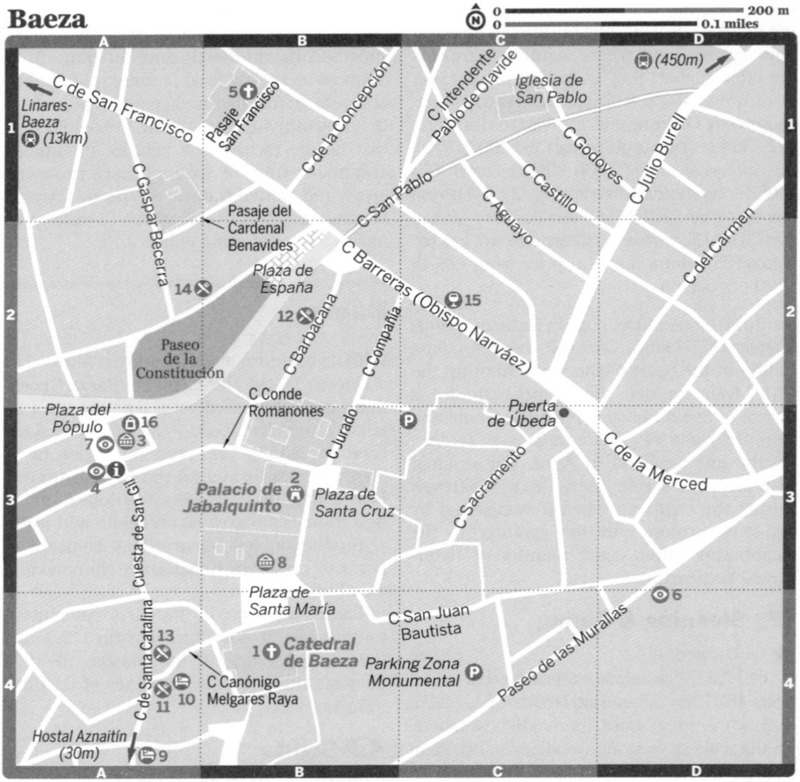

Baeza

Top Sights
1 Catedral de Baeza B4
2 Palacio de Jabalquinto B3

Sights
3 Antigua Carnicería A3
4 Arco de Villalar A3
Casa del Pópulo .... (see 4)
5 Convento de San Francisco B1
Fuente de los Leones .... (see 7)
6 Paseo de las Murallas D4
7 Plaza del Pópulo A3
Puerta de Jaén .... (see 4)
8 Seminario de San Felipe Neri B3

Sleeping
9 Hostal Aznaitín A4
10 Hotel Puerta de la Luna A4

Eating
11 Bar Pacos A4
12 El Arcediano B2
13 Palacio de Gallego A4
14 Taberna El Pájaro B2

Drinking & Nightlife
15 Café Teatro Central C2

Shopping
16 La Casa del Aceite A3

rose window. Inside, there's a clear transition from the nave's two easternmost bays, which are Gothic, with sinuous ceiling tracery, pointed arches and gargoyled capitals, to the Renaissance-style bays further west with their Corinthian capitals and classical square and circle designs. Audio guides in several languages are available for €1.

The broad Plaza de Santa María was designed to be a focus of Baeza's religious and civic life. On its north side you can look into the main patio of the 17th-century **Seminario**

de San Felipe Neri (9am-2pm Mon-Fri) FREE, a former seminary, which now houses part of the Universidad Internacional de Andalucía, teaching postgraduate courses.

★ Palacio de Jabalquinto PALACE
(Plaza de Santa Cruz; 10.30am-1pm & 4-6pm) FREE Baeza's most flamboyant palace was probably built in the late 15th century for a member of the noble Benavides clan. Its chief glory is the facade in decorative Isabelline Gothic style, with a strange array of naked humans clambering along the moulding over the doorway; above is a line of shields topped by helmets with mythical birds and beasts. The patio has a two-tier Renaissance arcade with marble columns, an elegant fountain, and a magnificent carved baroque stairway.

Plaza del Pópulo SQUARE
(Plaza de los Leones) This handsome square is surrounded by elegant 16th-century buildings. The central **Fuente de los Leones** (Fountain of the Lions) is made of carvings from the Ibero-Roman village of Cástulo and is topped by a statue reputed to represent Imilce, a local princess who became one of the wives of the famous Carthaginian general Hannibal.

The **Puerta de Jaén** on the plaza's west side was originally a city gate of Muslim Bayyasa, though it was reconstructed in 1526. Joined to it is the **Arco de Villalar**, erected by Carlos I the same year to commemorate the crushing of a serious insurrection in Castilla that had threatened to overthrow him.

On the southern side of the square, the lovely 16th-century **Casa del Pópulo** was formerly a courthouse and now houses the tourist office. It was built in the plateresque style, an early phase of Renaissance architecture noted for its decorative facades. Today the role of courthouse is played by the 1547 **Antigua Carnicería** (Old Butchery), on the eastern side of the square, which must rank as one of the world's most elegant ex-butcheries, with the shield of Carlos I emblazoned on its facade.

Paseo de las Murallas STREET
Heading southwest from Plaza del Pópulo, then looping back northeastward along the escarpment at the edge of town, this street and pedestrian promenade affords superb views across the olive groves to the distant mountains of the Sierra Mágina (south) and Sierra de Cazorla (east).

Convento de San Francisco CHAPEL
(Calle de San Francisco; 10.30am-1.45pm & 4-7pm Tue-Sat, 10.30am-1.45pm Sun) FREE This 16th-century monastery suffered grievously from an earthquake and Napoleonic sacking in the early 19th century. The main point of interest is the roofless **Capilla de Benavides** at the northeast end of its church – one of Andrés de Vandelvira's masterpieces, built in the 1540s as the funerary chapel of Baeza's powerful Benavides family. An arrangement of curved girders, erected during a semi-restoration in the 1980s, traces the outline of the chapel's majestic dome.

Festivals & Events

Semana Santa RELIGIOUS
(Mar/Apr) Baeza's Easter processions – numbering 19 between Palm Sunday and Easter Sunday – are solemn, grand and rooted very deep in the town's traditions.

Feria FERIA
(mid-Aug) The summer fair starts with a big Carnaval-style procession of *gigantones* (papier-mâché giants) and other colourful figures, and continues with five days of fireworks, a huge funfair, concerts and bullfights.

Sleeping

Hostal Aznaitín HOSTAL €€
(953 74 07 88; www.hostalaznaitin.com; Calle Cabreros 2; incl breakfast s €50-75, d €60-85;) Welcoming, bright Aznaitín is a far cry from the dreary *hostales* of old. Rooms are stylish and well sized, with good mattresses and large, appealing photos of Baeza sights. The recently opened in-house restaurant serves three-course dinners at bargain prices (€9.50 including a drink).

Hotel Puerta de la Luna HERITAGE HOTEL €€
(953 74 70 19; www.hotelpuertadelaluna.com; Calle Canónigo Melgares Raya 7; d €87-175; P) If they were to return today, Baeza's Renaissance-era nobility would doubtless stay at this luxurious hotel in a 17th-century mansion. Orange trees and a pool grace its elegant patio, complemented by beautifully furnished salons with welcoming fireplaces. The spacious rooms are enhanced by classical furnishings, artwork and large bathrooms. Buffet breakfast costs €15, and **Bar Pacos** (Calle de Santa Catalina; tapas & medias raciones €5-10; 1.30-4pm & 8.30pm-midnight) downstairs serves good tapas.

Eating & Drinking

Paseo de la Constitución and Plaza de España are lined with bar/cafe-restaurants that are great for watching local life, but most of the best finds are tucked away in the narrow old-town streets. As throughout the province, you'll get a free tapa with your drink in almost every bar.

★ **El Arcediano** TAPAS €
(Calle Barbacana 4; montaditos €3-7, raciones €7-15; ⏲8.30pm-midnight Thu, 1-4pm & 8.30pm-midnight Fri-Sun) Always buzzing with locals, this welcoming spot with dangling chandeliers, grapevines painted on the ceiling and tables on the narrow pedestrian lane out front serves up excellent large *montaditos* (slices of toasted bread with toppings). Scrumptious standouts such as thin-sliced Barbate tuna and smoked cod complement more standard offerings like pork, anchovies, assorted cheeses, or mashed tomato and olive oil.

Taberna El Pájaro ANDALUCIAN €€
(☎953 74 43 48; www.tabernaelpajaro.com; Paseo Portales Tundidores 5; mains €12-25; ⏲noon-5pm & 8pm-midnight) For an elegant dining experience, settle into El Pájaro's stone-walled, wood-beamed dining room and immerse yourself in its wide-ranging menu of Iberian specialities. Appetisers of cured sheep's-milk cheese, cod-stuffed artichokes and wild asparagus are followed up with plates of free-range rabbit risotto, garlic clams, grilled octopus, roast suckling pig and more.

★ **Palacio de Gallego** SPANISH €€€
(☎667 760184; www.palaciodegallego.com; Calle de Santa Catalina 5; mains €15-32; ⏲8-11pm Wed, 1.30-3.30pm & 8-11pm Thu-Mon) In the atmospheric setting of a 16th-century house, with tables on the delightful patio as well as in an old wood-beamed dining room, the Gallego serves up superb meat and fish dishes, barbecued and otherwise. There's a list of well over 100 Spanish wines, and you won't come across many starters better than their goat's cheese, orange and walnut salad.

★ **Café Teatro Central** BAR
(☎953 74 43 55; www.facebook.com/cafeteatrocentral; Calle Barreras 19; ⏲4pm-3am Sun-Thu, to 4am Fri & Sat; 📶) The most original and consistent nightspot in the province, with fascinatingly eclectic decor and determined support for live music, the Central fills up around midnight Thursday to Saturday with an arty-indie crowd. Live acts play to enthusiastic revellers amid the Buddha statues, historic instruments and coloured lighting. Their Facebook page lists upcoming shows.

Shopping

La Casa del Aceite FOOD
(☎953 74 80 81; www.casadelaceite.com; Paseo de la Constitución 9; ⏲10am-2pm & 5-8.30pm Mon-Sat, 10am-2pm Sun) Sells a big range of quality olive oil, plus other intriguing local products such as wild-boar or partridge pâté, olives and olive-based cosmetics.

Information

Tourist Office (☎953 77 99 82; www.andalucia.org; Plaza del Pópulo; ⏲9am-7.30pm Mon-Fri, 9.30am-3pm Sat & Sun) Housed in the 16th-century Casa del Pópulo.

Getting There & Around

BUS

Alsa (p235) runs services from the **bus station** (☎953 74 04 68; Avenida Alcalde Puche Pardo), 900m northeast of Plaza de España.

Destination	Cost (€)	Duration	Frequency
Cazorla	5	1¼-1½hr	3 daily
Córdoba	11.85	2½hr	2 daily
Granada	13.30	2-2½hr	7-9 daily
Jaén	4.60	45min-1¼hr	7-14 daily
Úbeda	1.20	15min	13-18 daily

CAR & MOTORCYCLE

Street parking in the centre is fairly restricted; two options are an **underground car park** (Calle Compañía; per 1/24hr €1.10/10; ⏲7.30am-11.30pm) and the free Parking Zona Monumental lot.

TRAIN

The nearest station is **Linares-Baeza** (www.renfe.com), 13km northwest of town, with a few daily trains to Almería, Córdoba, Jaén, Madrid and Seville. Alsa runs limited bus service to the station from Úbeda (€2.20, 30 to 50 minutes) and Baeza (€2.80, one hour). A taxi costs around €25.

Úbeda

POP 34,345 / ELEV 760M

Beautiful Renaissance buildings grace almost every street and plaza in the *casco antiguo* (old quarter) of World Heritage–listed Úbeda (*oo*-be-dah). Charming hotels in historic mansions, and some top-class restaurants and tapas bars, make a stay here a delight.

Úbeda's aristocratic lions jockeyed successfully for influence at the Habsburg court in the 16th century. Francisco de los Cobos y Molina became state secretary to King Carlos

DON'T MISS

OLIVE OIL: THE FACTS

You can't fail to notice that in the province of Jaén, the *olivo* (olive tree) rules. Over 66 million olive trees carpet 43% of the landscape, and the aroma of their oil perfumes memories of any visit. In an average year these trees yield about 500,000 tonnes of olive oil, meaning that Jaén accounts for more than 40% of Spain's, and up to 25% of the entire *world's*, production. Almost the whole population depends, directly or indirectly, on this one crop.

Olives are harvested from October until about February. They are taken straight to oil mills to be mashed into a pulp that is then pressed to extract the oil, which is then decanted to remove water. Oil that's good enough for consumption without being refined is sold as *aceite de oliva virgen* (virgin olive oil), and the best of that is *virgen extra*. Plain *aceite de oliva* – known in the trade as *lampante* (lamp oil) – is oil that has to be refined before it's fit for consumption. Oils are tested for chemical composition and tasted in International Olive Council laboratories before they can be labelled virgin or extra virgin.

A technological revolution has changed the face of the olive oil world since the late 20th century. On the way out, except in some smaller operations, are the traditional methods of harvesting (teams of people bashing the branches with poles), pulping (great conical stone rollers), pressing (squashing layers of pulp between esparto-grass mats) and decanting (four or five repeated processes taking eight or nine hours). Today's olives are shaken off the trees by tractor-driven vibrating machines; they are pulped mechanically; and centrifuge machines separate the liquids from the solids and do most of the decanting – all in a fraction of the time it used to take.

Olive oil's pivotal importance creates both opportunities and challenges for Jaén's economy. In December 2019, the European Union granted IGP 'protected origin' status to Jaén's extra virgin oil – making Jaén the first Spanish region to attain this honour, and allowing local producers to begin marketing their products under the 'IGP Aceite de Jaén' label. On the downside, Jaén remains susceptible to economic strains from beyond its borders, such as the tariffs imposed on Spanish olive oil by the US in October 2019, recent uncertainties brought on by Brexit and drop-offs in global prices due to overproduction. Largely in response to these challenges, oil output from Jaén province, which reached record-setting levels in 2018–19 (685,000 tons), was projected to fall off dramatically in 2019–20 to 455,000 tons.

Jaén is proud of its high-quality olive oil: many restaurants will offer you a few different types to try, soaked up with bread. Quality oil is sold in specialist shops and good groceries, and direct at some mills.

Oleícola San Francisco (953 76 34 15; www.oleoturismojaen.com; Calle Pedro Pérez, Begíjar; tours in Spanish €7.50, in English or French €8.50; tours in Spanish 11am & 5pm, in English or French 12.30pm & 4.30pm) These fascinating tours of a working oil mill near Baeza will teach you all you could want to know about the process of turning olives into oil, how the best oil is made and what distinguishes extra virgin from the rest. At the end you get to taste a few varieties, and you'll probably emerge laden with a bottle or two of San Francisco's high-quality product. Tours can be given in English or French (ring ahead to ensure availability). To get there, head west out of Baeza on the old Jaén road (A6109, formerly A316), turn right at the Begíjar signpost just before Km 5, then right again after 1.4km, immediately after the petrol station.

Centro de Interpretación Olivar y Aceite (953 75 58 89; www.centrodeolivaryaceite.com; Corredera de San Fernando 32; €2.80; 10am-2pm Tue-Sun year-round, plus 6-8.30pm Tue-Sat Jun-Sep, 5-7.30pm Tue-Sat Oct-May) Úbeda's olive-oil interpretation centre explains the area's olive-oil history and how the oil gets from the tree to your table, with the help of models, mill equipment and videos in English and Spanish. You get the chance to taste different oils, and to buy from a broad selection.

I, and his nephew Juan Vázquez de Molina succeeded him in the job and kept it under Felipe II.

High office exposed these men to the Renaissance aesthetic just then reaching Spain from Italy. Much of the wealth that they and a flourishing agriculture generated was invested in some of Spain's purest examples of Renaissance architecture. As a result, Úbeda (like its little sister Baeza) is one of the few places in Andalucía boasting stunning architecture that was *not* built by the Moors.

Úbeda

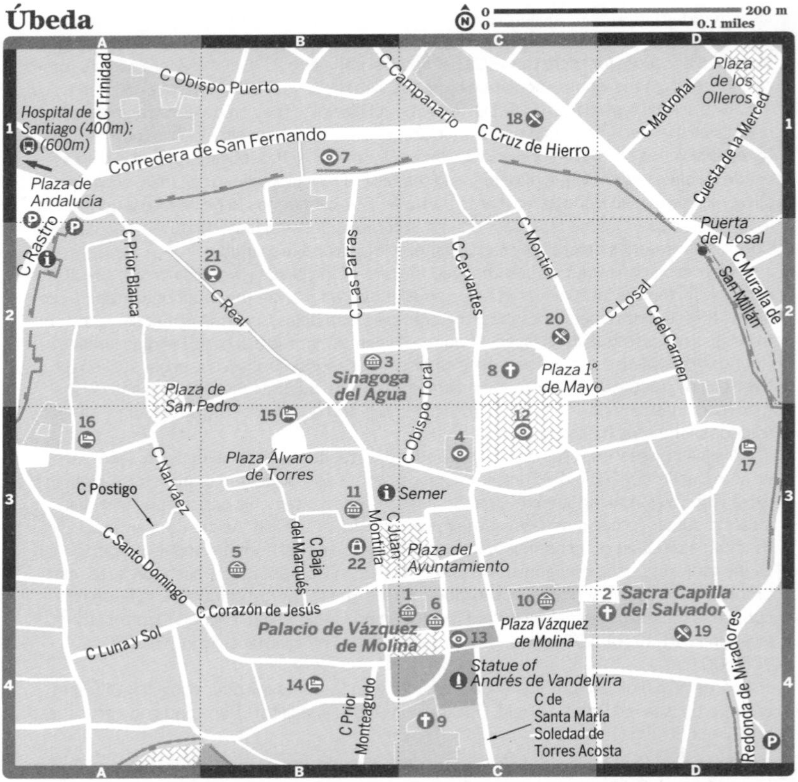

Úbeda

Top Sights
1 Palacio de Vázquez de Molina C4
2 Sacra Capilla del Salvador D4
3 Sinagoga del Agua B2

Sights
4 Antiguo Ayuntamiento C3
5 Casa Museo Andalusí B3
6 Centro de Interpretación Andrés de Vandelvira C4
7 Centro de Interpretación Olivar y Aceite B1
8 Iglesia de San Pablo C2
9 Iglesia de Santa María de los Reales Alcázares C4
10 Palacio del Deán Ortega C4
11 Palacio Vela de los Cobos B3
12 Plaza 1° de Mayo C3
13 Plaza Vázquez de Molina C4

Sleeping
14 Afán de Rivera B4
15 Hotel Álvaro de Torres B3
16 Hotel Ordóñez Sandoval A3
17 Las Casas del Cónsul D3
Parador de Úbeda .... (see 10)

Eating
18 Cantina La Estación C1
19 Llámame Lola D4
20 Misa de 12 .... C2

Drinking & Nightlife
21 La Bodega de Úbeda B2

Shopping
22 Alfarería Tito B3

Sights

Most of Úbeda's splendid buildings are in the web of narrow, winding streets and expansive squares that make up the *casco antiguo*, on the southern side of the mostly drab modern town. The old town is particularly beautiful at night with its wonderful plateresque facades floodlit gold against inky black skies.

Plaza Vázquez de Molina

The lovely Plaza Vázquez de Molina is the monumental heart of Úbeda's old town. An early case of Andalucian urban redevelopment, the plaza took on its present aspect in the 16th century when Úbeda's nobility decided to demolish existing buildings to make way for an assemblage of grand Renaissance buildings befitting their wealth and importance. Before 1507, the nobility had resided in Úbeda's Alcázar, a fortress-walled area immediately south of Plaza Vázquez de Molina, but this was demolished on Queen Isabel la Católica's orders to defuse power struggles involving the town's quarrelsome aristocrats.

★Sacra Capilla del Salvador CHAPEL

(Sacred Chapel of the Saviour; www.fundacionmedinaceli.org; adult/child incl audio guide €5/2.50; 9.30am-2.30pm & 4.30-7.30pm Mon-Sat, 11.30am-3pm & 4.30-7.30pm Sun Apr-Sep, to 6pm Mon-Sat, to 7pm Sun Oct-Mar) This famous chapel, built between 1536 and 1559, is the flagship of Úbeda Renaissance architecture. Commissioned by Francisco de los Cobos y Molina as his family's funerary chapel, it presents a marked contrast between the relatively sober proportions of the interior (by Diego de Siloé, architect of Granada's cathedral) and the more decorative western facade. The facade, a pre-eminent example of plateresque style, was designed by Andrés de Vandelvira, one of Siloé's stonemasons, who took over the project in 1540.

The chapel thus represents the first architectural commission obtained by Vandelvira, who went on to endow Úbeda, Baeza and Jaén with most of their outstanding Renaissance buildings. He worked in tandem with the French sculptor Esteban Jamete, who carved an orgy of classical sculpture depicting Greek gods on the underside of the facade arch, and scattered numerous skulls among the facade's decoration in a reminder that the building is a funerary chapel. Classical figures are also prominent in the sacristy (accessed from the northeast corner of the interior), another Vandelvira creation, but are absent from the main body of the chapel – where the Capilla Mayor sits beneath a stately dome painted in gold, blue and red, and features a grand 1560s altarpiece sculpture of the transfiguration by Alonso de Berruguete.

The Cobos family tombs lie beneath the floor of the chapel and aren't open to visitors. The chapel is still privately owned by the Seville-based Medinaceli ducal family, descendants of the Cobos. The audio guide is full of interesting information and anecdotes, and well worth listening to as you go round.

Next to the chapel stands what was originally its chaplain's residence, the **Palacio del Deán Ortega** (Plaza Vázquez de Molina) – another Vandelvira creation. The mansion is now Úbeda's luxurious *parador* hotel (p245).

★Palacio de Vázquez de Molina HISTORIC BUILDING

(Plaza Vázquez de Molina; 8am-8pm Mon-Fri, 10am-2pm & 5-7.30pm Sat & Sun) FREE Úbeda's *ayuntamiento* (town hall) is undoubtedly one of the most beautiful – if not *the* most beautiful – in Spain. It was built by Vandelvira in about 1562 as a mansion for Juan Vázquez de Molina, whose coat of arms surmounts the doorway. The perfectly proportioned, deeply Italian-influenced facade is divided into three tiers by slender cornices, with the sculpted caryatids on the top level continuing the lines of the Corinthian and Ionic pilasters on the lower tiers.

Two storeys of elegant arches surround the interior courtyard. In the basement is the **Centro de Interpretación Andrés de Vandelvira** (€3; 10am-2pm & 4-7.30pm Mon-Fri, to 8.30pm Sat) FREE – mainly photos but with some background on the great architect's work and life.

Iglesia de Santa María de los Reales Alcázares CHURCH

(www.santamariadeubeda.es; Plaza Vázquez de Molina; adult/child €4/1.50; 10.30am-1.30pm & 5-8pm May-Aug, 10.30am-1.30pm & 4-6.30pm Sep-Apr) Úbeda's grand parish church, founded in the 13th century on the site of Islamic Úbeda's main mosque, is a conglomerate of Gothic, Mudéjar, Renaissance, baroque and neoclassical styles. The main portico, facing Plaza Vázquez de Molina, is a beautiful late-Renaissance composition dating from 1604–12, with a relief sculpture showing the adoration of the shepherds.

Inside, the intricate Mudéjar-style *artesonado* (ceiling of interlaced beams) is the fruit of restoration work.

Other Areas

★Sinagoga del Agua HISTORIC BUILDING
(☎953 75 81 50; www.sinagogadelagua.com; Calle Roque Rojas 2; tours adult/child €4.50/3.50; ⊙tours every 45min 10.30am-1.30pm & 4.45-7pm Sep-Jun, 10.30am-1.30pm & 5.45-8pm Jul & Aug) The medieval Sinagoga del Agua was discovered in 2006 by a refreshingly ethical property developer who intended to build apartments here, only to discover that every swing of the pickaxe revealed some tantalising piece of an archaeological puzzle. The result is this sensitive re-creation of a centuries-old synagogue and rabbi's house, using original masonry whenever possible. Features include the women's gallery, a bodega with giant storage vessels, and a *miqvé* (ritual bath).

There is evidence of a sizeable Jewish community in medieval Islamic Úbeda, cohabiting peacefully with the considerably larger Muslim population. Tours are in Spanish, with printed translations available in English, French, German and Italian.

Palacio Vela de los Cobos HISTORIC BUILDING
(Calle Juan Montilla; tours €4; ⊙tours 1pm & 7pm Sep–mid-Jun, 1pm & 8pm mid-Jun–Aug) This fascinating Vandelvira-designed 16th-century mansion, elegantly restored in the 19th century, is still a private home, fully furnished and replete with paintings, antiques and books. **Semer** (☎953 75 79 16; www.semerturismo.com; Calle Juan Montilla 3; ⊙9.30am-2pm & 4.30-8pm Tue-Sat, 10am-1.30pm Sun), across the street, organises guided tours twice daily (available in English with advance notice).

Plaza 1° de Mayo SQUARE
Broad Plaza 1º de Mayo was originally Úbeda's market square and bullring. It was also the grisly site of Inquisition burnings, which local bigwigs used to watch from the gallery of the **Antiguo Ayuntamiento** (Old Town Hall) in the southwestern corner. The **Iglesia de San Pablo** (Plaza 1º de Mayo; donation €1; ⊙11am-1pm & 6-8pm Tue-Sat, 11am-1pm Sun), on the square's north side, has a particularly elaborate late-Gothic portal from 1511.

Hospital de Santiago HISTORIC BUILDING
(Avenida Cristo Rey; ⊙exhibition halls 11am-2pm & 5.30-9pm Tue-Sat) FREE Andrés de Vandelvira's last architectural project, completed in 1575, has been dubbed the Escorial of Andalucía in reference to the famous monastery outside Madrid, built in a similarly grand, austere late-Renaissance style. Standing outside the old town, 500m west of Plaza de Andalucía, the finely proportioned building has a broad, two-level, marble-columned patio, and a wide staircase with colourful original frescoes. It now acts as a cultural centre, housing a library, exhibition halls, and a concert hall in the chapel.

Festivals & Events

Semana Santa RELIGIOUS
(⊙Mar/Apr) Eighteen solemn brotherhoods carry sacred church statues through the town in atmospheric processions during the week leading up to Easter Sunday. Thursday and Friday see processions during the daytime as well as after dark.

Sleeping

★Las Casas del Cónsul HERITAGE HOTEL €€
(☎953 79 54 30; www.lascasasdelconsul.es; Plaza del Carmen 1; d Sun-Thu €65-70, Fri & Sat €80-90; ❄📶🏊) An attractive Renaissance mansion conversion, the welcoming 'Consul's Houses' has elegant, predominantly white rooms with old-time touches, and spacious common areas centred on a two-storey pillared patio – but what really sets it apart is the fabulous panoramic terrace (with pool) gazing over the olive groves to the distant mountains of Cazorla.

★Afán de Rivera HERITAGE HOTEL €€
(☎953 79 19 87; www.hotelafanderivera.com; Calle Afán de Rivera 4; incl breakfast s/d/tr Sun-Thu €50/70/90, Fri & Sat €56/110/120; ❄📶) This superb five-room hotel lies inside one of Úbeda's oldest buildings, predating the Renaissance. Expertly run by the amiable Jorge, it has beautifully historic common areas, and comfortable rooms that offer far more than is usual at these prices: shaving kits, fancy shampoos and tastefully eclectic decor combining the traditional and the contemporary.

Hotel Álvaro de Torres BOUTIQUE HOTEL €€
(AT Hotel; ☎953 75 68 50; www.hotelat.es; Plaza Álvaro de Torres 2; r €69-120; ❄📶) In a 16th-century mansion set round a charming stone-pillared, plant-draped patio, this is one of the best of Úbeda's ancient-meets-modern hotels. It's on a smallish, personal scale, with just eight all-different rooms that combine thick old stone walls with stylish contemporary fittings and comforts, including spacious walk-in showers. The excellent breakfast (€6) gets each morning off to a delightful start.

DON'T MISS

TOURING ÚBEDA'S HISTORIC MANSIONS

Úbeda's fascinating **Casa Museo Andalusí** (☎659 508766; www.vandelviraturismo.com; Calle Narváez 11; €4; ⊙tours 11.30am or by arrangement) comprises a 16th-century private home that was inhabited by *conversos* (Jews who converted to Christianity) and a huge, diverse collection of antiques assembled by owner Paco Castro. Informal guided tours of the house, led by his art historian daughter Eva Castro Martos, make it all come alive. The first hint that this is somewhere special is the original 16th-century heavy carved door. Ring the bell if it's closed, or schedule visits in advance via WhatsApp.

Above the central patio of this lovingly restored home are balconies and a painted Mudéjar-style ceiling and eaves. It's the ideal faded-grandeur setting for the family's collection of Renaissance doorways, 16th-century water jugs, antique bridal trunks, tapestries and artwork, gathered from all over Spain.

If Casa Museo Andalusí has whetted your appetite for more, ask about touring two other nearby mansions equally laden with aesthetic treasures – Casa Solar de los Granadas Venegas and Casa Sinagoga de Salomón; a visit to all three costs €12 and comes complete with fascinating historical commentary about Úbeda.

Hotel Ordóñez Sandoval HOTEL €€
(☎679 803942; www.hotelordonezsandoval.es; Calle Antonio Medina 1; r incl breakfast midweek/weekend €60/90; 📶) Housed in a dusky pink neoclassical mansion, this small hotel offers a peaceful and elegant refuge in the heart of Úbeda. Rooms are bright and spacious, with high ceilings, original antique furniture and private baths. Affable owner Pepe lovingly maintains the place and regales guests with fresh-squeezed orange juice at breakfast. Úbeda's sights are all within walking distance.

Parador de Úbeda HISTORIC HOTEL €€€
(Parador Condestable Dávalos; ☎953 75 03 45; www.parador.es; Plaza Vázquez de Molina; r €100-220; ❄📶) One of Spain's original *paradors* (opened in 1930), this plush hotel occupies a historic monument, the Palacio del Deán Ortega (p243), on the wonderful Plaza Vázquez de Molina. It has been comfortably modernised in period style and the rooms and common areas are appropriately luxurious. The best rooms have their own little garden patios. Breakfast costs €17.

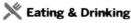

Eating & Drinking

The culinary hotspot of Jaén province; Úbeda's *andaluz*-fusion chefs are one reason why Spaniards flock here for weekend breaks.

★**Misa de 12** ANDALUCIAN €€
(☎953 82 81 97; www.facebook.com/MisaDe12Ubeda; Plaza 1º de Mayo 7; raciones €10-24; ⊙noon-4pm & 8.30pm-midnight Wed-Sun) Grab a table overlooking the plaza or hunker down in the cosy interior to sample a succession of succulent platters – from perfectly grilled slices of *presa ibérica* (a tender cut of Iberian pork) to *revuelto de pulpo y gambas* (eggs scrambled with octopus and shrimp). Despite the place's popularity, staff are always attentive and efficient.

★**Cantina La Estación** ANDALUCIAN €€
(☎687 777230; www.cantinalaestacion.com; Cuesta Rodadera 1; mains €15-24; ⊙1-3pm & 8pm-midnight Thu-Mon, 1-3pm Tue; 📶) The charming originality here starts with the design – three rooms with railway themes (the main dining room being the deluxe carriage). Seasonally inspired fusion dishes, such as wild boar in red-wine sauce, or octopus with garlic chips and paprika, share the menu with traditional Úbeda recipes like *andrajos* (a stew of meat and/or fish with tomatoes, peppers and spices).

Other whimsical touches include La Estación's ever-popular anchovy appetiser, served with a 'false olive' of cheese. Every dish is made with a different olive oil, and food presentation is a true art form here. Service is welcoming and attentive.

Llámame Lola ANDALUCIAN €€
(☎953 04 16 55; Calle Baja del Salvador 5; tapas €7-12, mains €12-20; ⊙noon-midnight; 🖉) With an inviting location under the trees near the Sacra Capilla del Salvador, Lola serves up good, creative *andaluz* fare with less fanfare than some other places. The *solomillo ibérico*, the octopus and the *revueltos* (scrambled-egg dishes) are all very tasty, as are the miniature fried shrimp from Cadiz.

La Bodega de Úbeda BAR
(☎667 565469; Calle Real 19; ⊙noon-1am Sun-Thu, to 2am Fri & Sat) Among the many bars and restaurants lining Úbeda's main pedestrian

JAÉN'S RENAISSANCE MASTER BUILDER

Most of the finest architecture that you see in Úbeda, Baeza and Jaén is the work of one man: Andrés de Vandelvira (1509–75), born in Alcaraz, Castilla-La Mancha, 150km northeast of Úbeda. Thanks largely to the patronage of Úbeda's Cobos and Molina families and the Benavides of Baeza, Vandelvira was able to endow Jaén province with some of Spain's finest Renaissance buildings. His work spanned all three main phases of Spanish Renaissance architecture – the ornamental early phase known as plateresque, as seen in Úbeda's Sacra Capilla del Salvador (p243); the purer line and classical proportions that emerged in the later Palacio de Vázquez de Molina (p243); and the austere late-Renaissance style (called Herreresque) of his last building, the Hospital de Santiago (p244). Relatively little is known about Vandelvira's life, but his legacy is a jewel of Spanish culture.

street, La Bodega stands out for its distinctive cellar, with low-lit vaulted stone walls sheltering a treasure trove of century-old ceramic urns once used to store oil and wine. It's an atmospheric spot to savour the Jaén tradition of free tapas with every round of drinks.

Shopping

Alfarería Tito CERAMICS
(☎953 75 13 02; www.alfareriatito.com; Plaza del Ayuntamiento 12; ⏰9.30am-2pm & 4-8pm) Juan Tito's distinctive style veers away from the classic green glaze, with intricate patterns and bright colours, especially blue. His large old-town showroom/workshop displays and sells a big range of covetable wares. You're looking at €30 or more for a decorative plate; the dazzling designs and artisanship are worth it.

Information

Oficina de Turismo (☎953 77 92 04; www.turismodeubeda.com; Plaza de Andalucía 5; ⏰9am-7.30pm Mon-Fri, 9.30am-3pm & 5-7.30pm Sat, 9.30am-3pm Sun) Helpful place on the northwest edge of the old town.

Getting There & Around

BUS

Alsa (p235) runs services from the **bus station** (☎953 79 51 88; Calle San José 6) is in the new part of town, 700m west of Plaza de Andalucía.

Destination	Cost (€)	Duration	Frequency
Baeza	1.20	15min	13-18 daily
Cazorla	4.35	1hr	3-5 daily
Córdoba	12.60	2½hr	4-5 daily
Granada	13.35	2-2¾hr	7-12 daily
Jaén	5.55	1-1¼hr	9-15 daily

CAR & MOTORCYCLE

Parking in the old town is free, but often difficult to find – the best bet is the car park on **Redonda de Miradores** (⏰24hr). The underground **Parking Plaza Andalucía** (per 1/24hr €1.50/17.50; ⏰7.30am-11.30pm) is also convenient.

TRAIN

The nearest station is **Linares-Baeza** (www.renfe.com), 21km northwest, which you can reach on four daily buses (€2.20, 30 to 50 minutes).

Destination	Cost (€)	Duration	Frequency
Almería	27	3¾hr	3 daily
Córdoba	20	1½hr	1 daily
Jaén	6.25	45min	3-4 daily
Madrid	24-33	3-4hr	6-7 daily
Seville	18-21	3¼hr	1 daily

Cazorla

POP 7441 / ELEV 826M

This picturesque, bustling white town sits beneath towering crags just where the Sierra de Cazorla rises up from a rolling sea of olive trees, 45km east of Úbeda. It makes the perfect launching pad for exploring the beautiful Parque Natural Sierras de Cazorla, Segura y Las Villas, which begins dramatically among the cliffs of Peña de los Halcones (Falcon Crag) directly above the town.

Sights

The heart of town is **Plaza de la Corredera**, with busy bars and the elegant *ayuntamiento*, in a 400-year-old former monastery, looking down from its southeast corner. Canyonlike streets lead south to the **Balcón de Zabaleta**. This little viewpoint is like a sudden window in a brick wall, with stunning views over the white houses up to the picturesque Castillo de la Yedra and the mountains beyond. From here another narrow street leads down to Cazorla's most picturesque square, **Plaza de Santa María**, dominated by the shell of the 16th-century Iglesia de Santa María.

★**Castillo de La Iruela** CASTLE
(Cuesta Santo Domingo, La Iruela; €1; ⏲10am-2pm & 4-8pm Wed-Mon) In a stunningly picturesque panoramic perch on a rocky pinnacle towering over pretty La Iruela village, this ancient fortification is worth the 3km drive or 1.5km uphill walk from central Cazorla. It was founded in early Islamic times though the keep and much of the walls date from after the castle's conquest by the Archbishop of Toledo in 1231. Brooding below is the shell of 16th-century Iglesia de Santo Domingo, torched by Napoleonic troops two centuries ago.

★**Castillo de la Yedra** CASTLE
(Museo del Alto Guadalquivir; EU/non-EU citizen free/€1.50; ⏲tours 10.30am, noon, 1.30pm, 4pm, 5.30pm & 7pm Tue-Sat, 10.30am, noon & 1.30pm Sun) Cazorla's dramatic Castle of the Ivy, a 700m walk above Plaza de Santa María, offers superb views and houses the interesting Museum of the Upper Guadalquivir, whose collections include traditional agricultural and kitchen utensils, religious art, models of an old olive mill, and a chapel featuring a life-size Romanesque-Byzantine crucifixion sculpture. Interior visits are by guided tour only. Of Muslim origin, it was comprehensively rebuilt in the 14th century after the Reconquista.

Iglesia de Santa María CHURCH
(Plaza de Santa María; church admission free, tour €2; ⏲9.30am-1.30pm & 4-8pm Tue-Sun Apr-Oct, to 7pm Nov-Mar) Nowadays housing Cazorla's tourist office (p248), this picturesque shell of a grand church, attributed to the great 16th-century Renaissance architect Andrés de Vandelvira, was wrecked by Napoleonic troops in reprisal for Cazorla's tenacious resistance. Guides at **Casa de la Luz** (www.almagaia.es; ⏲10.30am-1.30pm & 4.30-7.30pm), a few paces uphill, offer interesting 20-minute tours through the *bóvedas* (vaults) that channel the Río Cerezuelo underneath the church.

Activities

There are some great walks straight out of Cazorla town – all uphill to start with, but your reward is beautiful forest paths and fabulous panoramas of cliffs, crags and circling vultures. Agencies here offer a host of activities locally, including canyoning in the *parque natural* and an exciting via ferrata for climbers at the neighbouring village of La Iruela.

Sendero del Gilillo WALKING
(PRA313) The best walk for the fit and energetic is this full-day 21km loop (eight to nine hours) from Cazorla up to the Puerto del Gilillo pass (1100m higher than the town and with stupendous views) and back via Loma de los Castellones ridge, Puerto del Tejo pass, Prado Redondo forest house and the Ermita de la Virgen de la Cabeza chapel.

The trailhead is signposted about 200m uphill from Cazorla's Iglesia de Santa María. From here, the route ascends via the Ermita de San Sebastián chapel (2.2km, about 1½ hours return) and the Riogazas picnic area (3.5km, about three hours return), either of which makes a scenic there-and-back walk if you fancy something shorter. From the Puerto del Gilillo pass a short detour south to the 1848m summit of Gilillo (15 minutes from the pass) provides even more spectacular vistas. From the pass you can, if you like, return to Cazorla the way you came up, which takes about an hour less than the full loop route.

The route is well marked (despite occasionally being numbered PRA312 instead of PRA313) nearly all the way. Just note that when leaving the Puerto del Gilillo your route heads north, passing to the left of a ruined stone hut; and at the Puerto del Tejo you go left, initially downhill and curving to the right, instead of following GR247.3 and PRA314 signs to the right (which would bring you to the Parador de Cazorla). When you reach the Ermita de la Virgen de la Cabeza, follow the paved road downhill to meet another paved road opposite the Mirador Merenderos de Cazorla, then take the downhill path to the right of the mirador, leading down to Cazorla town.

Sendero de Ermitas y Monasterios WALKING
(SLA7) An 11km loop passing a few isolated chapels and monasteries in the hills, the SLA7 follows the PRA313 (Sendero del Gilillo) from Cazorla for 4km before continuing along the La Iruela–El Chorro road, then descending back to town via the Monasterio de Montesión. The route begins from Cazorla's Iglesia de Santa María and takes about 3½ hours.

Via Ferrata La Mocha CLIMBING
(La Iruela) This high-adrenaline challenge is a set of steel ladders, steps, cables and chains fixed into the precipitous rocky cone, La Mocha, above La Iruela village just outside Cazorla. It ascends 130m and includes a 'Tibetan bridge' – a set of horizontal cables strung across a precipice. **Tierraventura** (☎953 71 00 73; www.aventuracazorla.com; Carretera A319, Km 16.5, La Iruela; ⏲10am-2pm & 5-8pm Mon-Sat) offers guided climbs (€35 per person, about three hours).

Tours

Turisnat WILDLIFE WATCHING
(☎953 72 13 51; www.turisnat.es; Calle José Martínez Falero 11; tours per person €30-49; ⏲office 10am-2pm & 5-8pm Mon-Sat, to 2pm Sun) This highly experienced agency is a good option for 4WD trips along the forest tracks of the *parque natural*, with an emphasis on wildlife-spotting. English- or French-speaking guides are available at no extra cost.

Festivals

Bluescazorla MUSIC
(www.bluescazorla.com; ⏲Jul) Cazorla has a surprisingly cosmopolitan vibe for a remote country town and demonstrates it with this annual three-day blues fest, which sees international musicians and several thousand fans packing into town.

Sleeping & Eating

Casa Rural Plaza de Santa María CASA RURAL €
(☎953 72 20 87; www.plazadesantamaria.com; Callejón Plaza Santa María 5; s/d/ste incl breakfast €40/50/60, extra bed per person €13;) At this multilevel house in the heart of town, nine cheerily decorated rooms come complemented by a lovely garden-patio and a rooftop terrace with superb views over the plaza, the castle and the mountains beyond. It's well worth paying €10 extra for one of the three superior rooms with perks such as large windows, sitting rooms and/or panoramic views.

Molino La Farraga CASA RURAL €€
(☎696 697390, 953 72 12 24; www.molinolafarraga.com; Camino de la Hoz; d incl breakfast €65-100;) Featuring nine good-sized rooms with rustic wooden furnishings, this charming if somewhat faded guesthouse occupies an old water-driven flour mill on the edge of town in the verdant Río Cerezuelo valley. What's really special is the beautiful garden with fruit and nut trees, organic vegetables, rabbits, fish-and-lily pond and large open-air pool. Footpaths PRA313 and SLA7 run right outside the door.

To get there, go 250m from Plaza de Santa María up the street towards the Castillo de la Yedra, then fork left for 150m along a narrow lane. You have to walk the last steep bit uphill.

Antojitos Mexican Curious LATIN AMERICAN €
(☎644 908452; www.facebook.com/AntojitosMexicanCurious; Calle Sandoval 1; mains €4-8; ⏲9pm-midnight) Run by Mexican ex-pat Ulísses, this backstreet hole-in-the-wall sets a cheery tone with its flamboyant decor of *papel picado* (colourful Mexican paper cutouts) and Christmas lights. The Latin American *antojitos* (snacks) hit the spot, from ceviche to homemade tacos with authentic Mexican fillings like *carnitas* (shredded, slow-roasted pork). The margaritas, alas, miss the mark.

La Yedra ANDALUCIAN €
(☎953 71 02 92; Calle Cruz de Orea 51; mains €9-14; ⏲noon-midnight Mon-Sat) Rub elbows with the locals at this down-to-earth spot near Cazorla's market, where the lunchtime *menú del día* (including appetiser, main course, dessert and drink) goes for €11. Expect traditional country fare like *sopa de ajo* (garlic soup) followed by filling mains such as stewed pork with tomatoes, peppers and potatoes.

Mesón Leandro SPANISH €€
(☎953 72 06 32; www.mesonleandro.com; Calle Hoz 3; mains €10-28; ⏲1.30-4pm & 8.30-11pm Wed-Mon) Leandro is a step up in class from most other Cazorla eateries – professional but still friendly service in a bright dining room with lazy music, and only one set of antlers on the wall. The broad menu of nicely presented dishes ranges from partridge-and-pheasant pâté to *fettuccine a la marinera* and a terrific *solomillo de ciervo* (venison tenderloin).

Information

Oficina Municipal de Turismo (☎953 71 01 02; www.cazorla.es/turismo; Plaza de Santa María; ⏲10am-1pm & 4-8pm Tue-Sun Apr-Oct, to 7pm Nov-Mar) Inside the remains of Santa María church, with some information on the natural park as well as the town.

Punto de Información Cazorla (☎670 943880; Calle Martínez Falero 11; ⏲10am-2pm & 5.30-8.30pm Mon-Sat, 10am-2pm Sun Jul–mid-Sep, hours vary rest of year) Good for information on the *parque natural* as well as the town and surrounds.

Getting There & Around

BUS

Alsa (www.alsa.es) runs three to five daily buses to Úbeda (€4.35, one hour), Baeza (€5, 1¼ hours), Jaén (€9.50, two to 2½ hours) and Granada (€18.20, 3½ to four hours). The **bus station** (Calle de Hilario Marco) is 500m north of Plaza de la Corredera via Plaza de la Constitución.

CAR & MOTORCYCLE

Driving in the old, central part of town is tricky, but there's free street parking around its periphery.

Parking Plaza de Andalucía (Calle Cronista Lorenzo Polaino), just down from Plaza de la Constitución at the northern end of the centre, is Cazorla's most easily accessible parking garage. Alternatively, if you're willing to brave the tight wriggle through narrow streets to Plaza de Santa María, there's a free car park just off its western end on Calle de la Herrería.

Parque Natural Sierras de Cazorla, Segura y Las Villas

One of the biggest drawcards in Jaén province – and, for nature lovers, in all of Andalucía – is the mountainous, lushly wooded Parque Natural Sierras de Cazorla, Segura y Las Villas. This is the largest protected area in Spain: 2099 sq km of craggy mountain ranges, deep, green river valleys, canyons, waterfalls, remote hilltop castles and abundant wildlife, threaded by well-marked walking trails and forest roads, with a snaking, 20km-long reservoir, the Embalse del Tranco, in its midst. The abrupt geography, with altitudes varying from 460m up to 2107m at the summit of Cerro Empanadas, makes for dramatic changes in the landscape. The Río Guadalquivir, Andalucía's longest river, rises in the south of the park, and flows northwards into the Embalse del Tranco, before heading west across Andalucía to the Atlantic Ocean.

The best times to visit the park are spring and autumn, when the vegetation is at its most colourful and temperatures pleasant. The park is hugely popular with Spanish tourists and attracts several hundred thousand visitors each year. Peak periods are Semana Santa, July, August, and weekends from April to October.

Exploring the park is far easier if you have a vehicle. The network of paved and unpaved roads and footpaths reaches some remote areas and offers plenty of scope for panoramic day walks or drives. If you don't have a vehicle, you have the option of guided walks, 4WD excursions and wildlife-spotting trips with agencies based in Cazorla (p247) and elsewhere. Bus services are effectively nonexistent.

Information

Centro de Visitantes Torre del Vinagre (953 71 30 17; Carretera A319, Km 48; 10am-2pm & 5-8pm Jul–mid-Sep, hours vary rest of year) The park's main visitors centre is 16km north of Arroyo Frío. It sells maps, guides and souvenirs, and can provide information on walking routes and other attractions, though staff may not speak English.

Getting There & Away

BUS

Cazorla is the only park gateway with dependable bus service. To conveniently explore the park, you'll need your own wheels.

CAR & MOTORCYCLE

The A319 from Cazorla heads up through the centre of the park past the Embalse del Tranco almost to Hornos, where the A317 heads southeast to Santiago de la Espada. Roads feed into the north of the park from the N322 Úbeda–Albacete road. There are at least seven petrol stations in the park.

The South of the Park

The A319, heading northeast from Cazorla, passes through La Iruela then enters the *parque natural* 6km later at Burunchel, from where it winds 6km up to the 1200m **Puerto de las Palomas** pass. The **mirador** (P) here affords wonderful views northward down the Guadalquivir valley and can be a fine spot for observing raptors gliding the thermals. Three twisting kilometres downhill from here is **Empalme del Valle**, a junction where the A319 turns north to follow the Río Guadalquivir downstream to Arroyo Frío (6km) – the most commercialised of the park's villages, with a rash of restaurants, tour agencies and accommodation.

WALKING PREPARED

Printed maps and information in anything except Spanish are hard to come by, but the main routes are well signposted and waymarked. Editorial Penibetica's Sierra de Cazorla (€12) and Sierra de Segura y las Villas (€15) maps are useful and sold in some Cazorla shops, including Alma Gaia (www.almagaia.es; Calle Dr Muñoz 6; h10am-2pm & 5-8.30pm Mon-Sat), which also sells outdoor gear. The website www.sierrasdecazorlaseguraylasvillas.es is a useful resource in English, with some walk descriptions and maps.

When walking, be sure to equip yourself with enough water and appropriate clothes. Temperatures up in the hills are generally several degrees lower than down in the valleys, and the wind can be cutting at any time. In winter the park is often blanketed in snow; summer temperatures can easily reach into the 40°C range.

Sierra de Cazorla

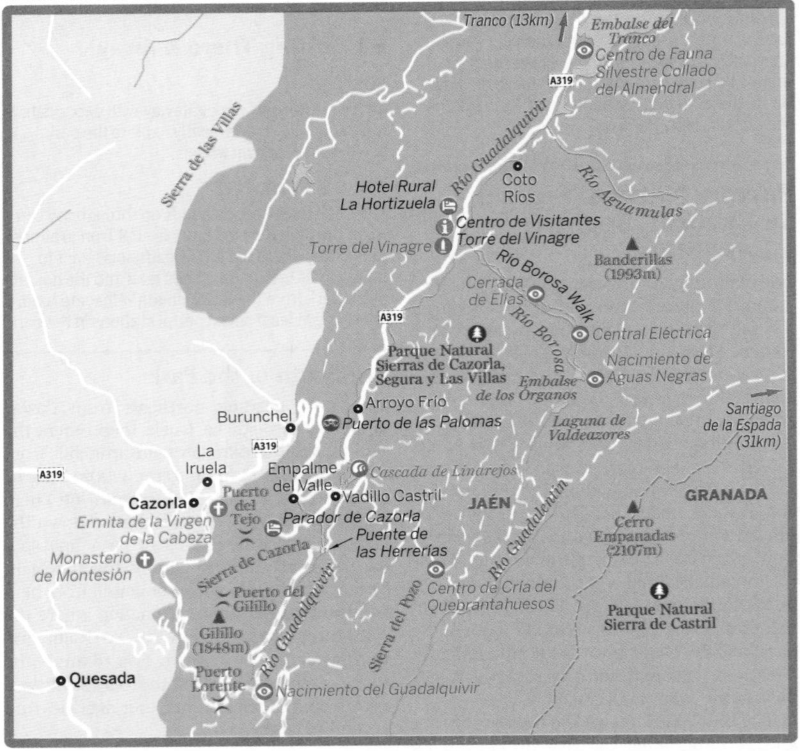

Past Arroyo Frío, the A319 continues 16km along the valley to the Torre del Vinagre visitors centre and the turn-off for the wonderful Río Borosa walk. After another 10km the **Embalse del Tranco** (P) reservoir opens out beside the road. Several miradors offer panoramas over its waters – often a vivid turquoise colour – as the road continues to the dam holding back the reservoir at Tranco village. From here you have the option of continuing north to Hornos and/or Segura de la Sierra.

Sights & Activities

Nacimiento del Guadalquivir SPRING

An interesting detour from Empalme del Valle will take you past Vadillo Castril village to the Puente de las Herrerías bridge (7km) and then 11km on southward along a good gravel-and-dirt road through the forests to the Source of the Guadalquivir, where Andalucía's longest river begins its 657km journey to the Atlantic Ocean as a pool in a shady green nook of the hills.

Centro de Fauna Silvestre Collado del Almendral NATURE RESERVE

(☎953 82 52 67; www.parquecinegeticocolladodelalmendral.com; Carretera A319, Km 60; adult/reduced €9/7; ⊙from 10am Tue-Sun; P) You can view ibex, mouflon, deer, eagles, owls and falcons in semi-liberty at this 1-sq-km enclosed animal park. Visits are by mini train along 5km of road through the park, followed by a 1.5km walk taking in three miradors. Set on a spur of land between the A319 and the Embalse del Tranco, 7km north of Coto Ríos; closing times range from 5pm in winter to 9pm in summer, with last tours one hour earlier.

★ **Río Borosa Walk** WALKING

The most popular walk in Cazorla follows the crystal-clear Río Borosa upstream to its source through scenery that progresses from the pretty to the majestic, via a gorge, two tunnels and a mountain lake. The walk is about 11km each way, with an ascent of about 600m, and takes six to seven hours there and back.

To reach the start, turn east off the A319 at the 'Sendero Río Borosa' sign opposite the Centro de Visitantes Torre del Vinagre (p249), and go 1.7km. The first section of the walk criss-crosses the tumbling, beautiful Río Borosa on a couple of bridges. After just over 3km, where the main track starts climbing to the left, take a path forking right, clearly signposted 'Cerrada de Elías'. This leads through a lovely 1.5km section where the valley narrows to a gorge, the **Cerrada de Elías**, and the path becomes a wooden walkway cantilevered out over the river. You re-emerge on the dirt road and continue 4km to the **Central Eléctrica**, a small hydroelectric station.

Beyond the power station, the path crosses a footbridge, after which a 'Nacimiento Aguas Negras, Laguna Valdeazores' sign directs you onward and upward. The path winds its way up the valley, getting gradually steeper as it climbs through increasingly dramatic scenery past a series of waterfalls. After about an hour, you enter the first of two tunnels cut through the rock for water flowing to the power station. It takes about five minutes to walk the narrow path through the first tunnel (the path is separated from the watercourse by a metal handrail), then there's a short section in the open air before a second tunnel, which takes about one minute to get through. You emerge just below the dam of the **Embalse de los Órganos** (Laguna de Aguas Negras), a small reservoir surrounded by forested hills. From the top of the dam, follow the trail along the reservoir's left bank and in five minutes you reach the **Nacimiento de Aguas Negras**, where the Río Borosa begins life welling out from under a rock. Enjoy your picnic beneath the spreading boughs of a large tree here, then head back down the way you came.

Due to its popularity, it's preferable to do this walk on a weekday. Do carry a water bottle: all the trackside springs are good and drinkable but the last is at the Central Eléctrica. A torch (headlamp) is comforting, if not absolutely essential, for the tunnels.

Sleeping & Eating

Casa Rural Los Parrales CASA RURAL €
(☎689 600091; www.cazorlaturismo.com; Carretera A319, Km 78, Tranco; s/d incl breakfast €45/60; ⏰Feb-Dec; P❄️📶🏊) Set on a rise among trees, Los Parrales makes a great, chilled-out base, with pine furnishings, terracotta-tile floors and wrought-iron bedheads. The pool and terraced garden enjoy spectacular Embalse del Tranco views, and excellent meals emphasising local products are available. It's 3km north of Tranco village along the A319. The GR247 long-distance footpath passes nearby. Advance reservations are essential.

Hotel Rural La Hortizuela HOTEL €
(☎953 71 31 50; www.hotellahortizuela.com; Carretera A319, Km 50.5, Coto Ríos; s €40-45, d €55-60, q €80-90; ⏰Mar-Oct; P📶🏊) The rooms here are well kept, but what really makes it special are the wooded 4 hectare grounds, fenced in to protect plants such as wild orchids and asparagus. Wildlife, including deer, boar and red squirrels, is plentiful in the surrounding woodlands. It's 1km west off the A319, 3km north of Torre del Vinagre visitors centre.

Parador de Cazorla HOTEL €€€
(Parador El Adelantado; ☎953 72 70 75; www.parador.es; Paraje El Sacejo, Sierra de Cazorla; d €75-170, incl breakfast €109-204, incl half board €167-262; ⏰Feb-Dec; P📶🏊) Despite its staid, old-fashioned 1960s vibe, Parador de Cazorla is comfortable and spacious, with a superb forest setting 25km from Cazorla, and panoramic mountain views. A highlight is the expansive lawned garden with large open-air pool. A number of trails pass nearby, including the SLA8 and GR247.3 from Cazorla. The in-house restaurant serves breakfast (€17) and set dinner menus (€29).

WILD THINGS

If you're a wildlife enthusiast, you have to get yourself to the Cazorla natural park. The chances of spotting wildlife are better here than almost anywhere else in Andalucía. Creatures such as red and fallow deer, ibex, wild boar, mouflon (a wild sheep) and red squirrels are all present in good numbers, and are surprisingly visible out on the trails (even along the roads in the case of deer). The autumn mating season (September and October for deer, November for mouflon and wild boar) is a particularly exciting time to observe the big mammals. The park is also home to some 180 bird species, including griffon vultures, golden eagles, peregrine falcons and the majestic *quebrantahuesos* (lammergeier, bearded vulture), which is being reintroduced here after dying out in the 1980s. In short, get walking and keep those binoculars at the ready!

BRINGING BACK THE BONE-BREAKERS

The lammergeier or bearded vulture, once widespread around Andalucía, was finally hunted and poisoned to extinction in the region in 1986 when the last lammergeier disappeared from the Cazorla mountains – at the time, its last refuge in Western Europe except the Pyrenees and Corsica. Today this giant bird with its 2.70m–2.90m wingspan, and downy yellowy-white leg and neck feathers, is flying again over the Sierra de Cazorla, thanks to a reintroduction program based at the **Centro de Cría del Quebrantahuesos** (Lammergeier Breeding Centre; 667 609925; Nava de San Pedro; tour per person €5; tours 5pm Thu, noon & 5pm Fri-Sun mid-May–Sep) deep in the forests of the Parque Natural Cazorla. A visit to the centre, possible outside the breeding season and with advance reservation, is a fascinating experience for any wildlife lover.

One of the weirdest things about the lammergeier is its main diet – animal bones, which it breaks into small, edible pieces by dropping them from the sky on to rocks below – hence its evocative Spanish name, *quebrantahuesos*, which means bone-breaker.

Reintroduction is a long, painstaking process. The birds typically don't start breeding till they are eight or nine years old. The breeding centre was established in 1996; the first young lammergeiers were released into the wild in 2006, and the total number of birds released has now surpassed 60. The first chick hatched in the wild in 2015, and by 2019 there were seven wild-hatched juveniles and two breeding pairs residing in these hills.

As of early 2020, the breeding centre sheltered 23 lammergeiers, including seven breeding pairs. On a visit here you'll see several of these spectacular birds (individuals unsuitable for release into the wild) in their large cages, and have the breeding, rearing and release process explained in detail. The centre is a 33km drive from Cazorla, the last 7km on a well-surfaced gravel-and-dirt road. Make it known when booking if you'd like a guide who speaks some English; also double-check the location as there's a possibility that it may move.

El Tranco ANDALUCIAN €€

(953 00 22 76; www.tranco.es; Centro Náutico, Carretera A319, Km 75, Tranco; mains €9-20; 1-4pm & 8.30-11.30pm mid-Jul–mid-Sep, hours vary rest of year) Highly popular El Tranco is quite avant-garde for this neck of the woods, providing a tasty contemporary take on traditional local ingredients, in generous portions. Dishes include venison in aromatic-herb sauce, trout-and-mushroom risotto, some creative salads, baked apple with crumble and olive-oil ice cream, and options like guacamole or sweet-chilli sauce to go with the charcoal-oven grills.

Hornos

POP 601 / ELEV 867M

Like better-known Segura de la Sierra, little Hornos is fabulously located. It sits atop a crag backed by a sweep of mountains, with marvellous views over the shimmering Embalse del Tranco and the lush, green countryside, richly patterned with olive, pine and almond trees and the occasional tossed dice of a farmhouse.

The castle on the crag was built by Christians in the mid-13th century, probably on the site of an earlier Muslim fortification. Don't expect colour-coordinated geraniums, souvenir shops or a tourist office: Hornos' unfussy charms lie in exploring its narrow, winding streets and admiring the view from several strategically placed miradors.

If you want to stride out, there are several trails including two of about 4km each to tiny outlying villages – the PRA152 south down to Hornos El Viejo and the PRA148 east up to La Capellanía – as well as the long-distance GR247 to El Yelmo or Tranco.

To get to Hornos, take the A319 12km north of the Tranco dam to a T-junction; from here the A317 winds 4km up to Hornos village.

Cosmolarium PLANETARIUM

(688 906165; www.cosmolarium.info; €3, incl planetarium €5; 10.30am-2pm & 5.30-8.30pm Jul-early Sep, hours vary rest of year) Hornos' panoramic medieval castle now houses, curiously enough, a modern astronomy interpretation centre and planetarium. Exhibits are devoted to the universe, galaxies, the solar system and the history of astronomy, with English or French audio guides included in the ticket price. The planetarium presents projections in Spanish and English on astronomical themes.

Apartamentos Raisa HOSTAL, APARTMENT €

(953 49 50 23; www.apartamentosraisa.es; Calle Puerta Nueva 35; incl breakfast s/d/apt €27/50/70;

) Friendly Raisa provides five straightforwardly clean and comfy rooms and three apartments with well-equipped kitchens. It also has a moderately priced all-day restaurant/cafe/bar downstairs, serving pizzas alongside mountain specialities such as homemade sausages, local *segureño* lamb chops and *lomo de orza* (garlicky marinated pork loin).

Segura de la Sierra

POP 1790 / ELEV 1145M

One of Andalucía's most picturesque and strategically placed historic villages, Segura de la Sierra perches on a steep hill crowned by a Reconquista castle. The village takes some of its character from its five Moorish centuries before the Knights of Santiago captured it in 1214, after which it became part of the Christian front line against the Almohads and then the Granada emirate.

As you drive up into the village, the **Puerta Nueva**, one of four gates of Islamic Saqura, marks the entrance to the old part of Segura. Signs to the Castillo lead you round to a junction on the northern side by the little walled bullring. Turn left here for the castle itself.

In the village below the castle, the sturdy 16th-century **Iglesia de Nuestra Señora del Collado** stands just below the main square, **Plaza de la Encomienda**. From here, continue downhill to the 12th-century **Baños Árabes** (Calle Baño Moro) FREE at the foot of the village. Nearby is the **Puerta Catena**, the best-preserved of Segura's Islamic gates.

★**Castillo de Segura** CASTLE
(627 877919; adult/child €4.50/3.50; 10.30am-2pm & 5-8.45pm mid-Jul–Aug, shorter hours rest of year) This lofty castle dates from Moorish times but was rebuilt after the Christian conquest in the 13th century. Abandoned in the 17th century, it was restored in the 1960s and has now become a 'frontier territory ' interpretation centre. The ticket office is also Segura's main tourist information point.

You can see the original Arab steam baths, visit the 13th-century Mudéjar chapel, climb the tower and walk round the battlements for a bird's-eye view of El Yelmo, 5km south, and the rocky crags and olive-tree-strewn lowlands all around. A series of videos (in Spanish with English subtitles) offers historical background on Segura and the castle.

It's a minimum 400m walk, plus 80 steps, from the nearest parking place to the castle entrance, though vehicles are allowed to drop passengers near the entrance then go back down to park. Note: the castle's opening hours are complicated; it's advisable to call ahead to check the schedule.

Apartamentos La Mesa Segureña APARTMENT €
(610 743725; Calle Cruz de Montoria 2; incl breakfast 2-person apt €50-65, 4-person apt €75-100;) Seven cosy apartments just below Segura castle, with great views, a touch of bright art, cast-iron trimmings, fireplaces and mini-kitchens.

La Mesa Segureña ANDALUCIAN €€
(953 48 21 01; Calle Postigo 2; mains €12-18; 10am-10pm Mon-Sat, to 5pm Sun) Hidden down a small lane between Segura's castle and the Arabic baths, La Mesa Segureña makes for a festive lunch break. Meaty mountain specialities – from pork chops to venison stew – are the star attractions, served by bustling black-clad waitresses in a dining room with cheerful orange-and-green walls.

El Yelmo

El Yelmo (1808m) is one of the highest and most panoramic mountains in the north of the park. A 5.5km road – paved all the way, but single-track in parts – goes right to the summit, which is disfigured by a rash of communications towers but has magnificent 360-degree views. El Yelmo is a favourite take-off point for paragliders and is the focus of a big fiesta of free-flying and other activities, the **Festival Internacional del Aire** (www.fiaelyelmo.com; hJun), which attracts thousands of people for three days every June (usually the first weekend of the month). For tandem flights contact **Olivair** (Segura Activa; 607 301716; www.facebook.com/olivairfly; Calle Francisco Quevedo s/n; tandem paragliding from €100, motorised paratrike from €80, mountain bike rental per day €30) by phone or at its Segura Activa office in Segura de la Sierra.

To drive to El Yelmo, take the A6305 from Hornos, winding your way east up into the mountain pine forests. Go left (signposted to Segura and Siles) at a junction after 13km, and in 1km you'll see a road taking off to the left, between a ruined building and a smaller intact one (El Campillo walkers' refuge). This is the road up to El Yelmo. If you'd prefer to walk up, take the path signed 'Derivación 2 Bosques del Sur' from the El Campillo refuge. It shortens the climb to 3km (about 1½ hours).

AT A GLANCE

POPULATION
919,000

CAPITAL
Granada

BEST ALHAMBRA VIEW
Mirador San Nicolás (p266)

BEST COUNTRY RETREAT
Las Chimeneas (p289)

BEST VEGETARIAN RESTAURANT
L'Atelier (p286)

WHEN TO GO

Apr–Jun
Spring festivals, warm weather (usually), countryside blooming; a fine time for Alpujarras walking.

Jul–Aug
Peak months for the beaches but also best for hiking in the high Sierra Nevada.

Dec–Apr
Enjoy Europe's most southerly ski resort, in the Sierra Nevada (snow permitting).

Alhambra (p258)
DAVID IONUT/SHUTTERSTOCK

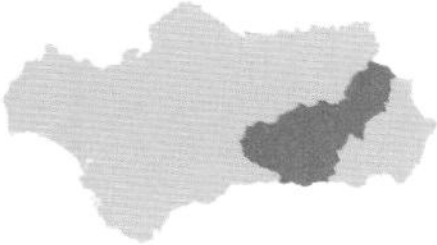

Granada Province

No city encapsulates the drama of Andalucía's past to more gripping effect than Granada. The lively provincial capital is home to Spain's greatest Moorish building, the Alhambra, and the influence of the Moorish era infuses the city. Meanwhile, monumental churches tower over teeming tapas bars, bold murals adorn back streets, and the flamenco scene simmers.

The peaks of the Sierra Nevada provide a magnificent backdrop and outdoor playground. Hiking possibilities abound, and skiers can enjoy Europe's southernmost resort.

Further afield, you can soak up the sun on the silver-pebble beaches of the Costa Tropical, seek out hidden villages, and explore cave houses amid the expanses of the Altiplano.

INCLUDES

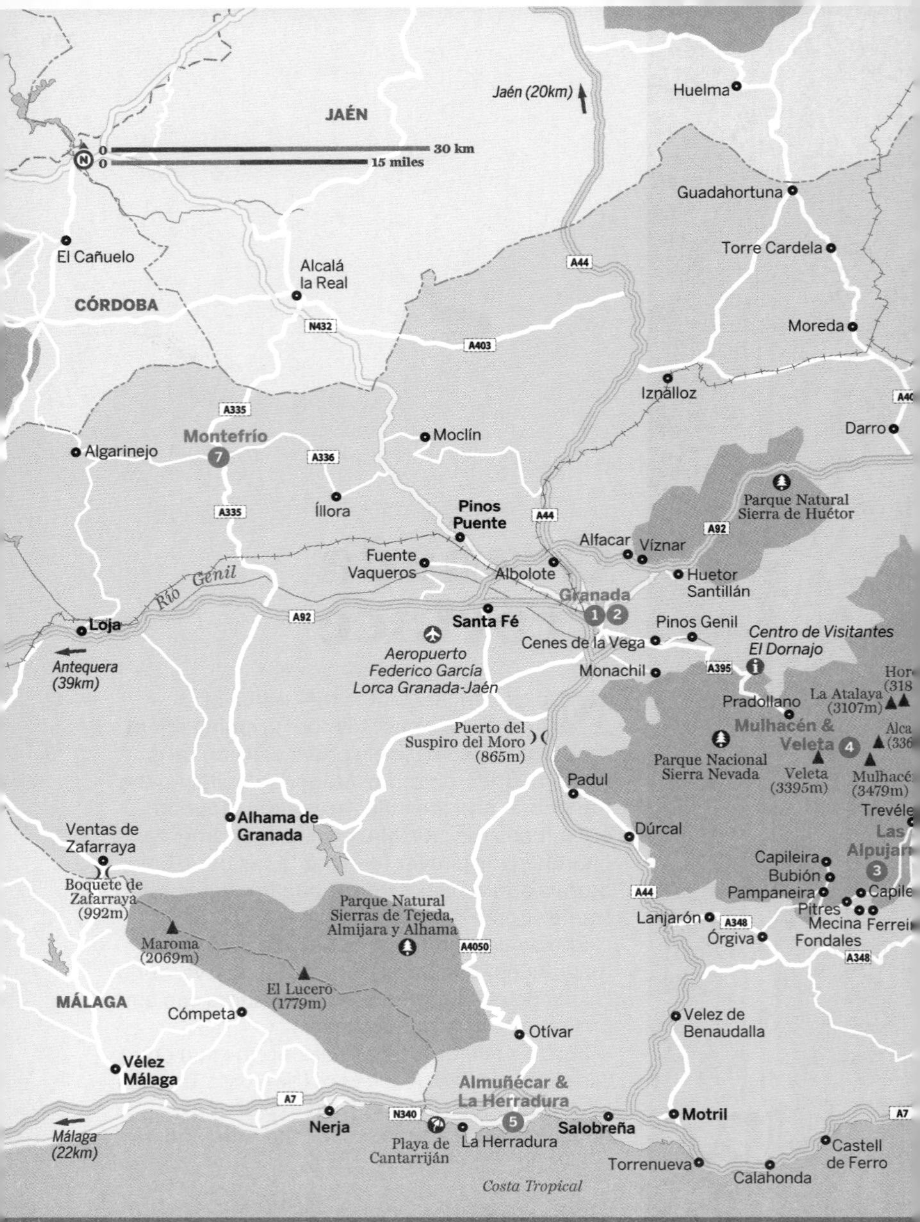

Granada Province Highlights

1 **Alhambra** (p258) Basking in the awe-inspiring majesty of Spain's most spectacular monument, a masterpiece of exquisite Moorish architecture.

2 **Granada** (p273) Meandering around the history-rich Albayzín and Sacromonte, then bar-crawling for free tapas and uncovering local wines.

3 **Las Alpujarras** (p282) Hiking through the white villages and vertiginous canyons of the Sierra Nevada's southern slopes.

4 **Mulhacén & Veleta** (p282) Summitting mainland

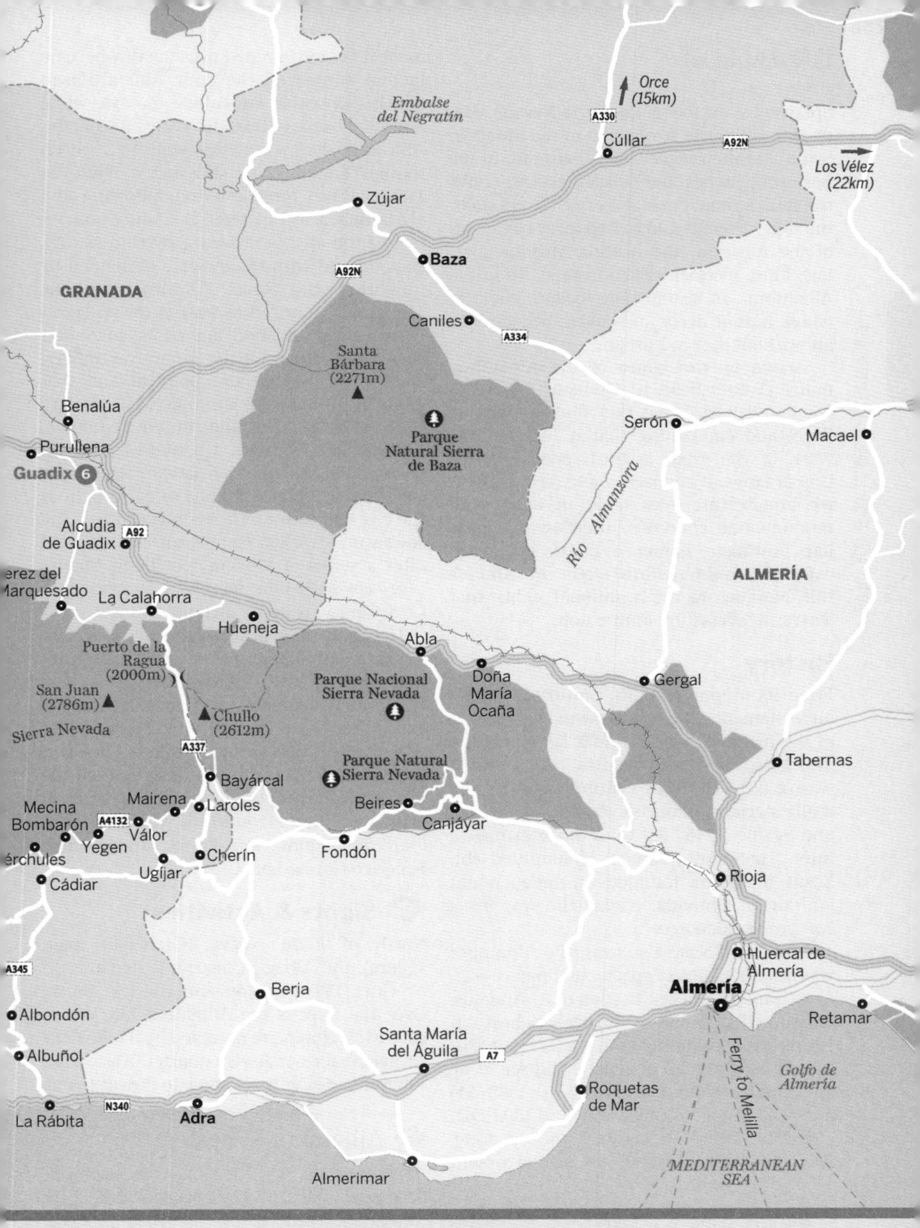

Spain's highest or third-highest peak, or hitting the Sierra Nevada ski pistes in winter.

5 **Almuñécar & La Herradura** (p292) Kicking back on pebble beaches, feasting on fresh seafood and tackling water sports on the Costa Tropical.

6 **Guadix** (p290) Going underground for a glimpse of cave life in this lively provincial town, packed with fuss-free tapas bars.

7 **Montefrío** (p279) Escaping into the province's little-visited northwest, where a cragtop castle-church awaits.

GRANADA

POP 227,631 / ELEV 680M

Sprawled at the foot of the Sierra Nevada, Granada was the last stronghold of the Moors in Spain and their legacy lies all around: in the horseshoe arches, the delicate artisan crafts, the spicy aromas emanating from street stalls, the sultry *teterías* and tucked-away *cármenes* of the Albayzín (the historic Muslim quarter). Most spectacularly, of course, it's in the Alhambra, an astonishing palace complex whose Islamic decor and landscaped gardens are without peer in Europe.

Drawn by the allure of the Alhambra, many visitors head to Granada unsure of what to expect. What they find is a city so lively and compelling that it inspired the work of the great Spanish poet Federico García Lorca. It's a place where serene Moorish architecture goes hand in hand with monumental churches, overflowing tapas bars, intimate flamenco clubs, bohemian cafes and counterculture street art. And it's this, as much as the traditional sights, that leaves such a lasting impression.

History

From its origins as a 5th-century-BC Iberian settlement, Granada grew to become one of the medieval world's great Islamic cities. The Muslims first arrived in 711 CE but it wasn't until the 13th century that the city really started to flourish. As Córdoba (1236) and Seville (1248) fell to Catholic armies, a minor potentate named Mohammed ibn Yusuf ibn Nasr founded an independent emirate in Granada, paving the way for a 250-year golden age.

Under the Nasrid sultans, the Alhambra was developed into a spectacular palace-fort, and Granada, the last bastion of Al-Andalus, blossomed into one of Europe's richest cities, its streets teeming with traders and artisans. Two centuries of artistic and scientific splendour peaked under Yusuf I (r 1333–54) and Mohammed V (r 1354–59 and 1362–91).

In the late 15th century, the economy stagnated and court politics turned violent as rival factions argued over the throne. One faction supported the emir Abu al-Hasan and his Christian concubine, Zoraya, while another backed Boabdil (Abu Abdullah), Abu al-Hasan's son by his wife Aixa – even though Boabdil was still just a child. In 1482 civil war broke out and, following Abu al-Hasan's death in 1485, Boabdil won control of the city. It proved a pyrrhic victory, though, and with the emirate weakened by infighting, the Reyes Católicos (Catholic Monarchs) pounced in 1491. After an eight-month siege, Boabdil agreed to surrender the city in return for the Alpujarras valleys, 30,000 gold coins, and political and religious freedom for his subjects. On 2 January 1492, Isabel and Fernando entered Granada.

What followed was a period of religious persecution as the Christian authorities sought to establish Catholic rule throughout the city and former Moorish territories. The Jews were expelled from Spain in 1492, and after a series of Muslim rebellions, Spain's *moriscos* (Muslims who had converted to Christianity) were thrown out in 1609.

Granada sank into a deep decline from which it only began to emerge in the mid-19th century, with interest aroused by the Romantic movement, in particular American writer Washington Irving's *Tales of the Alhambra* (1832). Granada suffered another dark period when the Nationalists took the city at the start of the Spanish Civil War: an estimated 4000 *granadinos* with left or liberal connections were killed, among them Federico García Lorca.

GRANADA CARD

The five-day Granada Card (adult €36 to €40, child €11; www.granadatur.com; ☎858 88 09 90) covers admission to 10 city monuments, including the Alhambra, and nine free trips on city buses.

Sights & Activities

North of Plaza Nueva (Granada's main square), the Albayzín district is demarcated by Gran Vía de Colón and the Río Darro. Over the river is the Alhambra hill, whose southwest slopes are occupied by the Realejo, Granada's former Jewish quarter. West of the Albayzín, the Centro is home to the cathedral.

Alhambra & Realejo

★Alhambra ISLAMIC PALACE

(Map p259; ☎958 02 79 71, tickets 858 95 36 16; www.alhambra-patronato.es; adult/12-15yr/under 12yr €14/8/free, Generalife & Alcazaba only adult/under 12yr €7/free; ⌚8.30am-8pm Apr–mid-Oct, to 6pm mid-Oct–Mar, night visits 10-11.30pm Tue & Sat Apr–mid-Oct, 8-9.30pm Fri & Sat mid-Oct–Mar) The Alhambra is Granada's – and Europe's – love letter to Moorish culture. Set against

Alhambra

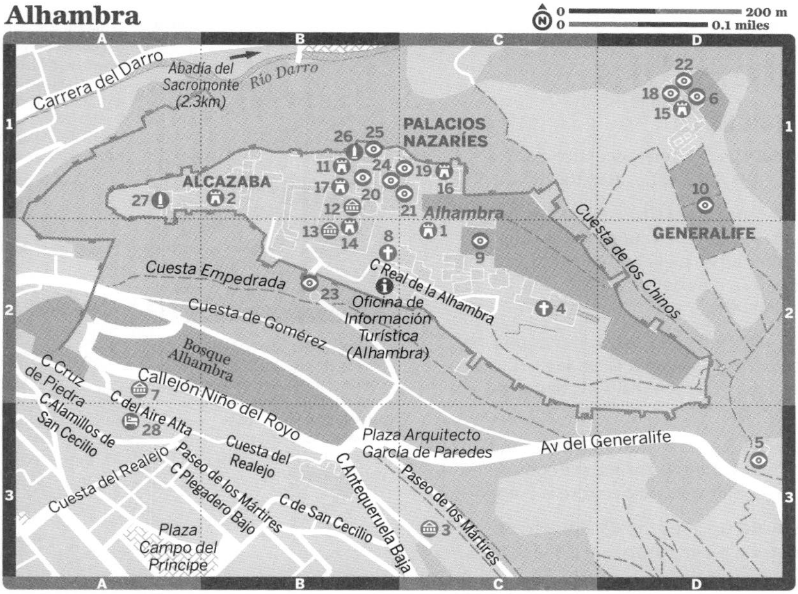

Alhambra

Top Sights

1 Alhambra C2

Sights

2 Alcazaba B1
3 Casa-Museo Manuel de Falla C3
4 Convento de San Francisco C2
5 Entrance Pavilion D3
6 Escalera del Agua D1
7 Fundación Rodríguez-Acosta A2
8 Iglesia de Santa María de la Alhambra B2
9 Jardines del Partal C2
10 Jardines Nuevos D1
11 Mexuar B1
Mirador de Daraxa .... (see 19)
12 Museo de Bellas Artes B1
13 Museo de la Alhambra B2
14 Palacio de Carlos V B2
15 Palacio del Generalife D1
16 Palacio del Partal C1
17 Palacios Nazaríes B1
18 Patio de la Acequia D1
19 Patio de la Lindaraja C1
20 Patio de los Arrayanes B1
21 Patio de los Leones C1
22 Patio del Ciprés de la Sultana D1
Patio del Cuarto Dorado .... (see 11)
23 Puerta de la Justicia B2
24 Sala de Dos Hermanas B1
25 Sala de la Barca B1
Sala de los Abencerrajes .... (see 21)
Sala de los Reyes .... (see 21)
Salón de los Embajadores .... (see 25)
26 Torre de Comares B1
27 Torre de la Vela A1

Sleeping

28 Carmen de la Alcubilla del Caracol A3
Parador de Granada .... (see 4)

Eating

Parador de Granada .... (see 4)

the brooding Sierra Nevada peaks, this fortified palace started life as a walled citadel before becoming the opulent seat of Granada's Nasrid emirs. Their showpiece palaces, the 14th-century Palacios Nazaríes, are among the finest Islamic buildings in Europe and, together with the Generalife gardens, form the Alhambra's great headline act. Tickets sell out, so book ahead (p263); you'll have to choose a time to enter the Palacios Nazaríes.

The origins of the Alhambra, whose name derives from the Arabic *al-qala'a al-hamra* (the Red Castle), are mired in mystery. The first references to construction in the area appear in the 9th century but it's thought that buildings may already

Alhambra

A TIMELINE

900 CE The first reference to *al-qala'a al-hamra* (the Red Castle) atop the Sabika hill.

1237 Mohammed I, founder of the Nasrid dynasty, moves his court to Granada. Threatened by belligerent Christian armies he builds a new defensive fort, the ① **Alcazaba**.

1302–09 Designed as a summer palace and country estate for Granada's rulers, the bucolic ② **Generalife** is begun by Mohammed III.

1333–54 Yusuf I initiates the construction of the ③ **Palacios Nazaríes**, still considered the highpoint of Islamic culture in Europe.

1350–60 Up goes the ④ **Palacio de Comares**, taking Nasrid lavishness to a whole new level.

1362–91 The second coming of Mohammed V ushers in even greater architectural brilliance, exemplified by the construction of the ⑤ **Patio de los Leones**.

1527 The Christians add the ⑥ **Palacio de Carlos V**. Inspired Renaissance palace or incongruous crime against Moorish art? You decide.

1829 The languishing, half-forgotten Alhambra is 'rediscovered' by American writer Washington Irving during a protracted sleepover.

1954 The Generalife gardens are extended southwards to accommodate an outdoor theatre.

TOP TIPS

➡ Booking tickets as far ahead as possible is essential; by phone or online.

➡ You can visit the general areas of the palace free of charge any time by entering through the Puerta de la Justicia.

➡ Within the Alhambra grounds, the lavish Parador de Granada is a fabulous (and pricey) place to stay, or just pop in for a drink or meal.

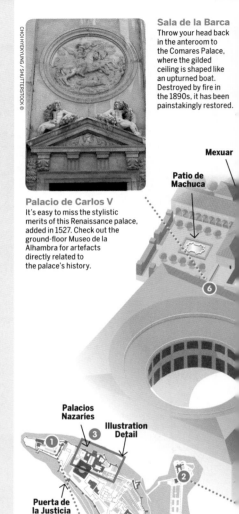

Sala de la Barca

Throw your head back in the anteroom to the Comares Palace, where the gilded ceiling is shaped like an upturned boat. Destroyed by fire in the 1890s, it has been painstakingly restored.

Palacio de Carlos V

It's easy to miss the stylistic merits of this Renaissance palace, added in 1527. Check out the ground-floor Museo de la Alhambra for artefacts directly related to the palace's history.

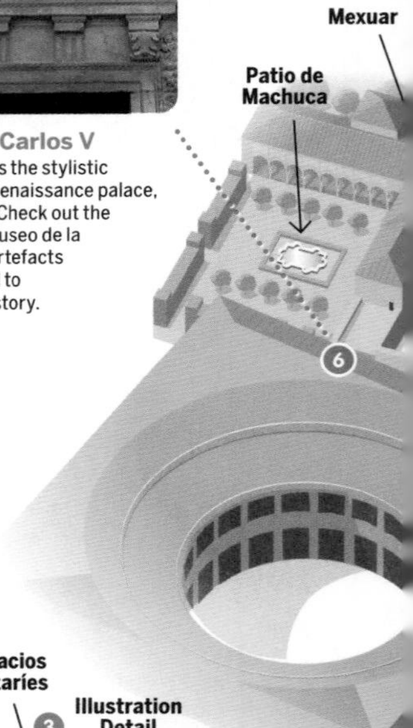

Alcazaba

Find time to explore the towers of the original citadel, the most important of which – the Torre de la Vela – takes you, via a winding staircase, to the Alhambra's best viewpoint.

Patio de los Arrayanes

If only you could linger longer beside the rows of *arrayanes* (myrtle bushes) that border this calming rectangular pool. Shaded porticos with seven harmonious arches invite further contemplation.

Palacio de Comares

The largest room in the Palacio de Comares, renowned for its rich geometric ceiling, is the Salón de los Embajadores – a negotiating room for the emirs and a masterpiece of Moorish design.

JOSE IGNACIO SOTO / SHUTTERSTOCK ©

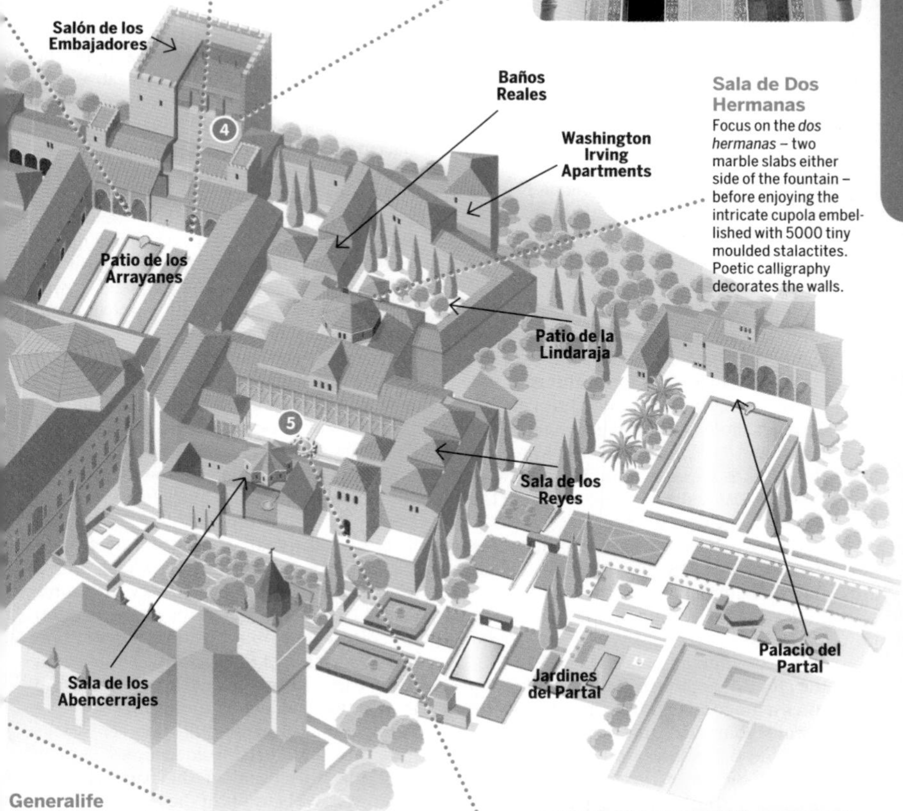

Sala de Dos Hermanas

Focus on the *dos hermanas* – two marble slabs either side of the fountain – before enjoying the intricate cupola embellished with 5000 tiny moulded stalactites. Poetic calligraphy decorates the walls.

Generalife

A coda to most people's visits, the 'architect's garden' is no afterthought. While Nasrid in origin, the horticulture is relatively new: the pools and arcades were added in the early 20th century.

Patio de los Leones

Count the 12 lions sculpted from marble, holding up a gurgling fountain. Then pan back and take in the delicate columns and arches built to signify an Islamic vision of paradise.

FOTOGRAFIECOR.NL / SHUTTERSTOCK©

HIDDEN SPACES

Each month the Alhambra authorities open a different, otherwise off-limits section of the monument to visitors, usually included in tickets. Ask for the Espacio del Mes (Space of the Month).

have been standing since Roman times. In its current form, it largely dates to the 13th and 14th centuries when Granada's Nasrid rulers transformed it into a fortified palace complex. Following the 1492 Reconquista (Christian reconquest), its mosque was replaced by a church and the Habsburg emperor Charles V had a wing of palaces demolished to make space for the huge Renaissance building that still bears his name. In the early 19th century, French Napoleonic forces destroyed part of the palace and attempted to blow up the entire site. Restoration work began in the mid-1800s and continues to this day.

➡ Palacio de Carlos V & Around

From the southeastern entrance pavilion, a signposted path leads into the core of the complex, passing the 15th-century **Convento de San Francisco**, now the Parador de Granada hotel (p271), where the bodies of Isabel and Fernando were laid to rest while their tombs were being built in the Capilla Real (p267). A short walk further on brings you to the **Iglesia de Santa María de la Alhambra** (⌚10am-1pm Tue-Sun & 4-6pm Tue-Sat), built between 1581 and 1618 on the site of the Alhambra's mosque.

Beyond the church, the Palacio de Carlos V clashes spectacularly with its surroundings. The hulking palace, begun in 1527 by the Toledo architect Pedro Machuca, features a monumental facade and a two-tiered circular courtyard ringed by 32 columns.

Inside the palace are two museums: the **Museo de la Alhambra** (⌚8.30am-8pm Wed-Sat, to 2.30pm Sun & Tue mid-Mar–mid-Oct, 8.30am-6pm Wed-Sat, to 2.30pm Sun & Tue mid-Oct–mid-Mar) FREE, which showcases an absorbing collection of Moorish artefacts, including the wood-carved door from the Sala de Dos Hermanas, and the excavated remains of the Acequia Real (Royal Water Channel); and the **Museo de Bellas Artes** (☎958 56 35 08; EU/non-EU citizen free/€1.50; ⌚9am-8pm Tue-Sat Apr–mid-Oct, 9am-6pm Tue-Sat mid-Oct–Mar, 9am-3pm Sun year-round), with 15th- to 20th-century artworks.

➡ Alcazaba

Occupying the western tip of the Alhambra are the martial remnants of the Alcazaba, the site's original 13th-century citadel. The **Torre de la Vela** (Watchtower) is famous as the tower where the cross and banners of the Reconquista were raised in January 1492. A winding staircase leads to the top where you can enjoy sweeping views over Granada's rooftops.

➡ Palacios Nazaríes

The Alhambra's stunning centrepiece, the palace complex known as the Palacios Nazaríes, was originally divided into three sections: the Mexuar, a chamber for administrative and public business; the Palacio de Comares, the emir's official and private residence; and the Palacio de los Leones, a private area for the royal family and harem. Access is limited to 300 people every half hour.

Entrance is through the **Mexuar**, a 14th-century hall where the council of ministers would sit and the emir would adjudicate citizens' appeals. Two centuries later, it was converted into a chapel, with a prayer room at the far end. Look up here and elsewhere to appreciate the geometrically carved wood ceilings and elegant tiling.

From the Mexuar, you pass into the **Patio del Cuarto Dorado**, a courtyard where the emirs gave audiences, with the **Cuarto Dorado** (Golden Room) on the left, looking out on the Albayzín. Opposite the Cuarto Dorado is the entrance to the **Palacio de Comares** through a beautiful facade of glazed tiles, stucco and carved wood. A dog-leg corridor (a common strategy in Islamic architecture to keep interior rooms private) leads through to the **Patio de los Arrayanes** (Courtyard of the Myrtles). This elegant patio, named after the myrtle hedges around its rectangular pool, is the central space of the palace built in the mid-14th century as Emir Yusuf I's official residence.

The southern end of the patio is overshadowed by the walls of the Palacio de Carlos V. To the north, in the 45m-high **Torre de Comares** (Comares Tower), the **Sala de la Barca** (Hall of the Boat), with its sculpted ceilings, leads into the **Salón de los Embajadores** (Chamber of the Ambassadors; also the Salón de Comares), where the emirs would have conducted negotiations with Christian emissaries. The room's domed marquetry ceiling contains more than 8000 cedar pieces in an intricate star pattern representing the seven heavens of Islam.

The Patio de los Arrayanes leads into the **Palacio de los Leones** (Palace of the Lions), built in the second half of the 14th century under Muhammad V. The palace rooms branch off the **Patio de los Leones** (Lion Courtyard), centred on an 11th-century fountain channelling water through the mouths of 12 marble lions. The courtyard layout, using the proportions of the golden ratio, demonstrates the complexity of Moorish geometric design – the 124 slender columns that support the ornamented pavilions are placed in such a way that they are symmetrical on numerous axes.

Of the four halls around the patio, the **Sala de los Abencerrajes**, on the south side, is the most impressive. Boasting a mesmerising octagonal stalactite ceiling, this is the legendary site of the murders of the noble Abencerraj family, whose leader, the story goes, dared to dally with Zoraya, Abu al-Hasan's favourite concubine.

At the eastern end of the patio is the **Sala de los Reyes** (Hall of the Kings), which has three leather-lined ceiling alcoves painted by 14th-century Christian artists. The central alcove is thought to depict 10 Nasrid emirs.

ALHAMBRA PRACTICALITIES

The Alhambra is Spain's second most visited tourist attraction (after Barcelona's Sagrada Família), drawing almost 2.5 million visitors a year. You'll need to book as far ahead as possible, even during low season, and choose a specific time to enter the Palacios Nazaríes section.

Tickets

Some parts of the Alhambra can be visited free of charge, but for the main areas you'll need a ticket.

General (€14) All areas.

Gardens, Generalife & Alcazaba (€7) Excludes the Palacios Nazaríes.

Night Visit Palacios Nazaríes (€8) Year-round.

Night Visit Gardens & Generalife (€5) April, May, September, October and, possibly, early November.

Dobla de Oro (€19.65) Covers the Alhambra and five sights in the Albayzín.

➡ You can buy tickets from two hours to three months in advance: online, by phone or at the Alhambra ticket office (some foreign cards might not work online). A few 'leftover' tickets *may* be available at the ticket office on the day, but this is rare.

➡ You can show your ticket on your phone, print it yourself or pick it up from the ticket machines at the Alhambra Entrance Pavilion ticket office, the information point (p279) next to the Palacio de Carlos V, or the Corral del Carbón (p269) in central Granada.

➡ All children's tickets must be collected at the Alhambra ticket office as you'll need to prove your kids' ages (take IDs).

Tours

Many local agencies offer private guided Alhambra tours, with tickets included, and guides can be invaluable. Note, however, that there have been complaints of tickets booked through some tour operators falling through at the very last minute – it's always best to book your own ticket through the official portal. Audio guides cost €6.

For Families

Strollers and prams are not permitted in the Palacios Nazaríes or the Generalife; you can leave them at the main ticket office or at the services pavilion next to the Puerta del Vino (which also lends baby carriers).

Getting There

By foot, walk 800m up Cuesta de Gomérez from Plaza Nueva through the woods to the Puerta de la Justicia; enter here if you already have your ticket or are able to collect it at the information point, otherwise continue to the main (southeastern) ticket office. Bus C30 runs to the ticket office from just off Plaza Isabel la Católica.

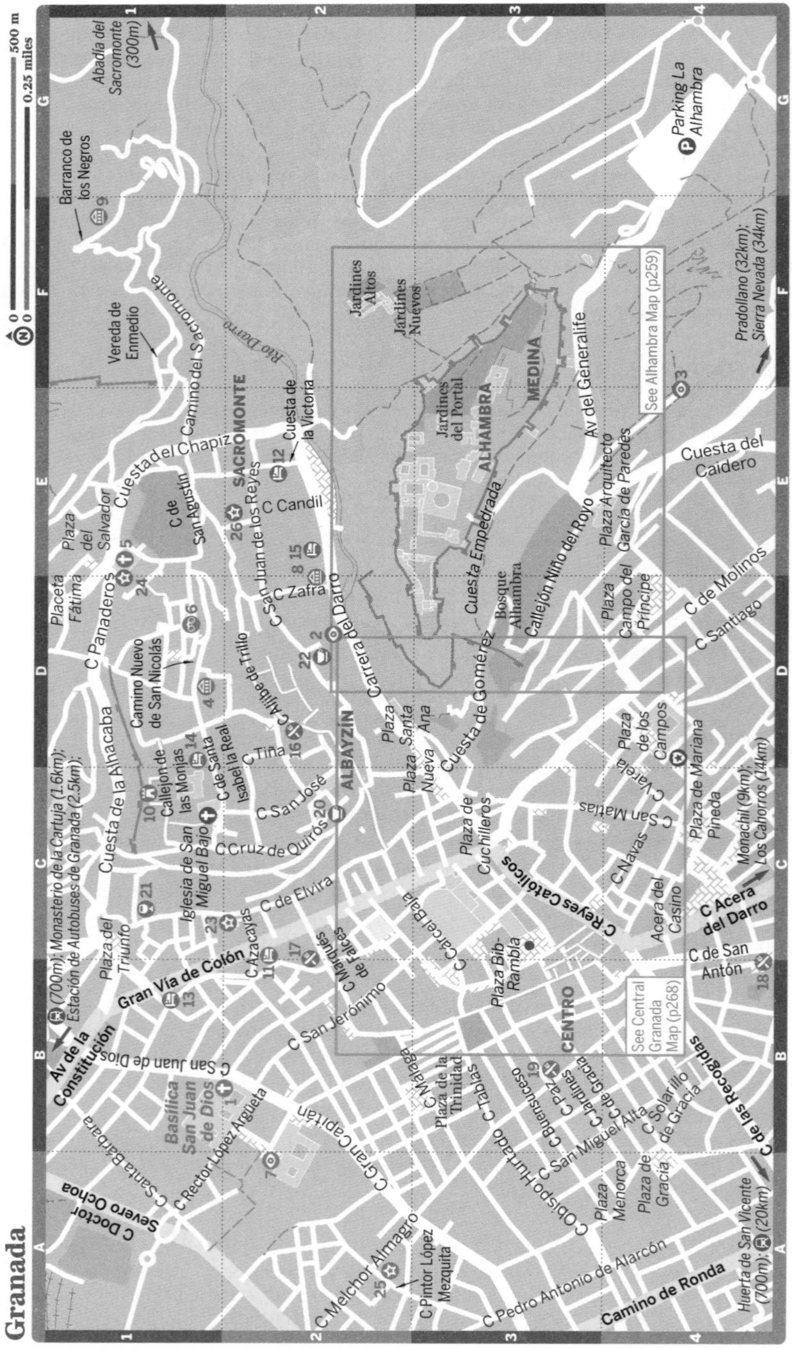
Granada
500 m
0.25 miles
Abadía del Sacromonte (300m)
Barranco de los Negros
Vereda de Enmedio
Camino del Sacromonte
Río Darro
Cuesta del Chapiz
Cuesta de la Victoria
SACROMONTE
Plaza del Salvador
Placeta Fátima
C de San Agustín
C Panaderos
C San Juan de los Reyes
C Candil
C Zafra
Camino Nuevo de San Nicolás
Cuesta de la Alhacaba
Callejón de las Monjas
C de Santa Isabel la Real
C Aljibe de Trillo
C Tiña
C San José
C Cruz de Quirós
ALBAYZÍN
Iglesia de San Miguel Bajo
Plaza del Triunfo
(700m); Monasterio de la Cartuja (1.6km); Estación de Autobuses de Granada (2.5km)
Gran Vía de Colón
C de Elvira
C Azacayas
C Marqués de Falces
Carrera del Darro
Plaza Santa Ana
Plaza Nueva
Cuesta de Gomérez
Plaza de Cuchilleros
Jardines Altos
Jardines Nuevos
Jardines del Portal
ALHAMBRA
MEDINA
Cuesta Empedrada
Bosque Alhambra
Callejón Niño del Royo
Av del Generalife
Plaza Arquitecto García de Paredes
Plaza Campo del Príncipe
See Alhambra Map (p259)
Parking La Alhambra
Pradollano (32km); Sierra Nevada (34km)
Cuesta del Caidero
C de Molinos
C Santiago
Plaza de los Campos
C Varela
C San Matías
C Navas
Plaza de Mariana Pineda
Monachil (9km); Los Cahorros (14km)
C Reyes Católicos
C Cárcel Baja
Plaza Bib-Rambla
Acera del Casino
C Acera del Darro
C de San Antón
CENTRO
See Central Granada Map (p268)
C San Jerónimo
Av de la Constitución
C San Juan de Dios
Basílica San Juan de Dios
C Rector López Argüeta
C Santa Bárbara
C Doctor Severo Ochoa
C Gran Capitán
C Melchor Almagro
C Pintor López Mezquita
C Málaga
Plaza de la Trinidad
C Tablas
C Obispo Hurtado
C Buensuceso
C Paz
C Jardines
C de Gracia
C San Miguel Alta
C Solarillo de Gracia
Plaza de Gracia
Plaza Menorca
C de las Recogidas
C Pedro Antonio de Alarcón
Camino de Ronda
Huerta de San Vicente (700m); (20km)
1
2
3
4
5
6
7
8
9
10
11
12
13
14
15
16
17
18
19
20
21
22
23
24
25
26
A
B
C
D
E
F
G

Granada

Top Sights

1 Basílica San Juan de Dios B2

Sights

2 Baños Árabes El Bañuelo D2
3 Carmen de los Mártires E4
4 Casa-Museo Max Moreau D1
5 Colegiata del Salvador E1
6 Mirador San Nicolás D1
7 Monasterio de San Jerónimo A2
8 Museo Arqueológico D2
9 Museo Cuevas del Sacromonte F1
10 Palacio de Dar-al-Horra C1

Sleeping

11 AC Palacio de Santa Paula C2
12 Casa Morisca E2
13 Eco Hostel B1
14 Santa Isabel la Real D1
15 White Nest E2

Eating

16 Café 4 Gatos D2
17 El Bar de Fede C2
18 La Fábula Restaurante B4
19 Poë B3

Drinking & Nightlife

20 Abaco Té C2
21 Al Sur de Granada C1
22 Tetería El Bañuelo D2

Entertainment

23 Eshavira C2
24 Jardines de Zoraya D1
25 La Tertulia A2
26 Peña La Platería E2

On the patio's northern side is the richly decorated **Sala de Dos Hermanas** (Hall of Two Sisters), probably named after the slabs of white marble flanking its fountain. It features a dizzying *muqarnas* (honeycomb-vaulted) dome with a central star and 5000 tiny cells, reminiscent of the constellations. The carved wood screens in the upper level enabled women (and perhaps others involved in palace intrigue) to peer down from hallways above without being seen. At its far end, the tile-trimmed **Mirador de Daraxa** (Daraxa Lookout) was a lovely place for palace denizens to look on the garden.

From the Sala de Dos Hermanas, a passageway leads through the **Estancias del Emperador** (Emperor's Chambers), built for Carlos V in the 1520s, and later used by the American author Washington Irving. From here descend to the **Patio de la Reja** (Patio of the Grille) and the **Patio de la Lindaraja**, where, in the southwest corner, you can peer into the **Baño Real de Comares** bathhouse, lit by star-shaped skylights.

You eventually emerge into the **Jardines del Partal**, an area of terraced gardens laid out at the beginning of the 20th century. Here a reflecting pool stands in front of the **Palacio del Partal**, a small porticoed building with its own tower (the Torre de las Damas) dating to the early 14th century.

➡ Generalife

The Generalife, the sultans' gorgeous summer estate, dates to the 14th century. A soothing ensemble of pathways, patios, pools, fountains, trees and, in season, flowers of every imaginable hue, it takes its name from the Arabic *jinan al-'arif,* meaning 'the overseer's gardens'.

A string of elegant rectangular plots with tinkling water features, the **Jardines Nuevos**, leads up to the whitewashed **Palacio del Generalife**, the emirs' summer palace. The courtyards here are particularly graceful: the first, the **Patio de la Acequia**, has gorgeous gardens and distant views of the Palacios Nazaríes, while in the second one, the **Patio de la Sultana**, the trunk of a 700-year-old cypress tree suggests the delicate shade that would once have graced the area. Beyond this courtyard, the **Escalera del Agua** is a delightful work of landscape engineering with water channels running down a shaded staircase.

Carmen de los Mártires GARDENS

(Map p264; ☎958 84 91 03; Paseo de los Mártires; ⏲10am-2pm & 6-8pm Mon-Fri, 10am-8pm Sat & Sun Apr-Oct, 10am-2pm & 4-6pm Mon-Fri, 10am-6pm Sat & Sun Nov-Mar) FREE A peaceful oasis on the hillside south of the Alhambra, these romantically dishevelled gardens sprawl around a restored 19th-century mansion, with uplifting views of the city and surrounding mountains. Over the years the site has hosted a prison, a chapel, a convent and more; today it's a great spot to escape the crowds.

Casa-Museo Manuel de Falla MUSEUM

(Map p259; ☎958 22 21 88; www.museomanueldefalla.com; Calle Antequeruela Alta; adult/reduced €3/1; ⏲10am-5pm Tue-Sat, to 3pm Sun Oct-May, 9am-2.30pm Tue-Sun Jun & Sep, 9am-2.30pm Wed-Sun Jul & Aug) Arguably Spain's greatest classical composer and an artistic friend of Lorca, Manuel de Falla (1876–1946) was born in Cádiz, but spent his key years in Granada until the civil war forced him into exile. Learn all about the man at the attractive Carmen del Ave María where he lived and composed; the sky-blue shutters were inspired by the Cádiz sea. Ring the bell to get in; visits are guided (Spanish, English, French).

Fundación Rodríguez-Acosta MUSEUM
(Map p259; ☎958 22 74 97; www.fundacionrodriguezacosta.com; Callejón Niño del Royo 8; tour adult/child €5/3, 2-5pm Sun free; ⏰10am-6.30pm Apr–mid-Oct, to 4.30pm mid-Oct–Mar) On the Realejo hill, the Carmen Blanco houses the Rodríguez-Acosta foundation in a building created in 1914 by the Granada-born modernist artist José María Rodríguez-Acosta (1878–1941). It's a whimsical place that borrows from several architectural genres including art deco, Nasrid, Greek and baroque. One-hour guided tours take you through the house's subterranean tunnels and a well-curated museum containing works by Francisco Pacheco, Alonso Cano and Francisco de Zurbarán.

Centro de la Memoria Sefardí MUSEUM
(Map p268; ☎610 060255; museosefardidegranada@gmail.com; Placeta Berrocal 5; tour €5; ⏰10am-2pm & 5-8pm Sun & Tue-Thu, 10am-2pm Fri Apr-Oct, 10am-2pm & 4-8pm Sun & Tue-Thu, 10am-2pm Fri Nov-Mar) Since being expelled en masse in 1492, there are very few Sephardic Jews left living in Granada. But this didn't stop one enterprising couple from opening a museum to their memory in 2013, the year the Spanish government began offering Spanish citizenship to any Sephardic Jew who could prove their Iberian ancestry. The owners also do Realejo tours on advance request.

Plaza Nueva & Around

Iglesia de Santa Ana CHURCH
(Map p268; Plaza Santa Ana; ⏰Mass 7pm Tue-Sat, 12.30pm & 7pm Sun Jun-Sep, 6pm Tue-Sat, 12.30pm & 6pm Sun Oct-May) Off the eastern corner of Plaza Nueva, Plaza Santa Ana is dominated by this 16th-century Mudéjar church whose bell tower incorporates the minaret of the mosque over which it stands; it was designed by Diego de Siloé. It's only open during Mass.

Hammam Al Ándalus HAMMAM
(Map p268; ☎958 22 99 78; www.granada.hammamalandalus.com; Calle Santa Ana 16; baths €38, with massage from €50; ⏰10am-midnight) With three pools of different temperatures, plus a steam room and the option of skin-scrubbing massages, this is the best of Granada's Moorish-style baths. Its dim, tiled rooms are suitably sybaritic and relaxing. Reservations required.

Albayzín

The Albayzín, Granada's old Muslim quarter, is sprawled over a hill facing the Alhambra. It's a fascinating, history-rich district of steep cobblestone streets, whitewashed *cármenes* and Alhambra views – you'll almost certainly get lost at some point. Bus C31 loops through the Albayzín in a circular route to/from Plaza Nueva, every eight to 15 minutes from 7am to 11pm (to 1am Friday and Saturday).

Mirador San Nicolás VIEWPOINT
(Map p264; Plaza de San Nicolás) For those classic sunset shots of the Alhambra sprawled along a wooded hilltop with the Sierra Nevada mountains looming in the background, wander up through the Albayzín to this well-known lookout (reached via Callejón de San Cecilio). Expect pastel-hued sunsets and crowds of camera-toting tourists, students and buskers; it's also a haunt of pickpockets and bag-snatchers, so keep your wits about you. Other fab viewpoints pop up across the surrounding streets.

Colegiata del Salvador CHURCH
(Map p264; ☎958 27 86 44; Plaza del Salvador; ⏰Mass 8pm Mon-Fri, 11.30am Sun Apr-Oct, 7pm Mon-Fri, noon Sat & Sun Nov-Mar) Dominating the Plaza del Salvador near the top of the Albayzín, the 16th-century Colegiata del Salvador rests on the site of the Albayzín's former mosque, the patio of which still survives, with its original *aljibe* (cistern) and horseshoe arches. It's only open during Mass.

Museo Arqueológico MUSEUM
(Map p264; ☎600 143141; www.museosdeandalucia.es; Carrera del Darro 43; EU/non-EU citizen free/€1.50; ⏰9am-8.45pm Tue-Sat, to 3pm Sun) Relaunched in 2018 after an eight-year restoration, Granada's archaeology museum is spread across the 16th-century Casa de Castril, with its elaborate Renaissance facade. The small, thoughtfully presented collection (in Spanish and English) shows off 120 pieces unearthed in Granada province, from the Palaeolithic to late-Moorish times. The star is the 1.4-million-year-old Orce tooth (p291) – Europe's most ancient human remain. Other finds include a 4th-century-BCE alabaster urn from Almuñécar, a 15th-century marquetry casket and a 1481 Granada-made Moorish astrolabe.

Baños Árabes El Bañuelo ARCHITECTURE
(Map p264; Carrera del Darro 31; €5, Sun free; 9.30am-2.30pm & 5-8.30pm May–mid-Sep, 10am-5pm mid-Sep–Apr) Sitting by the Río Darro, this well-preserved Moorish bathhouse dates to the 11th or 12th century. Light beams into its vaulted brick rooms through octagonal star-shaped shafts, illuminating columns, capitals and marble-tiled floors. The ticket includes entrance to the Palacio de Dar-al-Horra.

Casa-Museo Max Moreau MUSEUM
(Carmen de los Geranios; Map p264; 958 29 33 10; Camino Nuevo de San Nicolás 12; 10.30am-1.30pm & 6-8pm Tue-Sat) FREE Get a rare (and free) glimpse of one of Granada's secret *cármenes* (p272) at the former home of 20th-century Belgian portrait painter and composer Max Léon Moreau. His attractive house, dotted with terraces and gardens, has been converted into a museum displaying his former living quarters and study, along with a gallery showcasing his finest portraits.

Palacio de Dar-al-Horra PALACE
(Map p264; 671 563553; Callejón de las Monjas; €5, Sun free; 9.30am-2.30pm & 5-8.30pm May–mid-Sep, 10am-5pm mid-Sep–Apr) Up high in the Albayzín – down a lane off Placeta de San Miguel Bajo and Callejón del Gallo – this 15th-century Nasrid palace was the home of sultana Aixa, the mother of Boabdil, Granada's last Muslim ruler. It's surprisingly intimate, with rooms set around a central courtyard and fabulous views across the surrounding neighbourhood and over to the Alhambra. After the Reconquista, it was incorporated into the adjacent Monasterio de Santa Isabel la Real. Admission includes entry to the El Bañuelo Moorish baths.

Centro

★**Capilla Real** HISTORIC BUILDING
(Map p268; 958 22 78 48; www.capillarealgranada.com; Calle Oficios; adult/child €5/free; 10.15am-6.30pm Mon-Sat, 11am-6pm Sun) The Royal Chapel is the last resting place of Spain's Reyes Católicos, Isabel I de Castilla (1451–1504) and

LORCA'S LEGACY

Spain's greatest poet and playwright, Federico García Lorca (1898–1936) epitomised many of Andalucía's potent hallmarks – passion, ambiguity, exuberance and innovation. Born in Fuente Vaqueros, 17km northwest of Granada, he won international acclaim in 1928 with *El romancero gitano* (Gypsy Ballads), a collection of verses on Roma themes, full of startling metaphors yet crafted with the simplicity of a flamenco song. Between 1933 and 1936 he wrote the three tragic plays for which he's best known: *Bodas de sangre* (Blood Wedding), *Yerma* (Barren) and *La casa de Bernarda Alba* (The House of Bernarda Alba) – brooding, dramatic works dealing with themes of entrapment and liberation. In 1922 Lorca helped organise Granada's flamenco-reviving Concurso de Cante Jondo (p347) as part of the local El Rinconcillo group of poets, writers and musicians.

Lorca was killed at the start of the civil war in August 1936. It's generally held that he was executed by military authorities loyal to Franco for his perceived left-wing political views and his homosexuality. Despite ongoing searches, his remains have never been found.

Near the cathedral, the **Centro Federico García Lorca** (Map p268; 958 27 40 62; www.centrofedericogarcialorca.es; Plaza de la Romanilla; 10am-2pm & 5-9pm Tue-Sat mid-Mar–mid-Sep, 10am-2pm & 4-8pm Tue-Sat mid-Sep–mid-Mar, 11am-2pm Sun year-round) FREE houses the Lorca foundation, with exhibitions and cultural events. Lorca's early-20th-century summer house, the **Huerta de San Vicente** (958 84 91 12; www.huertadesanvicente.com; Calle Virgen Blanca; adult/child €3/1, Tue free; 9am-3pm Tue-Sun Jun–mid-Sep, 9.30am-5pm Tue-Sun mid-Sep–May), sits amid the modern Parque Federico García Lorca, 1.5km west of the centre; visits are by 30-minute guided tour, in Spanish or English.

In Fuente Vaqueros, the **Museo Casa Natal Federico García Lorca** (958 51 64 53; www.patronatogarcialorca.org; Calle Poeta Federico García Lorca 4; adult/child €3/1.50, Wed free; tours hourly 10am-1pm Tue-Sat year-round, 4-5pm Oct-Mar, 5-6pm Apr-Jun) displays photos, posters and costumes for the writer's plays; visits are by guided tour in Spanish. Famous Granada street artist El Niño de las Pinturas (p273) adorned its facade with a vibrant mural in early 2020. **Ureña** (953 22 01 71; www.urena.es) has buses to Fuente Vaqueros (€2, 25 minutes, hourly to two-hourly) from Avenida de Andalucía, 1.5km southwest of Granada bus station.

Central Granada

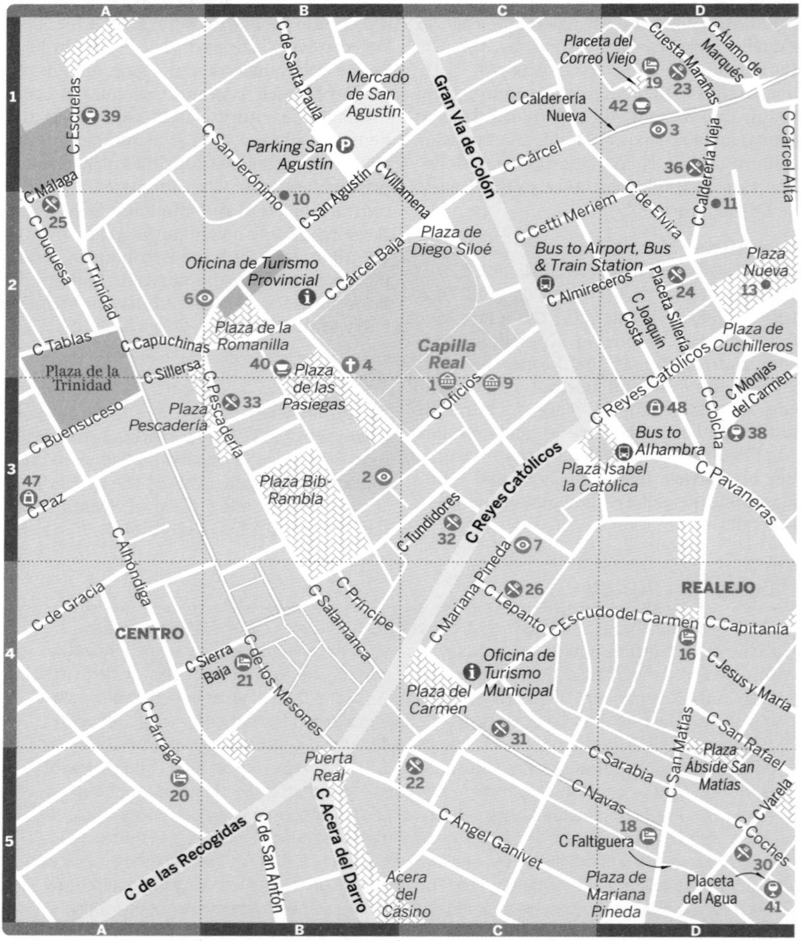

Fernando II de Aragón (1452–1516), who commissioned the elaborate Isabelline-Gothic-style mausoleum that was to house them. Commenced in 1505, it wasn't completed until 1517, hence the royals' interment in the Alhambra's Convento de San Francisco (p258) until 1521. Their monumental marble tombs (and those of their heirs) lie behind a 1520 gilded wrought-iron screen by Bartolomé de Jaén.

The tombs are just for show, however, as the monarchs actually lie in simple lead coffins in the crypt beneath the chancel. Also here are the coffins of Isabel and Fernando's unfortunate daughter, Juana la Loca (Juana the Mad); her husband Felipe el Hermoso (Philip the Handsome); and Miguel, Prince of Asturias, who died as a boy.

The sacristy contains a small but impressive museum, with Fernando's sword and Isabel's silver sceptre, crown and personal art collection, which is mainly Flemish but also includes Botticelli's *Prayer in the Garden*. Felipe Vigarny's two early-16th-century wood-carved statues of the Catholic Monarchs at prayer are also here. Audio guides included.

Catedral de Granada CATHEDRAL
(Map p268; ☎958 22 29 59; www.catedraldegranada.com; Plaza de las Pasiegas; adult/child €5/free;

⌚10am-6.30pm Mon-Sat, 3-5.45pm Sun) From street level, it's difficult to appreciate the immensity of Granada's cavernous, boxed-in cathedral. But it's nonetheless a monumental work of architecture, and one of Spain's largest cathedrals. Built atop Granada's former mosque, it was originally intended to be Gothic, but over the two centuries of its construction (1523–1704) it underwent major modifications. Most notably, architect Diego de Siloé changed its layout to a Renaissance style, and Alonso Cano added a magnificent 17th-century baroque facade.

Cano was also responsible for two wooden busts of Adam and Eve in the Capilla Mayor (main chapel), which sit above small praying statues of the Reyes Católicos, who rest in the adjacent Capilla Real (p267). The cathedral's interior is vast with 20 huge white piers rising from a black-and-white tiled floor to a ceiling capped by a 30m-high dome.

Palacio de la Madraza HISTORIC BUILDING
(Map p268; ☎676 385600; Calle Oficios; tour €2; ⌚10.30am-7.45pm) Easily recognisable by the trompe l'oeil on its facade, La Madraza was founded in 1349 by Yusuf I as a school and university – and still belongs to Granada University. Since extensive renovations in the early 2010s, you can wander in to view its interesting, and sometimes contradictory, mix of Moorish, Mudéjar and baroque architecture. Highlights include an elaborate *mihrab* (prayer niche), a baroque dome and some coloured stucco. Student guides lead 15-minute tours in multiple languages.

Alcaicería STREET
(Map p268; off Calle Oficios) This skinny street lined with gaudy souvenir shops is all that's left of what was once Granada's great bazaar (the Alcaicería), a claustrophobic warren of alleyways packed with stalls selling silks, spices and much more. The original bazaar was destroyed by fire in the 19th century and rebuilt in a much reduced form.

Corral del Carbón COURTYARD
(Map p268; Calle Mariana Pineda; ⌚9am-8pm) FREE Just east of Calle Reyes Católicos, an elaborate horseshoe arch leads through to the 14th-century Corral del Carbón, a cobbled, much-restored courtyard with a well and surrounded by two storeys of brick galleries. Initially, this was a Nasrid-era corn exchange, but in subsequent centuries it was used as an inn for coal dealers (hence its name, Coal Yard) and later as a theatre.

Outside the Centre

★**Basílica San Juan de Dios** BASILICA
(Map p264; ☎958 27 57 00; www.basilicasanjuandedios.es; Calle San Juan de Dios 19; adult/child €5/free; ⌚10am-8pm Mon-Sat, 2-8pm Sun Jun-Sep, to 7pm Oct-May) Built between 1737 and 1759, this spectacular basilica unveils a blinding display of opulent baroque decor. Barely an inch of its interior lacks embellishment, most of it in gleaming gold and silver. Frescoes by Diego Sánchez Sarabia and Italian artists Corrado Giaquinto and Tomás Ferrer adorn the ceilings and side chapels, while up above the basilica's dome soars to

Central Granada

50m. The highlight, however, is the extraordinary gold altarpiece in the Capilla Mayor. Audio guides bring the details to life.

Monasterio de San Jerónimo MONASTERY
(Map p264; ☎958 27 93 37; Calle Rector López Argüeta 9; €4; ⏲10am-1.30pm & 4-7.30pm Apr-Oct, 10am-1.30pm & 3-6.30pm Nov-Mar) With Gothic cloisters, fragrant orange trees and a lavishly decorated interior, this 16th-century monastery is one of Granada's most stunning Catholic buildings. Behind a plateresque entrance by Diego de Siloé, the church mixes late-Gothic and Renaissance styling, and reveals a profusion of painted sculptures and vivid colours, most spectacularly on the apse's immense eight-level gilt retable.

Gonzalo Fernández de Córdoba, the Reyes Católicos' military man known as El Gran Capitán, is entombed in the church.

Courses

Escuela Delengua LANGUAGE
(Map p268; ☎958 20 45 35; www.delengua.es; Calle Caldereria Vieja 20; single private class €31, 2-week course from €275) This Spanish-language school in the heart of the Albayzín runs a range of courses, individual lessons and extracurricular activities, including guided tours, tapas nights and visits to traditional craft-workers. It's also actively involved in the local community and supports young non-Spanish-speaking immigrants in Granada.

Tours

Spain Food Sherpas FOOD
(☎644 329806; www.spainfoodsherpas.com; tour/cooking class €69/71) Join a local gastronomy expert for a fabulous small-group wander off the usual trail. The spotlight is on Granada's glorious produce, speciality dishes and intriguing backstory: you might taste mango-infused *salmorejo* (chilled soup), zesty *remojón* (cod, orange and olive salad) or *jamón* (ham) croquettes, with Alpujarras wines (and vegetarian/vegan options). Also does wine tastings, paella classes and more.

Granada Tapas Tours FOOD
(☎619 444984; www.granadatapastours.com; tours per person €40) Engaging guides lead small-group food tours (in Spanish, English, French, Italian or German) delving into Granada's gastronomic history and specialities, with plenty of extra recommendations, as well as walks through the Albayzín and craft-beer jaunts. Routes can cater for vegan, vegetarian and gluten-free diets.

Walk in Granada WALKING
(Map p268; ☎630 070893; www.walkingranada.com; Plaza Nueva) This energetic operation runs three pay-what-you-like tours: the central-Granada sights at 11am daily, and thoughtful afternoon walks around the Sacromonte or the Albayzín. Other fixed-price options include Lorca-themed walks and adapted itineraries for wheelchair users.

Cicerone CULTURAL
(Map p268; ☎607 691676, 958 56 18 10; www.ciceronegranada.com; Calle San Jerónimo 10; group tours from €23) Offers a range of private and small-group walking tours, as well as thematic itineraries and guided Alhambra visits.

Festivals & Events

Semana Santa RELIGIOUS
(Mar/Apr) The two most striking events in Granada's Holy Week are Los Gitanos (Wednesday), when members of the *fraternidad* (brotherhood) parade to the Abadía del Sacromonte (p278), and El Silencio (Thursday), when the street lights are turned off for a silent candlelit march.

Feria del Corpus Christi RELIGIOUS
(May/Jun) The most spectacular of Andalucía's Corpus Christi celebrations, this is Granada's big annual party. Held approximately 60 days after Easter, it involves a week of dancing (including flamenco), parades and processions. Bullfighting is also part of it – but there is growing opposition from animal rights activists (p349).

Festival Internacional de Música y Danza MUSIC, DANCE
(www.granadafestival.org; Jun & Jul) For three weeks in June and July, first-class classical and modern performances are staged at the Alhambra and other historical sites.

Sleeping

Granada's accommodation scene is a delight, with everything from excellent hostels to centuries-old mansions to flashy five-stars. Some of the prettiest lodgings are in the sloping Albayzín, though many aren't accessible by vehicle; the Realejo has some characterful picks too. The few hotels near the Alhambra are scenic but a hassle for sightseeing elsewhere. Rates are highest in spring and autumn, spiking over Easter.

Alhambra & Realejo

Gar-Anat BOUTIQUE HOTEL €€
(Map p268; ☎958 22 55 28; www.hotelgaranat.com; Placeta de los Peregrinos 1; d €88-190;) Gleaming, literary-themed boutique style runs through this sharply repurposed 16th-century house (later a pilgrims' hostel), set around a courtyard where a metallic wishing tree awaits. The 15 contemporary-design rooms (some with hot tubs) are inspired by greats in music and literature; there's even one with Alhambra glimpses. Breakfast (€9.50) happens in the 17th-century *aljibe*.

Hotel Palacio de Los Navas HERITAGE HOTEL €€
(Map p268; ☎958 21 57 60; www.hotelpalaciodelosnavas.com; Calle Navas 1; incl breakfast s €72-150, d €85-195;) A glassed-in atrium, terracotta-tiled floors and smooth cream styling set the tone at this gorgeously revamped 16th-century building, strung around a classic columned patio just off a busy tapas street. The 19 rooms have wrought-iron bedheads and an instantly soothing feel; those on the top floor are attic-style with sloping wood-beamed ceilings. Staff are charmingly helpful and there's complimentary *merienda* (afternoon tea).

★**Carmen de la Alcubilla del Caracol** B&B €€€
(Map p259; ☎958 21 55 51; www.alcubilladelcaracol.com; Calle Aire Alta 12; r €149-185; closed mid-Jul–Aug; P) A painstakingly restored traditional 1880s *cármen* (p272), this much-sought-after, utterly charming hideaway sits on the Alhambra's southern slopes, in the upper Realejo. Homey decor, antiques and seven quietly refined rooms washed in pale pastels are complemented by the warm welcome from knowledgeable host Manuel. Outside, bask in fabulous views from the spectacular terraced gardens of palms, bougainvillea and citrus trees.

Parador de Granada HERITAGE HOTEL €€€
(Map p259; ☎958 22 14 40; www.parador.es; Calle Real de la Alhambra; r €225-420; P)

Few Andalucian moments rival waking up within the walls of the dazzling Alhambra (p258). Granada's luxurious *parador* (state-run-hotel) is housed in a 15th-century convent (also a former Moorish palace), in which you can still see 14th-century tilework and the Reyes Católicos' original tombs, but rooms are smartly updated in creams, greys or silvers. It's mega-popular (obviously), as is the modern-Andalucian **restaurant** (mains €15-25; ⏲1-4pm & 8-11pm; 🖉).

Albayzín

Oasis Backpackers Hostel HOSTEL €
(Map p268; ☎958 21 58 48; www.oasisbackpackershostels.com; Placeta Correo Viejo 3; dm €16-23, d €70; ❄📶) Bohemian Oasis is one of Granada's original, most successful hostels (now also in Seville and Málaga), occupying a historical building with tiled floors and a central patio, just off Calle de Elvira. Dorms (mixed or women-only) sleep four to 10, with individual plugs, lights and lockers; some have balconies. Perks include a well-equipped kitchen, group excursions and a roof terrace.

White Nest HOSTEL €
(Map p264; ☎958 99 47 14; www.nesthostelsgranada.com; Calle Santísimo 4; dm €11-20, d €80; ❄📶) A beautiful old building graced by a pillared patio, marble floors, wood-carved doors and dangling textiles has been reimagined as a colourfully contemporary budget bolthole at the foot of the Albayzín. Dorms (including one women-only) have personal lights, lockers and plugs. It's a welcoming, popular place, and the lively social scene runs from free Sacromonte tours to mojito nights.

GRANADA'S CÁRMENES

Granada's *cármenes* (from the Arabic *karm* for 'vine') are quiet, private houses, many of them adapted from Moorish homes post-Reconquista, with high walls that conceal beautiful terraced gardens of fruit trees, vines, fountains and scented flowers. The Albayzín, with its awe-inspiring Alhambra views, has the richest concentration of *cármenes*.

Most remain true to their original concept – private and hidden – though a few are open to visitors, including the gardens of the Carmen de los Mártires (p265) opposite the Alhambra. A handful have been converted into museums, such as the Fundación Rodríguez-Acosta (p266), while others, like the Realejo's Carmen de la Alcubilla del Caracol (p271), have been reborn as intimate hotels.

El Ladrón del Agua BOUTIQUE HOTEL €€
(Map p268; ☎958 21 50 40; www.ladrondeagua.com; Carrera del Darro 13; r €111-200; ❄📶) A sensitively restored 16th-century mansion overlooking the Río Darro, in the lower Albayzín, family-run El Ladrón centres on a marble-clad patio with a fountain and original pillars. A creative theme fills the 15 tastefully updated rooms, which are named for poems by Juan Ramón Jiménez and decorated with lovely tiling and antique desks. Breakfasts are served in the arched *aljibe*.

Casa del Capitel Nazarí HERITAGE HOTEL €€
(Map p268; ☎958 21 52 60; www.hotelcasacapitel.com; Cuesta Aceituneros 6; s €71-90, d €89-161; ❄📶) Another slice of Albayzín magic in a 1503 Renaissance palace that's as much architectural history lesson as three-star hotel. The sound of trickling water follows you through columned courtyards to 18 traditional, low-ceilinged rooms clad in tiles, bricks, beams, murals and *artesonado* (ceiling of interlaced beams with decorative insertions), and there's free tea, coffee and cakes mid-afternoon. Just off Plaza Nueva at the foot of the Albayzín.

★ **Casa Morisca** HERITAGE HOTEL €€€
(Map p264; ☎958 22 11 00; www.hotelcasamorisca.com; Cuesta de la Victoria 9; d €131-231; ❄📶) Live like a Nasrid emir at Granada's original boutique hotel, an exquisite late-15th-century mansion in the lower Albayzín lovingly restored by architect owners. Atmosphere and history are laid on thick in the form of timber-beamed ceilings, brick columns, original stuccowork and an enchanting turquoise-tiled courtyard. Of the 14 intimate, attractive and individually decorated rooms, the best have Alhambra views.

★ **Hotel Casa 1800 Granada** BOUTIQUE HOTEL €€€
(Map p268; ☎958 21 07 00; www.hotelcasa1800.com; Calle Benalúa 11; r €148-210, ste €229-350; ❄📶) Hidden in a venerable 16th-century building, the Casa de los Migueletes, this elegant 25-room boutique property charms with its delightful old-world-inspired decor: beds with gilded headboards, coffered ceilings, exposed-stone walls, original *artesonado*, a lovely courtyard overlooked

DON'T MISS

GRANADA STREET ART: EL NIÑO DE LAS PINTURAS

While the UK has Banksy, Granada has El Niño de las Pinturas (real name Raúl Ruíz), a street artist whose creative graffiti have become a defining symbol of the city. Larger-than-life, lucid and thought-provoking, El Niño's murals, many of which are dotted around the Realejo, often juxtapose vivid close-ups of human faces with short poetic stanzas in highly stylised lettering. Over the last two decades, El Niño has become a famous underground personality in Granada. Although he risks criticism and occasional fines for his work, most *granadinos* agree that his art brings creative colour and a contemporary edge to the streets of their ancient city. Seek out El Niño's work at vegan restaurant Hicuri and bar Candela (p277) opposite; at his old home at Calle de Molinos 44; on the wall beside the Hotel Molinos; and, as of early 2020, on the facade of Federico García Lorca's birthplace in Fuente Vaqueros (p267), 17km northwest of Granada.

by wood-balustraded balconies. Service is warm and efficient, and complimentary *merienda* appears each afternoon.

Santa Isabel la Real HERITAGE HOTEL €€€
(Map p264; ☎958 29 46 58; www.hotelsantaisabellareal.com; Calle de Santa Isabel la Real 19; r €115-210; ❄📶) Up in the Albayzín, this welcoming small hotel occupies a whitewashed 16th-century home that was once a *casa de vecinos* (house lived in by different families). Many original architectural features endure, from marble columns to flagstone floors to the fountain-studded patio. Each of the 11 rooms is adorned with embroidered pictures and handwoven rugs.

Centro

Eco Hostel HOSTEL €
(Map p264; ☎958 29 29 24; www.ecohostel.es; Gran Vía de Colón 53; dm/d from €17/50; 📶) Inhabiting a gracefully restored 1920s Gran Vía building, this minimal-chic hostel is a maze of tiled floors, open-brick walls, bright murals and upcycled furnishings, with a vegan cafe, a shared kitchen and no single-use plastics. Dorms of four or six (including a women-only) have personal lockers, lights and plugs; family rooms sleep up to four. The helpful team organises free walking tours, yoga, paella dinners, club nights and more.

Párragasiete BOUTIQUE HOTEL €€
(Map p268; ☎958 26 42 27; www.hotelparragasiete.com; Calle Párraga 7; s €45-65, d €70-115; ❄📶) With its blonde-wood floors, smart furniture and clean modern lines, this warmly styled hotel feels more Scandinavia than southern Spain. But Granada pops up in wall sketches of local monuments, a glassed-in interior patio, and a sleek downstairs bar-restaurant, Vitola – popular with *granadinos* and ideal for breakfast or tapas.

Room Mate Leo HOTEL €€
(Map p268; ☎958 53 55 79; www.room-matehotels.com; Calle de los Mesones 15; r €71-145; ❄📶) Granada's outpost of the popular, youthful and ecosensitive Room Mate chain opens through a jazzy lobby filled with crimson sofas and splashes of sparkle. Stylish yet unfussy rooms (some with terraces) channel a fun, colourful design, with lots of gold, black and antique-inspired flourishes. Great value in a super-central shopping area, just steps from Plaza Bib-Rambla.

AC Palacio de Santa Paula HERITAGE HOTEL €€€
(Map p264; ☎958 80 57 40; www.marriott.co.uk; Gran Vía de Colón 31; s €140-200, d €193-300; P❄📶) The modern frontage of this super-central five-star gives no hint of what lies behind. A cobbled cloister (where you can sip a Granada *vino*) forms the elegant centrepiece of what was once a 16th-century convent but is now a luxe, glossy hotel with subtly stylish rooms, a contemporary-Andalucian restaurant, a gym, a sauna and a Turkish bath.

Eating

Eating out in Granada is all about the joys of tapas, traditional Andalucian fare and, increasingly, contemporary creativity, with fresh ingredients from across the province starring on most menus. Moroccan cuisine is another speciality, particularly in the Albayzín. Granada is also one of Spain's most vegetarian- and vegan-friendly cities.

Alhambra & Realejo

Hicuri Art Restaurant VEGAN €
(Map p268; ☎858 98 74 73; www.restaurantehicuriartvegan.com; Plaza de los Girones 3; mains

WORTH A TRIP

CORTIJO DEL MARQUÉS

Hidden in a sea of olive groves, gorgeous **Cortijo del Marqués** (958 34 00 77; www.cortijodelmarques.com; Albolote; r incl breakfast €129-189; mid-Mar–early Nov; P), dating to the 16th century, has been beautifully restored by welcoming Dutch-Austrian owners and makes for a fabulous escape. The main building is strung around a cobbled patio, the pool gazes out on rolling hills, and the 15 individually styled rooms blend country elegance with original features. It's 25km north of Granada (4km off the A44).

€7.50-10, menú del día €14; noon-11pm Mon-Sat;) Granada's leading street artist, El Niño de las Pinturas (p273), has been let loose inside Hicuri, creating a psychedelic backdrop to the wonderful vegan food and organic wines served at this easy-going, hugely popular restaurant. Zingy salads, creative veggie burgers and curried seitan sit alongside plant-based renditions of Andalucian faves, like shiitake croquettes or *pisto* (ratatouille) with *patatas a lo pobre* (poor man's potatoes).

Papaupa TAPAS €

(Map p268; 958 99 18 44; www.facebook.com/papauparetrofusionfood; Calle de los Molinos 16; raciones €7-12, 3-course menú del día €9.95; 1-4pm & 8pm-midnight Mon, 12.30-4pm & 8pm-midnight Wed, 12.30pm-midnight Thu-Sun;) With brick arches, a marble-top bar and a subtle bohemian edge, this Realejo hideaway specialises in self-styled 'retro-fusion food'. Inventive dishes marry Spanish, Latin American and Asian flavours – yuca croquettes, tuna tacos, *arepas* (corn-based round bread) – and pair well with a glass of vermouth or, perhaps, *manzanilla* (sherry from Sanlúcar de Barrameda).

El Piano VEGAN €

(Map p268; 858 81 56 40; www.facebook.com/elpiano.granada; Calle Santiago 2; 4-dish plate €11.95; noon-11.30pm;) Punchy world-wandering dishes like coconut dhal accompany plant-based twists on Andalucian classics such as tortilla, *arroces* (rice dishes) and *albóndigas* (meatballs) at this cheery, good-value vegan and gluten-free deli-restaurant. Mango-yellow walls, Mexican place mats and ceramic plates add colour. Also hosts yoga classes.

★ **Picoteca 3Maneras** ANDALUCIAN €€

(Map p268; 958 22 68 18; www.facebook.com/picoteca3maneras; Calle Santa Escolástica 19; mains €12-17; 1-4.30pm & 8pm-midnight Tue-Sat, 1-4.30pm Sun;) Glorious fresh produce, spot-on service, chic whitewashed decor, excellent Spanish wines and a deliciously creative approach to local cuisine make Picoteca a Realejo gem. South American and various Asian flavours infuse ambitiously reimagined dishes such as pork-and-wild-mushroom risotto, pear-and-pancetta gnocchi, and tuna in orange sauce; every Sunday there's a special *arroz*.

La Botillería SPANISH €€

(Map p268; 958 22 49 28; www.labotilleriagranada.es; Calle Varela 10; mains €10-20; 12.30pm-midnight) La Botillería continues to get rave local reviews thanks to its imaginatively presented food, thoughtful wine list and smart-casual modern design. Dine on starters of Cantabrian anchovies and Trevélez ham, followed by original mains such as *milhoja de presa ibérica* (millefeuille with pork and avocado).

Cisco y Tierra TAPAS €€

(Map p268; 694 504906; www.facebook.com/ciscoytierra1920; Calle Lepanto 3; raciones €8-18, mains €12-19; 1pm-midnight Thu-Tue, 1-4pm & 8pm-midnight Wed) Beamed ceilings, a marble bar and barrels of homemade vermouth grace the spruced-up 1920s interior of this tiny tapas bar. Seasonal produce fuels the menu, which marries traditional recipes with contemporary creativity in elegantly prepped plates like octopus parmentier and Iberian-pork *pluma* in mushroom sauce, but also stars classic cheese and meat boards.

Los Diamantes TAPAS €€

(Map p268; 958 227 070; www.barlosdiamantes.com; Calle Navas 26; raciones €10-14; 12.15-5.30pm & 7.15pm-midnight) A Granada institution, going strong since 1942, this scruffy, always-busy joint is one of the best tapas hang-outs on bar-packed Calle Navas. It's standing room only, but the seafood – fried squid, grilled prawns, *boquerones* (anchovies) – is excellent and there's a sociable scene. Branches around town, including on Plaza Nueva.

Damasqueros ANDALUCIAN €€€

(Map p268; 958 21 05 50; www.damasqueros.com; Calle Damasqueros 3; tasting menu €40, with wine €59-89; 1-3.30pm & 8.30-10.30pm Mon-Sat, 1-3.30pm Sun;) *Granadina* chef Lola

Marín, who trained at some of Spain's top restaurants, unveils her gourmet, market-based cuisine in a tucked-away, white-tablecloth corner of the Realejo. Granada-rooted tasting menus change weekly, with seasonal ingredients taking centre stage, paired with wines from across the province and beyond.

Plaza Nueva & Around

Bodegas Castañeda TAPAS €

(Map p268; ☎958 21 54 64; www.facebook.com/BodegasCastaNeda; Calle Almireceros 1; tapas €2-6; ⊙11.30am-1am Mon-Thu, to 2am Fri-Sat) At this traditional, forever-popular tapas bar, crowds of hungry punters jostle for food under hanging hams. Don't expect any experimental nonsense here: just classic tapas and *raciones* (full servings of tapas items) of paella, tortilla, bean stew, *ibérico* ham, Andalucian cheeses and more, all served lightning-fast, with vermouth, sherries and wines poured from big wall-mounted casks.

Albayzín

Café 4 Gatos CAFE €

(Map p264; ☎958 22 48 57; www.cafe4gatos.com; Placeta Cruz Verde 6; breakfasts €2-7; ⊙8.30am-4pm Mon, Tue & Thu, to 8pm Wed & Fri, 9am-8pm Sat, 9am-4pm Sun, closed Aug) A buzzy box-sized cafe, with terrace tables and old black-and-white Granada photos, 4 Gatos has a friendly neighbourhood vibe and terrific Granada-style breakfasts. Gracing the menu are artisan jams, homemade cakes, and enormous organic *tostadas* topped with Manchego cheese, *escalivada* (smoky grilled vegetables) or other goodies, as well as local wines and craft beers.

Casa Torcuato ANDALUCIAN €

(☎958 28 81 48; www.casatorcuato.com; Calle Pagés 31; raciones €4-15; ⊙noon-10.30pm Mon, to 6pm Tue, to midnight Sat, to 5pm Sun, 9am-10.30pm Thu, to midnight Fri) Crowds spill out into a pretty plaza from a blue-and-white-tiled interior at long-running, fourth-generation Casa Torcuato in the upper Albayzín. Delectable, smartly traditional tapas swing from fresh gazpacho and aubergines with honey to succulent seafood including grilled prawns, squid and *boquerones*. The *arroz* tapa is famous, while wines include Granada picks.

Arrayanes MOROCCAN €€

(Map p268; ☎958 22 84 01, 619 076862; www.rest-arrayanes.com; Cuesta Marañas 7; mains €10-17; ⊙1.30-4.30pm & 7.30-11.30pm Wed-Sun, closed mid-Jan–mid-Feb;) Granada hosts some excellent Moroccan kitchens, especially in the Albayzín, and long-established Arrayanes is one of its best. Tinkling fountains, ceramic tiles and ornate arches set the stage for superb North African staples, from *bisara* split-pea soup to steaming tagines and flaky *pastelas* (savoury pies). No alcohol, but the mint lemonade is perfect.

Samarkanda LEBANESE €€

(Map p268; ☎958 21 00 04; www.facebook.com/RestauranteLibanesSamarkanda; Calle Calderería Vieja 3; mains €8-16; ⊙1-4.30pm & 7.30-11.30pm Thu-Tue;) Despite the rather tired decor, this friendly family-run Lebanese restaurant cooks up a tempting menu of traditional mainstays in the backstreets of the Albayzín. Kick off with hummus, *labneh* and falafel before digging into a bowl of *kafta* (ground beef baked and served with potatoes and a sesame sauce), steaming couscous, or rice with almonds and raisins.

Centro

Poë TAPAS €

(Map p264; ☎985 43 67 81; www.barpoe.com; Calle Verónica de la Magdalena 40; tapas €1.50, raciones €5; ⊙8pm-12.30am;) It might not look much from the outside, but 'El Poë' is a whole different world once you walk through the door. Students, *granadinos* and visitors mingle over globe-trotting tapas such as Brazilian *feijoada* (black bean and pork stew), chickpea salad, Portuguese-style cod and spicy-hot Thai chicken, courtesy of well-travelled owners Ana and Matt.

★ **El Bar de Fede** ANDALUCIAN €€

(Map p264; ☎958 28 88 14; www.facebook.com/ElbardeFede1; Calle Marqués de Falces 1; raciones €9-15; ⊙9am-2am Mon-Thu, to 3am Fri & Sat, 11am-2am Sun) 'Fede' refers to hometown poet Federico García Lorca, whose free, creative spirit seems to hang over this chicly styled, gay-friendly bar. Patterned wallpaper, stone arches and high tables set around a ceramic-tiled island create a casual feel, and the food is a joy. Standouts include aubergines drizzled with honey, chicken in orange sauce and perfect garlic-parsley squid.

Más Que Vinos TAPAS €€

(Map p268; ☎958 56 09 86; www.restaurantemasquevinos.es; Calle Tundidores 10; raciones €9-19; ⊙noon-5pm & 8pm-midnight Sun-Fri, noon-1am Sat;) Down an alley just off Plaza Bib-Rambla, the rustic-modern tavern Más

FREE TAPAS

Granada is one of the last bastions of the highly civilised practice of serving a free tapa with every drink. Place your drink order at the bar and a plate will magically appear with a generous portion of something delicious-looking on it. The process is repeated with every round you buy, and many places now let you pick your tapa and even do vegetarian options if you ask. Packed shoulder-to-shoulder with tapas institutions, Calle de Elvira and Calle Navas are popular central strips, but these days heavily touristed. You'll find many excellent spots sprinkled around west and south of the cathedral, in the Realejo and the Albayzín, and in outer *barrios* (districts).

Que Vinos puts the spotlight on Granada province's wonderful produce and up-and-coming wines. Fried aubergines are drizzled with Motril honey, chunky tortilla is filled with local potatoes, and other delights include garlic-fried squid, *payoyo* cheese from Cádiz and croquettes stuffed with cured ham.

Alameda ANDALUCIAN €€

(Map p268; 958 22 15 07; www.alameda.com.es; Calle Rector Morata 3; mains €12-25; noon-1am;) A glassed-in, split-level gastrobar and strong wine list sets the contemporary-cuisine tone at elegant Alameda, where traditional, seasonal Andalucian and Spanish flavours and ingredients are given a creative twist. Croquettes arrive stuffed with oxtail or wild mushroom, cod cheeks are cooked in *pil pil* sauce, and steaming *arroz* is laced with *pluma ibérica* (a fine pork loin cut).

Botánico MEDITERRANEAN €€

(Map p268; 958 27 15 98; www.botanicocafe.es; Calle Málaga 3; mains €11-19; 1pm-1am Mon-Thu, to 2am Fri & Sat, to 6pm Sun;) Casual restaurant at lunch, cafe at *merienda* time, and buzzing bar come evening, Botánico wears plenty of hats. Amid sleek orange-on-white decor, the fusion kitchen plates up Mediterranean dishes with hints of Asia and Latin America (lamb tagine, pumpkin tagliatelle, seitan or chicken fajitas), and does a market-fired weekday *menú del día* (daily set menu; €13).

Oliver SEAFOOD €€

(Map p268; 958 26 22 00; www.restauranteoliver.com; Plaza Pescadería 12; raciones €6-15, mains €11-22; 9am-4pm & 8pm-midnight Mon-Sat) One of the best of the seafood bar-restaurants that throng central Granada's Plaza Pescadería. Everyone from lunching professionals to curious visitors packs in to devour *raciones* of garlicky shrimps, grilled mushrooms, Galician-style octopus and fried seafood treats at the mobbed bar or terrace tables.

★**La Fábula Restaurante** GASTRONOMY €€€

(Map p264; 958 25 01 50; www.restaurantelafabula.com; Calle de San Antón 28, Hotel Villa Oniria; mains €23-30, tasting menus €80-125; 2-3.30pm & 8.30-10.30pm) A formal fine-dining restaurant set in a stylishly restored 1909 *palacete* (now the Hotel Villa Oniria), La Fábula is the domain of star chef Ismael Delgado López, whose artfully composed plates of contemporary-Spanish cuisine with strong, seasonal Granada flavours impress: fresh fish from Motril, *ibérico* pork cheeks, Riofrío caviar, smoked-cheese ravioli with garlic and honey. The terrace garden is lovely for a drink.

Drinking & Nightlife

Scruffy Calle de Elvira, Carrera del Darro at the base of the Albayzín, touristed Calle Navas, the area just off northern Gran Vía, and the streets of the Realejo are hotspots, but you'll find drinking dens all over the place.

Taberna La Tana WINE BAR

(Map p268; 958 22 52 48; www.facebook.com/TabernaLaTana; Placeta del Agua 3; 12.30-4pm & 8.30pm-midnight, closed Sat & Sun Jul & Aug) With bottles stacked to the rafters, hanging strings of garlic and a small wood-and-brick interior, friendly La Tana is one of Granada's greatest wine bars. It specialises in Spanish labels (over 400 of them!), backed up with some beautifully paired tapas. Ask about the wines of the month.

La Finca COFFEE

(Map p268; 658 852573; www.facebook.com/lafincacoffee; Calle Colegio Catalino 3; 9am-8pm Mon-Fri, from 10am Sat & Sun;) Bringing third-wave, Granada-roasted coffee to the city with astounding success, this small rustic-chic cafe sources its fair-trade speciality beans directly from growers. The expertly poured espresso goes perfectly with the fresh cakes, cookies and pastries, amid open-stone walls and dangling fairy lights.

Al Sur de Granada WINE BAR

(Map p264; 958 27 02 45; www.facebook.com/alsurdegranadagram; Calle de Elvira 150;

⏲9.30am-11.30pm Mon-Sat, from 10am Sun) Shelves laden with fragrant olive oils, coffee from roaster La Finca, organic produce and other Andalucian goodies tempt you through the door. Al Sur specialises in local natural wines, best enjoyed with a platter of artisanal cheese or *jamón* cured in the Sierra Nevada, or a tapa from the seasonal, daily changing menu. Wine-and-tapas-pairing sessions at 7pm (book ahead).

El Bar de Eric BAR
(Map p268; ☎958 27 63 01; www.facebook.com/elbardeeric; Calle Escuelas 8; ⏲8pm-2am Mon-Thu, 1pm-3am Fri-Sun) Strewn with old posters and framed photos of musical heroes, from Debbie Harry to Jim Morrison, this laid-back bar is the creation of Spanish drummer Eric Jiménez of indie rock band Los Planetas. Get into the swing with fusion tapas, and check online for upcoming gigs, tastings and theatre.

Casa de Vinos La Brujidera WINE BAR
(Map p268; ☎958 22 25 95; www.facebook.com/casadevinoslabrujidera; Calle Monjas del Carmen 2; ⏲1-4pm & 8.30pm-1am Sun-Thu, 1-5pm & 8.30pm-2am Fri & Sat) A cosy wood-panelled bar with hams in the window and an astonishing collection of wines (per glass €3 to €4) from all over Spain – everything from organic Granada reds and Jerez sherries to Galician *albariño* and Catalan Penedès chardonnay. Fuss-free tapas (€4 to €7) range from tortilla to goat's cheese with onion confit.

Candela BAR
(Map p268; ☎958 22 70 10; www.facebook.com/barelcandela; Calle Santa Escolástica 9; ⏲1-4pm & 8.30pm-1am) Murals by local street artist El Niño de las Pinturas (p273) adorn the walls and shutters at this lively, well-established neighbourhood bar in the lower Realejo, with low-key ambient beats and a steady supply of beer and tapas.

☆ Entertainment

★Peña La Platería FLAMENCO
(Map p264; ☎958 21 06 50, 603 473228; www.laplateria.org.es; Placeta de Toqueros 7) Founded in 1949, La Platería claims to be Spain's oldest flamenco club. Unlike some of Andalucía's more private clubs, it regularly opens its doors to non-members for soulful, foot-stomping performances on Thursday nights at 10pm, as well as on other sporadic occasions. Tapas and drinks are available. Book ahead!

Jardines de Zoraya FLAMENCO
(Map p264; ☎958 20 62 66; www.jardinesdezoraya.com; Calle Panaderos 32; show €20, with dinner from €49; ⏲shows 8pm & 10.30pm; 👪) Up in the Albayzín, this *cármen*-turned-restaurant appears, on first impression, to be a tourist-focused *tablao* (choreographed flamenco show). But reasonable entry prices, talented performers and a highly atmospheric patio, where Mediterranean meals are served (kids'

GRANADA'S TEAHOUSES

Granada's *teterías* (teahouses) have proliferated in recent years, but there's still something inviting about their dimly lit interiors, stuffed with lace veils, stucco and low cushioned seats. Most serve a long list of aromatic teas and infusions and Arabic sweets, and many still offer *cachimbas* (hookah pipes). Souk-like **Calle Caldereria Nueva** (Map p268) in the Albayzín is Granada's famous '*tetería* street'.

Abaco Té (Map p264; www.abacote.com; Calle Álamo de Marqués 5; ⏲3-9.30pm; 📶) Hidden up in the Albayzín, outrageously popular Abaco puts an arty contemporary spin on the traditional *tetería* (no hookahs). Choose from an encyclopaedic list of infusions (€2.50 to €4), fresh juices, excellent cakes and vegetarian snacks (crepes, salads, *montaditos* – mini open sandwiches). The roof terrace is irresistible.

Tetería Dar Ziryab (Map p268; ☎655 446775; Calle Caldereria Nueva 11; ⏲1pm-1am) Duck into the dimly lit interior, adorned with tiling, cushioned benches and Moorish latticework arches, to puff on a *cachimba* and drink herbal tea (€2.50 to €4) from ornately decorated glasses. One of Granada's original tearooms, it also occasionally hosts cultural events.

Tetería El Bañuelo (Map p264; Calle Bañuelo 5; ⏲11am-11pm) Just off Carrera del Darro, this minimalist *tetería* is loved by both *granadinos* and visitors for its tucked-away, vine-shaded roof terrace looking out on the Alhambra above. Rustle up a silver pot of steaming, fresh mint tea (€3 to €4), best with honey- or pistachio-infused Moroccan sweets.

menus available), make it a worthwhile stop for any aficionado.

Flamenco Los Olvidados FLAMENCO
(Map p268; ☎958 19 71 22; www.flamencolosolvidados.com; Cuesta de Santa Inés 6; adult/child €18/12; ⏱shows 8.15pm & 9.30pm) As the sun sets, the Albayzín's 16th-century Palacio de los Olvidados (also, inexplicably, a museum of Spanish Inquisition torture instruments) morphs into an intimate flamenco space, with quality performers stomping their stuff in the courtyard.

Casa del Arte Flamenco FLAMENCO
(Map p268; www.casadelarteflamenco.com; Cuesta de Gomérez 11; shows €20; ⏱shows 7.30pm & 9pm) A small flamenco venue that is neither a *tablao* nor a *peña* (private club), but something in between. The performers are invariably top-notch, managing to conjure a highly charged mood in the intimate space.

Eshavira JAZZ, FLAMENCO
(Map p264; ☎958 29 08 29; https://eshaviraclub.wordpress.com; Calle Póstigo de la Cuna 2; €6-18; ⏱10pm-6am) Just off Calle Azacayas, this is one of Granada's historic jazz and flamenco haunts, staging a regular program of gigs, jam sessions and flamenco performances; check the website for schedules.

La Tertulia LIVE PERFORMANCE
(Map p264; ☎674 037595; www.tertuliagranada.com; Calle Pintor López Mezquita 3; ⏱8pm-2am Tue & Thu, to 1am Wed, 7pm-2am Fri & Sat, to 11pm Sun) A *tertulia* is an artistic gathering, and that's what you generally get at this bohemian bar where the emphasis is on the stage – film screenings, poetry jams, book presentations and, every Tuesday, free tango sessions.

Shopping

Many shops in Granada play on the city's Moorish heritage: bags of spices, curly-toed slippers and handmade leather bags. A local craft speciality to look out for is *taracea* (marquetry), with shell, silver or mother-of-pearl inlay, applied to boxes, tables and more; just a few specialist workshops continue this intricate art that has flourished in Granada since around the 14th century.

★La Oliva FOOD & DRINKS
(Map p268; ☎650 182358, 958 22 57 54; www.laoliva.eu; Calle Virgen de Rosario 9; ⏱11am-2.30pm & 7-10pm Mon-Fri, 11am-2.30pm Sat) By day, La Oliva sells fine Spanish wines, high-end olive oils and other gourmet treats. By night, the tables come out and multilingual owner Francisco welcomes a handful of guests to dine on his €38.50 tasting menu (bookings essential; cash only).

La Cata Con Botas WINE
(Map p268; ☎958 37 27 37; www.lacataconbotas.com; Calle Paz 4; ⏱11am-2.15pm & 5-9pm Mon-Fri, 11am-2.15pm Sat Sep-Jul, 10.30am-2.30pm Mon-Fri Aug) Perfectly pairing with its clever name (a *vino*-themed pun on Puss in Boots), this bright wine specialist stocks almost exclu-

SACROMONTE

The Sacromonte, Granada's historical Roma neighbourhood, sits northeast of the neighbouring Albayzín (p266). Renowned for its flamenco traditions and cave-houses, it draws tourists to late-night shows and aficionados to music schools, yet still feels like the fringes of the city. Some of the caves dug out of its hillside date back to the 14th century, but many were devastated by floods in the early 1960s, after which some of the Sacromonte's Roma community were forced to relocate. The caves were then forgotten until the 1980s, when an international hippie crowd began to trickle in. Today around 500 people live here, including immigrants and Roma dancers and musicians.

Centred on the Camino del Sacromonte, the area unveils some of Granada's best views, particularly from the Vereda de Enmedio lookout and the San Miguel Alto chapel, which both overlook the Alhambra and Albayzín. At the **Museo Cuevas del Sacromonte** (Map p264; ☎958 21 51 20; www.sacromontegranada.com; Barranco de los Negros; €5; ⏱10am-8pm mid-Mar–mid-Oct, to 6pm mid-Oct–mid-Mar) you can see what a traditional cave-home once looked like, while at the hillside **Abadía del Sacromonte** (☎958 22 14 45; www.sacromonteabbey.com; Abadía del Sacromonte; adult/child €5/free; ⏱10.30am-5.30pm), towards the *barrio*'s eastern end, you can explore catacombs and underground cave-chapels. Several local companies run guided walks of the Sacromonte, such as the sensitive tours with Walk in Granada (p271).

WORTH A TRIP

MONTEFRÍO

Around 50km northwest of Granada, in a little-visited pocket of the province near the Córdoba and Jaén borders, Montefrío (pop 4073) is one of the region's most wonderfully scenic villages. Surrounded by softly rolling hills of olive trees, it makes a rewarding detour on the drive between Granada and Córdoba or Antequera, with whitewashed, tile-roofed homes cascading down the hillside from a cragtop castle.

Opposite the **tourist office** (958 33 60 04; www.montefrio.org; Plaza de España; 10am-2pm Mon-Fri, 10am-2pm & 4-6pm Sat & Sun) stands the imposing 18th-century neoclassical **Iglesia Mayor de la Encarnación** (Plaza de España; 10am-1.30pm Mon-Fri, 10am-1.30pm & 4-6pm Sat & Sun), whose striking circular form and 29.5m-high dome were inspired by Rome's Pantheon. From here, a steep 10-minute climb brings you to the hilltop **Fortaleza Árabe** (€2; 10.30am-2pm Tue-Fri, 10.30am-2pm & 4-6 Sat & Sun). All that remains of the original Nasrid fortress, built in 1382 (supposedly by the great architect behind the Alhambra), is its ruined defensive wall. Montefrío was taken by the Christians in 1486, and after the Reconquista the Reyes Católicos commissioned a looming church, the Iglesia de la Villa, within the castle complex; it combines Mudéjar, Renaissance and Gothic styles, and Diego de Siloé had a hand in its creation. The best views of Montefrío are from the **Mirador National Geographic**, 800m south of town on the A335.

sively drops from Granada province. Renowned local labels like Anchurón (p288), Pago de Almaraes and Cuatro Vientos (p288) grace the shelves.

Tienda Librería de la Alhambra BOOKS
(Map p268; 958 22 78 46; www.alhambratienda.es; Calle Reyes Católicos 40; 9.30am-8.30pm) A fabulous shop for Alhambra aficionados, with a great collection of books dedicated to the monument, its art and its history. You'll find everything from simple guidebooks to glossy coffee-table tomes on Islamic art, plus quality gifts including hand-painted fans, stylish stationery, Alhambra-scented candles and stunning photographic prints.

Artesanías González ARTS & CRAFTS
(Map p268; Cuesta de Gomérez 12; 11am-8pm) Specialising in the ancient art of *taracea* since 1920, this artisan shop is a great place to pick up a small piece of Granada: handcrafted inlaid boxes, coasters, chess sets and beautiful backgammon boards.

Gil de Avalle MUSIC
(Map p268; 625 619201; www.gildeavalle.com; Plaza del Realejo 15; 10am-1.30pm & 5-8pm Mon-Fri, 10.30am-1.30pm Sat) The workshop of master guitar-maker Daniel Gil de Avalle is a paradise for aficionados, with a range of exquisite handmade flamenco and classical guitars, as well as castanets and sheet music. It also offers guitar lessons (from €30).

Information

Oficina de Información Turística (Alhambra) (Map p259; 958 02 79 71; www.granadatur.com; Calle Real de la Alhambra; 7.30am-8.30pm May-Oct, to 6.30pm Nov-Apr)

Oficina de Turismo Municipal (Map p268; 958 24 82 80; www.granadatur.com; Plaza del Carmen 9; 9am-6pm Mon-Sat, to 2pm Sun) City information.

Oficina de Turismo Provincial (Map p268; 958 24 71 28; www.turgranada.es; Calle Cárcel Baja 3; 9am-8pm Mon-Fri Mar-Oct, to 7pm Nov-Feb, 10am-7pm Sat, 10am-3pm Sun year-round) For Granada province.

Oficina de Turismo Regional (Map p268; 958 57 52 02; www.andalucia.org; Calle Santa Ana 2; 9am-7.30pm Mon-Fri, 9.30am-3pm Sat & Sun) Covers the whole of Andalucía.

Getting There & Away

AIR

The **Aeropuerto Federico García Lorca Granada-Jaén** (913 211000; www.aena.es) is 17km west of Granada, just south of the A92. Flights connect with airports across Spain (including Madrid, Barcelona, Tenerife and Mallorca), as well as Berlin, Bordeaux, Milan, Naples, London Gatwick and Manchester. Airlines include easyJet, Vueling and Iberia.

BUS

Granada's **bus station** (Avenida Juan Pablo II) is 3km northwest of the city centre. **Alsa** (902 42 22 42; www.alsa.es) runs buses across the region, including to/from Las Alpujarras (p283), and has one to two daily direct connections to Madrid's Barajas airport (€47, 4¾ hours).

Alsa Buses from Granada

Destination	Cost (€)	Time	Frequency (daily)
Almuñécar	8.58	1¼-1¾hr	8-9
Córdoba	12-18	2¾-3¾hr	12-13
Guadix	5.65	45min	10-15
Jaén	9.13	1-1¼hr	15
Málaga	11-14	1½-1¾hr	24-25
Seville	23-30	3-4½hr	9

TRAIN

The train station is 1.5km northwest of the centre. A new high-speed line between Granada and Antequera was inaugurated in 2019, linking with the high-speed Madrid–Córdoba–Málaga AVE line.

Trains from Granada

Destination	Cost (€)	Time (hr)	Frequency (daily)
Algeciras	32	4¼-5	3
Almería	21	2½-3	4
Barcelona	36-75	6¼-7½	3
Córdoba	15-49	1¼-2	7-9
Madrid	37-81	3¼	3
Seville	29-62	2¼-4	9

Getting Around

TO/FROM THE AIRPORT

Alsa (p279) buses run from the airport to the city centre (€3, 20 to 40 minutes) at 6am and then roughly hourly between 9.20am and 10pm. They stop at various points, including **Gran Vía de Colón** (Map p268) near the cathedral. Returns are roughly timed with flights. Taxis to/from Granada centre cost around €25 to €30.

BICYCLE

Rent-a-Bici (www.rent-a-bici.com; 1- or 2-day hire €50)

BUS

One-way tickets (€1.40; €1.50 at night) can be bought on buses (cash only). Useful lines:

C30 Plaza Isabel II–Alhambra (via Realejo)
C31 Plaza Nueva–Albayzín
C34 Plaza Nueva–Sacromonte
4 Gran Vía–Train station
33 Gran Vía–Bus station

CAR & MOTORCYCLE

Driving in central Granada is frustrating and best avoided; central car parks cost €20 to €25 per night. Arrive by bus or train, or park on the outskirts and hop in by public transport.

METRO

Granada's **metro** (www.metropolitanogranada.es) runs between Albolote in the north and Armilla in the southwest. It serves 26 stations, running from 6.30am to 11pm Sunday to Thursday and to 2am on Friday and Saturday. Single tickets cost €1.35; one-day unlimited-travel tickets cost €4.50.

TAXI

Taxis (958 28 00 00; www.granadataxi.com) congregate in Plaza Nueva and at the train and bus stations.

SIERRA NEVADA

Providing Granada's dramatic backdrop, the wild snowcapped peaks of the Sierra Nevada range are home to the highest point in mainland Spain (Mulhacén, 3479m) and Europe's most southerly ski resort at Pradollano. The Sierra Nevada extends about 75km from west to east, with 15 peaks over 3000m. The lower southern reaches, peppered with bucolic white villages, are collectively known as Las Alpujarras.

Some 862 sq km are encompassed by the Parque Nacional Sierra Nevada, Spain's largest national park, designated in 1999. This vast protected area is home to 2100 of Spain's 7000 plant species, including unique types of crocus, narcissus, thistle, clover and poppy, as well as Andalucía's largest ibex population (around 15,000). Bordering the national park at lower altitudes is the 864-sq-km Parque Natural Sierra Nevada.

From July to early September, the higher mountains offer wonderful multiday trekking and day hikes. Outside of this period there's a risk of inclement weather, but the lower Alpujarras are always welcoming, and the ski scene swings into action from around November to April.

Pradollano

POP 233 / ELEV 2100M

The modern village of Pradollano is the gateway to Europe's most southerly ski resort. In summer, skiing gives way to mountain biking in the **Sierra Nevada Bike Park** (www.sierranevadabikepark.com; day pass €22; lifts

Sierra Nevada & Las Alpujarras

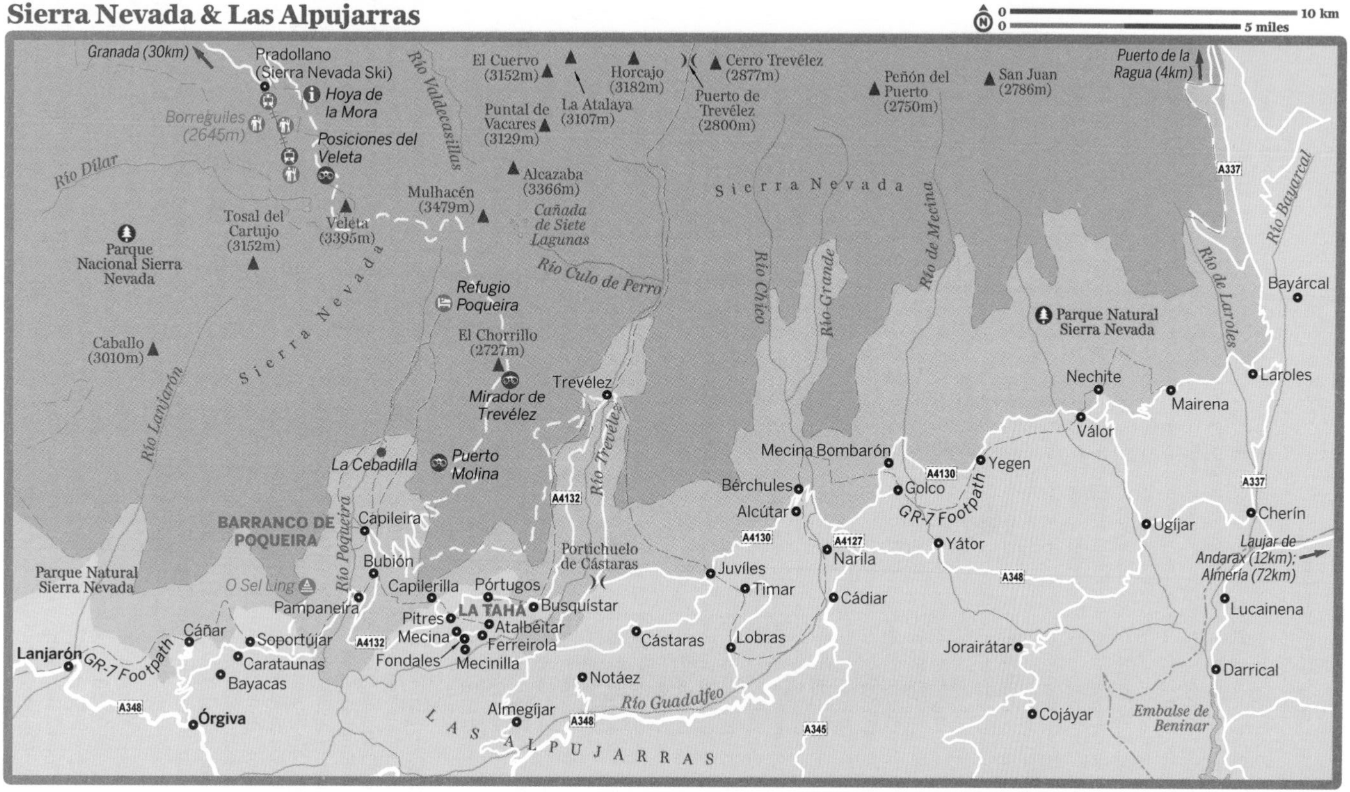

WORTH A TRIP

MULHACÉN & VELETA

Tempting thrill-seekers across Spain, the Sierra Nevada's two highest peaks – Veleta (3395m) and Mulhacén (3479m; the highest mountain in mainland Spain) – stand on the western end of the range. Both can be summited from a national park post at **Hoya de la Mora** (2512m) on the mountains' northern flank, accessible by road from Granada and the Pradollano ski resort, which is 3km away. For information and maps (p285), contact the **Centro de Visitantes El Dornajo** (☎958 34 06 25; www.juntadeandalucia.es; A395, Km 23; ⏲8am-3pm Wed-Sun mid-Jun–mid-Sep, 9am-3pm Wed-Fri, 10am-5pm Sat & Sun mid-Sep–mid-Jun), 23km southeast from Granada on the road to/from Pradollano.

The Hoya de la Mora post sits by the entrance to a mountain pass that runs over to the Alpujarras village of Capileira on the southern side. However, the top road is closed to private vehicles and the mountains' upper reaches can only be accessed by a national park shuttle bus that's operational between late June and October (snow permitting). It's always best to check availability and schedules for the shuttle buses ahead. Weather permitting, bicycles are permitted to use the top road freely.

To climb Mulhacén or Veleta from the north, the easiest approach is to take the **shuttle bus** (☎671 564407; www.reservatuvisita.es; one way/return €6/10; ⏲8am-6pm Jun-Oct) from the Albergue Universitario at Hoya de la Mora. This drops you at the Posiciones del Veleta (3100m), from where it's a 4km trek (1½ hours) to the top of Veleta or 14km (four to five hours) to the summit of Mulhacén.

To tackle Mulhacén from the south side, base yourself in Capileira (p286). From the village's Servicio de Interpretación de Altas Cumbres office (p286) you can catch a summer shuttle bus (one way/return €13/9) to the **Mirador de Trevélez** (2710m; also called El Chorrillo), from where it's around a three-hour hike to the summit (5.1km, 800m ascent). To make the trip into an overnight excursion, you can bunk down at the **Refugio Poqueira** (☎958 34 33 49; www.refugiopoqueira.com; adult/child €18/7), which has bunks and home-cooked meals at 2500m (cash only; book ahead by phone). From the Mirador de Trevélez, it's 3.3km to the *refugio*, then 4.4km to the top of Mulhacén (six to seven hours total). You can also summit Mulhacén on a demanding hike from the Alpujarras village of Trevélez (p287; 24km, 10 to 12 hours return).

The routes described here are suitable for walkers of good to moderate fitness. However, in winter they should only be attempted by experienced mountaineers or with a guide. Always check on weather forecasts beforehand and be prepared for changing conditions and possible high winds. Good sources of information include Sierra Nevada Guides (www.sierranevadaguides.co.uk), Nevadensis (p285) and Spanish Highs (p284), all of which also run guided hikes.

9.30am-6pm late Jun-early Sep), with 18.5km over four routes. It's about 30km southeast of Granada, along the A395.

From December to April, **Autocares Tocina** (☎958 46 50 22; www.autotransportetocina.es) has buses to Pradollano from Granada's bus station (€5, one hour) at 8am, 10am and 5pm (plus 3pm on weekends), returning at 9am, 4.30pm and 6.30pm (plus 1pm on weekends). Outside ski season there's one daily bus (9am from Granada, returning at 5pm). Taxis to/from Granada cost €60.

Sierra Nevada Ski SKIING
(☎958 70 80 90; www.sierranevada.es; ski pass adult €47-52, child €31-34; ⏲Nov-Apr) The southernmost ski resort in Europe is popular with day-trippers from Granada and beyond and gets supremely busy on winter weekends. It caters to all levels with 110km of pistes ranging from tough black descents to mild green runs, plus cross-country trails, many on the flanks of the mighty Veleta (3395m). Gear rental is available for around €25 per day.

LAS ALPUJARRAS

A 70km stretch of valleys and deep gorges extending across the southern flank of the Sierra Nevada, Las Alpujarras is famed for its picturesque white villages, which cling to the steep hillsides, their Berber-style flat-roofed houses recalling the region's past as a refuge for Moors escaping the Christian conquest of Granada. The Moorish influence lingers today in the local architecture, crafts and cuisine. Between the villages, terraced farmlands made fertile by snow-fed mountain waters sit amid woodlands and rocky, arid slopes, with well-trodden footpaths criss-crossing the hills for superlative hiking, and local wineries (p288) blossoming. These days, many villages host a mixed population of *alpujarreños* and expats.

Lanjarón

POP 3218 / ELEV 659M

The main gateway to the western Alpujarras, Lanjarón is an attractive, leafy mountain town best known for its therapeutic spa waters, which have long been a major source of income and still draw coach-loads of visitors. It also profits from its pure spring water, bottled and sold across Spain, and its air-cured *jamón serrano*. It's 45km south of Granada, along the A44 and A348.

Caballo Blanco HORSE RIDING

(☎627 794891; www.caballoblancotrekking.com; 2/4hr rides €40/70, full day incl picnic €95) This well-established outfit offers horse-riding lessons and treks into the surrounding hills and mountains, including multi-day trips; book ahead. English, Spanish, German and a little French are spoken. It's about 5km east of Lanjarón.

Arca de Noé SPANISH €€

(☎958 77 00 27; www.facebook.com/arcadenoe gustavorubio; Avenida de la Alpujarra 38; raciones €6-18; 10am-3.30pm & 6.30-10.30pm Mon-Sat, 10am-3pm Sun) The orderly rows of hanging hams and shelves laden with wine bottles, conserves and marinated goodies give the game away. This deli-eatery is the place to sample the celebrated local *jamón,* as well as a smorgasbord of regional delicacies: spicy sausages, goat's cheese and tomato salads.

Getting There & Away

Lanjarón has Alsa (p279) buses to/from Granada (€4.40, one to 1½ hours, six to nine daily), Málaga (€13, 4½ hours, one daily Monday to Saturday) and Motril (€4.13, 1¼ hours, two daily Monday to Friday, one Saturday).

Órgiva

POP 3589 / ELEV 450M

Surrounded by citrus and olive trees, Órgiva, the main town of the western Alpujarras, is a bit scruffier and considerably larger than neighbouring villages, with 68 different nationalities living here and a fertile hippie scene. The alternative lifestyle community of Beneficio sits in the woodlands north of town and its inhabitants regularly pop in to sell their wares at the Thursday market. British visitors might recognise Órgiva from Chris Stewart's best-selling book *Driving Over Lemons.*

Casa Rural Jazmín CASA RURAL €€

(☎621 223140; www.casaruraljazmin.com; Calle Ladera de la Ermita; d incl breakfast €53-70; P❄📶🏊) A warm welcome awaits at this peaceful sanctuary hidden behind a swirl of bougainvillea in the upper part of town. It's a cosy set-up with four colourful, homey rooms, each decorated in a different style and some larger than others. Outside, there's a tucked-away flower-filled garden where breakfast is served in summer and you can splash around in the pool.

LAS ALPUJARRAS BUSES TO/FROM GRANADA

DESTINATION	COST (€)	TIME (HR)	FREQUENCY (DAILY)
Bubión	6.26	2-2½	3
Cádiar	9	2¾	3
Capileira	6.30	2-3	3
Lanjarón	4.40	1-1½	6-9
Órgiva	5.26	1½-1¾	6-9
Pampaneira	6.22	1¾-2¼	3
Pitres	7	2¾-3¼	2
Trevélez	8.21	2¾-3¾	3
Válor	11	3½	2
Yegen	10	3½	2

DON'T MISS

WALKING IN LAS ALPUJARRAS

The alternating ridges and valleys of Las Alpujarras are criss-crossed by a network of mule paths, irrigation ditches and hiking routes, providing a near-infinite number of walks between villages or into the wild – all amounting to some of Andalucía's (and Spain's) outstanding hiking. The best months are April to mid-June and mid-September to early November, when temperatures are just right and the flora is at its most colourful.

The three villages in the Barranco del Poqueira – Pampaneira, Bubión and Capileira – are the most popular starting points, but even here, you'll pass few other hikers on the trail. Colour-coded routes, ranging from 4km to 23km (two to eight hours), run up and down the gorge, and you can also summit Mulhacén (p282) from Capileira as well as from Trevélez further east. Get maps and advice at long-running Nevadensis in Pampaneira or Sierra Nevada Outdoor in Órgiva; many local hotels provide their own maps with walk descriptions. Otherwise, handy maps showing most of the trails include those by Editorial Alpina and Discovery Walking Guides. Nevadensis also organises guided hikes, as do reputable **Spanish Highs** (www.spanishhighs.co.uk; guided day hike from €45 per person) and many Alpujarras hotels.

Of the long-distance footpaths that traverse Las Alpujarras, the GR7 (well signposted by red-and-white markers) follows the most scenic route – you can walk it from Lanjarón to Válor (80km) in around five days. Buses serve all these villages, allowing you to alternatively split it into shorter walks, such as the steep Bubión–Pitres section (4.5km, 1½ hours).

The 300km, relatively well signposted GR240 (known as the Sulayr) circuits the Sierra Nevada at a higher altitude than the GR7; it takes 15 to 19 days to walk in its entirety.

Tetería Baraka INTERNATIONAL €€
(☎958 78 58 94; www.teteria-baraka.com; Calle Estación 12; snacks €2-8, mains €5-14; ⏲10am-11pm; 📶✎) A laid-back local haunt, especially on market days, Baraka whips up zingy hummus, falafel wraps, tofu burgers, Moroccan tagines, tortilla omelettes and other delights, amid tiled tables and cosy corners. Teas are sweetened with Alpujarras honey and most ingredients are local and organic, including Órgiva olive oil, while home-baked treats spin from vegan brownies to Moroccan sweets.

Information

Sierra Nevada Outdoor (☎958 78 41 11; www.sierranevadaoutdoor.es; Avenida González Robles 14D; ⏲10am-2pm & 5-8pm Mon-Fri, 10am-2pm Sat) Helpful outdoor shop with maps, books and advice on hikes.

Barranco de Poqueira

The Barranco de Poqueira (Poqueira Gorge) is home to three of Las Alpujarras' most celebrated and most visited villages: Pampaneira, Bubión and Capileira, respectively 14km, 18km and 20km northeast of Órgiva along the A4132 and A4129. Seen from a distance they resemble flecks of white paint flicked Jackson Pollock–style on the vertiginous green landscape above the Río Poqueira. Up close, they're textbook models of the charming, steeply stacked white villages for which the Alpujarras are so famous, with their arches, irrigation channels and *tinaos* (passageways beneath houses).

The valley is also known for its handicrafts and you'll find shops selling leather goods, woven rugs and tilework (some still made according to age-old methods), as well as locally produced ham, jam, cheese, honey, mushrooms, grapes and more.

Paths fan out from all three villages, with many routes doable in a day. The 9km Sendero Pueblos de Poqueira runs up the gorge from Pampaneira to Capileira (around four hours) via Bubión.

Pampaneira

POP 275 / ELEV 1060M

The lowest of Barranco de Poqueira's three villages, Pampaneira is also one of the Alpujarras' most obviously tourist-driven. The snow-white centre, set around the Plaza de la Libertad and its 16th-century Mudéjar **church** (Plaza de la Libertad; ⏲10.30-11.30am), is packed with bars, restaurants and handicraft shops selling coarsely woven Alpujarran rugs. The GR7 hiking route passes through town.

Activities

★Nevadensis ADVENTURE SPORTS
(☎659 109662, 958 76 31 27; www.nevadensis.com; Plaza de la Libertad; ⏲10am-2pm Mar, Jul, Aug & Nov, 10am-2pm & 4-6pm Apr-Jun, Sep & Oct, 10am-2pm Fri-Sun Dec-Feb) The Alpujarras' most knowledgeable, all-encompassing outdoor adventure specialists have an office opposite the church on Pampaneira's main square, which also serves as a local tourist information hub. The professional guides offer expert advice and maps, plus a huge range of activities, from mountaineering courses, skiing classes, vie ferrate sessions and canyoning to guided hikes and 4x4 tours.

Sleeping & Eating

Estrella de las Nieves HOTEL €€
(☎958 76 39 81; www.estrelladelasnieves.com; Calle Huertos 21; s/d/ste €50/75/100; P 🛜 ≋) At the top of town, this dazzling-white complex offers elegant, understated modern rooms with local artwork, hydromassage showers or baths, and terraces overlooking the rooftops and mountains. Pleasant gardens, home-cooked mountain meals, a hillside pool, organic orchard, and terraces fresh with geraniums add to its charisma.

Bodega El Lagar ANDALUCIAN €
(☎673 636394; Calle Silencio; raciones €10; ⏲11am-5pm & 8pm-midnight) Hidden on a winding side street behind Plaza de la Libertad, this tiny bodega is one of Pampaneira's best spots to eat. Decked out with rough white walls, farm tools and wicker baskets, it cooks up huge helpings of reassuring farmhouse food, including char-grilled steaks, delicate almond soups and the *plato alpujarreño*, plus a €10 set lunch.

Casa Julio ANDALUCIAN €
(☎958 76 33 22; Avenida Alpujarra 9; mains €7-9; ⏲1-4.30pm & 8.30-11pm) Just above the main road and south of Pampaneira's church, rustic-style Casa Julio is a warm, family-owned favourite for lovingly prepared, home-cooked Alpujarras classics, from *patatas a lo pobre* and local ham to *migas alpujarreñas* (fried breadcrumbs with sausages and green pepper) and rabbit in almond sauce.

Shopping

Abuela Ili Chocolate CHOCOLATE
(☎958 56 57 84; www.abuelailichocolates.com; Plaza de la Libertad 1; ⏲9am-2pm & 3-6pm Mon-Fri, 9am-8pm Sat & Sun) With branches also in Capileira and Granada, this cosy shop has been making artisan chocolates since the 1990s. You'll find wacky flavours such as chocolate with goat's cheese or pepper, alongside the traditional stuff, and, in winter, delicious bites made with local oranges.

Bubión

POP 279 / ELEVATION 1350M

The smallest and quietest of the Barranco del Poqueira villages, Bubión is an impossibly picturesque spot with Moorish backstreets, whitewashed arches, flat-roofed houses, and a 16th-century Mudéjar **church** (Plaza Doctor Pérez Ramón; ⏲noon-1pm) built on the site of an old mosque. The GR7 cross-continental footpath bisects the village.

Hilacar ArtesAna WORKSHOP
(☎658 106576; www.jarapahilacar.com; Calle Carretera 29; ⏲11am-7pm Thu-Tue, hours vary) FREE At the top of town, this is the Alpujarras' only remaining artisan workshop of *jarapas*, those colourful rugs you'll spot all over the Poqueira villages. You can see the 200-year-old loom in action, buy handmade *jarapas* (from €45) or even make your own in a two-hour workshop (enquire ahead).

Teide ANDALUCIAN €
(☎958 76 30 37; www.restauranteteide.com; Calle Carretera 1; mains €6-17; ⏲1-4pm & 7.30-10.30pm Wed-Mon, closed 2 weeks Feb) With shaded outdoor tables and a large wood-beamed dining hall, long-running roadside Teide serves up generous, home-cooked *alpujarreño* dishes, such as goat with garlic and almonds, roast leg of lamb, trout with *patatas a lo pobre*, and local *jamón*.

SIERRA NEVADA & LAS ALPUJARRAS MAPS

The best maps for the Sierra Nevada and Las Alpujarras are Editorial Alpina's *Sierra Nevada, La Alpujarra* (1:40,000) and Editorial Penibética's *Sierra Nevada* (1:40,000). Both come with booklets describing walking, cycling and skiing routes, and are available at the Centro de Visitantes El Dornajo (p282) near Pradollano. *Walking and Trekking in the Sierra Nevada* (Cicerone; 2017) by Richard Hartley is a great resource, as is the Discovery Walking Guides map/booklet.

DON'T MISS

L'ATELIER

Set in a traditional 350-year-old house in the hamlet of Mecina Fondales, 4km south of Pitres, long-established, candlelit **L'Atelier** (958 85 75 01; www.facebook.com/latelierveg restaurant; Calle Alberca 21, Mecina; mains €11-14; 1-4pm & 7.30-10pm;) is worth the trip, unveiling a feast of globetrotting vegetarian and plant-based dishes: spiced couscous, hummus shawarma, wild-mushroom risotto, coconut tofu curry. Book ahead, particularly outside summer. Local produce fuels the kitchen, and the French owners also run cooking courses on request.

L'Atelier doubles as a fuss-free B&B (d incl breakfast €56;), with a couple of cheerful, homey rooms.

Capileira

POP 550 / ELEV 1436M

Overlooked by a lily-white 18th-century church, Capileira is the highest, largest and prettiest village in the Barranco de Poqueira (and Las Alpujarras' most touristed). It also has the valley's best restaurants, accommodation and leather goods, and is a departure point for high-altitude hikes up and around Mulhacén (p282).

Sights & Activities

A popular walk, signposted from the top of town, is the PRA69 loop to the abandoned hamlet of La Cebadilla (7.1km, 3½ hours).

Casa-Museo Pedro Antonio de Alarcón MUSEUM
(958 76 30 51; Calle Mentidero; €1; 11am-2pm Sat & Sun) An ancient village home with a modest exhibition on local farming and living utensils, and the life and work of the Guadix-born novelist Pedro Antonio de Alarcón, whose 1872 book *La Alpujarra* detailed his travels in the region.

Sleeping & Eating

★**Hotel Real de Poqueira** HOTEL €€
(958 76 39 02; www.hotelespoqueira.es; Plaza Panteón Viejo; s €50, d €55-95; mid-Feb–mid-Jan;) Occupying a typical old house opposite Capileira's church, this terrific three-star is the pick of several village accommodations run by the same welcoming family. Rooms are elegantly minimalist and modern, with smart bathrooms and shimmery bedding, and there's a small pool, garden bar and a restaurant.

El Corral del Castaño ANDALUCIAN €€
(958 763 414; Plaza del Calvario 16; mains €8-23; 1-4pm & 8-10pm Thu-Tue;) Enjoy a lovely plaza setting and excellent Andalucian cooking with creative, international influences at this welcoming village restaurant. The menu roams from traditional Alpujarras classics like the meaty *plato alpujarreño* to inventive numbers such as Moroccan-style veg-stuffed *pastela* or pork cheeks in red wine, plus home-baked pizzas and desserts.

Taberna Restaurante La Tapa ANDALUCIAN, MOROCCAN €€
(618 307030; Calle Cubo 6; mains €8-18; noon-4pm & 8pm-midnight;) The distinctive flavours of the Alpujarras' culinary micro-region are skilfully melded with the area's Moorish past at pint-sized La Tapa, snugly ensconced in a classic whitewashed house. With locally sourced ingredients and pops of flavours like almond, plum and rosemary, dishes might include *raciones* of mountain cheeses, chorizo and ham, organic gazpacho and the signature couscous and casseroles.

Shopping

J Brown FASHION & ACCESSORIES
(958 76 30 92; tallerbrown@gmail.com; Calle Doctor Castilla 7; 10am-2pm & 5-8pm) Don't miss J Brown's excellent leatherwork, including bags, belts and Western-style hats, all handcrafted by artisan José Manuel Moreno and family. Bank on at least €70 for a bag and €40-plus for hats.

Information

Servicio de Interpretación de Altas Cumbres (SIAC, High Summits Interpretation Service; 671 564406; www.reservatuvisita.es; Carretera de Sierra Nevada, Capileira; 10am-2pm & 5-8pm approx Easter-early Dec) Next to the bus stop in Capileira. Information about the national park and Las Alpujarras in general, plus national park summer minibus services (p282) up into the high Sierra Nevada.

La Tahá

POP 653

In La Tahá, the beautiful valley immediately east of the Barranco del Poqueira, life slows and the number of tourists drops noticeably.

The area, still known by the Arabic term *taha* for the administrative districts into which the Nasrid emirate of Granada divided the Alpujarras, consists of Pitres (6.5km east of Pampaneira on the A4132) and its outlying villages – Mecina, Capilerilla, Mecinilla, Ferreirola, Fondales and Atalbéitar.

Ancient paths (usually labelled 'Sendero Local Pitres–Ferreirola') link the hamlets, wending their way through woods and orchards, while the tinkle of running water provides the soundtrack. About 1.5km below Mecina Fondales (a 20-minute walk), a Moorish-era bridge spans the deep gorge of the Río Trevélez. The GR142 runs through the bottom of the valley, and there's a clutch of lovely places to stay and eat.

Sierra y Mar B&B €
(958 76 61 71; www.sierraymar.com; Calle Albaicín 3, Ferreirola; s/d/tr incl breakfast €42/69/90; Feb-Nov;) With eight rooms across several houses around a lush terraced garden, this *casa rural* complex has been welcoming guests to the soothingly quiet hamlet of Ferreirola, 4km southeast of Pitres, since 1985. Behind a sky-blue door, whitewashed walls, rustic decor, scattered terraces and uplifting mountain views combine to make a wonderfully relaxing base, with a kitchen, library and fire.

★ **Casa Ana** B&B €€
(678 298497; www.casa-ana.com; Calle Artesa 7-9, Ferreirola; incl breakfast s €55-70, d €95; Mar-Dec;) A beautifully restored 400-year-old house in tiny Ferreirola, 4km southeast of Pitres, Casa Ana has just 10 rustic-chic rooms (handmade tiles, chestnut beams, rain showers) set around gardens of lavender and wisteria. Writing, painting, yoga and other creative retreats are the speciality. British owner Anne organises walking holidays with author Chris Stewart.

Hotel Fuente Capilerilla HOTEL €€
(686 888076; www.fuentecapilerilla.com; Calle Fuente Escarda 5, Capilerilla; r €63-140; Feb–mid-Dec;) Total tranquillity, mountain views and 12 smartly rustic rooms (some with terraces) await at this Spanish-Belgian-owned hideaway in Capilerilla, La Tahá's highest hamlet at 1350m. Massages, steam baths, a sparkling pool, guided hikes and wellness retreats add to the appeal, and breakfast (€5 to €12), tapas and dinners are available. It's 1.5km up a steep road from Pitres.

Trevélez

POP 724 / ELEV 1476M

To gastronomes, Trevélez is celebrated for its *jamón serrano,* one of Spain's finest cured hams, which matures perfectly in the crisp, rarefied mountain air. To hikers it's a spaghetti junction of hiking paths and the gateway to high mountain trails, including one of the main routes up Mulhacén (p282), mainland Spain's highest peak. To statisticians it's the second-highest village in Spain after Valdelinares in Aragón.

Sited 10km north of Busquístar on the almost treeless slopes of the Barranco de Trevélez, the village is divided into three *barrios*: the *alto* (high) part, which is older and more labyrinthine, and commands the best views; the *medio* (middle) part; and the *bajo* (low) part, with the bulk of tourist facilities.

Activities

Trevélez is the starting point for a challenging 24km (return) ascent of Mulhacén via Siete Lagunas, possible in around 10 to 12 hours round trip if you're mega-fit (elevation gain is over 1900m); you can descend via the Mirador de Trevélez to make a circuit. An easier hike follows the Trevélez river valley from the top of town to just below El Horcajo pasture (around 14km, 4½ to five hours), and the GR7 passes through town.

Sleeping & Eating

Hotel La Fragua II HOTEL €€
(958 85 86 26; www.hotellafragua.com; Calle Posadas; d/tr/q €76/95/125; Mar-Dec;) With a smart alpine look, a white-and-stone exterior, potted flowers, and 10 spacious, sun-filled rooms (with kettles and balconies), La Fragua II makes a cosy upper-Trevélez base. Outside, you can revel in mountain views by the pool. It's something of a mini-chain, along with a snug attached *alpujarreño* **restaurant** (958 85 85 73; mains €9-14; 12.30-4pm & 8-10.30pm Mar-Dec;) and the more modest **Hotel La Fragua I** (Calle San Antonio 4; s/d €38/55; Mar-Dec;).

Mesón Joaquín ANDALUCIAN €€
(958 85 85 14; www.jamonestrevelez.com; Carretera A4132, Km 22; mains €8-20; 12.30-4.30pm Mar-Dec) No prizes for spotting the star ingredient at this casual restaurant at the village's southern entrance: scores of cured hams hang from the ceiling in the

arch-filled, ceramic-tiled interior. Expertly prepared plates of thinly sliced *jamón*, oil-dressed tomatoes or Trevélez trout showcase all-local ingredients.

Shopping

Jamones Cano González FOOD
(958 85 86 32; www.jamonescanogonzalez.com; Calle Pista del Barrio Medio 18; 10am-2pm & 5-7pm Mon-Fri, 11am-2pm & 4-8pm Sat, 11am-2pm Sun) Load up on Trevélez *jamón* at this shop bursting with cured meats, local cheeses, organic olive oil and Alpujarras wines.

Eastern Alpujarras

The eastern reaches of Granada's Alpujarras reveal a harsher, barer, more open landscape. The small villages here – Bérchules, Cádiar, Mecina Bombarón, Yegen, Válor, Mairena – provide oases of greenery, but for the most part this is tough, isolated mountain country, with Ugíjar its main town. Significantly fewer visitors make it this far, and those who do are often on long, solitary hiking expeditions – the long-distance GR7 path traverses the area.

Cádiar

POP 1183 / ELEV 950M

Cádiar is one of the bigger Alpujarras villages, down in the lowlands by the Río Guadalfeo, 8km south of Bérchules on the A348. The town celebrates its four-day early-October **feria** (Plaza de la Iglesia) by opening the taps on its Fuente del Vino (Wine Fountain). Ceramics and esparto-grass craft pieces are local specialities, and the GR7 and GR142 pass through town.

★ **Alquería de Morayma** HOTEL €€
(958 34 32 21, 605 051841; www.alqueriamorayma.com; Carretera A348, Km 50; s €52, d €70-78, 4-person apt €120; P) On a 40-hectare estate of organic vineyards, fruit trees and woodland, this comfortably rustic farmstead makes a gorgeous rural retreat. Wood-beamed ceilings, stone-flagged floors and colour-painted arches adorn the all-different rooms and apartments (some in outlying buildings). Own-label wines (p288) and olive oil feature in the wonderful season-inspired **restaurant** (raciones €8-12, mains €11-16; 8.30-11am, 1.30-4.30pm & 7.30-11pm;), and there's a library plus hikes from the doorstep. It's 2km south of Cádiar.

GRANADA WINES

Though wine has been produced across Granada for centuries, it was, until fairly recently, typically for personal consumption. But with the establishment of the Vinos de Granada Denominación de Origen Protegida (DOP; Denomination of Origin; www.dopvinosdegranada.es) in 2018, Granada wines are having something of a renaissance. The two main wine-growing areas are Guadix and El Altiplano, where vines grow at up to 1500m and produce deliciously rich reds, and the Contraviesa–Alpujarras area (between the Mediterranean and the Sierra Nevada), whose high-altitude grapes yield reds, whites and rosés. Many bodegas now welcome visitors.

Alquería de Morayma (p288) Just south of Cádiar, this enchanting, eco-aware estate makes its own organic reds and whites, which you can sample in the excellent restaurant.

Dominio Buenavista (Vinos Veleta; 958 76 72 54; www.vinosveleta.com; Ugíjar; tours €12; 11am-2pm & 5-8pm) Produces some of the Alpujarras' best wines, inspired by California's Napa Valley, along with delicious olive oil. Call ahead for a tour and tasting. It's just east of Ugíjar, 7km southeast of Válor.

Bodega Cuatro Vientos (616 407250; www.bodegacuatrovientos.es; Murtas; tours €12; 10am-6pm Sat & Sun) The winery behind the Alpujarras' smooth Malafollá reds, with its own restaurant; book ahead. It's about 18km southeast of Cádiar.

Bodega Anchurón (958 27 77 64; www.anchuron.es; Darro; tour €12) A family-owned operation powered by renewable energy, Anchurón specialises in single-origin wines (mostly rich reds) grown at 1000m. Book for tastings and tours. It's 23km northwest of Guadix.

Yegen

POP 396 / ELEV 1000M

The tranquil whitewashed village of Yegen is best known as the home of British writer Gerald Brenan, a peripheral Bloomsbury Group member whose *South from Granada* depicted life here in the 1920s. A plaque marks Brenan's former house, just off the plaza below the main road, and you can explore Yegen's dramatically eroded landscape on the 1.9km **Sendero Gerald Brenan trail**. Yegen is 6km east of Mecina Bombarón.

Espacio Brenan MUSEUM
(Carretera A4130) FREE On the main road, the old Fonda de Manuel Juliana is where Gerald Brenan stayed upon first arriving in Yegen in the 1920s. It's now a small, fascinating museum filled with photos of village life between the 1950s and 1990s by Danish photographer Vagn Hansen (Juan El Dinamarca). No official opening hours; if next-door bar El Tinao is open, pop in for a coffee and ask for the key.

El Rincón de Yegen ANDALUCIAN €€
(642 890243; www.elrincondeyegen.com; Calle de las Eras 2; mains €8-20; 9am-midnight Wed-Mon, closed 2 weeks Jan;) On the northern edge of the village, this cosy country restaurant centres on a wood-beamed dining room with tables around a stone fireplace. Dishes reflect the setting, featuring local specialities such as the meaty *plato alpujarreño* alongside vegetarian specials.

El Rincón also has colourfully styled, balcony-equipped rooms (double €45) and two-floor apartments for four to six people (from €63), all with a communal pool.

Válor

POP 507 / ELEV 900M

A typical Alpujarras village with a 16th-century Mudéjar church, Válor has an important history. It was the birthplace of Aben Humeya, a *morisco* who led a 1568 rebellion against Felipe II's repressive policies banning Arabic names, dress and even language. Two years of guerrilla mountain warfare ended only after Don Juan of Austria, Felipe's half-brother, was brought in to quash the insurrection and Aben Humeya was assassinated by his cousin Aben Aboo. The historical clash is celebrated with a well-known autumn festival, **Moros y Cristianos** (Moors and Christians; 12-15 Sep). It's 6km northeast of Yegen and on the GR7 route.

Balcón de Válor APARTMENT €
(958 85 18 21; www.balcondevalor.com; 4-person casita €100-130; P) Designed like a traditional Alpujarras *finca* (rural estate), with flat roofs, wood beams, beautiful hand-painted tiles and a big shared pool, this cluster of pristine, modern-rustic, one- to four-bedroom *casitas* (cottages) enjoys sprawling views across Válor and the mountains. It's a welcoming, self-catering family operation. The owners also run the simple nearby **Hostal Las Perdices** (958 85 18 21; www.hlasperdices.com; Carretera A4130; r €48;).

Restaurante Aben Humeya ANDALUCIAN €
(958 85 18 10; Calle Los Bolos; raciones €8-15; 10am-late) Sample Válor specials like goat's cheese, olive oil and partridge at this cosy bar-restaurant downhill from the main road. Seasonal treats might include local mushrooms or scrambled asparagus, while regional staples range from *conejo al ajillo* (rabbit in a garlic sauce) and delicate croquettes to enormous salads and *bocadillos* (filled rolls) stuffed with tortilla or *jamón*.

Mairena

POP 157 / ELEV 1082M

Even in this silent mountain country, tiny Mairena feels remote. One of four villages in the Nevada municipality, it sits 7km east of Válor off the main A4130, basking in soul-stirring views and a timeless sense of calm, and overlooked by a 16th-century church.

★**Las Chimeneas** CASA RURAL €€
(659 137461, 958 76 00 89; www.laschimeneas.com; Calle Amargura 6; d incl breakfast €90; closed Christmas & Jan;) A solar-powered 800-year-old village house, this rustic-chic bolthole makes a dreamy walking base. The nine rooms exude character with antiques, timber beams, grey-blue shutters and some of the Alpujarras' best views, while the outstanding **restaurant** (3-course dinner €25; 7.30-11pm;) serves Andalucian specialities made with organic homegrown vegetables and local produce and wines. British owners David and Emma are a mine of information.

Winery visits, hiking holidays and yoga, cooking and baking retreats are also hosted.

Getting There & Away

Alsa (p279) buses go to Almería (€8.41, 3½ hours) via Válor at 7.50am on Monday, returning at 2.30pm. For Granada, go to Válor.

LA VEGA & EL ALTIPLANO

Surrounding Granada is a swath of fertile land known as La Vega, a patchwork of woods, shimmering poplar groves and cultivated farmlands. Northeast of the city, the landscape becomes increasingly hilly and arid until it tops out in a sparsely populated highland plain, El Altiplano, well known for its palaeontological riches. This vast tract of barren semidesert is a hauntingly scenic place, made all the more dramatic by the mighty Sierra Nevada peaks looming on its southern horizon; much of it is protected within the 4722-sq-km Unesco **Geoparque de Granada**. The A92 runs from near Granada through the Parque Natural Sierra de Huétor to Guadix, a handsome town famed for its cave houses. Continuing northeast brings you to Baza, Orce and the Altiplano proper.

Guadix

POP 16,400

A lively provincial town, Guadix (gwah-deeks) is best known for its cave dwellings, many of which are still lived in by local townsfolk. Often (undeservedly) overlooked by visitors, the town is also graced by a handsome historic core centred on an imposing cathedral, and has some excellent tapas bars. The surrounding geopark is a Mars-like semi-desert landscape, dotted with a few walking trails and wineries (p288). Guadix is 50km northeast of Granada, near the northern foothills of the Sierra Nevada.

Sights

Guadix' old quarter is an attractive place with its impressive cathedral, 11th-century **Alcazaba** (Calle Barradas 3), late-16th-century Renaissance **Plaza de la Constitución** and distinctive sandstone architecture.

Catedral de Guadix CATHEDRAL
(958 66 51 08; www.catedraldeguadix.es; Paseo de la Catedral; adult/child €6/4.50; 10.30am-2pm & 5-7.30pm Jun-Sep, hours vary rest of year) Its flamboyant sandstone exterior set against the rich blue sky, Guadix' cathedral was built between the 16th and 18th centuries on the site of the former main mosque, and mixes Gothic, Renaissance and baroque styles. You can climb the tower for terrific views, including of the excavated 1st-century Roman theatre nearby. Tickets include multi-language audio guides detailing highlights such as the beautifully carved walnut-wood choir stalls and a collection of books from the 15th to 18th centuries.

Barrio de las Cuevas ARCHITECTURE
Around 2000 dwellings are burrowed into the rocky terrain of Guadix' main cave district, 1.2km south of the centre – a weird, other-worldly place where stumpy chimneys, antennae, white walls and doors emerge from undulating yellow-brown hillocks. The oldest caves are thought to have been inhabited since early Moorish times, though most date from the 15th or 16th centuries.

The **Centro de Interpretación Cuevas de Guadix** (958 66 55 69; Plaza del Padre Poveda; €2.60; 10am-2pm & 4-6pm Mon-Fri, 10am-2pm Sat) has displays on cave-house life in a sprawling, eight-room cave-house dating back 300 to 400 years; the whitewashed church opposite conceals a **cave-chapel** (hours vary).

Castillo de La Calahorra CASTLE
(667 038523, 958 67 70 98; www.lacalahorra.es; La Calahorra; 10am-1pm & 4-6pm Wed) FREE This forbidding castle guards the northern Sierra Nevada from a hilltop looming over the sleepy village of La Calahorra, 16km southeast of Guadix. Built between 1509 and 1512, on the ruins of a Moorish fortress, its four cylindrical towers and blank outer wall enclose a lavish Renaissance interior, with an elegant courtyard and a staircase of Italian Carrara marble. Visits are by 30-minute guided tour (in Spanish and, sometimes, English).

Sleeping & Eating

YIT Abentofail BOUTIQUE HOTEL €€
(958 66 92 81; www.hotelabentofail.com; Calle Abentofail; s €41-57, d €49-97; P ❄) Boutique style at bargain prices, just off Plaza de la Constitución, makes this characterful and friendly hideaway the best deal in town. Contemporary-design rooms beneath beamed ceilings are set around a columned patio. Breakfast (€5) is served in the attached **Taberna El Búho** (mains €12 to €18).

★ **La Bodeguilla** TAPAS €
(Calle Doctor Pulido 4; tapas €1-4; 9am-3.30pm & 6.30pm-late) No frills, precious few tables: this old-school hang-out just off the main Avenida Medina Olmos is one of Guadix' best and oldest tapas bars (since 1904).

WORTH A TRIP

ORCE & EL HOMBRE DE ORCE

A dusty outpost on Granada's parched Altiplano, Orce (population 1020) owes its place on the map to the remarkable local palaeontological finds – digs in several hamlets here have unearthed evidence of human activity dating back almost 1.5 million years, as well as bones from long-extinct local fauna that once included mammoths and sabre-toothed tigers.

In 1982 Catalan palaeontologist Josep Gibert made international headlines when he announced he had unearthed a human skull fragment at Venta Micena. He put its age at between 0.9 and 1.6 million years old, making it potentially the oldest such fragment ever discovered in Europe. However, subsequent studies threw doubt on his claims, holding that the fragment was more likely from a horse or donkey – turning the Orce Man into the Orce Donkey. Gibert died in 2007, but the debate rages on. Archaeologists made a second major find in 2002 at Barranco León: a 10-year-old child's milk tooth dated at 1.4 million years old, the oldest human remain ever found in Europe. Orce's modern **Centro de Interpretación Primeros Pobladores de Europa 'Josep Gibert'** (958 74 61 71; Camino de San Simón; €2; 11am-2pm Tue-Thu & Sun, 11am-2pm & 4-6pm Fri & Sat) displays the area's finds.

Orce is 90km northeast of Guadix off the A92. Alsa (p279) runs a daily bus to/from Granada (€13, three hours) and one to three daily buses to/from Baza (€3.02, 45 minutes).

Whitewashed arches, dangling hams and a tiled bar create a suitably rustic setting for tucking into plates of olives, homemade cold cuts or local cheese, accompanied by sherry straight from the barrel.

Information

Oficina de Turismo (958 66 28 04; otguadix@gmail.com; Plaza de la Constitución 15; 9am-2pm & 4-6pm Mon-Fri, 10am-2pm & 4-6pm Sat, 10am-2pm Sun)

Getting There & Away

Alsa (p279) buses run to/from Granada (€5.65, one hour, seven to 11 daily), Almería (€9.65, 1½ to two hours, two to three daily) and Málaga (€19, three to 3½ hours, three daily). The **bus station** (Calle Santa Rosa) is off Avenida Medina Olmos, 700m southeast of the centre.

There are four trains daily to Granada (€9.85, one hour) and six to Almería (€11 to €13, 1½ to two hours). The station is 2km northeast of town.

COSTA TROPICAL

There's a hint of Italy's Amalfi Coast about the Costa Tropical, Granada province's 80km coastline. Named for its subtropical microclimate (which produces mangoes, bananas, avocados, custard apples and more), it's far less developed than Málaga's Costa del Sol to the west, and often dramatically beautiful, with dun-brown mountains cascading into the sea and whitewashed villages huddled into bays. The main resorts of Almuñécar and Salobreña are popular summer destinations with long pebble beaches, hilltop castles and handsome historic centres, while La Herradura is a water-sports hub.

Salobreña

POP 9090

Like many other Andalucian coastal towns, Salobreña is split in two: the main historical town with its attractive hillside centre, white-cube houses and formidable Moorish castle, and, about a kilometre away, the seafront district centred on two long grey-sand beaches, **Playa de la Guardia** and **Playa de la Charca**. Around 8km west of Motril and 15km east of Almuñécar, the town is a fairly quiet, low-key place, but in August it bursts into life for the summer season. During Nasrid times, Salobreña was an important hub and sugar-cane producer.

Casco Antiguo OLD TOWN

Salobreña's historic centre (west of the modern town) comprises the *barrios* that once huddled inside its medieval walls. Slender cobbled lanes meander up the steep hillside, past whitewashed houses and bursts of bougainvillea, to the 12th-century **castle** (Calle Andrés Segovia; €4; 10am-2pm & 4-6pm Jun-Aug, 10am-1.30pm & 5.30-8pm Sep-May) and Mudéjar **Iglesia del Rosario** (Calle Bóveda; hours vary).

Hostal San Juan HOSTAL €

(958 61 17 29; www.hostalsanjuan.com; Calle Jardines 1; s €47-61, d €52-68, f €65-75; Mar–mid-Dec;) A tiled, plant-filled patio with

sky-blue arches welcomes guests at this *hostal* on a quiet street in the old town. Ceramic tiling, a sunny roof terrace, Andalucian breakfasts (€4) and 11 colourful rustic rooms make for a good-value package. There are also a couple of two-person studios (from €320 to €480 per week).

Aráis TAPAS, ANDALUCIAN €€
(☎958 61 17 38; www.facebook.com/restaurante.arais; Calle Granada 11; tapas €9-18, mains €12-25; ⊙11am-midnight Tue-Sun) Take your pick: tapas-style food in the laid-back, contemporary-design bar or updated Andalucian cooking in the sharply designed restaurant, all seasonally sourced and courtesy of chef Francisco Izquierdo. The bar focuses on creative international-inspired dishes, including *huevos rotos* (fried eggs) and zingy guacamole, while the restaurant impresses with artful culinary compositions such as *arroz negro* or paella (order ahead).

Information

Turismo Salobreña (☎958 61 03 14; www.turismosalobrena.com; Plaza de Goya; ⊙10am-2pm & 5-8pm daily Jul & Aug, 10am-5.30pm Mon-Sat Sep-Jun) In the modern part of town.

Getting There & Around

From the bus stop, 200m northeast of the tourist office on the north side of the N340, Alsa (p279) runs to/from Almuñécar (€1.37, 15 minutes, 13 to 19 daily), Nerja (€4.16, 50 minutes, 10 or 11 daily), Órgiva (€3.38, one hour, 4.45pm Monday to Saturday), Málaga (€8.81, 1¾ to 2¼ hours, five daily), Granada (€6.91, one to two hours, eight daily) and Almería (€10.48, 2½ to 3¼ hours, two daily).

WORTH A TRIP

PLAYA DE CANTARRIJÁN

Hemmed in by rocky cliffs and the glittering Mediterranean, gorgeous grey-pebble Cantarriján is one of Andalucía's original and favourite nudist beaches. All are welcome, and the main naturist section is around the corner at the southern end. It's 7km west of La Herradura and 1.4km off the N340; from mid-June to mid-September park at the top and catch a shuttle bus (€1).

Beachfront *chiringuito* **La Barraca** (☎958 34 92 87; www.facebook.com/restaurantelabarracacantarrijan; Playa de Cantarriján, mains €9-20; ⊙10am-midnight May-Sep, noon-6.30pm Oct-Apr; 🅥) is open all year and cooks up super-fresh fish and delicious paellas (including vegetarian).

Almuñécar

POP 17,900

The Costa Tropical's main resort town, Almuñécar heaves in summer as crowds of Spanish holidaymakers and northern European sun-seekers flock to its palm-fringed esplanade and two pebble beaches. It's not an obviously attractive place back from the seafront, but beyond the dreary high-rises you'll uncover a picturesque *casco antiguo* (old town) filled with narrow lanes, whitewashed homes and bar-flanked plazas, and topped by a striking Moorish castle.

Sights

Life in Almuñécar centres on its two pebbly beaches: **Playa de San Cristóbal** to the west, which catches the sun well into the evening, and **Playa Puerta del Mar** to the east, backed by high-rise tower blocks.

Castillo de San Miguel CASTLE
(☎650 027584; Explanada del Castillo; combined ticket Museo Arqueológico adult/child €2.35/1.60, 10am-1pm Fri free; ⊙10am-1.30pm & 6.30-9pm Tue-Sat, 10am-1pm Sun Jul–mid-Sep, shorter hours mid-Sep–Jun) Almuñécar's impressive hilltop castle was built over Islamic, Roman and Phoenician fortifications by the conquering Christians in the 16th century, was severely damaged during the Napoleonic Wars, and later became the town's cemetery until the 1980s. The hot, circuitous climb through the *casco antiguo* rewards with excellent views and an informative little museum; tickets include Almuñécar's small **archaeology museum** (☎958 83 86 23; Calle San Joaquín; ⊙10am-1.30pm & 6.30-9pm Tue-Sat, 10am-1pm Sun Jul–mid-Sep, shorter hours mid-Sep–Jun), set in a series of 1st-century vaulted underground cellars.

Parque Botánico El Majuelo PARK, RUINS
(Avenida de Europa; ⊙8am-10pm) FREE A lush park built around the remains of a Carthaginian and Roman fish-salting workshop, where *garum* (fermented fish sauce) was produced before being shipped across the empire. Subtropical plants shade a series of free-standing sculptures by Syrian artists.

Sleeping & Eating

Almuñécar hosts an inordinate number of buzzing tapas bars and drinking spots, particularly around Plaza Kelibia, Plaza de la Rosa and Paseo del Altillo. There are good beachfront *chiringuitos* (snack bars) too, and fresh seafood is an obvious speciality.

Hotel Casablanca HOTEL €€
(958 63 55 75; www.hotelcasablancaalmunecar.com; Plaza de San Cristóbal 4; s €48-90, d €57-124;) Convenient for both the beach and Almuñécar's lively centre, this welcoming family-run hotel is dressed in neo-Moorish style, with smartly contemporary rooms in calming pastel tones (the best have balconies and sea views). Breakfasts (€7), afternoon drinks and Andalucian meals happen in the ground-floor terrace bar-restaurant.

★ **Los Geráneos** ANDALUCIAN €€
(958 63 40 20; www.facebook.com/losgeraneos; Plaza de la Rosa 4; menú del día €15; 1-5pm & 7.30-11pm Tue-Sat, 1-5pm Sun;) With tables on a cobbled plaza beneath sky-blue windows or amid wood beams and dangling onions in the charmingly rustic interior, Los Geráneos is a packed Almuñécar favourite. The excellent-value homestyle *menú* is a delight of zingy salads (potatoes with garlic-lemon dressing), superb fresh grilled fish and meats, and homemade desserts or local oranges.

Information

Oficina de Turismo Palacete de La Najarra
(958 63 11 25; www.turismoalmunecar.es; Avenida de Europa; 9.30am-1.30pm & 4.30-7pm) In the 19th-century neo-Moorish Palacete de la Najarra.

Getting There & Away

Almuñécar's **bus station** (Avenida Juan Carlos I 1) is 600m north of the town centre. Alsa (p279) runs to/from Granada (€8.60, 1½ to two hours, nine daily), Málaga (€7.65, 1½ to two hours, eight or nine daily), Almería (€12.20, two to 3½ hours, five daily), Salobreña (€1.37, 15 minutes, 13 to 19 daily) and Nerja (€3, 25 to 45 minutes, 13 to 15 daily). **Fajardo** (958 88 27 62; www.grupofajardo.es) goes to/from La Herradura (€1.50, 15 minutes, five to 10 daily). For Las Alpujarras, Alsa goes to Órgiva (€4.82, 1¼ hours) at 4.30pm Monday to Saturday, returning at 8.20am Monday to Saturday.

La Herradura

POP 4215

Catering to a lively crowd of windsurfers, divers, kayakers and other water-sports fans, the shimmering horseshoe-shaped bay at La Herradura feels like Almuñécar's more active, less touristed sister. It's 7km west of Almuñécar and has a subtle castaway vibe, a lengthy pebble beach, and plenty of holiday apartments and seafront *chiringuitos*.

Windsurf La Herradura WATER SPORTS
(958 64 01 43; www.windsurflaherradura.com; Paseo Marítimo 34; windsurf/paddleboard/kayak hire from €20/10/7; beach stand 10.30am-8pm Easter-Oct, shop 10.30am-2pm & 5.30-8.30pm year-round) An established La Herradura all-rounder renting windsurfing gear, kayaks and paddleboards, and offering classes (one-hour windsurf class €40), courses, SUP yoga sessions (€12; June to August), and guided kayaking and paddleboarding excursions to sea caves (two hours, €20).

Buceo La Herradura DIVING
(958 82 70 83; www.buceolaherradura.com; Puerto Deportivo Marina del Este; single dive incl equipment €48; 9am-2pm & 4-7pm daily year-round, to 8.30pm Mon-Fri Jun-Sep) This long-established outfit runs dives, 'baptisms' (€70) and PADI courses (four-day Open Water €320). It's 3km east of central La Herradura.

Getting There & Away

Fajardo has five to 10 daily buses to/from Almuñécar (€1.50, 15 minutes). Alsa (p279) serves destinations including Málaga (€6.73, 1½ hours, five daily) and Granada (€9, 1½ to two hours, five to six daily).

AT A GLANCE

POPULATION
728,000

CAPITAL
Almería

BEST REBORN GHOST TOWN
Rodalquilar (p310)

BEST INDIANA JONES FILM LOCATION
Playa de Mónsul (p313)

BEST FLAMINGOS
Salinas de Cabo de Gata (p308)

WHEN TO GO

Apr–May
Good, not-too-hot time for exploring the arid interior (at its most colourful) and coastal walking.

Jun–Sep
Main beach season; lower prices and fewer crowds in June and September than July-August.

Dec–Feb
Plenty of sunshine makes Almería good for a winter break; hotel rates are a bargain.

Las Negras, Parque Natural de Cabo de Gata-Níjar (p311)
CABRERAFOTO/SHUTTERSTOCK

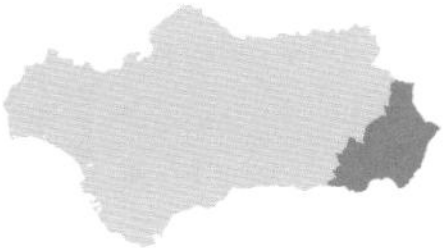

Almería Province

Silent mountain valleys, sublime beaches and vast tracts of semidesert scrubland – Almería province is an area of haunting natural beauty. Despite this, and its 3000 hours of annual sunshine, it remains relatively unknown outside Spain. Its obvious drawcard is its glorious coastline, with thrilling beaches along the Parque Natural de Cabo de Gata-Níjar, and lively, good-time resort Mojácar. But the unsung capital, Almería city, is well worth a visit, for one of Andalucía's mightiest fortresses, some excellent museums and a great tapas trail. And there's plenty to explore in the sparsely populated, other-worldly hinterland: the spaghetti-western badlands of Desierto de Tabernas, underground treasures in the Sorbas caves, white villages and a fairy-tale castle at Vélez Blanco.

INCLUDES

Almería Province Highlights

1 Parque Natural de Cabo de Gata-Níjar (p307) Hopping around the heavenly beaches and plunging cliffs of Andalucía's southeastern coastline.

2 Alcazaba (p298) Patrolling Almería's formidable hilltop fort, once one of the most powerful in Moorish Spain.

3 Cuevas de Sorbas (p305) Going underground in this other-worldly cave complex.

4 Los Vélez (p315) Taking to the remote forests and rocky peaks of the Sierra de María in the province's far north.

5 Desierto de Tabernas (p304) Touring the cinematic Wild West landscapes of this barren semidesert.

6 Mojácar (p312) Soaking up the *playa*'s summer beach vibe, and basking in sweeping vistas from the quaint hilltop *pueblo* (village).

7 La Geoda de Pulpí (p316) Contemplating the dazzling crystals of the world's second largest geode.

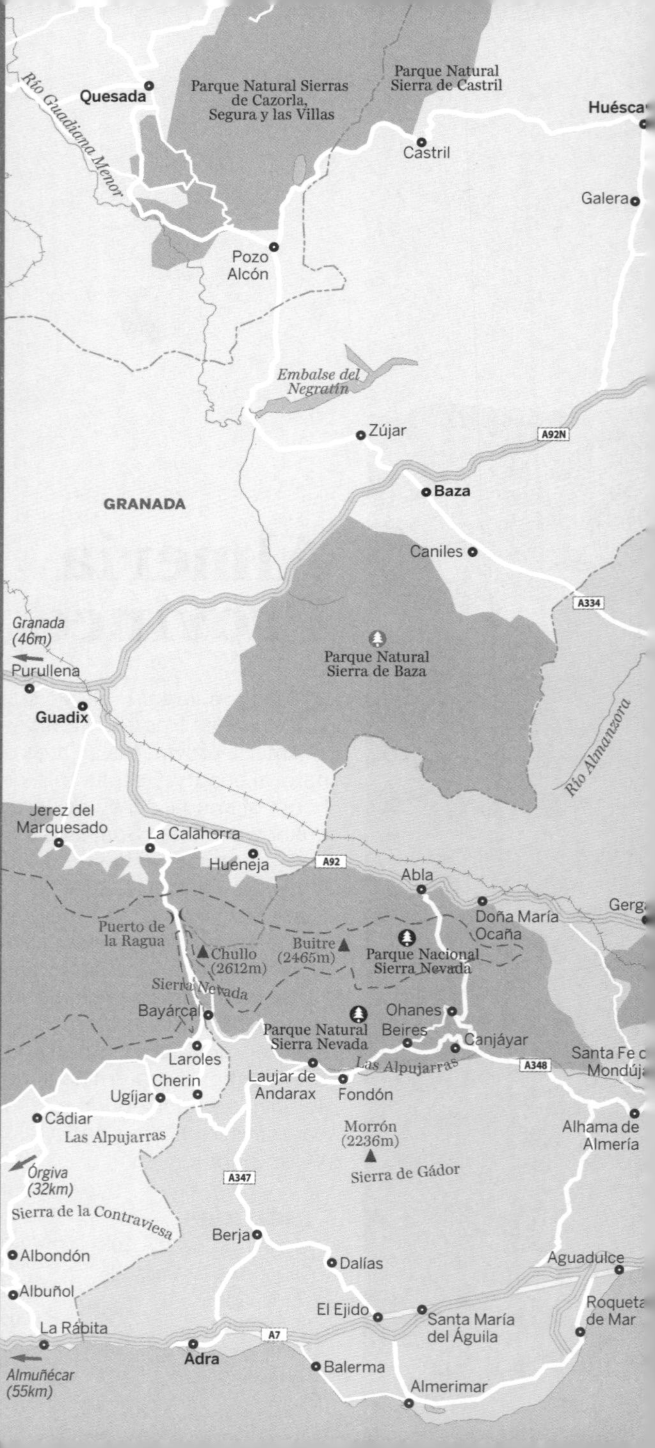

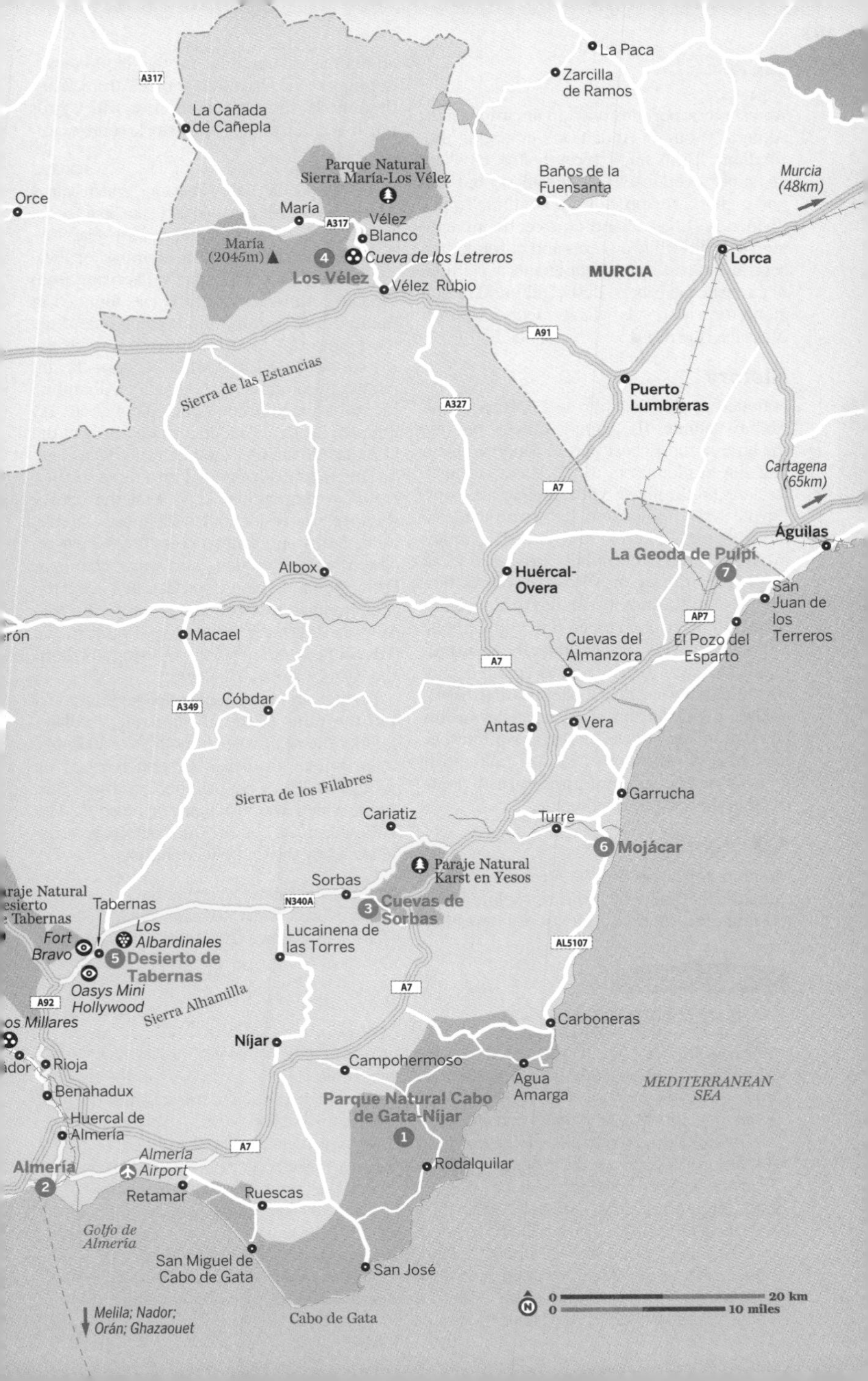

La Paca
Zarcilla de Ramos
La Cañada de Cañepla
A317
Parque Natural Sierra María-Los Vélez
Baños de la Fuensanta
Murcia (48km)
Orce
María
Vélez Blanco
María (2045m)
4
Cueva de los Letreros
Los Vélez
Vélez Rubio
MURCIA
Lorca
A91
Sierra de las Estancias
Puerto Lumbreras
A327
Cartagena (65km)
A7
Águilas
La Geoda de Pulpí
7
Albox
Huércal-Overa
San Juan de los Terreros
AP7
rón
Macael
Cuevas del Almanzora
El Pozo del Esparto
A349
Cóbdar
Antas
Vera
Sierra de los Filabres
Garrucha
Cariatiz
Turre
6
Mojácar
Paraje Natural Karst en Yesos
Sorbas
araje Natural esierto Tabernas
Tabernas
N340A
3
Cuevas de Sorbas
Fort Bravo
Los Albardinales
Lucainena de las Torres
AL5107
5
Desierto de Tabernas
Oasys Mini Hollywood
A92
Sierra Alhamilla
os Millares
Carboneras
Níjar
ador
Rioja
Campohermoso
Agua Amarga
Benahadux
MEDITERRANEAN SEA
Parque Natural Cabo de Gata-Níjar
Huercal de Almería
1
Almería
Almería Airport
Rodalquilar
2
Retamar
Ruescas
Golfo de Almería
San Miguel de Cabo de Gata
San José
0
20 km
0
10 miles
Melila; Nador; Orán; Ghazaouet
Cabo de Gata

ALMERÍA

POP 198,533

An energetic port city with an illustrious past, Almería is one of Andalucía's emerging destinations. Until fairly recently the city was generally overlooked by travellers, but ongoing efforts to spruce it up continue to pay dividends. It has a handsome centre, punctuated by palm-fringed plazas and old churches, several interesting museums and a plethora of fantastic tapas bars. Best of all – and reason alone for a visit – is its spectacular Moorish Alcazaba (fortress).

History

Founded in AD 955 by the Córdoba caliph Abd ar-Rahman III, Almería quickly became the largest and richest port in Moorish Spain and the headquarters of the Umayyad fleet. Its streets thronged with merchants from Egypt, Syria, France and Italy, who came to buy silk, glass, marble and glazed ceramics in Al-Andalus. It eventually lost its trading supremacy during a Christian occupation from 1147 to 1157 but it remained a significant Moorish city until conquered by the Catholic Monarchs in 1489. It subsequently went into rapid decline – a 1658 census counted only 500 inhabitants – due to devastating earthquakes, the expulsion of Andalucía's Muslim population and attacks by Barbary pirates. In the late 20th century its fortunes took a turn for the better as agriculture and tourism flourished in the surrounding region.

Sights

Almería's top sights are the Alcazaba and the cathedral, both of which can be explored in a morning, but there are plenty of interesting additional distractions in the city's meandering streets. Orientate yourself from Paseo de Almería, the city's main drag, which runs north–south through the historic centre.

★Alcazaba FORTRESS
(☎950 80 10 08; Calle Almanzor; ⏲9am-3pm & 7-10pm Tue-Sat mid-Jun–mid-Sep, 9am-8pm Tue-Sat Apr–mid-Jun, 9am-6pm Tue-Sat mid-Sep–Mar, 9am-3pm Sun year-round) FREE A looming fortification with great curtain-like walls rising from the cliffs, Almería's Alcazaba was founded in the mid-10th century and became one of the most powerful Moorish fortresses in Spain. It's survived well and while it lacks the intricate decoration of Granada's Alhambra, it's still a magnificent sight. Allow about 1½ hours to explore. Pick up a guide leaflet at the kiosk inside the four-arch entrance gate.

The Alcazaba is divided into three distinct *recintos* (compounds). The lowest, the **Primer Recinto**, was residential, with houses, streets, wells, baths and other necessities – now replaced by lush gardens and water channels. From the battlements, you can look over the city's huddled rooftops and down to the **Muralla de Jayrán**, a fortified wall built in the 11th century to defend the outlying northern and eastern parts of the city.

Further up in the **Segundo Recinto** you'll find the ruins of the Muslim rulers' palace, built by the *taifa* ruler Almotacín (r 1051–91), under whom medieval Almería reached its peak, as well as a chapel, the **Ermita de San Juan**, which was originally a mosque. The highest section, the **Tercer Recinto**, is a castle added by the Catholic Monarchs.

★Catedral de la Encarnación CATHEDRAL
(☎605 396483; www.catedralalmeria.com; Plaza de la Catedral 8, entrance Calle Velázquez; €5; ⏲10am-

DON'T MISS

THE OLD MEDINA

Sprawled at the foot of the Alcazaba, the maze-like Almedina is one of Almería's most atmospheric neighbourhoods. This was the area occupied by the original Almería – a walled medina (city), bounded by the Alcazaba to the north, the sea to the south, and what are now Calle de la Reina and Avenida del Mar to the east and west. At its heart was the city's main mosque – whose *mihrab* (a prayer niche indicating the direction of Mecca) survives inside the **Iglesia de San Juan** (Calle General Luque; ⏲open for Mass 8pm Apr-Sep, 7pm Oct-Mar, closed Tue & Fri) FREE – with the commercial area of markets and warehouses spread around it. Calle de la Almedina still traces the line of the old main street running diagonally across the medina.

An excellent place for refreshment is Tetería Almedina (p302), a friendly tea-house-restaurant. Also worth seeking out is the **Plaza de Pavía market** (Plaza de Pavía; ⏲9am-2pm Mon-Sat), at its liveliest on Saturdays, with stalls selling everything from cheap shoes to churros (delicious, fat, tubular doughnuts).

7pm Mon-Fri, 10am-2.30pm & 3.30-7pm Sat, 1.30-7pm Sun Apr-Sep, to 6.30pm Oct-Mar) Almería's formidable, six-towered cathedral, begun in 1525, was conceived both as a place of worship and a refuge for the population from frequent pirate raids from North Africa. It was originally Gothic-Renaissance in style, but baroque and neoclassical features were added in the 18th century. The Gothic interior, entered through a fine neoclassical cloister, is an impressive spectacle with its sinuous, ribbed ceiling, 16th-century walnut choir stalls and monumental Capilla Mayor (chancel).

Outside, in a suite of rooms off the cloister, you can browse the cathedral's small collection of paintings, vestments and ceremonial silverware. On the building's exterior, note the cute stone lions around the northwest tower and the exuberant Sol de Portocarrero, a 16th-century relief of the sun (now the city's symbol) on the cathedral's eastern end.

Museo de Almería MUSEUM
(Museo Arqueológico; ☎950 01 62 56; www.museosdeandalucia.es/museodealmeria; Calle Hermanos Pinzón 91; ⊙9am-9pm Tue-Sat, to 3pm Sun) FREE Almería's excellent archaeology museum focuses on two local prehistoric cultures – Los Millares (3200–2250 BC), probably the Iberian Peninsula's first metalworking culture, and El Argar (2250–1550 BC), which ushered in the Bronze Age. Artefacts are well displayed and accompanied by Spanish and English explanatory panels. The 3rd floor features finds relating to the area's Roman and Islamic past.

Museo de la Guitarra MUSEUM
(☎950 27 43 58; Ronda del Beato Diego Ventaja; adult/reduced €3/2; ⊙10.30am-1.30pm Tue-Sun year-round, plus 6-9pm Tue-Sat Jun-Sep, 5-8pm Tue-Sat Oct-May) It's worth establishing two important facts before you enter this absorbing museum. First: the word 'guitar' is derived from the Andalucian-Arabic word *qitara,* hinting at its Spanish roots. Second: all modern acoustic guitars owe a huge debt to Almerian guitar-maker Antonio de Torres (1817–92), to whom this museum is dedicated. The museum itself details the history of the guitar and pays homage to Torres' part in it.

Refugios de la Guerra Civil HISTORIC SITE
(Civil War Shelters; ☎950 26 86 96; Plaza de Manuel Pérez García; adult/reduced €3/2; ⊙tours 10.30am & noon Tue-Sun year-round, plus 6pm & 7.30pm Tue-Sat Jun-Sep, 5pm & 6.30pm Tue-Sat Oct-May) During the civil war, Almería was the Republicans' last holdout in Andalucía, and was repeatedly and mercilessly bombed. The attacks prompted a group of engineers to design and build the Refugios, a 4.5km-long network of concrete shelters under the city. Visits – by 1¼-hour guided tour, in Spanish – take you through 1km of the tunnels, including the re-created operating theatre and storerooms. An engaging 10-minute film (in Spanish with English subtitles) features local survivors recounting their personal experiences in the shelters.

HEAVENLY HAMMAMS

Hammam Aire de Almería (☎950 28 20 95; www.beaire.com; Plaza de la Constitución 5; 1½hr session Mon-Thu €29, Fri-Sun €35; ⊙9am-10.30pm) This luxurious and spacious *hammam* exudes a feeling of tranquillity throughout its marble and brick interior. It offers three baths – the frigidarium (16°C), tepidarium (36°C) and caldarium (40°C) – as well as a range of aromatherapy and other massages. Reservations are advisable.

Hammam Almeraya (☎950 23 10 10; www.almeraya.info; Calle Perea 9; 1½hr session incl aromatherapy €18; ⊙sessions 11am, 1pm, 4pm, 6pm & 8pm Wed-Sun) This small *hammam* has hot and cold baths, a 'Turkish' steam bath and a beautiful marble-and-tiled interior. It also offers massages, and has a relaxing tetería (www.almeraya.info; Calle Perea 9; ⊙4pm-midnight Wed-Mon). Reservations required.

Centro de Interpretación Patrimonial MUSEUM
(☎671 099981; Plaza de la Constitución; ⊙10am-8.30pm Tue-Sat, to 2pm Sun) FREE A good place to get your historical bearings and set the city's sights in context, this informative museum has three floors of historical exhibits as well as a panoramic roof terrace.

Centro Andaluz de la Fotografía GALLERY
(Andalucian Photography Centre; ☎950 18 63 60; www.centroandaluzdelafotografia.es; Calle Pintor Díaz Molina 9; ⊙11am-2pm & 5.30-9.30pm) FREE Anyone interested in photography should visit this excellent centre, which puts on top-class exhibitions of work by Spanish and international photographers. They vary dramatically in theme but are invariably thought-provoking.

Aljibes Árabes de Jayrán HISTORIC SITE
(☎950 27 30 39; Calle Tenor Iribarne; ⊙10.30am-1.30pm Tue-Sun year-round, plus 6-9pm Fri & Sat Jun-Sep, 5-8pm Fri & Sat Oct-May) FREE These

Almería

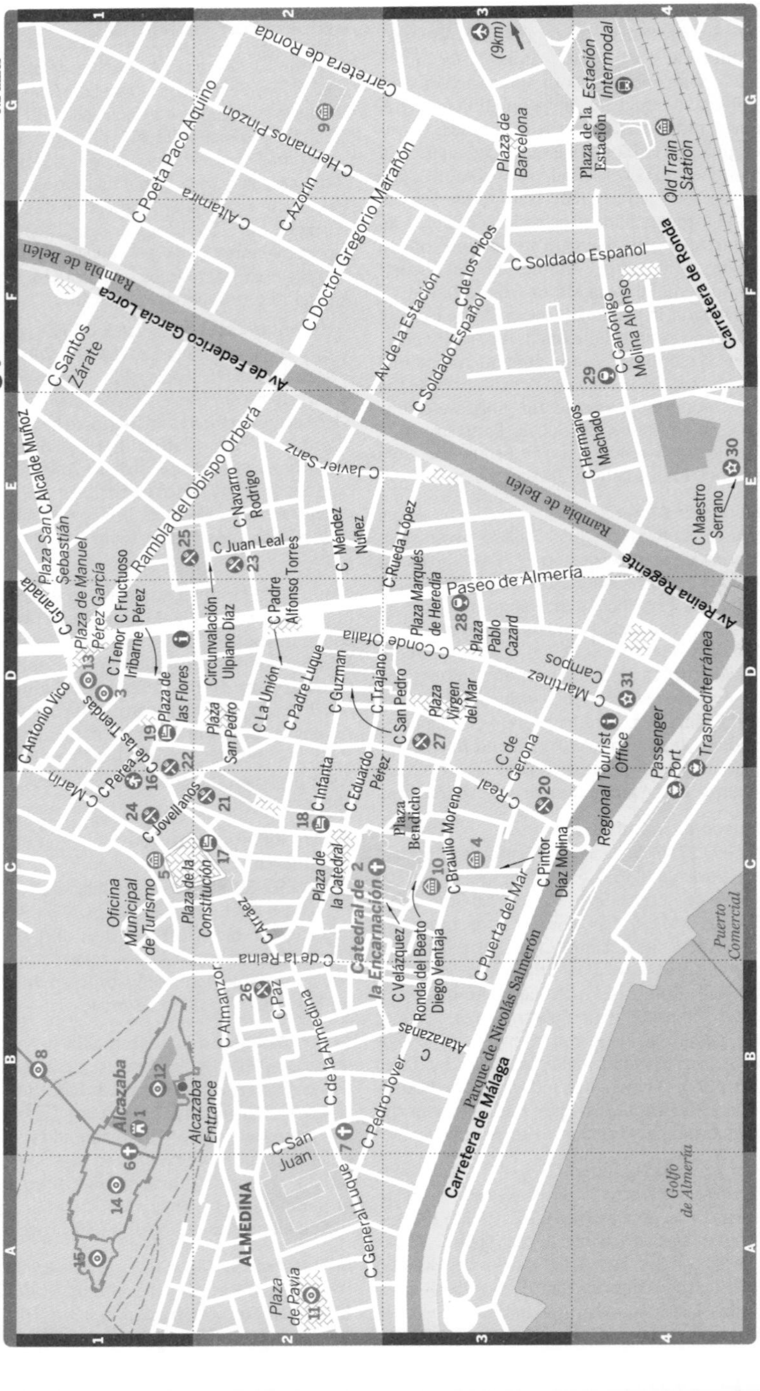
0.2 miles
400 m
Alcazaba
Alcazaba Entrance
ALMEDINA
Plaza de Pavía
C San Juan
C General Luque
C Pedro Jover
C de la Almedina
C Almanzor
C Paz
C de la Reina
Catedral de la Encarnación
C Velázquez
Ronda del Beato Diego Ventaja
C Atarazanas
Parque de Nicolás Salmerón
Carretera de Málaga
C Puerta del Mar
C Pintor Díaz Molina
Plaza de la Constitución
Oficina Municipal de Turismo
Plaza de la Catedral
C Jovellanos
C Marín
C Perea
C de las Tiendas
C Antonio Vico
C Infanta
C Eduardo Pérez
Plaza Bendicho
C Braulio Moreno
C Real
C de Gerona
Plaza Virgen del Mar
C San Pedro
C Trajano
C Guzman
C Padre Luque
C La Unión
Plaza San Pedro
Plaza de las Flores
Circunvalación Ulpiano Díaz
C Tenor Iribarne
C Fructuoso Pérez
Plaza de Manuel Pérez García
C Granada
Plaza San Sebastián
C Alcalde Muñoz
C Santos Zárate
Rambla del Obispo Orberá
C Navarro Rodrigo
C Juan Leal
C Padre Alfonso Torres
C Méndez Núñez
C Rueda López
Plaza Marqués de Heredia
Paseo de Almería
C Conde Ofalia
Plaza Pablo Cazard
C Martínez Campos
Regional Tourist Office
Passenger Port
Trasmediterránea
Puerto Comercial
Golfo de Almería
Av Reina Regente
Rambla de Belén
C Maestro Serrano
C Hermanos Machado
C Javier Sanz
Av de Federico García Lorca
Av de la Estación
C Soldado Español
C de los Picos
C Canónigo Molina Alonso
Carretera de Ronda
C Doctor Gregorio Marañón
C Azorín
C Altamira
C Poeta Paco Aquino
C Hermanos Pinzón
Plaza de Barcelona
Plaza de la Estación
Estación Intermodal
Old Train Station
(9km)
1 2 3 4
A B C D E F G
1 3 4 5 6 7 8 9 10 11 12 13 14 15 16 17 18 19 20 21 22 23 24 25 26 27 28 29 30 31

brick-vaulted underground cisterns, built in the early 11th century to help supply the city's water, are well preserved. During the day, they're open to the public for visits; by night, the legendary Peña El Taranto stages occasional flamenco shows here (alas, generally closed to non-members).

Festivals & Events

Feria de Almería FIESTA

(www.feriadealmeria.es; Aug) Nine days and nights of live music, fairground rides, exhibitions and full-on partying in the second half of August.

Sleeping

Hotel Nuevo Torreluz HOTEL €

(950 23 43 99; www.torreluz.com; Plaza de las Flores 10; s/d from €45/58; P) A polished four-star enjoying a superb location on a small square in the historic centre. Carpeted corridors lead to smallish but comfortable rooms sporting parquet floors and modern pearl-grey tones. Unlimited fresh-squeezed orange juice is a highlight of the optional breakfast (€7). The hotel also runs a trio of cafes and restaurants around the square. Parking is available for €11.90.

★Aire Hotel & Ancient Baths BOUTIQUE HOTEL €€

(950 28 20 96; www.airehotelalmeria.com; Plaza de la Constitución 4; d €99-159, ste €149-179;) Attached to the plush Hammam Aire de Almería (p299), this elegant hideaway is perfectly situated on beautiful Plaza de la Constitución, just steps from some of the city's top tapas bars. Its slick, contemporarily attired rooms come with high ceilings, polished wood floors and vast photo-walls of local sights such as Cabo de Gata.

Hotel Catedral BOUTIQUE HOTEL €€€

(950 27 81 78; www.hotelcatedral.net; Plaza de la Catedral 8; r €120-190;) In a prime location overlooking the cathedral, this debonair four-star occupies a handsome 1850s building. Inside, the decor slickly marries the old and the new, combining clean contemporary lines with Gothic arches and an *artesonado* (coffered) ceiling in the restaurant. Rooms are large and high-ceilinged, and the roof terrace offers heady cathedral views.

Eating

Fresh off its 2019 stint as Spain's official culinary capital (Capital Española de la Gastronomía), Almería is a fabulous place to eat. The city is awash with restaurants and tapas bars, ranging from old-school bodegas to trendy modern hang-outs.

Mercado Central MARKET €

(Circunvalación Ulpiano Díaz; 8am-3pm Mon-Sat year-round, plus 5-8.30pm Mon-Fri mid-Sep–mid-Jun) Almería's central market occupies a grand

ALMERÍA TAPAS TOUR

The area between Paseo de Almería and Plaza de la Constitución is packed with busy and atmospheric tapas bars, frequented as much by locals as by out-of-towners. Many maintain the civilised tradition of serving a free tapa with your drink. As a rule, portions are generous, and for the hungry – or to share – almost everywhere offers *raciones* and *medias raciones* (full- and half-sized plates of tapas items). Two perennial favourites are Casa Puga and Jovellanos 16, but there are plenty more to choose from.

Nuestra Tierra (www.tabernanuestratierra.com; cnr Calles Jovellanos & Marín; tapas €2-6, raciones €14-25; ⏲7.30am-noon Mon, to midnight Tue-Thu, to 1am Fri, 8.30am-1.30am Sat, noon-midnight Sun) Head to this good-looking modern eatery on bar-heavy Calle Jovellanos for creative tapas made with seasonal Andalucian ingredients. Showstoppers include IGP Sierra de los Filabres lamb with caramelised peppers, and octopus grilled to buttery softness.

El Quinto Toro (☎950 23 91 35; www.facebook.com/elquintotoroalmeria; Calle Juan Leal 6; tapas from €1.50, raciones €7-18; ⏲noon-5pm Mon-Sat & 8pm-midnight Mon-Fri) Keep it traditional at this old-school bar near the central market. Don't expect culinary fireworks, just tried-and-tested staples such as *chorizo ibérico* (spicy sausage) and *albóndigas* (meatballs) in wine sauce.

Tortillería La Mala (☎619 350816; www.facebook.com/tortillerialamala; Calle Real 69; tapas €1.20-5, tortillas €9-12, raciones €8-18; ⏲noon-4pm Tue, noon-4pm & 8pm-1am Wed-Sun) This buzzing corner bar fills quickly on weekend evenings. With its boho decor and young crowd, it's a great spot to try a genuine Spanish tortilla (omelette), here prepared with everything from tuna to prawns and chilli.

Cervecería Las Tiendas (☎640 684947; Calle de las Tiendas; tapas €1.20-5, raciones €8-18; ⏲10am-4pm Mon-Wed, to midnight Thu-Sat) Every seafood tapa imaginable is yours for a song at this streetside venue. Patrons sip beers throughout the evening as waiters sling plates of steamed mussels, grilled tuna, fried squid, sardines, octopus and more.

1890s building near the top of Paseo de Almería. Go early to see squid so fresh they're still changing colour, as well as a profusion of fruit and veg grown in greenhouses across the province.

★Tetería Almedina — MOROCCAN €€

(☎629 277827; Calle Paz 2, off Calle de la Almedina; mains €10-15, fixed-price menús €17-30; ⏲noon-11pm Tue-Sun; ✎) For a break from tapas, this welcoming little tearoom-restaurant is the answer. Hidden in a backstreet below the Alcazaba, it serves a reassuring menu of homestyle Moroccan staples – tagines, tabbouli, couscous and lightly spiced legume soups, with many vegetarian options in the mix. To drink, a herbed tea or infusion is the way to go.

The restaurant is run by a local group dedicated to revitalising the old town, with its many Moroccan immigrants, and reviving the culture of Al-Andalus.

★Casa Puga — TAPAS €€

(☎950 23 15 30; www.barcasapuga.es; Calle Jovellanos 7; tapas from €1.70, raciones €7-18; ⏲noon-4pm & 8pm-midnight Mon-Sat) For an authentic tapas experience, make a beeline for this long-standing favourite, on the go since 1870. Shelves of ancient wine bottles and walls plastered with lottery tickets and ancient maps set the scene while well-practised waiters work the bar, dishing out classical tapas prepared at the tiny cooking station. Arrive early or expect crowds.

★Jovellanos 16 — TAPAS €€

(☎660 547354; www.facebook.com/jovellanos16; Calle Jovellanos 16; tapas €1.80, raciones €10-18; ⏲12.30-4.30pm & 8pm-midnight Tue-Sat, 12.30-4.30pm Sun) With friendly service and a prime people-watching location opposite Plaza Constitución, Jovellanos 16 is a rising star on Almería's 'tapas row'. Don't miss their *hamburguesa Jovellanos* (a scrumptious mini-burger with bacon, cheese and tomato on a crunchy roll) or the *secreto ibérico con ajo verde* (pork with garlicky green sauce), both served with crispy, perfectly salted fried potatoes.

Casa Joaquín — SEAFOOD €€€

(☎950 26 43 59; Calle Real 111; raciones €12-30; ⏲noon-3.30pm & 9-11pm Mon-Fri, noon-3.30pm Sat) Fresh seafood is the draw at this historic Almería bodega, classically attired with hanging hams and rustic clutter. What's on offer depends on the day's catch but regular crowd-pleasers include juicy *gambas rojas* (red prawns) cooked a la plancha (grilled on a hotplate), and fried *calamares* (squid).

Drinking & Entertainment

The old-town tapas bars are many people's chosen drinking spots. The city's nightlife epicentre is the Cuatro Calles area around the intersection of Calles Real, Trajano and Eduardo Pérez. Within a couple of blocks you'll find several pubs, bars and clubs, generally with free admission. Many places don't hit their stride until around midnight.

Almería has an active cultural scene, with everything from flamenco performances to theatrical drama, classical music concerts, jazz and rock. Check www.almeriacultura entradas.es for upcoming events.

La Cueva PUB
(950 08 25 21; www.lacueva-almeria.com; Calle Canónigo Molina Alonso 23; 4pm-4am) Craft beer goes hand-in-hand with jam sessions and live music at this laid-back pub. The subdued lighting and walls plastered with posters and concert flyers create an intimate vibe for everything from blues and rock to punk, rap and heavy metal. Gigs typically cost between €3 and €7.

Burana BAR
(www.facebook.com/mollygroup; Paseo de Almería 56; 3pm-3am Sun-Thu, to 4am Fri & Sat) With its terrace in the portals of the neoclassical Teatro Cervantes and a disco-lit interior, this is a fashionable spot for an afternoon coffee or late-night cocktail. The vibe is upmarket trendy, with regular DJ sets at weekends.

Clasijazz JAZZ
(640 581457; www.clasijazz.com; Calle Maestro Serrano 9; shows €3-35) Located in a bland shopping centre, Clasijazz is a thriving music club that stages four or five weekly gigs – ranging from jam sessions to jazz, flamenco, big band and classical concerts – in a clean, contemporary space. Check the website for upcoming events.

MadChester LIVE MUSIC
(661 696930; www.facebook.com/madchester-club; Parque de Nicolás Salmerón 9; cover €8-16; 11pm-late Thu-Sat, 6-11pm Sun) This club venue hosts Spanish and international DJs and regular gigs by bands playing indie, rock and electronica.

Information

Oficina Municipal de Turismo (950 21 05 38; www.turismodealmeria.org; Paseo de Almería 12; 9am-2pm & 4-7pm Mon-Fri, 10am-2pm & 4-7pm Sat, 10am-2pm Sun Sep-Jun, 10am-2pm & 5-8pm Jul & Aug)

Regional Tourist Office (950 17 52 20; www.andalucia.org; Parque de Nicolás Salmerón; 9am-7.30pm Mon-Fri, 9.30am-3pm Sat & Sun)

Getting There & Away

AIR

Almería's small **airport** (913 21 10 00; www.aena.es) is 9km east of the city centre. **EasyJet** (902 59 99 00; www.easyjet.com) and **Ryanair** (www.ryanair.com) fly direct to/from various English airports; Ryanair also flies from Dublin, Milan and Brussels. **Iberia** (901 11 15 00; www.iberia.com) and **Vueling** (902 80 80 05; www.vueling.com) serve Spanish destinations.

BOAT

Trasmediterránea (902 45 46 45; www.trasmediterranea.es) sails from Almería's **passenger port** (950 23 68 20; www.apalmeria.com) to the North African ports of Melilla (from €38, 5½ to eight hours) and Nador, Morocco (from €45, seven hours), at least once daily, and to the Algerian cities of Ghazaouet (€90, eight hours) and Orán (€90, nine hours) at least once weekly.

BUS

Buses and trains share the **Estación Intermodal** (950 17 36 02; Plaza de la Estación), just east of the centre. **Bus Bam** (902 22 72 72; www.busbam.com) runs eight daily buses to/from Madrid (€30, 6¼ to 7¼ hours). Most other intercity services are operated by **Alsa** (902 42 22 42; www.alsa.es).

Destination	Cost (€)	Duration (hr)	Frequency (daily)
Córdoba	30	5	1
Granada	15-18	2-4¾	9
Guadix	9.65	1½-2	3
Jaén	20-24	3-5¼	6
Málaga	19-23	2½-5½	8
Murcia	14	2¾-4	8
Seville	38-47	5½-8½	5

TRAIN

From the Estación Intermodal (p303), there are trains to Granada (€21, three hours, four daily), Seville (€43, seven hours, four daily) and Madrid (€25 to €85, 6¾ to 7¾ hours, three daily). Note that at the time of research, RENFE was providing train passengers with alternate bus transport on the segments between Almería and Huércal-Viator and between Granada and Osuna due to ongoing track improvement work.

Getting Around

TO/FROM THE AIRPORT

Surbus (☎950 17 00 50; www.surbusalmeria.es) city bus 30 (€1.05, 35 minutes) runs from the airport to the city centre every 25 to 35 minutes (less frequently on Sunday), stopping at the main Estación Intermodal (p303), among other places. Services run between 7.15am and 11pm daily.

Taxis between the airport and city centre cost approximately €15 to €20. There are several rental car agencies at the airport, including Europcar, Hertz and Thrifty.

CAR & MOTORCYCLE

The A7/E15 runs a large ring around Almería; the easiest access to the centre is along the seafront (Carretera de Málaga) from the west, or the AL12 (Autovía del Aeropuerto) from the east.

Underground car parks dotted around the city centre area cost about €18 for 24 hours.

TAXI

Catch a taxi at ranks on Paseo de Almería, or call **Radio-Taxi Almería** (☎950 22 22 22; www.radiotaxialmeria.com) or **Tele Taxi Almería** (☎950 25 11 11; www.teletaxialmeria.com).

NORTH OF ALMERÍA

Desierto de Tabernas

Travel 30km north of Almería and you enter another world. The Desierto de Tabernas (Tabernas desert) is a strange and haunting place, a vast, sun-baked scrubland of shimmering, dun-coloured hills scattered with tufts of tussocky brush. In the 1960s the area was used as a film location for Sergio Leone's famous spaghetti westerns (*A Fistful of Dollars; For a Few Dollars More; The Good, the Bad and the Ugly;* and *Once Upon a Time in the West*), and still today film-makers come to shoot within its rugged badlands. Many of its 'Western' sets have now been incorporated into Wild West theme parks, which make for a fun family day out. The main town in the area is Tabernas, on the N340A road.

Sights & Activities

Oasys Mini Hollywood AMUSEMENT PARK
(☎950 36 52 36; www.oasysparquetematico.com; Carretera N340A, Km 464; adult/child €22.90/13.60; ⏲10am-7.30pm Jun & Sep, to 9pm Jul & Aug, to 6pm Oct-May, closed Mon-Fri Nov–mid-Apr; P) Tabernas' best known and most expensive Wild West park provides good family entertainment. The set itself is in decent condition, and the well-kept zoo has some 800 animals, including lions, giraffes, tigers and hippos. Children usually enjoy the 20-minute shoot-outs, while adults may prefer the clichéd can-can show (or at least the beer) in the saloon. There are also two summer pools, restaurants and cafes. Take sunscreen and a hat: there's little shade.

Fort Bravo AMUSEMENT PARK
(Texas Hollywood; ☎902 07 08 14; www.fortbravo.org; Carretera N340A, Km 468; adult/child €19.40/9.90; ⏲9am-7.30pm Mar-Sep, to 6pm Oct-Feb; P) Situated in the desert outside Tabernas, this popular Wild West theme park has a certain dusty charm with its movie sets – which are still used for filming – and daily cowboy and can-can shows. There's a pool (in summer only), buggy rides and horse treks; plus you can stay overnight in a log cabin. The park is 1km off the N340A, signposted 31km from Almería.

Malcaminos TOURS
(☎652 022582; www.malcaminos.com; Avenida de las Angustias, Tabernas) Malcaminos' enthusiastic local guides offer tours of Tabernas' cinematic landscape – not just its filmic geography but also its history and geology. Packages include a two-hour 4WD tour (€30) of the area's movie locations. Meet at the Bar Portichuelo, across from Tabernas' tourist office.

Eating

★**Los Albardinales** ANDALUCIAN €€
(☎950 61 17 07; www.losalbardinales.com; Carretera N340, Km 474; mains €16-23; ⏲cafe 9am-6pm, lunch 1.30-4pm Fri-Wed; P) Los Albardinales is an award-winning organic olive-oil producer. At this, their roadside mill, you can see how the oil is pressed and sample it at their excellent farmhouse restaurant. Expect earthy regional cuisine, prepared with locally sourced ingredients and accompanied by fine organic wines. It's 2km east of Tabernas.

Las Eras Antonio Gázquez ANDALUCIAN €€
(☎950 36 52 69; www.antoniogazquez.net; Paraje Las Eras, Tabernas; menú del día €13.50; ⏲1-6pm Sun-Fri; P) This big, barn-like restaurant, hidden behind a petrol station at the northern entrance to town, is ideal for a filling lunch. Everyone from local labourers to British expats to smartly dressed office workers pack

WORTH A TRIP

SORBAS

Dramatically perched on a rocky gorge overlooking the Río de Adeguar, Sorbas is a small, attractive town known for its traditional pottery. Its main drawcard is its network of caves, the Cuevas de Sorbas, protected as part of the 24-sq-km Paraje Natural Karst en Yesos de Sorbas (Sorbas Gypsum Karst Natural Area). The **Centro de Visitantes Los Yesares** (☎677 116877; Calle Terraplén; ⊙10am-2pm Thu-Sun) FREE, at the town entrance, has tourist information.

By road, Sorbas is 60km northeast of Almería, 36km west of Mojácar and 33km northeast of Níjar. Two daily Alsa (p303) buses (one on Saturday) run between Almería and Sorbas (€4.75, one hour).

The rare and spectacular **Cuevas de Sorbas** (☎950 36 47 04; www.cuevasdesorbas.com; basic tour adult/child €15/10.50; ⊙tours 11am, 1pm & 4pm Oct-May, 10am-8pm Jun-Sep; P), 2km east of Sorbas, are part of a vast network of underground galleries and tunnels. Guided visits lead through the labyrinthine underworld, revealing glittering gypsum crystals, tranquil ponds, stalactites, stalagmites and dark, mysterious tunnels. The basic tour, suitable for everyone from children to seniors, lasts about 1½ hours. Tours need to be reserved at least one day ahead; English- and German-speaking guides are available.

Tranquil hideaway **Almond Reef** (☎950 36 90 97; www.almondreef.co.uk; Calle Los Josefos, Cariatiz; s/d/f/ste incl breakfast €40/60/77/99; P 📶 ❄) sits in the sleepy hamlet of Cariatiz, 8km northeast of Sorbas. Run by an English couple, it's a cosy spot with seven rustic rooms in a whitewashed farmhouse, a small pool, and a four-bed cottage to rent. As well as breakfast, dinner is also available.

in for three courses of homey cooking, from soup starters to grilled meat mains to refreshing fruit salads.

Getting There & Away

Tabernas is about 35km north of Almería, accessible via the A7 and N340A roads.

Up to six weekday Alsa (p303) buses run from Almería to Tabernas (€2.70, 40 minutes). Weekend services are much reduced (two on Saturday, three on Sunday).

Níjar

POP 30,663

Níjar, a pristine white town in the foothills of the Sierra Alhamilla, is best known for its glazed pottery and handwoven rugs known as *jarapas*. These are widely available in shops and showrooms on the main drag, Avenida García Lorca, and in the old potters' quarter, the Barrio Alfarero. Shopping apart, the town has a quaint old town, centred on leafy **Plaza La Glorieta**, and huge views from its signature monument, the **Atalaya watchtower**.

La Tienda de los Milagros CERAMICS
(☎950 36 03 59; www.latiendadelosmilagros.com; Callejón del Artesano 1; ⊙10.30am-9.30pm) This is the workshop of British ceramicist Matthew Weir and Spanish artisan Isabel Hernández, who produces artistic *jarapa* (cotton-rag) rugs. As well as quality ceramics, Matthew makes woodblock prints and works with stoneware and porcelain. The workshop is just off Calle Las Eras in the Barrio Alfarero.

Information

Oficina Municipal de Turismo (☎950 36 00 12; www.turismonijar.es; Plaza del Mercado 1; ⊙10am-2pm daily & 4-6pm Mon-Sat) Centrally located tourist office.

Getting There & Away

Níjar is 4km north of the A7, 30km northeast of Almería. There are parking bays all the way up Avenida Lorca.

Bus M-211, operated by **Consorcio de Transporte Metropolitano** (www.ctal.es), runs two to four times daily from Almería's Estación Intermodal to Níjar (€2, 1¼ to 1½ hours).

LAS ALPUJARRAS DE ALMERÍA

The Almerian part of Las Alpujarras (the Sierra Nevada's southern foothills and valleys) is much less visited than its Granada counterpart. It's admittedly less spectacular, but still a very pretty part of the world. White villages, clustered around large churches that are mostly former mosques, are strung along the

OFF THE BEATEN TRACK

OHANES

The drive up to Ohanes – an isolated, whitewashed hamlet wedged into vertiginous, terraced slopes – is as worthwhile as the visit itself. The snaking road up from the A348 winds past stark red rock until it curves around a ridge into the upper Ohanes valley, where the scenery changes completely, to green terraces and flourishing vineyards. Continuing past the village down the steep west side of the valley, you'll enjoy further splendid views of the terraced fields. This route back to the A348 is shorter than the ascent, but slightly more nerve-racking, dwindling to one lane as it zigzags down through the fields. It comes out just west of Canjáyar.

valley of the Río Andarax between the mountains of the Sierra Nevada to the north and Sierra de Gádor to the south. Approaching from Almería, the landscape is at first rather barren, but the land gradually becomes more lush, with lemon and orange orchards and vineyards producing plenty of Almerian wine.

Los Millares ARCHAEOLOGICAL SITE
(☎677 903404; AL3411; ⊙10am-2pm Wed-Sun; P) FREE Los Millares, reckoned one of Europe's most important Copper Age sites, occupies a plateau above the Río Andarax some 20km north of Almería. Dusty and exposed, it contains the scant remains of a fortified metalworking settlement that stood here between 3200 and 2200 BC. Excavations, which began in the early 20th century, have unearthed outlines of defensive walls, stone houses and domed graves. Also of note is a series of re-created huts and workshops.

Before heading onto the site, bone up on its history at the small **interpretation centre** by the entrance. To get here, turn off the A348 about 4km east of Alhama de Almería. then follow the signs another 1km east.

Laujar de Andarax

POP 1536 / ELEV 920M

Overlooked by foreboding hills and surrounded by vineyards, Laujar de Andarax is the 'capital' of the Almería Alpujarras. It was here that Boabdil, the last emir of Granada, settled briefly after losing Granada, and where Aben Humeya, the leader of the doomed 1568–70 *morisco* uprising (Christians converted from Islam), had his main base. These days, Laujar is a laid-back wine town with a handsome town hall and a formidable 17th-century church, the towering **Iglesia de la Encarnación**.

Sights & Activities

To sample and buy local wines, head west of town to **Bodegas Valle de Laujar** (☎950 51 42 00; www.bodegasvallelaujar.es; Carretera AL5402; ⊙8am-2pm & 3.30-7pm; P) FREE, or visit the nearby organic winery **Cortijo El Cura** (☎950 52 40 26; www.cortijoelcura.com; ⊙tours & tastings noon Sat & Sun or by appointment; P) .

Mirador de Laujar VIEWPOINT
A hairy drive up a steep, snaking road leads to this terrific viewing platform 3.2km above town. From here you can look down on the full sweep of the valley – and beyond to the remote mountains that curtain it. To get to the site from the western end of town, follow signs to the Recreation Area ('Área Recreativa') and, shortly after, to the mirador.

El Nacimiento Waterfalls WATERFALL
(P) Just east of Laujar's main plaza, a signposted road heads 1.5km north to El Nacimiento, a shaded recreation area set around a series of waterfalls. It's not at its best in high summer or autumn – the water can dry up then – but for the rest of the year it's a popular weekend haunt.

Sendero del Aguadero WALKING
Starting 1km from El Nacimiento waterfalls, this lovely path (signposted PRA37) winds through woodlands of alder, pine and chestnut. The whole trail is a circular route of 14km (five to six hours), climbing and descending more than 600m, but you can double back whenever you like. Look out for wild boar and hoopoes (black-and-white birds with elaborate orange crests).

Sleeping & Eating

Hotel Almirez HOTEL €
(☎950 51 35 14, 655 573204; www.hotelalmirez.es; Carretera AL5402; s €43, d €56-60, q €100-112; P) A friendly, family-run hotel set in its own grounds off Laujar's western access road. Its spotless, spacious rooms are plainly furnished, but each comes with a terrace offering lovely views of the verdant surrounds.

Patio Andaluz ANDALUCIAN €€
(☎648 488946; Plaza Mayor de la Alpujarra 3; menú del día €12.50; ⊙1-3.30pm Thu-Mon) For a home-

cooked Andalucian lunch, head for this sweet spot behind the tourist office. The *menú del día* features hearty mains – *carrilleras* (pork cheeks), *migas* (breadcrumbs with chorizo), *costillas a la brasa* (grilled ribs) – followed by traditional desserts like *arroz con leche* (rice pudding), all served on a flowery whitewashed patio with trickling fountain, or by the fireside in winter.

Information

Centro de Visitantes Laujar de Andarax (☎950 51 55 35; Carretera AL5402; ⊙10am-2pm Thu-Sun) This office 1.5km west of the town centre provides info on nearby Parque Natural Sierra Nevada.

Oficina de Turismo (☎950 51 31 03; Plaza Mayor de la Alpujarra 9; ⊙10.30am-1pm Mon-Thu, 10am-2pm & 4-6pm Fri & Sat, 10am-2pm Sun) Laujar de Andarax' brand-new downtown tourist office offers town maps and other handouts, plus an interpretive centre with excellent displays on local history and hiking opportunities.

Getting There & Away

Three Alsa (p303) buses run from Almería to Laujar (€6.60, two to 2¼ hours) Monday to Friday, and one on Saturday and Sunday. To continue on to the Granada Alpujarras you'll have to travel via Berja (€2.20, 40 to 55 minutes, two daily Monday to Friday, one daily Saturday and Sunday), south of Laujar; it's most practical if you start on the 7.50am bus (Monday to Friday only) from Laujar to Berja.

COSTA DE ALMERÍA

Almeria's coastline is one of Andalucía's great natural wonders. Encompassing heavenly beaches, plunging cliffs and wild tracts of arid scrubland, it has largely escaped unsightly development and remains an unspoilt and relatively unexplored part of the region. Hotspots include the Parque Natural de Cabo de Gata-Níjar to the southeast and, to the north, Mojácar, a quaint hilltop *pueblo* with a vibrant beachfront scene.

Parque Natural de Cabo de Gata-Níjar

Extending southeast of Almería, the Parque Natural de Cabo de Gata-Níjar (www.degata.com/en) has some of Spain's most flawless and least crowded beaches. The park, which stretches from Retamar in the west up to Agua Amarga in the east, encompasses 340 sq km of dramatic cliff-bound coastline and stark semidesert terrain punctuated by remote white villages and isolated farmsteads. Adding to the often eerie atmosphere are the abandoned mines and bizarre rock formations that litter the landscape.

There is plenty to do in the area besides enjoying the beaches and walking: diving, snorkelling, kayaking, sailing, cycling, horse riding, and 4WD and boat tours are all popular. A host of operators offers these activities from the coastal villages during Easter and

ALMERÍA: THE GREENHOUSE OF EUROPE

As much a feature of Almería's landscape as its arid badlands and remote beaches are the plastic-covered *invernaderos* (greenhouses) that sprawl across the province. West of Almería city, for example, the entire 35km-long coastal plain from Roquetas de Mar to Adra is coated in grey-white polythene. Such is the size of this sea of plastic that sunbeams reflected off it are said to have caused the local climate to cool.

Almería province has long supported agriculture. Its mountainsides have been farmed for centuries after the Moors built a complex system of terraces and irrigation channels a millennium or so ago. But it wasn't until the introduction of year-round greenhouse cultivation in the late 20th century that this previously dirt-poor part of Spain started to profit from its agricultural endeavours. Now produce grown in the province accounts for nearly 40% of Spain's vegetable exports, including around half its tomato sales, with a value of €2.6 billion annually.

Given this, it's not surprising that tomatoes are a staple on menus across the region. In summer, mountain-grown, sun-ripened tomatoes are delectable. In winter, look out for *tomate Raf*, a greenish heirloom variety with a sweet taste and segmented surface.

But away from the restaurants and supermarkets, there's another, less savoury, side to the story. Reports in the international press have highlighted the plight of greenhouse workers, drawing attention to the exploitation of the largely immigrant labour force and the appalling living and working conditions endured by many labourers.

from July to September; a few carry on year-round. The park's main hub is San José, a popular resort on the east coast.

El Cabo a Fondo BOATING
(☎637 449170; www.elcaboafondo.es; 1½hr tour adult/child €25/20) Some of the most spectacular views of the Cabo de Gata coast are from the sea – a perspective you'll get on Cabo a Fondo's outings, which start from La Isleta del Moro, Las Negras or La Fabriquilla. Tours run up to seven times daily and are offered year-round, weather permitting (minimum numbers may be needed in low season). Reservations required.

Information

Centro de Información (☎950 38 02 99; www.cabodegata-nijar.com; Avenida San José 27; ⊙10am-2pm & 6-9pm Apr-Oct, 10am-2pm & 4.30-6pm Nov-Mar) Park information centre in San José.

Centro de Interpretación Las Amoladeras (☎950 16 04 35; Carretera Retamar-Pujaire, Km 7; ⊙10am-2pm Jul-Sep, hours vary rest of year) The park's main visitor centre, 2km west of Ruescas on the main road from Almería.

Getting There & Away

Alsa (p303) runs one daily bus from Almería's Estación Intermodal to Las Negras (€2.95, 1¼ hours) and Rodalquilar (€2.95, 1½ hours).

Autocares Bernardo (☎950 25 04 22; www.autocaresbernardo.com) runs buses from Almería to San José (€2.95, 1¼ hours, two to four daily).

Autocares Frahermar (☎950 29 02 12; www.frahermar.com) operates three buses daily from Almería to Agua Amarga (€2.90, 1¼ hours) in July and August. Service is reduced to two buses Monday, Wednesday and Friday and one bus Saturday and Sunday the rest of the year.

San Miguel de Cabo de Gata & Around

Faro de Cabo de Gata LIGHTHOUSE
(P) Marking the southwest point of the promontory, this photogenic lighthouse commands stirring views of a jagged volcanic reef known as the **Arrecife de las Sirenas** (Reef of the Mermaids), after the monk seals that used to lounge here. A side road runs 3km up to **Torre Vigía Vela Blanca**, an 18th-century watchtower boasting even more coastal vistas.

Salinas de Cabo de Gata LAGOON
(P) Southeast of San Miguel de Cabo de Gata, some of Spain's last surviving salt-extraction lagoons draw flocks of migrating flamingos and other waterbirds between spring and autumn: by late August there can be a thousand flamingos there. To spy on them, search out the strategically sited birdwatching hides, accessible along the east side of the main road just north of Almadraba de Monteleva.

San José

POP 849

The main beach resort in Parque Natural de Cabo de Gata-Níjar, San José makes a wonderful base for exploring the area. It's well set up with hotels and restaurants and the surrounding coastline harbours a string of sublime beaches, most within easy striking distance.

Activities

The cold, clear waters off Cabo de Gata offer superlative diving (and snorkelling), rivalled in southern Spain only by Cabo de Palos in Murcia. The posidonia seagrass meadows are proof of water cleanliness; along with caves, rocks and canyons they provide a habitat for many marine animals, including eagle rays, sunfish, moray and conger eels, grouper, angelfish and barracuda. A highlight for experienced divers is the wreck *El Vapor,* 1.8km off Faro de Cabo de Gata. There are several dive centres in the area, including **Isub** (☎950 38 00 04; www.isubsanjose.com; Calle Babor 8; ⊙8.30am-2pm & 4-7pm Mon-Sat, 8.30am-2pm Sun Mar-Dec) and **MedialunAventura** (☎667 224861; www.medialunaventura.com; Calle del Puerto 7; rental per hour/day kayak €12/40, double kayak €18/60, SUP €12/45, bike hire per half-day/day €15/20; ⊙9am-2pm & 5-8pm, to 10pm summer) in San José, and **Buceo en Cabo de Gata** (☎664 534200; www.buceoencabodegata.es; Calle Cala Stay 1, La Isleta del Moro; ⊙9am-8pm) in La Isleta del Moro.

Sleeping

You'll need to book early for the peak periods of Semana Santa, July and August. Many places close for a few months in winter; most offer deep discounts outside high season.

Hostal El Dorado HOSTAL €€
(☎950 38 01 18; www.hostaleldorado.es; Camino del Aguamarina; d €55-95; ❄️📶🏊) Perched on a hillside about 500m inland from San José's waterfront, El Dorado offers an appealing combination of affordable rates and fine sea views. There's nothing fancy about the 27 rooms, but most face the Mediterranean, and all come with balconies or terraces. A rooftop swimming pool sweetens the deal.

Parque Natural de Cabo de Gata-Níjar

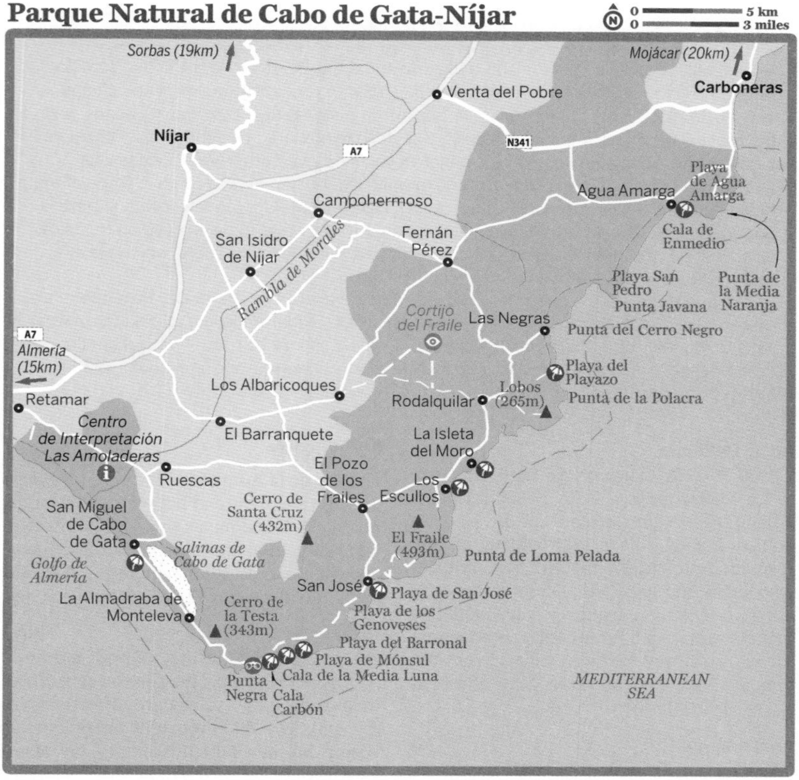

MC San José BOUTIQUE HOTEL €€

(☎950 61 11 11; www.hotelesmcsanjose.com; Calle Faro 2; r incl breakfast €75-188; ⏲Apr-Oct; P ❄ ☎ ≋) The MC offers the best of both worlds – warm family hospitality and a chic, designer look. Inside, it's all sharp modern furniture, cool whites and slate-greys, while outside the plant-lined terrace and small pool are ideal for basking in the sun. Come the evening, you can relax over a glass of local Almería wine at the in-house wine cellar.

Eating & Drinking

La Góndola PIZZA €€

(☎950 38 01 80; Calle Correo 11; pizza €7-17, pasta €9-12; ⏲1-4pm & 8-11pm Jul & Aug, shorter hours rest of year) La Góndola offers a welcome break from standard Andalucian fare. The Neapolitan-style pizza is the real deal, thin-crusted with excellent tomato sauce, and the desserts – including homemade *panna cotta* and *tiramisù* – are worth saving room for.

Casa Miguel SPANISH €€

(☎950 38 03 29; www.casamiguelentierradecine.es; Avenida de San José 43; mains €9-26; ⏲1-4.30pm & 7.30-11.30pm Tue-Sun) Service and food are reliably good at this long-standing San José favourite, one of several places with outdoor seating on the main drag. There's plenty to choose from on the extensive menu but you'll rarely go wrong with the grilled fish of the day.

★4 Nudos SEAFOOD €€€

(☎620 938160; www.4nudosrestaurante.com; Club Náutico, Puerto Deportivo; mains €16-25; ⏲1.30-4pm & 8-11pm Tue-Sun Mar-Oct, 1.30-4pm Tue-Sun Nov-Feb) Of San José's various seafood restaurants, the 'Four Knots' is the star performer. Aptly housed in the Club Náutico at the marina, it serves classic Spanish dishes – paella included – alongside more innovative creations such as baby-prawn ceviche and tuna marinated in soy sauce, ginger and rosemary. Reservations advised except at the quietest times.

WALKING THE CABO DE GATA COAST

An extensive network of roads and trails runs for about 50km along the coast from San Miguel de Cabo de Gata to Agua Amarga. The full hike requires three days and should only be attempted in spring or, even better, autumn (when the sea is warm), as the summer heat is fierce and there is no shade. But you can embark on sections of the walk for a day or afternoon, and some of the beaches you'll pass are otherwise inaccessible.

Southwest from San José it's a fine 9km walk of about 2½ hours (passing some of the best beaches) to the Torre Vigía Vela Blanca (p308), an old lookout tower with superb panoramas. Northeast from San José, there are further views to be enjoyed on the fairly level 8km hike to the tiny beach settlement of **Los Escullos**. The route, which partly follows old mining roads, skirts the ancient volcano **El Fraile**.

Another good stretch is from Rodalquilar along the valley to **Playa del Playazo**, then up the coast along scenic cliff edges to **Las Negras** (6km from Rodalquilar). It's another 3km to the real prize: Playa San Pedro (p313) – inaccessible by road – with its small settlement of boho-travellers. You can also drive to Las Negras and walk to Playa San Pedro from there.

★La Gallineta FUSION €€€

(☎950 38 05 01; Carretera Níjar-San José, El Pozo de los Frailes; mains €15-30; ⏰1.30-3.30pm & 9-11pm) An elegant restaurant in El Pozo do los Frailes village, 4km north of San José, La Gallineta is a hit with city escapees who make the drive out for its innovative, outward-looking cuisine. Menu highlights include tuna with Cambodian spices and carpaccio of red prawns with citrus and mango. Book two or three days ahead at Easter or in summer.

Abacería Avesivá BAR

(☎950 38 01 73; Calle del Puerto 3; ⏰11am-3.30pm & 7-11.30pm Wed-Mon) Search out this cosy bar for a taste of the local wine. It looks the part with its burgundy walls, blackboards and high wooden stools, and has a decent selection of Almería labels and craft beers – best enjoyed with a side plate of cheese and cured ham.

Rodalquilar

Until not long ago the tiny inland village of Rodalquilar was a ghost town, its few residents hanging on among the shells of abandoned gold mines. However, since the 1990s it has undergone something of a makeover, thanks in part to the transfer here of the *parque natural's* headquarters, and nowadays it attracts a steady stream of visitors. Most come to explore its former gold mine but it also has an excellent botanical garden and many buildings sport large murals, lending it something of a bohemian air.

Sights

Mirador de la Amatista VIEWPOINT

(P) On the main road between La Isleta del Moro and Rodalquilar, this viewpoint commands breathtaking views of the vertiginous, unspoilt coastline. From here the road snakes down into the basin of the Rodalquilar valley.

Gold Mines RUINS

(P) Set amid the Martian red-rock terrain at the top of the village, the skeletal remains of Rodalquilar's gold mines are an eerie sight. The complex, which was fully operational as recently as the mid-20th century, lies abandoned – and you're free to explore its former crushing towers and decantation tanks.

To get an insight into the area's mining history, stop first at **La Casa de los Volcanes** (Calle Apartadero; ⏰10am-2pm Thu-Sat; P) FREE, a small museum with Spanish-language displays (some translated into English) on the mines and the geology of Cabo de Gata.

Beyond the mines, a rough dirt road continues through the hills, pocked with abandoned mines and the ruined miners' hamlet of **San Diego**. Rather than attempt this road by car, you'd be better off taking the **Sendero Cerro del Cinto**, an 11km walking trail that traverses the striking post-industrial landscape.

Jardín Botánico El Albardinal GARDENS

(☎671 561226; Calle Fundición; ⏰10am-1pm & 6-8.30pm Tue-Sun Jun-Aug, 9am-2pm Tue-Fri, 10am-2pm & 4-6pm Sat & Sun Sep-May; P) FREE Rodalquilar's extensive botanical gardens showcase the vegetation of Andalucía's arid southeast. It's well planned, with every plant, tree and shrub identified. There's also a charming *huerta* (vegetable garden), complete with jam recipes and a scarecrow.

El Cortijo del Fraile HISTORIC BUILDING

(P) This abandoned farmstead on a windswept plain 6km northwest of Rodalquilar was the scene of the tragic, true-life love-and-revenge story that inspired Federico García Lorca's best-known play, *Blood Wedding*. In 1928, in what's known as El Crimen de Níjar (the Níjar Crime), a woman due to be married here disappeared with another man, who was then shot dead by the brother of the jilted groom. The romantically ruined 18th-century buildings are now fenced off but maintain a suitably doom-laden aura.

Take the ALP824 road (which soon becomes a dirt track) 5km east from Los Albaricoques.

Sleeping & Eating

★Oro y Luz RESORT €€

(☎722 789973; www.oroyluz.com; Paraje Los Albacetes; ste €89-177; 📶) Backed by olive trees, palms and Cabo de Gato's rugged coastal landscape, this whitewashed villa near the turn-off for beautiful Playa del Playazo offers seven stand-alone suites with private entrances and terraces. The welcoming new Italian owners have added a dose of designer flair, and the on-site **restaurant** (☎950 80 88 19; www.oroyluz.com; Paraje Los Albacetes; mains €14-24; ⏱1.30-4pm Mon, 1.30-4pm & 8-10.30pm Wed-Sun) is one of the province's best.

El Jardín de los Sueños CASA RURAL €€

(☎950 38 98 43, 669 184118; www.eljardindelos suenos.es; Calle Los Gorriones; incl breakfast s €65-85, d €80-118, ste €110-150; P❄📶🏊) Just outside Rodalquilar, signposted off the main road, this year-round retreat is ideal for getting away from it all. The main farmhouse is surrounded by a beautiful garden of dry-climate plants and fruit trees, some of which contribute to the substantial breakfasts. Inside, the rooms are notable for bright colours, original art, private terraces and the absence of TVs.

Las Negras

Camping La Caleta CAMPGROUND €

(☎950 52 52 37; www.campinglacaleta.com; sites per adult/tent & car €6.60/14.20, d/q bungalow €75/115; P📶🏊) This secluded campground is tucked into a cove 1km south of Las Negras. Signposted from the entrance of the village, it offers tent pitches and bungalows (the latter have a two-night minimum stay) plus a decent range of facilities, including an on-site shop, restaurant and pool.

Restaurante La Palma SEAFOOD €€

(☎950 38 80 42; Calle Bahía de Las Negras 21; mains €10-25; ⏱9am-11.30pm Tue-Sun) Waves breaking on the pebble beach provide the soundtrack to meals at this jaunty seafront restaurant in Las Negras. Seafood is an obvious highlight, ideally eaten on the outdoor terrace, but you can also dine on roast meats and rice dishes.

Agua Amarga

POP 376

A tiny fishing village turned low-key resort, Agua Amarga is a favourite with Spanish urbanites and Scandinavian sun-seekers. It's a sleepy spot for much of the year but bursts into life in July and August, when holidaymakers flock to its fine, sandy beach and casual seafront restaurants.

LIGHTS, CAMERA, ACTION

International film-makers have long been drawn to Almería's harsh desert landscapes. Most famously, director Sergio Leone teamed up with Clint Eastwood et al in the mid-1960s to shoot his spaghetti westerns in the Desierto de Tabernas (p304). But the Italian wasn't the first to film in the area. A few years earlier, David Lean had brought the production of his 1962 epic *Lawrence of Arabia* to the province, filming at various locations including the Playa de los Genoveses (p313). A second beach, the Playa de Mónsul (p313), later featured in *Indiana Jones and the Last Crusade* (1989), serving as the backdrop for a scene in which Sean Connery brings down a plane with a flock of birds.

Almería city has also staged its fair share of drama. It doubled as Palermo and Messina in the WWII classic *Patton* (1970) and has hosted shoots for *Game of Thrones* – the Alcazaba (p298) appears as Sunspear, the capital of Dorne.

Other movies filmed in the province include *Cleopatra* (1963); *2001: A Space Odyssey (1968); Conan the Barbarian* (1982); *Never Say Never Again* (1983); and *The Girl with the Dragon Tattoo* (2009).

★MiKasa BOUTIQUE HOTEL €€€
(☎950 13 80 73; www.mikasasuites.com; Carretera Carboneras 20; d incl breakfast €160-300; P❄📶🏊) In the heart of Agua Amarga village, MiKasa is an enchanting retreat. A few blocks back from the beach (within easy walking distance), it's a lovely villa set up with charming, individually styled rooms, two pools, Jacuzzi, spa, well-stocked honesty bar and a variety of comfy common areas. Rates drop considerably outside August.

★La Frontera TAPAS €
(☎950 13 03 44; www.facebook.com/bar.lafrontera; Avenida de Garrucha 4, Carboneras; tapas €1.50, medias raciones/raciones from €6/10) For top-notch seafood tapas in a low-key local setting, head 15 minutes up the coast from Agua Amarga to this roadside bar in Carboneras. Small plates of paella, grilled shrimp and sardines, fried squid and smoked tuna are yours for €1.50 each – or free with each drink you order. For larger appetites, reasonably priced *raciones* (full servings of tapas items) are also available.

La Palmera SEAFOOD €€
(☎restaurant 950 13 82 08, rooms 676 726819; www.hostalrestaurantelapalmera.com; Calle Aguada 4; mains €11-20; ⏱noon-11pm mid-Mar–early Nov; ❄) Seafood on the beach is one of Agua Amarga's specialities and this breezy, beachfront restaurant is ideally situated to provide it. Bag a table on the terrace and dig into hearty bowls of mussels and grilled cuttlefish. The restaurant also has several simple sea-facing guest rooms (€110 to €140).

Restaurante La Villa MEDITERRANEAN €€€
(☎950 13 80 90; Carretera Carboneras 18; mains €15-25; ⏱8pm-midnight Jun-Sep, shorter hours rest of year) Reserve ahead for this sophisticated Agua Amarga restaurant with its romantically lit dining room and elegant poolside terrace. Dishes – from pasta to steak tartare and gourmet black-Angus burgers – are original and artfully presented, complemented by a stellar line-up of cocktails.

Mojácar

POP 6403

Both a massively popular beach resort and a charming hill town, Mojácar is divided into two quite separate parts: Mojácar Pueblo, the attractive historic centre, a picturesque jumble of white-cube houses daubed down an inland hilltop; and 3km away on the coast, Mojácar Playa, its young offspring, a modern low-rise resort fronting a 7km-long beach.

As recently as the 1960s, Mojácar was decaying and almost abandoned. But a savvy mayor managed to resurrect its fortunes by luring artists and travellers to the area with offers of free land – which brought a distinct bohemian air that endures to this day.

Sights

The main sight is Mojácar's hilltop *pueblo*, with its whitewashed houses, charming plazas, bars and cafes centred on the fortress-like Iglesia de Santa María. Beach lovers should head down to Mojácar Playa, which boasts 7km of mainly sandy beach. To reach the *pueblo* from the *playa* turn inland at the roundabout by the Parque Comercial, a large shopping centre towards the north end of the beach. Regular buses also connect the two.

With some 7km of sands, Mojácar Playa has room for everyone, as well as some excellent beachfront bars and restaurants. The best sands are at the southern end, which also has a pleasant seafront promenade.

South of the main beach, a 1.25km stretch of rocks gives onto a second, 1.25km-long beach overlooked by an 18th-century watchtower, the **Castillo de Macenas** (Mojácar Playa; P). From the *castillo* an unpaved track runs 3km along the coast passing several small coves, some of which have nudist beaches. Along the way you can climb the **Torre Pirulico** (P) FREE, a 13th-century defensive tower.

Mirador del Castillo VIEWPOINT
(Plaza Mirador del Castillo, Mojácar Pueblo) Perched on the highest point in town – originally the site of a castle – this hilltop *mirador* (viewpoint) looks down to the sea and over a hazy brown-green landscape studded with white buildings and stark volcanic cones just like the one Mojácar occupies.

Casa La Canana HOUSE
(☎950 16 44 20; Calle Esteve 6, Mojácar Pueblo; adult/child €2.50/1; ⏱10.30am-2.30pm daily, plus 5-8pm Tue, Wed, Fri & Sat) Beautifully maintained and thoughtfully interpreted by the owners (who live upstairs), this house-museum re-creates a well-to-do villager's dwelling from the early 20th century. Much of the interior decor – including furniture, tiles, bedspreads, fireplaces and everyday household items – is original to the house. Bilingual information panels, photos, tools and model animals illustrate the lifestyle of the time.

Fuente Pública FOUNTAIN
(Public Fountain; Calle La Fuente, Mojácar Pueblo) Hidden near the foot of the hilltop *pueblo*,

CABO DE GATA BEACHES

Cabo de Gata's best beaches are strung along the south and east coasts. Some of the most beautiful lie southwest of San José, reached by a dirt road signposted 'Playas' and/or 'Genoveses/Mónsul'. Note that from mid-June to mid-September, the road is closed to cars once the beach car parks (€5) fill up, typically by about 10am, but a bus (€1 one way) runs from town every half hour from 9am to 9pm.

The first beach outside of San José is **Playa de los Genoveses** (P), a 1km stretch of sand where the Genoese navy landed in 1147 to help the Christian attack on Almería. A further 2.5km on, pristine **Playa de Mónsul** (P) is another glorious spot – you may recognise the large free-standing rock on the sand from the film *Indiana Jones and the Last Crusade*. Tracks behind the large dune at Mónsul's east end lead down to nudist **Playa del Barronal**, 600m from the road. If you bear left just before Barronal and work your way over a little pass just left of the highest hillock, you'll come to **El Lance del Perro**. This beach, with striking basalt rock formations, is the first of four gorgeous, isolated beaches called the **Calas del Barronal**. Tides permitting, you can walk round the foot of the cliffs from one to the next.

A little west of Playa de Mónsul, paths lead from the road to two other less-frequented beaches, **Cala de la Media Luna** and **Cala Carbón**.

San José has a busy sandy beach of its own, and to the northeast there are reasonable beaches at **Los Escullos** and **La Isleta del Moro**. Much finer is **Playa del Playazo** (P), a broad, sandy strip between two headlands 3.5km east of Rodalquilar (the last 2km along a drivable track from the main road) or 2.5km south of Las Negras via a coastal footpath.

With its own part-sandy, part-stony beach, **Las Negras** is also a gateway to the fabulous **Playa San Pedro**, 3km to the northeast. Set between dramatic headlands and home to a small New Age settlement, this fabled beach can be reached only on foot or by boat (€12 return) from Las Negras.

Further up the coast, the small resort of **Agua Amarga** is fronted by a popular sandy beach. A short but steep 1.5km trek to the southwest leads to **Cala de Enmedio**, a pretty, secluded beach enclosed between eroded rocks.

this historic fountain is a village landmark. Locals and visitors come to fill containers with the water that pours out of 13 spouts into marble troughs and tinkles along a courtyard below colourful plants. A plaque states that in 1488 this was where the envoy of the Reyes Católicos (the Catholic Monarchs Fernando and Isabel) met Mojácar's last Moorish mayor, Alavez, to negotiate the village's surrender.

Festivals & Events

Moros y Cristianos CULTURAL

(weekend nearest 10 Jun) Mojácar's big three-day annual event sees locals don costumes in dances, processions and other festivities commemorating the town's Christian reconquest.

Noche de San Juan FIESTA

(Mojácar Playa; 23 Jun) Expect bonfires and dawn-to-dusk eating, drinking and dancing at this big summer solstice beach party.

Sleeping

★**Hostal El Olivar** HOSTAL €

(950 47 20 02; www.hostalelolivar.es; Calle Estación Nueva 11, Mojácar Pueblo; d incl breakfast €53-70;) Friendly owners Alberto and Michaela have completely revamped this stylish boutiquey hostal, with new paint, curtains, bedspreads, mini-fridges, handmade furniture and a massage room. Three rooms have balconies, and there's a delightful sun terrace for lounging or lingering over breakfast. An olive theme runs throughout, with olive oil soaps and a tree whose 'leaves' are handwritten notes from past guests.

★**Hostal Arco Plaza** HOSTAL €

(647 846275, 950 47 27 77; www.hostalarcoplaza.es; Calle Aire 1, Mojácar Pueblo; s €30, d €39-45, tr €45-50;) Right in the heart of the action, this friendly, excellent-value *hostal* has attractive sky-blue rooms with wrought-iron beds and terracotta-tiled floors. The best have private balconies overlooking Plaza Nueva, though you can enjoy the same views from the communal rooftop terrace. The plaza can be noisy in the evening but generally quiets down after midnight.

Hotel El Puntazo HOTEL €€

(950 47 82 65; www.hotelelpuntazo.com; Paseo del Mediterráneo 257, Mojácar Playa; 4-star d €80-141,

Mojácar Pueblo

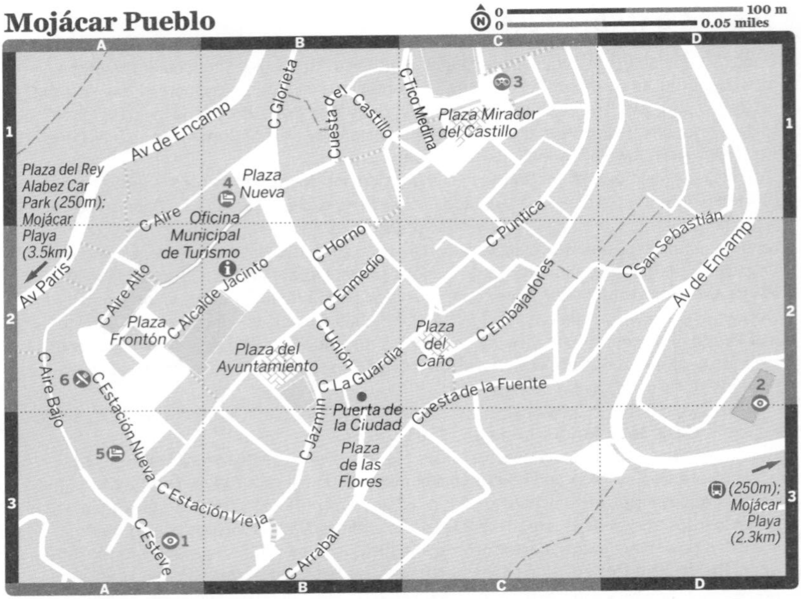

Mojácar Pueblo

Sights
1 Casa La Canana....................A3
2 Fuente Pública....................D2
3 Mirador del Castillo....................C1

Sleeping
4 Hostal Arco Plaza....................B1
5 Hostal El Olivar....................A3

Eating
6 Viento Norte....................A2

1-star d €50-90; P ❄ 📶 🏊) A big seafront set-up in Mojácar Playa, El Puntazo is made up of two hotels, one a four-star, the other a more basic one-star. Rooms in the four-star are bright and spacious, decked out in summery whites and greens; in the one-star they're smaller and more modestly furnished. All have access to the on-site swimming pool.

Eating & Drinking

Both *pueblo* and *playa* have a good range of restaurants serving varied cuisines (Spanish, Mexican, Italian), though some close from about November to March.

In summer, especially August, Mojácar nightlife is hopping, with a number of friendly, lively bars tucked into small houses in the *pueblo*. Down at the *playa*, action is centred on the many beachfront bars and clubs.

Tito's Cantina MEXICAN €
(☎950 47 88 41; www.facebook.com/lacantina.mojacar; Paseo del Mediterráneo, Mojácar Playa; mains €8-14; ⏱7pm-midnight Apr-Oct; 📝) 🍃 Founder and local legend Tito has passed away, but his legacy lives on at this festive cane-canopied cantina under the palms along Mojácar's beachfront. Expect all the old favourites – enchiladas, quesadillas, fajitas, tacos and guacamole – plus enough tequila and Mexican beer to ensure a grand old time. The colourful decor will make you feel like you're in Mexico.

Viento Norte BASQUE €€
(www.vientonorte.es; Plaza Frontón 2, Mojácar Pueblo; mains €10-18; ⏱noon-4pm & 8pm-midnight Jul & Aug, shorter hours rest of year; 📝) Bringing a touch of Spain's Basque Country to the Andalucian coast, the 'North Wind' entices with red-and-white checked tablecloths and a blackboard menu that runs the gamut from grilled octopus to *txistorra* (garlicky Basque sausage). The lunchtime *menú del día* (€12 for a first and second course, bread, wine and dessert) is good value.

Neptuno ANDALUCIAN €€
(☎616 005387; www.neptunomojacar.com; Paseo del Mediterráneo 62E, Mojácar Playa; mains €10-

21, plato del día €8; ⏲10am-5pm & 7pm-midnight, closed evenings Sun-Thu Oct-May) One of the smartest, busiest and best regarded of the *chiringuitos* (beach restaurants) in Mojácar Playa. Specialities of the house are its barbecued meats and fresh fish, but there's also a decent selection of salads and rice dishes.

Information

Oficina Municipal de Turismo (☎950 61 50 25; www.mojacar.es; Plaza Frontón, Mojácar Pueblo; ⏲9.30am-2pm & 4.30-7pm Mon-Fri, 10am-2pm & 4.30-7pm Sat, 10am-2pm Sun) Up in Mojàcar's hilltop *pueblo*.

Tourist Information Point (www.mojacar.es; Playa Villazar, Mojácar Playa; ⏲10am-2pm daily & 4.30-7pm Mon-Sat) Down on the beach in front of the Parque Comercial (shopping centre).

Getting There & Around

BUS

Intercity buses stop at various spots around the Parque Comercial roundabout in Mojácar Playa and on Avenida de Andalucía in Mojácar Pueblo.

Alsa (p303) runs buses to/from Almería (€7.90, 1¼ to 1¾ hours, two to four daily) and Murcia (€9.25, 2½ to three hours, two daily). Buy tickets at **Mojácar Tour** (☎950 47 57 57; www.viajesmojacar.grupoairmet.com; Centro Comercial Montemar, Avenida de Andalucía, Mojácar Playa; ⏲10am-1.30pm & 5.30-8pm).

A local bus (€1.20) runs a circuit from Mojácar Pueblo along the full length of the beach and back again, roughly every half hour from 9.15am to 11.35pm June to September, and until 9.15pm from October to May.

CAR & MOTORCYCLE

Follow the main road through the *pueblo* for two free parking lots on the western edge of town. The main Plaza del Rey Alabez car park hosts a weekly market on Wednesday mornings (so, no parking).

TAXI

Taxis wait in the *pueblo's* Plaza Nueva, or call ☎950 88 81 11.

LOS VÉLEZ

The beautiful mountain landscape of the remote Los Vélez district, in the northernmost part of Almería, is greener and more forested than most of the province. Three small towns nestle in the shadow of the stark Sierra de María range, part of the Parque Natural Sierra María-Los Vélez. There's good walking in the area, as well as some celebrated rock art at the Cueva de los Letreros.

Vélez Rubio is the largest town, with an enormous 18th-century baroque church, but Vélez Blanco has more charm.

Getting There & Away

Alsa (p303) runs one afternoon bus from Almería to Vélez Rubio (€15.25, 3½ hours), Vélez Blanco (€15.75, 3¾ hours) and María (€16.50, four hours). The return service starts from María at 6.30am (6.30pm on Sundays).

From Vélez Rubio, Alsa also runs buses to Granada (€14.50, two to three hours, three to four daily).

Parque Natural Sierra María-Los Vélez

Encompassing 226 sq km of verdant mountain terrain in the north of Almería province, the Parque Natural Sierra María-Los Vélez is a glorious wilderness. Its rocky peaks are cloaked in forests of pine and holm oaks while overhead golden eagles and peregrine falcons patrol the silent skies.

The area offers wonderful walking, with waymarked trails at their best in spring or autumn; pick up information at Vélez Blanco's visitor centre (p316). A good circular trail is the 13km **Sendero Solana de Maimón**, which runs through the Sierra de Maimón hills southwest of Vélez Blanco.

Just west of the tiny upland town of María, off the A317, the 40-hectare **Jardín Botánico Umbría de la Virgen** (⏲9am-3pm Tue-Sun May-Sep, 10am-4pm Tue-Sun Oct-Apr) FREE highlights the unique flora of the area and the Altiplano of Granada. From here, you can follow the circular, fairly easy 3km **Sendero Umbría de la Virgen**; figure on 1¾ hours.

Vélez Blanco

At 1070m, with its scramble of red-roofed houses, fairy-tale castle and sensational valley views, Vélez Blanco is the most appealing base among Los Vélez' three villages. On Wednesday mornings you can browse its lively street market on the central Calle Corredera.

Cueva de los Letreros CAVE
(☎694 467136; adult/child €2/1; ⏲guided tours 6.30pm Wed & Sat, 11am Sun Jun-Aug, 4pm Wed & Sat, noon Sun Sep-May; P) Of the several Unesco-protected cave-painting locations in the area, this Stone Age ceremonial site is the star. The reddish drawings, made before 5500 BC, show animals, a horned figure dubbed *El Hechicero* (The Witchdoctor) and the *indalo,*

WORTH A TRIP

ALMERÍA'S GARGANTUAN GEODE

In 2019 the world's second-largest geode, **La Geoda de Pulpí** (950 96 27 27; www.geodapulpi.es; Calle Sierra de los Filabres, Los Jurados, Pulpí; adult/child €22/10; 9am-2pm & 4-9pm), opened to the public in Sierra del Aguilón. Measuring an astounding 8m long by 2m tall, this rare geological marvel was discovered by Madrid-based mineralogists in the abandoned Mina Rica, where iron, lead and silver were mined until the Spanish Civil War. Guided tours (half hourly; book in advance on the website) lead visitors 60m underground down corridors and metal steps, culminating with a chance to clamber inside the geode and view its dazzling collection of translucent gypsum crystals.

a stick-person with outspread arms connected by an arc (possibly a bow), among other things. Visits are by guided tour only, departing from the entrance of Camping Pinar del Rey, 1km south of Vélez Blanco off the A317.

Castillo de Vélez Blanco CASTLE
(10am-2pm & 5-8pm Wed-Sun Apr-Sep, 10am-2pm & 4-6pm Wed-Sun Oct-Mar; P) FREE The Disneyesque castle rising on a pinnacle high above Vélez Blanco's tiled roofs confronts the great sphinx-like butte La Muela (The Molar Tooth) across the valley as if in a bizarre duel. From the outside, the 16th-century castle is all Reconquista fortress, but inside it's pure Renaissance palace – or was until 1904, when the carved marble arcades, columns, doorways, window frames, statues and friezes were sold off by the impoverished owners.

American millionaire George Blumenthal ended up with the entire marble patio and later donated it to the Metropolitan Museum of Art in New York, where it's on permanent display. There is an ongoing project to make a copy of the patio and reinstall it.

El Palacil APARTMENT €€
(950 41 50 43; www.elpalacil.com; Calle Molino Cantarería; 2-/4-/6-person apt €70/140/210; P) Enjoying a tranquil streamside setting in Vélez Blanco, El Palacil offers spacious apartments for up to six people, with rustic homey decor and big kitchens. It also has a decent **restaurant** (pizzas €8-11, mains €12-23; 1-4pm & 8-11pm Tue-Sun) serving pizzas, salads, grilled meats and seafood.

★**Asador Espadín** ANDALUCIAN €€€
(950 41 25 34; www.restauranteasadorespadin.com; Calle Almez 2, Vélez Rubio; mains €16-24; noon-4pm Thu-Tue) Long before you reach the front door, delicious smoky aromas greet you at this ever-popular Vélez Rubio lunch spot. Formally dressed old-school waiters proffer plates of olive oil–drizzled roasted peppers stuffed with capers and anchovies, followed by massive fire-grilled steaks, pork cutlets and lamb chops. On weekends you'll need advance reservations for a table in the cavernous circular dining room.

Information

Centro de Visitantes Almacén del Trigo
(648 140091; Avenida Marqués de los Vélez; 10am-2pm Thu-Sun) Has useful information on the Parque Natural Sierra María-Los Vélez.

Cuevas del Almanzora

With its formidable, art-rich castle and handsome architecture, the busy agricultural centre of Cuevas del Almanzora merits a brief visit. The town, whose name is a nod to the many caves that pit the surrounding landscape, has ancient origins but took on its current form in the 19th century, when it flourished as a base for the silver mines in the nearby Sierra Almagrera hills.

Castillo del Marqués de los Vélez CASTLE
(950 54 87 07; Plaza de la Libertad; €2.50; 9am-2pm Tue-Sat mid-Jun–mid-Sep, 10am-1.30pm & 4-6.30pm Tue-Sat, 10am-1.30pm Sun mid-Sep–mid-Jun) Presiding over the old town, this 16th-century castle houses the **Museo Antonio Manuel Campoy**, showcasing the celebrated Spanish art critic's superb modern art collection, with works by the likes of Picasso and Miró. Your ticket also grants admission to the adjacent **gallery of Goya lithographs**, a small **archaeology museum** devoted to the El Argar Bronze Age culture, and the **Cueva Museo**, a nearby reconstruction of a mid-20th-century cave house filled with vintage furniture, tools and evocative old photos.

Getting There & Away

By car, Cuevas del Almanzora is just east of the main A7 road, 24km north of Mojácar. Or, take one of three daily buses Alsa (p303) runs from Almería (€9.55, 1¾ to 2¼ hours).

Understand Andalucía

History

A beacon of culture in medieval Europe, the hub of a transcontinental empire, a destitute backwater in decline and a booming tourism destination – Andalucía has seen it all. Set at a meeting point of continents and oceans, its cross-currents have yielded a culture unique in the world. From Islamic palaces to Christian cathedrals and the rhythms of the flamenco guitar, Andalucía cherishes its heritage, and you will sense the past in the fabric of the present everywhere you go.

Andalucía's Early Innovators

It was prehistoric Andalucians, especially in the east, who introduced many early technological advances to the Iberian Peninsula, perhaps thanks to contact with more advanced societies around the Mediterranean.

The Cueva de los Letreros near Vélez Blanco, with paintings of animals and human and mythological figures, is among the finest of many Neolithic (New Stone Age) rock-art sites scattered up the Mediterranean side of Spain. The Neolithic reached Spain from Egypt and Mesopotamia around 6000 BC, bringing the revolution of agriculture – the plough, crops, domesticated livestock – and with it pottery, textiles and villages. Some 3500 years later the people of Los Millares, near Almería, learned how to smelt and shape local copper deposits and became Spain's first metalworking culture. Around the same time, people near Antequera were constructing Spain's most impressive dolmens (megalithic tombs, made of large rocks covered in earth), during the same era as the megalithic age in France, Britain and Ireland.

About 1900 BC the people of El Argar (Almería province) learned to make bronze, an alloy of copper and tin that is stronger than copper – ushering the Bronze Age into the Iberian Peninsula.

Earlier, Andalucía may have been home to the last Neanderthal humans. Excavations at Gorham's Cave in Gibraltar show that Neanderthals were probably still hanging on there until at least 26,000 BC. Neanderthals had begun their terminal decline around 35,000 BC as a result of climate change and the arrival of Europe's first *Homo sapiens*, probably from North Africa. Like 21st-century tourists, early European

Prehistoric Andalucía

Cueva de la Pileta (Benaoján, near Ronda; p183)

Dolmen de Menga and Dolmen de Viera (Antequera; p191)

Orce (Granada province; p291)

Los Millares (Almería province; p306)

Cueva de Nerja (p198)

Museo de Almería (p299)

TIMELINE

18,000–14,000 BCE

Palaeolithic hunter-gatherers paint quarry such as aurochs, stags, horses and fish in the Cueva de la Pileta (near Ronda), Cueva de Ardales and Cueva de Nerja.

1000–800 BCE

Olives, grapevines and donkeys arrive in Andalucía with Phoenician traders, who establish coastal colonies such as Gadir (Cádiz) and Onuba (Huelva).

700–600 BCE

Iron replaces bronze as the most important metal around the lower Guadalquivir valley. The Tartessos culture that develops here is later mythologised as a source of fabulous wealth.

Homo sapiens gravitated to Andalucía's relatively warm climate, which permitted varied fauna and thick forests to develop, and made hunting and gathering somewhat easier. Between 20,000 and 16,000 years ago they left impressive rock paintings of some of the animals they hunted in Andalucian caves such as the Cueva de Ardales near Bobastro, the Cueva de la Pileta near Ronda and the Cueva de Nerja.

Ancient stone tools and a milk tooth, found near Orce in Granada province, reveal the presence of an early version of humanity cohabiting with mammoths, rhinoceroses, sabre-tooth tigers and giant hyenas an estimated 1.4 million years ago. At that age, the tooth would be the oldest confirmed human remnant in Western Europe.

Traders & Invaders

As history dawned, Andalucía's rich resources and settled societies attracted seafaring traders from around the Mediterranean. Later, the traders were replaced by invaders as imperialistic states emerged in the Mediterranean and sought not just to tap local wealth but also to exert political control. All these newcomers – Phoenicians, Greeks, Carthaginians, Romans and Visigoths – left indelible marks on Andalucian life and identity.

Phoenicians, Greeks & Tartessos

By about 1000 BCE, a flourishing culture rich in agriculture, animals and metals arose in western Andalucía. This attracted Phoenician traders (from present-day Lebanon), who came to exchange perfumes, ivory, jewellery, oil, wine and textiles for Andalucian silver and bronze. The Phoenicians set up coastal trading settlements at places such as Cádiz (which they called Gadir), Huelva (Onuba) and Almuñécar (Ex or Sex). As a result Cádiz, founded around 1100 BCE, has a good claim to be the oldest continuously inhabited settlement in Europe. In the 7th century BCE Greeks arrived, too, trading much the same goods. The Phoenicians and Greeks brought with them the potter's wheel, writing and three quintessential elements of the traditional Andalucian landscape: the olive tree, the vine and the donkey.

The Phoenician- and Greek-influenced culture of western Andalucía in the 8th and 7th centuries BCE is known as the Tartessos culture. The Tartessians developed advanced methods of working gold, but it was iron that replaced bronze as the most important metal. Tartessos was described centuries later by Greek, Roman and biblical writers as the source of fabulous riches. Whether it was a city or just a region no one knows. Some argue that it was a trading settlement near Huelva; others believe it may lie beneath the lower Guadalquivir marshes.

Ancient Andalucía

Museo Arqueológico (Seville; p66)

Museo de Huelva (p92)

Museo de Cádiz (p116)

Museo Arqueológico (Almuñécar; p292)

Carthage & Rome

A former Phoenician colony in modern Tunisia, Carthage came to dominate trade around the western Mediterranean from the 6th century BCE. Unhappily for the Carthaginians, the next new Mediterranean power was Rome. Carthage was defeated by Rome in the First Punic War (264–241 BCE), fought for control of Sicily. Later, Carthage occupied southern

206 BCE

Roman legions under General Scipio Africanus defeat the army of Carthage at Ilipa, near Seville. Itálica, the first Roman town in Spain, is founded near the battlefield.

100 BCE–300 CE

Andalucía becomes one of the wealthiest, most civilised areas of the Roman Empire, with Corduba (Córdoba) its most important city. Christianity arrives in the 3rd century CE.

98–138 CE

The Roman Empire is ruled by two successive emperors from Itálica in Andalucía: Trajan (98–117 CE) and Hadrian (117–138 CE).

552 CE

Byzantium, capital of the eastern Roman Empire, conquers Andalucía. The Visigoths, a Christian Germanic people now controlling the Iberian Peninsula, drive the Byzantines out in 622.

Spain, and the Second Punic War (218–201 BC) saw Carthaginian general Hannibal march his elephants over the Alps from Spain to threaten Rome. But the Romans opened a second front by sending legions to Spain, and their victory at Ilipa near modern Seville in 206 BC gave them control of the Iberian Peninsula. The first Roman town in Spain, Itálica, was founded near the battlefield soon afterwards.

As the Roman Empire went from strength to strength, Andalucía became one of its wealthiest and most civilised areas. Rome imported Andalucian crops, metals, fish and *garum* (a spicy seasoning derived from fish, made in factories whose remains can be seen at Bolonia and Almuñécar). Rome brought the Iberian Peninsula aqueducts, temples, theatres, amphitheatres, baths, Christianity, a sizeable Jewish population (Jews spread throughout the Mediterranean areas of the empire) – and the peninsula's main languages (Castilian Spanish, Portuguese, Catalan and Galician are all descended from the colloquial Latin spoken by Roman colonists).

Roman Andalucía

- *Itálica (Santiponce, near Seville; p78)*
- *Baelo Claudia (Bolonia; p148)*
- *Necrópolis Romana (Carmona; p79)*
- *Museo de la Ciudad de Antequera (p192)*
- *Roman Amphitheatre (Málaga; p165)*
- *Puente Romano (Córdoba; p211)*
- *Museo Histórico Municipal (Écija; p84)*

The Visigoths

When the Huns erupted into Europe from Asia in the late 4th century CE, displaced Germanic peoples moved westwards across the crumbling Roman Empire. One group, the Visigoths, took over the Iberian Peninsula in the 6th century, with Toledo, in central Spain, as their capital. The long-haired Visigoths, numbering about 200,000, were, like their relatively sophisticated Hispano-Roman subjects, Christian, but their rule was undermined by strife among their own nobility. After a 552 invasion, parts of present-day Andalucía spent some decades as an outpost of the Byzantine empire before coming back under Visigothic sway in 624.

Moorish Spain Reads

- *Moorish Spain (Richard Fletcher; 1992)*
- *The Ornament of the World (María Rosa Menocal; 2002)*
- *Andalus (Jason Webster; 2004)*

Heartland of Islamic Spain

Andalucía was under Islamic rule, wholly or partly, for nearly eight centuries from 711 to 1492 – a time span much longer than the five centuries that have passed since 1492. For much of those eight centuries Andalucía was the most cultured and economically advanced region in a Europe that for most part was going through its 'dark ages'. The Islamic centuries left a deep imprint that still permeates Andalucian life, and a legacy of unique monuments: Granada's Alhambra, Córdoba's great Mezquita and Seville's Alcázar are windows into the splendours of the age and essential Andalucian cultural experiences.

Arabs carried Islam through the Middle East and North Africa following the death of the Prophet Mohammed in 632. Legend has it they were ushered onto the Iberian Peninsula by the sexual exploits of the last Visigothic king, Roderic. Chronicles relate how Roderic seduced young Florinda, the daughter of Julian, the Visigothic governor of Ceuta in North Africa, and how Julian sought revenge by approaching the Arabs

711

Muslim forces from North Africa thrash the Visigothic army near the Río Guadalete in Cádiz province. Within a few years, the Muslims overrun almost the whole Iberian Peninsula.

756–929

The Muslim emirate of Córdoba, under the Umayyad dynasty founded by Abd ar-Rahman I, rules over most of the Iberian Peninsula. The name Al-Andalus is given to Muslim-controlled areas.

785

The Mezquita (Mosque) of Córdoba, one of the world's wonders of Islamic architecture, opens for prayer.

929–1031

The caliphate of Córdoba: ruler Abd ar-Rahman III declares himself caliph; Al-Andalus attains its greatest power; and Córdoba becomes Western Europe's biggest city.

with a plan to invade Spain. In reality, Roderic's rivals may just have been seeking support in the endless struggle for the Visigothic throne.

In 711 Tariq ibn Ziyad, the Muslim governor of Tangier, landed at Gibraltar with around 10,000 men, mostly indigenous North African Berbers. They decimated Roderic's army, probably near the Río Guadalete in Cádiz province, and Roderic is thought to have drowned as he fled. Within a few years, the Muslims had taken over the whole Iberian Peninsula except for small areas in the Asturian mountains in the far north. The name given to the Muslim-ruled territories was Al-Andalus. From this comes the modern name of the region that was always the Islamic heartland on the peninsula – Andalucía.

Al-Andalus' frontiers shifted constantly as the Christians strove to regain territory, but until the 11th century the small Christian states developing in northern Spain were too weak to pose much of a threat to Al-Andalus.

In the main cities, the Muslims built beautiful palaces, mosques and gardens, opened universities and established public bathhouses and bustling *zocos* (markets). The Moorish (as it's often known) society of Al-Andalus was a mixed bag. The ruling class was composed of various Arab groups prone to factional friction. Below them was a larger group of Berbers, some of whom rebelled on numerous occasions. Jews and Christians had freedom of worship, but Christians had to pay a special tax, so most either converted to Islam or left for the Christian north. Christians living in Muslim territory were known as Mozarabs (*mozárabes* in Spanish); those who adopted Islam were *muwallads (muladíes).* Before long, Arab, Berber and local blood merged, and many Spaniards today are partly descended from medieval Muslims.

Moorish Andalucía

Alhambra (Granada; p258)

Mezquita (Córdoba; p206)

Albayzín (Granada; p266)

Medina Azahara (Córdoba; p217)

Giralda (Seville; p50)

Castillo de Gibralfaro (Málaga; p165)

Alcazaba (Almería; p298)

Mezquita (Almonaster la Real; p110)

Bobastro (near El Chorro; p190)

The Cordoban Emirate & Caliphate

The first centre of Islamic culture and power in Spain was the old Roman provincial capital Córdoba. In 750 the Umayyad dynasty of caliphs in Damascus, supreme rulers of the Muslim world, was overthrown by a group of revolutionaries, the Abbasids, who shifted the caliphate to Baghdad. One of the Umayyad family, Abd ar-Rahman, escaped the slaughter and somehow made his way to Morocco and then to Córdoba, where in 756 he set himself up as an independent emir (prince). Abd ar-Rahman I's Umayyad dynasty kept Al-Andalus more or less unified for over 250 years.

In 929 Abd ar-Rahman I's descendant Abd ar-Rahman III (r 912–61) gave himself the title caliph to assert his authority in the face of the Fatimids, a growing Muslim power in North Africa. Thus he launched the caliphate of Córdoba, which at its peak encompassed three quarters of the Iberian Peninsula and some of North Africa. Córdoba became the biggest, most dazzling and cultured city in Western Europe. Astronomy, medicine, mathematics, philosophy, history and botany flourished, and

Most if not all of Córdoba's Umayyad rulers had Spanish mothers – concubine slaves from the north. Caliph Abd ar-Rahman III is said to have had red hair and blue eyes, and to have been the grandson of a Basque princess.

1091–1140

The strict Muslim rulers of Morocco, the Almoravids, conquer Al-Andalus and rule it as a colony. Their power crumbles in the 1140s.

1160–73

The Almoravids' successors in Morocco, the Almohads, in turn take over Al-Andalus, making Seville their capital and promoting arts and learning.

1212

The armies of three northern Spanish Christian kingdoms, Castilla, Aragón and Navarra, defeat a large Almohad force at Las Navas de Tolosa in northeastern Andalucía – the beginning of the end for Al-Andalus.

1227–48

Castilla's King Fernando III (El Santo, the Saint) conquers the west and north of Andalucía, culminating in the capture of Seville in 1248.

Abd ar-Rahman III's court was frequented by Jewish, Arabian and Christian scholars.

Later in the 10th century, the fearsome Cordoban general Al-Mansur (or Almanzor) terrorised the Christian north with 50-odd *razzias* (forays) in 20 years. In 997 he destroyed the cathedral at Santiago de Compostela in northwestern Spain – home of the cult of Santiago Matamoros (St James the Moor-Slayer), a key inspiration to Christian warriors. But after Al-Mansur's death, the caliphate disintegrated into dozens of small kingdoms known as *taifas,* ruled by local potentates (often Berber generals).

The Almoravids & Almohads

Seville, in the wealthy lower Guadalquivir valley, emerged as the strongest *taifa* in Andalucía in the 1040s. By 1078 the writ of its Abbadid dynasty ran all the way from southern Portugal to Murcia (southeast Spain), restoring a measure of peace and prosperity to the south.

Meanwhile, the northern Christian states were starting to raise their game. When one of them, Castilla, captured Toledo in 1085, a scared Seville begged for help from the Almoravids, a strict Muslim sect of Saharan Berbers who had conquered Morocco. The Almoravids came, defeated Castilla's Alfonso VI, and ended up taking over Al-Andalus, too, ruling it from Marrakesh as a colony and persecuting Jews and Christians. But the charms of Al-Andalus seemed to relax the Almoravids' austere grip: revolts spread across the territory from 1143 and within a few years it had again split into *taifas.*

In Morocco, the Almoravids were displaced by another strict Muslim Berber sect, the Almohads, who in turn took over Al-Andalus by 1173. Al-Andalus was by now considerably reduced from its 10th-century heyday: the frontier ran from south of Lisbon to north of Valencia. The Almohads made Seville capital of their whole realm and revived arts and learning in Al-Andalus.

In 1195, the Almohad ruler Yusuf Yakub al-Mansur thrashed Castilla's army at Alarcos, south of Toledo, but this only spurred other Christian kingdoms to join forces with Castilla against him. In 1212 the combined armies of Castilla, Aragón and Navarra routed the Almohads at Las Navas de Tolosa, a victory that opened the gates of Andalucía. With the Almohad state riven by a succession dispute after 1224, Castilla, Aragón and two other Christian kingdoms, Portugal and León, expanded southwards down the Iberian Peninsula. Castilla's Fernando III took strategic Baeza (near Jaén) in 1227, Córdoba in 1236, and Seville, after a two-year siege, in 1248.

Jewish Andalucía

Centro de Interpretación Judería de Sevilla (p61)

Palacio de los Olvidados (Granada; p278)

Sinagoga del Agua (Úbeda; p244)

Casa de Sefarad (Córdoba; p213)

Sinagoga (Córdoba; p213)

Centro de la Memoria Sefardí (Granada; p266)

The Nasrid Emirate of Granada

The Granada emirate was a wedge of territory carved out of the disintegrating Almohad realm by Mohammed ibn Yusuf ibn Nasr, from whom

1249–1492
The emirate of Granada, ruled by the Nasrid dynasty from the lavish Alhambra palace, sees the final flowering of medieval Muslim culture on the Iberian Peninsula.

1250–80
Fernando III's son Alfonso X of Castilla, known as El Sabio (the Learned), makes Seville one of his several capitals and launches a cultural revival there.

1350–69
Castilian king Pedro I, 'El Cruel', creates the most magnificent section of Seville's Alcázar palace, but reputedly has a dozen relatives and friends murdered in his efforts to keep the throne.

January 1492
After a 10-year war Granada falls to the armies of Castilla and Aragón, which are now united through the marriage of their rulers Isabel and Fernando, the 'Catholic Monarchs'.

it's known as the Nasrid emirate. Comprising essentially the modern provinces of Granada, Málaga and Almería, it held out for nearly 250 years as the last Muslim state on the Iberian Peninsula.

The Nasrids ruled from the lavish Alhambra palace in Granada, which witnessed the final flowering of Islamic culture in Spain. Their emirate reached its peak in the 14th century under emirs Yusuf I and Mohammed V, authors of the Alhambra's greatest splendours. The Nasrids' final downfall was precipitated by two things: one was Emir Abu al-Hasan's refusal in 1476 to pay any further tribute to Castilla; the other was the unification in 1479 of Castilla and Aragón, Spain's biggest Christian states, following the marriage of their monarchs Isabel and Fernando. The Reyes Católicos (Catholic Monarchs), as the pair is known, launched the final crusade of the Reconquista (Christian reconquest) against Granada in 1482.

Harem jealousies and other feuds among Granada's rulers degenerated into a civil war that allowed the Christians to push across the emirate. They captured Málaga in 1487, and Granada itself, after an eight-month siege, on 2 January 1492.

The surrender terms were fairly generous to the last emir, Boabdil, who received the Alpujarras valleys, south of Granada, as a personal fiefdom. He stayed only a year, however, before departing to Africa. The Muslims were promised respect for their religion, culture and property, but this didn't last long.

Reconquista Andalucía

- *Real Alcázar (Seville; p56)*
- *Capilla Real (Granada; p267)*
- *Castillo de Guzmán (Tarifa; p149)*
- *Fuente Pública (Mojácar; p312)*
- *Castillo de Santa Catalina (Jaén; p232)*
- *Castillo de La Iruela (Cazorla; p247)*
- *Castillo de Segura de la Sierra (p253)*

Christians in Control

The relatively uniform culture of modern Andalucía has its roots in the early centuries of Christian rule. In their zeal to establish Christianity in the conquered territories, Andalucía's new rulers enforced increasingly severe measures that ended with the expulsion of two of the three religious groups that had cohabited in Al-Andalus.

In areas that fell under Christian control in the 13th century, Muslims who stayed on (known as Mudéjars) initially faced no reprisals. But in

PATH OF KNOWLEDGE

Al-Andalus was an important conduit of classical Greek and Roman learning into Christian Europe, where it would exert a profound effect on the Renaissance, which got under way in 14th-century Italy. The Arabs had absorbed the philosophy of Aristotle, the mathematics of Pythagoras, the astronomy of Ptolemy and the medicine of Hippocrates during their conquests in the eastern Mediterranean and Middle East. Al-Andalus was one of the few places where Islamic and Christian worlds met, enabling this knowledge to find its way northward. Particularly influential was the Cordoban Averroës (1126–98), whose commentaries on Aristotle tried to reconcile religious faith with science and reason.

April 1492

Under the influence of Grand Inquisitor Tomás de Torquemada, Isabel and Fernando expel from Spain all Jews who refuse Christian baptism. Some 200,000 Jews leave for other Mediterranean destinations.

August 1492

Christopher Columbus, funded by Isabel and Fernando, sails from Palos de la Frontera and after 70 days finds the Bahamas, opening up a whole new hemisphere of opportunity for Spain.

1500

Persecution of Muslims in the former Granada emirate sparks rebellion. Afterwards, Muslims are compelled to adopt Christianity or leave. Most, an estimated 300,000, undergo baptism.

1503

Seville is granted a monopoly on Spanish trade with the Americas and becomes the cosmopolitan hub of world trade, with its population jumping from 40,000 to 150,000 by 1600.

1264 the Mudéjars of Jerez de la Frontera rose up against new taxes and rules that required them to celebrate Christian feasts and live in ghettos. After a five-month siege they were expelled to Granada or North Africa, along with the Mudéjars of Seville, Córdoba and Arcos.

The Spanish Inquisition was established by the Reyes Católicos (Catholic Monarchs; Isabel and Fernando) in 1478. Of the estimated 12,000 deaths for which it was responsible in its three centuries of existence, 2000 took place in the 1480s.

Large tracts of southern Spain were handed to nobility and knights who had played important roles in the Reconquista. These landowners turned much of their vast estates over to sheep, and by 1300 rural Christian Andalucía was almost empty. The nobility's preoccupation with wool and politics allowed Jews and foreigners, especially Genoese, to dominate Castilian commerce and finance.

Fernando III's son Alfonso X (r 1252–84) made Seville one of Castilla's capitals and launched something of a cultural revival there, gathering scholars around him, particularly Jews, who could translate ancient texts into Castilian Spanish. But rivalry within the royal family, and challenges from the nobility, plagued the Castilian monarchy right through till the late 15th century, when the Catholic Monarchs took things in hand.

Persecution of the Jews

After the Black Death and several bad harvests in the 14th century, discontent found its scapegoat in the Jews, who were subjected to pogroms around Christian Spain in the 1390s. As a result, many Jews converted to Christianity (they became known as *conversos*); others found refuge in Muslim Granada. In the 1480s the *conversos* became the main target of the new Spanish Inquisition, founded by the Catholic Monarchs, which accused many *conversos* of continuing to practise Judaism in secret.

IN ISLAMIC FOOTSTEPS

The medieval Islamic era left a profound stamp on Andalucía. The great architectural monuments, such as Granada's Alhambra and Córdoba's Mezquita, are the stars of this Islamic heritage, but the characteristic tangled, narrow street layouts of many towns and villages also date from Islamic times, as do the Andalucian predilections for fountains, running water and decorative plants. Flamenco music, though brought to its modern form by Roma people in more recent times, has clear influences from medieval Andalucian Islamic music.

The Muslims developed Spain's Hispano-Roman agricultural base by improving irrigation and introducing new fruits and crops, many of which are still widely grown, often on the same irrigated terraces created by the Moors. The Spanish language contains many common words of Arabic origin, including the names of some of those new crops – *naranja* (orange), *azúcar* (sugar) and *arroz* (rice). Nowadays you can experience a taste of Moorish life in luxurious *hammams* – bathhouses with the characteristic three pools of cold, warm and hot water – and Middle Eastern–style *teterías* (teahouses) that have opened in several Andalucian cities.

1568–70

Persecution of the *moriscos* (converted Muslims) leads to a two-year revolt centred on the Alpujarras valleys, south of Granada. Felipe III expels the *moriscos* from Spain altogether between 1609 and 1614.

1590–1680

Seville plays a leading part in Spain's artistic Siglo de Oro (Golden Age), as a base for artists such as Velázquez, Zurbarán and Murillo and sculptors such as Martínez Montañés.

17th century

The boom engendered by American trade fizzles out as silver shipments slump, and epidemics and bad harvests kill 300,000 Andalucians.

19th century

Andalucía sinks into economic depression, with landless labourers and their families making up three-quarters of the population.

In 1492 Isabel and Fernando ordered the expulsion of every Jew who refused Christian baptism. Around 50,000 to 100,000 converted, but some 200,000 left for other Mediterranean destinations – the Sephardic (Iberian Peninsula Jewish) diaspora. A talented middle class was decimated.

Morisco Revolts & Expulsion

The task of converting Granada's Muslims to Christianity was handed to Cardinal Cisneros, overseer of the Inquisition. He carried out forced mass baptisms, burnt Islamic books and banned the Arabic language. As Muslims found their land being expropriated, too, a revolt in Las Alpujarras in 1500 spread right across the former Granada emirate. Afterwards, Muslims were ordered to convert to Christianity or leave. Most converted, becoming known as *moriscos* (converted Muslims), but after the fanatically Catholic King Felipe II (r 1556–98) forbade the Arabic language, Arabic names and *morisco* dress in 1567, a new Alpujarras revolt spread across southern Andalucía and took two years to put down. The *moriscos* were then deported to western Andalucía and more northerly parts of Spain, before being expelled altogether from Spain by Felipe III between 1609 and 1614.

The Catholic Monarchs, pious Isabel and machiavellian Fernando, united Spain under one rule for the first time since Roman days – a task completed when Fernando annexed Navarra in 1512, eight years after Isabel's death.

Seville & the Americas: Boom & Bust

If Islamic Andalucía's golden age was the 10th-century Cordoban caliphate, its Christian counterpart was 16th-century Seville.

In April 1492 the Catholic Monarchs granted the Genoese sailor Christopher Columbus (Cristóbal Colón to Spaniards) funds for a voyage across the Atlantic in search of a new trade route to the Orient. Columbus found the Americas instead – and opened up a whole new hemisphere of opportunity for Spain, especially for the river port of Seville.

During the reign of Carlos I (r 1516–56), the first ruler of Spain's new Habsburg dynasty, the ruthless but brilliant conquerors Hernán Cortés and Francisco Pizarro subdued the Aztec and Inca empires respectively with small bands of adventurers, and other Spanish conquerors and colonists occupied further vast tracts of the American mainland. The new colonies sent huge quantities of silver, gold and other treasure back to Spain, where the crown was entitled to one-fifth of the bullion (the *quinto real*, or royal fifth).

Seville became the hub of world trade, a cosmopolitan melting pot of money seekers, and remained the major city in Spain until late in the 17th century, even though a small country town called Madrid was named the national capital in 1561. The prosperity was shared to some extent by Cádiz, and less so by inland cities such as Jaén, Córdoba and Granada.

But Spain never developed any strategy for investing the American windfall, spending too much on European wars and opulent palaces, cathedrals and monasteries, while wasting any chance of becoming an early industrial power. Grain had to be imported, while sheep and cattle

The American Adventure

Lugares Colombinos (near Huelva; p95)

Columbus' Tomb (Seville Cathedral; p53)

Archivo General de Indias (Seville; p61)

Patio de la Montería (Real Alcázar, Seville; p57)

1805

In the Napoleonic Wars, Spanish sea power is terminated when a combined Spanish–French navy is defeated by the British fleet, under Admiral Nelson, off Cabo de Trafalgar, south of Cádiz.

1810–12

With most of Spain under Napoleonic occupation, Cádiz survives a two-year siege. In 1812 the Cádiz parliament adopts Spain's first constitution, 'La Pepa', proclaiming sovereignty of the people.

1873

During Spain's chaotic, short-lived First Republic, numerous cities and towns declare themselves independent states. Seville and the nearby town of Utrera even declare war on each other.

1891–1919

Impoverished Andalucian rural workers launch waves of anarchist strikes and revolts. Powerful anarchist union the CNT is founded in Seville in 1910 and gains 93,000 members in Andalucía by 1919.

roamed the countryside. The ensuing centuries of neglect and economic mismanagement would turn Andalucía into a backwater, a condition from which it didn't start to emerge until the 1960s.

In the 17th century, silver shipments from the Americas shrank disastrously and the lower Río Guadalquivir, Seville's lifeline to the Atlantic, became increasingly silted up. In 1717 control of commerce with the Americas was transferred to the seaport of Cádiz, which enjoyed its heyday in the 18th century.

The Battle of Trafalgar (1805), in which Spanish sea power was terminated by Admiral Nelson's British fleet, was fought off a small headland, Cabo de Trafalgar, in the town Los Caños de Meca (Cádiz province). A plaque commemorating those who died was erected at the cape in 2005, the bicentenary.

The Great 19th-Century Wealth Gap

The 18th century saw a few economic advances in Andalucía such as a new road from Madrid to Seville and Cádiz, new lands planted with wheat and barley, and new settlers from elsewhere in Spain, who boosted Andalucía's population to about 1.8 million by 1787. But Spain's loss of its American colonies in the early 19th century was desperate news for the port of Cádiz, which had been totally reliant on trade with them. As the 19th century wore on, Andalucía declined into one of Europe's most backward, socially polarised regions.

The Disentailments of 1836 and 1855, when church and municipal lands were auctioned off to reduce the national debt, were a disaster for the peasants, who lost grazing lands. At one social extreme were a small population of rich aristocratic landowners and bourgeoisie; at the other, a very large number of impoverished *jornaleros* – landless agricultural day labourers who were without work for a good half of the year. Illiteracy, disease and hunger were rife.

Andalucian peasants began to stage uprisings, always brutally quashed. Many favoured the anarchist strategy of strikes, sabotage and revolts as the path to spontaneous revolution and a free society, governed by voluntary cooperation. Powerful anarchist union the Confederación Nacional del Trabajo (CNT; National Labour Confederation) was founded in Seville in 1910.

Civil War Reads

- *For Whom the Bell Tolls* (Ernest Hemingway; 1940)
- *The Spanish Holocaust* (Paul Preston; 2012)
- *The Spanish Civil War* (Hugh Thomas; 1961)
- *Soldiers of Salamis* (Javier Cercas; 2001)

The Civil War

The polarisation of Andalucian society and politics in the 19th century was mirrored in Spain at large. As the 20th century progressed, divisions deepened and a large-scale conflagration looked increasingly inevitable. It came with the devastating Spanish Civil War of 1936–39.

The Prelude: Dictatorship & Republic

In 1923 an eccentric Andalucian general from Jerez de la Frontera, Miguel Primo de Rivera, launched a comparatively moderate military dictatorship with the cooperation of the big socialist union, the Unión General de Trabajadores (UGT; General Union of Workers). Primo was unseated

1931–36

The Second Republic: King Alfonso XIII goes into exile and Spain is ruled first by the left, then the right, then the left again, with political violence spiralling.

1933–36

Granada-born Federico García Lorca writes his three great tragedies, *Blood Wedding*, *Yerma* and *The House of Bernarda Alba* – probably the greatest achievements of Andalucian literature.

17 July 1936

The Spanish garrison at Melilla (North Africa) revolts against the government, starting the Spanish Civil War. The plot is led by five 'Nationalist' generals, including Francisco Franco.

1936–39

Western Andalucía falls early in the civil war to the Nationalists, who also take Málaga in February 1937. Much of eastern Andalucía remains in Republican hands until the end of the war.

in 1930 as a result of an economic downturn and discontent in the army. When Spain's burgeoning Republican movement scored sweeping victories in local elections in 1931, King Alfonso XIII departed for exile in Italy.

The ensuing Second Republic (1931–36) was a tumultuous period of mounting confrontation between left and right. National elections in 1931 brought in a mixed government including socialists, centrists and Republicans, but the next elections in 1933 were won by the right. By 1934 violence was spiralling out of control, and the left, including the emerging communists, was calling increasingly for revolution. In the February 1936 elections a left-wing coalition narrowly defeated the right-wing National Front. Violence continued on both sides of the political spectrum, the anarchist CNT had over a million members and the peasants were on the verge of revolution.

But when the revolt came, on 17 July 1936, it came from the other end of the political spectrum. On that day the Spanish military garrison at Melilla in North Africa revolted against the leftist government, followed the next day by some garrisons on the mainland. The leaders of the plot were five generals. The Spanish Civil War had begun.

By most estimates, about 350,000 Spaniards died in the civil war, although some writers put the figure as high as 500,000.

The War

The civil war split communities, families and friends. Both sides committed atrocious massacres and reprisals, especially in the early weeks. The rebels, who called themselves Nationalists, shot or hanged tens of thousands of supporters of the republic. Republicans did likewise to those they considered Nationalist sympathisers, including some 7000 priests, monks and nuns.

The basic battle lines were drawn very early. Cities whose military garrisons backed the rebels (most did) often fell immediately into Nationalist hands, as happened at Cádiz, Córdoba and Jerez. Seville was in Nationalist hands within three days and Granada within a few more. The Nationalists killed an estimated 4000 people in and around Granada after they took the city, including the great writer Federico García Lorca. There was slaughter in Republican-held areas too. An estimated 2500 were murdered in anarchist-controlled Málaga. The Nationalists then executed thousands in reprisals when they and their fascist Italian allies took the city in February 1937. Eastern Andalucía remained in Republican hands until the end of the war.

By late 1936 General Francisco Franco emerged as the undisputed Nationalist leader, calling himself Generalísimo (Supreme General). The Republicans had the support of some Soviet planes, tanks, artillery and advisers, and 25,000 or so French soldiers fought with them, along with a similar number of other foreigners in the International Brigades – but

In Republican-held areas during the civil war, anarchists, communists or socialists ran many towns and cities. Social revolution followed. In Andalucía this was often anarchist-led, with private property abolished and churches and convents wrecked. Large estates were occupied by peasants and around 100 agrarian communes were established.

1939–75

The Franco dictatorship: his opponents continue to be killed and jailed after the civil war; no political opposition is tolerated; the Catholic Church gains a privileged position in society.

1950–60

Some 1.5 million Andalucians leave to find work elsewhere in Spain or Europe. New mass tourism on Andalucía's Costa del Sol helps to stimulate some economic recovery.

1969

Andalucía's first national park, the Parque Nacional de Doñana, is declared. By 2017, environmentally protected areas cover 30% of Andalucian territory, the biggest such program in Spain.

1969–77

Flamenco singer El Camarón de la Isla and guitarist Paco de Lucía record nine albums in the greatest flamenco partnership of modern times – if not all time.

the scales of the war were tipped in the Nationalists' favour by weapons, planes and 92,000 troops from Nazi Germany and fascist Italy.

The Republican government moved from besieged Madrid to Valencia in late 1936, then to Barcelona in 1937. The USSR withdrew from the war in 1938, and the Nationalists took Barcelona in January 1939 and Madrid in March. Franco declared the war won on 1 April 1939.

Franco's Spain

After the civil war, instead of reconciliation, more bloodletting ensued and an estimated 100,000 Spaniards died in prison or were killed. Franco ruled absolutely. He was commander of the army and leader of the only political party, the Movimiento Nacional (National Movement). Army garrisons were maintained outside every large city, strikes and divorce were banned, and church weddings became compulsory.

A few communists and Republicans continued their struggle after the civil war in small guerrilla units in Andalucía's mountains and elsewhere. *Between Two Fires: Guerrilla War in the Spanish Sierras* (2011) by David Baird is a fascinating chronicle of their activity around Frigiliana (near Nerja) in 1940–50.

Spain stayed out of WWII but afterwards suffered a UN-sponsored trade boycott that helped turn the late 1940s into the *años de hambre* (years of hunger) – particularly in poor areas such as Andalucía where, at times, peasants subsisted on soup made from wild herbs.

In an effort to relieve Andalucian poverty, mass foreign tourism was launched on the Costa del Sol in the late 1950s. But 1.5 million hungry people still left Andalucía in the 1950s and '60s to look for work in Madrid, northern Spain and other countries. By the 1970s many Andalucian villages still lacked electricity, reliable water supplies and paved roads, and the education system was pathetically inadequate. Today a surprising number of rural Andalucians over 50 are still illiterate.

The New Democracy

Spain, and Andalucía, have come a very long way in the four and a half decades since Franco died in 1975. Democracy has taken root, society has been liberalised beyond recognition, and living standards, despite the knock they took from the post-2008 economic crisis, have climbed. High-speed trains, fast highways, shiny shopping malls, one-child families, same-sex marriage, thinly populated churches and heavily populated universities are just a few of the things that would amaze 1970s Andalucians today if they returned after being away for 40 years.

Franco's chosen successor, Alfonso XIII's grandson Prince Juan Carlos, took the throne two days after Franco's death. Much of the credit for Spain's transition to democracy goes to Juan Carlos and his prime minister, Adolfo Suárez. A new parliamentary system was introduced, and political parties, trade unions and strikes were all legalised. Spain enjoyed a rapid social liberation: contraceptives, homosexuality and divorce were legalised, adultery was decriminalised, and a wave of hedonism was unleashed.

1975–78

Following Franco's death, King Juan Carlos I and Prime Minister Adolfo Suárez engineer a transition to democracy. The 1978 constitution makes Spain a parliamentary monarchy with no official religion.

1982–96

Under Spain's new regional autonomy system, Andalucía gets its own parliament in Seville, with the social-democratic PSOE presiding over an economic boom after Spain joins the EU in 1986.

1992

Hundreds of thousands of people visit Expo '92 in Seville, and the superfast AVE (Alta Velocidad Española) Madrid–Córdoba–Seville rail link opens. Andalucian roads get a major upgrade, too.

1996–2004

Spain is governed by the right-of-centre Partido Popular (PP). Andalucian unemployment nearly halves (to 16%), thanks to a construction boom, tourism and industrial growth, and EU subsidies.

In 1982 Spain made a final break with the Franco era by voting the left-of-centre Partido Socialista Obrero Español (PSOE; Spanish Socialist Workers' Party) into power. The PSOE's leader, Felipe González, a young lawyer from Seville, was to be prime minister for 14 years, and his party's young, educated leadership included several other Andalucians. The PSOE made improvements in education, launched a national health system and basked in an economic boom after Spain joined the European Community (now the EU) in 1986.

For nearly four decades the PSOE dominated Andalucía's regional government in Seville, the Junta de Andalucía. It eradicated the worst of Andalucian poverty in the 1980s and early 1990s with grants, community works schemes and a relatively generous dole system. It also gave Andalucía Spain's biggest network of environmentally protected areas.

The PSOE lost power nationally in 1996 to the centre-right Partido Popular (PP; People's Party), which presided over eight years of economic progress – and the economic sun continued to shine after the PSOE regained national power in 2004. By 2007 Andalucía had never had it so good. A decade-long boom in construction and property prices, massive EU funds for agriculture, and a constant flow of tourists saw unemployment down to 13%, the lowest in memory. Instead of Andalucians emigrating for jobs, hundreds of thousands of immigrants were coming to work in Andalucía.

Everything fell apart in 2008 when the global economic crisis hit Europe, a blow from which Andalucía recovered more slowly than other regions of Spain. Andalucía's unemployment rate hovered near 23% in 2018 – 8% higher than the national average – while youth unemployment was a whopping 45% – 11.5% higher than in Spain overall, and 7% above 2008 levels.

Economic anxiety contributed in part to an earth-shattering political development in December 2018. For the first time since 1982 – when Spain moved to its current system of regional autonomy – the social-democratic PSOE failed to win a majority in Andalucía's parliamentary elections. This led to the formation of a right-wing government presided over by the PP and Ciudadanos parties, with support from the far-right Vox party.

Vox – whose policies towards Muslims, immigrants and women mark a radical departure from those espoused by the PSOE – consolidated its newfound regional strength in Spain's November 2019 general elections, claiming 20% of Andalucian votes and 12 of the 61 Andalucian seats in the national Congress of Deputies.

Andalucía has long been the home of the controversial activity of bullfighting. Spain's first official bullfighting school, the Escuela de Tauromaquia de Sevilla, was established in Seville by King Fernando VII in the 1830s.

Andalucía's regional government, the Junta de Andalucía, controls many policy areas and services including health, schools, environment, town planning and agriculture. It has an annual budget of over €30 billion and more than 250,000 direct employees, about 80% of those being teachers or health workers.

2003

The Museo Picasso opens in Málaga, which joins Barcelona, Paris and New York as cities with major collections of the art of Pablo Picasso, born in Málaga in 1881.

2008–13

Andalucía is savaged by economic recession; unemployment leaps from 13% to 36%. The PP returns to power nationally in 2011 with an austerity program to tackle the crisis.

2014

King Juan Carlos abdicates, with his health and the monarchy's popularity declining, making way for his son, Felipe VI.

2019

For the first time since attaining regional autonomy, Andalucía is ruled by a right-wing government after December 2018 elections in which the long-ruling PSOE loses seats to the PP, Ciudadanos and Vox.

Andalucian Architecture

From the noble Renaissance palaces of Úbeda and Baeza to the finely carved stucco work that beautifies the Alhambra, Andalucía's architecture is a study in grace, skilled artisanship and unique cultural interchange. Hybridisation is almost a hobby here. Wander the region's towns and cities, and you'll see mosques converted into churches, Moorish arches held up by Roman columns, and minarets refashioned as belfries. Spared the carpet bombing that plagued other European cities in WWII, Andalucía's historic buildings are remarkably well preserved.

Moorish Factor

Architecturally speaking, Spain – and in particular Andalucía – is different from the rest of Europe. The reason? The Moorish factor. The conquering Christian armies may have disposed of the emirs and government of Al-Andalus (the Muslim-controlled parts of the Iberian Peninsula) by 1492, but, tellingly, they didn't have the heart to flatten all of its most iconic buildings. While they knocked down some mosques and replaced them with churches, other mosques were simply repurposed for the new religion. Fortresses, palaces and mansions were often reused and adapted as the centuries went by. Córdoba's Mezquita still stands, as do Seville's Giralda and Granada's Palacios Nazaríes. As a result, Andalucía's architecture is a story of layers, hybrids and Christian–Moorish intermixing. Even today, more than 500 years since the fall of Granada, the impact of the Islamic centuries is never far from the surface. In villages across the region, and in the hearts of cities (as in Granada's Albayzín), intricate tangles of streets are redolent of North African medinas. Similarly, the Islamic love of ornate, scented gardens with flowing or trickling water – hidden inner sanctums that safeguarded residents from prying eyes – can be seen in patios, courtyards and the carefully manicured greenery that embellishes Andalucía's Moorish-influenced houses and palaces. The resulting picture is as inspiring as it is complicated. Indeed, one might even come to the conclusion that European architectural design reached its highpoint in the 1350s in a palace complex at the foot of the Sierra Nevada called the Alhambra.

Islamic Fortresses

Alcazaba (Almería; p298)

Alcazaba (Antequera; p192)

Alhambra (Granada; p258)

Castillo de Gibralfaro (Málaga; p165)

Castillo de Guzmán el Bueno(Tarifa; p149)

Torre del Oro (Seville; p63)

Islamic Architecture

The period of Islamic architectural dominance began with the Umayyads, the Muslim invaders who kick-started eight centuries of Islamic rule in 711 and ushered in an era that bequeathed the region, more than anywhere else in Europe, a strong sense of the exotic. Elaborate monuments on an unprecedented scale – Córdoba's Mezquita and Granada's Alhambra, for example, which stand like bookends to the Moorish era – were the means by which the rulers of Al-Andalus brought architectural sophistication to Europe. They remain the most visible legacy of Andalucía's Islamic past.

Umayyads

When the Umayyad caliphs of Damascus were overthrown by the revolutionary Abbasids in 750, one young member of the Umayyad clan, Abd ar-Rahman ibn Muawiya, managed to escape the carnage and flee to Morocco and then Spain. In 756 he set himself up as an independent emir, Abd ar-Rahman I, in Córdoba, launching a dynasty that lasted until 1031 and made Al-Andalus, at the western extremity of the Islamic world, the last outpost of Umayyad culture.

Mezquita of Córdoba

Abd ar-Rahman I was responsible for founding Córdoba's Mezquita (p206) in 784 CE, a building that was – and still is – the epitome of Islamic architecture's grace and pleasing unity of form. This sense of harmony is all the more remarkable given the significant alterations carried out over the centuries. Zealous Christian architects darkened the original light-filled interior by building thick outer walls, and in the middle of the 16th century an incongruous Christian cathedral was plonked right in the middle of the former mosque.

In its original form, the Mezquita was a square split into two rectangular halves: a covered prayer hall, and an open courtyard where the faithful performed their ritual ablutions before entering the prayer hall. This early structure drew on the essential elements of Umayyad architecture. It maintained, for example, the 'basilical' plan of some early Islamic buildings by having a central 'nave' of arches, broader than the others, leading to the *mihrab,* the niche indicating the direction of Mecca (and thus of prayer) that is key to the layout of any mosque. But the Mezquita's prayer hall broke away from the verticality of earlier landmark Umayyad buildings, such as the Great Mosque of Damascus and the Dome of the Rock in Jerusalem. Instead, it created a broad horizontal space that evoked the yards of desert homes that formed the original Islamic prayer spaces. It also conjured visions of palm groves with mesmerising lines of two-tier, red-and-white-striped arches in the prayer hall.

As Córdoba grew into its role as the increasingly sophisticated capital of Al-Andalus, later emirs left their personal stamp on Al-Andalus' landmark building. Later enlargements extended the lines of arches to cover an area of nearly 120 sq metres, making it one of the biggest of all mosques. These arcades afford ever-changing perspectives, vistas disappearing into infinity and interplays of light and rhythm that rank among the Mezquita's most arresting features.

It was the caliph Al-Hakim II (r 961–76) who endowed the Mezquita with its most splendid flourishes. Al-Hakim II created a magnificent new *mihrab,* decorated with superb Byzantine mosaics that imitate those of the Great Mosque of Damascus. In front of the *mihrab* Al-Hakim II added

HORSESHOE ARCH

The Visigoths are an often-overlooked civilisation who, on the Iberian Peninsula, had the historical misfortune to fall between the Romans and the Moors. But they did contribute at least one indelible architectural legacy: the horseshoe arch – so called because it curves inwards at the bottom like a horseshoe and unlike pure semicircle arches. The horseshoe arch was taken up by the Umayyads, who had used a less exaggerated version of it on the Great Mosque of Damascus and then found it adorning various Visigothic churches, most notably in Córdoba. The Mezquita in Córdoba displays the best early horseshoe arches, but the style endured to become a hallmark of Spanish Islamic architecture, passed down through the Almoravids, Almohads and Nasrids and, ultimately, to Mudéjar architects employed by the Christians.

a new royal prayer enclosure, the *maksura,* whose multiple interwoven arches and lavishly decorated domes were much more intricate and technically advanced than anything previously seen in Europe. The *maksura* formed part of a second axis to the building, an aisle running along in front of the wall containing the *mihrab* – known as the *qiblah* wall because it indicates the *qiblah,* the direction of Mecca. This transverse axis creates the T-plan that features strongly in many mosques. In its 'final' 10th-century form the Mezquita's roof was supported by 1293 columns.

The Almohads

As the centuries wore on, competing North African dynasties turned their attention to the glittering prize of Al-Andalus. Some, such as the Almoravids – a Berber dynasty from Morocco from the late 11th to mid-12th centuries – created few notable buildings in Spain. But the second wave of Moroccan Berbers to conquer Al-Andalus, the Almohads, more than made up for the Almoravids' lack of architectural imagination.

The Mezquita at Almonaster la Real (p110) in Huelva province is like a miniature version of Córdoba's Mezquita, with rows of arches forming five naves, the central one leading to a semicircular *mihrab*.

Late in the 12th century, the Almohads built huge Friday mosques in the main cities of their empire, with Seville especially benefiting from their attention. The design of the mosques was simple and purist, with large prayer halls conforming to the T-plan of the Córdoba Mezquita, but the Almohads introduced some important and beautiful decorative innovations. The bays where the naves meet the *qiblah* wall were surmounted by cupolas or by stucco *muqarnas* (stalactite or honeycomb vaulting), an architectural style with its origins in Iran or Syria. On walls, large brick panels with designs of interwoven lozenges were created. Tall, square, richly decorated minarets were another Almohad trademark.

The Giralda, the minaret of Seville's Great Mosque, is the masterpiece of Almohad buildings in Spain, with its beautiful brick panels. The mosque's prayer hall was demolished in the 15th century to make way for the city's cathedral, but its ablutions courtyard (the Patio de los Naranjos), and its northern gate, the handsome Puerta del Perdón, survive.

With defence a primary preoccupation due to Christian advances in the north, the Almohads went on a fortress-building spree in the 12th and early 13th centuries. Cities with bolstered defences included Córdoba, Seville and Jerez de la Frontera. Seville's primary Almohad creation – aside from its mosque – was the river-guarding Torre del Oro, still there today. Further outstanding Almohad creations are Jerez' austere Alcázar, Tarifa's Castillo de Guzmán el Bueno and the city walls of historic Niebla.

Nasrids

With the armies of the Reconquista (Christian reconquest) continuing their seemingly inexorable march south, the last emirate of Islamic Al-Andalus, the Nasrid stronghold of Granada (1249–1492), could have been forgiven for having its mind on nonarchitectural matters. But in a recurring theme that resonates through Andalucian history, it was architecture that best captured the spirit of the age. The Alhambra is at once an expansive fortification that reflected uncertain times and an extraordinary palace of last-days opulence.

Alhambra

Granada's magnificent Alhambra (p258) is the only surviving large medieval Islamic palace complex in the world. It's a palace-city in the tradition of Córdoba's Medina Azahara, but it's also a fortress, with 2km of walls, 23 towers and a fort within a fort, the Alcazaba. Within the Alhambra's walls were seven separate palaces, mosques, garrisons, houses, offices, baths, a summer residence (the Generalife) and exquisite gardens.

The Alhambra's designers were supremely gifted landscape architects, integrating nature and buildings through the use of pools, running water,

ANDALUCÍA'S FORMAL GARDENS

Paradise, according to Islamic tradition, is a garden. It's an idea that architects took to heart during Moorish times and later, surrounding some of Andalucía's loveliest buildings with abundant greenery, colour, fragrance and the tinkle of water.

Generalife gardens, Alhambra, Granada Landscaping of near-perfect sophistication. (p265)

Alcázar gardens, Seville A classic palace pleasure garden. (p56)

Alcázar de los Reyes Cristianos, Córdoba Terraces with abundant water and vegetation. (p212)

Parque de María Luisa, Seville Sprawling greenery in the heart of Seville. (p66)

Palacio de Viana, Córdoba Formal gardens with an emphasis on symmetry. (p214)

Carmen de los Mártires, Granada Little-known 19th-century oasis of tranquillity on the hillside south of the Alhambra.

Alcazaba, Almería Terraced gardens overlooking the Mediterranean.

meticulously clipped trees and bushes, vista-framing windows, carefully placed lookout points, interplays between light and shadow, and contrasts between coolness and heat. The juxtaposition of fountains, pools and gardens with domed reception halls reached a degree of perfection suggestive of the paradise described in the Quran. In keeping with the Alhambra's partial role as a sybarite's delight, many of its defensive towers also functioned as miniature summer palaces.

A huge variety of densely ornamented arches adorns the Alhambra. The Nasrid architects refined existing decorative techniques to new heights of delicacy, elegance and harmony. Their media included sculptured stucco, marble panels, carved and inlaid wood, epigraphy (with endlessly repeated inscriptions of 'There is no God but Allah') and colourful tiles. Plaited star mosaic tile patterns have since covered walls throughout the Islamic world, and Nasrid Granada is the dominant artistic influence in the Maghrib (northwest Africa) even today.

Although strongly associated with Andalucía, Mudéjar architecture originated in Castilla and Aragón during the 12th and 13th centuries. The best Andalucian Mudéjar buildings are in Seville.

Mudéjars & Mozarabs

Islam's architectural legacy lived on even after Christian conquest. Gifted Muslim artisans were frequently employed by Christian rulers and the term Mudéjar – meaning 'domesticated' and which was used to describe Muslims who stayed on in areas reconquered by the Christians – came to stick as an architectural label.

One hallmark of the Mudéjar style is geometric decorative designs in brick or stucco, often further embellished with tiles. Elaborately carved timber ceilings are also a mark of the Mudéjar hand. *Artesonado* is the word used to describe ceilings with interlaced beams leaving regular spaces for decorative insertions. True Mudéjar *artesonados* generally bear floral or simple geometric patterns.

You'll find Mudéjar or part-Mudéjar churches and monasteries all over Andalucía (Mudéjar is often found side by side with the Christian Gothic style). Andalucía's classic Mudéjar building is the exotic Palacio de Don Pedro, built in the 14th century inside the Alcázar of Seville for the Christian king Pedro I of Castilla. Pedro's friend, Mohammed V, the Muslim emir of Granada, sent many of his best artisans to work on Pedro's palace, and, as a result, the Palacio de Don Pedro is effectively a Nasrid building, and one of the best of its kind. Nowhere is this more evident than in the beautiful Patio de las Doncellas at its heart, with its sunken garden surrounded by exquisite arches, tiling and plasterwork.

Renaissance Architecture

Palacio de la Condesa de Lebrija (Seville; p62)

Casa de Pilatos (Seville; p62)

Catedral de la Asunción (Jaén; p232)

Catedral de Baeza (p237)

Palacio de Vázquez de Molina (Úbeda; p243)

The term Mozarab, from *musta'rib* (Arabised), refers to Christians who lived, or had lived, in Muslim-controlled territories in the Iberian Peninsula. Mozarabic architecture was, unsurprisingly, much influenced by Islamic styles and includes, for instance, the horseshoe arch. The majority of Mozarabic architecture is found in northern Spain; the most significant remaining Mozarabic structure in Andalucía is the rock-cut church at Bobastro (Málaga province).

Christian Architecture

The churches and monasteries built by the Christian conquerors, and the palaces and mansions of their nobility, are a superb part of Andalucía's heritage. But there is, as always, a uniquely Andalucian twist: after the Christian reconquest of Andalucía (1214–1492), Islamic buildings were often simply repurposed for Christian ends. Many Andalucian churches occupy converted mosques (most famously at Córdoba), several church towers began life as minarets, and the zigzagging streets of numerous old towns – such as Granada's Albayzín district – originated in labyrinthine Islamic-era street plans.

Andalucian Gothic

- *Catedral de Sevilla (p50)*
- *Capilla Real (Granada; p267)*
- *Palacio de Jabalquinto (Baeza; p239)*
- *Catedral de San Salvador (Jerez de la Frontera; p125)*
- *Iglesia de San Pablo (Úbeda; p244)*

Andalucian Gothic

Christian architecture reached northern and western Andalucía with the Reconquista during the 13th century. The prevailing architectural style throughout much of Christian Europe at the time was Gothic, with its distinctive pointed arches, ribbed ceilings, flying buttresses and fancy window tracery. Dozens of Gothic or part-Gothic churches, castles and mansions are dotted throughout Andalucía. Some of these buildings combine Gothic with Mudéjar style, while others have Gothic mixed with later styles and so have ended up as a stylistic hotchpotch.

The final flourish of Spanish Gothic was Isabelline Gothic, from the time of Queen Isabel la Católica. Isabelline Gothic features sinuously curved arches and tracery, and facades with lacelike ornament and low-relief sculptures (including lots of heraldic shields).

Small-town Architecture

- *Vejer de la Frontera*
- *Arcos de la Frontera*
- *Baeza*
- *Osuna*
- *Priego de Córdoba*
- *Écija*
- *Setenil de las Bodegas*

Clean Lines of the Renaissance

The Renaissance in architecture was an Italian-originated return to classical ideals of harmony and proportion, dominated by columns and shapes such as the square, circle and triangle. Many Andalucian Renaissance buildings feature elegant interior courtyards lined by two tiers of wide, rounded arcades. Whereas the Gothic period left its most striking mark on church architecture, the Renaissance period was an era in which the gentry built themselves gorgeous urban palaces with

MEDINA AZAHARA

The Córdoba caliphate's 'brilliant city', the Medina Azahara (p217), was as architecturally lavish as it was ephemeral. The pet project of Caliph Abd ar-Rahman III, it was conceived as the caliphate's new capital and laid out from scratch 8km west of the city of Córdoba, starting in 940 CE. Naming it after his favourite wife, Az-Zahra, the caliph planned his retreat as a royal residence, palace and seat of government, set away from the hubbub of the city in the same manner as the Abbasid royal city of Samarra, north of Baghdad. Its chief architect was Abd ar-Rahman III's son, Al-Hakim II, who later embellished the Córdoba Mezquita so superbly. In contrast to Middle Eastern palaces, where the typical reception hall was a domed *iwan* (hall opening to a forecourt), Medina Azahara's reception halls had a 'basilical' plan, each with three or more parallel naves – similar to mosque architecture. Although it was wrecked during the collapse of the Córdoba caliphate less than a century after it was built, the remaining imposing horseshoe arches, exquisite stucco work and extensive gardens demonstrate how large and lavish it was.

delightful patios surrounded by harmonious arched galleries. Many such mansions now serve as beautifully located museums or hotels.

Spanish Renaissance architecture had three phases. First came plateresque, taking its name from the Spanish for silversmith, *platero*, because it was primarily a decorative genre, with effects resembling those of silverware. Round-arched portals were framed by classical columns and stone sculpture. Next came a more purist style whose ultimate expression is the Palacio de Carlos V within Granada's Alhambra, while the last and plainest phase was Herreresque, after Juan de Herrera (1530–97), creator of the austere palace-monastery complex of El Escorial, near Madrid, and Seville's Archivo de Indias.

All three phases of Renaissance architecture were spanned in Jaén province by the legendary master architect Andrés de Vandelvira (1509–75), who gave the town of Úbeda one of the finest ensembles of Renaissance buildings in Spain. Vandelvira was much influenced by Burgos-born Diego de Siloé (1495–1563), who was primarily responsible for the cathedrals of Granada, Málaga and Guadix.

Alonso Cano (1601–67) was a sculptor, architect and painter from Granada whose creative talents were as vivid as his famous temper. He's sometimes called the Spanish Michelangelo, and his most celebrated work is the elaborate baroque facade of Granada's cathedral.

Baroque Backlash

An inevitable reaction to Renaissance sobriety came in the colours and dramatic sense of motion of baroque. This style really seemed to catch the Andalucian imagination, reaching its peak of elaboration here in the 18th century with ornamental facades and interiors chock-full of ornate stucco sculpture. *Retablos* – the large, sculptural altarpieces that adorn many Spanish churches to illustrate Christian stories and teachings – reached extremes of gilded extravagance. The most hyperbolic baroque work is termed Churrigueresque after a Barcelona family of sculptors and architects named Churriguera.

Seville has probably more baroque churches per square kilometre than any city in the world. However, the church at Granada's Monasterio de La Cartuja, by Francisco Hurtado Izquierdo (1669–1725), is one of the most lavish baroque creations in all Spain, with its multicoloured marble, golden capitals and profuse sculpture. Hurtado's followers also adorned the small town of Priego de Córdoba with seven or eight baroque churches.

Modern Andalucian Architecture

In the 19th century, Andalucía acquired some neo-Gothic and neo-baroque architecture, but most prevalent were neo-Mudéjar and neo-Islamic styles, harking back to an age that was now catching the fancy of the Romantic movement. Mansions such as the Palacio de Orleans y Borbon in Sanlúcar de Barrameda, and public buildings ranging from train stations in Seville to markets in Málaga and Tarifa, were constructed in colourful imitation of past Islamic architectural styles. For the 1929 Exposición Iberoamericana, fancy buildings in almost every past Andalucian style were concocted in Seville, chief among them the gaudy Plaza de España ensemble by local architect Aníbal González.

During the Franco dictatorship, drab Soviet-style blocks of workers' housing were erected in many cities, while Andalucía's decades-long tourism boom engendered, for the most part, architecture that ranged from the forgettable to the downright hideous. The 21st century has sparked a little more imagination, most notably in Seville, where a trio of big architectural projects – the Metropol Parasol, the Cajasol tower and the Pabellon de la Navegación – has added culture *and* controversy to the urban framework.

Andalucía's architects have demonstrated greater flair in restoring older edifices to serve as hotels, museums or other public buildings. Projects such as Málaga's Museo Picasso and Jaén's Palacio de Villardompardo are both 16th-century urban palaces that have been turned into top-class modern museums.

Hotels in Historic Architecture

Parador de Granada (p270)

Parador de Úbeda (p243)

Riad (Tarifa; p150)

La Casa del Califa (Vejer de la Frontera; p144)

Casa del Capitel Nazarí (Granada; p272)

Las Casas del Cónsul (Úbeda; p244)

Landscape & Wildlife

Andalucía is better known internationally for its history and culture than its wilderness. That 30% of the land is environmentally protected comes as a surprise to many visitors, who end up wishing they'd planned their trips with more nature in mind. Icons to rival the Alhambra include the snowcapped Sierra Nevada and the precious Doñana wetlands, both national parks. These stellar landscapes are backed up by 240 more protected areas and sites, most of them eminently accessible and enjoyable.

Landscape

Andalucía has mountains in abundance, from the relatively low hills of the Sierra Morena to the heights of the Sierra Nevada. The Sierra Morena, which rarely rises higher than 1000m, rolls across the north of Andalucía like the last outpost of rugged southern Spain before it yields to the sweeping flat lands and distant horizons of Spain's central *meseta* (plateau). Very sparsely populated, the Sierra Morena is extremely beautiful in its own subtle way, divided between evergreen oak woodlands, scrub, rough grazing pasture, river valleys and scattered old stone villages.

Closer to the coast, the Cordillera Bética was pushed up by the pressure of the African tectonic plate on the Iberian subplate 15 to 20 million years ago. This band of jagged mountains widens out from its beginnings in southwestern Andalucía to a breadth of 125km or so in the east. It includes the 75km-long Sierra Nevada southeast of Granada, with several 3000m-plus peaks (including 3479m Mulhacén, the highest mountain in mainland Spain). The cordillera continues east from Andalucía across Spain's Murcia and Valencia regions, before re-emerging from the Mediterranean as the Balearic islands of Ibiza and Mallorca. Much of it is composed of limestone, yielding some wonderful karstic rock formations.

Apart from the coastal plain, which varies in width from 50km in the west to a sliver in parts of Granada and Almería provinces, the fertile valley of the 660km-long Río Guadalquivir is Andalucía's other major geographical feature. Andalucía's longest river, the Guadalquivir, rises in the Cazorla mountains of Jaén province, flows westward through Córdoba and Sevilla, and enters the Atlantic at Sanlúcar de Barrameda. Before entering the ocean, the river splits into a marshy delta known as Las Marismas del Guadalquivir, which includes the Parque Nacional de Doñana.

Andalucía contains both Spain's wettest town (Grazalema in Cádiz province, with up to 200cm of rain annually) and its driest area (the Desierto de Tabernas in Almería province, with a mere 14cm annually).

Andalucía's Main Parks & Protected Areas

Andalucía has the biggest environmental-protection program in Spain. More than 240 areas, covering some 27,000 sq km, are included within regional, national or international protection networks, amounting to 30% of Andalucian territory. All this habitat conservation, as well as some specific recovery programs, has helped bring about a highly encouraging recovery in the numbers of some iconic endangered species such as the Iberian lynx and the black vulture. Ventana del Visitante (Visitor's Window; www.juntadeandalucia.es/medioambiente/servtc5/ventana) is the comprehensive and very useful official website for information about visiting Andalucía's protected areas, with much of the information in English as well as Spanish.

Parques Nacional & Natural de Doñana

In the Guadalquivir delta, Parque Nacional de Doñana and its *parque natural* buffer embrace Europe's largest wetlands, a crucial area for over 350 migratory and resident bird species and 37 types of mammal, including herds of deer, wild boar and the rare Iberian lynx. Explore the area by 4WD, on horseback or on foot.

Donaña, established in 1969, was Spain's sixth national park; the Sierra Nevada, established in 1999, was the 12th.

Parque Nacional & Natural Sierra Nevada

The national park covers the upper reaches of mainland Spain's highest mountain range – a great summer hiking and winter skiing challenge – while the surrounding *parque natural* includes timeless white villages and many walking, mountain-biking and horse-riding routes, especially in the Alpujarras valleys on the Sierra Nevada's southern slopes.

Parque Natural Sierra de Andújar

A medium-sized park in the Sierra Morena in the northwest of Jaén province, Andújar is notable for its rare mammals and birds. It contains Andalucía's largest population of Iberian lynx, endangered black vultures, black storks and Spanish imperial eagles.

The mountain La Veleta, in the Sierra Nevada, sports Europe's highest paved road, which climbs to an altitude of 3380m, just 15m below the summit. The road is not, however, open to private vehicles.

Parque Natural de Cabo de Gata-Níjar

Flamingo colonies, volcanic cliffs and sandy beaches make for a combination unlike any other protected area in Andalucía. One of the region's driest corners, the eastern park showcases a semidesert terrain, and promises a range of activities, including swimming, birdwatching, walking, horse riding, diving and snorkelling.

Parque Natural Sierras Subbéticas

Consisting of a set of craggy, green hills and canyons in Córdoba province, and sprinkled with caves, springs and streams, this park offers good hiking and some charming old villages and country hotels around its periphery. The best bases are Zuheros and Priego de Córdoba.

PARKS & PROTECTED AREAS

Andalucía's protected areas fall into two main categories.

Parques nacionales (national parks) are areas of exceptional importance for their fauna, flora, geomorphology or landscape, and their conservation is considered to be in the national interest. These are the most strictly protected areas and may include reserve areas closed to the public, or restricted areas that can only be visited with permission. Spain has just 15 *parques nacionales;* two of them – Doñana and Sierra Nevada – are in Andalucía.

Parques naturales (natural parks) are intended to protect cultural heritage as well as nature, and to promote economic development (including tourism) that's compatible with conservation. Many include roads and villages and accommodation available within the park. There are 24 *parques naturales* in Andalucía; they account for most of its protected territory and include nearly all of its most spectacular country.

Other types of protected areas in Andalucía include *parajes naturales* (natural areas; there are 35 of these) and *reservas naturales* (nature reserves; numbering 28). These are generally smaller, little-inhabited areas, with much the same goals as natural parks. There are also 49 *monumentos naturales* (natural monuments), protecting specific features such as waterfalls, forests or dunes.

Then there are areas protected under various international agreements, which often overlap with the regionally or nationally protected areas. They include 226 sites in the Natura 2000 European network of conservation areas, and 25 Ramsar wetland areas.

Parque Natural Sierra de Grazalema

Ibex, griffon vultures and other species inhabit this beautiful, damp, hilly region that is notable for its vast sweeps of Mediterranean woodlands and stands of rare Spanish firs. Archetypal white Andalucian villages serve as gateways to fantastic hiking trails, and you can also climb, canyon and paraglide to your heart's content.

Parque Natural Sierra de las Nieves

Spectacular vistas and deep valleys characterise this mountain region deep in Málaga province's interior. With iconic examples of Andalucian flora (Spanish firs) and fauna (ibex), as well as other species, the park is a good choice for hiking in off-the-beaten-track Andalucian wilds.

Parque Natural Sierra de Aracena y Picos de Aroche

Woodlands, evergreen oak pastures, old stone villages and imposing castles populate this charming tract of the Sierra Morena in far western Andalucía. An extensive network of well-maintained walking trails provides some of the most delightful rambling in Andalucía.

Parque Natural Sierras de Cazorla, Segura y Las Villas

Abundant, easily visible wildlife, craggy mountains, deep valleys and thick forests – it's difficult to overestimate the charms of this beautiful park, Spain's largest (2099 sq km), in Jaén province. Red and fallow deer, wild boar, mouflon and ibex provide the wildlife interest. Hike or explore on horseback or by 4WD.

Paraje Natural Torcal de Antequera

Striking limestone formations are what most visitors remember about this mountainous natural area close to Antequera in Málaga province. It contains some of the strangest landforms in Andalucía and has a handful of walking trails. It also draws climbers.

Parque Natural Sierras de Tejeda, Almijara y Alhama

Popular with walkers, this park encompasses a large area of mountains and valleys not far back from the coast of Málaga and Granada provinces. Ibex roam the higher altitudes and wild boar the valleys. Nerja, Cómpeta and Almuñécar all make good bases.

The Parque Natural Sierras de Cazorla, Segura y Las Villas, at 2099 sq km, is the largest protected area in Spain and the second largest in Europe.

Wildlife

Andalucía is a haven for wildlife that is hard or impossible to find elsewhere, and wildlife enthusiasts, if they know where to look, are unlikely to return home disappointed.

Signature Mammals

Several large mammal species that once roamed across Western Europe are now confined to small, isolated populations surrounded by an ever-expanding sea of humanity. That they survive in Andalucía is thanks to the region's varied, often untamed terrain, and admirable nature-conservation policies, but even here they remain at risk.

Andalucía's most celebrated mammal, the Iberian lynx, has been recovering well in the last decade thanks to a successful captive breeding and release program. The species is still endangered, but, with patience and a bit of luck, it's no longer impossible to see a lynx in the wild.

Wolves *(lobos)* are in a far more precarious situation, possibly down to single figures (or none at all), in and around Jaén province's Parque Natural Sierra de Andújar. Wolf numbers have increased in recent years in Spain as a whole, to about 2000, but almost all of these are in the northwest of the country.

Hunting throughout the 20th century, and traps and poison put out by livestock farmers, are among the reasons that lynx and wolf populations declined so alarmingly.

One of the region's most easily spotted mammals is the ibex *(cabra montés)*, a stocky wild mountain goat whose males have distinctive long, curved horns. The ibex spends its summer hopping with amazing agility around high-altitude precipices; it descends to lower elevations in winter. Nearly 40,000 ibex live in Andalucía, with the largest populations found in the Sierra Nevada; the Parque Natural Sierras de Cazorla, Segura y Las Villas; and the Sierras de Tejeda, Almijara, Mágina, Grazalema and Nieves (all protected as *parques naturales*). It's in no apparent danger of extinction, although its numbers sometimes plummet due to outbreaks of scabies.

One of Spain's most unusual wildlife-watching experiences is the sight of Barbary apes, the only wild primates in Europe, clambering around Gibraltar's heights.

Just as the sight of Barbary apes can seem like an apparition of Africa on European soil, whales *(ballenas)* and dolphins *(delfines)* are more often associated with the open waters of the Atlantic than with the Mediterranean. Even so, the Bahía de Algeciras and Strait of Gibraltar harbour plenty of common, striped and bottlenose dolphins, as well as some pilot, killer and even sperm whales. You can get close to them on whale-and-dolphin-watching trips from Tarifa.

More common, less iconic mammals abound. Although some are nocturnal, those you may come across once you leave behind well-trodden trails include the wild boar *(jabalí)*, red deer *(ciervo)*, roe deer *(corzo)*, fallow deer *(gamo)*, genet *(gineta)*, Egyptian mongoose *(meloncillo)*, red squirrel *(ardilla)*, badger *(tejón)* and otter *(nutria)*.

Endangered Lynx

The Iberian (or pardel) lynx (*lince ibérico* to Spaniards; *Lynx pardina* to scientists) – a separate species from the larger Eurasian lynx found elsewhere in Europe – is, at the time of writing, a remarkable success story. The species once ranged across almost the whole Iberian Peninsula (the Hispanic Legions of the Roman Empire wore breastplates adorned with it) and a century ago there were perhaps 100,000 Iberian lynx in the wild. So plentiful was the lynx that the Spanish government classed it as vermin, encouraging hunters to kill it. By 1960 there were only an estimated 500 left. By 1973, the species was officially protected, but this did little to slow the lynx's precipitous decline, prompting fears that it would become the first cat species to become extinct since the sabre-toothed tiger, 10,000 years ago.

By the early 21st century, numbers were down to little over 100, chiefly in two separate areas of Andalucía – in and around the Parque Nacional de Doñana, and in the Sierra Morena in northern Jaén province – with a few more in the Montes de Toledo of Castilla-La Mancha. Since then a captive breeding program, initially launched at El Acebuche in Doñana in 1992 and later extended to other centres in Andalucía, with young lynx being released into the wild, has proved a big success. By 2015 numbers had risen to about 400 and the Iberian lynx was taken off the International Union for Conservation of Nature's 'critically endangered' list. As of 2018 there were estimated to be 686 Iberian lynx in the wild, 450 of them in Andalucía – roughly 350 in the Parque Natural Sierra de Andújar and other areas of the Sierra Morena in Jaén and Córdoba provinces, and nearly 100 in the Doñana area. Lynx have also been released in the Montes de Toledo, the south of Extremadura and southern Portugal.

The Iberian lynx still faces threats from road accidents and epidemics that kill off large numbers of rabbits (its main prey), but its future certainly looks far rosier than it did a decade ago.

Live film of lynx in the breeding program is displayed on a screen at Doñana's El Acebuche visitor centre, though the breeding centre itself is closed to the public. Chances of sighting a wild lynx are highest in the Parque Natural Sierra de Andújar.

Birdwatcher's Paradise

Andalucía is something of a last refuge for several highly endangered raptor species. When it comes to migratory bird species, however, Andalucía is a veritable superhighway.

Andalucía has 13 resident raptor species, as well as a handful of summer visitors from Africa. Glowering in the almost-sinister manner of its kind, the rare and vulnerable black vulture *(buitre negro)* – Europe's biggest bird – has established a stronghold in the Sierra Morena, with around 400 pairs (doubled since 2001) scattered from Huelva's Sierra Pelada to Jaén's Sierra de Andújar. As this is probably the world's biggest population of black vultures, the bird's survival here is critical to the viability of the species.

An excellent English-language source of information on Andalucian fauna and flora is Iberianature (www.iberianature.com).

More easily spotted and just as impressive is the 2.5m-wingspan griffon vulture *(buitre leonado)*, whose numbers approach 3400 breeding pairs in Andalucía. You are virtually guaranteed sightings in places such as the Garganta Verde in the Parque Natural Sierra de Grazalema, the Peñón de Zaframagón near Olvera, and the hills around the town of Cazorla.

Also emblematic and very rare is the Spanish imperial eagle *(águila imperial ibérica)*, found in no other country. Its total numbers have increased tenfold over the past half century, helped by an active government protection plan operative since 2001. There were 112 nesting pairs in Andalucía at last count – mostly in the Sierra Morena, with nine pairs in the Doñana area. Poisoned bait put out by farmers or hunters is the imperial's greatest enemy.

The bearded vulture or lammergeier *(quebrantahuesos)*, with its majestic 2.7m to 2.9m wingspan, disappeared from Andalucía – its last refuge in Spain except for the Pyrenees – in 1986. But a breeding centre was established in the Parque Natural Sierras de Cazorla, Segura y Las Villas in 1996; the first young lammergeiers were released into the wild in 2006; the first chick hatched in the wild in 2015; and by 2019 there were seven wild-hatched juveniles and two breeding pairs residing in the Cazorla mountains.

Other large birds of prey in Andalucía include the golden eagle *(águila real)* and the Egyptian vulture *(alimoche)*, all found in mountain regions.

If Andalucía's raptors lend gravitas to birdwatching here, the waterbirds that visit Andalucía add a scale rarely seen in Europe, mainly thanks to extensive wetlands along the Atlantic coast, such as those at the mouths of the Guadalquivir and Odiel Rivers. Hundreds of thousands of migratory birds, including an estimated 80% of Western Europe's wild ducks, winter in the Doñana wetlands of the Guadalquivir delta, and many more call in during spring and autumn migrations.

Laguna de Fuente de Piedra, near Antequera, sees as many as 20,000 greater flamingo *(flamenco)* pairs rearing chicks in spring and summer. This beautiful pink bird can also be seen in several other places, including San Miguel de Cabo de Gata, El Rocío on the edge of the Parque Nacional de Doñana, and the Paraje Natural Marismas del Odiel; these last two have extensive wetlands that serve as a haven for many other waterbirds.

The large, ungainly white stork *(cigüeña blanca)*, actually black and white, nests from spring to summer on electricity pylons and in trees and towers (sometimes right in the middle of towns) across western Andalucía. Much rarer and less sociable is the black stork *(cigüeña negra)*, which prefers cliff ledges. Both birds are mainly migrant visitors, crossing the Strait of Gibraltar from Africa to breed in Spain, although a few of them stay year-round.

For more information on Andalucía's bird life, including where to see particular species, check out the websites of SEO/BirdLife (www.seo.org) and the Andalucia Bird Society (www.andaluciabirdsociety.org).

Arts & Culture

For significant parts of Spanish history, Andalucía has stood at the forefront of the nation's artistic and cultural life. Halcyon eras have come and gone, often ebbing and flowing with the power of Spain in world affairs. Though all the arts are well represented in Andalucía, the region has produced a particularly rich seam of talented painters, including two of the most influential masters to put brush to canvas: Diego Velázquez and Pablo Picasso. Meanwhile, flamenco – reflective but uplifting, raw but layered, pure yet loaded with complexity – is proudly and unequivocally a product of Andalucía.

Arts

Córdoba Caliphate

The most populous and culturally vibrant city in Europe at the time, Córdoba of the 8th to 11th centuries was an intellectual powerhouse, replete with libraries, schools and a university that competed with the rival caliphate of Baghdad to promote the global spread of ideas. Emir Abd ar-Rahman II (r 822–52) was a strong patron of the arts who maintained a close relationship with the influential Arabic poet and musician Ziryab; Abd ar-Rahman III (r 912–61) filled his city Medina Azahara with the finest Islamic art, crafts and mosaics, much of it copied from Byzantine artists; while Al-Hakim II (r 961–76) was an avid reader who collected and catalogued hundreds of thousands of books. Many of the great works of Greek philosophy were later translated and reinterpreted in medieval Córdoba by scholarly polymaths such as Averroës (1126–98), Maimonides (1135–1204) and Ibn Tufail (1105–85).

Though Córdoba's influence declined after its reconquest by the Christians in 1236, the invaders from the north subtly absorbed many of the city's ideas. It was partly through this intellectual inheritance that Western Europe attained the know-how and inspiration that sparked the Renaissance in Italy two centuries later.

Nasrid Flowering

The Nasrid emirate established in Granada in 1232 was more of a defensive entity than an outward-looking culture-spreader in the mould of Córdoba. However, its foppish rulers were vociferous appreciators of the arts, in particular poetry. Several of the emirate's sultans became acclaimed poets, most notably the yearningly romantic Yusuf III (r 1408–17). The high point of the Granadan flowering came during the illustrious reigns of Yusuf I (1333–54) and Mohammed V (1354–91), the two great builders of the Alhambra. Both sultans established literary circles in their courts. Yusuf employed Arabic poet and historian Ibn al-Khatib (1313–74), whose verse was set to music and whose lyrical poems remain inscribed on the walls of Alhambra's palaces and fountains. Mohammed V installed al-Khatib as his *vizier* (political adviser), a position that stoked much political controversy at the time and possibly cost al-Khatib his life: in 1374, according to one version of the story, al-Khatib's student and fellow poet Ibn Zamrak (1333–93) hired assassins to kill him. Ibn Zamrak subsequently became court poet to Mohammed V, during an era

Novels Set in Andalucía

- *The Blind Man of Seville*, Robert Wilson
- *Encarnita's Journey*, Joan Lingard
- *The Hand of Fatima*, Ildefonso Falcones
- *Leo the African*, Amin Maalouf
- *A Manuscript of Ashes*, Antonio Muñoz Molina
- *The Seville Communion*, Arturo Perez
- *A Vineyard in Andalusia*, María Dueñas
- *The Wind from the East*, Almudena Grandes

when poetry and cultural exchange with Morocco and Egypt had created a healthy cross-continental flow of ideas.

Miguel de Cervantes, creator of Don Quijote, was not Andalucian, but he did spend 10 troubled years in the region procuring oil and wheat for the Spanish navy and as a collector of unpaid taxes. Some of his short *Novelas ejemplares* (Exemplary Novels) chronicle life in turbulent 16th-century Seville.

Golden Age

For a glittering 50 years during Spain's artistic Siglo de Oro (Golden Age), which ran from the late 16th to late 17th centuries, Andalucian painters pretty much defined world art. The mantle rested chiefly on the shoulders of three Sevillan giants. Bartolomé Esteban Murillo (1617–82) was a baroque master with a delicate touch and a penchant for documentary and religious painting. The mystically inclined Francisco de Zurbarán (1598–1664), born in Extremadura but resident in and around Seville for most of his life, was a more restrained exponent of the Italian art of chiaroscuro (the technique of contrasting light and dark elements in a painting to create a dramatic effect). Diego Velázquez (1599–1660) was known as an artist's artist; his exacting methods and subtle use of colour and tone ultimately opened the door to Impressionism. He was born and started his artistic career in Seville but moved to Madrid to become a court painter in 1623. Velázquez' most celebrated work, *Las meninas* (Maids of Honour), is a revolutionary masterpiece of viewpoint in which the artist depicts himself contemplating his invisible subjects, King Felipe IV and Queen Mariana of Spain, whose faces appear reflected in a mirror. *Las meninas* hangs today in Madrid's El Prado. Three centuries after Velázquez' death, an enamoured Picasso made 58 abstract attempts to reinterpret this great work.

Both Velázquez and Zurbarán were employed by the royal court of Felipe IV, while Murillo was favoured by the Catholic Church. Murillo painted several works for Seville's cathedral and produced dozens of depictions of the Virgin Mary's immaculate conception.

Velazquez' friend Alonso Cano (1601–72), from Granada, was a gifted painter, sculptor and architect noted for an uncontrollable temper. In the course of his turbulent life he also found work at Felipe IV's court. Much of his best work hangs in Seville's Museo de Bellas Artes, along with strong representations of Zurbarán's and Murillo's art.

Generation of '98

Spain's humiliation in the Spanish-American War of 1898, when it lost its last colonies, was a key moment for the group of critical writers known as the Generación de '98. Their writings, flecked with rebellion and realism, aimed to offset the cultural malaise and re-establish the nation's literary prominence. The circle's leading poet, Seville-born Antonio Machado (1875–1939), chided the nation for being asleep, adrift in a sea of mediocrity. Machado spent most of his adult life outside Andalucía, except for a few years as a teacher in Baeza, where he completed *Campos de Castilla,* a set of poems evoking the landscape of Castilla and ruminating on the national malaise. Machado's friend Juan Ramón Jiménez (1881–1958),

PICASSO RECLAIMED

Born in Málaga in 1881 to Don José Ruíz y Blasco (also an artist) and María Picasso y López, Pablo Picasso lived in Málaga until he was 10. In 1891 he moved with his family to A Coruña in Galicia and then, in 1895, to Barcelona, where he ultimately established his artistic reputation. Since he never returned permanently to Málaga, Picasso's connection with Andalucía was long underemphasised; you'll find better exhibitions of his art in Barcelona and Paris. But with Málaga undergoing a cultural awakening in recent decades, the city took steps to reclaim him. The Picasso Foundation was established in 1988 in his Casa Natal (birth house) in Plaza de la Merced, and, in 2003, after 50 years of on-off planning, the excellent Museo Picasso Málaga was opened in a 16th-century palace.

from Moguer near Huelva, touchingly and amusingly brought to life his home town in *Platero y yo* (Platero and I), a prose poem telling of his childhood wanderings with his donkey and confidant, Platero. Winner of the 1956 Nobel literature prize, Juan Ramón stands as a kind of bridge between the Generation of '98 and the next great wave of Andalucian writers in the Generation of '27.

Around the same time, classical music found a cohesive Iberian voice in a group of four Spanish composers, two of whom were from Andalucía. Both Manuel de Falla (1876–1946) from Cádiz and Joaquín Turina (1882–1949) from Seville used influences absorbed from Parisian Impressionists Debussy and Ravel to craft operas, ballet scores, songs and chamber music that resonated with echoes of Andalucian folklore.

Generation of '27

Spain's great literary blossoming took place during the relatively calm 1920s dictatorship of Primo de Rivera, between the social unrest of the early 20th century and the tumultuous years leading to the Spanish Civil War in the 1930s. In 1927 in Seville, a key group of 10 poets came together to mark the 300th anniversary of the death of lyrical baroque master Luis de Góngora. Of the 10, six were born in Andalucía, including the peerless Federico García Lorca (from Granada), the romantic turned polemicist poet Rafael Alberti (from El Puerto de Santa María) and the surrealist wordsmith Vicente Aleixandre (from Seville).

Unlike the more pessimistic Generación de '98, which had criticised the conformism of Spain after the restoration of the monarchy in 1874, the 27ers were less damning of what had gone before in their exploration of classic themes such as love, death, destiny and the beauty of images. Obsessed by the work of Góngora, they espoused wider poetic expressionism and free verse, combining elements of the new surrealism with echoes from Spain's ancient folkloric tradition (in particular, flamenco). The movement was ultimately shattered and dispersed by the civil war, an event that killed Lorca and sent many of the others into a long exile. The last surviving member of the Generación de '27, Francisco Ayala from Granada, died in 2009 aged 103. Ayala spent many years in exile in Argentina and Puerto Rico after his father and brother were murdered by Nationalists in the civil war.

Lorca – Man of Many Talents

Andalucía's (and arguably Spain's) greatest writer, Granada-born Federico García Lorca (1898–1936), is best known for his poems and plays and – more tragically – his senseless murder at the hands of Spanish fascists at the start of the civil war. But Lorca's talents went beyond writing. He was an accomplished pianist, an actor with a rural theatre troupe, a director of his own and other people's plays, and a deft cultural organiser (along with classical composer Manuel de Falla, he was instrumental in conceiving flamenco's Concurso de Cante Jondo (p347) in 1922). In collaboration with Falla, Lorca also co-composed an opera – sadly, unfinished – called *Lola, la comedianta;* inspired by another friend, Salvador Dalí, he demonstrated his skill for art: his drawings and paintings were published in books and displayed at exhibitions. Lorca once even drafted a surrealistic film screenplay entitled *Viaje a la luna* (Trip to the Moon, which wasn't filmed until 1998).

Dead by the age of 38, Lorca squeezed his achievements into a fertile two decades between 1918 and 1936, when he was shot and slung into an unmarked grave just outside Granada. Not surprisingly, his legacy is massive and regularly refuelled by the ongoing search for his remains. They are thought to lie somewhere near the village of Viznar, beneath the pastoral Vega he loved so dearly.

Anglophone Andalucía

- *Lord Byron, Don Juan*
- *Washington Irving, Tales of the Alhambra*
- *Laurie Lee, A Rose for Winter*
- *Gerald Brenan, South from Granada*
- *Chris Stewart, Driving Over Lemons*
- *Steven Nightingale, Granada: The Light of Andalucia*

The 2008 British-Spanish film *Little Ashes* (*Cenicitas*) is based on long-standing rumours of a 1920s love affair between Federico García Lorca and Salvador Dalí.

Flamenco

Part *cante flamenco,* part hymn of adoration, part outpouring of grief, *saetas* are unaccompanied songs typically offered to images of Christ or the Virgin Mary during Semana Santa processions. You'll hear them drifting from upper-floor balconies as religious floats pass beneath, or intoned by a lone singer standing in rapt devotion along the parade route.

Basics

One of the beauties of flamenco is its lack of straightforwardness, though a handful of basic points offer some clarity. First, flamenco is an expressive art, incorporating more than just music. In the early days it was a realistic reflection of the lives of those who sang it – the oppressed – and they carried it with them everywhere: in the fields, at work, at home and in their famed *juergas* (Roma parties). Second, it is very much a 'live' spectacle and – for purists, at least – a necessarily spontaneous one. The preserve of the Roma until the 19th century, performances were never rehearsed or theatrical, and the best ones still aren't. Third, flamenco hinges on the interaction between its four basic elements: the *cante* (song), the *baile* (dance), the *toque* (guitar), and an oft-forgotten fourth element known as the *jaleo* (handclaps, shouts and audience participation/appreciation). The *cante* sits centre stage, as the guide. In its earliest incarnations, flamenco didn't have regular dancers, and guitars weren't added until the 19th century. Some flamenco forms, such as *martinetes* and *carceleras,* remain voice only. In traditional flamenco performances, players warm up slowly, tuning their guitars and clearing their throats while the gathered crowd talk among themselves. It is up to the dancers and musicians to grab the audience's attention and gradually lure them in.

Flamenco Palos (Musical Forms)

The purist expression of flamenco is known as *cante jondo* (literally 'deep song'), a primitive collection of *palos* (musical forms) that includes *soleares* (a quintessential form with a strong, strict rhythm), the tragic and expressive *siguiriyas*, and *tientos*, *martinetes* and *carceleras*. *Cante jondo* is considered to be the main building block of flamenco and good singers – whose gravelly, operatic voices can sound like a cross between Tom Waits and Pavarotti – are required to sing as if their lives depended upon it, and leave a piece of their soul in every stanza. The raw emotion and almost religious absorption of these powerful performers can be rather unnerving to the uninitiated. The ideal is to inspire *duende* – the musical spirit that reaches out and touches your soul during an ecstatic live performance. But *duende* can be elusive. The poet Federico García Lorca, in his many commentaries on the subject, often alluded to its intangibility. Thus, it is up to the singer to summon it up, amalgamating yearning, superstition, anguish and fervour into a force that is both intimate and transcendental.

Best Peñas (Flamenco Clubs)

- *Peña La Platería, Granada*
- *Peña Flamenca La Perla, Cádiz*
- *Peña Juan Breva, Málaga*
- *Centro Cultural Flamenco Don Antonio Chacón, Jerez de la Frontera*

Cantes Chicos

The other main grouping of flamenco songs is called *cantes chicos* (little songs), *palos* that are more light-hearted and accessible derivatives of *cante jondo*. Popular *cantes chicos* are the upbeat *alegrías* from Cádiz, descended from sailor's jigs; the fast but tongue-in-cheek *bulerías* from Jerez; and the ubiquitous *tangos* made popular by the great Sevillan singer La Niña de los Peines.

Cantes Andaluces

A third, more nebulous, group of *palos* (sometimes called *cantes andaluces*) exists outside what most aficionados would call 'pure' flamenco. This consists mainly of *fandangos* that are descended from Spanish folk music, with each region broadcasting its own variation. The most famous are the strident *fandangos de Huelva,* enthusiastically danced during the Romería del Rocío religious pilgrimage. *Verdiales,* an ancient Arabic-style song/dance, are a type of *fandango* from Málaga, a province that also concocted the freer and easier (and undanced) *malagueñas.*

ANDALUCÍA'S GUITAR LEGACY

It's not just flamenco – the Spanish guitar itself has its roots in Andalucía. The *vihuela*, an early guitar-shaped instrument with six pairs of strings, was already being played here in the mid-15th century, when the rest of Europe was still strumming pear-shaped lutes. But the guitar really came into its own four centuries later, when Almería-born artisan Antonio de Torres (1817–92) introduced design innovations that transformed earlier iterations into the Spanish classical guitar we know today. Inspired by conversations with his friend, Almerian guitarist and composer Julián Arcas, Torres equipped his instruments with a thinner, lighter arched soundboard anchored by symmetrical fan-bracing, thus significantly enhancing the guitar's resonant, sonorous quality. His mastery of the craft paved the way for generations of future Andalucía-born guitar virtuosos, including Andrés Segovia, Pepe Romero, Juan Francisco Padilla, Niño Ricardo, Rafael Riqueni, Tomatito, Vicente Amigo, Manolo Sanlúcar, Pepe Habichuela and Niño Josele.

Granaínas are an ornamental and introspective *fandango* offshoot from Granada with no set rhythm; *tarantas* are an earthier, sparser version of the form from the mining communities of the Levante (Almería).

Historical Roots

The long-time preserve of marginalised and culturally oppressed people (most of whom were illiterate), it was neither written about nor eulogised in its early days. Instead, the music was passed through bloodlines by word of mouth. No published testimonies exist before 1840.

The genesis of the art as we now know it took place in Andalucía some time in the early 15th century, among disparate groups of Roma, Jews, Moors and perhaps other Spaniards. Anthropological evidence suggests that the Roma had begun a 400-year westward migration from the Indian subcontinent in the 11th century, settling all over Europe, with a southern contingent reaching Andalucía in the early 15th century. The Roma brought with them a dynamic form of musical expression – a way of performing that encouraged embellishment, virtuosity and improvisation – and they blended this rich musicality with the songs and melodies of the regions in which they settled. In Andalucía, they found natural allies among the Jews and Moors recently disenfranchised by the Reconquista (Christian reconquest). The collision of these three distinct cultures and the subsequent marinating of their music and culture over three or four centuries resulted in what we now know as *cante jondo,* or pure flamenco.

Modern Writers

José Manuel Caballero (b. Jerez de la Frontera, 1926)

Salvador Compán (b. Úbeda, 1949)

Emilio Lledó (b. Seville, 1927)

Antonio Muñoz Molina (b. Úbeda, 1956)

Elvira Navarro (b. Huelva, 1978)

Felix J Palma (b. Sanlúcar de Barrameda, 1968)

A Tale of Three Cities

Flamenco's documented history begins in the early 19th century and is essentially a tale of three cities in western Andalucía: Seville, Cádiz and Jerez de la Frontera, and their respective Roma neighbourhoods. Jerez has often been called the 'cradle of flamenco', primarily because its densely packed Roma quarters of Santiago and San Miguel have produced so many great artists. Today, the city is home to Andalucía's main flamenco centre and school and hosts two major festivals: the Festival de Jerez (in February or early March) and the Fiestas de Otonõ (in September). Flamenco in Cádiz grew up in the Santa María neighbourhood, while in Seville its font was the riverside Roma district of Triana. A few other towns with strong flamenco traditions lie in Sevilla province: Morón de la Frontera, Utrera and Lebrija. Together with Seville, Jerez and Cádiz, they make up Andalucía's so-called flamenco triangle.

The first real flamenco singer of note was the mysteriously named El Planeta (Antonio Monge Rivero), a Roma blacksmith born in either Jerez or Cádiz around 1785. El Planeta wasn't a performer in the modern sense, but he soon became well known for his passionate singing voice,

Best Festivals & Museums

Festival de Jerez, Jerez de la Frontera

Noche Blanca del Flamenco, Córdoba

Bienal de Flamenco, Seville

Museo del Baile Flamenco, Seville

Centro Flamenco Fosforito, Córdoba

Museo de Arte Flamenco, Málaga

which gave birth – allegedly – to such early flamenco *palos* as *martinetes* and *livianas*. El Planeta sits at the head of a flamenco family tree of interrelated singers, musicians and dancers that has carried on to the present day. His immediate heir was El Fillo (Francisco Ortega Vargas), whose naturally gravelly voice became the standard against which all others were compared, and whose name lived on in the term used to describe that type of voice – *voz afillá*.

Golden Age

Flamenco's 'golden age' began in the late 1840s and lasted until around 1915. In the space of 70 years, the music metamorphosed from an esoteric Roma art practised spontaneously at raucous *juergas* into a professional and increasingly popular form of public entertainment that merged *cante jondo* with other forms of Spanish folkloric music. It was during this fertile epoch that the modern musical forms took shape. Other innovations included the more complex choreography of flamenco dance and the emergence of the guitar as the de rigueur accompanying instrument.

The catalysts for change were the famous *cafés cantante* that took root in many Spanish cities, especially in Andalucía. Decorated with mirrors, bullfighting posters, gilded stages, and tables where patrons could enjoy alcoholic beverages, these became the engine rooms of a dramatic musical cross-fertilisation. The first cafe opened in Seville in 1842, and the establishments gradually spread, reaching their apex in the 1880s with prestigious venues such as the Café Silverio in Seville. Presiding over this conflation was Silverio Franconetti, proprietor of Seville's Café Silverio and soulful inheritor of El Fillo's hoarse, cracked *voz afillá*. Yet, despite his lifelong penchant for *siguiriyas* and *soleares,* Franconetti couldn't stop the bastardisation of the music he loved as it moved from the *juergas* into the cafes, substituting tragic harshness for tuneful palatability. Unwittingly, he had created the conditions for flamenco's jump from music of the Roma to popular property.

Slide into Decadence

By 1920 pure flamenco, threatened by changing public tastes and impending political crises, was an endangered species. Fearing oblivion, Andalucian aesthetes Federico García Lorca and Manuel de Falla organised a competition in Granada in 1922 to try to save the art – the Concurso de Cante Jondo. But with the civil war approaching, the die was cast. The music entered an era known as *ópera flamenco,* when *cante jondo* was diluted further by folk music and greater commercialisation. The controversial figure of the era was Pepe Marchena (1903–76), flamenco's first well-paid superstar, who broke with tradition by singing lighter *fandangos* and *cantes de ida y vuelta* (musical forms sugar-frosted with Latin American influences before being 'returned' to Spain), often backed by an orchestra. Purists were understandably leery, while others saw it as the natural evolution of a music that had leapt into the public domain. Just below the radar, *cante jondo* survived, in part because it was still performed by Roma singers such as Manuel Torre and La Niña de los Peines, the greatest male and female voices of their age.

The traditional flamenco costume – shawl, fan and long, frilly *bata de cola* (tail gown) for women, and flat Cordoban hats and tight black trousers for men – is based on Andalucian fashions in the late 19th century.

Rebirth

By the 1950s, the re-evaluation of *cante jondo* fell to Antonio Mairena (1909–83), an impassioned Roma *cantaor* (singer) from Sevilla province and the first real flamencologist to historically decipher the art. Mairena insisted on singing only old forms of *palos,* such as *siguiriyas* and *martinetes,* many of which he rescued from almost certain extinction. Through his stubborn refusal to pander to commercial tastes, he provided a lifeline between the golden age and the revival that was to come.

CONCURSO DE CANTE JONDO, 1922

On an ethereal summer's evening in June 1922, a little-known Andalucian poet named Federico García Lorca welcomed 4000 guests to the Concurso de Cante Jondo (competition of 'deep song'), a flamenco singing contest he had organised at Granada's Alhambra in collaboration with the distinguished Spanish classical composer Manuel de Falla.

Between them, these two great avant-garde artists had struggled relentlessly to elevate flamenco – and in particular *cante jondo* – into a serious art form, a dynamic cultural genre of half-forgotten Andalucian folkloric traditions, in the face of a growing popular penchant for watered-down forms of flamenco 'opera'.

Amassed inside the atmospheric confines of the Alhambra were an impressive array of intellectuals, writers, performers, musicians and flamenco purists. One 72-year-old *cantaor* (singer) named Tio Bermúdez had walked 100km from his village to be there, and stunned the audience with his interpretations of old-style *siguiriyas*. Another, an old blind woman of Roma stock, found by Lorca, sang an unaccompanied *liviana,* a flamenco form long thought to be dead. A 12-year-old boy named Manolo Ortega, aka 'El Caracol' ('The Snail'), so impressed the judges that he walked off with first prize. Gathered beneath the cypress trees in a courtyard filled with the aroma of jasmine and lavender, young men swapped guitar *falsetas* (riffs), ladies stood up and danced *soleares*, while others listened to the virtuosity of established stars such as Ramón Montoya and Manuel Torre. The complex – observers later reported – seemed to be alive with a magical energy.

Whether the *concurso* ultimately 'saved' flamenco is open to debate. While the music gained some short-lived prestige, and sporadic recordings and revivals ensued, its golden age was over. An era of decadence followed, hastened by the onset of the civil war and the repressive Franco dictatorship. Flamenco's modern rebirth ultimately had to wait for a second *concurso* in Córdoba in 1956, and the subsequent rise of more groundbreaking innovators over a decade later.

By the 1960s, nascent *tablaos* – nightclubs staging professional flamenco shows – had filled the vacuum left by the closure of the *cafés cantante* in the 1920s. Some *tablaos,* particularly those in the new resort towns on the coast, were fake and insipid, while others played a role in re-establishing *cante jondo* alongside the newer *palos*. Flamenco's ultimate revival was spearheaded, however, not by venues but by the exciting performers who frequented them. Two in particular stood out. Paco de Lucía from Algeciras was a guitarist so precocious that by age 14 he had absorbed everything any living musician could teach. His muse and foil was Camarón de la Isla, a Roma singer from the town of San Fernando (known as La Isla), who by the early 1970s had attained the kind of godlike status normally reserved for rock stars and bullfighters. Between them, Camarón and de Lucía took flamenco to a different level, injecting it with out-of-the box innovations (such as electric guitars and keyboards) while, at the same time, carefully safeguarding its purity.

Best Tablaos

- *Tablao Cardenal, Córdoba*
- *Jardines de Zoraya, Granada*
- *Puro Arte, Jerez de la Frontera*
- *La Cava, Cádiz*

Modern Flamenco

In the 1970s musicians began mixing flamenco with jazz, rock, blues, rap and other genres. The purists loathed these changes, but this *nuevo flamenco* greatly broadened flamenco's appeal. The seminal recording was a 1977 flamenco-folk-rock album, *Veneno* (Poison), by the group of the same name centred on Kiko Veneno and Raimundo Amador, both from Seville.

The group Ketama, whose key members were all from Granada's Montoya flamenco family, was crucial in bringing flamenco to a younger audience in the 1980s and '90s, mixing the music with African, Cuban, Brazilian and other rhythms. *Songhai* (1987) and *Songhai II* (1995) –

FLAMENCO LEGENDS

El Planeta (1785–1850) Legendary Roma blacksmith who purportedly invented many unaccompanied *cantes* (songs).

El Fillo (1829–78) Protégé of El Planeta and famed for his gravelly voice, dubbed the *voz afillá.*

Silverio Franconetti (1831–89) Non-Roma who met El Fillo in Morón de la Frontera. Became an accomplished singer and set up Spain's most famous *café cantante* in Seville.

Antonio Chacón (1869–1929) Non-Roma singer with a powerful voice. Hired by Franconetti to sing in his Seville *café cantante* in the 1890s.

Ramón Montoya (1880–1949) Accompanist to Chacón from 1922 onwards – he put the guitar centre stage in flamenco.

La Niña de los Peines (1890–1969) Dynamic Roma singer from Seville who sang with Chacón and provided a vital link between the golden age and the 1950s revivalists.

El Caracol (1909–73) Discovered at age 12 at the Concurso de Cante Jondo in 1922. Went on to become one of the greatest, yet most self-destructive, flamenco singers of all time.

Carmen Amaya (1913–63) Her dynamic dancing and wild lifestyle made her the Roma dance legend of all time. From Barcelona.

Camarón de la Isla (1950–92) Performed in a club owned by El Caracol; this modern flamenco 'god' from San Fernando (La Isla) lived fast, died young and dabbled in bold experimentation.

Paco de Lucía (1947–2014) Guitar phenomenon from Algeciras who became Camarón's main accompanist, and successfully crossed over into jazz and classical music.

collaborations with Malian *kora* (harp) player Toumani Diabaté – were among their best albums.

Flamenco today is as popular as it has ever been and probably more innovative. New generations continue to increase flamenco's audience. Among the most popular are José Mercé from Jerez, whose big-selling albums have included *Lío* (Entanglement; 2002) and *Mi única llave* (My Only Key; 2012), and El Barrio, a 21st-century urban poet from Cádiz.

Some say that Madrid-born Diego El Cigala (b 1968) is Camarón de la Isla's successor, although he turns his talent as much to flamenco-Latin crossover as to pure flamenco. This powerful singer launched himself onto the big stage with the extraordinary *Lágrimas negras* (2003), a wonderful collaboration with Cuban virtuoso Bebo Valdés that mixes flamenco with Cuban influences.

Another innovative singer, whose untimely death in 2010 was mourned by a generation of flamenco aficionados, was Granada's Enrique Morente (1942–2010). While careful not to alienate flamenco purists, Morente, through numerous collaborations across genres, helped lay the foundations for *nuevo flamenco*. His daughter Estrella Morente (internationally best known for being the 'voice' behind the 2006 film *Volver*) has also carved out a niche in the first rank of performers.

Flamenco dance has reached its most adventurous horizons in the person of Joaquín Cortés, born in Córdoba in 1969. Seemingly indefatigable, Cortés fuses flamenco with contemporary dance, ballet and jazz in spectacular shows all over the world with music at rock-concert amplification. Top-rank, more purist dancers include Sara Baras and Antonio Canales.

On the guitar, modern virtuosos include Manolo Sanlúcar from Cádiz, Tomatito from Almería (who used to accompany Camarón de la Isla) and Vicente Amigo from Córdoba. A rising guitar star, from Málaga, is Daniel (Dani) Casares (b 1980).

Bullfighting

There is no more controversial activity in Spain than bullfighting. Already effectively banned in Catalonia and the Canary Islands – and temporarily banned in the Balearic Islands before a court order reinstated it in 2019 – this deeply rooted traditional activity has faced mounting opposition in recent years. It's unlikely, however, that Andalucía will cave in any time soon, as this is the region where modern bullfighting was invented, and it has produced the lion's share of the nation's legendary matadors.

For & Against

Supporters of bullfighting emphasise its historical legacy and high-profile place in Spanish culture. Some claim that *corridas* (bullfights) are less cruel than slaughterhouses; fighting bulls, they argue, live longer in better conditions than domestic beasts. For its opponents, however, bullfighting is an intolerably cruel, violent spectacle that sees many thousands of bulls slowly and painfully killed in public every year, and it is a blight on Spain's conscience in these supposedly more enlightened times.

A recent national opinion poll found that only 19% of Spaniards aged between 16 and 65 supported bullfighting, while 58% opposed it. Among 16- to 24-year-olds, the level of support was just 7%. But the anti-bullfighting lobby is bigger and more influential in northern Spain than it is in Andalucía, Madrid, Castilla y León or Castilla-La Mancha, and the pro-bullfighting lobby is powerful. Political parties including Ciudadanos, the Partido Popular and Vox often still glorify bullfighting as a centrepiece of Spain's cultural heritage, and King Felipe VI has praised the spectacle as a cohesive element of Spanish society.

That there is a debate at all about the morality of bullfighting owes much to Spain's growing integration with the rest of Europe since its return to democracy in the late 1970s. Much of the anti-bullfighting impetus has come from groups beyond Spanish shores, among them PETA (www.peta.org.uk) and World Animal Protection (www.worldanimalprotection.org.uk). But home-grown Spanish anti-bullfighting, pro-animal-rights organisations are ever more active, including a political party, PACMA (www.pacma.es), the parliamentary grouping APDDA (www.apdda.es), the vets-against-bullfighting association AVATMA (www.avatma.org) and the animal-rights NGO ADDA (www.addaong.org).

The number of bullfights in Spain has fallen dramatically, from 3651 in 2007 to 1521 in 2018 (of which 241 took place in Andalucía), according to government figures. The bullfighting industry attributes the decline partly to economic factors, but statistics also show that the younger generation is losing interest in this age-old tradition.

History

Some historical testimonies suggest that it was Roman emperor Claudius who introduced bullfighting to Spain. However, it was the Moors who refined what was then an unregulated spectacle by adding ritualistic moves and the use of horses. The practice was largely the preserve of the horse-riding nobility until the early 18th century, when an Andalucian from Ronda named Francisco Romero got down from his mount, feinted a few times with a cape and killed the bull with a sword. Francisco's methods quickly gained popularity and he became the first professional bullfighter and head of Ronda's famous Romero dynasty. His son Juan Romero evolved bullfighting further by adding the *cuadrilla* (bullfighting team). Third in line, Pedro (Francisco's grandson) remains the most celebrated bullfighter of all time, with more than 5000 bulls slain in a 60-year career. Pedro introduced theatrics to bullfighting and established it as a serious pursuit. His methods remained commonplace for nearly a century.

An *espontáneo* is a bullfight spectator who illegally jumps into the ring and attempts to fight the bull. Famous matador 'El Cordobés' controversially launched his career this way. Ironically, years later, one of his own fights was interrupted by a less lucky *espontáneo* who was fatally gored.

Bullfighting's 'golden age' came in the 1910s, when it was transformed into a breathtaking show of aesthetics and technicality with a minuscule margin for error. The change was prompted by two famous matadors: Juan Belmonte and Joselito 'El Gallo'. Regarded as the two greatest bullfighters in history, they were born within three years of each other in Sevilla province. Juan Belmonte (1892–1962) had deformed legs, so, unable to move like other matadors, he elected to stand bolt upright and motionless in the ring until the bull was nearly upon him. This startling new technique kept the audience's hearts in their mouths and resulted in Belmonte getting gored more than 20 times; yet he lived. Joselito (1895–1920) was a child prodigy who adapted Belmonte's close-quarter methods; the two quickly became rivals and their duels between 1914 and 1920 are unlikely to be replicated. The rivalry came to an end when Joselito was fatally gored in 1920.

Doused in tradition, bullfighting has changed little in essentials since Joselito's demise. Manolete (1917–47), a notoriously serious bullfighter from Córdoba, added some of the short, close passes with the *muleta* (matador's cape) that are now common, while his fellow Cordoban 'El Cordobés' combined flamboyance inside the ring with equally flamboyant antics outside it.

Bullfighting Books

- *Death in the Afternoon* (1932), by Ernest Hemingway
- *Into the Arena: The World of the Spanish Bullfight* (2011), by Alexander Fiske-Harrison
- *Death and Money in the Afternoon* (1999), by Adrian Shubert
- *On Bullfighting* (1999), by AL Kennedy
- *Making Sense of Bullfighting* (2017), by Reza Hosseinpour

The Fight

Bullfights are bloody spectacles, involving considerable pain and distress for the animals involved. The bull's back and neck are repeatedly pierced by lances and harpoon-like prods, and the bull gradually becomes weakened through blood loss before the matador delivers the final sword thrust. If this is done with precision, the bull dies instantly – but if the *coup de grâce* is not delivered accurately, the animal sometimes dies an excruciatingly slow death.

As a rule, in a professional *corrida* (bullfight) three different matadors will fight two bulls each. Each fight takes about 20 minutes. The *matador* (literally, 'killer') – more often called the *torero* (bullfighter) in Spanish – is the leader of the team, adorned in a glittering *traje de luces* (suit of lights). A complex series of events takes place in each clash. *Peones* (the matador's 'footmen') dart about with grand capes in front of the bull to test its strength; horseback picadors drive lances into the bull's withers; and *banderilleros* (flagmen) charge headlong at the bull in an attempt to stab its neck. Finally, when the bull seems tired out, the matador, facing the animal head-on, aims to sink a sword cleanly into its neck for an instant kill – the *estocada*. A skilful, daring performance followed by a clean kill will have the crowd on its feet, perhaps waving handkerchiefs in an appeal to the fight president to award the matador an ear of the animal.

Survival Guide

Directory A–Z

Accessible Travel

Accessibility in Andalucía is improving as new buildings (including hotels) meet regulations requiring them to have wheelchair access. Many midrange and top-end hotels are now adapting rooms and creating better access for wheelchair users; accessibility tends to be poorer at some budget accommodation.

If you call a taxi and ask for a 'eurotaxi', you should be sent one adapted for wheelchair users.

International organisations can usually offer advice (sometimes including Andalucía-specific info).

Accessible Spain Travel (www.accessiblespaintravel.com; Pujades 152, 3-1, Barcelona) Organises accessible tours, transport and accommodation in Córdoba, Granada, Málaga and Seville for travellers with limited mobility.

Mobility International USA (☎in USA 541-343-1284; www.miusa.org; 132 E Broadway, No 343, Eugene; ⏰9am-5pm Mon-Fri) Advises travellers with disabilities on mobility issues and runs an educational exchange program.

Accommodation

During peak season (ie around Easter, Christmas and in July and August), it is best to book accommodation in advance. Many travellers use online sites like booking.com to reserve rooms, though you can often save money while supporting local business by booking directly with the property.

Hostales Small family-run hotels ranked from one to three stars.

Casas rurales Rural houses run as B&Bs, or independent longer-term lets.

Hotels From modern chains in big cities to opulent *paradores* (luxury state-owned hotels) in historic buildings.

Hostels Cheap backpacker accommodation with dorm rooms.

Hostels & Hostales

In Spain, it is important to make a distinction between hostels and *hostales*. Hostels offer standard backpacker accommodation with dorm beds, kitchen facilities, communal lounges, shared bathrooms and bags of local information for budget travellers. Prices vary according to room size and, to a lesser extent, season, but start at around €15 for a shared dorm room. Dorms typically have between four and 10 beds, and many hostels offer double rooms and/or family rooms as well, usually with shared bathrooms.

Hostales are small family-run hotels where basic but adequate facilities are provided in single, double or triple rooms rather than dorms. Double rooms rarely go for more than €60. Travellers can usually expect private bathrooms and more personal service.

In Andalucía, hostels are normally confined to the main cities such as Seville, Granada and Málaga, although there's a handful of Hostelling International (HI) hostels in smaller villages such as El Bosque (in the Parque Natural Sierra de Grazalema), Cortes de la Frontera and Cazorla. The privately run **Oasis Hostels** (www.oasisbackpackershostels.com) is an excellent non-HI bet. It runs hostels in Granada and Málaga, as well as two in Seville (one of which is in an old palace). All are centrally located and offer heaps of freebies such as tapas tours, drink vouchers, bike hire and pancake breakfasts.

For more information on hostels or to make online bookings, see www.hostelworld.com, www.hostel

> **BOOK YOUR STAY ONLINE**
>
> For more accommodation reviews by Lonely Planet authors, check out http://lonelyplanet.com/hotels/. You'll find independent reviews, as well as recommendations on the best places to stay. Best of all, you can book online.

bookers.com or **Andalucia Youth Hostels** (☎955 18 11 81; www.inturjoven.com).

Hotels

Andalucía's hotels range from spruce business-style operations to the state-run *parador* chain of luxury hotels inhabiting old historic buildings. Boutique hotels are well on the rise; in Andalucía they often cleverly combine historical features with dynamic contemporary design. Seville, Granada and Córdoba host some of the finest boutique hotels, though a number of *pueblos blancos* (white villages) also have spectacular options, particularly Vejer de la Frontera.

Campgrounds

Andalucía has approximately 150 campgrounds, accommodating both caravans and tents. Cádiz province leads the way with 32 facilities, while Sevilla province has a select five. Rural areas offer the most idyllic camping spots. Highlights include the Costa de la Luz, with more than 20 campgrounds; the areas abutting the Parque Nacional de Doñana marshes; the steep Las Alpujarras valleys in the Sierra Nevada; the Cazorla mountains; and the Cabo de Gata coastline. Campgrounds in Spain are graded 1st class, 2nd class or 3rd class, and facilities are generally very good. Even a 3rd-class campground will have hot showers, electrical hook-ups and a cafe; top-notch places, meanwhile, often have minimarkets and swimming pools.

Campgrounds normally charge separately per adult, child and car. Average prices are rarely higher than €7.50, €6 and €6 respectively. Many facilities also rent cabins or bungalows from approximately €50 a night depending on size and season.

The **Federación Española de Clubes Campistas** (FECC; www.guiacampingfecc.com) is Spain's main camping club. Its website is an excellent information resource; from it you can access the websites of individual campgrounds, and most allow you to make reservations online and provide further contact info. It also publishes the annual *Guía Camping*, available in bookshops in Spain.

Self-Catering Apartments & Casas Rurales

Self-catering apartments and houses are relatively easy to procure in Andalucía and are particularly popular in coastal resort areas. Basic one-bedroom apartments start at around €40 per night, while a luxury pad with a swimming pool somewhere like Marbella will set you back up to €400 a night for four people.

Casas rurales are usually old renovated farmhouses run as B&Bs or as more independent short-term holiday lets. They exist predominantly in smaller towns and villages. Prices for double rooms run from €50 to €100, though many people opt for longer-term bookings, thus saving money.

The agencies listed here all offer online bookings. In the peak summer months (June to August) and around holiday periods (Semana Santa and Easter) it's best to book at least a month ahead.

Agencies include the following:

Escapada Rural (www.escapadarural.com)

Owners Direct (www.ownersdirect.co.uk)

Ruralka (www.ruralka.com)

Rustic Rent (www.rusticrent.com)

Secret Places (www.secretplaces.com)

SLEEPING PRICE RANGES

The following price ranges refer to a double room with private bathroom in high season.

€ less than €65

€€ €65–€140

€€€ more than €140

Discount Cards

Many museums and other attractions offer discounts for students, young people, children, families and/or seniors.

Seniors Reduced prices for people over 60 or 65 (depending on the place) at various museums and attractions (sometimes restricted to EU citizens) and occasionally on transport. Proof of age (passport or other official ID) is generally sufficient.

Student cards Discounts on museums, transport and more for students. You will need some kind of identification (eg an International Student Identity Card; www.isic.org) to prove student status.

Youth cards Travel, sights and accommodation discounts available to young people 30 and under with the European Youth Card (www.eyca.org) – known as Carné Joven in Spain – and the International Youth Travel Card

EATING PRICE RANGES

The following price ranges refer to a main course at dinner, excluding drinks. The service charge is included in the price.

€ less than €12

€€ €12–€20

€€€ more than €20

(IYTC) issued by ISIC (www.isic.org) and sold at outlets such as STA Travel (www.statravel.com).

Electricity

Type C
230V/50Hz

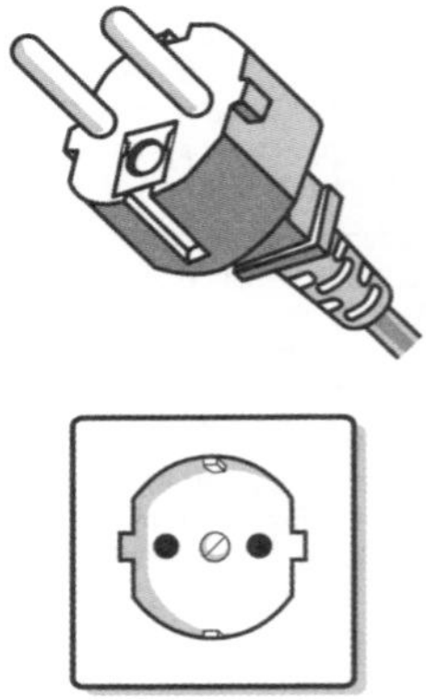

Type F
230V/50Hz

Health

For emergency treatment, go straight to the *urgencias* (casualty) section of the nearest hospital, or call 061 for an ambulance.

Good health care is readily available and *farmacias* (pharmacies) offer valuable advice and sell over-the-counter medication. In Spain, a system of *farmacias de guardia* (duty pharmacies) operates so that each district has one open all the time. When a pharmacy is closed, it posts the name of the nearest open one on the door.

Tap water is generally safe to drink in Andalucía and throughout Spain. Do not drink water from rivers or lakes as it may contain harmful bacteria.

Health Insurance

If you're an EU citizen, or a citizen of Norway, Iceland, Liechtenstein or Switzerland, the free **EHIC** (European Health Insurance Card; ☎in UK 0300 330 1350; www.ehic.org.uk) covers you for most medical care in Spain, including maternity care and care for chronic illnesses such as diabetes (though not for emergency repatriation). However, you will normally have to pay for medicine bought from pharmacies, even if prescribed, and perhaps for some tests and procedures. The EHIC does not cover private medical consultations and treatment in Spain; this includes nearly all dentists, and some of the better clinics and surgeries. For more information on applying for an EHIC from your home country, follow the appropriate link on the European Commission website (http://ec.europa.eu/social/main.jsp?catId=563). Citizens of the UK remain eligible for EHIC coverage through 31 December 2020. Non-EU citizens – including UK citizens starting in 2021 – should check with their home country health insurance provider to see if it offers any coverage in Spain.

Insurance

A travel-insurance policy to cover theft, loss and medical problems is a good idea. Travel agents will be able to make recommendations. Check the small print: some policies specifically exclude 'dangerous activities', which can include scuba diving, motorcycling or even trekking. Strongly consider a policy that covers you for the worst possible scenario, such as an accident requiring an ambulance or emergency flight home. Find out in advance if your insurance plan will make payments to doctors or hospitals directly, rather than your having to pay on the spot and claim later. The former option is generally preferable, as it doesn't leave you out of pocket. If you have to claim later, make sure you keep all documentation.

Buy travel insurance as early as possible. If you buy it in the week before you leave home, you may find, for example, that you are not covered for delays to your trip caused by strikes.

Paying for your airline ticket with a credit card often provides limited travel-accident insurance, and you may be able to reclaim payment if the operator doesn't deliver.

Worldwide travel insurance is available at www.lonelyplanet.com/travel-insurance. You can buy, extend and claim online any time – even if you're already on the road.

Internet Access

Nearly all hotels in Andalucía offer free wi-fi, and signal strength has improved in recent years. Many cafes also offer free wi-fi, as do airports, libraries and other public buildings.

A convenient and more universally reliable alternative to wi-fi – especially if you're travelling outside the cities – is to purchase a Spanish SIM card for your phone. Many local prepaid plans include generous data allowances at surprisingly low rates.

PARADORES: HISTORIC LUXURY

The state-run *parador* hotels were founded by King Alfonso XIII in the 1920s. There are 16 of them in Andalucía, all rated three or four stars. Prices range from €100 to nearly €400, but check the www.parador.es website for significant discounts. Occupying some astounding locations, these are possibly the best accommodation options around if you're up for a splurge. Most of the following occupy fine historical buildings:

Parador de Arcos de la Frontera (p137) Andalucía's smallest *parador* inhabits a former palace (the Casa del Corregidor) in Arcos de la Frontera's main square. The cliff-top views are stunning.

Parador de Granada (p271) Andalucía's and Spain's most celebrated (and expensive) *parador* is encased in a 15th-century convent inside the walls of the Alhambra, Granada.

Parador Castillo de Santa Catalina (p234) Newly refurbished and reopened in 2020, Jaén's medieval-style *parador* was built in the 1960s on the site of a 13th-century Christian castle. It sits atop a hill overlooking the city and the surrounding Sierra Morena.

Parador Málaga Gibralfaro (p171) On a hill next to the 14th-century Castillo de Gibralfaro and adjacent Alcazaba, this *parador* overlooks the whole spread of Málaga's city centre.

Parador de Ronda (p186) In the former town hall next to Ronda's gaping gorge; the town hall was the location of a real-life civil war massacre, fictionalised by Hemingway in *For Whom the Bell Tolls*.

Parador de Úbeda (p245) A luxury *parador* in one of Úbeda's trademark 16th-century Renaissance palaces.

Parador de Mazagón (p100) The natural setting is the star attraction at this *parador* perched above an endless sweep of cliff-fringed beach at the edge of Parque Nacional de Doñana.

Language Courses

Privately run language schools are scattered all over Spain and many of them are excellent. But, with most courses requiring a minimum of one week's study, it's important to find the right location. Seville is a beautiful city in which to linger for a week or two and has an abundance of top-notch language schools. If you'd prefer a slightly smaller city with instant access to history and beaches, try Cádiz, where a couple of good schools are located in the old quarter. For a more rural experience in a diminutive hilltop town close to the coast, you can't beat Vejer de la Frontera.

The best schools running language courses:

CLIC (International House; Map p58; ☎954 50 21 31; www.clic.es; Calle Albareda 19, Seville) Schools in Seville and Cádiz.

Escuela Delengua (Map p268; ☎958 20 45 35; www.delengua.es; Calle Calderería Vieja 20; single private class €31, 2-week course from €275) 🍃 Centre in student-heavy city of Granada.

Instituto Picasso (Map p166; ☎952 21 39 32; www.instituto-picasso.com; Plaza de la Merced 20; 1-/2-/3-/4-week course €160/320/460/590) Individual and small group instruction in Málaga.

K2 Internacional (Map p118; ☎956 21 26 46; www.k2internacional.com; Plaza Mentidero 19) School in Cádiz.

Legal Matters

- Spain has some of Europe's more liberal laws on marijuana, but note that it is legal for personal use only – which means small amounts in your own home. Public consumption, sale or purchase of any illicit drug – including cannabis – remains illegal. It would be very unwise to smoke cannabis in hotel rooms or guesthouses. Travellers entering Spain from Morocco, especially with a vehicle, should be prepared for intensive drug searches.
- Spain's drink-driving laws are relatively strict: the blood-alcohol limit is 0.05%, or 0.01% for new drivers.
- Under the Spanish constitution, anyone who is arrested must be informed immediately, in a manner understandable to them, of their rights and the grounds for the arrest. Arrested people are entitled to the assistance of a lawyer (and, where required, an interpreter) during police inquiries or judicial investigations. For many foreign nationals, including British citizens, the police are also obliged to inform an arrested person's consulate immediately. Arrested people may not be compelled to make a statement. Within 72 hours of arrest, the person must be brought before a judge or released.

Police

Spain has three main types of police:

Policía Nacional (National Police; ☎091) Covers cities and bigger towns, sometimes forming special squads dealing with drugs, terrorism and the like. A further contingent is to be found in bunker-like police stations called *comisarías*.

Policía Local (Local Police; ☎092) Also known as Policía Municipal; is controlled by city and town halls and deals mainly with minor matters such as parking, traffic and by-laws. Officers wear blue-and-white uniforms.

Guardia Civil (Civil Guard; ☎062) The responsibilities of the green-uniformed Guardia Civil include roads, the countryside, villages and international borders.

If you need to go to the police (for example, if you're the victim of petty theft), any of these services will do, but your best bets are the Policía Nacional or Policía Local.

LGBTIQ+ Travellers

Spain is one of the most progressive countries in the world for LGBTIQ+ travellers. Openly gay people have been able to serve in the Spanish military since 1979, antidiscrimination laws were introduced in the 1990s, and in 2005 Spain became the third country in the world to legalise same-sex marriage.

Andalucía's liveliest gay scene is in Torremolinos, closely followed by the scenes in Málaga, Seville and Granada, but there are gay- and lesbian-friendly bars and clubs in all major cities. Some cities produce special leaflets, guides and maps advertising gay-specific sights, such as Seville's *Municipios Orgullosos de la Provincia de Sevilla* (downloadable from www.turismosevilla.org). Ask at tourist information offices.

Seville hosts Andalucía's largest pride festival, **Orgullo de Andalucía** (http://orgullolgtbiandalucia.es) in late June. It features a week-long program of concerts, exhibitions and parties, culminating in a carnivalesque parade to the Alameda de Hércules on the final Saturday.

The websites www.travelgay.com and www.patroc.com have helpful listings of gay and gay-friendly accommodation, bars, clubs, beaches, cruising areas, health clubs and associations. Both have special sections for Seville and Torremolinos. Other useful websites include www.gayseville4u.com and www.gaytorremolinos4u.com.

The **Federación Andaluza Arco Iris** (☎615 773089; www.federacionarcoiris.blogspot.com) is an organisation based in Málaga that campaigns for equal opportunities for LGBTIQ+ people.

Maps

If you're going to do any walking in Andalucía you should arm yourself with the best possible maps, especially as trail markings can be patchy.

Spain's **Centro Nacional de Información Geográfica** (CNIG; www.cnig.es), the publishing arm of the Instituto Geográfico Nacional (IGN), produces a useful *Mapa Guía* series of national and natural parks, mostly at 1:25,000. The CNIG also covers Andalucía in its 1:50,000 *Mapa Topográfico Nacional* maps, most of which are up to date. Andalucía's eight provinces can be studied separately in the *mapas provinciales* series (1:200,000). CNIG maps may be labelled CNIG, IGN or both.

The CNIG website lists where you can buy CNIG maps (click on 'Puntas de Venta') or you can buy online. There are sales offices in Seville, Granada, Málaga, Almería and Jaén.

Good commercially published series, all usually accompanied by guide booklets, come from **Editorial Alpina** (www.editorialalpina.com), **Editorial Penibética** (www.penibetica.com) and Britain's **Discovery Walking Guides** (www.dwgwalking.co.uk).

Money

ATMs

Many credit and debit cards can be used for withdrawing money from *cajeros automáticos* (ATMs) that display the relevant symbols, such as Visa, MasterCard, Cirrus etc. Some Spanish banks such as Unicaja and Liberbank may offer ATM cash withdrawals free of charge, while others charge rather exorbitant fees (€5 to €7 per transaction); it pays to shop around. Note that your home bank may also assess a fee over and above whatever the Spanish bank charges.

Cash

Most banks will exchange major foreign currencies and offer better rates than exchange offices at the airport. Ask about commissions – these can vary from bank to bank – and take your passport.

Credit & Debit Cards

You can generally get by very well in Andalucía with a credit or debit card enabling you to make purchases and withdraw euros from ATMs.

Not every establishment accepts payment by card, but most do. You should be able to make payments by card in midrange and top-end accommodation and restaurants, and larger shops, but you cannot depend on this elsewhere. When you pay by card, you may occasionally be asked for ID such as your passport. Don't forget to memorise your PIN, as you may have to key it in as you pay, and keep a note of phone numbers to call for reporting a lost or stolen card.

American Express (Amex) cards are much less widely accepted than Visa and MasterCard.

Taxes & Refunds

Visitors are entitled to a refund of the 21% IVA on purchases costing more than €90.15 from any shop, if they are taking them out of the EU within three months.

As of 2019, Spain has instituted a new electronic tax refund system known as DIVA. Ask the shop for an official DIVA refund form showing the price and IVA paid for each item, and identifying the vendor and purchaser. Upon arrival at your departure airport, get your refund forms electronically stamped by scanning them at a DIVA kiosk, or have them manually stamped by a customs agent. You can then present the stamped forms at tax-free kiosks in the boarding area to get your refund.

Tipping

Restaurants A service charge is usually included in the bill, but most people leave some small change if they're satisfied – 5% is usually plenty.

Hotels Tip porters around €1.

Taxis Tipping isn't necessary, but a little rounding up won't go amiss.

PRACTICALITIES

Newspapers UK and some other European newspapers are sold at kiosks wherever large numbers of expats and tourists are found. The centre-left *El País* (www.elpais.es) is Spain's biggest-selling newspaper. Every sizeable Andalucian city has at least one daily paper of its own. The Costa del Sol's *Sur in English* (www.surinenglish.com) is an excellent English-language news weekly.

Radio For radio stations *El País* publishes province-by-province wavelength guides in its *Cartelera* (What's On) section. Among the several stations of Radio Nacional de España (RNE), RNE3 plays a variety of pop and rock, and Radio Clásica is classical.

Weights and measures Spain uses the metric system.

Post

Stamps are sold at *estancos* (tobacconist shops with 'Tabacos' in yellow letters on a maroon background) as well as at *oficinas de correos* (post offices; www.correos.es). Mail to or from other Western European countries normally arrives within a week; to or from North America within 10 days; and to or from Australia and New Zealand within two weeks.

Public Holidays

Everywhere in Spain has 14 official holidays a year – some are holidays nationwide, some only in one village. The list of holidays in each place may change from year to year. If a holiday date falls on a weekend, sometimes the holiday is moved to the Monday or replaced with another at a different time. If a holiday falls on the second day following a weekend, many Spaniards take the intervening day off, too, a practice known as making a *puente* (bridge).

The two main periods when Spaniards go on holiday are Semana Santa (Holy Week, leading up to Easter Sunday) and the six weeks from mid-July to the end of August. At these times accommodation in resorts can be scarce and transport heavily booked.

There are usually nine official national holidays:

Año Nuevo (New Year's Day) 1 January

Viernes Santo (Good Friday) 2 April 2021, 15 April 2022

Fiesta del Trabajo (Labour Day) 1 May

La Asunción (Feast of the Assumption) 15 August

Fiesta Nacional de España (National Day) 12 October

Todos los Santos (All Saints' Day) 1 November

Día de la Constitución (Constitution Day) 6 December

La Inmaculada Concepción (Feast of the Immaculate Conception) 8 December

Navidad (Christmas) 25 December

In addition, regional governments normally set three holidays, and local councils a further two. The three regional holidays in Andalucía are usually the following:

Epifanía (Epiphany) or **Día de los Reyes Magos** (Three Kings' Day) 6 January

Día de Andalucía (Andalucía Day) 28 February

Jueves Santo (Maundy Thursday) Easter

The following are often selected as holidays by local councils:

Corpus Christi Around two months after Easter

Día de San Juan Bautista (Feast of St John the Baptist, King Juan Carlos II's saint's day) 24 June

Día de Santiago Apóstol (Feast of St James the Apostle, Spain's patron saint) 25 July

Safe Travel

Most visitors to Andalucía never feel remotely threatened, but a sufficient number have unpleasant experiences to warrant an alert. Be careful, but don't be paranoid.

➡ The main thing to be wary of is petty theft. Keep a close eye on your bag(s) in busy public areas, especially parks, plazas and bus/train stations.

➡ Be wary of pickpockets in areas heavily frequented

GIBRALTAR PRACTICALITIES

Border crossings The border is open 24 hours. Bag searches at **customs** (Map p157; ☎20078879; Customs House; ⏰24hr) are usually perfunctory.

Electricity Electric current is the same as in Britain: 220V or 240V, with plugs of three flat pins. You'll need an adaptor (available from electronics shops on Main St) to use your Spanish-plug devices.

Emergency ☎190, ☎112

Money Currencies are the interchangeable Gibraltar pound (£) and pound sterling. You can spend euros, but conversion rates are poor. Change unspent Gibraltar currency before leaving. Banks (mostly on Main St) open weekdays from 8.30am to 4pm.

Telephone To phone Gibraltar from other countries, dial the international access code, then 350 (Gibraltar's country code) and the eight-digit local number. To call Spain from Gibraltar, dial 0034, then the nine-digit number.

Visas and documents To enter Gibraltar, you need a passport or EU national identity card. American, Canadian, Australian, New Zealand and EU passport holders are among those who do not need visas for Gibraltar. For further information, contact Gibraltar's **Civil Status and Registration Office** (Map p158; ☎20076948; www.gibraltar.gov.gi; 2-8 Secretary's Lane).

by tourists, such as Seville's crowded streets and squares during Semana Santa processions.

➡ Beware of extreme heat and always carry water when hiking in the high summer (July and August).

Telephone

Phones from anywhere within the EU can be used in Spain without roaming charges. If you're bringing an unlocked phone from outside the EU, you'll often save money by purchasing a local SIM card. Other economical options include calling from your computer using an internet-based service such as Skype or from your mobile phone using Whatsapp.

Mobile Phones

Pre-paid Spanish SIM cards can be used in any unlocked European or Australian phone, and in most newer phones brought from elsewhere (Spain uses GSM 900/1800, which is compatible with the rest of Europe and Australia but not with the North American or Japanese systems, so you'll need a tri- or quad-band phone if travelling from these latter regions).

The leading Spanish mobile-phone companies (MoviStar, Orange, Vodafone and Yoigo) all offer *prepagado* (prepaid) accounts for mobiles. A SIM card costs from €10, and promotional offers including start-up amounts of calls, texts and data are widely available. You can top up your account as needed at phone company shops or outlets such as *estancos* (tobacconists) and newspaper kiosks. Smaller providers such as Pepephone (www.pepephone.com) are another option.

If you're from the EU, there is now EU-wide roaming so that call and data plans for mobile phones from any EU country should be valid in Spain without any extra roaming charges. If you're from elsewhere and want to use your home country phone plan in Spain, check with your mobile provider for information on roaming charges.

Phone Codes & Useful Numbers

Spain has no telephone area codes. Every phone number has nine digits and for any call within Spain you just dial all those nine digits. The first digit of all Spanish fixed-phone numbers is 9. Numbers beginning with 6, 7 or 8 are mobile phone numbers. Phone numbers in Gibraltar have eight digits.

Calls to Spanish numbers starting with 800 or 900 are free. Numbers starting with 901 to 906 are pay-per-minute numbers and charges vary. The same applies to numbers starting with 803, 806 and 807. For a rundown on these numbers, visit www.andalucia.com/travel/telephone/numbers.htm.

International access code ☎00

Spain's country code ☎34

Time

➡ Mainland Spain is on GMT/UTC plus one hour during winter, and GMT/UTC plus two hours during the country's daylight saving period, which runs from the last Sunday in March to the last Sunday in October.

➡ Most Western European countries have the same time as Spain year-round, the major exceptions being Britain, Ireland and Portugal. Add one hour to these three countries' times to get Spanish time.

➡ Spanish time is normally US eastern time plus six

hours, and US Pacific time plus nine hours.

➡ In the Australian winter subtract eight hours from Sydney time to get Spanish time; in the summer subtract 10 hours (the difference is nine hours for a few weeks in March).

➡ Morocco is on GMT/UTC year-round, so it's two hours behind Spain during Spanish daylight saving time, and one hour behind at other times of the year.

➡ Note that the European Parliament has voted to abolish daylight saving time effective in 2021, with EU member states choosing to stay on either permanent summer or winter time. Spain's decision is pending – stay tuned!

Toilets

➡ Public toilets are almost nonexistent; the exceptions are some tourist offices, large tourist-oriented beaches (eg Torremolinos) and all bus and train stations.

➡ It's OK to use the toilet at bars and cafes, but you're usually expected to order something.

➡ It's worth carrying some toilet paper with you, as many toilets lack it.

Tourist Information

All cities and many smaller towns and villages in Andalucía have at least one *oficina de turismo* (tourist office). Staff are generally knowledgeable and increasingly well versed in foreign languages; they can help with everything from town maps and guided tours to opening hours for major sights and, sometimes, bus timetables. Offices are usually well stocked with printed material. Opening hours vary widely (and seasonally).

Tourist offices in Andalucía may be operated by the local town hall, by local district organisations, by the government of whichever province you're in or by the Junta de Andalucía (regional government). There may also be more than one tourist office in larger cities: in general, regional tourist offices offer information on the city and the wider region, while municipal offices deal just with the city and immediate surrounds. The Junta de Andalucía's Consejería de Medio Ambiente (environmental department) also has visitor centres located in many environmentally protected areas (*parques naturales* and so on). Many present interesting displays on local flora and fauna and carry information on hiking routes.

Many tourist offices have Bluetooth information points that allow you to download town maps, guided tours and event listings directly to your mobile phone.

Visas

Spain is one of 26 member countries of the Schengen Agreement, under which 22 EU countries (all but Bulgaria, Croatia, Cyprus, Ireland and Romania) plus Iceland, Norway, Liechtenstein and Switzerland have abolished checks at common borders.

The visa situation for entering Spain is as follows:

➡ For citizens or residents of EU and Schengen countries, no visa is required.

➡ For citizens or residents of Australia, Canada, Israel, Japan, New Zealand, the USA and most Latin American countries, no visa is required for tourist visits of up to 90 days. However, starting in 2022, nationals of the above countries will require prior authorisation to enter Spain under the new European Travel Information and Authorisation System (ETIAS; www.etias.com). Travellers can apply online; the cost is €7 for a three-year, multi-entry authorisation. With ETIAS pre-authorisation, travellers can stay in Spain visa-free for 90 days within any given 180-day period. The same conditions are likely to apply to British nationals post-Brexit, though the exact terms were being negotiated at the time of research.

➡ For other countries, check with a Spanish embassy or consulate.

➡ To work or study in Spain a special visa may be required; contact a Spanish embassy or consulate before travel.

➡ Remember that Gibraltar is not part of Schengen and if you do not have permission to enter the UK, you may not enter Gibraltar.

Women Travellers

Women travellers in Spain will rarely experience harassment, although you may find yourself subjected to stares, catcalls and comments from time to time. Skimpy clothes are the norm in many coastal resorts, but people tend to dress more modestly elsewhere. Some women travellers have reported feeling more comfortable at the front of public transport. Remember the word for help *(socorro)* in case you need to use it.

Each province's national police headquarters has a special Servicio de Atención a la Mujer (SAM; literally 'Service of Attention to Women'). The national **Comisión para la Investigación de Malos Tratos a Mujeres** (Commission for Investigation into Abuse of Women; ☎emergency 900 100009; www.malostratos.org; ⊙9am-9pm Mon-Fri) maintains an emergency line for victims of physical abuse anywhere in Spain. In Andalucía the **Instituto Andaluz de la Mujer** (☎900 200999; www.juntadeandalucia.es/institutodelamujer; ⊙24hr) also offers help.

Transport

GETTING THERE & AWAY

Andalucía is a top European holiday destination and is well linked to the rest of Spain and Europe by air, rail and road. Regular hydrofoils and car ferries run to and from Morocco, and there are also ferry links to Algeria. Flights, tours and rail tickets can be booked online at lonelyplanet.com/bookings.

Entering the Region

Immigration and customs checks usually involve a minimum of fuss, although there are exceptions. Spanish customs look for contraband duty-free products designed for illegal resale in Spain, in particular from people arriving from Morocco. Expect long delays at this border, especially in summer.

Passport

Citizens of EU member states, as well as those from Norway, Iceland, Liechtenstein and Switzerland, can travel to Spain with their national identity card alone.

DEPARTURE TAX

Departure tax is always included in the price of your ticket.

All other nationalities must carry a valid passport.

In the aftermath of the UK's departure from the EU, British citizens, like citizens of the US and elsewhere, are allowed to enter Spain visa-free for stays of up to 90 days only. Check with your local Spanish embassy or consulate for the latest rules.

By law you are supposed to carry your passport or ID card with you in Spain at all times.

Air

Getting to Andalucía by air is easy. Dozens of regular and charter airlines fly into the region's five airports from elsewhere in Europe, especially the UK, and a couple also fly from the UK to Gibraltar. Andalucía's busiest airport, Málaga, also has flights from Morocco. The region is well connected by domestic flights to other Spanish cities. From outside Europe, you'll normally need to change planes en route – usually at Madrid or Barcelona or in another European country – though there are a few direct charter flights to Málaga from places such as Montreal, Canada.

High season is generally mid-June to mid-September, although flights can also be fully booked (and prices higher) during Semana Santa (Holy Week; the week leading up to Easter Sunday).

Airports

Málaga Airport (AGP; ☎952 04 84 84; www.aena.es) is the main international airport in Andalucía and Spain's fourth busiest, with almost 60 airlines connecting the city to Spain, Europe and beyond.

Seville (Aeropuerto de Sevilla; ☎91 321 10 00; www.aena.es; A4, Km 532), **Granada** (☎91 321 10 00; www.aena.es), **Jerez de la Frontera** (☎956 15 00 00; www.aena.es; Carretera A4) and **Almería** (☎91 321 10 00; www.aena.es) also have connections to other Spanish and European cities, although flights from the latter three airports are far more limited than from Seville. To see which airlines fly into your chosen airport, visit www.aena.es, choose the airport from the pull-down menu, then click on 'Airlines' for a full list. The website also has detailed information on facilities at each airport.

Gibraltar (Map p157; ☎20 012345; www.gibraltarairport.gi) also receives a small number of flights direct from the UK and Morocco.

Land

If you're coming from Morocco, journey times are increased by a couple of hours by border formalities, which are notoriously strict at the ferry departure and arrivals terminals. There are usually

CLIMATE CHANGE & TRAVEL

Every form of transport that relies on carbon-based fuel generates CO_2, the main cause of human-induced climate change. Modern travel is dependent on aeroplanes, which might use less fuel per kilometre per person than most cars but travel much greater distances. The altitude at which aircraft emit gases (including CO_2) and particles also contributes to their climate change impact. Many websites offer 'carbon calculators' that allow people to estimate the carbon emissions generated by their journey and, for those who wish to do so, to offset the impact of the greenhouse gases emitted with contributions to portfolios of climate-friendly initiatives throughout the world. Lonely Planet offsets the carbon footprint of all staff and author travel.

long queues at customs on both sides of the Strait of Gibraltar.

Bus

Andalucía is well connected by bus with the rest of Spain. Although there are direct bus services from many European countries, it rarely works out cheaper than flying and takes a whole lot longer.

Destinations that may be more economical to reach by bus include Lisbon and Morocco. **Alsa** (☎902 422242; www.alsa.es) has regular daily services to Seville from Lisbon (six to seven hours), and also runs several weekly buses between Moroccan cities such as Casablanca, Marrakesh and Fès, and Andalucian destinations such as Seville, Marbella, Málaga, Granada, Jerez de la Frontera and Almería, via the Algeciras–Tangier ferries. Journey times can be quite long; for example, the Málaga–Marrakesh trip takes about 18½ hours.

Buses run to most Andalucian cities and medium-sized towns from elsewhere in Spain, with the largest selection leaving from Madrid's Estación Sur de Autobuses. The trip from Madrid to Seville, Granada or Málaga takes around six hours. There are also services down the Mediterranean coast from Barcelona, Valencia and Alicante to Almería, Granada, Jaén, Córdoba, Seville, Málaga and the Costa del Sol. The best bus companies serving Andalucía from other parts of Spain are Alsa and **Secorbus/Socibus** (☎902 229292; www.socibus.es).

Car & Motorcycle

Drivers can reach Andalucía from just about anywhere in Spain in a single day on the country's good-quality highways. The main routes run down the centre of the country from Madrid and along the Mediterranean coast from Barcelona. Popular vehicle ferries run from the UK to Bilbao and Santander in northern Spain, from where you can drive to Andalucía via Madrid. Ferry routes also connect Andalucía with Tangier and Nador in Morocco and with Ceuta and Melilla, the Spanish enclaves on the Moroccan coast.

The main highway from Madrid to Andalucía is the A4/AP4 (also known as Autovía del Sur) to Córdoba, Seville and Cádiz. For Jaén, Granada, Almería or Málaga, turn off at Bailén. In the east, the AP7/A7 leads all the way down the Mediterranean side of Spain from La Jonquera on the French border as far as Algeciras.

Given Andalucía's southerly location, visitors from elsewhere in Europe often find that it works out cheaper (and quicker) to fly here and hire a car upon arrival.

In the UK, further information on driving in Europe is available from the AA (www.theaa.com).

Train

Renfe (Red Nacional de los Ferrocarriles Españoles, Spanish National Railways; ☎91 232 03 20; www.renfe.es) is the excellent national Spanish train system that runs services in Andalucía. It has benefited from massive investment in recent years, meaning journeys are fast, efficient and comfortable.

IN SPAIN

The fastest train to Andalucía is Renfe's Alta Velocidad Española (AVE), capable of reaching speeds approaching 300km/h. These trains connect Madrid to Córdoba (one way from €40, 1¾ hours), Seville (from €48, 2½ hours) and Málaga (from €44, 2¾ hours) in not much more time than travelling by plane. Direct multigauge Alvia trains also run from Madrid three or four times daily to Cádiz and once daily to Huelva. From most other parts of Spain you can reach Andalucía by train in one day, usually with a connection in Madrid or Barcelona.

Most long-distance trains have *preferente* (1st-class) and *turista* (2nd-class) carriages. They go under various names indicating standards of comfort and time of travel.

The most common services consist of AVEs on the Madrid–Seville, Madrid–Córdoba–Málaga, Madrid–Granada, Barcelona–Seville, Barcelona–Córdoba–Málaga, Barcelona–Granada and Valencia–Seville routes and

Alvia on the Madrid–Cádiz and Madrid–Huelva routes.

Buy your ticket in advance as trains can get fully booked, especially in July and August. You can buy tickets in English by phone and online. Phone-booked tickets must be collected and paid for at a Renfe ticket office within 72 hours of booking and more than 24 hours before the train's departure. Internet tickets can be paid for online. The first time tickets are purchased online by credit card, they must be picked up at a Renfe ticket office at least one hour before the train's departure; subsequent tickets with the same card can be printed online.

Some fare discounts are available:

➡ Return fares on long-distance trains are 20% less than two one-way fares.

➡ Children aged under four travel free (including on high-speed trains when sharing a seat with an adult).

➡ Children aged four to 13 get 40% off the cost of seats and couchettes.

➡ The European Youth Card (www.eyca.org) entitles holders to 20% off long-distance and regional train fares.

OUTSIDE SPAIN

If you're coming from elsewhere in Europe and can afford to take at least a day to arrive, there are rail routes to Andalucía, always involving a change of train. The best routing is through Barcelona Sants station (roughly 5½ hours from Seville or six hours from Málaga), where you can catch direct trains to Paris. In Paris there are connections on to Amsterdam, the UK and Germany. Alternatively, take a train from Barcelona to Geneva (changing in Valence), where there are connections to Italy. For more details on these and other routes, check **The Man in Seat 61** (www.seat61.com).

Sea

You can sail to Andalucía from the Moroccan ports of Tangier and Nador, as well as Ceuta or Melilla (Spanish enclaves on the Moroccan coast), and Oran and Ghazaouet (in Algeria). The routes are: Melilla–Almería, Nador–Almería, Oran–Almería, Ghazaouet–Almería, Tangier–Motril, Nador–Motril, Al-Hoceima–Motril, Melilla–Málaga, Tangier–Algeciras, Ceuta–Algeciras and Tangier–Tarifa.

All routes usually take vehicles as well as passengers and the most frequent sailings are to/from Algeciras. Usually at least 12 sailings a day ply the routes between Algeciras and Tangier (1½ hours), and 10 run between Algeciras and Ceuta (one hour). Extra services are added at busy times, especially during the peak summer period (mid-June to mid-September), when hundreds of thousands of Moroccan workers return home from Europe for holidays. If you're taking a car, book well ahead for July, August or Easter travel, and expect long queues and customs formalities.

The following are the main ferry companies; there's little price difference between them.

Trasmediterránea (www.trasmediterranea.es)

Intershipping (www.intershipping.es)

FRS (www.frs.es)

Naviera Armas (www.navieraarmas.com)

GETTING AROUND

Air

There are few regular flights between airports within Andalucía. The one exception is the daily flight between Seville and Almería with Air Nostrum, a franchise of Iberian Airlines.

Bicycle

Andalucía is good biking territory, with wonderful scenery and varied terrain. While some mountain roads (such as those through the Sierra de Grazalema or Sierra Nevada) are best left to professional cyclists, there aren't too many corners of Andalucía that keen and reasonably fit cyclists can't reach. Plenty of lightly trafficked country roads, mostly in decent condition, enable riders to avoid the busy main highways. Road biking here is as safe as anywhere in Europe, provided you make allowances for some drivers' love of speed. Day rides and touring by bike are particularly enjoyable in spring and autumn, as you'll avoid weather extremes.

➡ It's often possible to take your bike on a bus (you'll usually just be asked to remove the front wheel).

➡ You can take bikes on most regional and suburban trains. On long-distance and high-speed trains, bikes must usually be folded or disassembled and enclosed in a box or carrier. Check at the train station for any special conditions before buying tickets.

➡ Bicycles are available for hire in main cities, coastal resorts, and inland towns and villages that attract tourism. They're often *bicis todo terreno* (mountain bikes). Prices range from €10 to €20 a day. Seville is easily the region's most cycle-friendly city.

➡ Bike lanes on main roads are rare, but cyclists are permitted to ride in groups up to two abreast.

➡ Helmets are obligatory outside built-up areas.

Boat

There's a regular catamaran service (p123) between Cádiz and El Puerto de Santa María.

Bus

Buses in Andalucía are mostly modern, comfortable and inexpensive, and run almost everywhere – including along some unlikely mountain roads – to connect remote villages with their nearest towns. The bigger cities are linked to each other by frequent daily services. On the quieter routes, services may be reduced (or nonexistent) on Saturday and Sunday.

- Alsa's luxurious 'Supra' buses have wi-fi, free drinks and snacks, toilets and single seats available.
- Larger towns and cities usually have one main *estación de autobuses* (bus station) where all out-of-town buses stop. In smaller places, buses tend to operate from a particular street or square, which may be unmarked. Ask around; locals generally know where to go.
- During Semana Santa (Holy Week) and July and August it's advisable to buy most bus tickets a day in advance.
- On a few routes, a return ticket is cheaper than two singles.
- Travellers aged under 26 should ask about discounts on intercity routes.
- Buses on main intercity routes average around 70km/h, and cost a bit less than €1 per 10km.

Car & Motorcycle

Andalucía's excellent road network and inexpensive rental cars make driving an attractive and practical way of getting around.

Bringing Your Own Vehicle

Bringing your own car to Andalucía is possible. Roads are generally good, although driving and finding parking in cities can be tiresome. Petrol (around €1.30 to €1.35 per litre in Spain) is widely available. In the event of breakdowns, every small town and many villages will have a garage with mechanics on-site.

If the car is from the UK or Ireland, remember to adjust the headlights for driving in mainland Europe (motor-accessory shops sell stick-on strips that deflect the beams in the required direction).

Driving Licence & Documentation

All EU countries' licences (pink or pink and green) are accepted in Spain. Licences from other countries are technically supposed to be accompanied by an International Driving Permit – valid for 12 months and available from your home country automobile club – but in practice your national licence will usually suffice for renting cars or dealing with traffic police.

When driving a private vehicle in Europe, proof of ownership (a Vehicle Registration Document for UK-registered vehicles), driving licence, roadworthiness certificate (MOT), and either an insurance certificate or a Green Card should always be carried. Also ask your insurer for a European Accident Statement form, which can greatly simplify matters in the event of an accident.

Hire

If you plan to hire a car in Andalucía, it's a good idea to organise it before you leave home. As a rule, local firms at Málaga airport or on the Costa del Sol offer the cheapest deals. You can normally get a four-door, air-con, economy-class car from local agencies for around €150 a week in August, or considerably less in winter. Many local firms offer internet booking and have a desk in or just outside the airport. In general, rentals away from the holiday *costas* (coasts) are more expensive.

Well-established local firms with branches at Andalucian airports and/or major

MAIN BUS COMPANIES

COMPANY	WEBSITE	TELEPHONE	MAIN DESTINATIONS
Alsa	www.alsa.es	902 422242	Almería, Córdoba, Granada, Jaén, Málaga, Seville
Casal	www.autocarescasal.com	954 99 92 90	Seville, Carmona
Comes	www.tgcomes.es	956 80 70 59	Cádiz, Algeciras, Granada, Jerez, Málaga, Ronda, Seville
Damas	www.damas-sa.es	959 25 69 00	Huelva, Ayamonte, Seville
Los Amarillos	www.losamarillos.es	902 210317	Cádiz, Jerez, Málaga, Ronda, Seville
Avanza/Portillo	http://malaga.avanzagrupo.com	955 03 86 65	Málaga, Costa del Sol, Algeciras, Ronda
Autocares Carrera	www.autocarescarrera.es	957 50 03 02	Córdoba province

rail stations (such as Málaga and Seville) include the following:

Centauro (☎966 36 03 60; www.centauro.net)

Crown Car (☎965 79 00 10; www.crowncarhire.com)

Helle Hollis (☎952 24 55 44; www.hellehollis.com)

Marbesol (☎952 23 49 16; www.marbesol.com)

Niza Cars (☎952 23 61 79; www.nizacars.es)

Pepecar.com (☎902 996666; www.pepecar.com)

Major international rental companies are also usually available:

Avis (☎902 180854; www.avis.es)

Enterprise (☎902 100101; www.enterprise.es)

Europcar (☎91 150 50 00; www.europcar.es)

Hertz (☎91 749 90 69; www.hertz.es)

To rent a car you need to be aged at least 21 (23 with some companies) and to have held a driving licence for a minimum of one year (sometimes two years). Under-25s have to pay extra charges with many firms.

Insurance

Third-party motor insurance is a minimum requirement throughout Europe. Before leaving home, check with your existing motor insurance company to see if it provides automatic third-party cover for your vehicle throughout the EU, and to determine whether you will also be covered for medical or hospital expenses or accidental damage to your vehicle. You might have to pay an extra premium if you want the same protection abroad as you have at home. A European breakdown-assistance policy is a good investment, providing services such as roadside assistance, towing, emergency repairs and 24-hour telephone assistance in English.

If you're renting a vehicle in Andalucía, the routine insurance provided may not go beyond basic third-party requirements. For cover against theft or damage to the vehicle, or injury or death to driver or passengers, you may need to request extra coverage. Always read the fine print and don't be afraid to ask.

Parking

Street parking can be hard to find in larger cities during working hours (about 9am to 2pm Monday to Saturday and 5pm to 8pm Monday to Friday). You'll often have to use underground or multistorey car parks, which are common enough in cities, and well-enough signposted, but not cheap (typically around €1.50 to €2.50 per hour or €15 to €18 for 24 hours). City hotels with their own parking usually charge for the right to use it, at rates similar to or slightly cheaper than those of underground car parks.

Blue lines along the side of the street usually mean you must pay at a nearby meter to park during working hours (typically around €0.50 to €1 an hour). Yellow lines mean no parking. A sign with a red line through a blue backdrop also indicates that parking is prohibited. It's inadvisable to park in prohibited zones, even if other drivers have done so (you risk having your car towed and paying a substantial fine to get it released).

Road Rules

- As elsewhere in continental Europe, drive on the right and overtake on the left.
- The minimum driving age is 18 years.
- Rear seatbelts, if fitted, must be worn and children under three must sit in child safety seats.
- The blood-alcohol limit is 0.05% (0.01% for drivers with a licence less than two years old) and breath-testing is carried out on occasion.
- The police can – and do – carry out spot checks on drivers, so it pays to have all your papers in order. Nonresident foreigners may be fined on the spot for traffic offences. For any questions relating to traffic-violation tickets, phone the Centro de Tratamiento de Denuncias Automatizadas (☎987 010 559).
- The speed limit is 50km/h in built-up areas, between 80km/h and 100km/h outside built-up areas, and 120km/h on *autopistas* (toll highways) and *autovías* (toll-free highways).
- In Spain it's compulsory to carry two warning triangles (to be placed 100m in front of and 100m behind your vehicle if you have to stop on the carriageway), and a reflective jacket, which must be donned if you get out of your vehicle on the carriageway or hard shoulder outside built-up areas.
- It's illegal to use hand-held mobile phones while driving.

Taxis & Ridesharing

Taxis are plentiful in larger places, and most villages have a taxi or two. Fares are reasonable – a €3 to €3.50 start rate and then around €1.05 per kilometre, with airport runs costing a bit extra. You don't have to tip taxi drivers, but rounding up the change is always appreciated.

Ridesharing companies such as Cabify (www.cabify.com) and Uber (www.uber.com) are increasingly popular in Andalucian cities such as Seville.

Train

Renfe (Red Nacional de los Ferrocarriles Españoles, Spanish National Railways; ☎91 232 03

Train Destinations

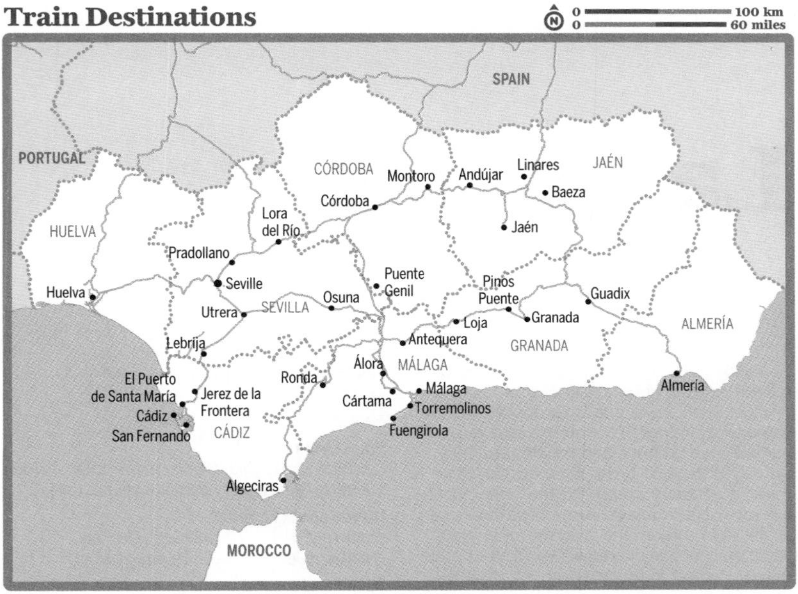

20; www.renfe.es) has an extensive and efficient rail system in Andalucía that links most of the main cities and many smaller places. Trains are at least as convenient, quick and inexpensive as buses on many routes.

➡ High-speed AVE trains run between Córdoba and Málaga, Córdoba and Seville, and Seville and Málaga.

➡ Generally, more frequent services between Andalucian destinations are provided by the cheaper (but slower) one-class *regional* and *cercanía* trains. *Regionales* run between Andalucian cities, stopping at many towns en route. *Cercanías* are commuter trains that link Seville, Málaga and Cádiz with their suburbs and nearby towns.

➡ Train tickets can be booked online with Renfe, which also lists full up-to-date timetables.

➡ Reservations are necessary on high-speed AVE trains but less important on shorter, slower routes.

➡ Regional trains average around 75km/h, for a cost of around €1 per 15km.

➡ Return fares on many routes operated by Renfe are 20% less than two one-way fares.

Language

Spanish *(español)* – also called Castilian *(castellano)* – is spoken throughout Andalucia.

Most Spanish sounds are pronounced the same as their English counterparts. If you read our coloured pronunciation guides as if they were English, you'll be understood. Note that the kh is a throaty sound (like the 'ch' in Scottish *loch*), r is strongly rolled, ly is pronounced as the 'lli' in 'million' and ny as the 'ni' in 'onion'. If you travel outside the region, you'll also notice that the 'lisped' th sound, which is typical of the pronunciation in the rest of Spain, is pronounced as s in Andalucia. In our pronunciation guides, the stressed syllables are in italics.

Where necessary in this chapter, masculine and feminine forms are marked as 'm/f', while polite and informal options are indicated by the abbreviations 'pol' and 'inf'.

BASICS

Hello.	*Hola.*	o·la
Goodbye.	*Adiós.*	a·*dyos*
How are you?	*¿Qué tal?*	ke tal
Fine, thanks.	*Bien, gracias.*	byen *gra*·syas
Excuse me.	*Perdón.*	per·*don*
Sorry.	*Lo siento.*	lo *syen*·to
Yes.	*Sí.*	see
No.	*No.*	no
Please.	*Por favor.*	por fa·*vor*
Thank you.	*Gracias.*	*gra*·syas

WANT MORE?

For in-depth language information and handy phrases, check out Lonely Planet's *Spanish Phrasebook*. You'll find it at **shop.lonelyplanet.com**, or you can buy Lonely Planet's iPhone phrasebooks at the Apple App Store.

You're welcome. *De nada.* de *na*·da

My name is ...
Me llamo ... me *lya*·mo ...

What's your name?
¿Cómo se llama Usted? *ko*·mo se *lya*·ma oo·*ste* (pol)
¿Cómo te llamas? *ko*·mo te *lya*·mas (inf)

Do you speak English?
¿Habla inglés? *a*·bla een·*gles* (pol)
¿Hablas inglés? *a*·blas een·*gles* (inf)

I don't understand.
No entiendo. no en·*tyen*·do

ACCOMMODATION

hotel	*hotel*	o·*tel*
guesthouse	*pensión*	pen·*syon*
youth hostel	*albergue juvenil*	al·*ber*·ge khoo·ve·*neel*
I'd like a ... room.	*Quisiera una habitación ...*	kee·*sye*·ra *oo*·na a·bee·ta·*syon* ...
single	*individual*	een·dee·vee·*dwal*
double	*doble*	*do*·ble
air-con	*aire acondicionado*	*ai*·re a·kon·dee·syo·*na*·do
bathroom	*baño*	*ba*·nyo
bed	*cama*	*ka*·ma
window	*ventana*	ven·*ta*·na

How much is it per night/person?
¿Cuánto cuesta por noche/persona? *kwan*·to *kwes*·ta por *no*·che/per·*so*·na

Does it include breakfast?
¿Incluye el desayuno? een·*kloo*·ye el de·sa·*yoo*·no

DIRECTIONS

Where's ...?
¿Dónde está ...? *don*·de es·*ta* ...

What's the address?
¿Cuál es la dirección? kwal es la dee·rek·*syon*

Can you please write it down?
¿Puede escribirlo, por favor? *pwe*·de es·kree·*beer*·lo por fa·*vor*

Can you show me (on the map)?
¿Me lo puede indicar (en el mapa)? me lo *pwe*·de een·dee·*kar* (en el *ma*·pa)

at the corner	*en la esquina*	en la es·*kee*·na
at the traffic lights	*en el semáforo*	en el se·*ma*·fo·ro
behind ...	*detrás de ...*	de·*tras* de ...
far away	*lejos*	*le*·khos
in front of ...	*enfrente de ...*	en·*fren*·te de ...
left	*izquierda*	ees·*kyer*·da
near	*cerca*	*ser*·ka
next to ...	*al lado de ...*	al *la*·do de ...
opposite ...	*frente a ...*	*fren*·te a ...
right	*derecha*	de·*re*·cha
straight ahead	*todo recto*	*to*·do *rek*·to

EATING & DRINKING

What would you recommend?
¿Qué recomienda? ke re·ko·*myen*·da

What's in that dish?
¿Que lleva ese plato? ke *lye*·va e·se *pla*·to

I don't eat ...
No como ... no *ko*·mo ...

Cheers!
¡Salud! sa·*loo*

That was delicious!
¡Estaba buenísimo! es·*ta*·ba bwe·*nee*·see·mo

Please bring us the bill.
Por favor, nos trae la cuenta. por fa·*vor* nos *tra*·e la *kwen*·ta

I'd like to book a table for ...	*Quisiera reservar una mesa para ...*	kee·*sye*·ra re·ser·*var oo*·na *me*·sa *pa*·ra ...
(eight) o'clock	*las (ocho)*	las (*o*·cho)
(two) people	*(dos) personas*	(dos) per·*so*·nas

Key Words

appetisers	*aperitivos*	a·pe·ree·*tee*·vos
bar	*bar*	bar
bottle	*botella*	bo·*te*·lya
bowl	*bol*	bol
breakfast	*desayuno*	de·sa·*yoo*·no
cafe	*café*	ka·*fe*
(too) cold	*(muy) frío*	(mooy) *free*·o
dinner	*cena*	*se*·na
food	*comida*	ko·*mee*·da
fork	*tenedor*	te·ne·*dor*
glass	*vaso*	*va*·so
highchair	*trona*	*tro*·na
hot (warm)	*caliente*	ka·*lyen*·te
knife	*cuchillo*	koo·*chee*·lyo
lunch	*comida*	ko·*mee*·da
main course	*segundo plato*	se·*goon*·do *pla*·to
market	*mercado*	mer·*ka*·do
(children's) menu	*menú (infantil)*	me·*noo* (een·fan·*teel*)
plate	*plato*	*pla*·to
restaurant	*restaurante*	res·tow·*ran*·te
spoon	*cuchara*	koo·*cha*·ra
supermarket	*supermercado*	soo·per·mer·*ka*·do
vegetarian food	*comida vegetariana*	ko·*mee*·da ve·khe·ta·*rya*·na

KEY PATTERNS

To get by in Spanish, mix and match these simple patterns with words of your choice:

When's (the next flight)?
¿Cuándo sale (el próximo vuelo)? *kwan*·do *sa*·le (el *prok*·see·mo *vwe*·lo)

Where's (the station)?
¿Dónde está (la estación)? *don*·de es·*ta* (la es·ta·*syon*)

Where can I (buy a ticket)?
¿Dónde puedo (comprar un billete)? *don*·de *pwe*·do (kom·*prar* oon bee·*lye*·te)

Do you have (a map)?
¿Tiene (un mapa)? *tye*·ne (oon *ma*·pa)

Is there (a toilet)?
¿Hay (servicios)? ai (ser·*vee*·syos)

I'd like (a coffee).
Quisiera (un café). kee·*sye*·ra (oon ka·*fe*)

I'd like (to hire a car).
Quisiera (alquilar un coche). kee·*sye*·ra (al·kee·*lar* oon *ko*·che)

Can I (enter)?
¿Se puede (entrar)? se *pwe*·de (en·*trar*)

Can you please (help me)?
¿Puede (ayudarme), por favor? *pwe*·de (a·yoo·*dar*·me) por fa·*vor*

Do I have to (get a visa)?
¿Necesito (obtener un visado)? ne·se·*see*·to (ob·te·*ner* oon vee·*sa*·do)

SIGNS

Abierto	Open
Cerrado	Closed
Entrada	Entrance
Hombres	Men
Mujeres	Women
Prohibido	Prohibited
Salida	Exit
Servicios/Aseos	Toilets

with	*con*	kon
without	*sin*	seen

Meat & Fish

beef	*carne de vaca*	*kar*·ne de *va*·ka
chicken	*pollo*	*po*·lyo
cod	*bacalao*	ba·ka·*la*·o
duck	*pato*	*pa*·to
lamb	*cordero*	kor·*de*·ro
lobster	*langosta*	lan·*gos*·ta
pork	*cerdo*	*ser*·do
prawns	*camarones*	ka·ma·*ro*·nes
salmon	*salmón*	sal·*mon*
tuna	*atún*	a·*toon*
turkey	*pavo*	*pa*·vo
veal	*ternera*	ter·*ne*·ra

Fruit & Vegetables

apple	*manzana*	man·*sa*·na
apricot	*albaricoque*	al·ba·ree·*ko*·ke
artichoke	*alcachofa*	al·ka·*cho*·fa
asparagus	*espárragos*	es·*pa*·ra·gos
banana	*plátano*	*pla*·ta·no
beans	*judías*	khoo·*dee*·as
beetroot	*remolacha*	re·mo·*la*·cha
cabbage	*col*	kol
(red/green) capsicum	*pimiento (rojo/verde)*	pee·*myen*·to (*ro*·kho/*ver*·de)
carrot	*zanahoria*	sa·na·o·rya
celery	*apio*	*a*·pyo
cherry	*cereza*	se·*re*·sa
corn	*maíz*	ma·*ees*
cucumber	*pepino*	pe·*pee*·no
fruit	*fruta*	*froo*·ta
grape	*uvas*	*oo*·vas
lemon	*limón*	lee·*mon*
lentils	*lentejas*	len·*te*·khas
lettuce	*lechuga*	le·*choo*·ga
mushroom	*champiñón*	cham·pee·*nyon*
nuts	*nueces*	*nwe*·ses
onion	*cebolla*	se·*bo*·lya
orange	*naranja*	na·*ran*·kha
peach	*melocotón*	me·lo·ko·*ton*
peas	*guisantes*	gee·*san*·tes
pineapple	*piña*	*pee*·nya
plum	*ciruela*	seer·*we*·la
potato	*patata*	pa·*ta*·ta
pumpkin	*calabaza*	ka·la·*ba*·sa
spinach	*espinacas*	es·pee·*na*·kas
strawberry	*fresa*	*fre*·sa
tomato	*tomate*	to·*ma*·te
vegetable	*verdura*	ver·*doo*·ra
watermelon	*sandía*	san·*dee*·a

Other

bread	*pan*	pan
butter	*mantequilla*	man·te·*kee*·lya
cheese	*queso*	*ke*·so
egg	*huevo*	*we*·vo
honey	*miel*	myel
jam	*mermelada*	mer·me·*la*·da
oil	*aceite*	a·*sey*·te
pepper	*pimienta*	pee·*myen*·ta
rice	*arroz*	a·*ros*
salt	*sal*	sal
sugar	*azúcar*	a·*soo*·kar
vinegar	*vinagre*	vee·*na*·gre

Drinks

beer	*cerveza*	ser·*ve*·sa
coffee	*café*	ka·*fe*
(orange) juice	*zumo (de naranja)*	*soo*·mo (de na·*ran*·kha)
milk	*leche*	*le*·che
red wine	*vino tinto*	*vee*·no *teen*·to
tea	*té*	te
(mineral) water	*agua (mineral)*	*a*·gwa (mee·ne·*ral*)
white wine	*vino blanco*	*vee*·no *blan*·ko

EMERGENCIES

Help!	*¡Socorro!*	so·*ko*·ro
Go away!	*¡Vete!*	*ve*·te

Call ...!	*¡Llame a ...!*	*lya*·me a ...
a doctor	*un médico*	oon *me*·dee·ko
the police	*la policía*	la po·lee·*see*·a

I'm lost.
Estoy perdido/a. es·*toy* per·*dee*·do/a (m/f)

I'm ill.
Estoy enfermo/a. es·*toy* en·*fer*·mo/a (m/f)

It hurts here.
Me duele aquí. me *dwe*·le a·*kee*

I'm allergic to (antibiotics).
Soy alérgico/a a (los antibióticos). soy a·*ler*·khee·ko/a a (los an·tee·*byo*·tee·kos) (m/f)

Where are the toilets?
¿Dónde están los servicios? *don*·de es·*tan* los ser·*vee*·syos

SHOPPING & SERVICES

I'd like to buy ...
Quisiera comprar ... kee·*sye*·ra kom·*prar* ...

I'm just looking.
Sólo estoy mirando. *so*·lo es·*toy* mee·*ran*·do

Can I look at it?
¿Puedo verlo? *pwe*·do *ver*·lo

I don't like it.
No me gusta. no me *goos*·ta

How much is it?
¿Cuánto cuesta? *kwan*·to *kwes*·ta

That's too expensive.
Es muy caro. es mooy *ka*·ro

Can you lower the price?
¿Podría bajar un poco el precio? po·*dree*·a ba·*khar* oon *po*·ko el *pre*·syo

There's a mistake in the bill.
Hay un error en la cuenta. ai oon e·*ror* en la *kwen*·ta

ATM	*cajero automático*	ka·*khe*·ro ow·to·*ma*·tee·ko
credit card	*tarjeta de crédito*	tar·*khe*·ta de *kre*·dee·to
internet cafe	*cibercafé*	see·ber·ka·*fe*
post office	*correos*	ko·*re*·os
tourist office	*oficina de turismo*	o·fee·*see*·na de too·*rees*·mo

TIME & DATES

What time is it?	*¿Qué hora es?*	ke *o*·ra es
It's (10) o'clock.	*Son (las diez).*	son (las dyes)
Half past (one).	*Es (la una) y media.*	es (la *oo*·na) ee *me*·dya
At what time?	*¿A qué hora?*	a ke *o*·ra
At ...	*A la(s) ...*	a la(s) ...

morning	*mañana*	ma·*nya*·na
afternoon	*tarde*	*tar*·de
evening	*noche*	*no*·che
yesterday	*ayer*	a·*yer*
today	*hoy*	oy
tomorrow	*mañana*	ma·*nya*·na

Monday	*lunes*	*loo*·nes
Tuesday	*martes*	*mar*·tes
Wednesday	*miércoles*	*myer*·ko·les
Thursday	*jueves*	*khwe*·bes
Friday	*viernes*	*vyer*·nes
Saturday	*sábado*	*sa*·ba·do
Sunday	*domingo*	do·*meen*·go

January	*enero*	e·*ne*·ro
February	*febrero*	fe·*bre*·ro
March	*marzo*	*mar*·so
April	*abril*	a·*breel*
May	*mayo*	*ma*·yo
June	*junio*	*khoo*·nyo
July	*julio*	*khoo*·lyo
August	*agosto*	a·*gos*·to
September	*septiembre*	sep·*tyem*·bre
October	*octubre*	ok·*too*·bre
November	*noviembre*	no·*vyem*·bre
December	*diciembre*	dee·*syem*·bre

TRANSPORT

Public Transport

boat	*barco*	*bar*·ko
bus	*autobús*	ow·to·*boos*
plane	*avión*	a·*vyon*
train	*tren*	tren
tram	*tranvía*	tran·*vee*·a
first	*primer*	pree·*mer*
last	*último*	*ool*·tee·mo
next	*próximo*	*prok*·see·mo

QUESTION WORDS

How?	*¿Cómo?*	*ko*·mo
What?	*¿Qué?*	ke
When?	*¿Cuándo?*	*kwan*·do
Where?	*¿Dónde?*	*don*·de
Who?	*¿Quién?*	kyen
Why?	*¿Por qué?*	por ke

NUMBERS

1	*uno*	*oo*·no
2	*dos*	dos
3	*tres*	tres
4	*cuatro*	*kwa*·tro
5	*cinco*	*seen*·ko
6	*seis*	seys
7	*siete*	*sye*·te
8	*ocho*	*o*·cho
9	*nueve*	*nwe*·ve
10	*diez*	dyes
20	*veinte*	*veyn*·te
30	*treinta*	*treyn*·ta
40	*cuarenta*	kwa·*ren*·ta
50	*cincuenta*	seen·*kwen*·ta
60	*sesenta*	se·*sen*·ta
70	*setenta*	se·*ten*·ta
80	*ochenta*	o·*chen*·ta
90	*noventa*	no·*ven*·ta
100	*cien*	syen
1000	*mil*	meel

I want to go to (Córdoba).
Quisiera ir a (Córdoba). kee·*sye*·ra eer a (*kor*·do·ba)

At what time does it arrive/leave?
¿A qué hora llega/sale? a ke o·ra *lye*·ga/*sa*·le

Is it a direct route?
¿Es un viaje directo? es oon *vya*·khe dee·*rek*·to

Does it stop at (Granada)?
¿Para en (Granada)? *pa*·ra en (gra·*na*·da)

Which stop is this?
¿Cuál es esta parada? kwal es *es*·ta pa·*ra*·da

Please tell me when we get to (Seville).
¿Puede avisarme cuando lleguemos a (Sevilla)? *pwe*·de a·vee·*sar*·me *kwan*·do lye·*ge*·mos a (se·*vee*·lya)

I want to get off here.
Quiero bajarme aquí. *kye*·ro ba·*khar*·me a·*kee*

a ... ticket	*un billete de ...*	oon bee·*lye*·te de ...
1st-class	*primera clase*	pree·*me*·ra *kla*·se
2nd-class	*segunda clase*	se·*goon*·da *kla*·se
one-way	*ida*	ee·da
return	*ida y vuelta*	ee·da ee *vwel*·ta
aisle/window seat	*asiento de pasillo/ ventana*	a·*syen*·to de pa·*see*·lyo/ ven·*ta*·na
bus/train station	*estación de autobuses/ trenes*	es·ta·*syon* de ow·to·*boo*·ses/ *tre*·nes
cancelled	*cancelado*	kan·se·*la*·do
delayed	*retrasado*	re·tra·*sa*·do
platform	*plataforma*	pla·ta·*for*·ma
ticket office	*taquilla*	ta·*kee*·lya
timetable	*horario*	o·*ra*·ryo

Driving & Cycling

I'd like to hire a ...	*Quisiera alquilar ...*	kee·*sye*·ra al·*kee*·lar ...
4WD	*un todo-terreno*	oon *to*·do·te·*re*·no
bicycle	*una bicicleta*	*oo*·na bee·see·*kle*·ta
car	*un coche*	oon *ko*·che
motorcycle	*una moto*	oo·na *mo*·to

child seat	*asiento de seguridad para niños*	a·*syen*·to de se·goo·ree·*da* *pa*·ra *nee*·nyos
diesel	*gasóleo*	ga·*so*·le·o
helmet	*casco*	*kas*·ko
mechanic	*mecánico*	me·*ka*·nee·ko
petrol	*gasolina*	ga·so·*lee*·na
service station	*gasolinera*	ga·so·lee·*ne*·ra

How much is it per day/hour?
¿Cuánto cuesta por día/hora? *kwan*·to *kwes*·ta por *dee*·a/*o*·ra

Is this the road to (Malaga)?
¿Se va a (Málaga) por esta carretera? se va a (*ma*·la·ga) por *es*·ta ka·re·*te*·ra

(How long) Can I park here?
¿(Por cuánto tiempo) Puedo aparcar aquí? (por *kwan*·to *tyem*·po) *pwe*·do a·par·*kar* a·*kee*

The car has broken down (at Cádiz).
El coche se ha averiado (en Cádiz). el *ko*·che se a a·ve·*rya*·do (en *ka*·dees)

I have a flat tyre.
Tengo un pinchazo. *ten*·go oon peen·*cha*·so

I've run out of petrol.
Me he quedado sin gasolina. me e ke·*da*·do seen ga·so·*lee*·na

Are there cycling paths?
¿Hay carril bicicleta? ai ka·*reel* bee·see·*kle*·ta

Is there bicycle parking?
¿Hay aparcamiento de bicicletas? ai a·par·ka·*myen*·to de bee·see·*kle*·tas

GLOSSARY

alameda – *paseo* lined (or originally lined) with *álamo* (poplar) trees
alcázar – Islamic-era fortress
artesonado – ceiling with interlaced beams leaving regular spaces for decorative insertions
autopista – toll highway
autovía – toll-free dual carriageway
AVE – Alta Velocidad Española; the high-speed train between Madrid and Seville
ayuntamiento – city or town hall
azulejo – tile

bahía – bay
bailaor/a – flamenco dancer
bandolero – bandit
barrio – district or quarter (of a town or city)
bodega – winery, wine bar or wine cellar
buceo – scuba diving
bulería – upbeat type of flamenco song
buzón – postbox

cajero automático – automated teller machine (ATM)
calle – street
callejón – lane
cambio – currency exchange
campiña – countryside (usually flat or rolling cultivated countryside)
campo – countryside, field
cantaor/a – flamenco singer
cante jondo – 'deep song', the essence of flamenco
capilla – chapel
capilla mayor – chapel containing the high altar of a church
carnaval – carnival; a pre-Lent period of fancy-dress parades and merrymaking
carretera – road, highway
carta – menu
casa rural – a village house or farmhouse with rooms to let
casco – literally 'helmet'; used to refer to the old part of a city *(casco antiguo)*
castellano – Castilian; the language also called Spanish
castillo – castle
caza – hunting
centro comercial – shopping centre
cercanía – suburban train
cerro – hill
cervecería – beer bar
chiringuito – small, often makeshift bar or eatery, usually in the open air
Churrigueresque – ornate style of baroque architecture named after the brothers Alberto and José Churriguera
cofradía – see *hermandad*
colegiata – collegiate church, a combined church and college
comedor – dining room
comisaría – station of the Policía Nacional (National Police)
converso – Jew who converted to Christianity in medieval Spain
cordillera – mountain chain
coro – choir (part of a church, usually in the middle)
corrida de toros – bullfight
cortes – parliament
cortijo – country property
costa – coast
coto – area where hunting rights are reserved for a specific group of people
cruce – cross
cuenta – bill (check)
cuesta – sloping land, road or street
custodia – monstrance (receptacle for the consecrated Host)

dehesa – woodland pastures with evergreen oaks
Denominación de Origen (DO) – a designation that indicates the unique geographical origins, production processes and quality of wines, olive oil and other products
duende – the spirit or magic possessed by great flamenco performers
duque – duke
duquesa – duchess

embalse – reservoir
ermita – hermitage or chapel
escalada – climbing
estación de autobuses – bus station
estación de esquí – ski station or resort
estación de ferrocarril – train station
estación marítima – passenger port
estanco – tobacconist
estrella – literally 'star'; also class of overnight train with seats, couchettes and sleeping compartments

farmacia – pharmacy
faro – lighthouse
feria – fair; can refer to trade fairs as well as to city, town or village fairs
ferrocarril – railway
fiesta – festival, public holiday or party
finca – country property, farm
flamenco – means flamingo and Flemish as well as flamenco music and dance
frontera – frontier
fuente – fountain, spring

gitano – the Spanish word for Roma people
Guardia Civil – Civil Guard; police responsible for roads, the countryside, villages and international borders. They wear green uniforms. See also *Policía Local, Policía Nacional*.

hammam – Arabic-style bathhouse
hermandad – brotherhood (which may include women), in particular one that takes part in religious processions; also *cofradía*
hospedaje – guesthouse
hostal – simple guesthouse or small place offering budget hotel-like accommodation

infanta – daughter of a monarch but not first in line to the throne
infante – son of a monarch but not first in line to the throne

jardín – garden
judería – Jewish barrio in medieval Spain
Junta de Andalucía – executive government of Andalucía

lavandería – laundry
librería – bookshop
lidia – the modern art of bullfighting on foot
lucio – pond or pool in the Doñana *marismas* (wetlands)

madrugada/madrugá – the 'early hours', from around 3am to dawn; a pretty lively time in some Spanish cities
marismas – wetlands, marshes
marisquería – seafood eatery
marqués – marquis
medina – Arabic word for town or inner city
mercadillo – flea market
mercado – market
mezquita – mosque
mihrab – prayer niche in a mosque indicating the direction of Mecca
mirador – lookout point
morisco – Muslim converted to Christianity in medieval Spain
moro – 'Moor' or Muslim (usually in a medieval context)
movida – the late-night bar and club scene that emerged in Spanish cities and towns after Franco's death; a *zona de movida* or *zona de marcha* is an area of a town where people gather to drink and have a good time
mozárabe – Mozarab; Christian living under Islamic rule in medieval Spain
Mudéjar – Muslim living under Christian rule in medieval Spain; also refers to their decorative style of architecture
muelle – wharf, pier
muladí – Muwallad; Christian who converted to Islam, in medieval Spain

nazareno – penitent taking part in Semana Santa processions
nieve – snow
nuevo – new

oficina de correos – post office
oficina de turismo – tourist office
olivo – olive tree

palacio – palace
palo – literally 'stick'; also refers to the categories of flamenco song
panadería – bakery
papelería – stationery shop
parador – one of the Paradores Nacionales, a state-owned chain of luxurious hotels, often in historic buildings
paraje natural – natural area
parque nacional – national park
parque natural – natural park
paseo – avenue or parklike strip; walk or stroll
paso – literally 'step'; also the platform an image is carried on in a religious procession
peña – a club; usually for supporters of a football club or flamenco enthusiasts *(peña flamenca)*, but sometimes a dining club
pensión – guesthouse
pescadería – fish shop
picadero – riding stable
pícaro – dice trickster and card sharp, rogue, low-life scoundrel
pinsapar – forest of *pinsapo*
pinsapo – Spanish fir
piscina – swimming pool
plateresque – early phase of Renaissance architecture noted for its decorative facades
playa – beach
plaza de toros – bullring
Policía Local – Local Police; also known as Policía Municipal. Controlled by city and town halls, they deal mainly with minor matters such as parking, traffic and bylaws. They wear blue-and-white uniforms. See also *Guardia Civil, Policía Nacional.*
Policía Municipal – Municipal Police; see *Policía Local*
Policía Nacional – National Police; responsible for cities and bigger towns, some of them forming special squads dealing with drugs, terrorism and the like.
preferente – 1st-class carriage on a long-distance train
provincia – province; Spain is divided into 50 of them
pueblo – village, town
puente – bridge
puerta – gate, door
puerto – port, mountain pass
puerto deportivo – marina
puerto pesquero – fishing port
punta – point

rambla – stream
Reconquista – the Christian reconquest of the Iberian Peninsula from the Muslims (8th to 15th centuries)
refugio – shelter or refuge, especially a mountain refuge with basic accommodation for hikers
regional – train running between Andalucian cities
reja – grille; especially a wrought-iron one over a window or dividing a chapel from the rest of a church
Renfe – Red Nacional de los Ferrocarriles Españoles; Spain's national rail network
reserva – reservation, or reserve (eg nature reserve)
reserva nacional de caza – national hunting reserve
reserva natural – nature reserve
retablo – retable (altarpiece)
ría – estuary
río – river
romería – festive pilgrimage or procession
ronda – ring road

sacristía – sacristy, the part of a church in which vestments, sacred objects and other valuables are kept
salina – salt lagoon

Semana Santa – Holy Week; the week leading up to Easter Sunday
sendero – path or track
sevillana – a popular Andalucian dance
sierra – mountain range
Siglo de Oro – Spain's cultural 'Golden Century', beginning in the 16th century and ending in the 17th century

taberna – tavern
tablao – flamenco show
taifa – one of the small kingdoms into which the Muslim-ruled parts of Spain were divided during parts of the 11th and 12th centuries
taquilla – ticket window
taracea – marquetry
tarjeta de crédito – credit card
tarjeta telefónica – phonecard
teléfono móvil – mobile telephone
terraza – terrace; often means an area with outdoor tables at a bar, cafe or restaurant
tetería – Middle Eastern–style teahouse with low seats around low tables
tienda – shop, tent
tocaor/a – flamenco guitarist
torre – tower
trenhotel – sleek, expensive, sleeping car–only train
turismo – means both tourism and saloon car; *el turismo* can also mean the tourist office
turista – second-class carriage on a long-distance train

valle – valley

zoco – large market in Muslim cities

Behind the Scenes

SEND US YOUR FEEDBACK

We love to hear from travellers – your comments keep us on our toes and help make our books better. Our well-travelled team reads every word on what you loved or loathed about this book. Although we cannot reply individually to your submissions, we always guarantee that your feedback goes straight to the appropriate authors, in time for the next edition. Each person who sends us information is thanked in the next edition – the most useful submissions are rewarded with a selection of digital PDF chapters.

Visit **lonelyplanet.com/contact** to submit your updates and suggestions or to ask for help. Our award-winning website also features inspirational travel stories, news and discussions.

Note: We may edit, reproduce and incorporate your comments in Lonely Planet products such as guidebooks, websites and digital products, so let us know if you don't want your comments reproduced or your name acknowledged. For a copy of our privacy policy visit lonelyplanet.com/privacy.

WRITER THANKS

Gregor Clark

Muchísimas gracias to all of the many Andalucians and fellow travellers who shared their recommendations, expertise and enthusiasm for Spain's sunny south – especially Ramón, Laura, José Manuel, Michaela, Eva, Daniel, Alfredo, Alberto, John and Isabella. Across the Atlantic, *un gran abrazo* to Gaen, who makes every day a voyage of discovery, and coming home always the best part of the trip.

Duncan Garwood

I owe a lot of thanks, starting with Rachel, Steve, Robert and Nick, whose company in Seville was much enjoyed. Thanks also to fellow writers Isabella Noble and Gregor Clark, and, at LP, Tom Stainer, Darren O'Connell and Sandie Kestell. In Spain, *gracias* to Cristina Diaz, Félix, Paula Alcayada García, Salomé Rodríguez García, José Fabra Garrido, Ana Jimenez, José Peláez, María José Álvarez Rodríguez, Virginia Rivera, Miriam Toro and Tim. As always, a big hug to Lidia, Ben and Nick.

Isabella Noble

In Granada, thanks to Molly Piccavey, June Windon, Silvia Roth-Bruggers, Anne Hunt, Nancy Laforest, Lorrane Dean, and Emma and David Illsley. In Cádiz, *mil gracias* to James Stuart, Annie Manson, Barbara Seine and Víctor Vidal. And, of course, to the many tourism teams who handled my endless questions, and to my hard-working cowriters, Gregor and Duncan, for all the last-minute emails and wonderful tips. Thanks as always to the perfect research assistants, Jack and John Noble, and Andrew Brannan.

ACKNOWLEDGEMENTS

Climate map data adapted from Peel MC, Finlayson BL & McMahon TA (2007) 'Updated World Map of the Köppen-Geiger Climate Classification', Hydrology and Earth System Sciences, 11, 1633–44.

Cover photograph: Detail of stucco wall panels and tiles at the Alhambra in Granada, jacky chapman/Alamy Stock Photo ©

Illustrations pp54–5, 208–9 & 260–1 by Javier Zarracina

THIS BOOK

This 10th edition of Lonely Planet's *Andalucía* guidebook was researched and written by Gregor Clark, Duncan Garwood, Isabella Noble and John Noble. The previous edition was written by Gregor, Duncan, Isabella, John and Brendan Sainsbury. This guidebook was produced by the following:

Senior Product Editor Daniel Bolger, Sandie Kestell

Regional Senior Cartographer Anthony Phelan

Product Editors Will Allen, Angela Tinson

Book Designer Fergal Condon, Virginia Moreno

Assisting Editors James Appleton, Janet Austin, Carly Hall, Anne Mulvaney, Monique Perrin, Christopher Pitts

Cartographer Julie Dodkins

Cover Researcher Naomi Parker

Thanks to Karen Henderson, Rachel Imeson, Darren O'Connell, Charlotte Orr

Index

Map Pages **000**
Photo Pages **000**

Map Pages **000**
Photo Pages 000

Map Legend

Sights

- Beach
- Bird Sanctuary
- Buddhist
- Castle/Palace
- Christian
- Confucian
- Hindu
- Islamic
- Jain
- Jewish
- Monument
- Museum/Gallery/Historic Building
- Ruin
- Shinto
- Sikh
- Taoist
- Winery/Vineyard
- Zoo/Wildlife Sanctuary
- Other Sight

Activities, Courses & Tours

- Bodysurfing
- Diving
- Canoeing/Kayaking
- Course/Tour
- Sento Hot Baths/Onsen
- Skiing
- Snorkelling
- Surfing
- Swimming/Pool
- Walking
- Windsurfing
- Other Activity

Sleeping

- Sleeping
- Camping
- Hut/Shelter

Eating

- Eating

Drinking & Nightlife

- Drinking & Nightlife
- Cafe

Entertainment

- Entertainment

Shopping

- Shopping

Information

- Bank
- Embassy/Consulate
- Hospital/Medical
- Internet
- Police
- Post Office
- Telephone
- Toilet
- Tourist Information
- Other Information

Geographic

- Beach
- Gate
- Hut/Shelter
- Lighthouse
- Lookout
- Mountain/Volcano
- Oasis
- Park
- Pass
- Picnic Area
- Waterfall

Population

- Capital (National)
- Capital (State/Province)
- City/Large Town
- Town/Village

Transport

- Airport
- Border crossing
- Bus
- Cable car/Funicular
- Cycling
- Ferry
- Metro station
- Monorail
- Parking
- Petrol station
- S-Bahn/Subway station
- Taxi
- T-bane/Tunnelbana station
- Train station/Railway
- Tram
- U-Bahn/Underground station
- Other Transport

Routes

- Tollway
- Freeway
- Primary
- Secondary
- Tertiary
- Lane
- Unsealed road
- Road under construction
- Plaza/Mall
- Steps
- Tunnel
- Pedestrian overpass
- Walking Tour
- Walking Tour detour
- Path/Walking Trail

Boundaries

- International
- State/Province
- Disputed
- Regional/Suburb
- Marine Park
- Cliff
- Wall

Hydrography

- River, Creek
- Intermittent River
- Canal
- Water
- Dry/Salt/Intermittent Lake
- Reef

Areas

- Airport/Runway
- Beach/Desert
- Cemetery (Christian)
- Cemetery (Other)
- Glacier
- Mudflat
- Park/Forest
- Sight (Building)
- Sportsground
- Swamp/Mangrove

Note: Not all symbols displayed above appear on the maps in this book

OUR STORY

A beat-up old car, a few dollars in the pocket and a sense of adventure. In 1972 that's all Tony and Maureen Wheeler needed for the trip of a lifetime – across Europe and Asia overland to Australia. It took several months, and at the end – broke but inspired – they sat at their kitchen table writing and stapling together their first travel guide, *Across Asia on the Cheap*. Within a week they'd sold 1500 copies. Lonely Planet was born.

Today, Lonely Planet has offices in Tennessee, Dublin and Beijing, with a network of over 2000 contributors in every corner of the globe. We share Tony's belief that 'a great guidebook should do three things: inform, educate and amuse'.

OUR WRITERS

Gregor Clark

Huelva Province, Málaga Province, Jaén Province, Almería Province Gregor Clark is a US-based writer whose love of foreign languages and curiosity about what's around the next bend have taken him to dozens of countries on five continents. Chronic wanderlust has also led him to visit all 50 states and most Canadian provinces on countless road trips through his native North America. Since 2000, Gregor has regularly contributed to Lonely Planet guides, with a focus on Europe and the Americas. Destinations include Italy, France, Brazil, Costa Rica, Argentina, Portugal, Switzerland and Mexico. Gregor also wrote the Understand and Survival Guide sections.

Duncan Garwood

Sevilla Province, Córdoba Province From facing fast bowlers in Barbados to sidestepping hungry pigs in Goa, Duncan's travels have thrown up many unique experiences. These days he largely dedicates himself to Spain and Italy, his adopted homeland where he's been living since 1997. He's worked on around 50 Lonely Planet titles, including guidebooks to Spain, Italy, Rome, Sardinia, Sicily, and Portugal, and has contributed to books on world food and epic drives. He's also written on Italy for newspapers, websites and magazines.

Isabella Noble

Cádiz Province & Gibraltar, Granada Province English-Australian on paper but Spanish at heart, travel journalist Isabella has been wandering the globe since her first round-the-world trip as a one-year-old. Having grown up in an Andalucian village, she is a Spain specialist, but also writes extensively about India, Thailand, Greece, the UK and beyond for Lonely Planet, the *Daily Telegraph,* Etihad Airways' *Atlas* magazine and others. Isabella has written many Lonely Planet guides to Spain (including to Barcelona, Andalucía, the Balearic Islands, northern Spain and the Canary Islands) and is a *Telegraph Travel* Spain expert. She has also contributed to Lonely Planet guides to India, South India, Thailand, Southeast Asia, Great Britain and Greece. Find Isabella on Twitter and Instagram (@isabellamnoble). Isabella also wrote the Plan section.

John Noble

John has been travelling for Lonely Planet since the 1980s. The number of LP titles he's written is well into three figures, on numerous countries scattered around the globe. He's still as excited as ever about heading out to unfamiliar destinations, especially off-the-beaten-track ones. Above all, he loves mountains – from the Pyrenees to the Himalayas. See his pics on Instagram @johnnoble11.

Published by Lonely Planet Global Limited
CRN 554153
10th edition – Sep 2021
ISBN 978 1 78701 521 0

10 9 8 7 6 5 4 3 2 1
Printed in China